Shell Road Atlas
Great Britain

with special London Section

George Philip & Son Limited

Contents

Key Map   **1**

Sectional Maps of Great Britain   **2-64**
General Scale 5 miles = 1 inch

Sectional Maps of Approaches to London   **65-72**
Scale ¾ inch = 1 mile

Sectional Maps of Central London   **73-80**
Scale 5 inches = 1 mile

Index to Sectional Maps of Great Britain   **1-48**

Index to Sectional Maps of Central London   **49**
and Approaches to London

ISBN 0 540 05323 6

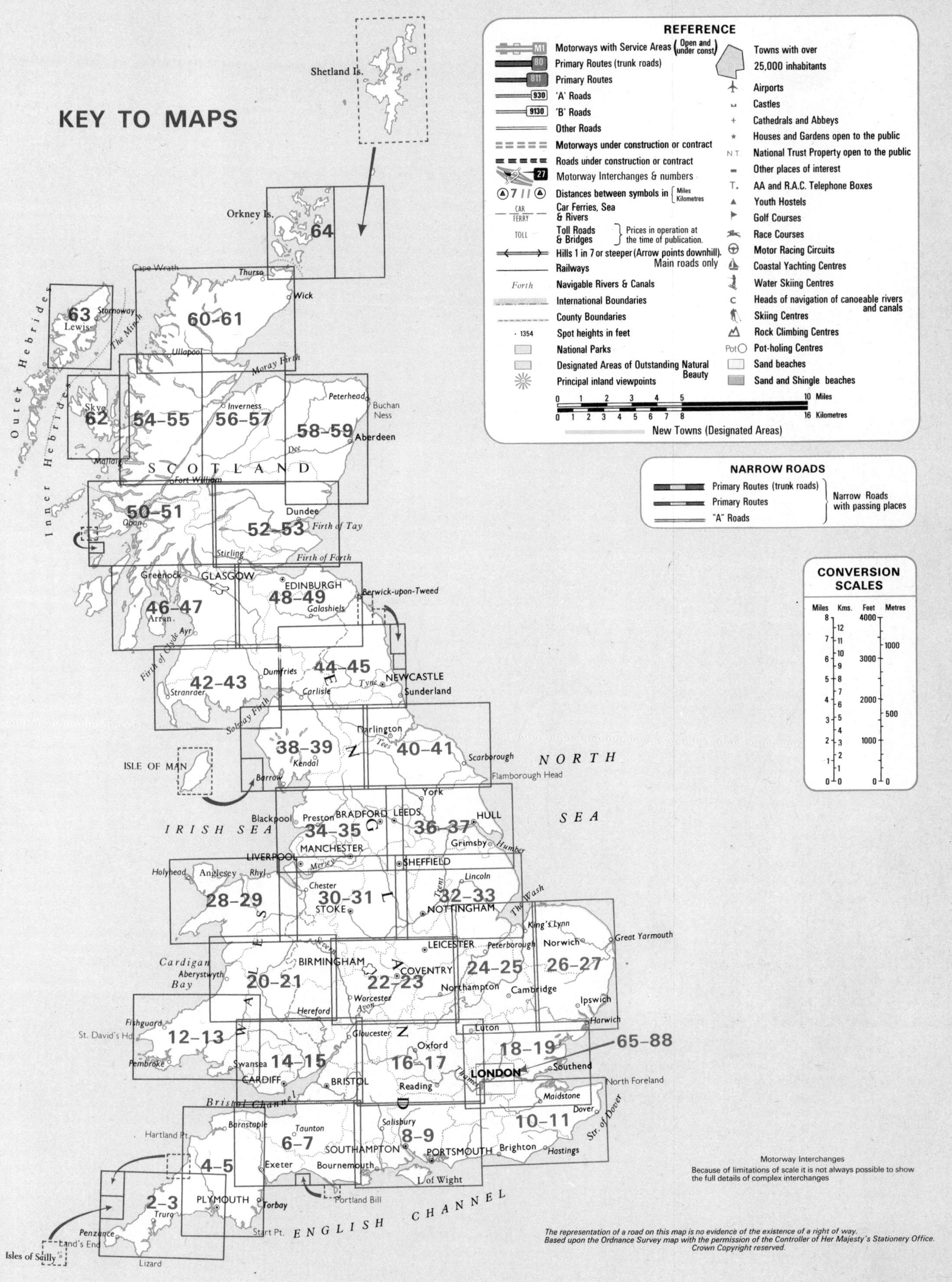

KEY TO MAPS

REFERENCE

Motorways with Service Areas (Open and under const)	Towns with over 25,000 inhabitants
Primary Routes (trunk roads)	Airports
Primary Routes	Castles
'A' Roads	Cathedrals and Abbeys
'B' Roads	Houses and Gardens open to the public
Other Roads	National Trust Property open to the public
Motorways under construction or contract	Other places of interest
Roads under construction or contract	AA and R.A.C. Telephone Boxes
Motorway Interchanges & numbers	Youth Hostels
Distances between symbols in Miles Kilometres	Golf Courses
Car Ferries, Sea & Rivers	Race Courses
Toll Roads & Bridges (Prices in operation at the time of publication)	Motor Racing Circuits
Hills 1 in 7 or steeper (Arrow points downhill). Main roads only	Coastal Yachting Centres
Railways	Water Skiing Centres
Navigable Rivers & Canals	Heads of navigation of canoeable rivers and canals
International Boundaries	Skiing Centres
County Boundaries	Rock Climbing Centres
Spot heights in feet · 1354	Pot-holing Centres
National Parks	Sand beaches
Designated Areas of Outstanding Natural Beauty	Sand and Shingle beaches
Principal inland viewpoints	

0 1 2 3 4 5 10 Miles
0 1 2 3 4 5 6 7 8 16 Kilometres

New Towns (Designated Areas)

NARROW ROADS

Primary Routes (trunk roads)	
Primary Routes	Narrow Roads with passing places
"A" Roads	

CONVERSION SCALES

Miles	Kms.	Feet	Metres
8	12	4000	
7	11		1000
6	10, 9	3000	
5	8, 7		500
4	6	2000	
3	5, 4		
2	3	1000	
1	2		
0	1, 0	0	0

Motorway Interchanges
Because of limitations of scale it is not always possible to show the full details of complex interchanges

The representation of a road on this map is no evidence of the existence of a right of way.
Based upon the Ordnance Survey map with the permission of the Controller of Her Majesty's Stationery Office.
Crown Copyright reserved.

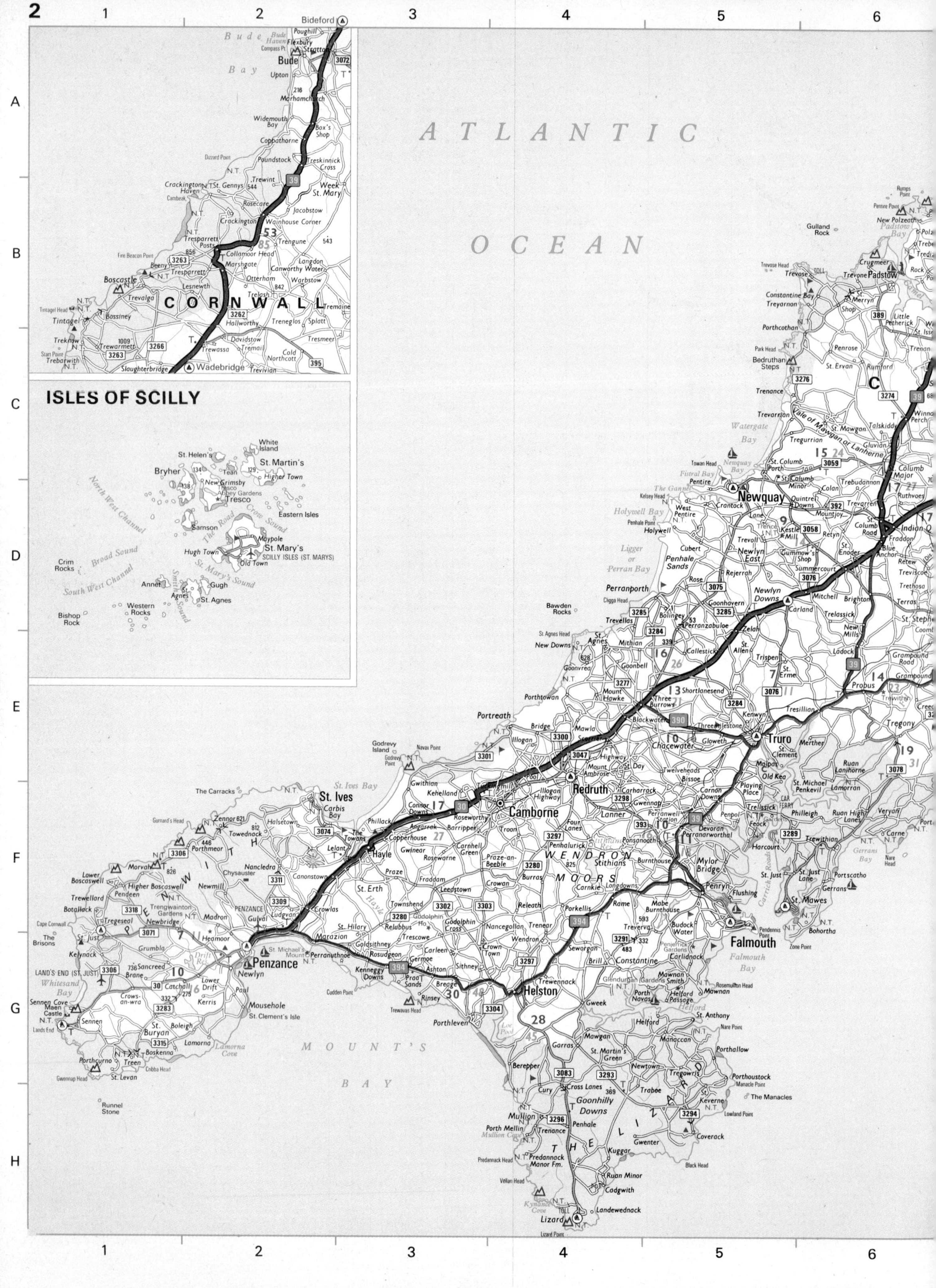
ATLANTIC
OCEAN
CORNWALL
ISLES OF SCILLY
Bideford
Bude
Bude Bay
Stratton
Widemouth Bay
Crackington Haven
Boscastle
Tintagel
Wadebridge
Slaughterbridge
Camelford
St. Martin's
Bryher
Tresco
St. Mary's
Hugh Town
St. Agnes
Annet
Western Rocks
Bishop Rock
Crim Rocks
Broad Sound
North West Channel
South West Channel
SCILLY ISLES (ST. MARYS)
Padstow
Newquay
Perranporth
St. Agnes
Redruth
Camborne
Truro
St. Ives
St. Ives Bay
Hayle
Penzance
Newlyn
Mousehole
St. Just
Sennen
St. Buryan
Marazion
Helston
Porthleven
Falmouth
Penryn
Mylor Bridge
St. Mawes
Lizard
Mullion
Coverack
MOUNT'S BAY
WENDRON MOORS
THE LIZARD
PENWITH
Goonhilly Downs
Land's End
Gulland Rock
Trevose Head
Watergate Bay
Fistral Bay
Holywell Bay
Ligger or Perran Bay
Godrevy Island
The Carracks
Runnel Stone
The Manacles
Falmouth Bay

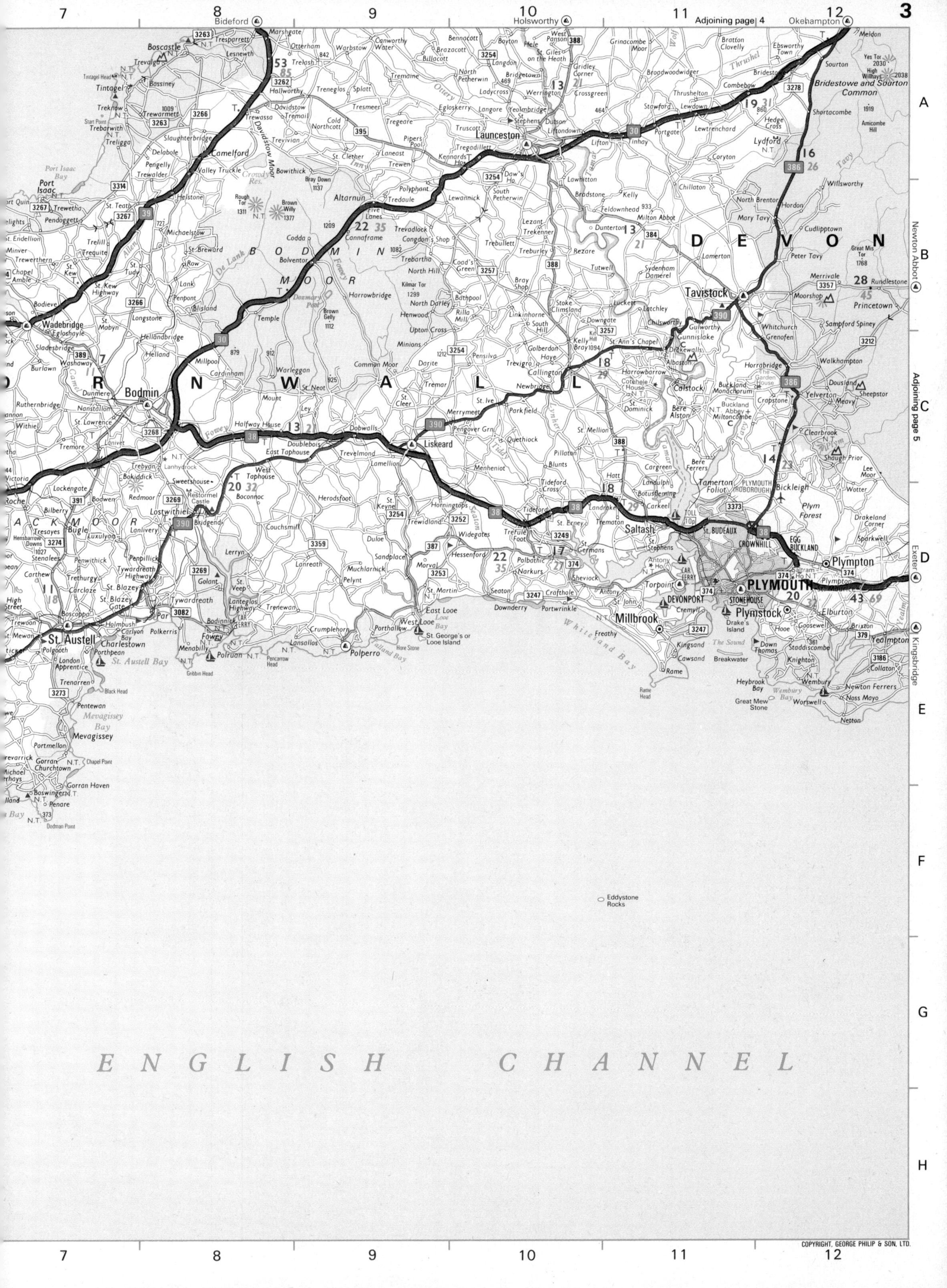

A

B

C

D

E

F

G

H

ENGLISH   CHANNEL

DEVON

CORNWALL

BODMIN MOOR

Okehampton

Bideford

Holsworthy

Launceston

Tavistock

Princetown

PLYMOUTH

Liskeard

Bodmin

Wadebridge

St. Austell

Mevagissey Bay

Boscastle

Camelford

Eddystone Rocks

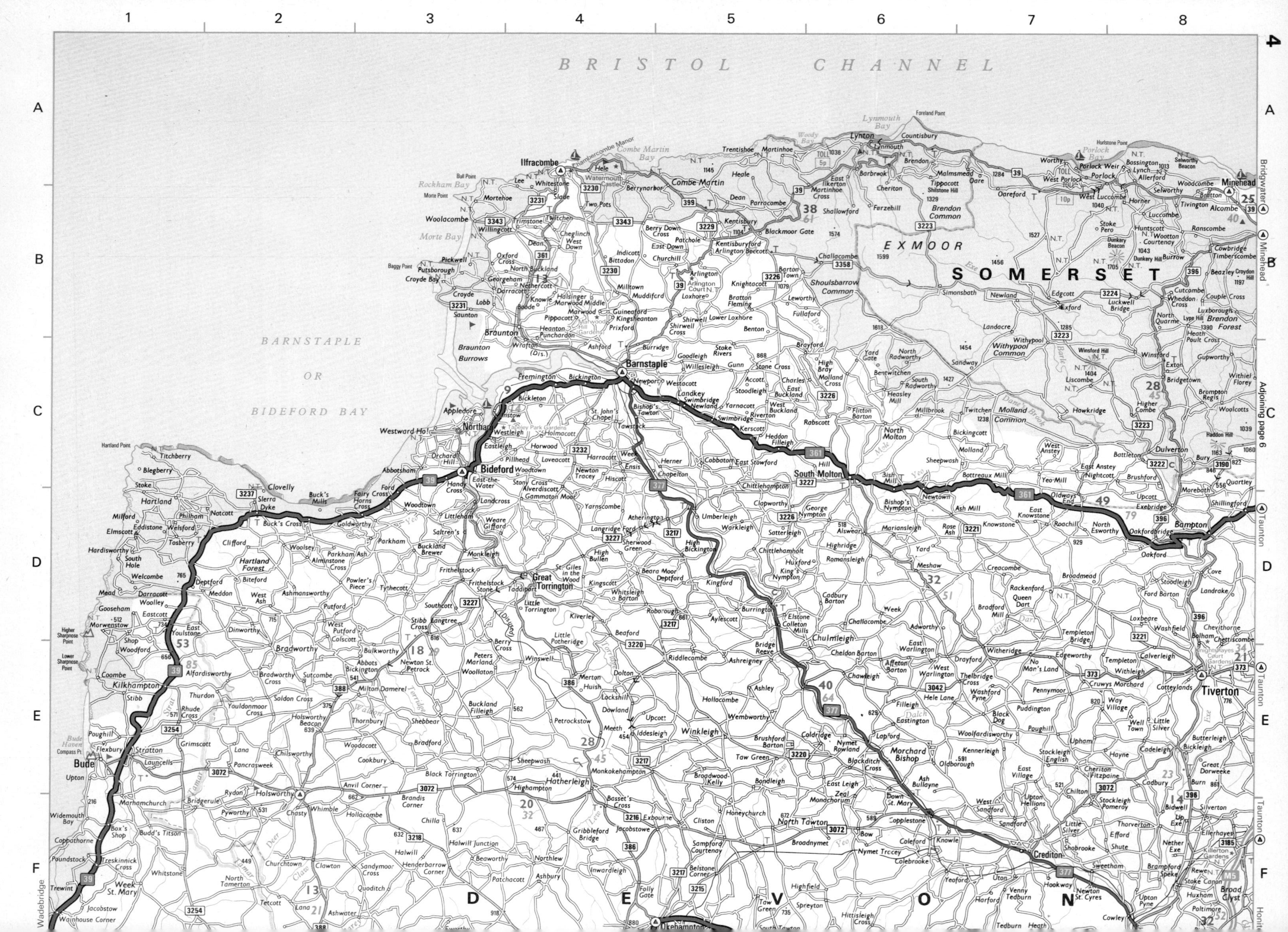
BRISTOL CHANNEL
BARNSTAPLE OR BIDEFORD BAY
EXMOOR
SOMERSET
DEVON
Adjoining page 6
Bridgwater
Minehead
Taunton
Wadebridge
Ilfracombe
Combe Martin
Lynton
Lynmouth
Porlock
Barnstaple
Bideford
Northam
Appledore
Westward Ho!
Braunton
Great Torrington
South Molton
Dulverton
Bampton
Tiverton
Crediton
Chulmleigh
Winkleigh
Hatherleigh
Holsworthy
Bude
Kilkhampton
Hartland
Clovelly
Morchard Bishop
North Tawton
Okehampton

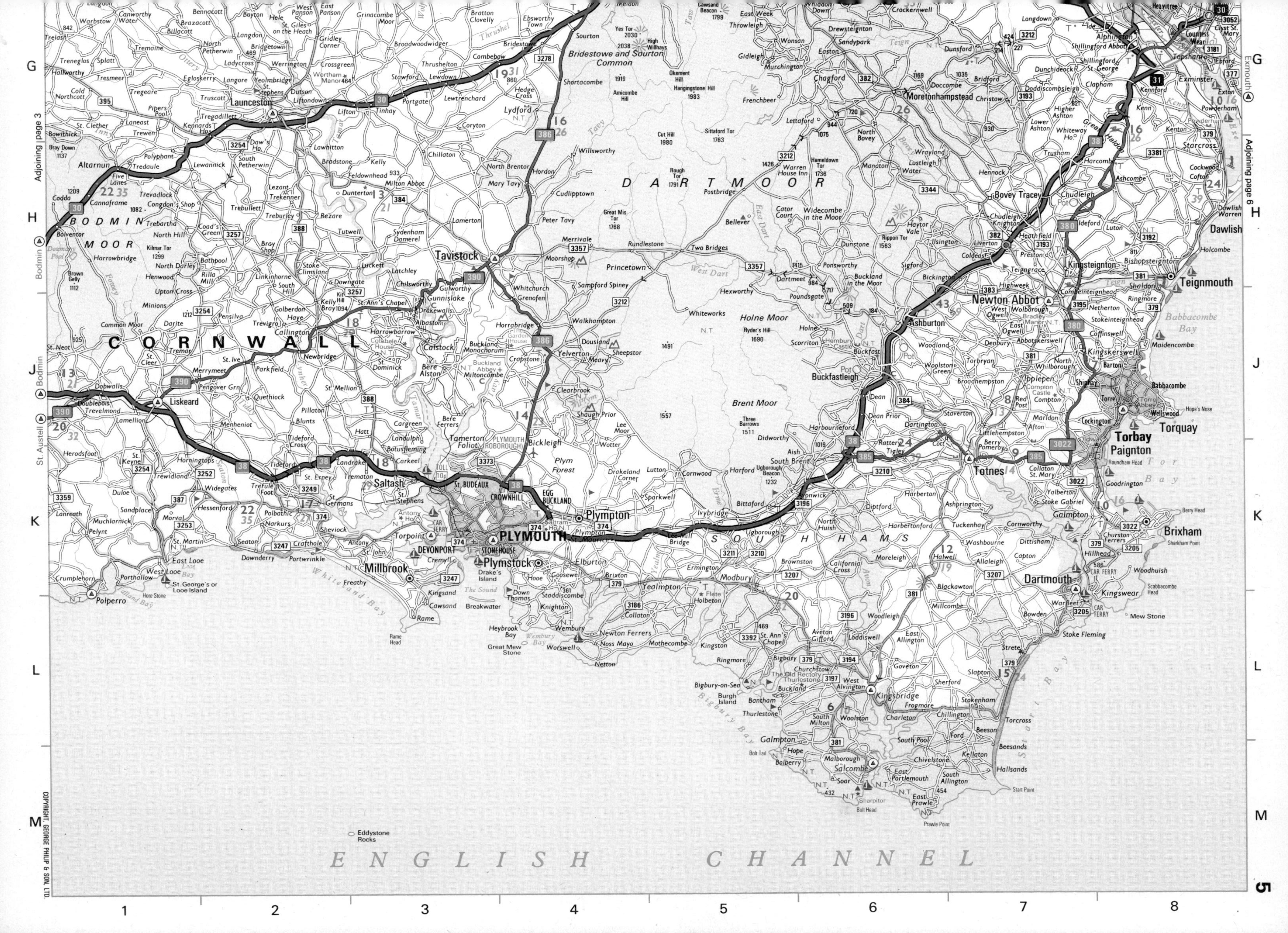
Adjoining page 6
Adjoining page 3
Exmouth
Bodmin
St. Austell
ENGLISH CHANNEL
DARTMOOR
CORNWALL
SOUTH HAMS
BODMIN MOOR
PLYMOUTH
Plympton
Plymstock
DEVONPORT
STONEHOUSE
Torquay
Torbay
Paignton
Brixham
Dartmouth
Totnes
Newton Abbot
Teignmouth
Dawlish
Bovey Tracey
Moretonhampstead
Ashburton
Buckfastleigh
Ivybridge
Tavistock
Launceston
Liskeard
Saltash
Torpoint
Millbrook
Kingsbridge
Salcombe
Modbury
Yealmpton
Princetown
Polperro
East Looe
West Looe
Start Bay
Bigbury Bay
Whitsand Bay
Tor Bay
Babbacombe Bay
Eddystone Rocks
Brent Moor
Holne Moor
Bridestowe and Sourton Common

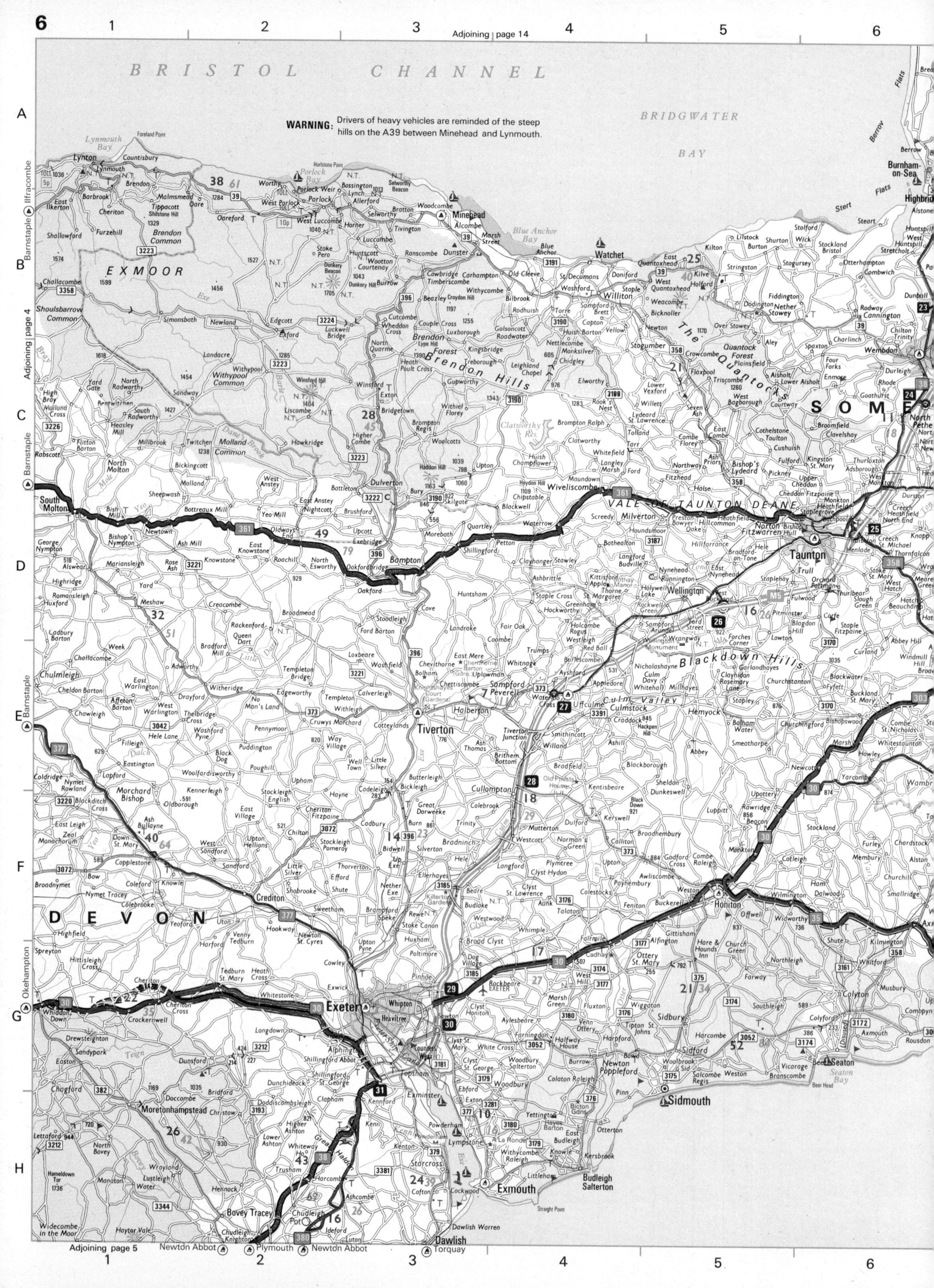

Adjoining page 14
BRISTOL CHANNEL
WARNING: Drivers of heavy vehicles are reminded of the steep hills on the A39 between Minehead and Lynmouth.
BRIDGWATER BAY
EXMOOR
Brendon Forest
Brendon Hills
The Quantock Hills
VALE OF TAUNTON DEANE
Blackdown Hills
Culm Valley
SOME
DEVON
Lynton
Lynmouth
Countisbury
Porlock
Minehead
Dunster
Watchet
Williton
Burnham-on-Sea
Dulverton
Bampton
Wiveliscombe
Milverton
Wellington
Taunton
South Molton
Tiverton
Cullompton
Honiton
Crediton
Exeter
Exmouth
Sidmouth
Budleigh Salterton
Dawlish
Bovey Tracey
Moretonhampstead
Chagford
Ottery St. Mary
Seaton
Colyton
Axminster
Adjoining page 4
Adjoining page 5
Newton Abbot
Plymouth
Torquay
Barnstaple
Ilfracombe
Okehampton

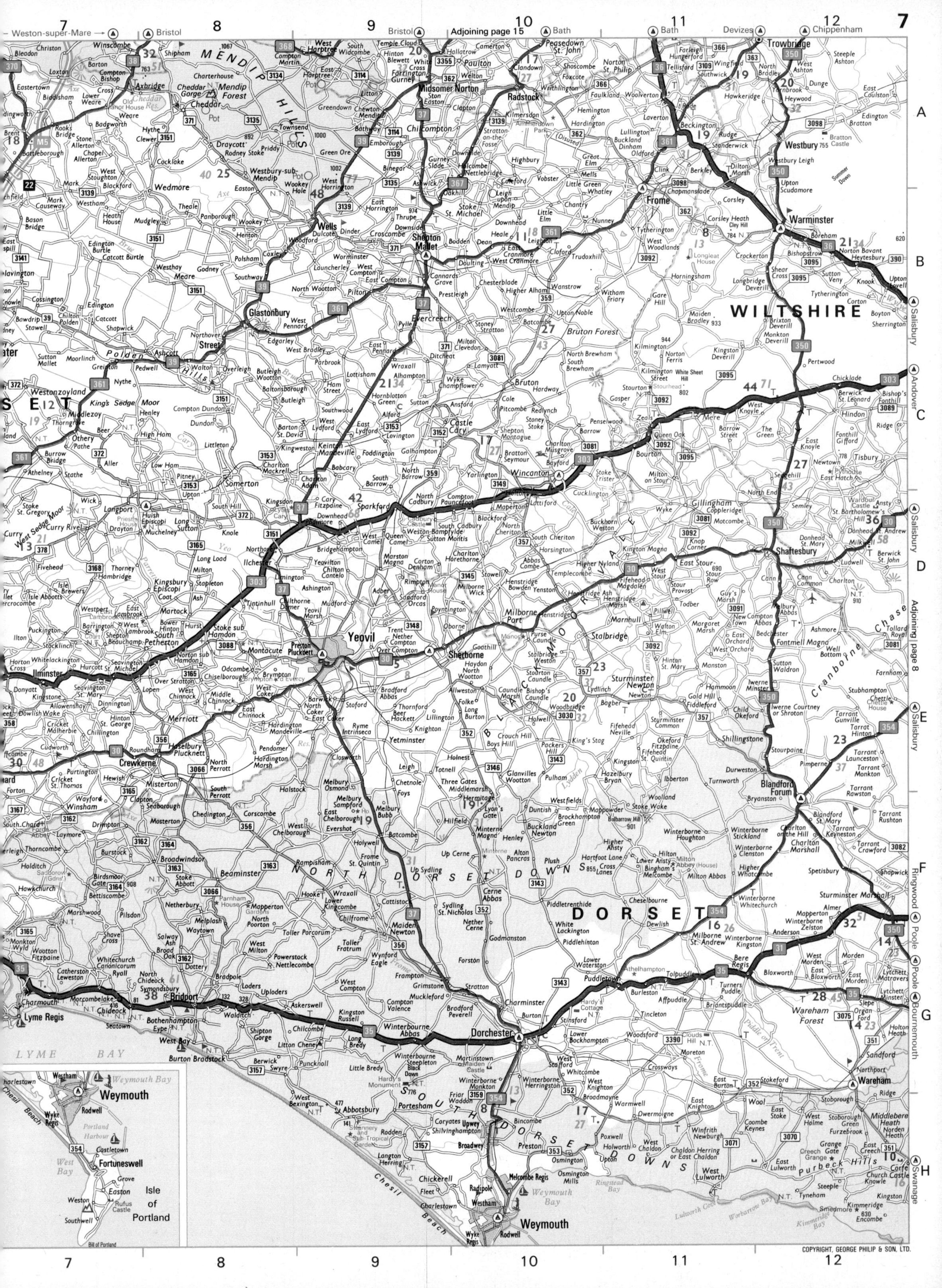

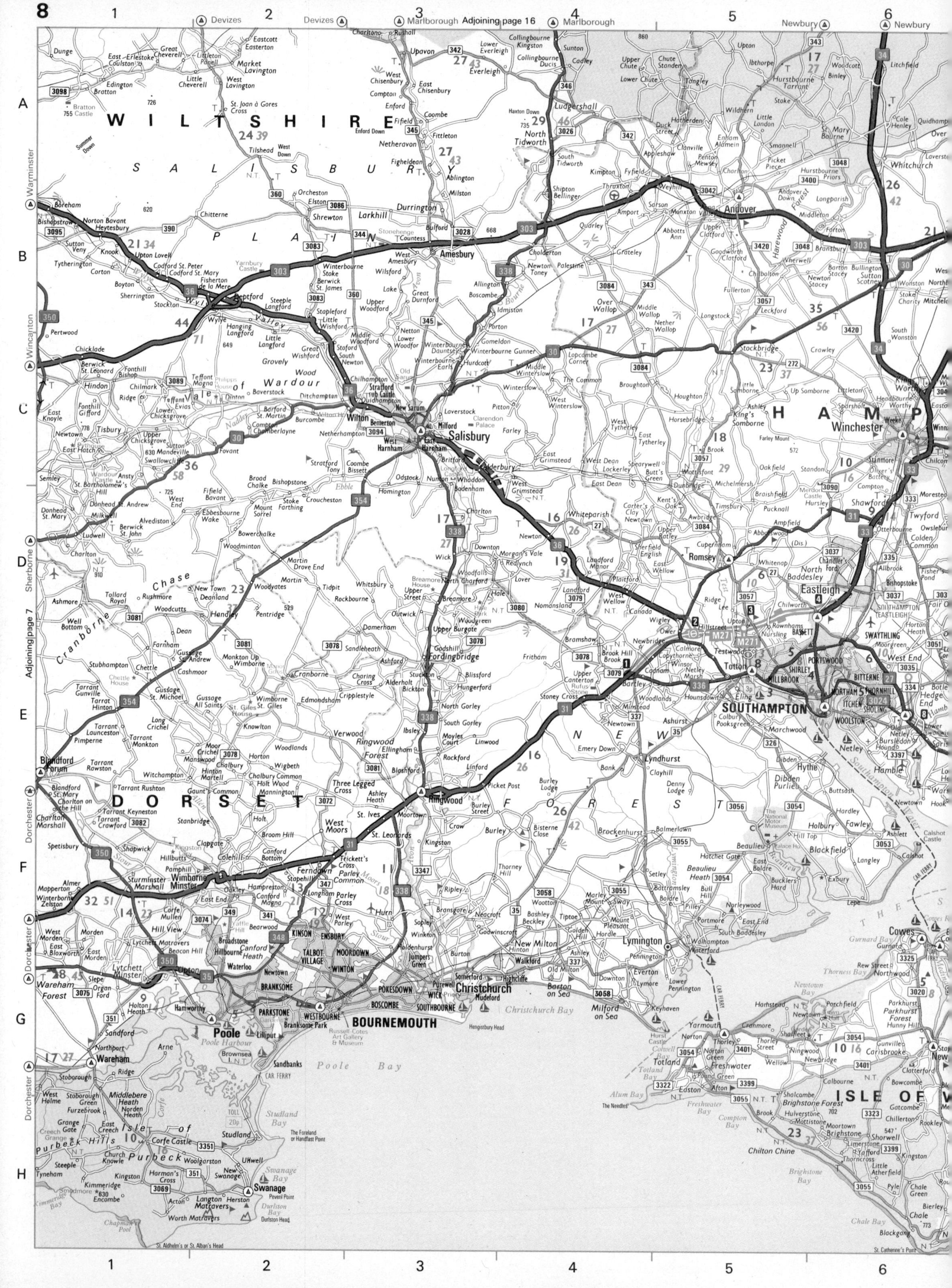

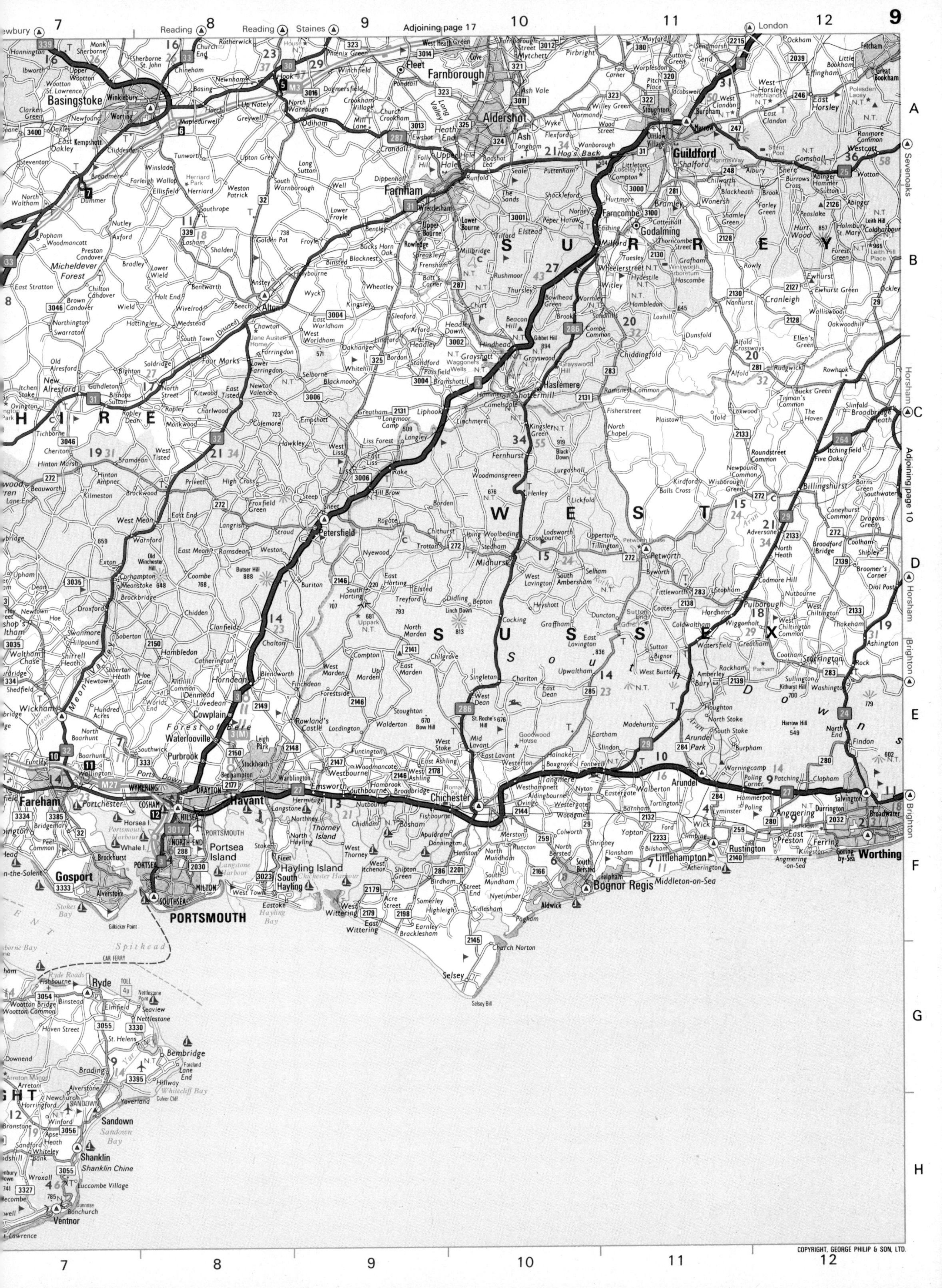

Reading
Staines
Adjoining page 17
London
Sevenoaks
Horsham
Adjoining page 10
Brighton
Basingstoke
Winklebury
Worting
Farnborough
Fleet
Aldershot
Farnham
Guildford
Godalming
Alton
Petersfield
Haslemere
Midhurst
Petworth
Chichester
Havant
Fareham
Gosport
Portsmouth
PORTSMOUTH
Portsea Island
Southsea
Hayling Island
Bognor Regis
Littlehampton
Worthing
Arundel
Selsey
Selsey Bill
Ryde
Sandown
Shanklin
Ventnor
Bembridge
Waterlooville
Cowplain
Cranleigh
Billingshurst
Pulborough
S U R R E Y
W E S T
S U S S E X
South Downs
Spithead
Forest of Bere
Chichester Harbour
Langstone Harbour
Sandown Bay
Whitecliff Bay

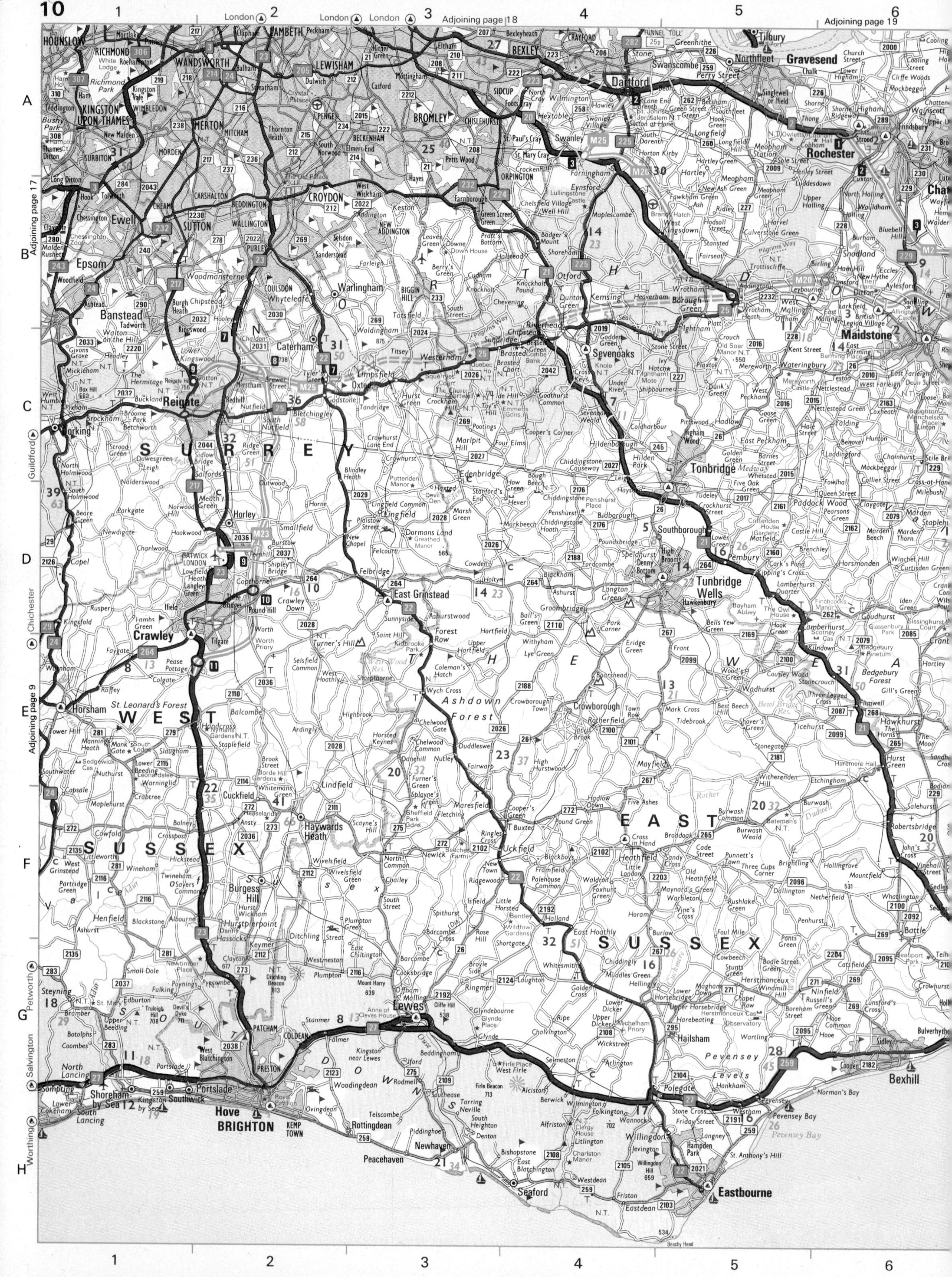
London
Adjoining page 18
Adjoining page 19
Adjoining page 17
Adjoining page 9
Guildford
Chichester
Petworth
Salvington
Worthing
HOUNSLOW
RICHMOND
WANDSWORTH
LAMBETH
LEWISHAM
BEXLEY
CRAYFORD
Tilbury
Gravesend
Northfleet
Dartford
KINGSTON UPON THAMES
WIMBLEDON
MERTON
MITCHAM
BROMLEY
CHISLEHURST
SIDCUP
Swanley
Rochester
Strood
CROYDON
SUTTON
Epsom
Ewell
ORPINGTON
NEW ADDINGTON
Warlingham
Caterham
Banstead
Reigate
Redhill
Oxted
Westerham
Sevenoaks
Otford
Kemsing
Maidstone
Dorking
S U R R E Y
Tonbridge
Edenbridge
Lingfield
Horley
Southborough
Tunbridge Wells
East Grinstead
Crawley
Horsham
W E S T
S U S S E X
Crowborough
Ashdown Forest
Haywards Heath
Cuckfield
Burgess Hill
Uckfield
Heathfield
Wadhurst
Hawkhurst
Robertsbridge
E A S T
S U S S E X
Battle
Lewes
Hailsham
Pevensey Levels
Bexhill
Pevensey Bay
Eastbourne
Beachy Head
Seaford
Newhaven
Peacehaven
Rottingdean
Hove
BRIGHTON
KEMP TOWN
Portslade
Southwick
Shoreham-by-Sea
Lancing
Steyning
Henfield
Polegate
Willingdon
M25
M23
M20
M26
M2

11
Adjoining page 19
7
8
9
10
11
12
A
B
C
D
E
F
G
H
Sheerness
Minster-on-Sea
Queenborough
Eastchurch
Warden
Leysdown-on-Sea
ISLE OF SHEPPEY
Elmley Island
Isle of Harty
The Swale
Medway
Sittingbourne
Milton Regis
Newington
Rainham
Faversham
Whitstable
Seasalter
Herne Bay
Reculver
Birchington
Westgate on Sea
Margate
Cliftonville
Broadstairs
North Foreland
Isle of Thanet
Ramsgate
Minster
Pegwell Bay
Sandwich Bay
Sandwich
Canterbury
Wingham
Deal
Walmer
Kingsdown
St. Margaret's-at-Cliffe
St. Margaret's Bay
South Foreland
Dover
Folkestone
Sandgate
Hythe
Cheriton
Lyminge
Elham
Wye
Ashford
Willesborough
Kennington
Charing
Lenham
Harrietsham
Hollingbourne
KENT
Tenterden
Biddenden
Headcorn
Bethersden
Smarden
Isle of Oxney
Rother Levels
Romney Marsh
Dymchurch
St. Mary's Bay
New Romney
Littlestone-on-Sea
Greatstone-on-Sea
Lydd
Lydd-on-Sea
Denge Marsh
Denge Beach
Dungeness
Walland Marsh
Royal Military Canal
Rye
Rye Harbour
Camber
Winchelsea
Winchelsea Beach
Rye Bay
West Road
East Road
Pett
Cliff End
Fairlight
Ore
Hastings
Icklesham
Guestling Green
Three Oaks
East Wear Bay
STRAIT OF DOVER
M2
M20
A2
A20
A299
A253
A259
A28
COPYRIGHT, GEORGE PHILIP & SON, LTD.

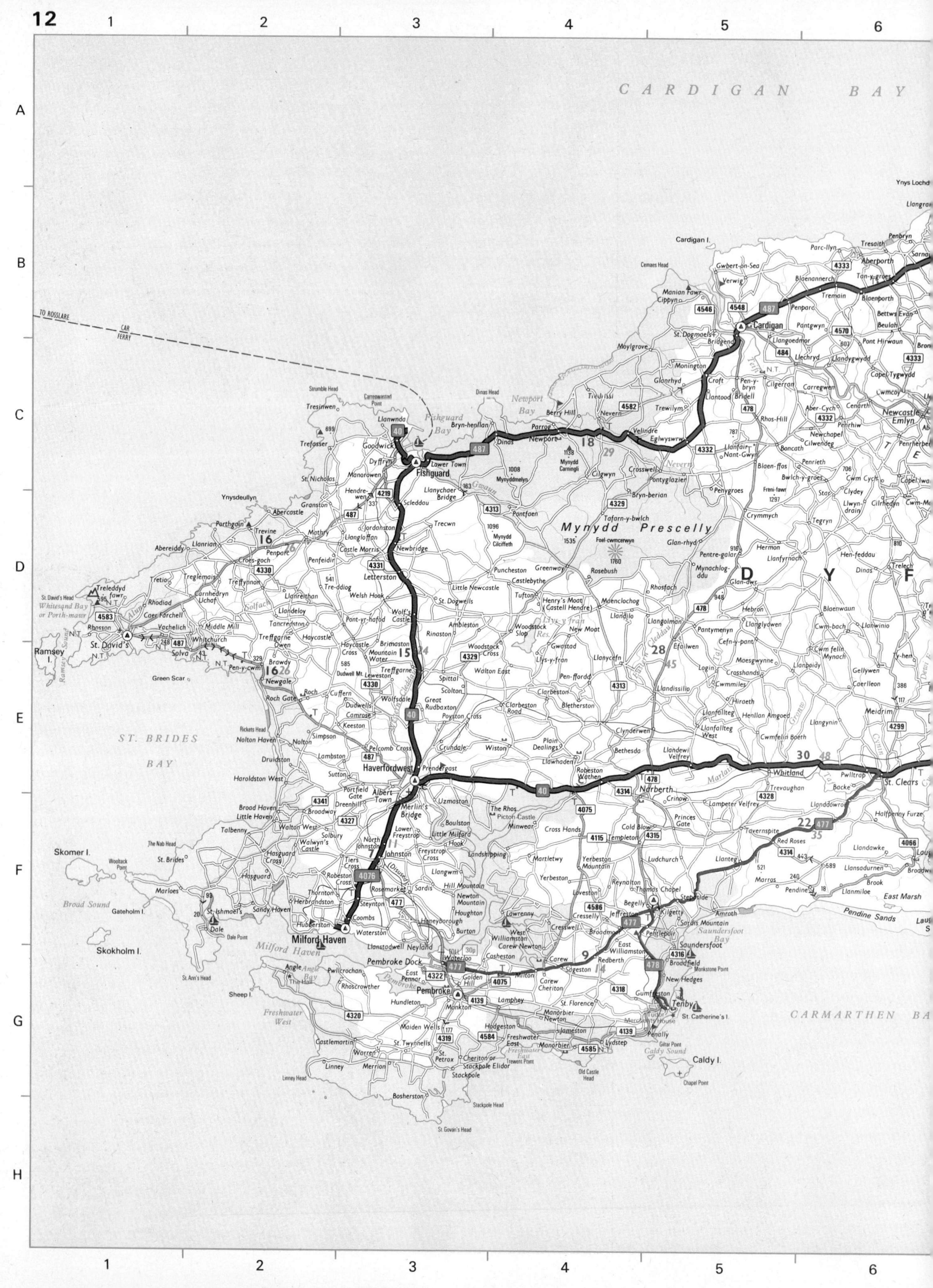

1
2
3
4
5
6
A
B
C
D
E
F
G
H
CARDIGAN BAY
Ynys Lochdyn
Cardigan I.
Cemaes Head
Gwbert-on-Sea
Verwig
Manian Fawr
Cippyn
Parc-llyn
Tresaith
Penbryn
Aberporth
Sarnau
Tan-y-groes
Blaenannerch
Tremain
Blaenporth
Penparc
Betws Evan
Beulah
Cardigan
St. Dogmaels
Bridgend
Pantgwyn
Llangoedmor
Pont Hirwaun
Moylgrove
Monington
Llechryd
Llandygwydd
Capel Tygwydd
Cwmcoy
Glanrhyd
Croft
Pen-y-bryn
Cilgerran
Carregwen
Llantood
Brideli
Trewilym
Aber-Cych
Cenarth
Newcastle Emlyn
Rhos-Hill
Penrhiw
Newchapel
Cilwendeg
Boncath
Llanfair-Nant-Gwyn
Eglwyswrw
Velindre
Nevern
Tredrissi
Berry Hill
Parrog
Newport
Newport Bay
Dinas Head
Dinas
Bryn-henllan
Fishguard Bay
Strumble Head
Carregwastad Point
Tresinwen
Llanwnda
Goodwick
Trefasser
Dyffryn
Lower Town
Fishguard
Manorowen
St. Nicholas
Hendre-wen
Llanychaer Bridge
Gwaun
Mynydd Carningli
Crosswell
Pontyglazier
Penygroes
Blaen-ffos
Penrieth
Bwlch-y-groes
Cwm Cych
Capel Iwan
Clydey
Freni-fawr
Llwyn-drain
Cilrhedyn
Star
Crymmych
Tegryn
Bryn-berian
Tafarn-y-bwlch
Mynydd Prescelly
Foel-cwmcerwyn
Glan-rhyd
Pontfaen
Scleddau
Granston
Abercastle
Ynysdeullyn
Porthgain
Trevine
Mathry
Jordanston
Llangloffan
Trecwn
Mynydd Cilciffeth
Abereiddy
Llanrian
Penparc
Castle Morris
Newbridge
Hermon
Hen-feddau
Croes-goch
Penfeidir
Letterston
Puncheston
Greenway
Castlebythe
Rosebush
Pentre-galar
Mynachlog-ddu
Llanfyrnach
Dinas
Trelech
St. David's Head
Treleddyd fawr
Whitesand Bay or Porth-mawr
Tretio
Treglemais
Treffynnon
Carnhedryn Uchaf
Rhodiad
Caer Farchell
Solfach
Llanreithan
Tre-ddiog
Welsh Hook
Little Newcastle
Tufton
Henry's Moat (Castell Hendre)
Maenclochog
Rhosfach
Glan-dwr
Llandeloy
St. Dogwells
Rhosson
Vachelich
Middle Mill
Tancredston
Pont-yr-hafod
Wolf's Castle
Ambleston
Woodstock Slop
Llys-y-fran Res.
New Moat
Llandilo
Llangolman
Hebron
Blaenwaun
Ramsey Sound
Ramsey I.
St. David's
Whitchurch
Solva
Treffgarne Owen
Haycastle
Haycastle Cross
Brimaston
Rinaston
Gwastad
Pantymenyn
Llanglydwen
Cwm-bach
Llanwinio
Pen-y-cwm
Mountain Water
Woodstock Cross
Llys-y-fran
Llanycefn
Efailwen
Cefn-y-pant
Cwm felin Mynach
Ty-hen
Green Scar
Newgale
Brawdy
Dudwell Mt.
Leweston
Treffgarne
Walton East
Pen-ffordd
Maesgwynne
Llanboidy
Gellywen
Crosshands
Cwmmiles
Caerlleon
Roch Gate
Roch
Cuffern
Spittal
Scolton
Clarbeston
Llandissilio
Hiraeth
Wolfsdale
Great Rudbaxton
Clarbeston Road
Bletherston
Llanfallteg
Henllan Amgoed
Llangynin
Meidrim
Dudwells
Camrose
Poyston Cross
Llanfallteg West
Keeston
Cwmfelin Boeth
Rickets Head
ST. BRIDES BAY
Nolton Haven
Nolton
Simpson
Clynderwen
Plain Dealings
Pelcomb Cross
Crundale
Wiston
Bethesda
Llandewi Velfrey
Druidston
Lambston
Llawhaden
Whitland
Marlais
St. Clears
Haverfordwest
Prendergast
Robeston Wathen
Haroldston West
Sutton
Narberth
Pwlltrap
Backe
Trevaughan
Portfield Gate
Albert Town
Crinow
Dreenhill
Uzmaston
Lampeter Velfrey
Llanddowror
Halfpenny Furze
Broad Haven
The Rhos
Picton Castle
Little Haven
Broadway
Merlin's Bridge
Boulston
Princes Gate
Minwear
Cross Hands
Talbenny
Walton West
Lower Freystrop
Little Milford
Cold Blow
Templeton
Tavernspite
Solbury
Walwyn's Castle
The Nab Head
North Johnston
Hook
Red Roses
Llandawke
Skomer I.
St. Brides
Hasguard Cross
Johnston
Freystrop Cross
Landshipping
Martletwy
Yerbeston Mountain
Ludchurch
Llanteg
Llansadurnen
Wooltack Point
Tiers Cross
Llangwm
Marros
Hasguard
Robeston Cross
Yerbeston
Reynalton
Llanmiloe
Broadway
Marloes
Thornton
Rosemarket
Sardis
Hill Mountain
Newton Mountain
Loveston
Thomas Chapel
Pendine
East Marsh
Broad Sound
Herbrandston
Houghton
Begelly
Stepaside
Gateholm I.
St. Ishmael's
Sandy Haven
Steynton
Lawrenny
Cresselly
Jeffreston
Kilgetty
Amroth
Pendine Sands
Dale
Hubberston
Coombs
Honeyborough
Burton
Cresswell
Broadmoor
Pentlepoir
Sardis Mountain
Saundersfoot Bay
Milford Haven
Waterston
West Williamston
Carew Newton
East Williamston
Saundersfoot
Dale Point
Skokholm I.
Llanstadwell
Neyland
Cosheston
Carew
Redberth
Broadfield
Pembroke Dock
Waterloo
Sageston
Monkstone Point
St. Ann's Head
Angle Bay
Angle
The Hall
Pwllcrochan
East Pennar
Golden Hill
Milton
Carew Cheriton
New Hedges
Sheep I.
Rhoscrowther
Pembroke
Lamphey
St. Florence
Gumfreston
Tenby
Hundleton
Monkton
Freshwater West
Manorbier Newton
St. Catherine's I.
CARMARTHEN BAY
Maiden Wells
Hodgeston
Jameston
Lydstep
Penally
Giltar Point
Castlemartin
St. Twynnells
Freshwater East
Manorbier
Caldy Sound
Caldy I.
Warren
St. Petrox
Cheriton or Stackpole Elidor
Trewent Point
Old Castle Head
Linney
Merrion
Stackpole
Chapel Point
Linney Head
Bosherston
Stackpole Head
St. Govan's Head
TO ROSSLARE
CAR FERRY

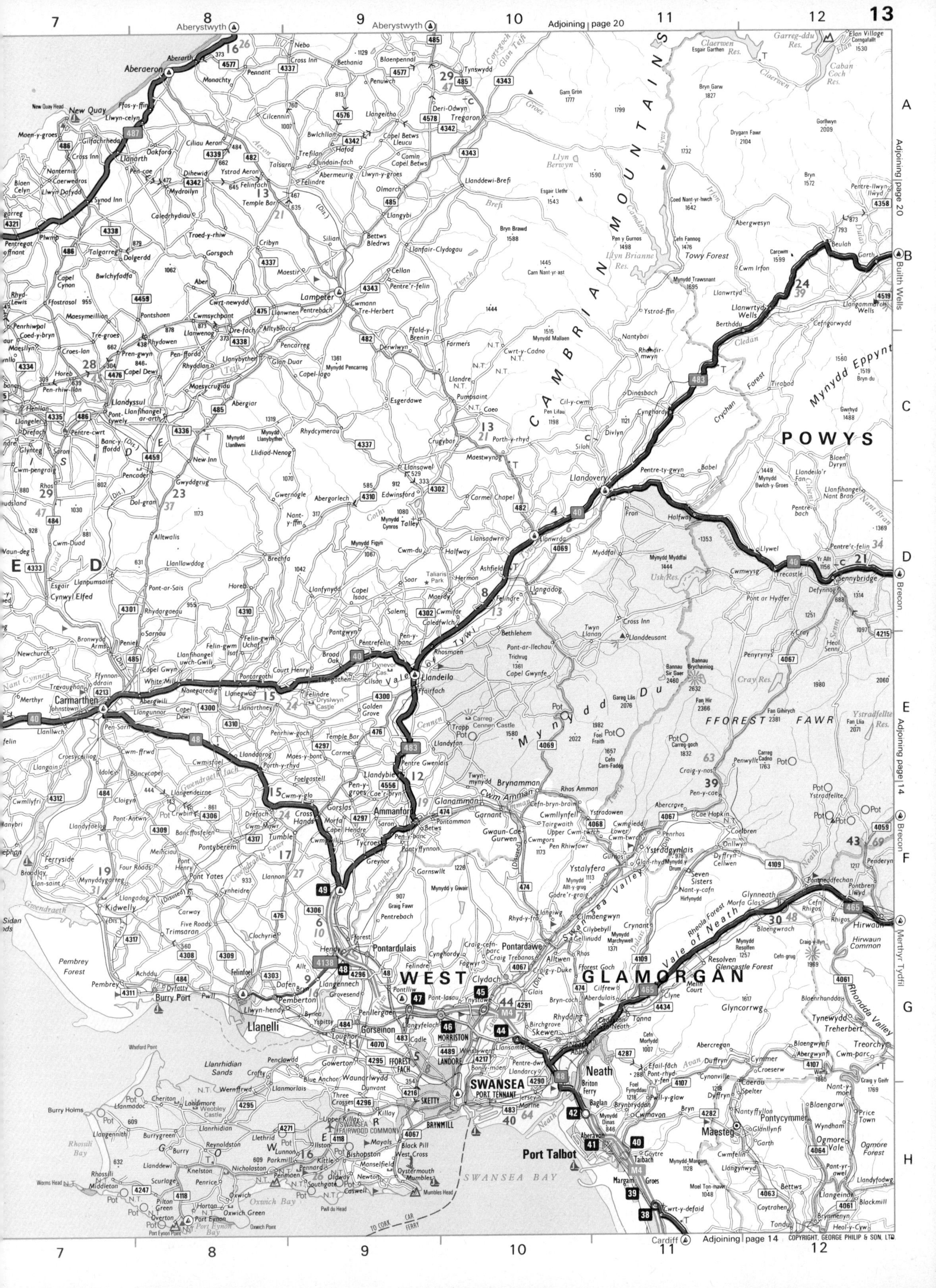

Adjoining page 20
Adjoining page 20
Adjoining page 14
Adjoining page 14
Aberystwyth
Builth Wells
Brecon
Merthyr Tydfil
Cardiff
CAMBRIAN MOUNTAINS
POWYS
WEST GLAMORGAN
DYFED
Mynydd Du
FFOREST FAWR
Mynydd Eppynt
Vale of Tywi
Vale of Neath
Swansea Valley
Towy Forest
Rheola Forest
Glencastle Forest
Pembrey Forest
Llyn Brianne Res.
Usk Res.
Cray Res.
Claerwen Res.
Garreg-ddu Res.
Caban Coch Res.
Elan Village
SWANSEA BAY
Oxwich Bay
Port Eynon Bay
Rhossili Bay
Aberaeron
New Quay
Lampeter
Tregaron
Llandovery
Llandeilo
Carmarthen
Ammanford
Llanelli
Burry Port
Pembrey
Kidwelly
Pontardulais
Gorseinon
SWANSEA
PORT TENNANT
MORRISTON
LANDORE
SKETTY
BRYNMILL
Mumbles
Neath
Port Talbot
Aberavon
Maesteg
Glynneath
Ystradgynlais
Ystalyfera
Pontardawe
Brynamman
Llandyssul
Newcastle Emlyn
Llanwrtyd Wells
Sennybridge
Trecastle
Hirwaun
Treorchy
Treherbert
Rhondda Valley
Swansea
Gower
Port Eynon
Rhossili
Worms Head
Burry Holms
Mumbles Head
Pwll du Head
Oxwich Point
Whitford Point
TO CORK CAR FERRY

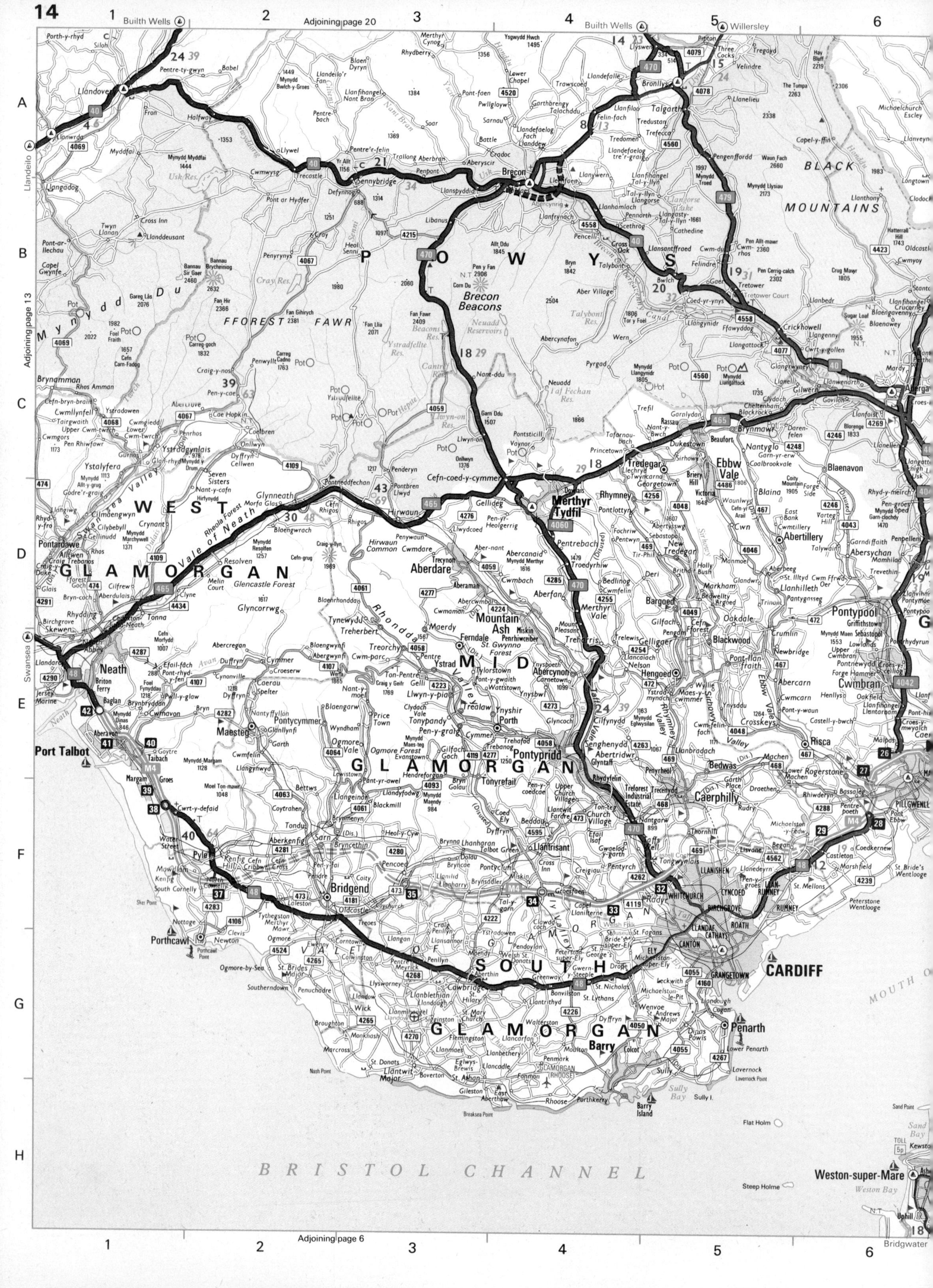

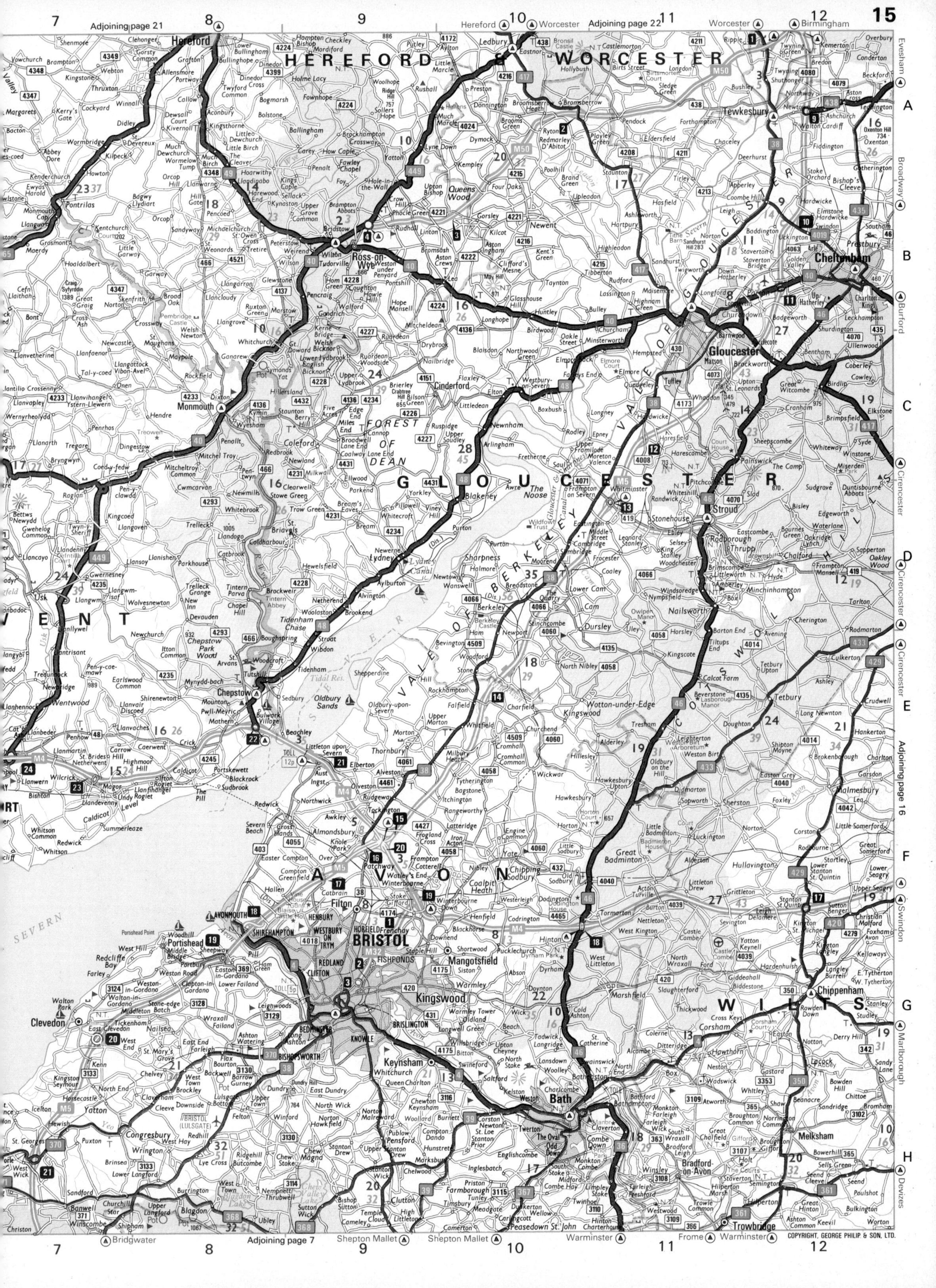

Evesham · Stratford-upon-Avon · Evesham · Adjoining page 22 · Warwick · Stratford-upon-Avon · Banbury

GLOUCESTER
OXFORD
WILTSHIRE
BERKSHIRE
HAMPSHIRE
Cheltenham
Cirencester
Swindon
Marlborough
Devizes
Calne
Hungerford
Newbury
Wantage
Didcot
Abingdon
Witney
Woodstock
Burford
Chipping Norton
Stow-on-the-Wold
Moreton-in-Marsh
Winchcombe
Faringdon
Lechlade
Fairford
Cricklade
Highworth
Northleach
Bourton-on-the-Water
Charlbury
Deddington
Kidlington
Eynsham
Bampton
Ramsbury
Pewsey
Lambourn
Chedworth Woods
Cleeve Common
Wychwood Forest
Savernake Forest
VALE OF WHITE HORSE
MARLBOROUGH DOWNS
BERKSHIRE DOWNS
HAMPSHIRE DOWNS
Vale of Pewsey
Lambourn Downs
Kennet and Avon Canal
Ridge Way
Wansdyke
Thames or Isis
Oxford Canal
WOLVERCOTE
SUMMERTOWN
OXFORD
NEW HINKSEY

Stroud · Gloucester · Adjoining page 15 · Stroud · Bath · Chippenham · Severn Bridge · Chippenham · Frome

Salisbury · Andover · Salisbury · Salisbury · Adjoining page 8 · Andover · Winchester

17
Towcester
Adjoining page 23
Northampton
Bedford
Adjoining page 25
Adjoining page 25
Baldock
Hertford
London
Adjoining page 18
London
London
London
Adjoining page 10
Basingstoke
Alton
Adjoining page 9
Guildford
COPYRIGHT, GEORGE PHILIP & SON, LTD.
B U C K S
B E D F O R D
H E R T F O R D
S U R R E Y
C H I L T E R N
Milton Keynes
Bletchley
Buckingham
Leighton Buzzard
Dunstable
LUTON
Hitchin
Letchworth
Harpenden
St. Albans
Hemel Hempstead
Aylesbury
Tring
Berkhamsted
Chesham
Amersham
Watford
Borehamwood
Princes Risborough
Thame
High Wycombe
Beaconsfield
Marlow
Henley-on-Thames
Maidenhead
Slough
Windsor
HARROW
HILLINGDON
EALING
HOUNSLOW
BRENT
READING
Wokingham
Bracknell
Staines
Camberley
Woking
Weybridge
Walton-on-Thames
Esher
Epsom
Leatherhead
Sunbury on Thames
KINGSTON UPON THAMES

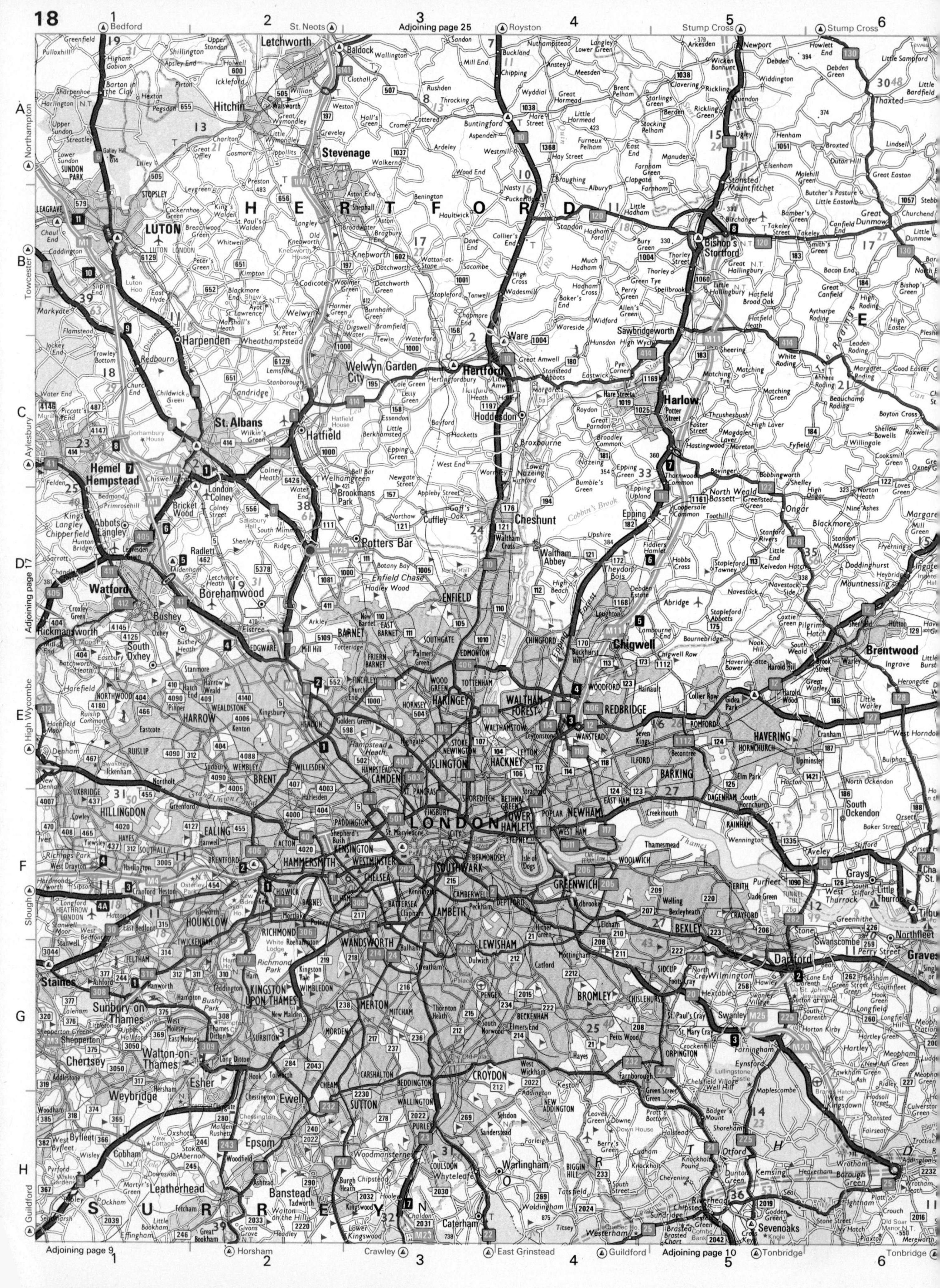

ing page 25
Adjoining page 27
Adjoining page 11
7
8
9
10
11
12
A
B
C
D
E
F
G
H
Haverhill
Sudbury
Sudbury
Ipswich
Felixstowe
Harwich
Dovercourt
Landguard Pt.
Shotley Gate
Parkeston
Ramsey
Wrabness
Bradfield
Mistley
Manningtree
Lawford
Dedham
Flatford Mill
Brantham
Cattawade
Stratford St. Mary
Nayland
Bures
Boxted
Langham
Boxted Cross
Little Horkesley
Great Horkesley
Wormingford
Mount Bures
Blacksmith's Corner
Ardleigh
Lamb Corner
Castle House
New Mistley
Bradfield Heath
Little Bromley
Horsley Cross
Horsley Cross Street
Wix
Little Oakley
Great Oakley
Stone's Green
Beaumont
Horsey I.
The Naze
Naze Park
Walton on the Naze
Kirby le Soken
Kirby Cross
Upper Kirby
Thorpe-le-Soken
Weeley
Weeley Heath
Frinton-on-Sea
Great Holland
Holland-on-Sea
Little Clacton
St. Osyth Heath
Great Clacton
Clacton on Sea
Rush Green
Jaywick
Seawick Sands
St. Osyth Marsh
St. Osyth
Colne Point
Brightlingsea
Tendring
Tendring Green
Little Bentley
Great Bentley
Great Bromley
Burnt Heath
Frating
Frating Green
Aingers Green
Thorrington
Alresford
Elmstead Market
Hare Green
Wivenhoe
Wivenhoe Cross
Fingringhoe
Rowhedge
Old Heath
Blackheath
The Hythe
Colchester
Crockleford Heath
Parson's Heath
Mile End
West Bergholt
Fordham
Wakes Colne
Colne Engaine
Earls Colne
Chappel
Great Tey
Fordstreet
Aldham
Eight Ash Green
Marks Tey
Stanway
Beacon End
Shrub End
Copford Green
Easthorpe
Layer-de-la-Haye
Birch
Birch Green
Hardy's Green
Messing
Inworth
Layer Marney
Layer Breton
Abberton
Abberton Res.
Langenhoe
Peldon
Great Wigborough
East Mersea
Mersea Island
West Mersea
Salcott
Tolleshunt D'Arcy
Tolleshunt Major
Tollesbury
Tiptree
Paternoster Heath
Oxley Green
Great Braxted
Little Braxted
Rivenhall End
Kelvedon
Feering
Coggeshall
Coggeshall Hamlet
Paycockes N.T.
Pattiswick Green
Broad Green
Stisted
Bocking
Bocking Churchstreet
Braintree
Rayne
Bradwell
Tye Green
Cressing
Silver End
Black Notley
Young's End
White Notley
Hawbush Green
Faulkbourne
Fairstead
Terling
Witham
Flack's Green
Fuller Street
Great Leighs
Little Leighs
Little Waltham
Hatfield Peverel
Wickham Bishops
Great Totham
Little Totham
Nounsley
Boreham
Broad Street Green
Langford
Heybridge
Heybridge Basin
Maldon
Beeleigh Abbey
Goldhanger
Blackwater
Osea I.
Northey I.
The Stone
Bradwell Waterside
Bradwell Lodge
Bradwell-on-Sea
St. Peter's Flat
Sales Point
Dengie Flat
Buxey Sand
St Lawrence
Tillingham
Steeple
Asheldham
Dengie
Dengie Marshes
Ray Sand
Mayland
Lower Mayland
Mundon Hill
Latchingdon
Southminster
Althorne
Ostend
Stoneyhills
Old Montsale
East Wick
Burnham-on-Crouch
Crouch
Foulness Point
Foulness Sands
Courtsend
Churchend
Canewdon
Paglesham
Eastend
Great Stambridge
Ballards Gore
Ashington
Potton I.
Foulness Island
Maplin Sands
Rochford
Barling
Little Wakering
Great Wakering
Samuel's Corner
North Shoebury
Shoeburyness
Shoebury Ness
Thorpe Bay
Southchurch
Bournes Green
Prittlewell
Southend Rochford
Eastwood
Southend-on-Sea
Westcliff on Sea
Leigh-on-Sea
Hadleigh
Leigh Beck
Canvey Island
Canvey
Coryton
Corringham
Fobbing
Stanford le Hope
Mucking
Thames
South Benfleet
Basildon
Vange
Pitsea
Bowers Gifford
Great Tarpots
Daws Heath
Thundersley
North Benfleet
Rayleigh
Stroud Green
Hockley
Hawkwell
Hullbridge
South Fambridge
North Fambridge
South Woodham Ferrers
Rettendon
Rettendon Place
Battlesbridge
Rawreth
Shotgate
Wickford
Runwell
Ramsden Bellhouse
Downham
Ramsden Heath
Crays Hill
Nevendon
South Hanningfield
Hanningfield Water
West Hanningfield
East Hanningfield
Coalhill
Stow Maries
Woodham Ferrers
Cold Norton
Purleigh
Cock Clarks
Bicknacre
Howe Green
Galleywood
Sandon
Great Baddow
Danbury
Little Baddow
Woodham Walter
Runsell Green
Woodham Mortimer
Springfield
Chelmer and Blackwater Navigation
Halstead
Gosfield
Gosfield Hall
Blue Bridge Ho
Sible Hedingham
Great Maplestead
Little Maplestead
Pebmarsh
Colne Valley
Greenstead Green
Blackmore End
Beazley End
High Garrett
Shalford
Shalford Green
Jasper's Green
Panfield
Great Saling
Wethersfield
Highstreet Green
Morris Green
Howe Street
Church End
Bannister Green
Row Green
Willows Green
Blyth Sands
Cliffe
St Mary's Hoo
Allhallows
Lower Stoke
Isle of Grain
Grain
Wallend
Cooling
Stoke
High Halstow
Sharnal Street
Church Street
Cooling Street
Cliffe Woods
Lower Higham
Mockbeggar
Chattenden
Hoo
Medway
Shorne Ridgeway
Higham
Wainscott
Upper Upnor
Frindsbury
Strood
Rochester
Brompton
Gillingham
Rainham Mark
Rainham
Chatham
Luton
Cuxton
North Halling
Wouldham
Halling
Burham
Bluebell Hill
Walderslade
Wayfield
Hempstead
Wigmore
Bredhurst
Dunn Street
Stockbury
Snodland
Eccles
Aylesford
New Hythe
Ditton
Larkfield
East Malling
Allington
Sandling
Boxley
Detling
Thurnham
Bearsted
Maidstone
Barming
East Barming
Roseacre
Shepway
Otham
Stoneacre
Broad Street
Hollingbourne
Eyhorne Street
Hucking
Bicknor
South Street
Wormshill
Frinsted
Wichling
Milstead
Doddington
Eastling
Newnham
Throwley
Throwley Forstal
Otterden Place
West Street
Leaveland
Badlesmere
Sheldwich
Painter's Forstal
Ospringe
Faversham
Preston
Goodnestone
Hernhill
Dunkirk
Boughton Street
Selling
Shottenden
Chilham
Old Wives Lees
Chartham
Chartham Hatch
Shalmsford Street
Nackington
Thanington
Harbledown
Canterbury
Bekesbourne
Patrixbourne
Bridge
Adisham
Littlebourne
Ickham
Wingham
Staple
Goodnestone
Chillenden
Eastry
Heronden
Marshborough
Ash
Guilton
Elmstone
Hooden
Preston
Ware
Westmarsh
Stodmarsh
East Stourmouth
West Stourmouth
Upstreet
Chislet
Hoath
Westbere
Sturry
Fordwich
Wickhambreaux
Hersden
Calcott
Broadoak
Tyler Hill
Blean
Rough Common
Honey Hill
Dargate
Yorkletts
Herne
Chestfield
Greenhill
Broomfield
Herne Bay
Swalecliffe
Eddington
Beltinge
Reculver
Hillborough
Birchington
Acol
Monkton
Minster
St. Nicholas at Wade
Boyden Gate
Sarre
Whitstable
Seasalter
Graveney
Goodnestone
Oare
Uplees
Conyer
Teynham
Teynham Street
Lynsted
Lewson Street
Rodmersham
Highsted
Tunstall
Bredgar
Silver Street
Borden
Bapchild
Sittingbourne
Murston
Milton Regis
Kemsley
Bobbing
Key Street
Danaway
Newington
Hartlip
Yelsted
Moor Street
Lower Halstow
Upchurch
Ham Green
Meresborough
Iwade
Elmley Island
Isle of Harty
The Swale
Isle of Sheppey
Queenborough
Sheerness
West Minster
Minster-on-Sea
Halfway Houses
Eastchurch
Warden
Leysdown-on-Sea
Ashford
Ashford
Dover
Margate
Ramsgate
S
E
X
K
E
N
T

Penrhyndeudraeth Adjoining page 28 Betws-y-coed Corwen
Adjoining page 29

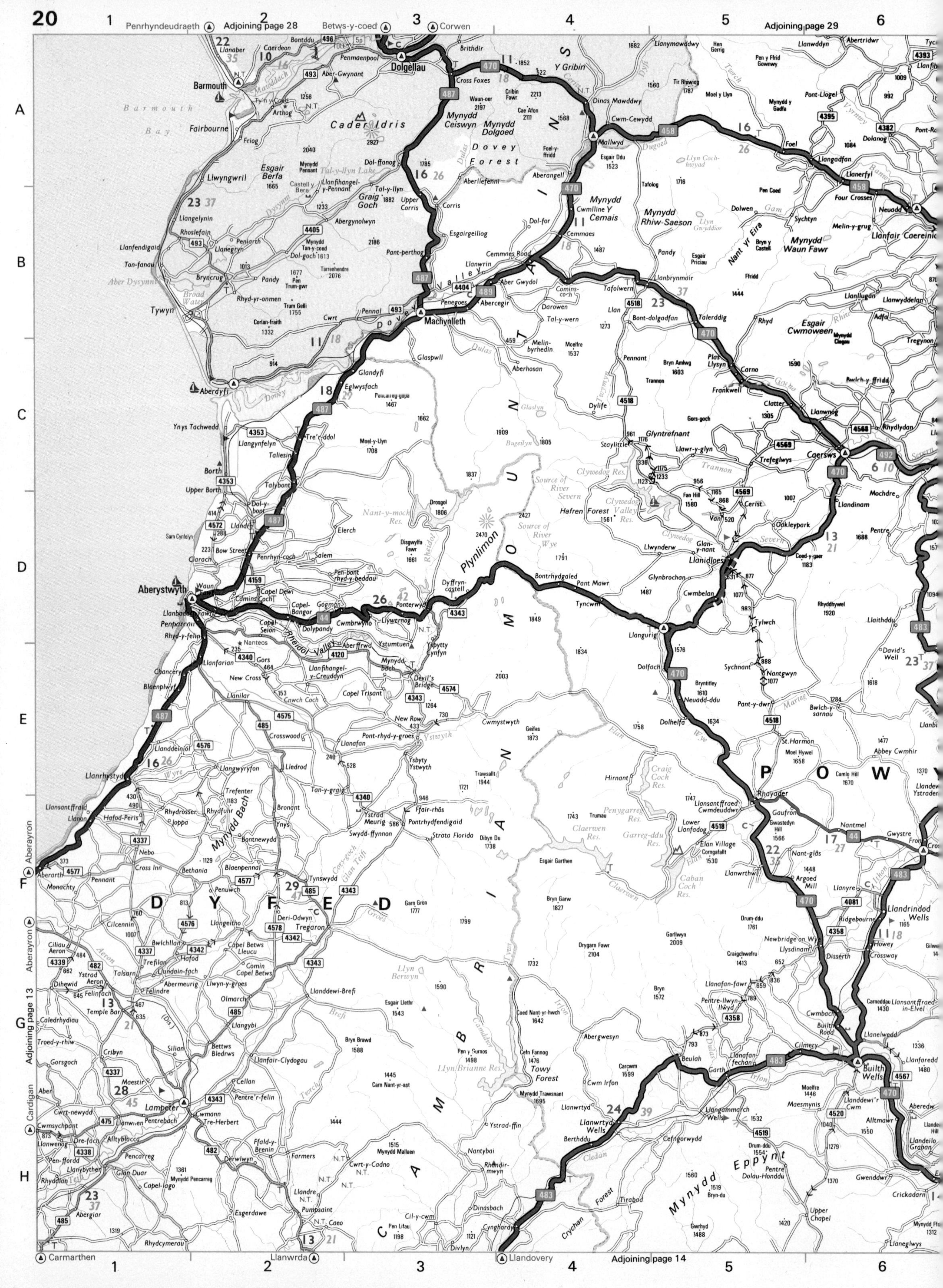

Adjoining page 14
Aberaeron Adjoining page 13 Cardigan

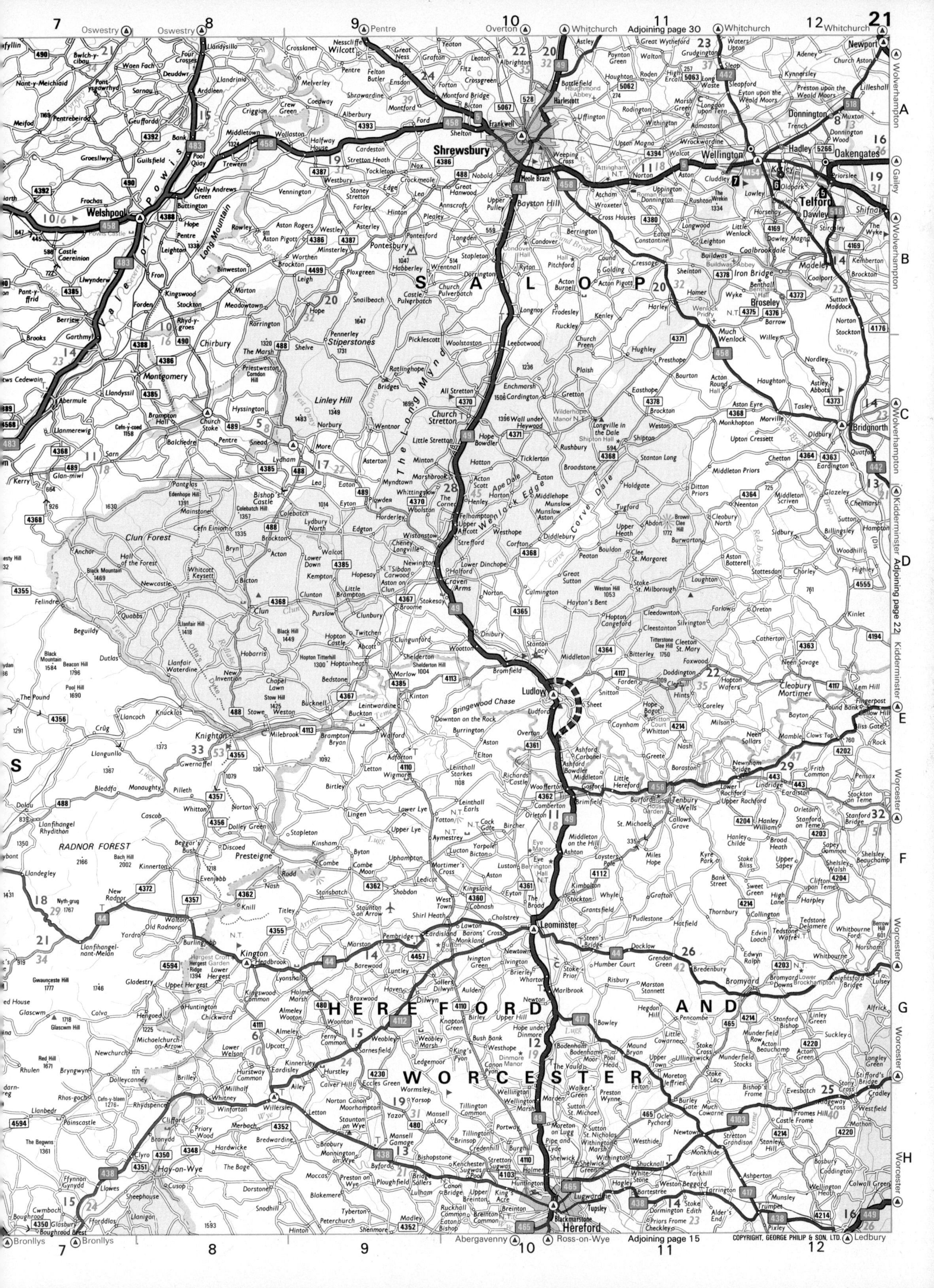
Adjoining page 30
Oswestry
Pentre
Overton
Whitchurch
Newport
Wolverhampton
Gailey
Kidderminster
Adjoining page 22
Worcester
Ledbury
Ross-on-Wye
Abergavenny
Bronllys
Adjoining page 15
SALOP
HEREFORD AND WORCESTER
Shrewsbury
Frankwell
Harlescott
Wellington
Oakengates
Telford
Dawley
Madeley
Iron Bridge
Broseley
Much Wenlock
Bridgnorth
Welshpool
Montgomery
Church Stoke
Bishop's Castle
Clun
Clun Forest
Craven Arms
Church Stretton
All Stretton
The Long Mynd
Stiperstones
Linley Hill
Long Mountain
Vale of Powis
Wenlock Edge
Ape Dale
Corve Dale
Ludlow
Bringewood Chase
Knighton
Presteigne
Kington
New Radnor
RADNOR FOREST
Leominster
Tenbury Wells
Cleobury Mortimer
Bromyard
Hereford
Hay-on-Wye
Weobley
Pembridge
Leintwardine
Bayston Hill
Pontesbury
Minsterley
Chirbury
Stokesay
Onibury
Bromfield
Woofferton
Richards Castle
Mortimer's Cross
Kingsland
Shobdon
Dilwyn
Wellington
Marden
Moreton on Lugg
Burghill
Credenhill
Bishopstone
Staunton on Wye
Clifford
Whitney
Eardisley
Letton
Lyonshall
Titley
Dolau
Llandegley
Beguildy
Felindre
Kerry
Newcastle
Mainstone
Lydham
Lydbury North
Aston on Clun
Hopton Castle
Bucknell
Brampton Bryan
Wigmore
Aymestrey
Orleton
Brimfield
Ashford Carbonel
Burford
Newnham Bridge
Stanford Bridge
Tupsley
Blackmarstone
Holmer
COPYRIGHT, GEORGE PHILIP & SON, LTD.

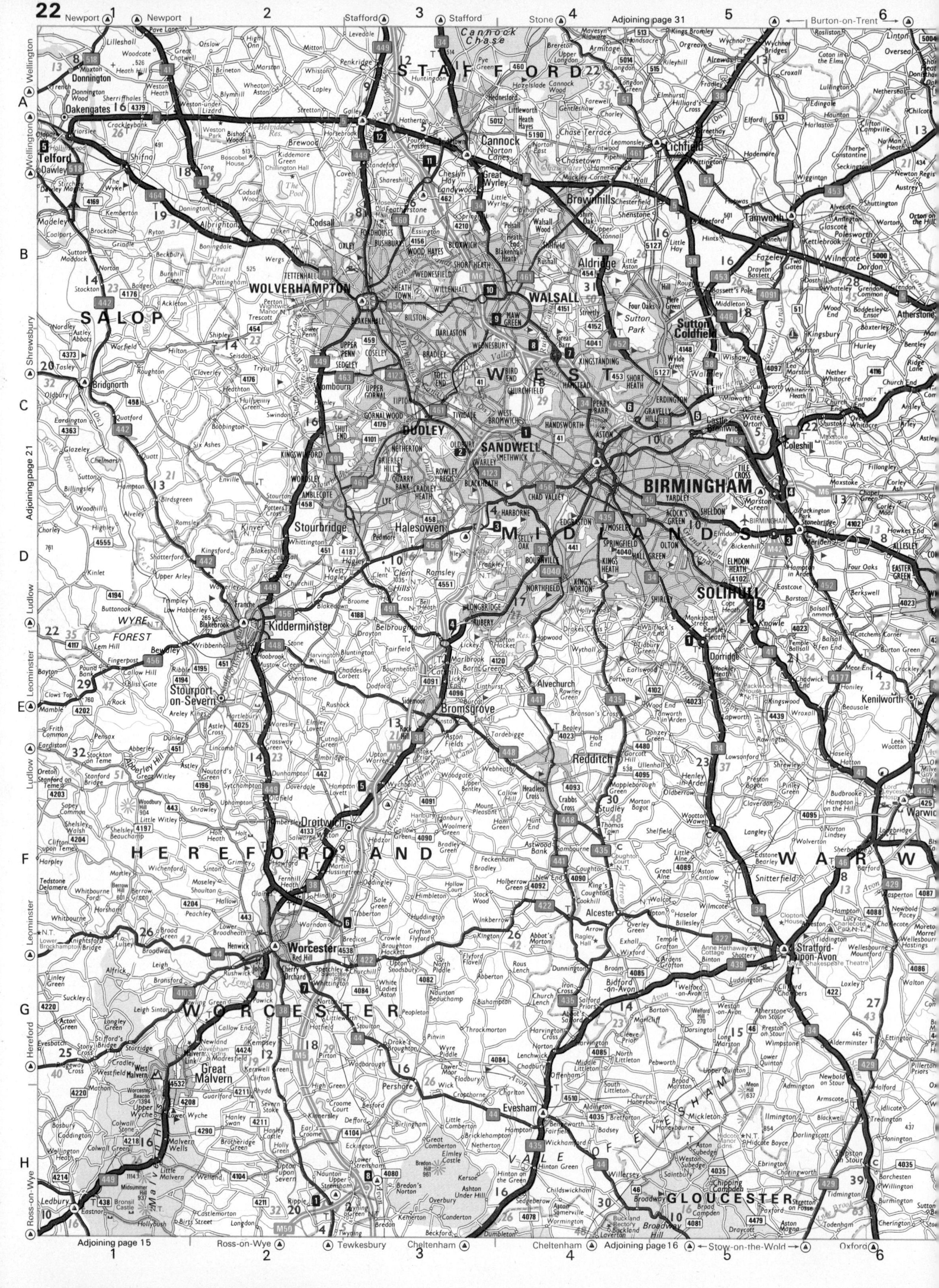
Newport
Newport
Stafford
Stafford
Stone
Adjoining page 31
Burton-on-Trent
Wellington
Wellington
Shrewsbury
Adjoining page 21
Ludlow
Leominster
Ludlow
Leominster
Hereford
Ross-on-Wye
Adjoining page 15
Ross-on-Wye
Tewkesbury
Cheltenham
Cheltenham
Adjoining page 16
Stow-on-the-Wold
Oxford
STAFFORD
SALOP
WEST MIDLANDS
HEREFORD AND WORCESTER
WARW
GLOUCESTER
Cannock Chase
WYRE FOREST
VALE OF EVESHAM
WOLVERHAMPTON
WALSALL
DUDLEY
SANDWELL
BIRMINGHAM
SOLIHULL
Telford
Oakengates
Donnington
Dawley
Madeley
Bridgnorth
Shifnal
Albrighton
Codsall
Cannock
Lichfield
Brownhills
Aldridge
Tamworth
Sutton Coldfield
Atherstone
Coleshill
Stourbridge
Halesowen
Kidderminster
Bewdley
Stourport-on-Severn
Bromsgrove
Redditch
Droitwich
Worcester
Great Malvern
Malvern Wells
Pershore
Evesham
Alcester
Studley
Stratford-upon-Avon
Kenilworth
Warwick
Chipping Campden
Broadway
Ledbury
Upton upon Severn

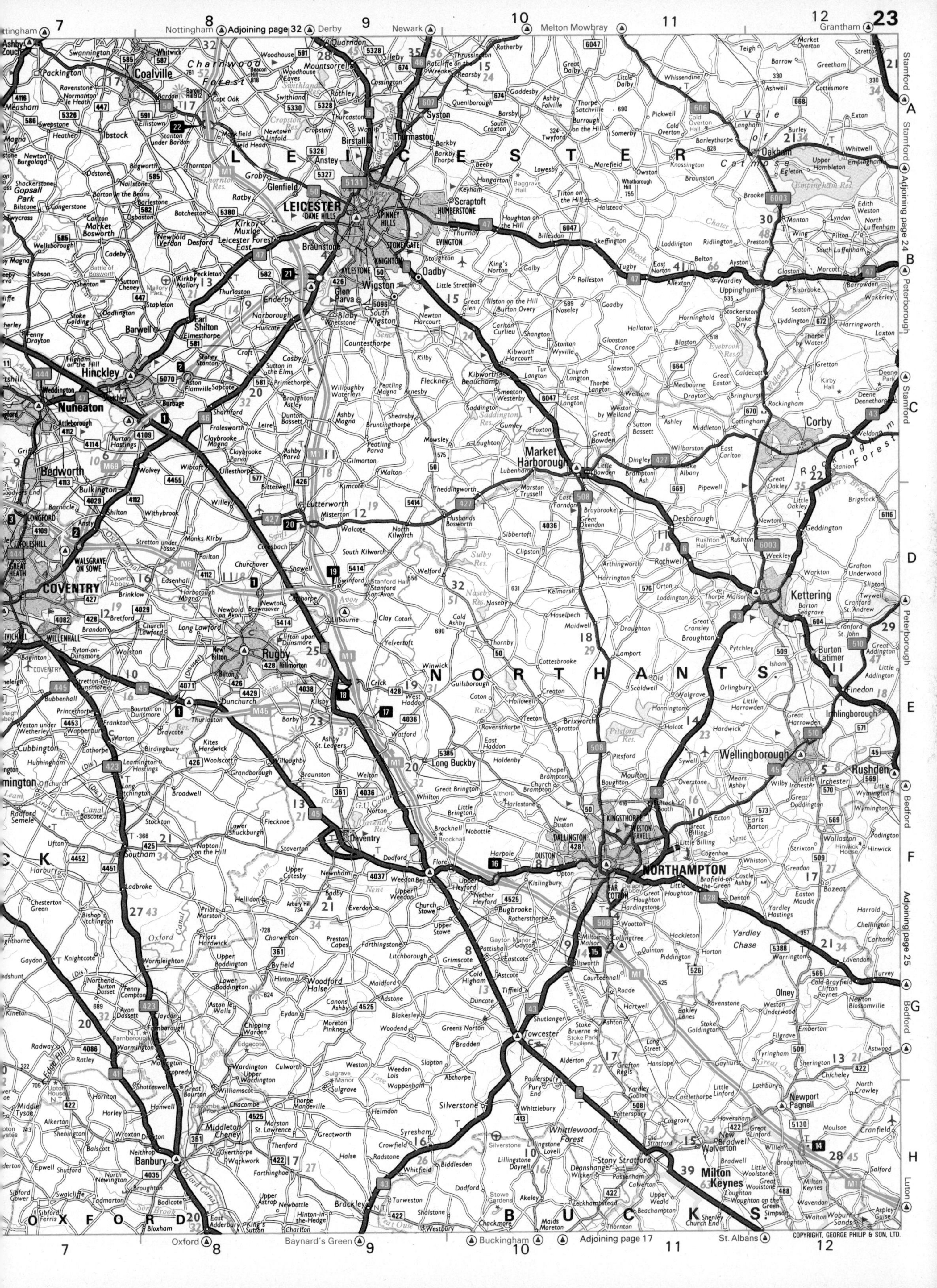

Nottingham
Adjoining page 32
Derby
Newark
Melton Mowbray
Grantham
Stamford
Adjoining page 24
Peterborough
Adjoining page 25
Bedford
Luton
Oxford
Baynard's Green
Buckingham
Adjoining page 17
St. Albans
LEICESTER
NORTHANTS.
OXFORD
BUCKS.
LEICESTER
NORTHAMPTON
COVENTRY
Coalville
Hinckley
Nuneaton
Bedworth
Rugby
Lutterworth
Market Harborough
Corby
Kettering
Wellingborough
Rushden
Daventry
Towcester
Banbury
Brackley
Milton Keynes
Newport Pagnell
Olney
Oakham
Uppingham
Melton Mowbray
Syston
Wigston
Oadby
Desborough
Rothwell
Long Buckby
Southam
Stony Stratford
Wolverton
Charnwood Forest
Rockingham Forest
Whittlewood Forest
Vale of Catmose
Yardley Chase
COPYRIGHT, GEORGE PHILIP & SON, LTD.

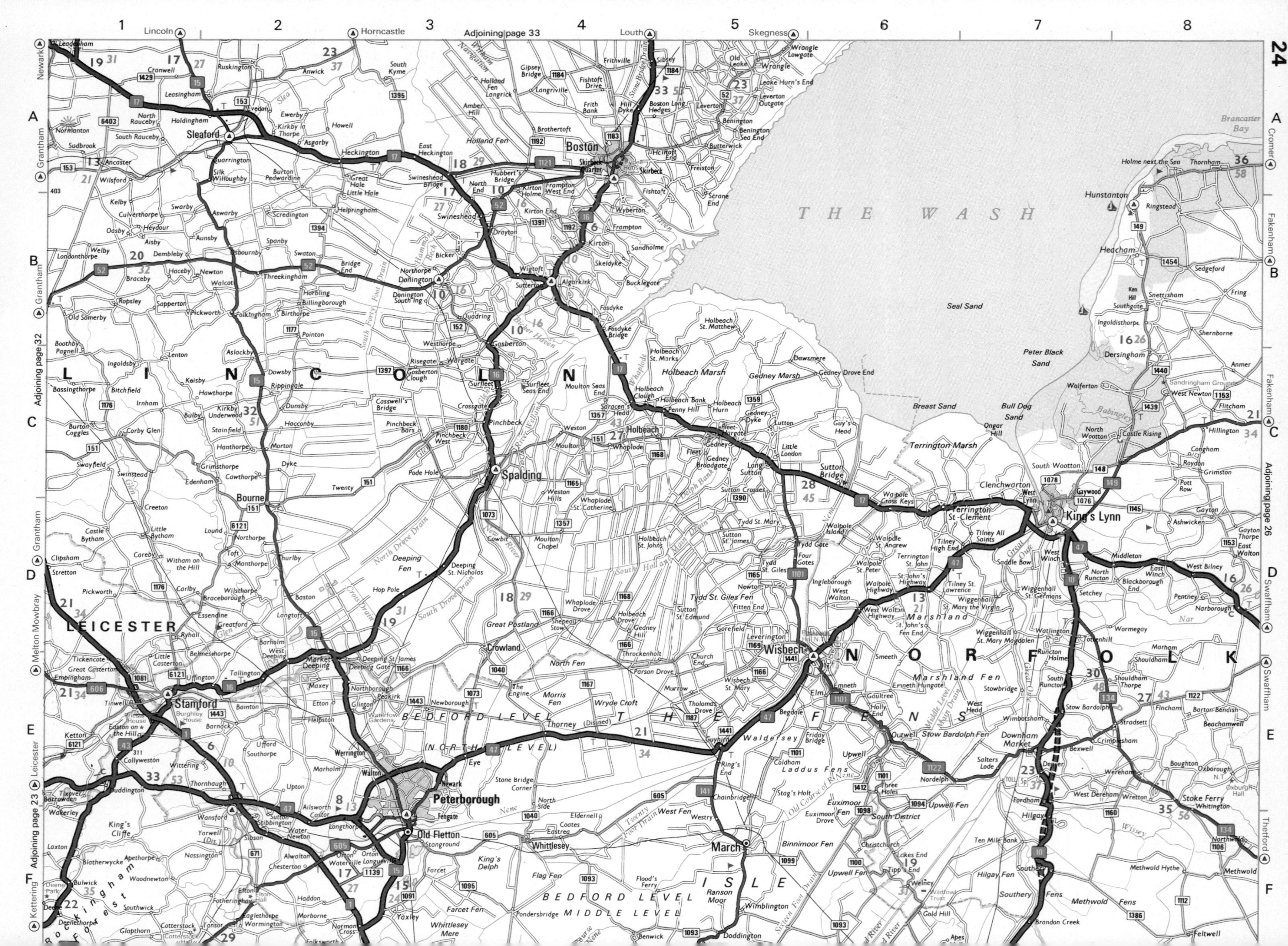
Lincoln
Horncastle
Adjoining page 33
Louth
Skegness
Newark
Grantham
Grantham
Adjoining page 32
Grantham
Melton Mowbray
Leicester
Adjoining page 23
Kettering
Cromer
Fakenham
Fakenham
Adjoining page 26
Swaffham
Swaffham
Thetford
THE WASH
Brancaster Bay
Seal Sand
Peter Black Sand
Breast Sand
Bull Dog Sand
LINCOLN
LEICESTER
NORFOLK
THE FENS
ISLE
BEDFORD LEVEL
(NORTH LEVEL)
BEDFORD LEVEL MIDDLE LEVEL
Rockingham Forest
Sleaford
Boston
Spalding
Bourne
Stamford
Market Deeping
Peterborough
Old Fletton
Crowland
Thorney
Whittlesey
March
Wisbech
Holbeach
Long Sutton
Sutton Bridge
King's Lynn
Hunstanton
Heacham
Dersingham
Castle Rising
Gaywood
Downham Market
Hilgay
Southery
Stoke Ferry
Methwold
Feltwell
Upwell
Outwell
Terrington St. Clement
Terrington Marsh
Clenchwarton
Holbeach Marsh
Gedney Marsh
Marshland
Marshland Fen
Deeping Fen
Deeping St. Nicholas
Donington
Swineshead
Heckington
Kirton
Gosberton
Pinchbeck
Ancaster
Holland Fen

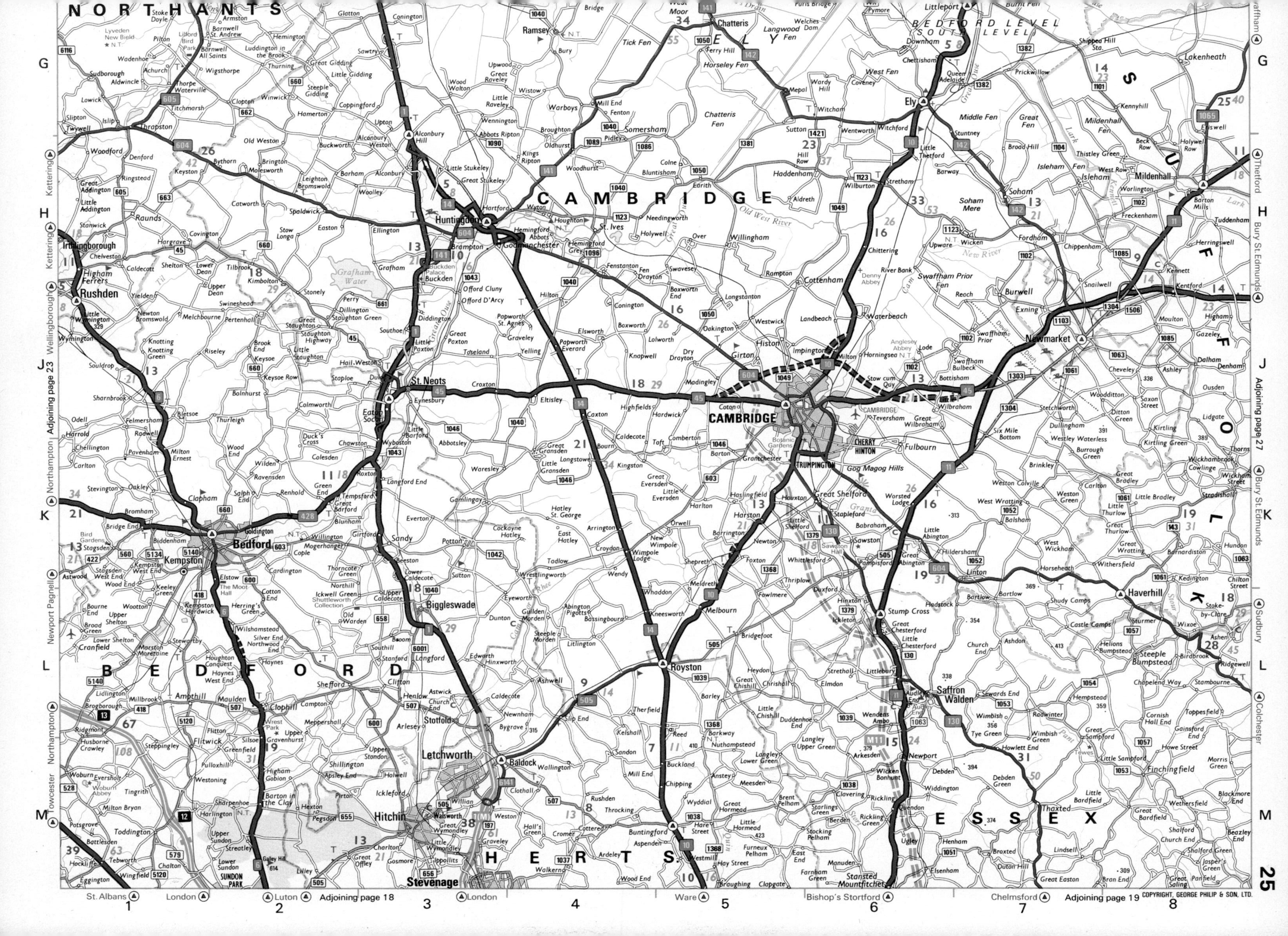

NORTHANTS
CAMBRIDGE
BEDFORD
HERTS.
ESSEX
SUFFOLK
ELY
BEDFORD LEVEL
SOUTH LEVEL
CAMBRIDGE
Huntingdon
St. Ives
St. Neots
Bedford
Kempston
Biggleswade
Letchworth
Hitchin
Stevenage
Baldock
Royston
Saffron Walden
Haverhill
Newmarket
Ely
Mildenhall
Soham
Chatteris
Ramsey
Rushden
Irthlingborough
Thrapston
Adjoining page 23
Adjoining page 18
Adjoining page 19
Adjoining page 27
St. Albans
London
Luton
Ware
Bishop's Stortford
Chelmsford
Thetford
Bury St. Edmunds
Sudbury
Colchester
Kettering
Wellingborough
Northampton
Newport Pagnell
Towcester
COPYRIGHT, GEORGE PHILIP & SON, LTD.

NORTH SEA

NORFOLK

THE BROADS

BRECKLAND

Hunstanton
Wells-next-the-Sea
Blakeney
Sheringham
Cromer
Mundesley
North Walsham
Fakenham
Holt
Aylsham
Reepham
Foulsham
North Elmham
East Dereham
Swaffham
Watton
Shipdham
Hingham
Wymondham
Attleborough
NORWICH
Acle
Hoveton
Horning
Martham
Hemsby
Caister-on-Sea
Great Yarmouth
Gorleston on Sea
Reedham
Loddon
Lowestoft
Beccles
King's Lynn
Wisbech

Adjoining page 24

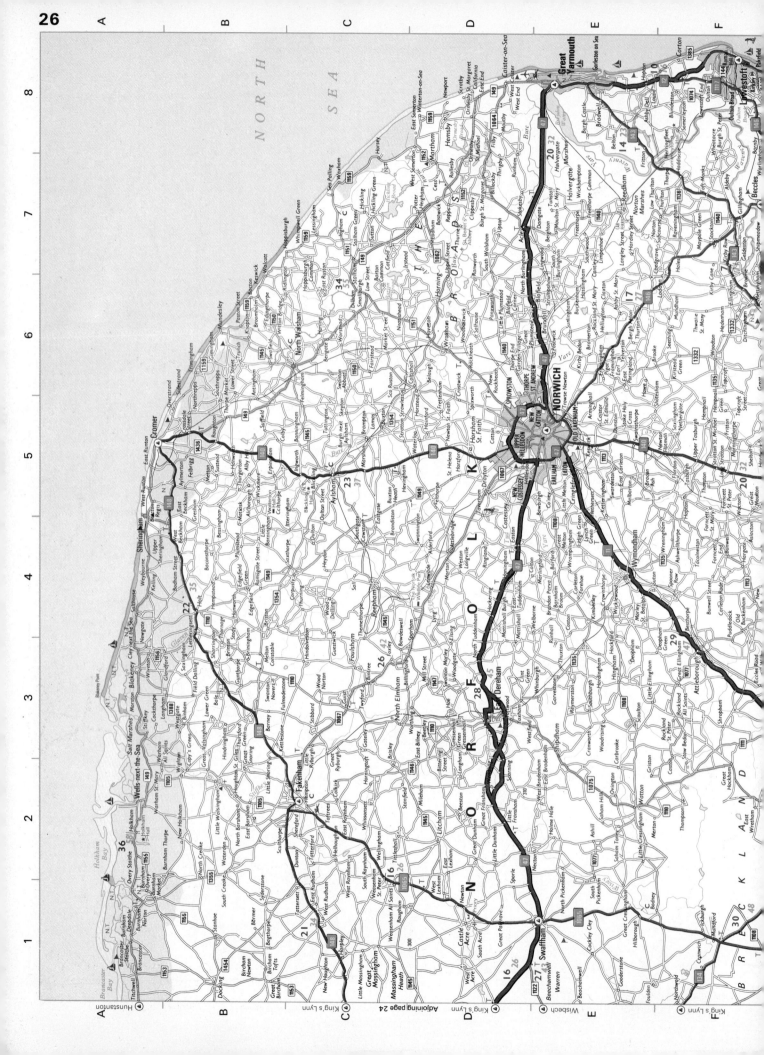

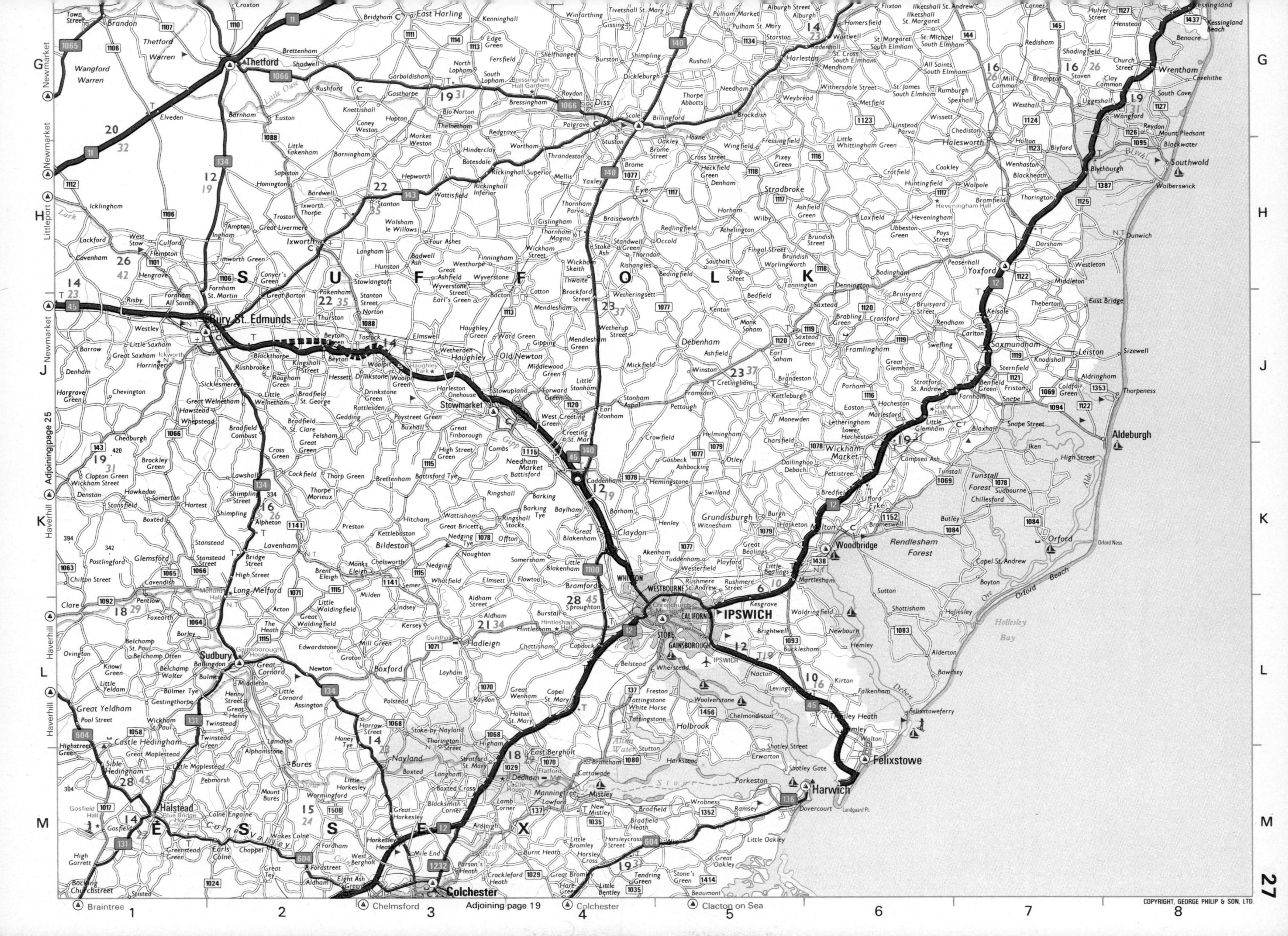

SUFFOLK
ESSEX
IPSWICH
Bury St. Edmunds
Colchester
Felixstowe
Harwich
Aldeburgh
Southwold
Stowmarket
Sudbury
Woodbridge
Thetford
Halstead
Framlingham
Saxmundham
Halesworth
Diss
Eye
Hadleigh
Rendlesham Forest
Hollesley Bay
Adjoining page 25
Adjoining page 19
Braintree
Chelmsford
Colchester
Clacton on Sea
Newmarket
Littleport
Haverhill

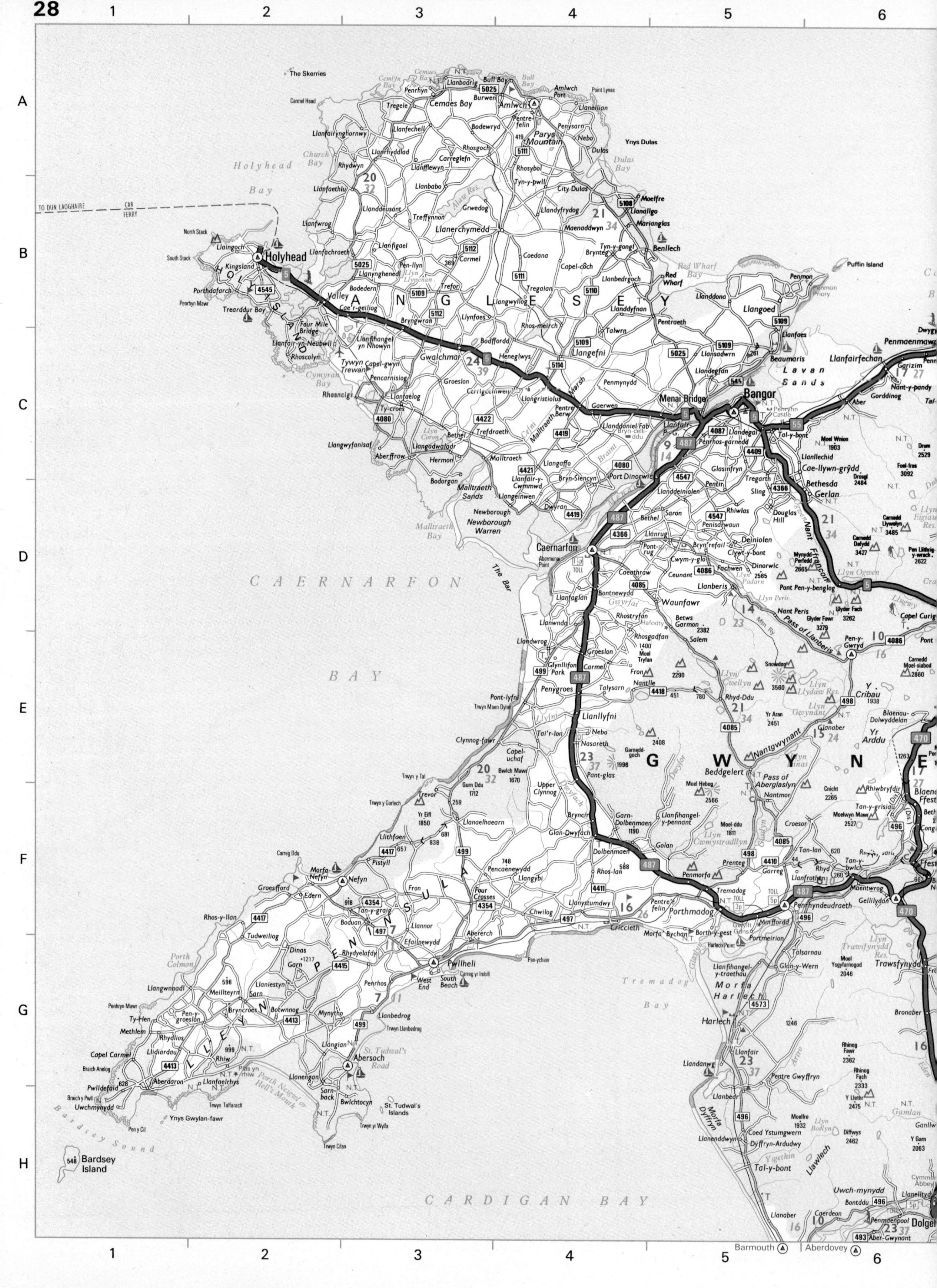

The Skerries
Carmel Head
Cemaes Bay
Bull Bay
Amlwch
Amlwch Port
Point Lynas
Llaneilian
Tregele
Llanfechell
Bodewryd
Parys Mountain
Penysarn
Nebo
Dulas
Ynys Dulas
Llanfairynghornwy
Church Bay
Holyhead Bay
Rhydwyn
Llanrhyddlad
Rhosgoch
Carreglefn
Llanfflewyn
Rhosybol
Dulas Bay
Llanfaethlu
Llanbabo
Tyn-y-pwll
City Dulas
Moelfre
Llanallgo
Marianglas
Llanddeusant
Alaw Res.
Grwedog
Llandyfrydog
TO DUN LAOGHAIRE
CAR FERRY
Llanfwrog
Treffynnon
Llanerchymedd
Maenaddwyn
North Stack
Llanfigael
Tyn-y-gongl
Benllech
Brynteg
Llaingoch
Holyhead
South Stack
Llanfachraeth
Kingsland
Pen-llyn
Carmel
Coedana
Capel-coch
Red Wharf Bay
Puffin Island
Llanynghenedl
Llanbedrgoch
Red Wharf
Penmon
Penmon Priory
Porthdafarch
Bodedern
Trefor
Tregaian
Penrhyn Mawr
Trearddur Bay
Valley
Caer-geiliog
ANGLESEY
HOLY ISLAND
Llanddona
Llangoed
Llangwyllog
Llanddyfnan
Bryngwran
Llynfaes
Rhos-meirch
Pentraeth
Four Mile Bridge
Llanfair-yn-Neubwll
Llanfihangel yn Nhowyn
Bodffordd
Talwrn
Llanfaes
Penmaenmawr
Llangefni
Llansadwrn
Beaumaris
Llanfairfechan
Rhoscolyn
Tywyn Trewan
Capel-gwyn
Gwalchmai
Heneglwys
Lavan Sands
Cymyran Bay
Pencarnisiog
Llandegfan
Garizim
Nant-y-pandy
Rhosneigr
Groeslon
Penmynydd
Bangor
Llanfaelog
Menai Bridge
Aber
Gorddinog
Ty-croes
Llangristiolus
Gaerwen
Penrhyn Castle
Pentre Berw
Malltraeth Marsh
Llyn Coron
Bethel
Trefdraeth
Llanddaniel Fab
Llanfair-P.G.
Llandegai
Tal-y-bont
Moel Wnion
Llangwyfan-isaf
Llangadwaladr
Bryn-celli-ddu
Penrhos-garnedd
Llanllechid
Aberffraw
Hermon
Malltraeth
Llangaffo
Cae-llywn-grŷdd
Foel-fras
Glasinfryn
Bodorgan
Llanfair-y-Cwmmwd
Bryn-Siencyn
Port Dinorwic
Pentir
Tregarth
Bethesda
Gerlan
Malltraeth Sands
Sling
Llanddeiniolen
Newborough
Llangeinwen
Dwyran
Newborough Warren
Rhiwlas
Douglas Hill
Malltraeth Bay
Saron
Penisarwaun
Bethel
Caernarfon
Llanrug
Deiniolen
Pont-rug
Bryn'refail
Clwyt-y-bont
Cwm-y-glo
Dinorwic
Abermenai Point
Fachwen
CAERNARFON BAY
The Bar
Caeathraw
Ceunant
Llyn Padarn
Llanberis
Nant Ffrancon
Llyn Ogwen
Pont Pen-y-benglog
Bontnewydd
Llanfaglan
Gwyrfai
Waunfawr
Llyn Peris
Nant Peris
Pass of Llanberis
Glyder Fawr
Glyder Fach
Capel Curig
Llanwnda
Rhostryfan
Hafodty
Betws Garmon
Rhosgadfan
Moel Tryfan
Salem
Pen-y-Gwryd
Pont
Llandwrog
Groeslon
Carmel
Glynllifon Park
Fron
Snowdon
Llyn Cwellyn
Llyn Llydaw Res.
BAY
Penygroes
Talysarn
Nantlle
Rhyd-Ddu
Yr Aran
Y Cribau
Moel-siabod
Pont-lyfni
Trwyn Maen Dylan
Llanllyfni
Llyn Gwynant
Blaenau-Dolwyddelan
Tai'r-lon
Nebo
Nasareth
Garnedd-goch
Glanaber
Yr Arddu
Clynnog-fawr
Capel-uchaf
Nantgwynant
GWYNEDD
Bwlch Mawr
Pant-glas
Dwyfor
Beddgelert
Pass of Aberglaslyn
Nantmor
Cnicht
Moel Hebog
Trwyn y Tal
Gurn Ddu
Upper Clynnog
Rhiwbryfdir
Blaenau Ffestiniog
Trevor
Tan-y-grisiau
Moelwyn Mawr
Trwyn y Gorlech
Yr Eifl
Llanaelhaearn
Bryncir
Garn-Dolbenmaen
Llanfihangel-y-pennant
Croesor
Moel-ddu
Llyn Cwmystradllyn
Glan-Dwyfach
Llithfaen
Golan
Tan-lan
Carreg Ddu
Pistyll
Dolbenmaen
Prenteg
Garreg
Rhyd
Tan-y-bwlch
Ffestiniog
Morfa-Nefyn
Nefyn
Pencaenewydd
Llangybi
Rhos-lan
Penmorfa
Llanfrothen
Maentwrog
Groesffordd
Edern
Fron
Four Crosses
Tremadog
Gellilydan
Tan-y-graig
Chwilog
Llanystumdwy
Pentrefelin
Porthmadog
Penrhyndeudraeth
Rhos-y-llan
Boduan
Llannor
Criccieth
Morfa Bychan
Borth-y-gest
Minffordd
Tudweiliog
Dinas
Efailnewydd
Abererch
Harlech Point
Portmeirion
Porth Colmon
Garn
Rhydyclafdy
Pwllheli
Pen-ychain
Talsarnau
Llyn Trawsfynydd Res.
Trawsfynydd
Llangwnnadl
Meillteyrn
Llaniestyn
Sarn
West End
South Beach
Carreg yr Imbill
Tremadog Bay
Llanfihangel-y-traethau
Glan-y-Wern
Moel Ysgyfarnogod
LLEYN PENINSULA
Penrhos
Morfa Harlech
Penhryn Mawr
Bryncroes
Botwnnog
Pen-y-groeslon
Mynytho
Llanbedrog
Trwyn Llanbedrog
Harlech
Bronaber
Ty-Hen
Methlem
Rhydlios
Llangian
Capel Carmel
Llidiardau
Rhiw
St. Tudwal's Road
Abersoch
Llanfair
Rhinog Fawr
Rhinog Fach
Llandanwg
Braich Anelog
Aberdaron
Llanfaelrhys
Porth Neigwl or Hell's Mouth
Llanengan
Sarn-back
Bwlchtocyn
Pentre Gwyffryn
Y Llethr
Pwlldefaid
Braich y Pwll
Uwchmynydd
Trwyn Talfarach
Ynys Gwylan-fawr
St. Tudwal's Islands
Trwyn yr Wylfa
Llanbedr
Morfa Dyffryn
Moelfre
Llyn Bodlyn
Diffwys
Y Garn
Gamlan
Bardsey Sound
Pen y Cil
Coed Ystumgwern
Dyffryn-Ardudwy
Llanenddwyn
Trwyn Cilan
Bardsey Island
Ysgethin
Llawlech
Tal-y-bont
Cymmer Abbey
CARDIGAN BAY
Uwch-mynydd
Bontddu
Llanelltyd
Llanaber
Caerdeon
Penmaenpool
Dolgellau
Aber-Gwynant
Barmouth
Aberdovey

29
Adjoining page 34
Southport
Preston
TO DUBLIN
LIVERPOOL
Bootle
WALLASEY
MERSEYSIDE
BIRKENHEAD
Hoylake
West Kirby
Bebington
Heswall
Neston
CHES.
Llandudno
Colwyn Bay
Conwy
Rhyl
Prestatyn
Abergele
St. Asaph
Holywell
Flint
Denbigh
Mold
Buckley
Ruthin
Wrexham
Llangollen
Ruabon
Chirk
Oswestry
Corwen
Bala
Llanrwst
Betws-y-coed
Cerrigydrudion
Llanfyllin
CLWYD
POWYS
SALOP
CAMBRIAN MOUNTAINS
Mynydd Hiraethog
Clocaenog Forest
Berwyn
Migneint
Brenig Res.
Alwen Res.
Llyn Celyn
Llyn Tegid or Bala Lake
Clwydian Range
Halkyn Mountain
Llantysilio Mountain
Eglwyseg Mountain
Valley of Conwy
Point of Air
Abergele Roads
Manchester
Warrington
Chester
Nantwich
Whitchurch
Overton
Shrewsbury
Machynlleth
Mallwyd
Welshpool
Adjoining page 30
Adjoining page 20
Adjoining page 21
COPYRIGHT, GEORGE PHILIP & SON, LTD.

Southport Preston Adjoining page 34 Wigan Manchester Manchester

SALFORD

MERSEYSIDE

Waterloo ORRELL ST. HELENS Haydock Glazebury Chat Moss Irlam Urmston M63
Seaforth Knowsley Eccleston Newton-Le-Willows Culcheth TRAFFORD
Bootle WALTON ON THE HILL Thatto Heath Collins Green Cadishead Partington MANCHESTER
New Brighton WEST DERBY PEASLEY CROSS SUTTON Burtonwood Croft Ashton upon Mersey Altrincham

WALLASEY EGREMONT **LIVERPOOL** Everton Prescot Rainhill Burtonwood Warrington Woolston Hollins Green Broadheath Hale
Hoylake MORETON Roby Whiston Clock Face Great Sankey Thelwall Dunham Bollington
West Kirby Greasby BIRKENHEAD Huyton Penketh Lymm Hale
Heswall Bebington Widnes Runcorn Stockton Heath Appleton Mere Knutsford
  Bromborough Frodsham Preston Brook Higher Whitley Over Tabley
Greenfield Neston Ellesmere Port Helsby Norton Lower Whitley Mobberley
Holywell Parkgate Overpool Manchester Ship Canal Comberbach Northwich Pickmere Plumley
Flint Childer Thornton Whitby Thornton-le-Moors Kingsley Weaverham Barnton Lostock Gralam
  Little Stanney Dunham-on-the-Hill Acton Bridge Hartford Lostock Green
Mold Connah's Quay Backford Picton Manley Cuddington Davenham Holmes Chapel
Buckley Queensferry Upton Mickle Trafford Ashton Kelsall Delamere Moulton Byley
Shotton Mancot **CHESTER** Hoole Guilden Sutton Oscroft Little Budworth Winsford Middlewich
Broughton Saltney Handbridge Christleton Kelsall Quarrybank Eaton Swettenham
Wrexham Bretton Rowton Waverton Tarporley Rushton Occleston Green Brereton Green
  Dodleston Saighton Hatton Heath Huxley Tiverton Rhuddall Heath Wettenhall Sandbach
Hope Pulford Aldford Milton Green Beeston Alpraham Calveley Church Minshull
Gresford Rossett Poulton Handley Burwardsley Bunbury Wardle Aston juxta Mondrum Crewe
Brymbo Marford Clutton Peckforton Spurstow Haughton Moss Poole Green Haslington
  Farndon Barton Broxton Bickerton Ridley Green Faddiley Burland Wistaston
Wrexham Holt Crewe Stretton Fuller's Moor Acton Willaston
  Acton Park Tilston Edge Green Duckington Chorley Ravensmoor Nantwich Shavington
Coedpoeth Bersham Horton Green Hampton Heath Bickley Moss Wrenbury Newtown Audlem
Rhostyllen Shocklach Chorlton Lane Malpas No Man's Heath Norbury Stapeley Betley
Johnstown Cross Lanes Cuddington Heath Bradley Green Marbury Hankelow Wybunbury Wrinehill
Ruabon Bangor-is-coed Worthenbury Threapwood Wirswall Combermere Newhall Checkley Madeley
Acrefair Eyton Hanmer Tallarn Green Grindley Brook Whitchurch Audlem Buerton Onneley
Cefn Mawr Overton Penley Holly Bush Higher Wych Redbrook Broughall Woore Pipe Gate
Newbridge Overton Bridge Horseman's Green Welshampton Fenn's Moss Ash Magna Wilkesley Knighton
Llangollen Erbistock Dudleston Bronington Tilstock Ightfield Adderley Norton in Hales Blackbrook
Froncysyllte Halton Knolton Fenn's Moss Sandy Bank Higher Heath Calverhall Muckleston Ashley
Chirk Pentre Street Dinas Dudleston Heath Coton Hall Prees Longslow Market Drayton Loggerheads
Glyn Ceiriog Chirk Green St. Martin's Bettisfield Whixall Northwood Moreton Say Hales Hookgate
Pandy New Marton Welshampton Lyneal Coton Hall Edstaston Longford Ternhill Chipnall
  Weston Rhyn Gobowen Welsh Frankton Lee Colemere Pressgreen Bletchley Bishops Wood
Chirk Gobowen Whittington Hordley Kenwick Wolverley Marchamley Wollerton Sutton Bishop's Offley
Llansilin Hindford Babbinswood Cockshutt English Frankton Loppington Aston Rosehill Cheswardine
Oswestry Middleton Rednal Lower Hordley Bagley Tilley Wem Stoke upon Tern Goldstone
Llangedwyn Morda Queen's Head Haughton Noneley Weston Hodnet Hodnet Hall Hinstock Adbaston
Trefonen Maesbury West Felton Petton Clive Stanton upon Hine Heath Peplow Ellerton Shebdon
  Maesbury Marsh Wykey Burlton Grinshill Ollerton Child's Ercall Knighton Woodseaves
Llanyblodwel Woolston Eardiston Weston Lullingfields Myddle Alderton High Ercall Sambrook Norbury
Llansantffraid-ym-Mechain Crickheath Stanwardine in the Field Clive Eaton upon Tern Meretown Sutton
  Llanymynech Sandford Shotatton Great Wytheford Rowton Edgmond **Newport** Chetwynd Aston
POWYS Crosslanes Knockin Ruyton Eleven Towns Preston Gubbals Hadnall Waters Upton Puleston Pave Lane
  Kinnerley Nesscliffe Little Ness Walford Heath Astley Crudgington Church Aston
Four Crosses Llandrinio Wilcott Kinton Leaton Albrighton Poynton Green Sleap Kynnersley
  Deuddwr Melverley Pentre Butler Ensdon Grafton Roden High Ercall Adeney

Neuadd Welshpool Shrewsbury Shrewsbury Shrewsbury Adjoining page 21 Wellington Wellington Wolverh'ton

CLWYD **CHESHIRE** **SALOP**

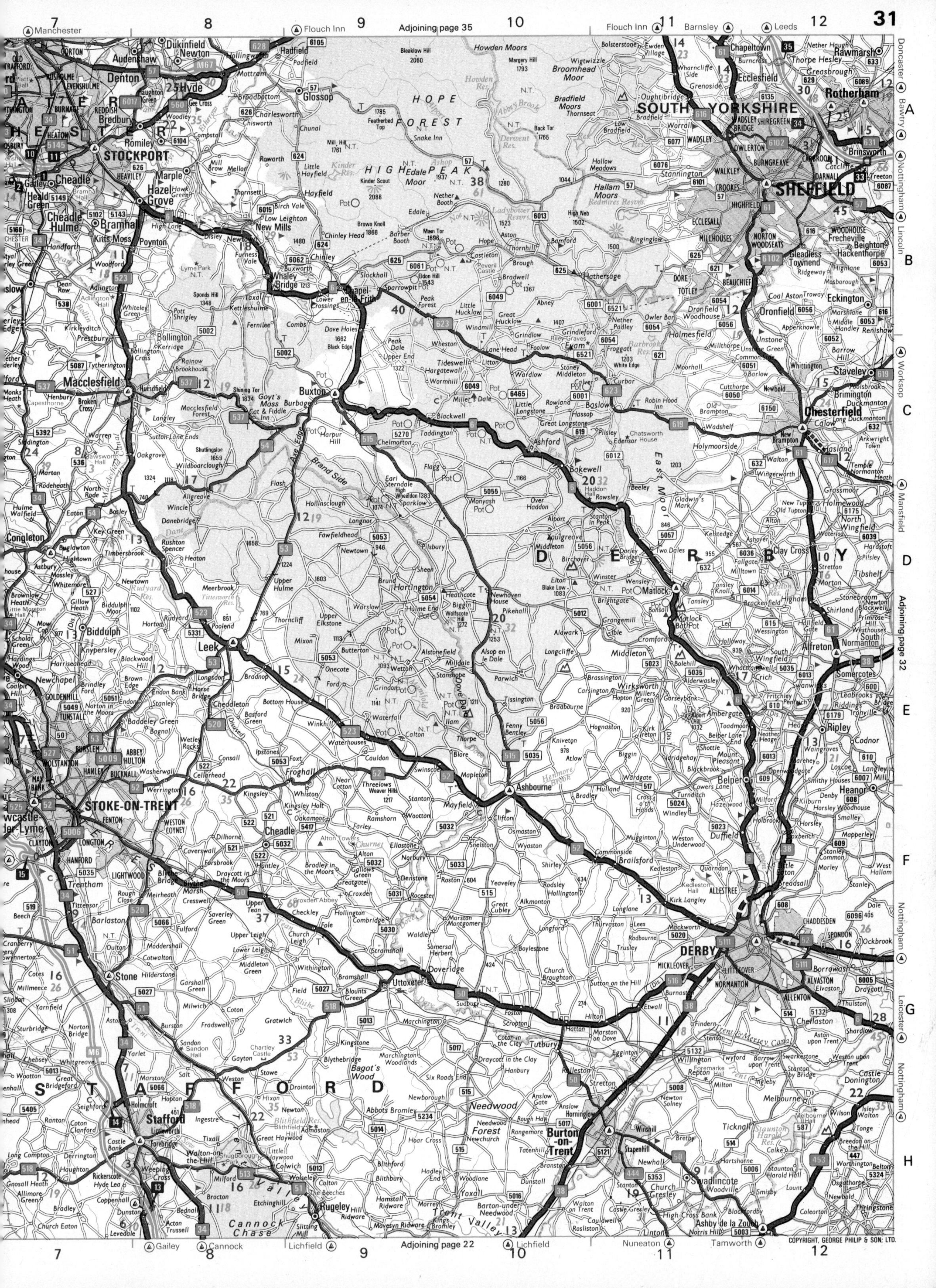

Adjoining page 35
Manchester
Flouch Inn
Barnsley
Leeds
Doncaster
Bawtry
Nottingham
Lincoln
Worksop
Mansfield
Adjoining page 32
Leicester
Adjoining page 22
Gailey
Cannock
Lichfield
Nuneaton
Tamworth
7
8
9
10
11
12
A
B
C
D
E
F
G
H
SOUTH YORKSHIRE
HOPE FOREST
HIGH PEAK
D E R B Y
S T A F F O R D
Audenshaw
Denton
Hyde
Glossop
Hadfield
Stockport
Cheadle
Hazel Grove
Bramhall
Marple
New Mills
Whaley Bridge
Chapel-en-le-Frith
Macclesfield
Buxton
Congleton
Biddulph
Leek
Stoke-on-Trent
Newcastle-under-Lyme
Stone
Stafford
Cheadle
Uttoxeter
Ashbourne
Rugeley
Burton-on-Trent
Swadlincote
Ashby de la Zouch
Derby
Belper
Matlock
Bakewell
Chesterfield
Sheffield
Rotherham
Dronfield
Clay Cross
Alfreton
Ripley
Heanor
Staveley
Kinder Scout
Edale Moor
Howden Moors
Broomhead Moor
Bradfield Moors
Hallam Moors
East Moor
Cannock Chase
Needwood Forest
Bagot's Wood
Trent Valley

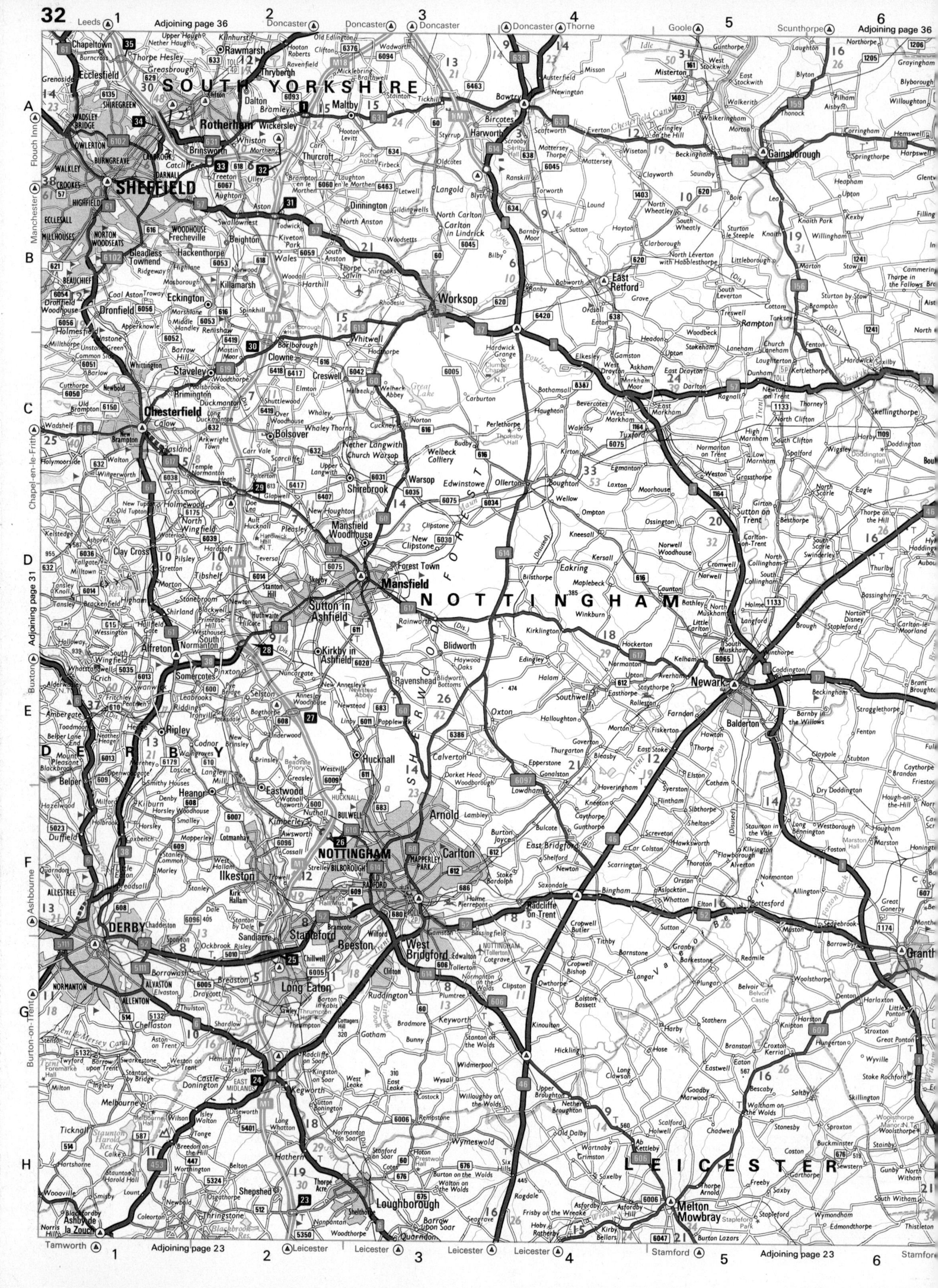
Adjoining page 36
Adjoining page 31
Adjoining page 23
Leeds
Doncaster
Thorne
Goole
Scunthorpe
Flouch Inn
Manchester
Chapel-en-le-Frith
Buxton
Ashbourne
Burton-on-Trent
Tamworth
Leicester
Stamford
SOUTH YORKSHIRE
NOTTINGHAM
DERBY
LEICESTER
SHEFFIELD
Rotherham
Chesterfield
Worksop
Mansfield
Sutton in Ashfield
Kirkby in Ashfield
Alfreton
Ripley
Heanor
Ilkeston
Eastwood
Hucknall
Arnold
Carlton
NOTTINGHAM
West Bridgford
Beeston
Stapleford
Long Eaton
DERBY
Belper
Duffield
Loughborough
Melton Mowbray
Ashby de la Zouch
Shepshed
Newark
Balderton
East Retford
Gainsborough
Bawtry
Harworth
Maltby
Dinnington
Staveley
Bolsover
Clowne
Shirebrook
Mansfield Woodhouse
Southwell
Bingham
Radcliffe on Trent
Dronfield
Eckington
Clay Cross
Tuxford
Ollerton
Edwinstowe
Blidworth
Ravenshead
Calverton
Keyworth
Kegworth
Castle Donington
Melbourne
Sherwood Forest
Grantham

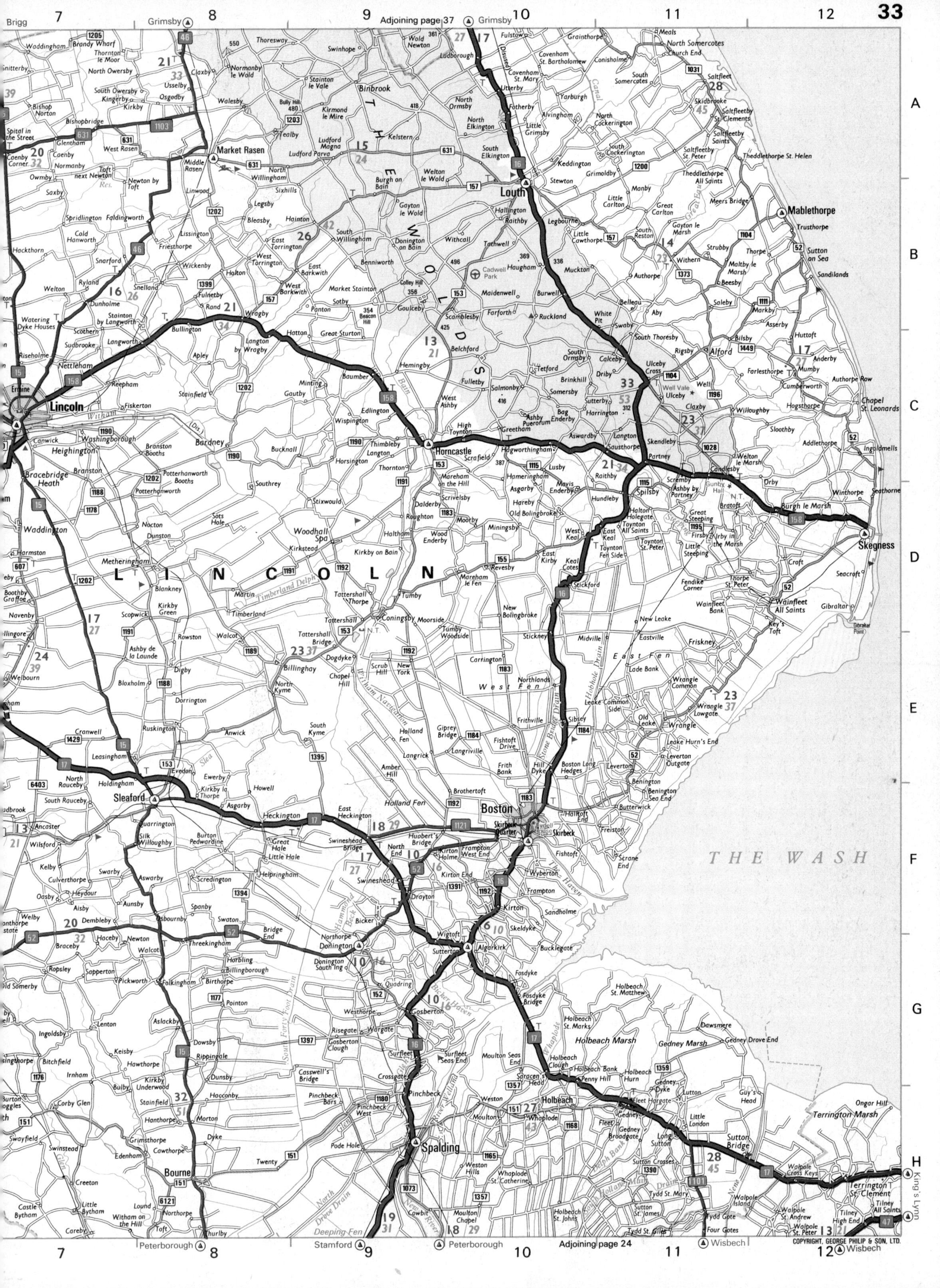
Adjoining page 37
Grimsby
Brigg
7
8
9
10
11
12
A
B
C
D
E
F
G
H
THE WOLDS
LINCOLN
THE WASH
Lincoln
Market Rasen
Louth
Mablethorpe
Sutton on Sea
Alford
Horncastle
Spilsby
Skegness
Woodhall Spa
Coningsby
Tattershall
Boston
Sleaford
Spalding
Holbeach
Bourne
Sutton Bridge
Wainfleet All Saints
Burgh le Marsh
Chapel St. Leonards
Saltfleet
Binbrook
Wragby
Billinghay
Heckington
Donington
Kirton
Swineshead
Pinchbeck
Long Sutton
Gedney
Terrington Marsh
Terrington St. Clement
King's Lynn
Waddington
Bracebridge Heath
Washingborough
Nettleham
Welton
Metheringham
Ruskington
Leasingham
Holbeach Marsh
Gedney Marsh
Holland Fen
East Fen
West Fen
Deeping Fen
Witham
Peterborough
Stamford
Wisbech
Adjoining page 24
COPYRIGHT, GEORGE PHILIP & SON, LTD.

Adjoining page 38
Adjoining page 39
Adjoining page 30
Kendal
Settle
Chester
Stoke-on-Trent
Isle of Walney
Biggar
Rampside
Roa Island
Piel Castle
Piel Island
Foulney Island
Sheep Island
South End
Morecambe
Heysham
Lancaster
Halton
Caton
Caton Moor
Claughton
Littledale
Clougha
Ward's Stone
Tatham Fells
Burn Moor
Mallowdale Fell
Croasdale Fell
Gisburn Forest
FOREST OF BOWLAND
Hawthornthwaite Fell
Sykes Fell
Bleasdale Moors
Slaidburn
Newton
Easington Fell
Sunderland
Glasson
Shoulder of Lune
Cockerham
Cockerham Sands
Pilling
Fleetwood
Knott End-on-Sea
Preesall
Cleveleys
Thornton
Garstang
Chipping
Longridge Fell
Waddington
Clitheroe
BISPHAM
BLACKPOOL
NORTH SHORE
SOUTH SHORE
Poulton-Le-Fylde
Kirkham
Longridge
Ribchester
Fulwood
PRESTON
Lytham St. Anne's
Lytham
Freckleton
Warton
Higher Penwortham
Walton-Le-Dale
Bamber Bridge
BLACKBURN
Great Harwood
Clayton-Le-Moors
Rishton
Church
Oswaldtwistle
Darwen
Haslingden
LANCASHIRE
Leyland
Chorley
Euxton
Anglezarke Moor
Hesketh Bank
Tarleton
Banks
Southport
Birkdale Sands
Ainsdale
Formby
Formby Hills
Ormskirk
Burscough Bridge
Skelmersdale
Up Holland
Standish
Wigan
Horwich
Adlington
Westhoughton
Hindley
Ince-in-Makerfield
Atherton
Leigh
Tyldesley
Walkden
Farnworth
BOLTON
GREATER MANCHESTER
Maghull
Crosby
LIVERPOOL BAY
Bootle
Kirkby
Rainford
ST. HELENS
Haydock
Newton-Le-Willows
Ashton-in-Makerfield
Golborne
Eccles
Worsley
Irlam
Urmston
Partington
Chat Moss
MERSEYSIDE
WALLASEY
LIVERPOOL
BIRKENHEAD
Hoylake
West Kirby
Huyton
Roby
Prescot
Whiston
Widnes
Warrington
Great Sankey
Penketh
Lymm
Thelwall
Stockton Heath
Halewood
Woolton
TO DOUGLAS
TO BELFAST
TO DUBLIN CAR FERRY

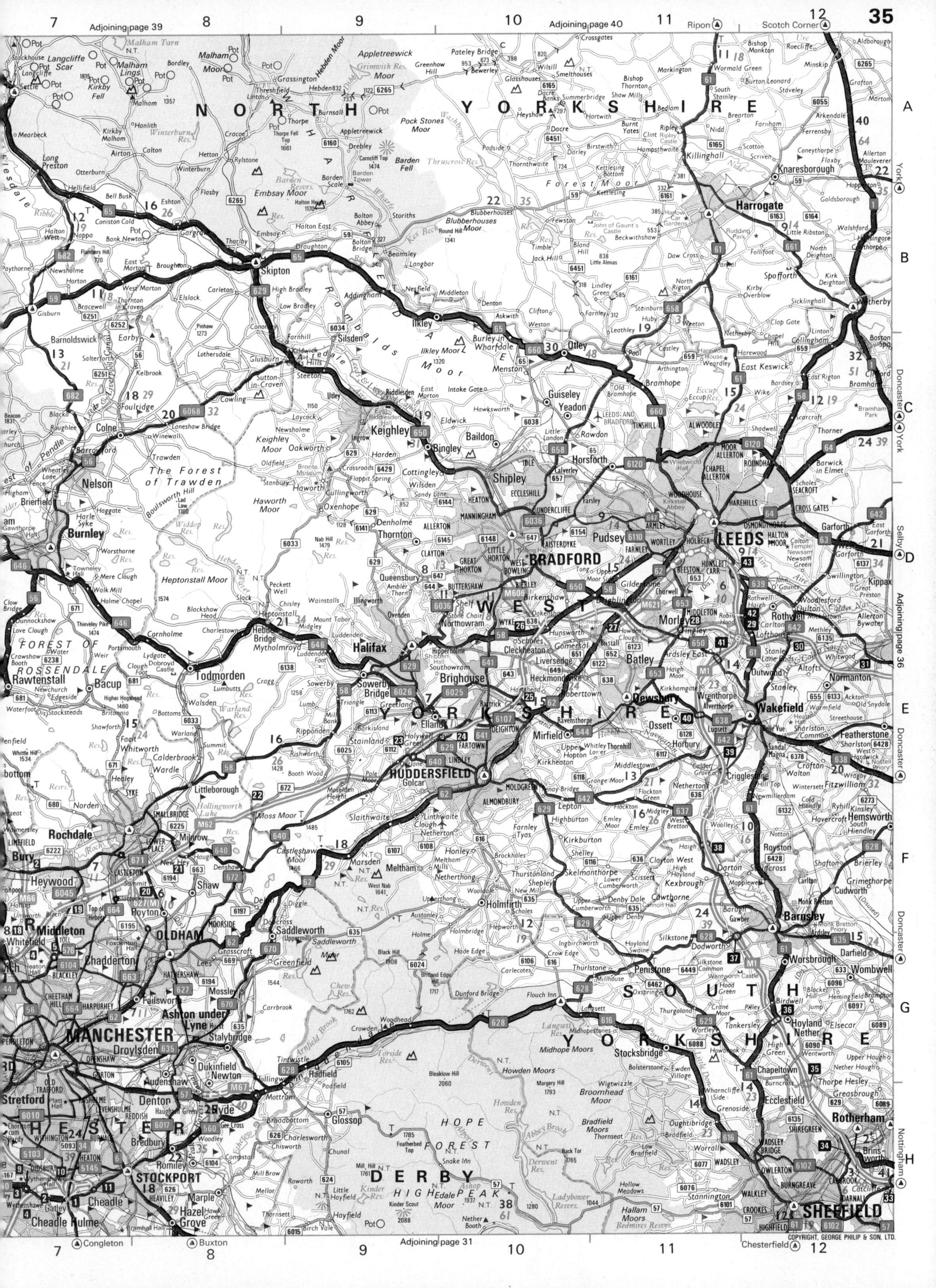

Adjoining page 39
Adjoining page 40
Adjoining page 36
Adjoining page 31
7
8
9
10
11
12
A
B
C
D
E
F
G
H
Ripon
Scotch Corner
York
Doncaster
Selby
Nottingham
Congleton
Buxton
Chesterfield
NORTH YORKSHIRE
WEST YORKSHIRE
SOUTH YORKSHIRE
DERBY
Settle
Malham
Grassington
Pateley Bridge
Skipton
Ilkley
Otley
Harrogate
Knaresborough
Wetherby
Keighley
Bingley
Shipley
Baildon
Guiseley
Yeadon
Horsforth
Pudsey
LEEDS
BRADFORD
Halifax
Brighouse
Huddersfield
Dewsbury
Batley
Morley
Rothwell
Wakefield
Ossett
Mirfield
Holmfirth
Penistone
Barnsley
Stocksbridge
Rotherham
SHEFFIELD
Todmorden
Hebden Bridge
Burnley
Nelson
Colne
Barnoldswick
Bacup
Rawtenstall
Rochdale
Littleborough
Milnrow
Heywood
Bury
Middleton
OLDHAM
Chadderton
Royton
Shaw
Saddleworth
Mossley
Ashton under Lyne
Stalybridge
Dukinfield
Hyde
Glossop
Denton
MANCHESTER
Droylsden
Stretford
STOCKPORT
Cheadle
Cheadle Hulme
Marple
Hazel Grove
Bredbury
Romiley
Featherstone
Normanton
Hemsworth
Garforth
Kippax
Castleford
Darfield
Wombwell
Hoyland Nether
Chapeltown
Ecclesfield
Sowerby Bridge
Elland
Cleckheaton
Heckmondwike
Liversedge
Horbury
Otley
Burley in Wharfdale
Menston
Forest of Rossendale
The Forest of Trawden
Rombalds Moor
Ilkley Moor
Haworth Moor
Heptonstall Moor
Hope Forest
High Peak
Bleaklow Hill 2060
Kinder Scout 2088
COPYRIGHT, GEORGE PHILIP & SON, LTD.

Adjoining page 40
Adjoining page 41
Adjoining page 32
Adjoining page 35

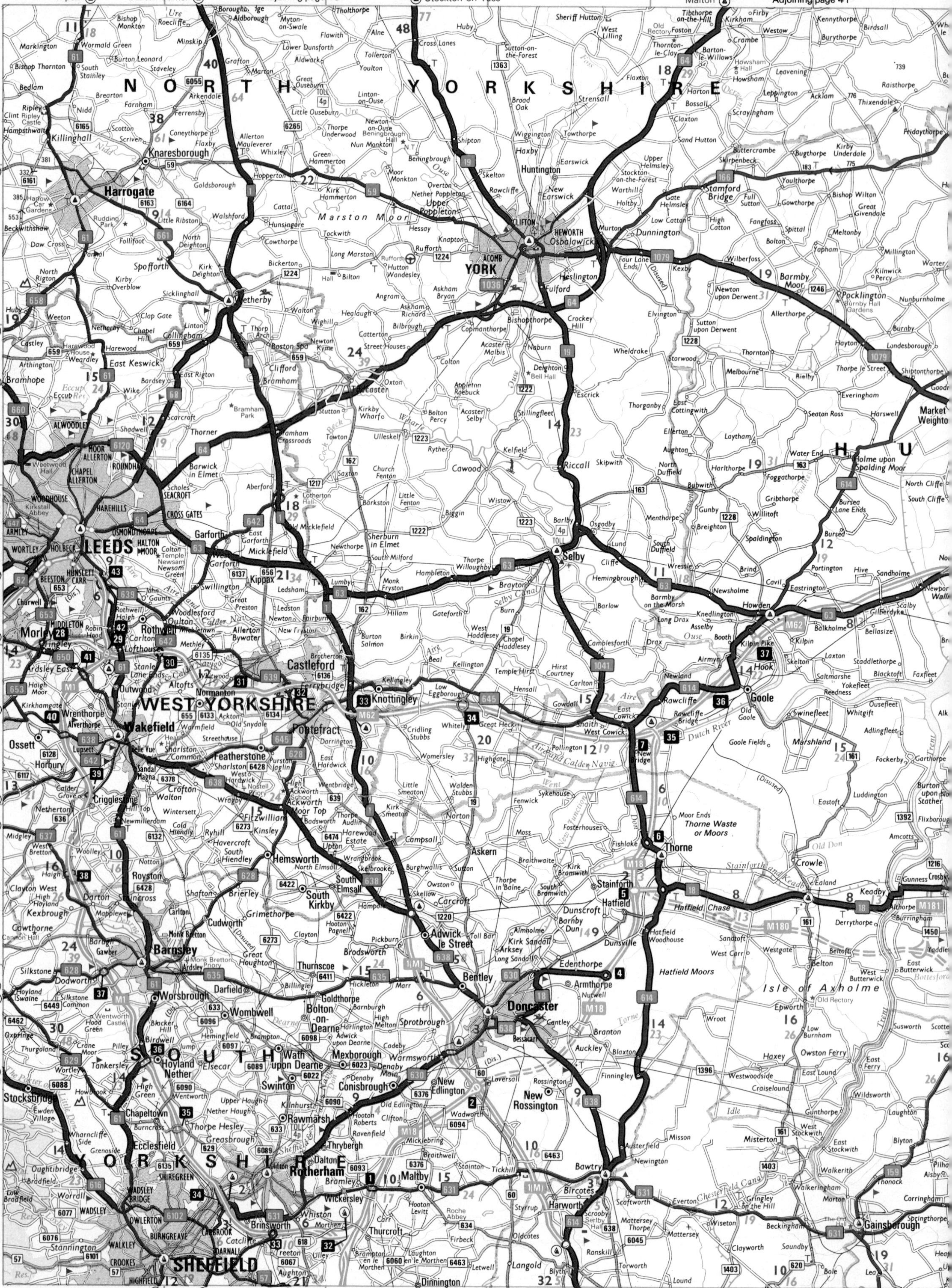

NORTH YORKSHIRE

WEST YORKSHIRE

SOUTH YORKSHIRE

HUMBERSIDE

YORK

LEEDS

Harrogate

Wakefield

Pontefract

Castleford

Selby

Goole

Doncaster

Thorne

Stainforth

Hatfield

Barnsley

SHEFFIELD

Rotherham

Morley

Ossett

Horbury

Knaresborough

Wetherby

Knottingley

Conisbrough

Mexborough

Swinton

Rawmarsh

Isle of Axholme

Stocksbridge

Chapeltown

Ecclesfield

Gainsborough

Market Weighton

Pocklington

Stamford Bridge

Ripon

Scotch Corner

Stockton-on-Tees

Malton

Chesterfield

Worksop

Nottingham

Lincoln

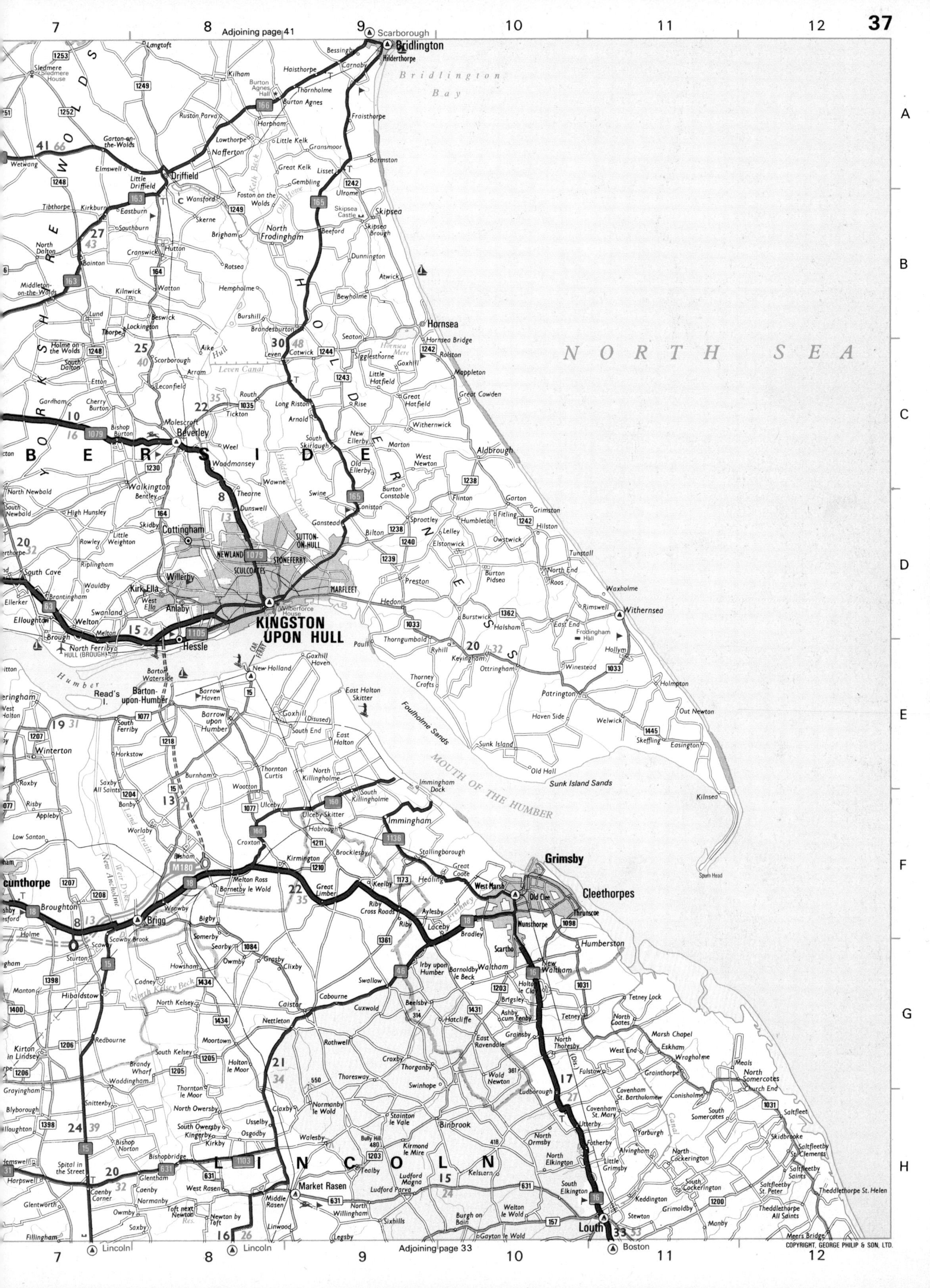

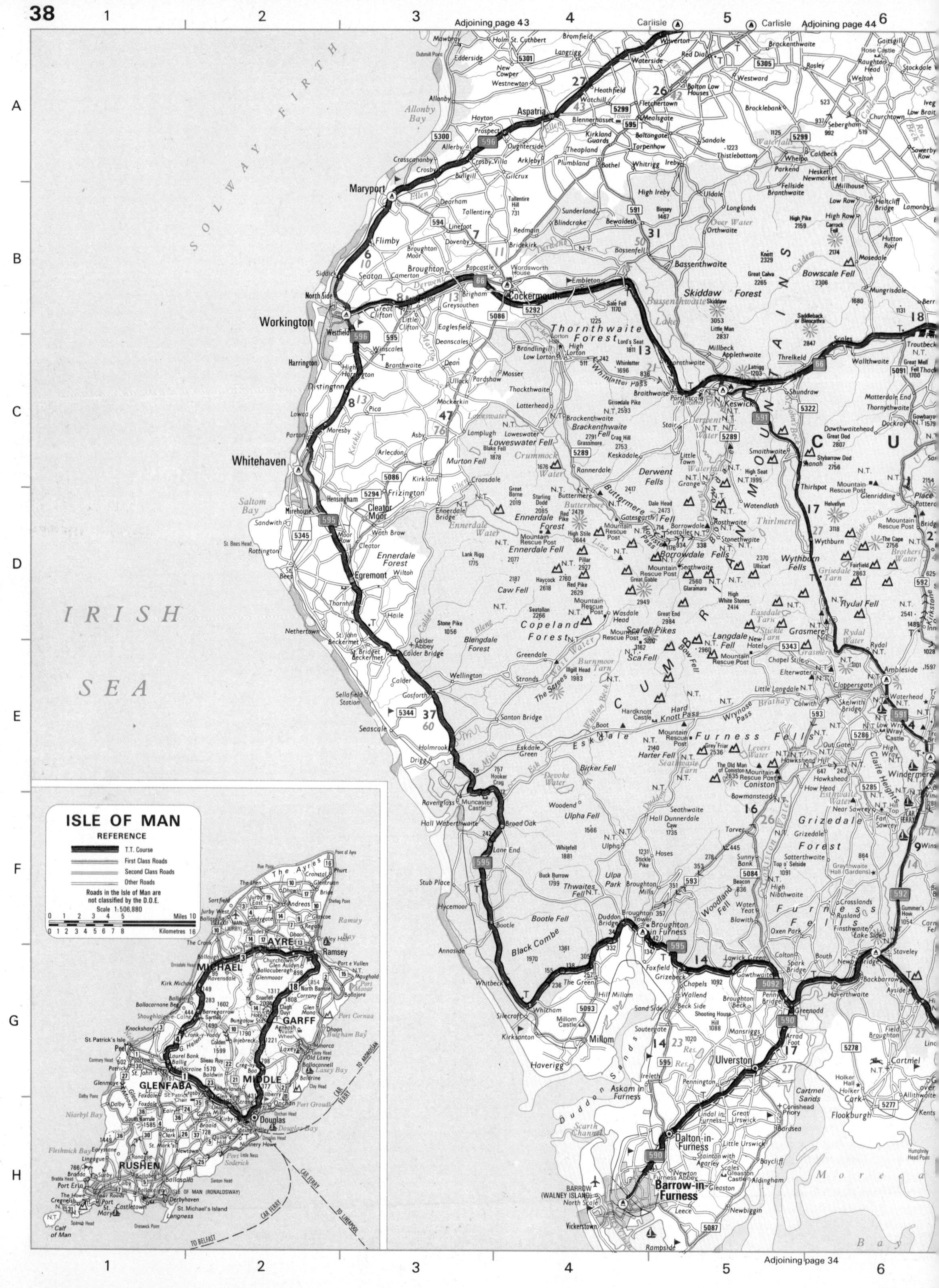

Adjoining page 43
Carlisle
Adjoining page 44
SOLWAY FIRTH
IRISH SEA
Allonby Bay
Maryport
Workington
Whitehaven
Harrington
Aspatria
Cockermouth
Keswick
Egremont
Cleator Moor
Seascale
Ravenglass
Millom
Ulverston
Dalton-in-Furness
Barrow-in-Furness
Ambleside
Windermere
Grasmere
Coniston
Thornthwaite Forest
Skiddaw Forest
Ennerdale Forest
Copeland Forest
Blengdale Forest
Loweswater Fell
Derwent Fells
Borrowdale Fells
Wythburn Fells
Furness Fells
Grizedale Forest
Scafell Pikes
Harter Fell
Ulpha Fell
Bootle Fell
Black Combe
Duddon Sands
Bowscale Fell
Rydal Fell
ISLE OF MAN
REFERENCE
T.T. Course
First Class Roads
Second Class Roads
Other Roads
Roads in the Isle of Man are not classified by the D.O.E.
Scale 1:506,880
Miles 10
Kilometres 16
AYRE
MICHAEL
GARFF
GLENFABA
MIDDLE
RUSHEN
Ramsey
Peel
Douglas
Port Erin
Castletown
Calf of Man
CAR FERRY
TO ARDROSSAN
TO BELFAST
TO LIVERPOOL
Adjoining page 34

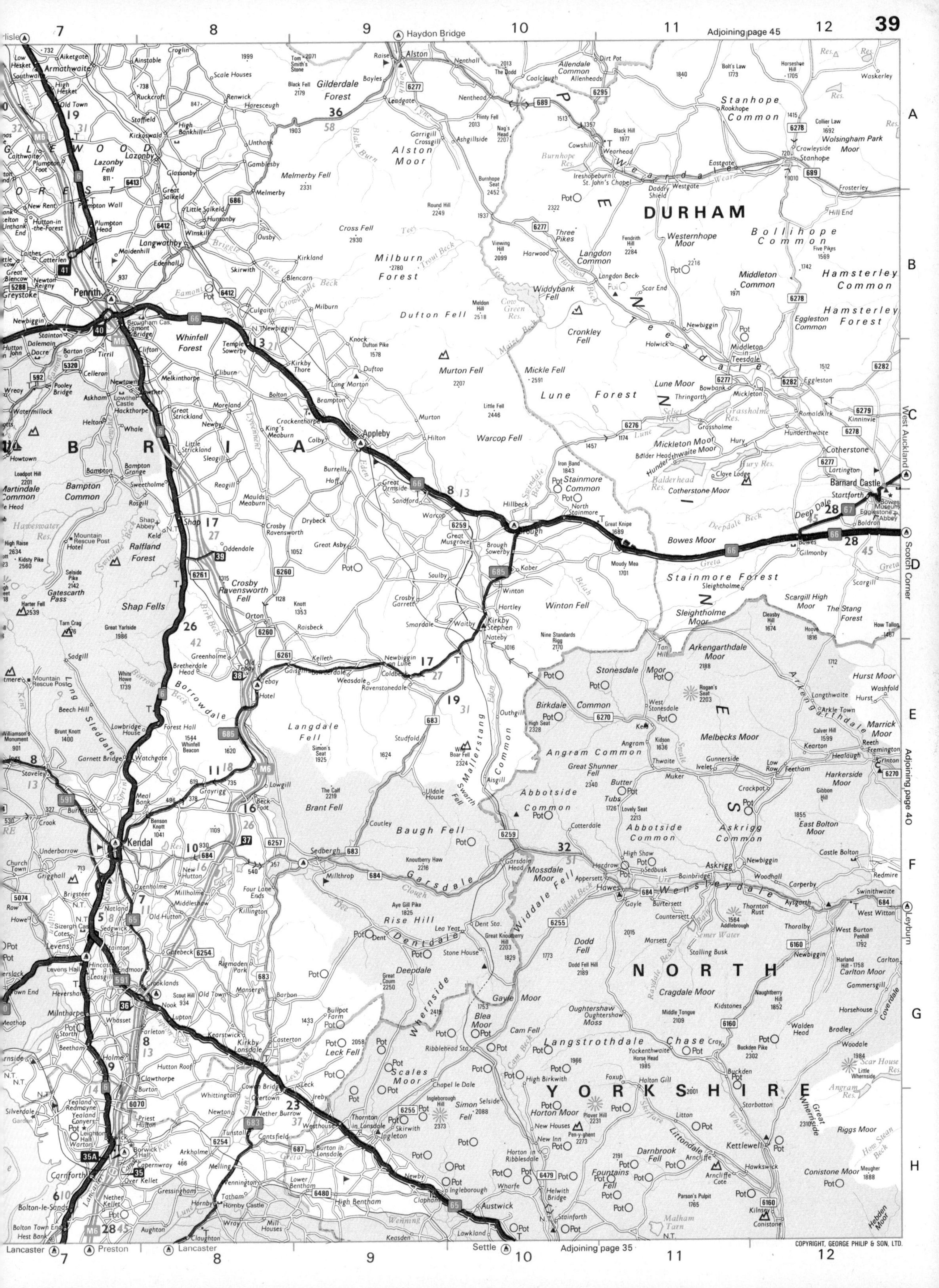

Adjoining page 45
Adjoining page 40
Adjoining page 35
Haydon Bridge
Carlisle
Lancaster
Preston
Settle
West Auckland
Scotch Corner
Leyburn
DURHAM
NORTH YORKSHIRE
CUMBRIA
PENNINES
INGLEWOOD FOREST
Penrith
Appleby
Kendal
Alston
Brough
Kirkby Stephen
Barnard Castle
Sedbergh
Hawes
Askrigg
Kirkby Lonsdale
Carnforth
Stanhope
Shap
Tebay
Orton
Middleton in Teesdale
Alston Moor
Cross Fell
Milburn Forest
Dufton Fell
Murton Fell
Lune Forest
Warcop Fell
Stainmore Forest
Bowes Moor
Shap Fells
Whinfell Forest
Langdale Fell
Baugh Fell
Garsdale
Dentdale
Wensleydale
Langstrothdale Chase
Ribblesdale
Weardale
Teesdale
Hamsterley Forest
Bollihope Common
Stanhope Common
Gilderdale Forest
Ingleborough
Whernside
Pen-y-ghent
Great Whernside
Kettlewell
Ingleton
High Bentham
Clapham
Austwick

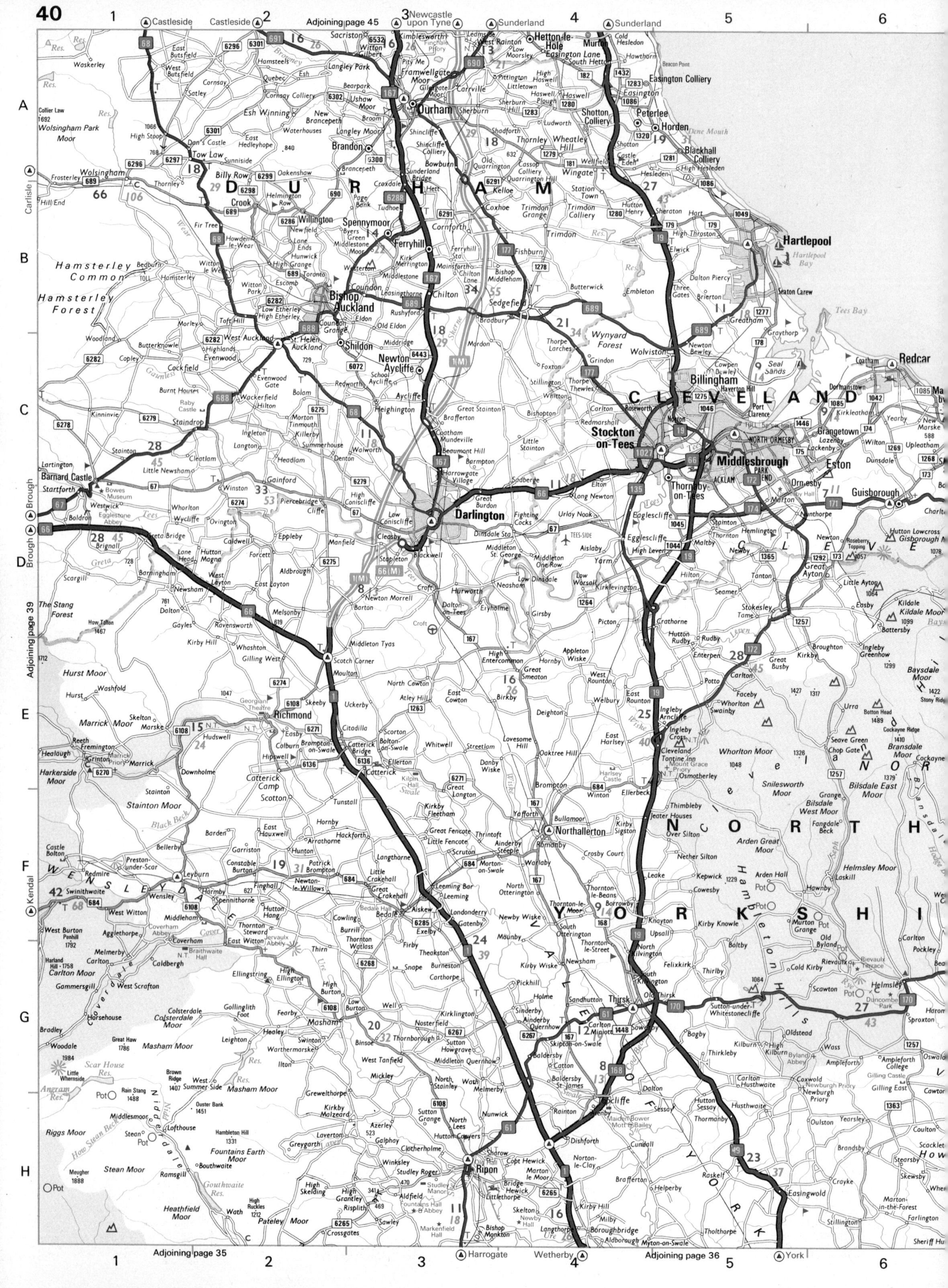

Adjoining page 45
Castleside
Newcastle upon Tyne
Sunderland
Adjoining page 39
Adjoining page 35
Adjoining page 36
Carlisle
Brough
Kendal
Harrogate
Wetherby
York
D U R H A M
C L E V E L A N D
N O R T H
Y O R K S H I
Durham
Hartlepool
Hartlepool Bay
Seaton Carew
Tees Bay
Redcar
Billingham
Stockton on-Tees
Middlesbrough
Thornaby-on-Tees
Darlington
Bishop Auckland
Spennymoor
Ferryhill
Newton Aycliffe
Shildon
Sedgefield
Peterlee
Horden
Easington Colliery
Blackhall Colliery
Hetton-le-Hole
Murton
Crook
Tow Law
Wolsingham
Barnard Castle
Staindrop
Richmond
Catterick
Catterick Camp
Scotch Corner
Leyburn
Middleham
Masham
Bedale
Northallerton
Thirsk
Ripon
Boroughbridge
Easingwold
Helmsley
Guisborough
Eston
Grangetown
Yarm
Stokesley
Great Ayton
Osmotherley
Hamsterley Common
Hamsterley Forest
Wolsingham Park Moor
Hurst Moor
Marrick Moor
Stainton Moor
Masham Moor
Fountains Earth Moor
Heathfield Moor
Riggs Moor
Stean Moor
Pateley Moor
Arden Great Moor
Snilesworth Moor
Whorlton Moor
Helmsley Moor
Bilsdale East Moor
Bilsdale West Moor
Kildale Moor
Baysdale Moor
Hambleton Hills
Cleveland Hills
W E N S L E Y D A L E
Nidderdale
Coverdale
Wynyard Forest
Seal Sands

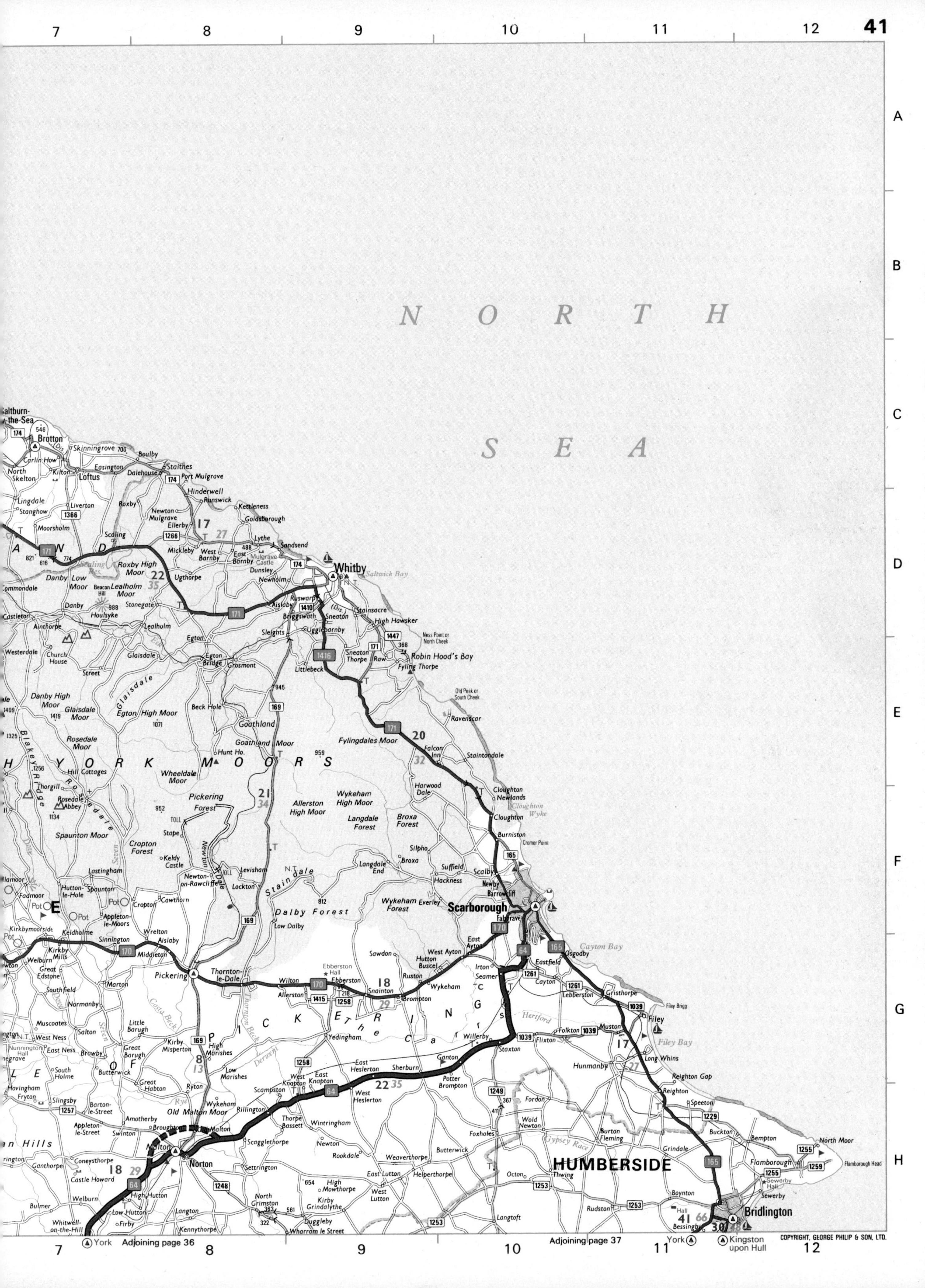

7
8
9
10
11
12
A
B
C
D
E
F
G
H
N O R T H
S E A
Saltburn-by-the-Sea
Brotton
Skinningrove
Carlin How
Kilton
Loftus
North Skelton
Easington
Boulby
Staithes
Dalehouse
Port Mulgrave
Hinderwell
Runswick
Lingdale
Stanghow
Liverton
Roxby
Newton Mulgrave
Kettleness
Goldsborough
Moorsholm
Scaling
Ellerby
Lythe
Sandsend
Mickleby
West Barnby
East Barnby
Mulgrave Castle
Dunsley
Whitby
Saltwick Bay
Scaling Res.
Roxby High Moor
Danby Low Moor
Beacon Hill
Lealholm Moor
Ugthorpe
Newholm
Commondale
Danby
Houlsyke
Stonegate
Aislaby
Ruswarp
Briggswath
Sneaton
Stainsacre
High Hawsker
Castleton
Ainthorpe
Lealholm
Sleights
Ugglebarnby
Ness Point or North Cheek
Westerdale
Church House
Glaisdale
Egton
Egton Bridge
Grosmont
Littlebeck
Sneaton Thorpe
Raw
Robin Hood's Bay
Fyling Thorpe
Street
Old Peak or South Cheek
Danby High Moor
Glaisdale Moor
Egton High Moor
Beck Hole
Ravenscar
Goathland
Goathland Moor
Fylingdales Moor
Falcon Inn
Staintondale
Rosedale Moor
Blakey Ridge
Hill Cottages
Hunt Ho.
Thorgill
Rosedale Abbey
Rosedale
Wheeldale Moor
YORK MOORS
Pickering Forest
Allerston High Moor
Wykeham High Moor
Langdale Forest
Broxa Forest
Harwood Dale
Cloughton Newlands
Cloughton Wyke
Cloughton
Burniston
Cromer Point
Spaunton Moor
Cropton Forest
Stape
Keldy Castle
Newton Dale
Silpho
Broxa
Lastingham
Newton-on-Rawcliffe
Levisham
Lockton
Staindale
Langdale End
Suffield
Hackness
Scalby
Newby
Barrowcliff
Hutton-le-Hole
Spaunton
Cropton
Cawthorn
Fadmoor
Appleton-le-Moors
Dalby Forest
Low Dalby
Wykeham Forest
Everley
Scarborough
Falsgrave
Kirkbymoorside
Keldholme
Sinnington
Wrelton
Aislaby
Middleton
Kirkby Mills
Welburn
Great Edstone
Pickering
Thornton-le-Dale
Wilton
Ebberston Hall
Ebberston
Allerston
Snainton
Sawdon
West Ayton
East Ayton
Hutton Buscel
Ruston
Wykeham
Brompton
Irton
Seamer
Cayton
Eastfield
Osgodby
Cayton Bay
Lebberston
Gristhorpe
Filey Brigg
Filey
Filey Bay
Marton
Southfield
Normanby
Muscoates
Salton
Little Barugh
West Ness
Nunnington Hall
East Ness
Brawby
Great Barugh
Kirby Misperton
High Marishes
Yedingham
Willerby
Staxton
Flixton
Folkton
Muston
Hunmanby
Long Whins
Reighton Gap
Reighton
Speeton
South Holme
Butterwick
Great Habton
Low Marishes
East Heslerton
Sherburn
Ganton
Potter Brompton
Hovingham
Fryton
Slingsby
Barton-le-Street
Ryton
Scampston
West Knapton
East Knapton
West Heslerton
Fordon
Wykeham
Old Malton Moor
Rillington
Amotherby
Broughton
Old Malton
Appleton-le-Street
Swinton
Malton
Norton
Thorpe Bassett
Wintringham
Scagglethorpe
Newton
Rookdale
Weaverthorpe
Butterwick
Foxholes
Wold Newton
Burton Fleming
Grindale
Buckton
Bempton
North Moor
Flamborough
Flamborough Head
Sewerby Hall
Sewerby
Coneysthorpe
Ganthorpe
Castle Howard
Settrington
East Lutton
Helperthorpe
HUMBERSIDE
Octon
Thwing
High Mowthorpe
West Lutton
Welburn
High Hutton
Bulmer
Low Hutton
Langton
North Grimston
Kirby Grindalythe
Boynton
Rudston
Hall
Bessingby
Bridlington
Whitwell-on-the-Hill
Firby
Kennythorpe
Duggleby
Wharram le Street
Langtoft
York
Adjoining page 36
Adjoining page 37
Kingston upon Hull

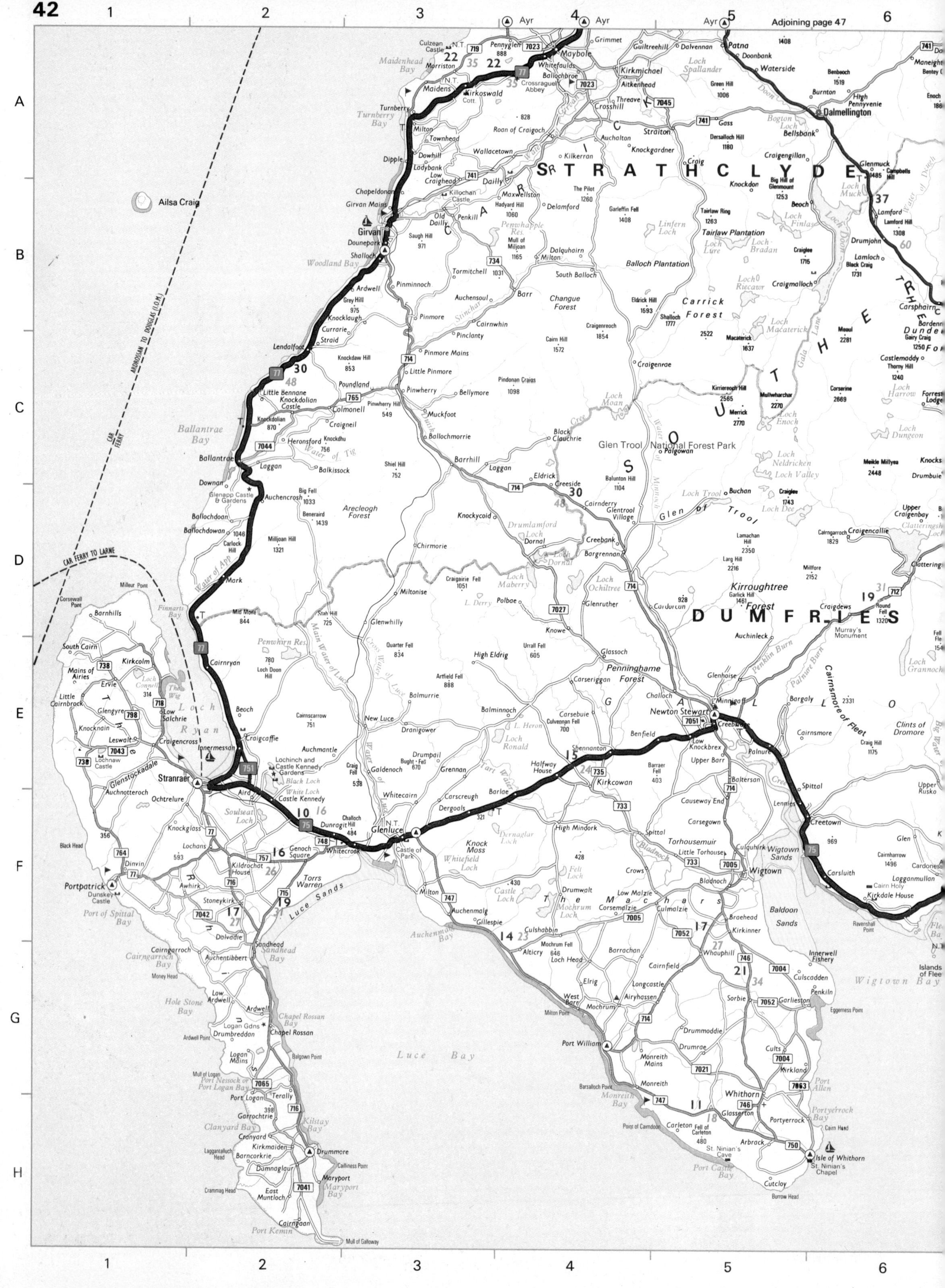

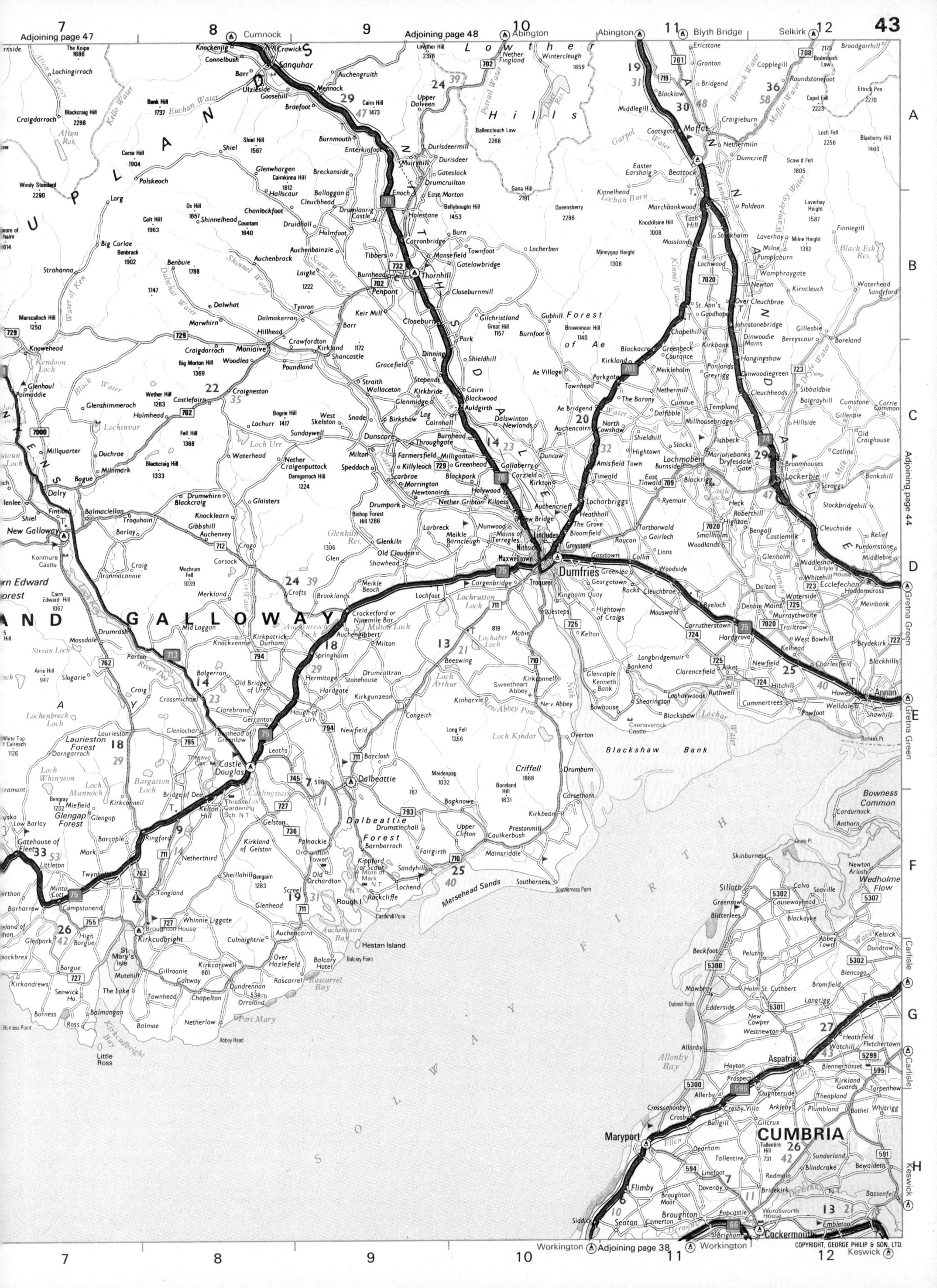

43
Adjoining page 47
Adjoining page 48
Adjoining page 44
Adjoining page 38
Cumnock
Abington
Blyth Bridge
Selkirk
Gretna Green
Carlisle
Keswick
Workington
Lowther Hills
UPLAND
DUMFRIES AND GALLOWAY
ANNANDALE
NITHSDALE
CUMBRIA
SOLWAY FIRTH
Sanquhar
Crawick
Kirkconnel
Mennock
Wanlockhead
Durisdeer
Thornhill
Penpont
Moniaive
Closeburn
Dumfries
Maxwelltown
Lincluden
Moffat
Beattock
Lockerbie
Lochmaben
Ecclefechan
Annan
Castle Douglas
Dalbeattie
New Galloway
Kirkcudbright
Gatehouse of Fleet
Dalry
Crocketford or Ninemile Bar
Kirkbean
Criffell
New Abbey
Caerlaverock Castle
Blackshaw Bank
Mersehead Sands
Hestan Island
Silloth
Maryport
Aspatria
Cockermouth
Flimby
Allonby Bay
Bowness Common
Forest of Ae
Glengap Forest
Dalbeattie Forest
Loch Ken
Loch Kindar
Lochrutton Loch
Milton Loch
Auchenreoch Loch
Carlingwark Loch
Lochar Water
Water of Ken
Scaur Water
Shinnel Water
Kinnel Water
Dryfe Water
Afton Water
Euchan Water
Rascarrel Bay
Kirkcudbright Bay
Auchencairn Bay
Southerness
COPYRIGHT, GEORGE PHILIP & SON, LTD.
7 8 9 10 11 12
A B C D E F G H

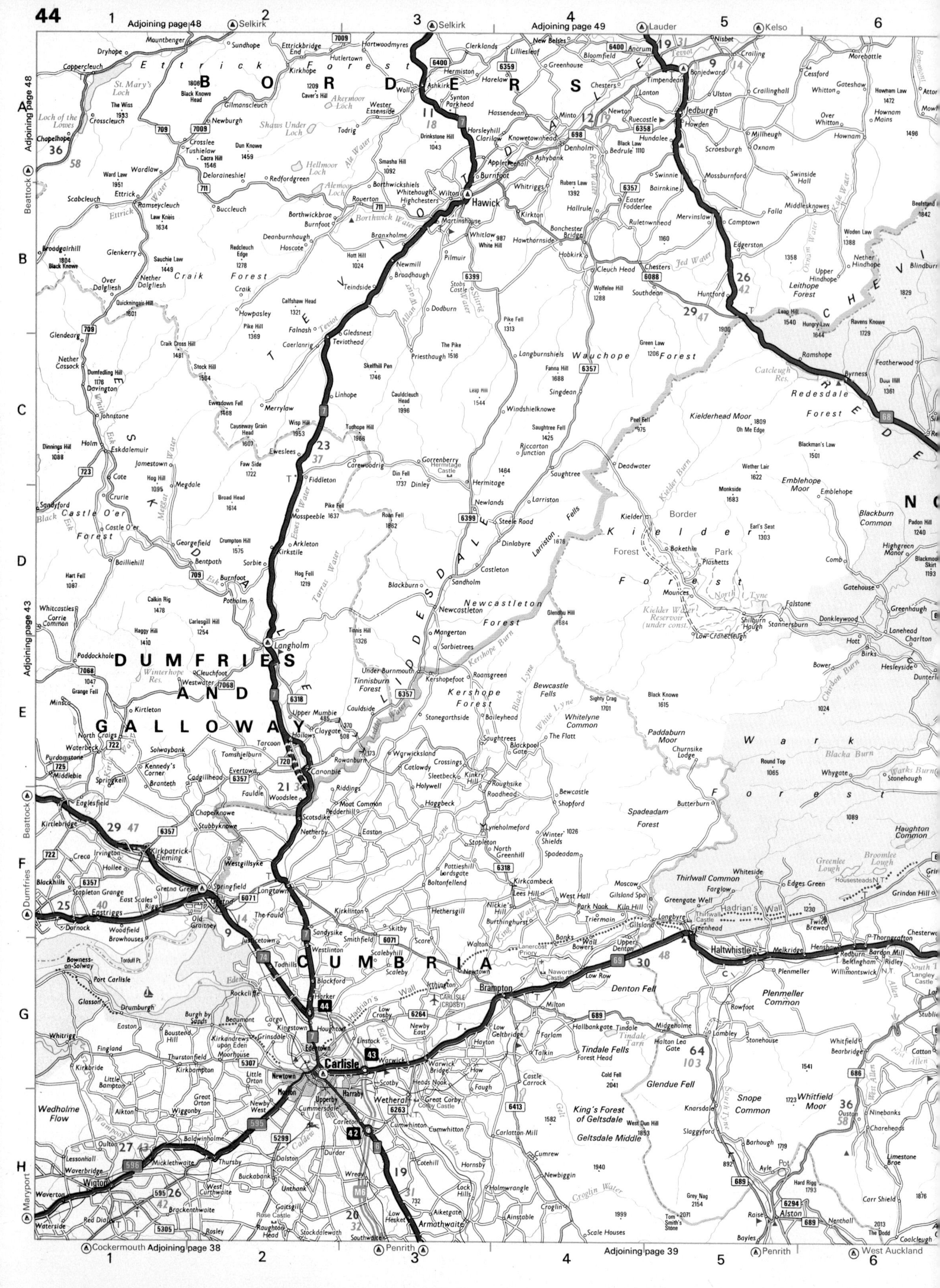
Adjoining page 48
Selkirk
Adjoining page 49
Lauder
Kelso
Adjoining page 43
Beattock
Dumfries
Maryport
Cockermouth Adjoining page 38
Penrith
Adjoining page 39
West Auckland
BORDERS
DUMFRIES AND GALLOWAY
CUMBRIA
Ettrick Forest
TEVIOTDALE
ESKDALE
LIDDESDALE
Craik Forest
Wauchope Forest
Kielder Forest Park
Border Forest Park
Newcastleton Forest
Kershope Forest
Wark Forest
Spadeadam Forest
Redesdale Forest
CHEVIOT
Dryhope
Mountbenger
Sundhope
Ettrickbridge End
Hartwoodmyres
Clerklands
Lilliesleaf
New Belses
Ancrum
Nisbet
Crailing
Morebattle
Cappercleuch
St. Mary's Loch
Black Knowe Head
The Wiss
Loch of the Lowes
Crosscleuch
Chapelhope
Kirkhope
Hutlertown
Ashkirk
Hermiston
Harelaw
Greenhouse
Bloomfield
Chesters
Timpendean
Bonjedward
Ulston
Cessford
Whitton
Gateshaw
Hownam Law
Caver's Hill
Akermoor Loch
Woll
Synton Parkhead
Hassendean
Minto
Newton
Lanton
Jedburgh
Crailinghall
Gilmanscleuch
Newburgh
Shaws Under Loch
Wester Essenside
Todrig
Drinkstone Hill
Horsleyhill
Clarilaw
Knowetownhead
Denholm
Ruecastle
Hundalee
Howden
Millheugh
Oxnam
Over Whitton
Hownam Mains
Hownam
Crosslee
Tushielaw
Cacra Hill
Dun Knowe
Hellmoor Loch
Smasha Hill
Appletreehall
Ashybank
Black Law
Bedrule
Scraesburgh
Wardlaw
Ward Law
Deloraineshiel
Redfordgreen
Alemoor Loch
Borthwickshiels
Whitehaugh
Burnfoot
Wilton
Hawick
Whitriggs
Rubers Law
Swinnie
Bairnkine
Mossburnford
Swinside Hall
Scabcleuch
Ettrick
Ramseycleuch
Buccleuch
Highchesters
Roberton
Easter Fodderlee
Hallrule
Law Kneis
Borthwickbrae
Borthwick Water
Martinshouse
Kirkton
Bonchester Bridge
Ruletownhead
Mervinslaw
Camptown
Falla
Middlesknowes
Beefstand Hill
Broadgairhill
Black Knowe
Glenkerry
Sauchie Law
Redcleuch Edge
Deanburnhaugh
Hoscote
Branxholme
Whitlaw
White Hill
Hawthornside
Hobkirk
Edgerston
Woden Law
Nether Hindhope
Over Dalgliesh
Nether Dalgliesh
Craik
Hott Hill
Newmill
Broadhaugh
Pilmuir
Stobs Castle
Cleuch Head
Chesters
Jed Water
Upper Hindhope
Blindburn
Leithope Forest
Teindside
Wolfelee Hill
Southdean
Huntford
Quickningair Hill
Calfshaw Head
Dodburn
Howpasley
Pike Hill
Falnash
Gledsnest
Teviothead
Caerlanrig
Pike Fell
Leap Hill
Hungry Law
Ravens Knowe
Glendearg
Craik Cross Hill
Langburnshiels
Green Law
The Pike
Priesthaugh
Nether Cassock
Dumfedling Hill
Davington
Stock Hill
Skelfhill Pen
Fanna Hill
Singdean
Ramshope
Catcleugh Res.
Featherwood
Byrness
Dour Hill
Linhope
Cauldcleuch Head
Merrylaw
Ewesdown Fell
Windshielknowe
Kielderhead Moor
Oh Me Edge
Johnstone
Causeway Grain Head
Wisp Hill
Tudhope Hill
Peel Fell
Saughtree Fell
Riccarton Junction
Blackman's Law
Dinnings Hill
Holm
Eskdalemuir
Eweslees
Gorrenberry
Hermitage Castle
Deadwater
Wether Lair
Emblehope Moor
Emblehope
Jamestown
Fiddleton
Carewoodrig
Din Fell
Dinley
Hermitage
Saughtree
Monkside
Cote
Hog Hill
Megdale
Faw Side
Crurie
Broad Head
Newlands
Larriston
Kielder
Blackburn Common
Padon Hill
Sandyford
Black Castle O'er Forest
Castle O'er
Mosspeeble
Roan Fell
Steele Road
Earl's Seat
Larriston Fells
Bakethin
Plashetts
Highgreen Manor
Georgefield
Crumpton Hill
Arkleton
Kirkstile
Dinlabyre
Castleton
Comb
Bailliehill
Hart Fell
Bentpath
Sorbie
Burnfoot
Hog Fell
Sandholm
Blackburn
Mounces
North Tyne
Gatehouse
Falstone
Whitcastles
Corrie Common
Calkin Rig
Potholm
Tarras Water
Newcastleton
Glendhu Hill
Kielder Water Reservoir (under const.)
Shilburn Haugh
Stannersburn
Donkleywood
Greenhaugh
Haggy Hill
Carlesgill Hill
Tinnis Hill
Mangerton
Low Cranecleugh
Lanehead
Hott
Charlton
Langholm
Sorbietrees
Kershope Burn
Birks
Paddockhole
Winterhope Res.
Cleuchfoot
Westwater
Under Burnmouth
Tinnisburn Forest
Kershopefoot
Roansgreen
Bower
Hesleyside
Dunterley
Grange Fell
Minsca
Kirtleton
Upper Mumbie
Cauldside
Bewcastle Fells
Sighty Crag
Black Knowe
Chirdon Burn
Claygate
Hollows
Stonegarthside
Baileyhead
Whitelyne Common
North Craigs
Waterbeck
Solwaybank
Tarcoon
Saughtrees
Blackpool Gate
The Flatt
Paddaburn Moor
Churnsike Lodge
Blacka Burn
Purdomstone
Middlebie
Kennedy's Corner
Tomshielburn
Wgrwicksland
Catlowdy
Crossings
Rowanburn
Canonbie
Sleetbeck
Kinkry Hill
Roughsike
Round Top
Whygate
Stonehaugh
Wark Burn
Springkell
Branteth
Cadgillhead
Evertown
Faulde
Woodslee
Riddings
Holywell
Roadhead
Bewcastle
Shopford
Butterburn
Eaglesfield
Chapelknowe
Moat Common
Pedderhill
Haggbeck
Kirtlebridge
Stubbyknowe
Scotsdike
Netherby
Easton
Lyneholmeford
Winter Shields
Haughton Common
Creca
Irvington
Kirkpatrick-Fleming
Hoillee
Westgillsyke
Stapleton
North Greenhill
Spadeadam
Greenlee Lough
Broomlee Lough
Blackhills
Stapleton Grange
East Scales
Rigg
Gretna Green
Springfield
Gretna
Longtown
Pattieshill
Lordsgate
Boltonfellend
Kirkcambeck
Lees Hill
West Hall
Moscow
Gilsland Spa
Thirlwall Common
Farglow
Whiteside
Edges Green
Housesteads
Grindon Hill
Eastriggs
Dornock
Woodfield
Browhouses
Old Graitney
The Fauld
Kirklinton
Hethersgill
Nickie's Hill
Burthinghurst
Park Nook
Kiln Hill
Triermain
Gilsland
Greengate Well
Longbyre
Thirlwall Castle
Greenhead
Hadrian's Wall
Twice Brewed
Chesterwood
Bowness-on-Solway
Torduff Pt.
Justicetown
Sandysyke
Smithfield
Skitby
Scare
Walton
Lanercost Priory
Banks
Wall Bowers
Upper Denton
Haltwhistle
Melkridge
Henshaw
Thorngrafton
Redburn
Bardon Mill
Bellingham
Ridley
Westlinton
Todhills
Scalebyhill
Scaleby
Newtown
Naworth Castle
Low Row
Denton Fell
Plenmeller
Willimontswick
Langley Castle
Port Carlisle
Rockcliffe
Blackford
Brampton
Plenmeller Common
Glasson
Drumburgh
Harker
Hadrian's Wall
Irthington
Carlisle (Crosby)
Milton
Rowfoot
Easton
Burgh by Sands
Beaumont
Cargo
Low Crosby
Newby East
Kingstown
Houghton
Hallbankgate
Tindale
Tindale Tarn
Midgeholme
Lambley
Stublick
Whitrigg
Finglnd
Boustead Hill
Kirkandrews upon Eden
Grinsdale
Moorhouse
Linstock
Edentown
Warwick
Low Geltbridge
Hayton
Farlam
Talkin
Tindale Fells
Forest Head
Halton Lea Gate
Stonehouse
Whitfield
Bearbridge
Catton
Kirkbride
Thurstonfield
Kirkbampton
Little Orton
Newtown
Carlisle
Warwick Bridge
How
Castle Carrock
Cold Fell
Little Bampton
Morton
Harraby
Upperby
Scotby
Heads Nook
Faugh
Glendue Fell
Wedholme Flow
Aikton
Great Orton
Wiggonby
Newby West
Cummersdale
Wetheral
Great Corby
Corby Castle
Carleton
King's Forest of Geltsdale
West Dun Hill
Geltsdale Middle
Snope Common
Knarsdale
Whitfield Moor
Ninebanks
Ouston
Baldwinholme
Cumwhinton
Carlatton Mill
Slaggyford
Chareheads
Oulton
Dalston
Durdar
Cotehill
Cumrew
Hornsby
Barhough
Limestone Brae
Lessonhall
Waverbridge
Mickleth waite
Thursby
Buckabank
Wreay
Newbiggin
Ayle
Hard Rigg
Wigton
West Curthwaite
Unthank
Lock Hills
Holmwrangle
Grey Nag
Waverton
Brackenthwaite
Gaitsgill
Rose Castle
Aiketgate
Croglin
Croglin Water
Tom Smith's Stone
Raise
Alston
Carr Shield
Red Dial
Waterside
Rosley
Raughton Head
Stockdalewath
Southwaite
Low Hesket
Armathwaite
Ainstable
Scale Houses
Nenthall
The Dodd
Coalcleugh
South Tyne
Eden
Liddel Water
Esk
Teviot
Ettrick Water
Ale Water
Rule Water
Slitrig Water
Allan Water
Ewes Water
Kielder Burn
King Water
Irthing
Lyne
Black Lyne
White Lyne
Gelt
Caldew
Wampool
Kirtle Water
Meggat Water
White Esk
Kale Water
Oxnam Water
Sark
Allen

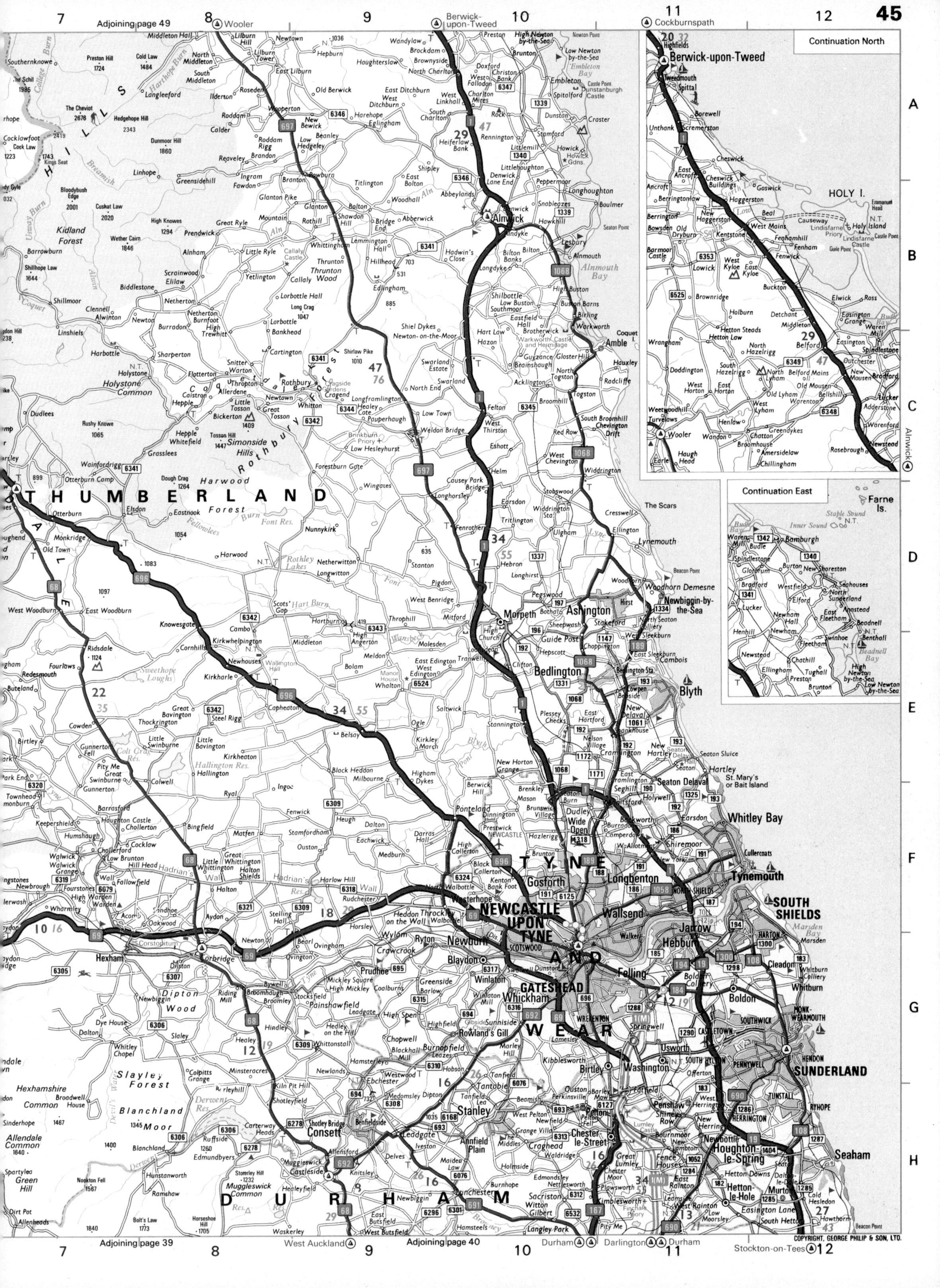

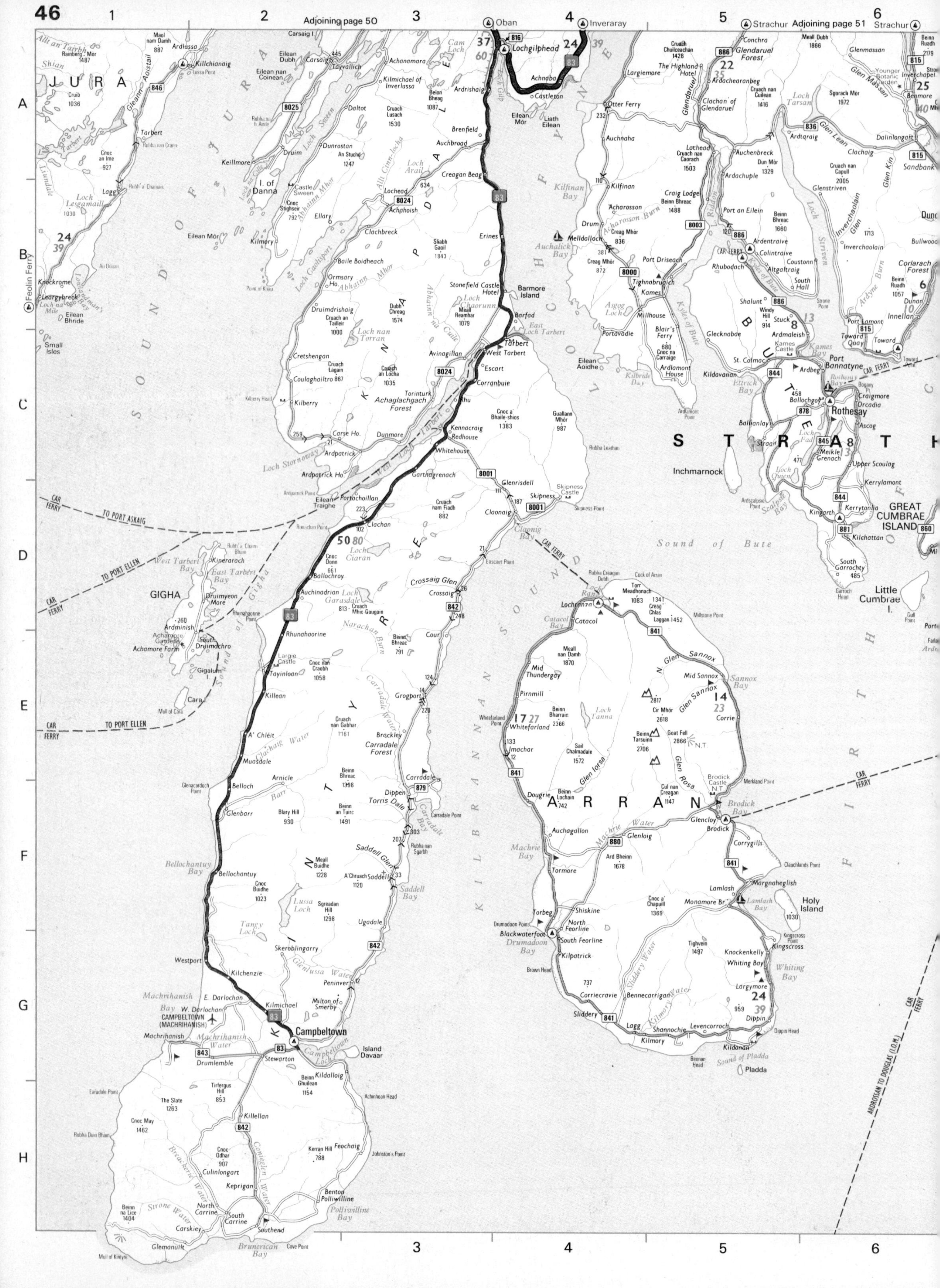

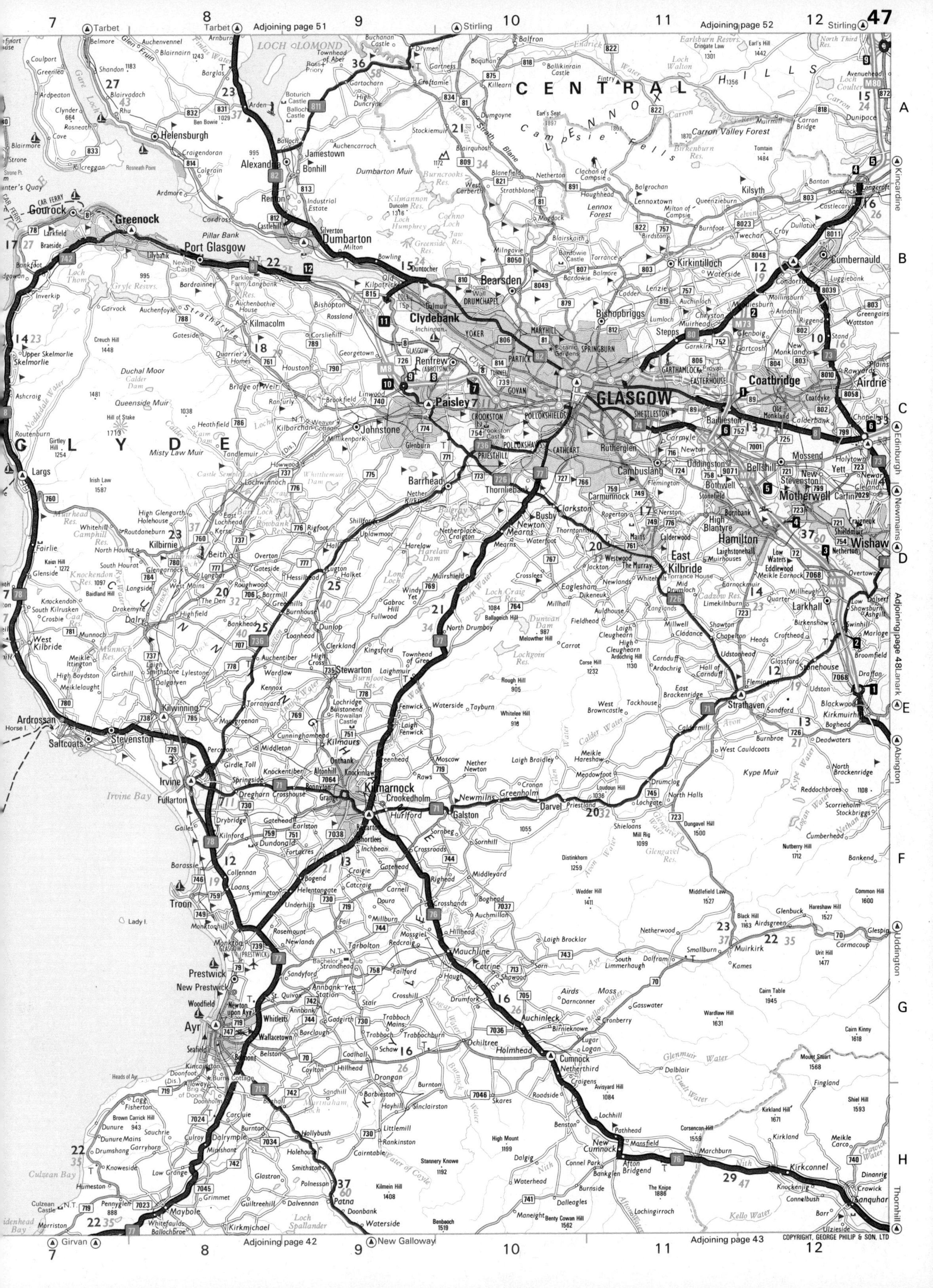

7
8
9
10
11
12
Tarbet
Adjoining page 51
Stirling
Adjoining page 52
A
B
C
D
E
F
G
H
Kincardine
Edinburgh
Newmains
Adjoining page 48
Lanark
Abington
Uddington
Thornhill
CENTRAL
Campsie Fells
Carron Valley Forest
LOCH LOMOND
Helensburgh
Alexandria
Dumbarton
Gourock
Greenock
Port Glasgow
Clydebank
Bearsden
Renfrew
Paisley
Johnstone
GLASGOW
Coatbridge
Airdrie
Cumbernauld
Kirkintilloch
Bishopbriggs
Rutherglen
Cambuslang
Motherwell
Wishaw
Hamilton
East Kilbride
Strathaven
Largs
Kilbirnie
Beith
Ardrossan
Saltcoats
Stevenston
Kilwinning
Irvine
Kilmarnock
Galston
Darvel
Troon
Prestwick
Ayr
Maybole
Girvan
Cumnock
New Cumnock
Auchinleck
Mauchline
Sanquhar
Kirkconnel
Lanark
C L Y D E
C U N N I N G H A M E
K Y L E
Irvine Bay
Culzean Bay
Adjoining page 42
New Galloway
Adjoining page 43
COPYRIGHT, GEORGE PHILIP & SON, LTD

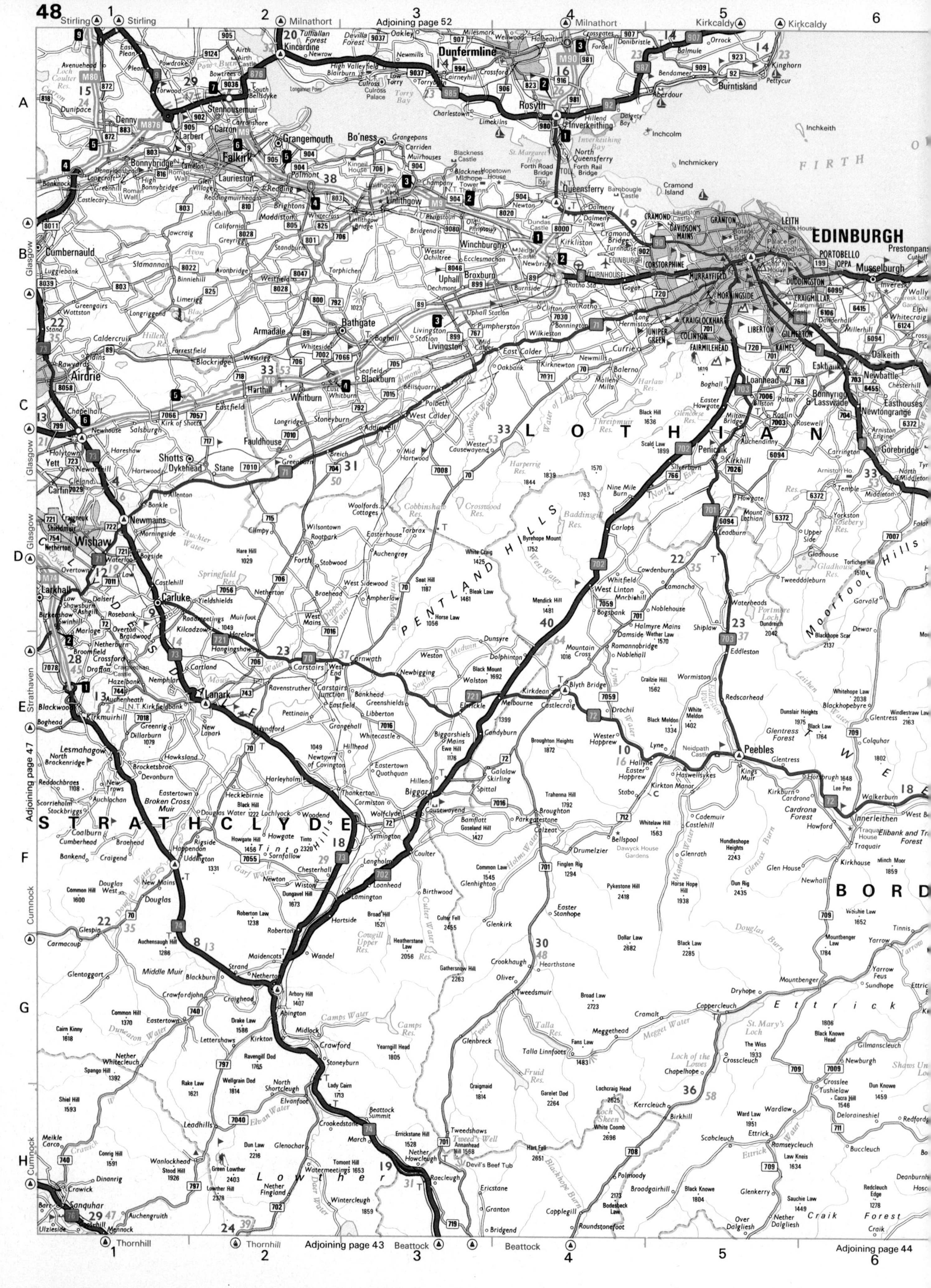

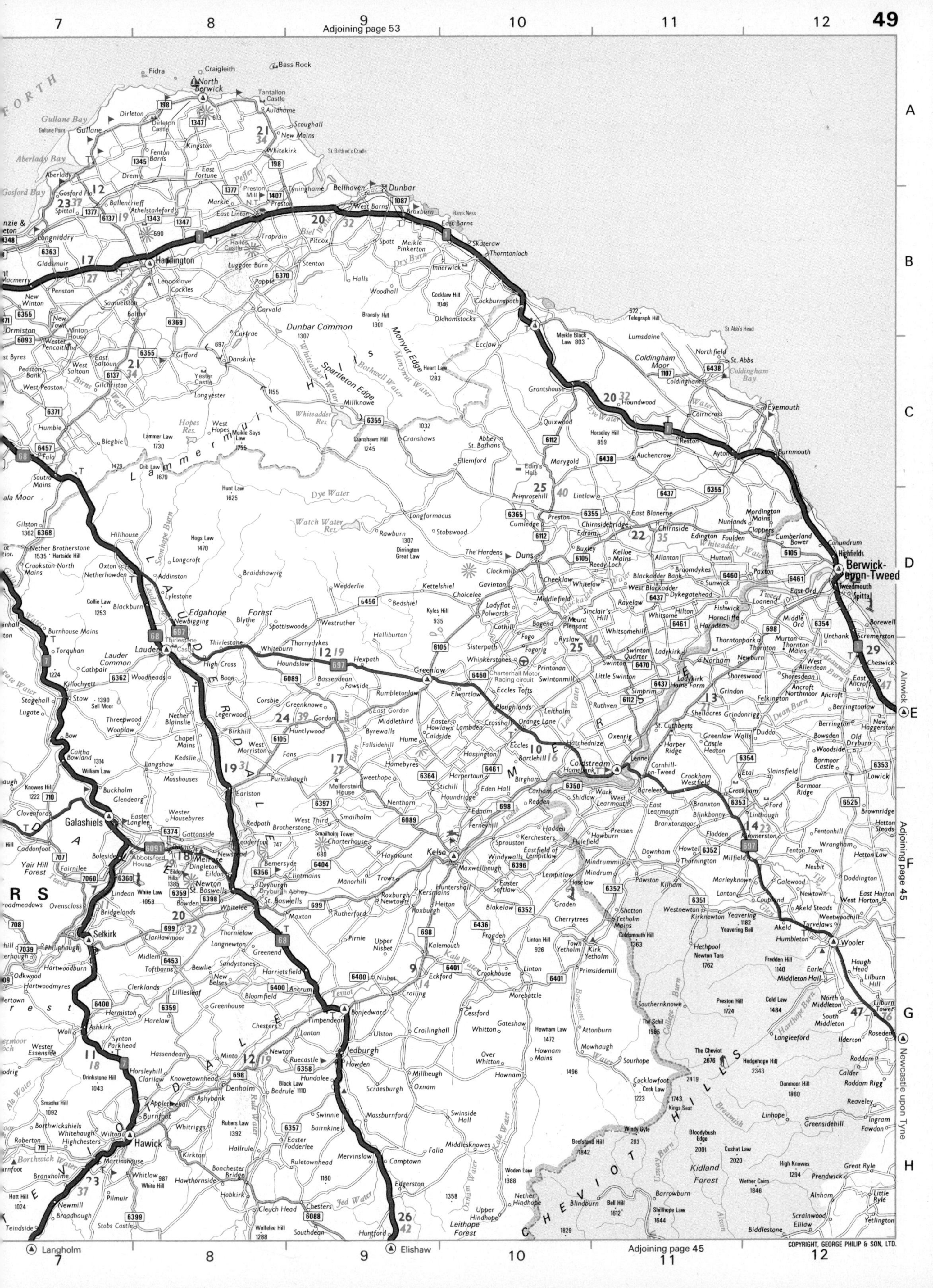

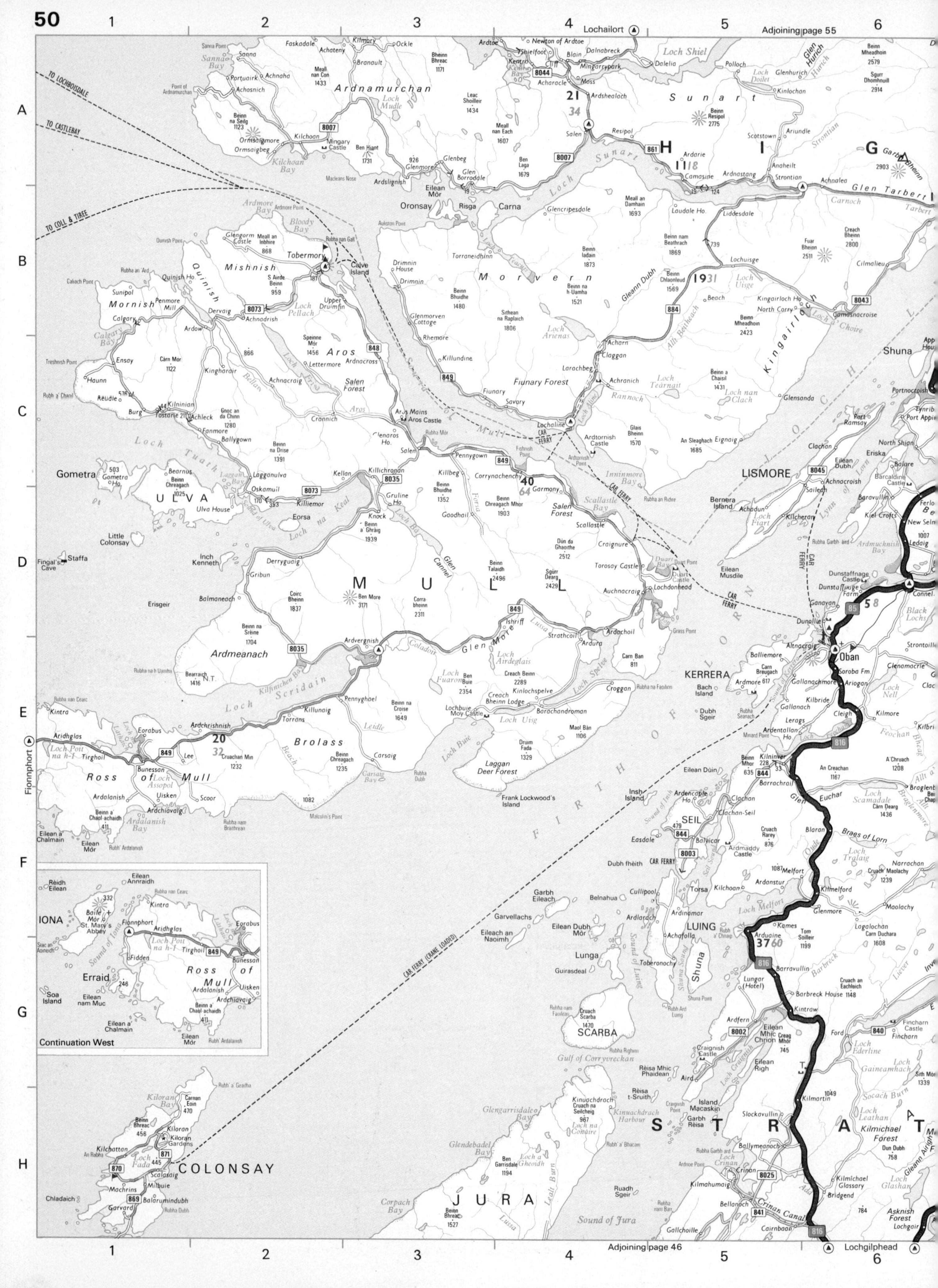
Lochailort
Adjoining page 55
Adjoining page 46
Lochgilphead
Fionnphort
TO LOCHBOISDALE
TO CASTLEBAY
TO COLL & TIREE
CAR FERRY
CAR FERRY (CRANE LOADED)
Ardnamurchan
Sunart
Morvern
Kingairloch
Mishnish
Mornish
Quinish
Aros
MULL
ULVA
LISMORE
KERRERA
SEIL
LUING
SCARBA
JURA
COLONSAY
STRAT
HIGH
FIRTH OF LORN
LOCH LINNHE
Sound of Mull
Loch Sunart
Loch Shiel
Loch Tuath
Loch na Keal
Loch Scridain
Loch Buie
Sound of Jura
Gulf of Corryvreckan
Crinan Canal
Sound of Iona
Ross of Mull
Brolass
Ardmeanach
Laggan Deer Forest
Salen Forest
Fiunary Forest
Glen More
Glen Tarbert
Tobermory
Calve Island
Dervaig
Calgary
Salen
Craignure
Lochaline
Kilchoan
Acharacle
Strontian
Oban
Connel
Kilmore
Kilninver
Kilmelford
Kilmartin
Crinan
Cairnbaan
Bunessan
Fionnphort
Staffa
Gometra
Inch Kenneth
Little Colonsay
Eorsa
Erraid
IONA
Kiloran
Scalasaig
Oronsay
Risga
Carna
Shuna
Easdale
Garvellachs
Belnahua
Lunga
Ben More 3171
Ben Hiant 1731
Beinn Resipol 2775
Garbh Bheinn 2903
Continuation West

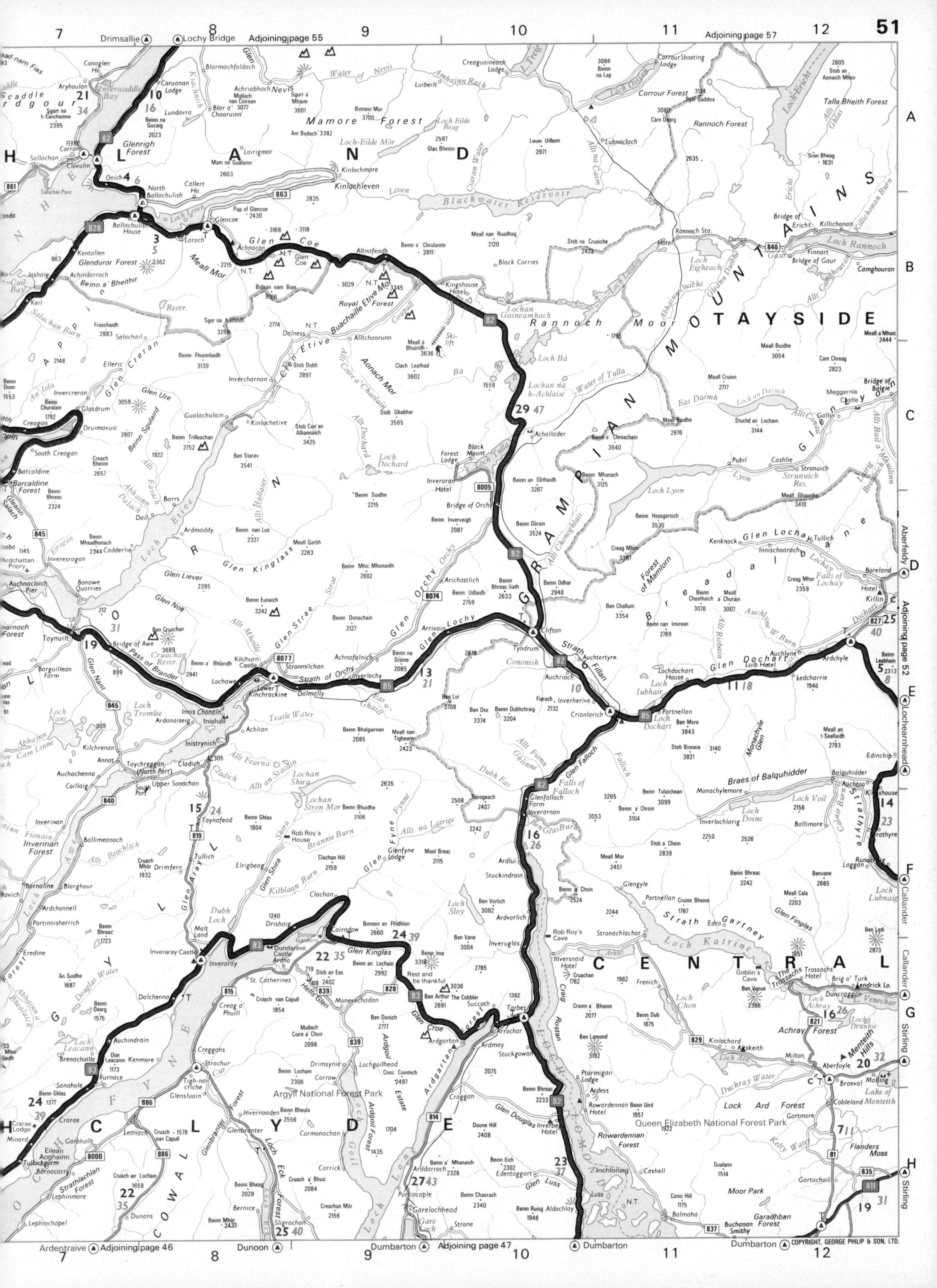
Drimsallie
Lochy Bridge
Adjoining page 55
Adjoining page 57
7
8
9
10
11
12
A
B
C
D
E
F
G
H
H L A N D
G R A M P I A N   M O U N T A I N S
T A Y S I D E
C E N T R A L
S T R A T H C L Y D E
Conaglen Ho.
Aryhoulan
Inverscaddle Bay
Coruanan Lodge
Lundavra
Glenrigh Forest
Blarmachfoldach
Achriabhach
Nevis
Water of Nevis
Mamore Forest
Loch Eilde Mòr
Am Bodach 3382
Binnein Mor 3700
Sgurr a' Mhàim 3601
Creaguaineach Lodge
Amhainn Rath
Luibeilt
L. Treig
Corrour Shooting Lodge
Corrour Forest
Loch Ossian
Rannoch Forest
Loch Ericht
Talla Bheith Forest
Stob an Aonaich Mhòir 2805
Sgòr Gaibhre 3124
Càrn Dearg 3080
Beinn na Lap 3066
Lubnaclach
Leum Uilleim 2971
Glas Bheinn 2587
Lairigmor
Mam na Gualainn 2603
Kinlochmore
Kinlochleven
Leven
Blackwater Reservoir
Ciaran Water
Allt na Caim
Sron Bheag 1631
Ericht
Killichonan Burn
Sallachan
Ferry
Corran
Clovulin
Onich
North Ballachulish
Callert Ho.
Sallachan Point
Loch Leven
Pap of Glencoe 2430
Ballachulish House
Glencoe
Laroch
Glen Coe
Achnacon
N.T.
Meall Mor 2215
Bidean nam Bian 3766
Altnafeadh
Beinn a' Chrulaiste 2811
Meall nan Ruadhag 2120
Black Corries
Stob na Cruaiche 2423
Rannoch Sta.
Hotel
Dunan
Loch Rannoch
Bridge of Ericht
Killichonan
Finnart
Bridge of Gaur
Gaur
Camghouran
Loch Eigheach
Loch Laidon
Kentallen
Glenduror Forest
Achindarroch
Beinn a' Bheithir
Inshaig
Keil
Salachan Burn
Buachaille Etive Mòr
Royal Forest
Kingshouse Hotel
Lochan Gainmheach
Rannoch Moor
Coupall
Sgor na h-Ulaidh 3258
Fraochaidh 2883
Salachail
Dalness
Alltchaorunn
Meall à Bhuiridh 3636
Ski-lift
Loch Bà
Lochan na h-Achlaise
Water of Tulla
Meall a' Mhuic 2444
Meall Buidhe 3054
Cam Chreag 2823
Meall Cruinn 2717
Bridge of Balgie
Meggernie Castle
Glen Lyon
Beinn Fhionnlaidh 3139
Elleric
Glen Creran
Glen Etive
Stob Dubh 2897
Aonach Mor
Clach Leathad 3602
Invercharnan
Glen Ure
Invercreran
Glasdrum
Gualachulain
Kinlochetive
Stob Coir' an Albannaich 3425
Stob Ghabhar 3565
Achallader
Meall Buidhe 2976
Stuchd an Lochain 3144
Gallin
Eas Daimh
Loch an Daimh
Creagan
Druimavuic
Beinn Sgulaird
Beinn Trilleachan 2752
Ben Starav 3541
Loch Dochard
Allt Dochard
Black Mount
Forest Lodge
Loch Tulla
Beinn a' Chreachain 3540
Beinn Mhanach 3125
Pubil
Cashlie
Stronuich
Stronuich Res.
South Creagan
Barcaldine
Barcaldine Forest
Creach Bheinn 2657
Abhainn Dalach
Barrs
Inveroran Hotel
Bridge of Orchy
Beinn Suidhe 2215
Beinn an Dòthaidh 3267
Beinn Dorain 3524
Loch Lyon
Meall Ghaordie 3410
Beinn Heasgarnich 3530
Loch Etive
Ardmoddy
Beinn nan Lus 2327
Meall Garbh 2283
Beinn Inverveigh 2087
Glen Kinglass
Allt Chonoghlais
Creag Mhor 3387
Kenknock
Glen Lochay
Tullich
Innischoarach
Forest of Mamlorn
Breadalbane
Aberfeldy
Boreland
Creag Mhor 2359
Falls of Lochay
Ardchattan Priory
Inveresragan
Cadderlie
Beinn Mheadhonach 2344
Achnacloich Pier
Bonawe Quarries
Glen Liever 2395
Beinn Mhic Mhonaidh 2602
Glen Orchy
Arichastlich
Beinn Udlaidh 2759
Beinn Bhreac-liath 2633
Beinn Odhar 2948
Ben Challum 3354
Beinn Cheathaich 3076
Meall Chuirn 3007
Killin
Adjoining page 52
Glen Noe
Beinn Eunaich 3242
Glen Strae
Beinn Donachain 2127
Arrivain
Glen Lochy
Clifton
Tyndrum
Cononish
Strath Fillan
Auchtertyre
Beinn nan Imirean 2769
Allt Riobain
Auchlyne
Auchlyne W. Burn
Dochart
Taynuilt
Bridge of Awe
Pass of Brander
Ben Cruachan 3689
Cruachan Resvr.
Beinn a' Bhùiridh 2941
Kilchurn Castle
Stronmilchan
Achnafalnich
Beinn na Sròine 2085
Inverlochy
Strath of Orchy
Dalmally
Lochawe
Lower Kinchrackine
Glen Nant
Barguillean Farm
Auchrioch
Inverherive
Crianlarich
Lochdochart House
Loch Iubhair
Glen Dochart
Luib Hotel
Ardchyle
Ledcharrie 1946
Beinn Leabhain 2312
Lochearnhead
Loch Tromlee
Innis Chonain
Ardanaiseig
Inishail
Teatle Water
Achlian
Ben Lui 3708
Ben Oss 3374
Beinn Dubhchraig 3204
Fiarach 2132
Portnellan
Loch Dochart
Ben More 3843
Stob Binnein 3821
Monachyle Glen
Meall an t-Seallaidh 2793
Edinchip
Loch Nant
Kilchrenan
Annat
Taychreggan
Cladich
Inistrynich
Beinn Bhalgairean 2085
Meall nan Tighearn 2423
Allt Fionn Ghlinne
Dubh Eas
Glen Falloch
Falloch
Braes of Balquhidder
Balquhidder
Auchtoo
Kingshouse
Auchachenna
Coillaig
Upper Sonachan
South Port
Lochan Shira
Lochan Stron Mor
Beinn Bhuidhe 3106
Troisgeach 2407
Glenfalloch Farm
Falls of Falloch
Inverarnan
Monachylemore
Loch Voil
Strathyre
Inverinan
Inverinan Forest
Ballimeanoch
Taynafead
Beinn Ghlas 1804
Rob Roy's House
Brannie Burn
Allt na Lairige
Ben Glas Burn
Beinn Tulaichean 3099
Beinn a' Chroin 3104
Inverlochlarig
Loch Doine
Ballimore
Cruach Mhòr 1932
Drimfern
Tullich
Elrigbeg
Glen Shira
Clachan Hill 2159
Glenfyne Lodge
Maol Breac 2115
Ardlui
Stuckindroin
Stob a' Choin 2839
Meall Mor 2451
Runachaig
Laggan
Barnaline
Blarghour
Ardchonnell
Portinnisherrich
Glen Aray
Dubh Loch
Kilblaan Burn
Clachan
Loch Sloy
Ben Vorlich 3092
Ardvorlich
Beinn a' Choin 2524
Glengyle
Portnellan
Beinn Bhreac 2242
Benvane 2685
Meall Cala 2203
Glen Finglas
Loch Lubnaig
Callander
Malt Land
Drishaig 1240
Cairndow
Binnein an Fhidhleir 2660
Rob Roy's Cave
Stronachlachar
Cruinn Bheinn 1787
Strath Gartney
Edra
Loch Katrine
Ben Ledi 2873
Eredine
Inveraray Castle
Dundarave Castle
Ardno
Glen Kinglas
Ben Vane 3004
Inveruglas
Beinn Ime 3318
Inversnaid Hotel
L. Arklet
Cruachan 1762
Inveraray
Stob an Eas 2402
Beinn an Lochain 2992
Rest and be thankful
The Cobbler 3036
Ben Arthur 2891
Succoth
Tarbet
Arrochar
Craig Rostan
Loch Lomond
Frenich
Loch Chon
Goblin's Cave
Ben Venue 2386
The Trossachs
Trossachs Hotel
Brig o' Turk
Lendrick Lo.
Loch Achray
L. Venechar
Duncraggan
An Suidhe 1687
Douglas Water
Dalchenna
St. Catherines
Hells Glen
Cruach nan Capull 1854
Creag a' Phuill
Monevechadan
Glen Croe
Ardgartan
Ardmay
Stuckgowan
Cruinn a' Bheinn 2077
Beinn Dub 1675
Achray Forest
Loch Drunkie
Stirling
Beinn Dearg 1575
Auchindrain
Loch Leacann
Dùn Leacainn 1173
Brenachoille
Kenmore
Furnace
Creggans
Strachur
Tigh-na-criche
Glensluain
Mullach Coire a' Chuir 2098
Ben Donich 2777
Lochgoilhead
Cnoc Coinnich 2497
Drimsynie
Corrow
Beinn Lochain 2306
Ardgoil
Ardgoil Estate
Ardgartan Forest
Ben Lomond 3192
Ptarmigan Lodge
Kinlochard
Aikskeith
Loch Ard
Milton
Aberfoyle
Menteith Hills
Duchray Water
Braeval
Malling
Lake of Menteith
Cobleland
Gartmore
Lock Ard Forest
Queen Elizabeth National Forest Park
Argyll National Forest Park
Sanahole
Beinn Ghlas 1377
Crarae Lodge
Crarae
Minard
Invernoaden
Beinn Bheula 2556
Leanach
Cruach nan Capull 1578
Glenbranter
Glenbranter Forest
Cormonachan
Craggan
Glen Douglas
Doune Hill 2408
Beinn Bhreac 2233
Ardess
Rowardennan Beinn Uird
Rowardennan Hotel 1957
Rowardennan Forest
Inverbeg Hotel
Loch Eck
Loch Goil
Ardgoil Forest
Eilean Aoghainn
Tullochgorm
Barnacarry
Garbhallt
Strathlachlan Forest
Lephinmore
Cruach an Lochain 1658
Beinn Bheag 2029
Cruach a' Bhuic 2084
Carrick
Ardentinny
Beinn a' Mhanaich 2328
Beinn Eich 2302
Edentaggart
Glen Luss
Inchlonaig
Cashell
Gualann 1514
Flanders Moss
Kelty Water
Gartachoil
Moor Park
Conic Hill 1175
Balmaha
Buchanan Smithy
Garadhban Forest
Luss
Beinn Chaorach 2340
Beinn Ruisg 1946
Aldochlay
Portincaple
Garelochhead
Gare Loch
Strone
Creachan Mòr 2156
Loch Long
Bernice
Beinn Mhòr 2433
Sligrachan
Dunans
Lephinchapel
C O W A L
Ardentraive
Adjoining page 46
Dunoon
Dumbarton
Adjoining page 47
COPYRIGHT, GEORGE PHILIP & SON, LTD.

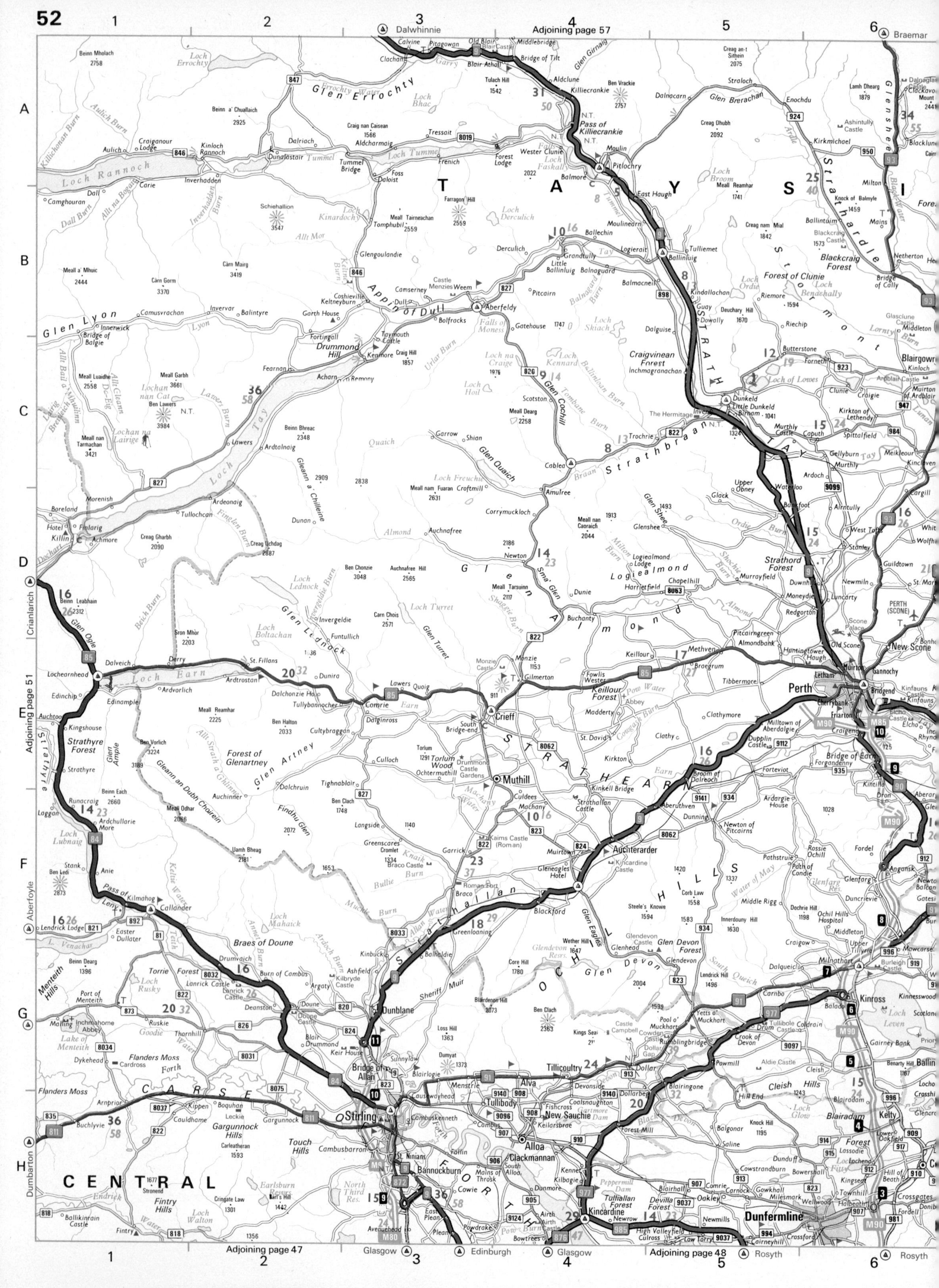

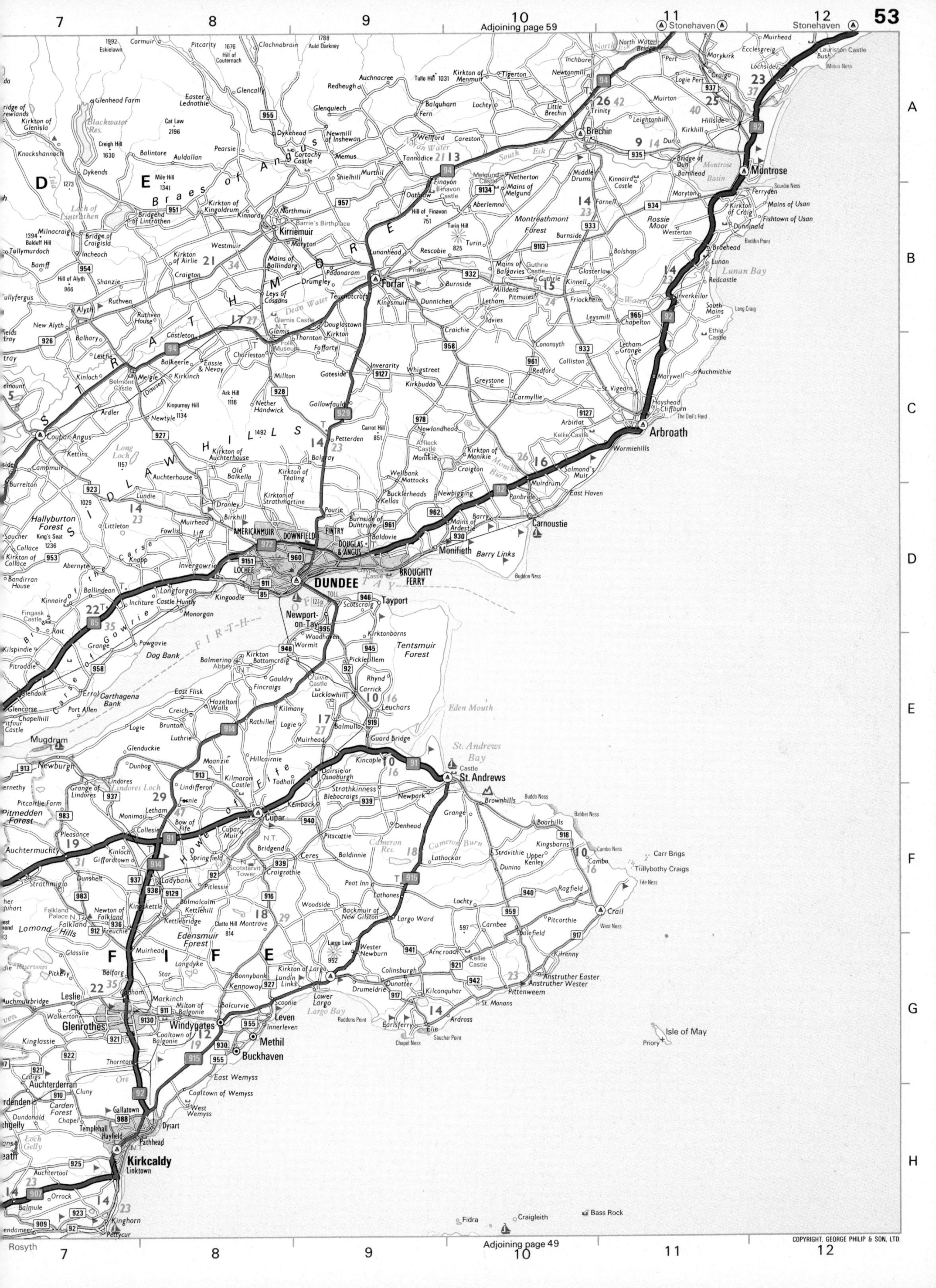

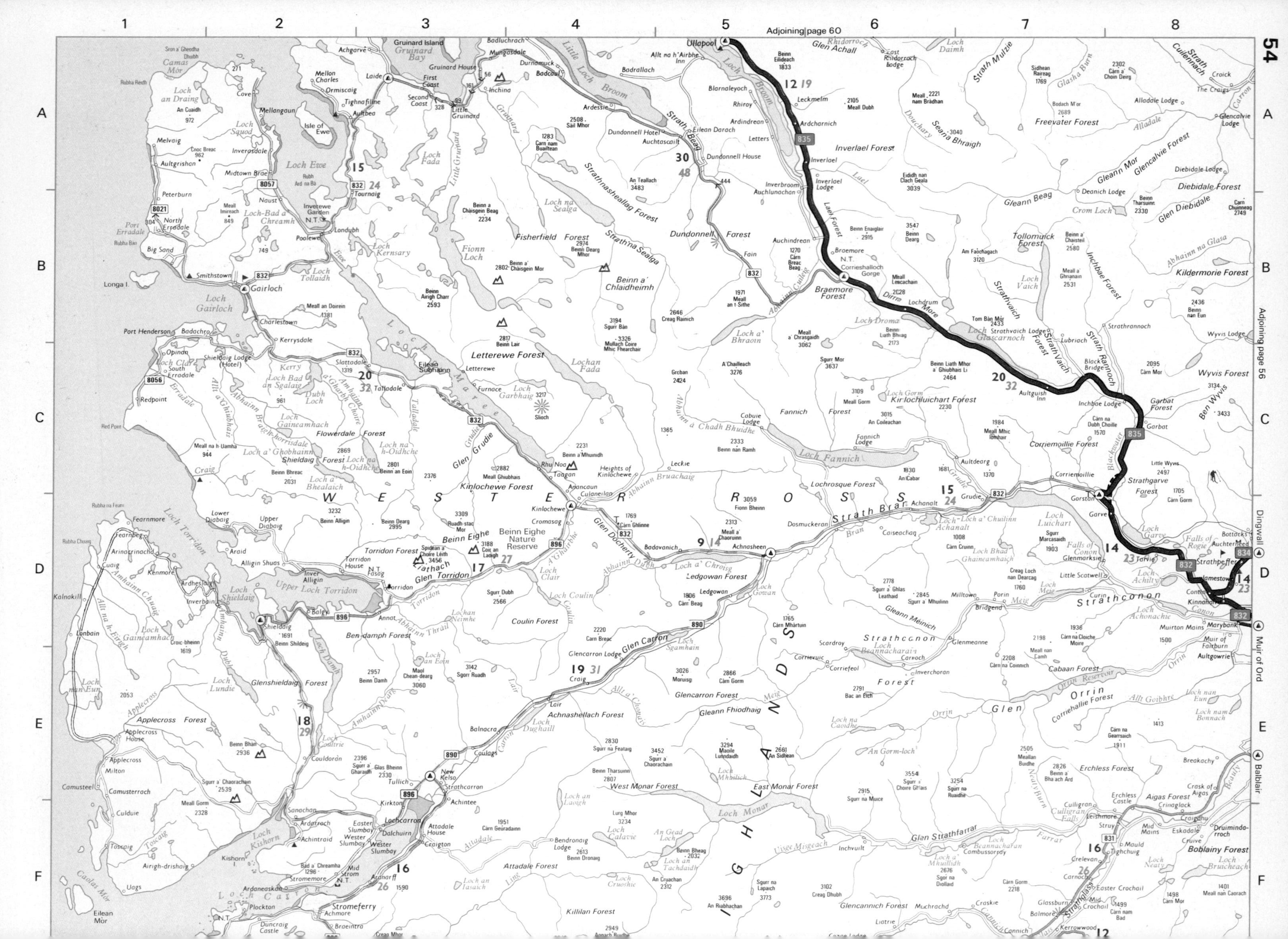

Adjoining page 60
Adjoining page 56
Dingwall
Muir of Ord
Balblair
Ullapool
Gairloch
Kinlochewe
Achnasheen
Lochcarron
Shieldaig
Applecross
Strathpeffer
Gorstan
Braemore
Loch Broom
Loch Maree
Loch Torridon
Loch Ewe
Loch Fannich
Loch Monar
Strath Bran
Glen Carron
Glen Docherty
Beinn Eighe Nature Reserve
Fisherfield Forest
Letterewe Forest
Applecross Forest
W E S T E R R O S S
H I G H L A N D S
835
832
896
890
8021
8056
8057

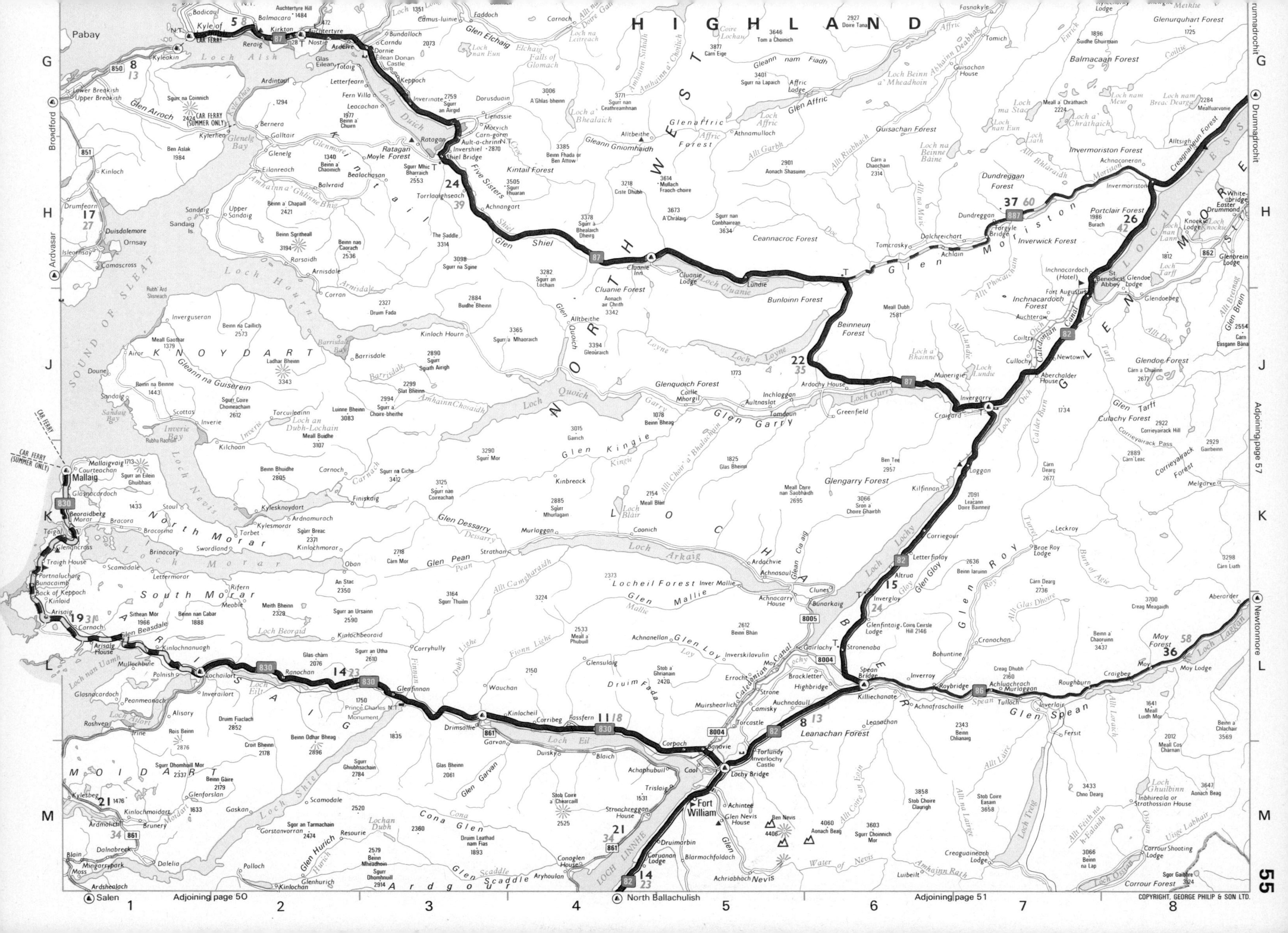

HIGHLAND
NORTH WEST
LOCHABER
KNOYDART
MOIDART
Ardgour
North Morar
South Morar
Loch Alsh
Kyle of Lochalsh
Kyleakin
Loch Duich
Dornie
Eilean Donan Castle
Five Sisters
Kintail Forest
Glen Shiel
Cluanie Inn
Loch Cluanie
Glen Moriston
Invermoriston
Loch Ness
Fort Augustus
Invergarry
Loch Garry
Glen Garry
Loch Quoich
Loch Hourn
Loch Nevis
Loch Morar
Mallaig
Arisaig
Lochailort
Glenfinnan
Loch Eil
Loch Arkaig
Loch Lochy
Spean Bridge
Glen Roy
Glen Spean
Loch Laggan
Fort William
Ben Nevis 4406
Loch Linnhe
Loch Shiel
Sound of Sleat
Caledonian Canal
Glen Affric
Adjoining page 57
Adjoining page 50
Adjoining page 51
Salen
North Ballachulish
Broadford
Ardvasar
Drumnadrochit
Newtonmore
CAR FERRY
CAR FERRY (SUMMER ONLY)
COPYRIGHT, GEORGE PHILIP & SON LTD.

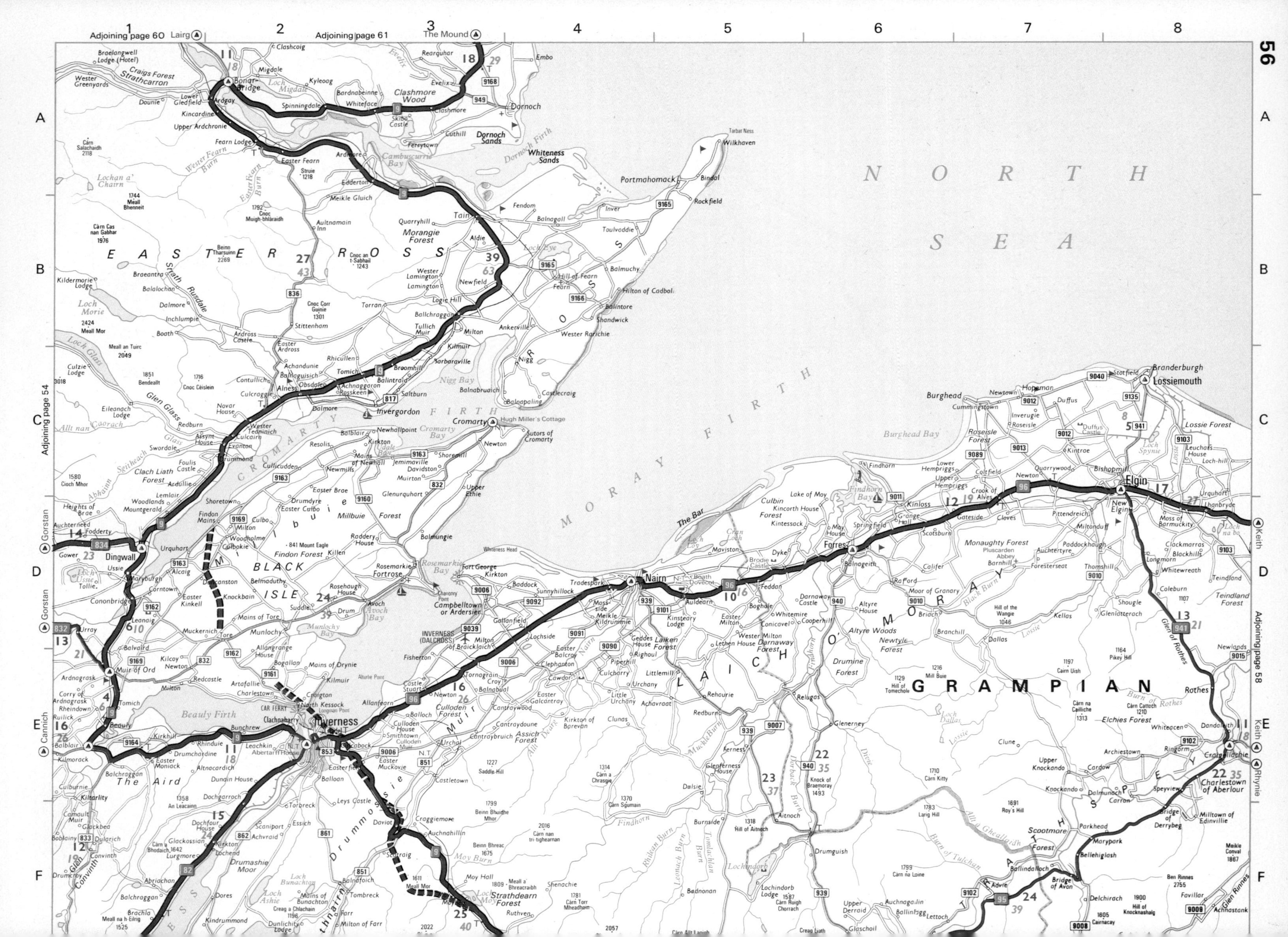

Adjoining page 60
Lairg
Adjoining page 61
The Mound
Adjoining page 54
Adjoining page 58
Keith
Rhynie
Gorstan
Cannich
NORTH SEA
MORAY FIRTH
CROMARTY FIRTH
EASTER ROSS
BLACK ISLE
GRAMPIAN
LAICH O' MORAY
Bonar Bridge
Dornoch
Dornoch Firth
Whiteness Sands
Tarbat Ness
Wilkhaven
Portmahomack
Tain
Invergordon
Cromarty
Dingwall
Fortrose
Inverness
Beauly
Beauly Firth
Nairn
Forres
Burghead
Burghead Bay
Lossiemouth
Branderburgh
Elgin
Rothes
Glen of Rothes
Charlestown of Aberlour
Culloden Forest
Strathdearn Forest
The Aird
Nigg Bay
Findhorn Bay
The Bar

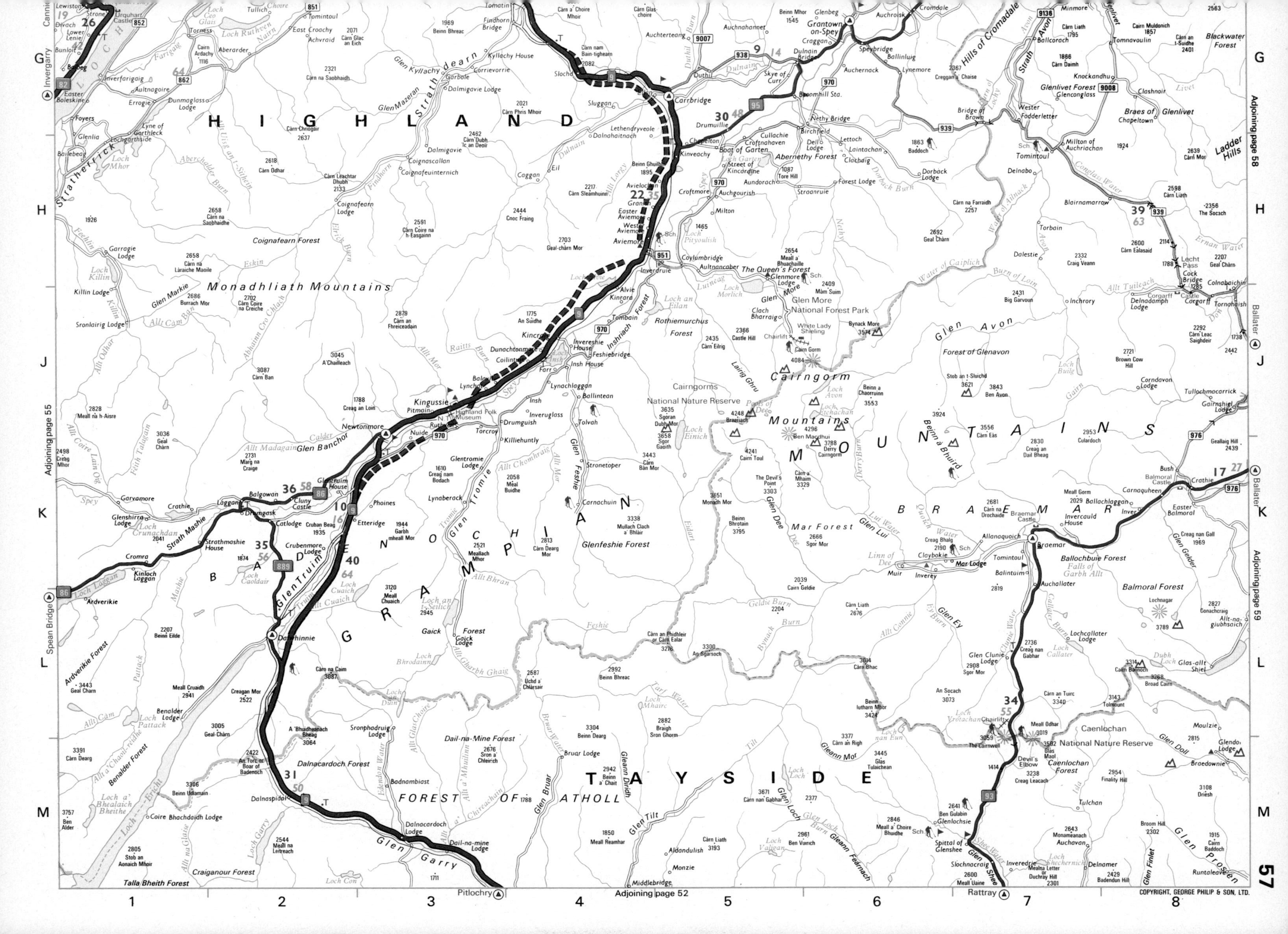
Adjoining page 58
Adjoining page 59
Ballater
Ballater
Adjoining page 52
Pitlochry
Rattray
Adjoining page 55
Spean Bridge
Invergarry
COPYRIGHT, GEORGE PHILIP & SON, LTD.
HIGHLAND
Monadhliath Mountains
GRAMPIAN
Cairngorm Mountains
MOUNTAINS
BRAEMAR
BADENOCH
TAYSIDE
FOREST OF ATHOLL
Cairngorms National Nature Reserve
Glen More National Forest Park
Caenlochan National Nature Reserve
Balmoral Forest
Mar Forest
Glenfeshie Forest
Gaick Forest
Rothiemurchus Forest
Abernethy Forest
Glenlivet Forest
Dalnacardoch Forest
Dail-na-Mine Forest
Coignafearn Forest
Ballochbuie Forest
Forest of Glenavon
Ben Macdhui
Cairn Gorm
Braeriach
Beinn à Bhuird
Ben Avon
Aviemore
Kingussie
Newtonmore
Grantown-on-Spey
Carrbridge
Dalwhinnie
Braemar
Tomintoul
Kincraig
Nethy Bridge
Boat of Garten
Strath Spey
Strathdearn
Glen Feshie
Glen Truim
Glen Garry
Glen Tilt
Glen Shee
Glen Doll
Glen Avon
Glen Ey
Glen Lui
Glen Dee
Glen Banchor
Hills of Cromdale
Ladder Hills
Braes of Glenlivet
Falls of Garbh Allt
Lochnagar
Balmoral Castle
Crathie
Spittal of Glenshee
Devil's Elbow
Linn of Dee
Inverey
Mar Lodge
Blair Atholl
Talla Bheith Forest
Ardverikie Forest
Benalder Forest
Craiganour Forest
Laggan
Strath Mashie
Loch Ness

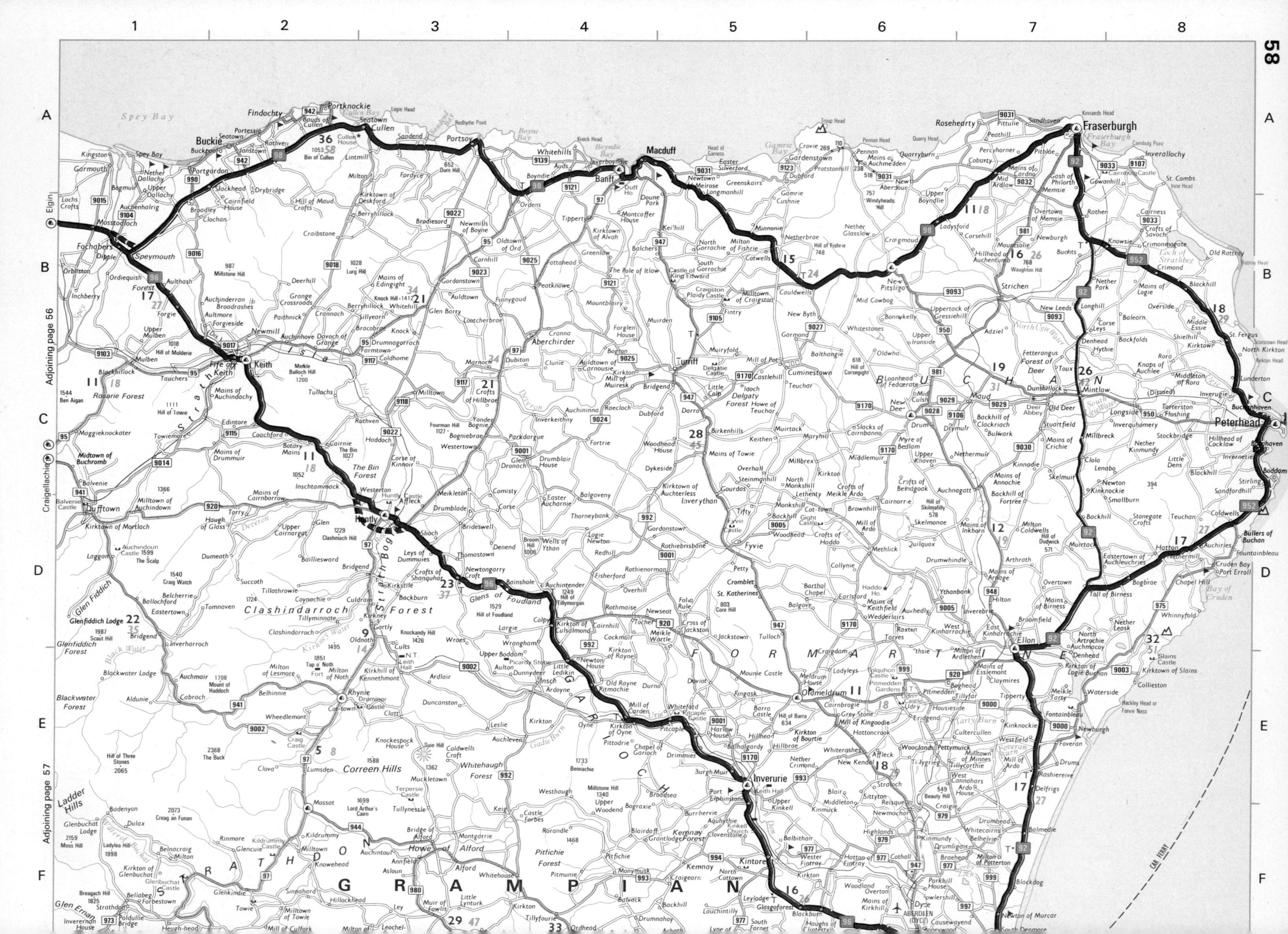
Fraserburgh
Peterhead
Macduff
Banff
Portsoy
Cullen
Buckie
Keith
Huntly
Turriff
Inverurie
Oldmeldrum
Ellon
Fyvie
New Deer
Maud
Mintlaw
New Pitsligo
Strichen
Aberchirder
Dufftown
Rhynie
Alford
Kintore
Fochabers
Rosehearty
Whitehills
Portknockie
Findochty
Spey Bay
Boyndie Bay
Bay of Cruden
Forest of Deer
Clashindarroch Forest
Correen Hills
The Bin Forest
Glens of Foudland
Adjoining page 56
Adjoining page 57
Elgin
Craigellachie
GRAMPIAN
BUCHAN
FORMARTINE
GARIOCH
STRATHDON

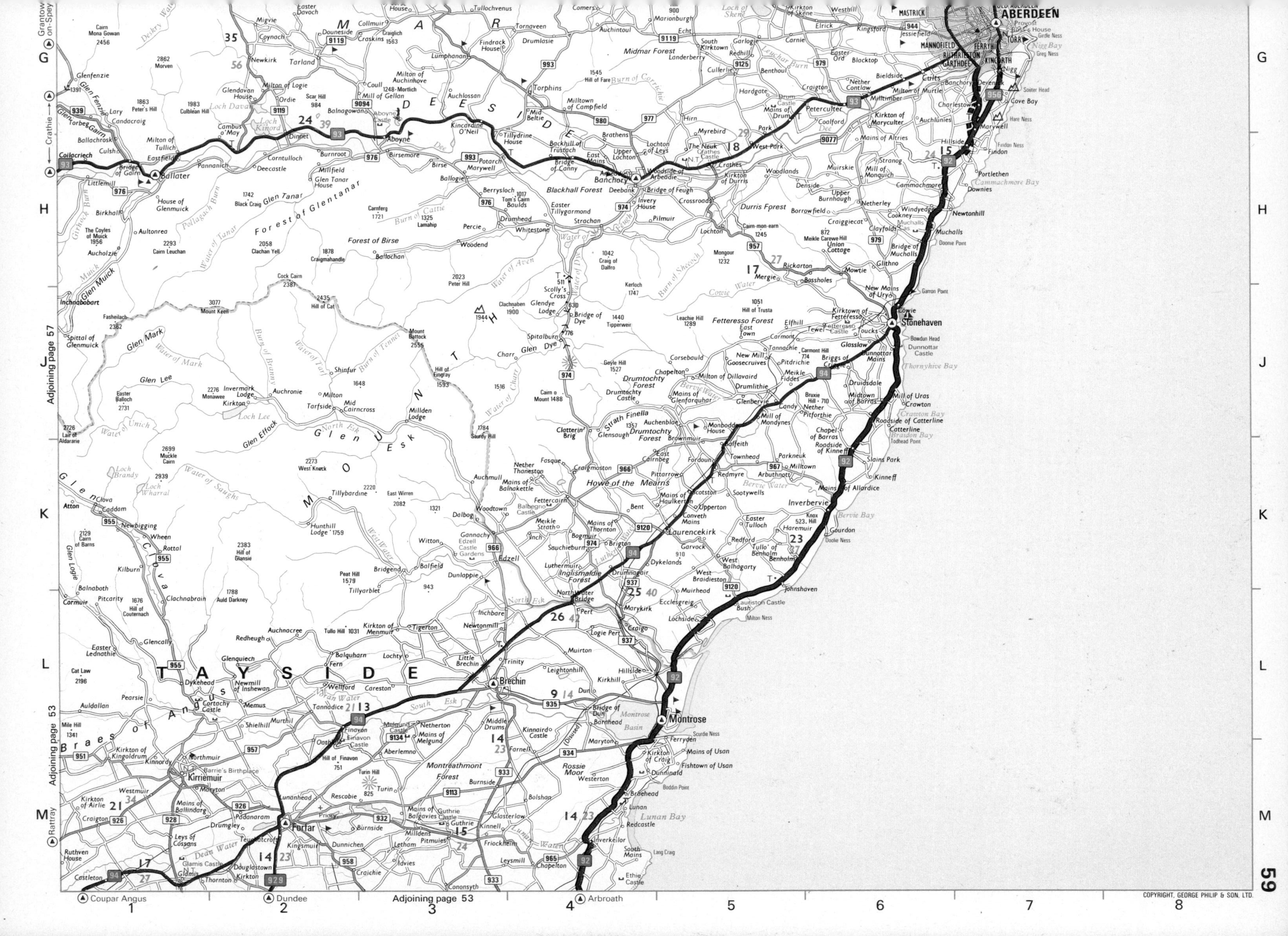
ABERDEEN
Stonehaven
Montrose
Brechin
Forfar
Kirriemuir
Banchory
Aboyne
Ballater
Inverbervie
Johnshaven
Laurencekirk
Edzell
Fettercairn
Durris Forest
Fetteresso Forest
Drumtochty Forest
Howe of the Mearns
Forest of Birse
Forest of Glentanar
Glen Esk
Glen Clova
Glen Muick
Lunan Bay
Montrose Basin
Peterculter
Portlethen
Newtonhill
Muchalls
Gourdon
Glamis Castle
DEESIDE
TAYSIDE
Arbroath
Dundee
Coupar Angus
Rattray
Crathie
Grantown on-Spey
Adjoining page 53
Adjoining page 57

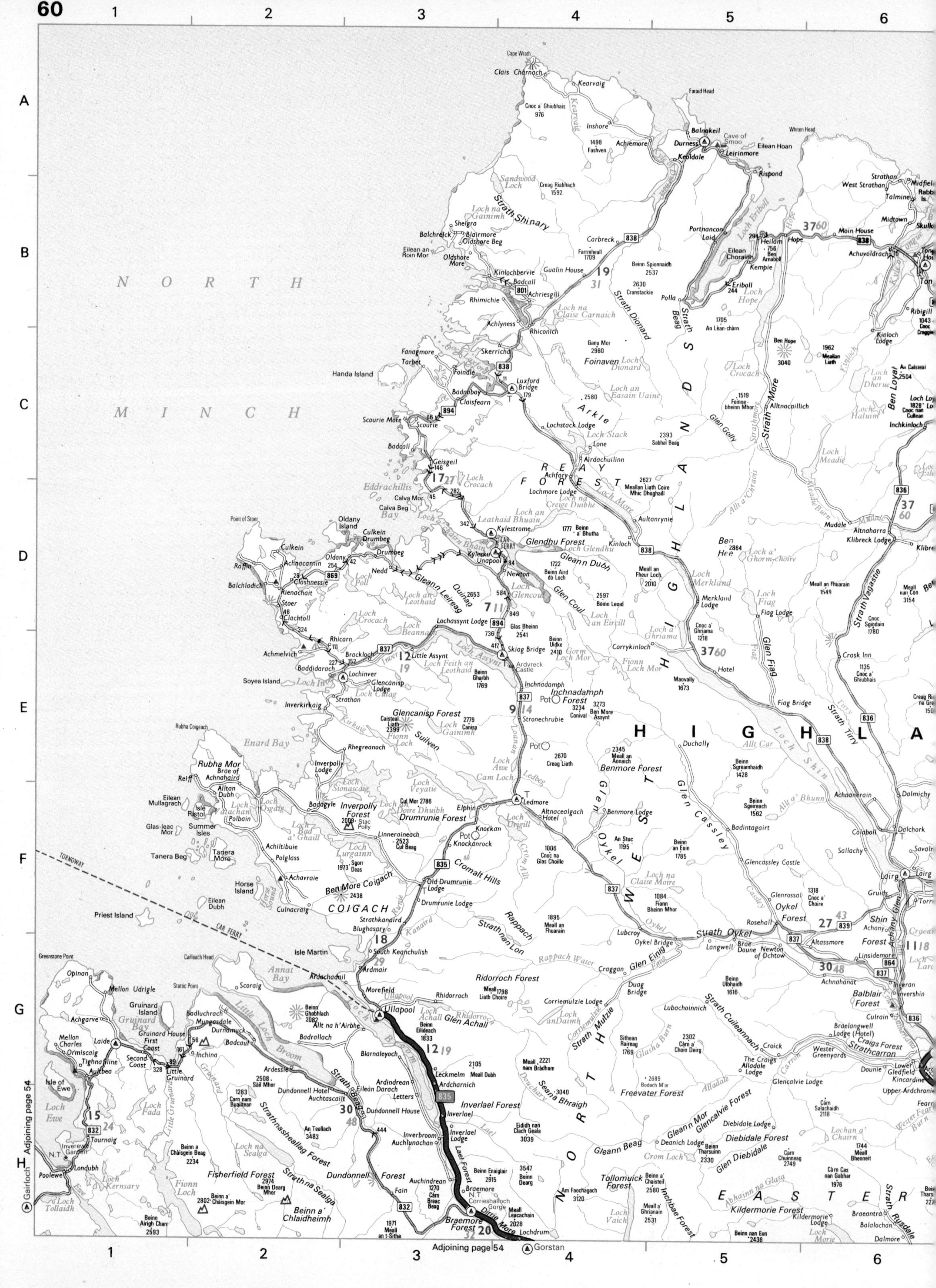

1
2
3
4
5
6
A
B
C
D
E
F
G
H
NORTH
MINCH
Cape Wrath
Clais Charnoch
Kearvaig
Cnoc a' Ghiubhais
976
Inshore
Achiemore
1498
Fashven
Faraid Head
Balnakeil
Durness
Cave of Smoo
Keoldale
Leirinmore
Eilean Hoan
Whiten Head
Rispond
Sandwood Loch
Creag Riabhach
1592
Strath Shinary
Loch na Gainimh
Sheigra
Balchreick
Blairmore
Oldshore Beg
Eilean an Roin Mor
Oldshore More
Kinlochbervie
Badcall
Achriesgill
Rhimichie
Achlyness
Rhiconich
Gualin House
Carbreck
838
Farrmheall
1709
Beinn Spionnaidh
2537
2630
Cranstackie
Strath Dionard
Loch na Claise Carnaich
19
31
Portnancon
Laid
Loch Eriboll
Eilean Choraidh
Kempie
Eriboll
244
Polla
Strath Beag
Loch Hope
1705
An Lean-charn
Heilam
Hope
Ben Arnaboll
756
Strathan
West Strathan
Midfield
Talmine
Rabbit Is.
Midtown
Skullomie
Moin House
Achuvoldrach
Tongue
Ribigill
Kinloch Lodge
Ben Hope
3040
1962
Meallan Liath
Strath More
Loch an Dherue
Ben Loyal
An Caisteal
2504
Loch Loyal
Loch Crocach
1519
Feinne-bheinn Mhor
Alltnacaillich
Loch Haluim
Inchkinloch
Fanagmore
Tarbet
Handa Island
Skerricha
Foindle
Badnabay
Luxford Bridge
Claisfearn
Scourie More
Scourie
894
Ganu Mor
2980
Foinaven
Loch Dionard
2580
Loch an Easain Uaine
Arkle
Lochstack Lodge
Loch Stack
Lone
Airdachuilinn
Achfary
REAY
FOREST
Lochmore Lodge
Loch More
Loch na Creige Duibhe
2393
Sabhal Beag
2627
Meallan Liath Coire Mhic Dhughaill
Glen Golly
Strathmore
Loch Meadie
Badcall
Geisgeil
146
17
27
Loch Crocach
Eddrachillis Bay
Calva Mor
Calva Beg
Point of Stoer
Oldany Island
Culkein Drumbeg
Culkein
Achnacarnin
Raffin
Oldany
Drumbeg
Nedd
Clashnessie
869
Balchladich
Rienachait
Stoer
Clachtoll
Leathaid Bhuain
Loch an Leathaid Bhuain
Kylestrome
CAR FERRY
Kylesku
Unapool
1777
Beinn a' Bhutha
Glendhu Forest
Loch Glendhu
Gleann Dubh
Kinloch
Aultanrynie
Allt a' Chraois
Ben Hee
2864
Loch a' Ghorm-choire
Mudale
Altnaharra
Klibreck Lodge
Klibreck
836
37
60
Gleann Leireag
Quinag
2653
Loch an Leothaid
Loch Poll
Newton
Loch Glencoul
Glen Coul
1722
Beinn Aird da Loch
2597
Beinn Leoid
Meall an Fheur Loch
2010
Loch Merkland
Merkland Lodge
Loch Fiag
Fiag Lodge
Meall an Fhuarain
1549
Strath Vagastie
Meall nan Con
3154
Loch Crocach
Loch Beannach
Lochassynt Lodge
7
11
849
Glas Bheinn
2541
Loch an Eircill
Loch a' Ghriama
Cnoc a' Ghriama
1218
Glen Fiag
Cnoc Sgiodain
1780
Rhicarn
Achmelvich
Baddidarach
Brackloch
837
Little Assynt
12
19
Loch Assynt
Skiag Bridge
Ardvreck Castle
Beinn Uidhe
2410
Gorm Loch Mor
Corrykinloch
Fionn Loch Mor
37
60
Hotel
Crask Inn
1135
Cnoc a' Ghiubhais
Soyea Island
Loch Inver
Lochinver
Glencanisp Lodge
Loch Feith an Leothaid
Beinn Gharbh
1769
Inchnadamph
Inchnadamph Forest
3234
Conival
3273
Ben More Assynt
Maovally
1673
Fiag Bridge
Strath Tirry
Inverkirkaig
Strathan
Loch Culag
Glencanisp Forest
Caisteal Liath
2399
2779
Canisp
Loch Gainimh
9
14
Stronechrubie
Rubha Coigeach
Enard Bay
Suilven
Fionn Loch
Kirkaig
Rhegreanoch
Pot
2670
Creag Liath
HIGHLANDS
HIGHLA
2345
Meall an Aonaich
Benmore Forest
Duchally
Allt Car
Loch Shin
Beinn Sgreamhaidh
1428
Rubha Mor
Reiff
Brae of Achnahaird
Altan Dubh
Inverpolly Lodge
Loch Sionascaig
Loch Veyatie
Loch Awe
Cam Loch
Ledbeg
Ledmore
Altnacealgach Hotel
Benmore Lodge
Glen Oykel
Glen Cassley
Beinn Sgeireach
1562
Allt a' Bhunn
Achnanerain
Dalmichy
Eilean Mullagrach
Isle Ristol
Polbain
Loch Osgaig
Badagyle
Inverpolly Forest
2009
Stac Polly
Cul Mor 2786
Loch Doire Dhuibh
Drumrunie Forest
Elphin
Loch Urigill
Glas-leac Mor
Summer Isles
Loch Bad a' Ghaill
Linneraineach
2523
Cul Beag
Knockan
Knockanrock
An Stuc
1195
Beinn an Eoin
1785
Badintagairt
Colaboll
Dalchork
Tanera Beg
Tanera More
Achiltibuie
Polglass
Loch Lurgainn
1973
Sgorr Deas
835
Cromalt Hills
1006
Cnoc na Glas Choille
Glencassley Castle
Sallachy
TORNOWAY
Achavraie
Horse Island
Horse Sound
Ben More Coigach
2438
Old Drumrunie Lodge
Crom Allt
Loch na Claise Moire
1084
Fionn Bheinn Mhor
Glenrossal
1318
Cnoc a' Choire
Lairg
Gruids
Eilean Dubh
Culnacraig
COIGACH
Drumrunie Lodge
Rappach
1895
Meall an Fhuarain
Oykel Forest
43
Shin
Priest Island
CAR FERRY
Strathkanaird
Blughasary
Kanaird
Strath nan Lon
Lubcroy
Oykel Bridge
Strath Oykel
Rosehall
27
839
Achany
Forest
Achany Glen
Langwell
Brae
Doune
Newton of Ochtow
Altassmore
Linsidemore
11
18
864
Greenstone Point
Cailleach Head
Isle Martin
18
South Keanchulish
29
Rappach Water
Craggan
Glen Einig
Annat Bay
Ardmair
Ardachadail
Ridorroch Forest
Opinan
Mellon Udrigle
Static Point
Scoraig
Morefield
Rhidorroch
Meall Liath Choire
1798
Corriemulzie Lodge
Duag Bridge
Beinn Ulbhaidh
1616
30
48
Achnahanat
Balblair Forest
Inveran
Invershin
Gruinard Island
Gruinard Bay
Achgarve
Badluchrach
Mungasdale
Dundonnell
Beinn Ghobhlach
2082
Allt na h' Airbhe
Ullapool
Loch Achall
Beinn Eilideach
1833
Glen Achall
Loch an Daimh
Strath Mulzie
Lubachoinnich
Strath Cuileannach
Culrain
Mellon Charles
Ormiscaig
Laide
Gruinard House
First Coast
Second Coast
Tighnafiline
Aultbea
Inchina
Little Gruinard
Badcaul
Badrallach
Little Loch Broom
Loch Broom
Blarnaleyoch
12
19
Sithean Rairaig
1769
2302
Carn a' Choin Deirg
Croick
Alladale Lodge
The Craigs
Wester Greenyards
Braelangwell Lodge (Hotel)
Craigs Forest
Strathcarron
Isle of Ewe
Loch Ewe
Ardessie
2508
Sail Mhor
Dundonnell Hotel
Auchtascailt
Strath Beag
Eilean Darach
Ardindrean
Letters
2105
Meall Dubh
Leckmelm
Ardcharnich
Meall nam Bradham
2221
Seana Bhraigh
3040
2689
Bodach M'or
Freevater Forest
Glencalvie Lodge
Glencalvie Forest
Dounie
Lower Gledfield
Kincardine
Upper Ardchronie
15
24
832
Tournaig
1283
Carn nam Buailtean
Loch Fada
Strathnasheallag Forest
An Teallach
3483
Dundonnell House
Inverbroom
Auchlunachan
Inverlael Forest
Inverlael
Inverlael Lodge
Eididh nan Clach Geala
3039
Gleann Mor
Diebidale Lodge
Diebidale Forest
Deanich Lodge
Beinn Tharsuinn
2330
Glen Diebidale
Carn Salachaidh
2118
Lochan a' Chairn
1744
Meall Bhenneit
Inverewe Gardens
N.T.
Londubh
Poolewe
Beinn a Chaisgein Beag
2234
Loch na Sealga
Fisherfield Forest
Strath na Sealga
Dundonnell Forest
Lael Forest
Gleann Beag
Crom Loch
Carn Chuinneag
2749
Carn Cas nan Gabhar
1976
Loch Kernsary
Fionn Loch
Beinn a' Chaisgein Mor
2802
2974
Beinn Dearg Mhor
Beinn a' Chlaidheimh
Auchindrean
Fain
1270
Carn Breac Beag
Beinn Enaiglair
2915
3547
Beinn Dearg
Braemore
N.T. Corrieshalloch Gorge
Meall Leacachain
2028
Am Faochagach
3120
Tollomuick Forest
Beinn a' Chaisteil
2580
Inchbae Forest
Abhainn na Glasa
EASTER
Kildermorie Forest
Kildermorie Lodge
Braeantra
Balalochan
Dalmore
Strath Rusdale
Loch Tollaidh
Beinn Airigh Charr
2593
1971
Meall an t-Sitha
Braemore Forest
Dirrie More
Lochdrum
32
20
Loch Vaich
Meall a' Ghrianain
2531
Beinn nan Eun
2436
Loch Morie
Gairloch
Adjoining page 54
Gorstan
NORTH
WEST

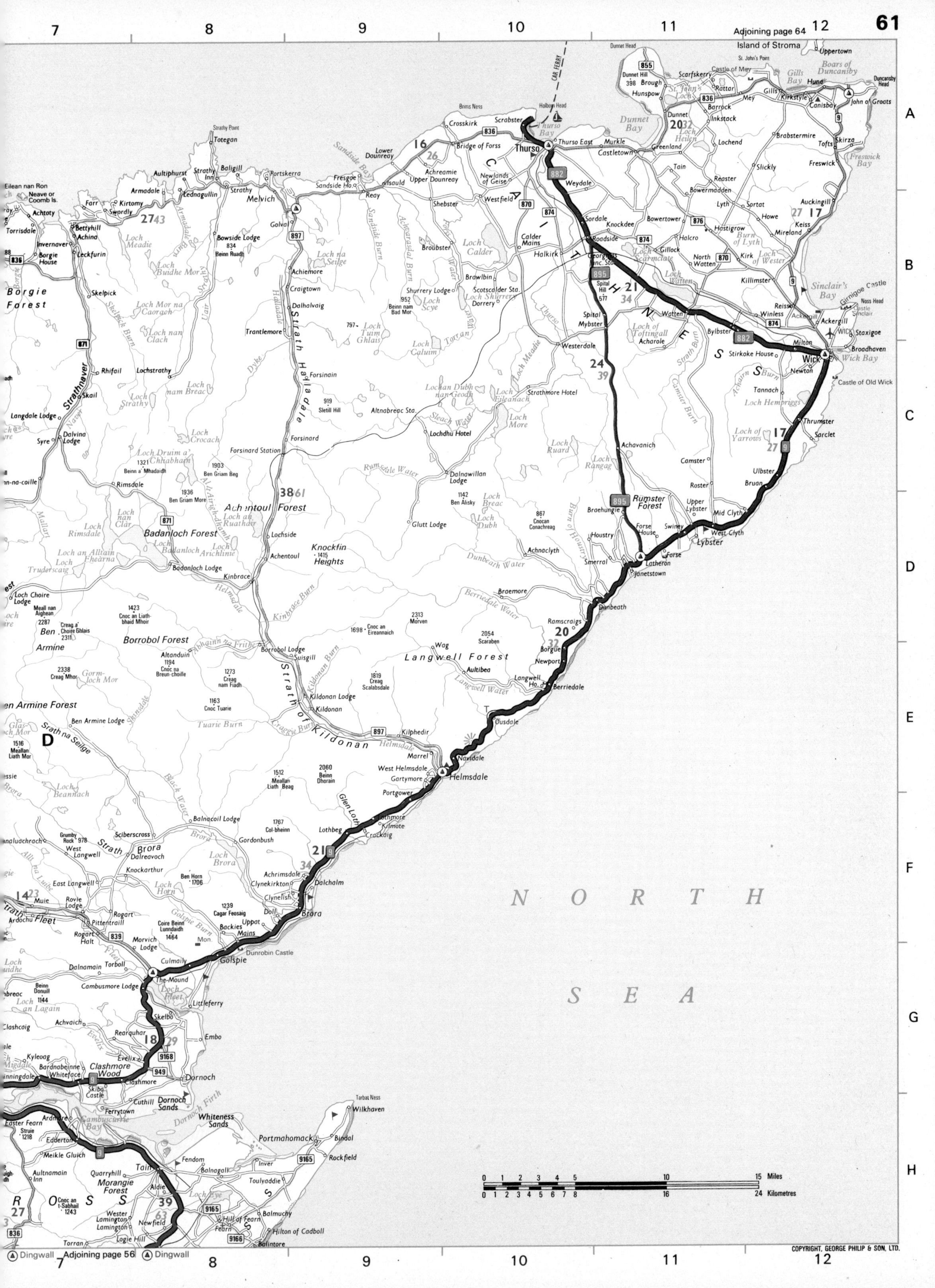

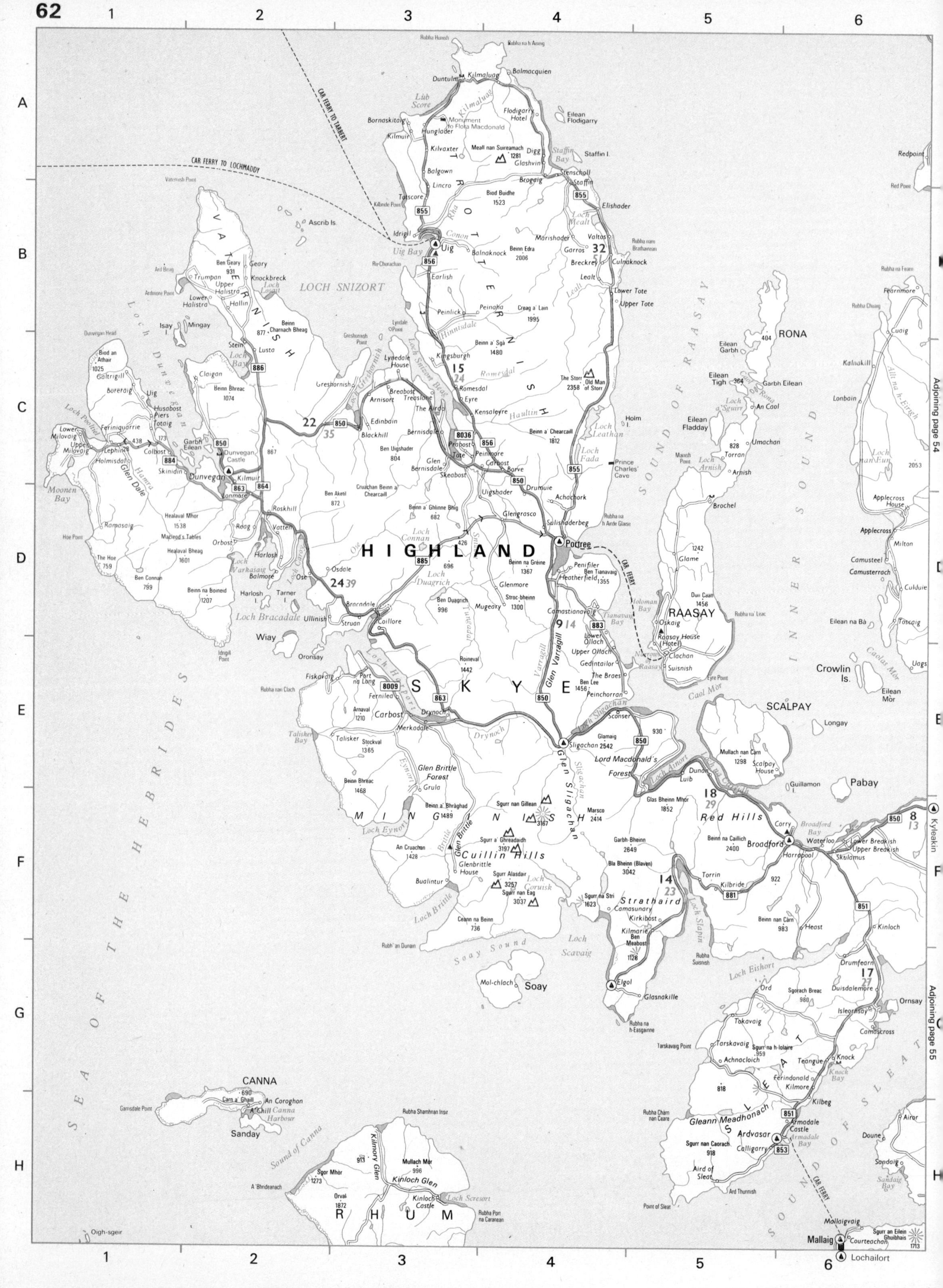
HIGHLAND
SKYE
TROTTERNISH
VATERNISH
MINGINIS
SLEAT
RAASAY
RONA
SCALPAY
CANNA
RHUM
Soay
Sanday
SEA OF THE HEBRIDES
SOUND OF RAASAY
INNER SOUND
SOUND OF SLEAT
LOCH SNIZORT
Cuillin Hills
Red Hills
Portree
Dunvegan
Uig
Broadford
Mallaig
Kyleakin
Adjoining page 54
Adjoining page 55
CAR FERRY TO LOCHMADDY
CAR FERRY TO TARBERT

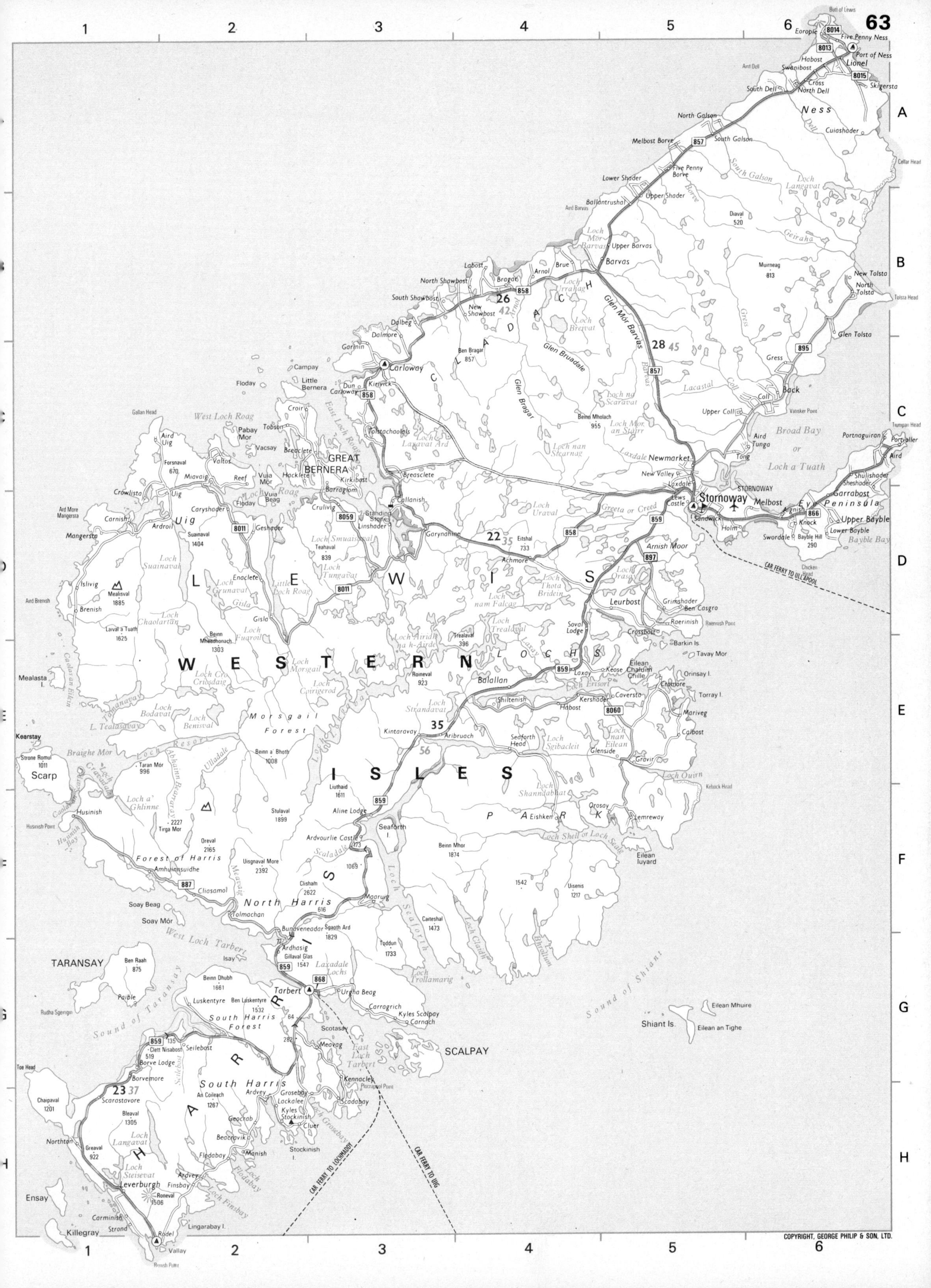

WESTERN ISLES
LEWIS
HARRIS
North Harris
South Harris
Stornoway
Barvas
Carloway
Tarbert
Leverburgh
Rodel
Uig
GREAT BERNERA
Callanish
Balallan
Ness
Lionel
Port of Ness
Butt of Lewis
Eye Peninsula
Broad Bay or Loch a Tuath
West Loch Roag
East Loch Roag
Morsgail Forest
Forest of Harris
South Harris Forest
West Loch Tarbert
East Loch Tarbert
Sound of Taransay
Sound of Shiant
Shiant Is.
TARANSAY
SCALPAY
Scarp
Kearstay
Ensay
Killegray
Loch Seaforth
Loch Erisort
Loch Shell or Loch Sealg
PARK
LOCHS
CLADACH
Clisham 2622
Mealisval 1885
CAR FERRY TO ULLAPOOL
CAR FERRY TO UIG
CAR FERRY TO LOCHMADDY

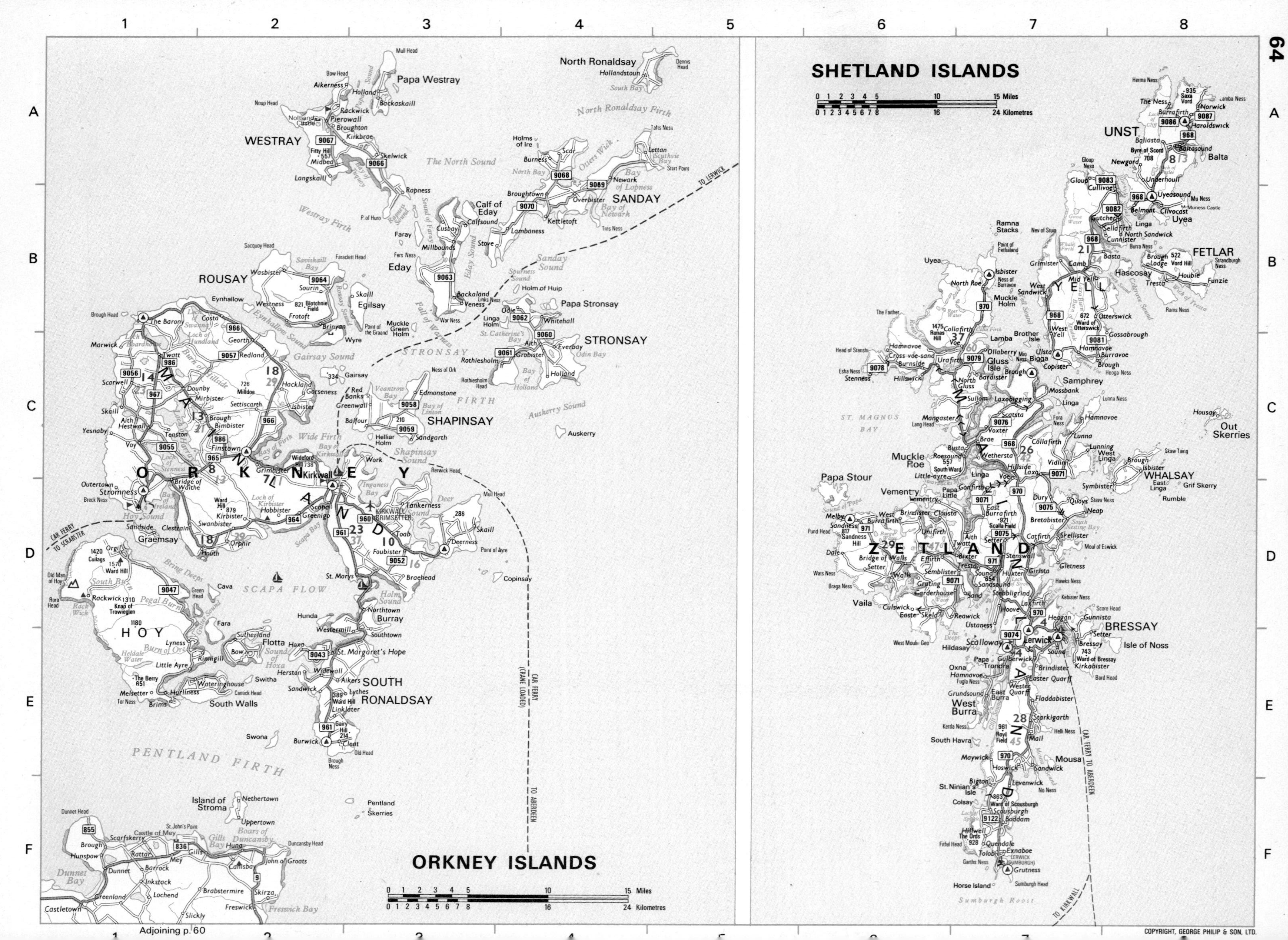

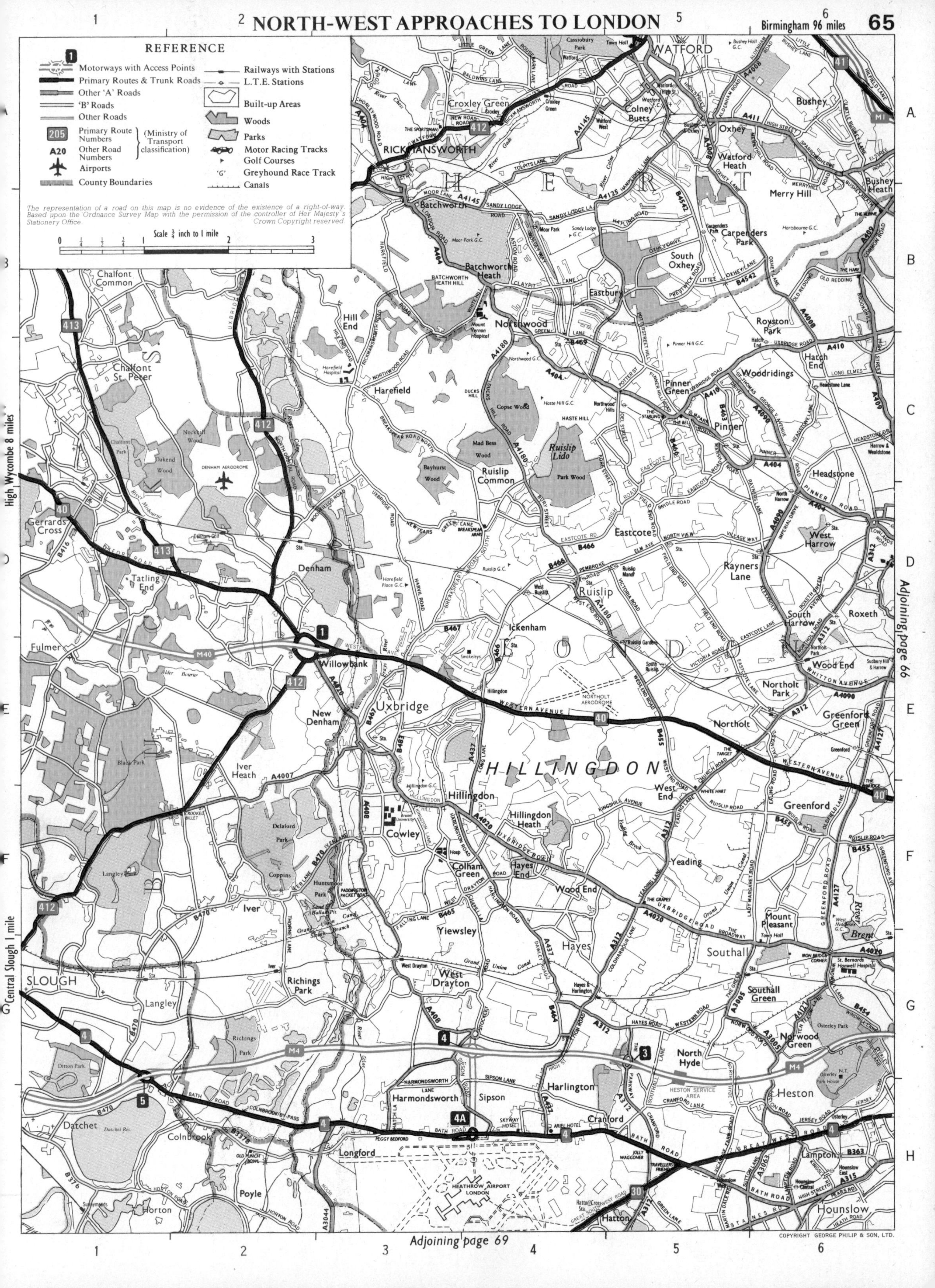
REFERENCE
Motorways with Access Points
Primary Routes & Trunk Roads
Other 'A' Roads
'B' Roads
Other Roads
Primary Route Numbers
Other Road Numbers
(Ministry of Transport classification)
Airports
County Boundaries
Railways with Stations
L.T.E. Stations
Built-up Areas
Woods
Parks
Motor Racing Tracks
Golf Courses
Greyhound Race Track
Canals
The representation of a road on this map is no evidence of the existence of a right-of-way. Based upon the Ordnance Survey Map with the permission of the controller of Her Majesty's Stationery Office. Crown Copyright reserved.
Scale 3/4 inch to 1 mile
WATFORD
Bushey
Oxhey
Watford Heath
Merry Hill
Bushey Heath
Croxley Green
Colney Butts
RICKMANSWORTH
Batchworth
Batchworth Heath
Carpenders Park
South Oxhey
Eastbury
Northwood
Royston Park
Hatch End
Chalfont Common
Chalfont St. Peter
Hill End
Harefield
Pinner Green
Woodridings
Pinner
Headstone
Ruislip Lido
Ruislip Common
Eastcote
West Harrow
Gerrards Cross
Tatling End
Denham
Rayners Lane
Ruislip
Roxeth
South Harrow
Ickenham
Fulmer
Willowbank
Wood End
Northolt Park
Uxbridge
New Denham
Northolt
Greenford Green
HILLINGDON
Iver Heath
Hillingdon
West End
Greenford
Hillingdon Heath
Cowley
Colham Green
Hayes End
Yeading
Wood End
Iver
Yiewsley
Mount Pleasant
Hayes
Southall
SLOUGH
Richings Park
West Drayton
Langley
Southall Green
Norwood Green
North Hyde
Heston
Harlington
Harmondsworth
Sipson
Datchet
Colnbrook
Cranford
Longford
Lampton
Poyle
HEATHROW AIRPORT LONDON
Horton
Hatton
Hounslow
High Wycombe 8 miles
Central Slough 1 mile
Adjoining page 66
Adjoining page 69
COPYRIGHT GEORGE PHILIP & SON, LTD.

1
2
3
4
5
6
A
C
D
E
F
G
H
St. Albans 7 miles
Peterborough 69 miles
Hatfield 8 miles
Adjoining page 65
Adjoining page 69
Adjoining page 70
ELSTREE AERODROME
Aldenham Park
Hilfield Reservoir
Aldenham Reservoir
Elstree
Borehamwood
Rowley Bank
Arkley
Barnet Gate
Totteridge
Cockfosters
New Barnet
East Barnet
Oakleigh Park
Whetstone
Friern Barnet
North Finchley
Palmers Green
New Southgate
Bushey Heath
Brockley Hill
SCRATCHWOOD SERVICE AREA
Moat Mount
Highwood Hill
B A R N E T
Stone Grove
Stanmore
Canons Park
Edgware
Mill Hill
Colney Hatch
Finchley
Hatch End
Harrow Weald
Belmont
Burnt Oak
H A R R O W
Queensbury
Colindale
Church End
Holders Hill
Wealdstone
Hendon
East Finchley
Muswell Hill
Headstone
Kingsbury
The Hyde
Hornsey
Harrow
Greenhill
Kenton
Kingsbury Green
Golders Green
West Harrow
Harrow on the Hill
Preston
B R E N T
Brent Reservoir
Highgate
Roxeth
Neasden
Hampstead Heath
Wembley
Cricklewood
Hampstead
Wood End
Willesden Green
Kentish Town
Greenford Green
Willesden
Brondesbury
C A M D E N
Camden Town
Alperton
Harlesden
Brondesbury Park
Kilburn
Perivale
Greenford
Park Royal
Kensal Green
Kensal Rise
St. John's Wood
Maida Vale
REGENT'S PARK
Somers Town
Hanger Hill
E A L I N G
Elthorne Heights
Drayton Green
Ealing
WORMWOOD SCRUBS
Paddington
Marylebone
Bloomsbury
Notting Hill
Bayswater
Soho
Acton
East Acton
HYDE PARK
Mayfair
Hanwell
Shepherd's Bush
KENSINGTON
KENSINGTON AND CHELSEA
Hammersmith
Brook Green
Brompton
WESTMINSTER
Little Ealing
GUNNERSBURY PARK
Gunnersbury
Belgravia
Brentford
Chiswick
Pimlico
Osterley
Kew
Spring Grove
H O U N S L O W
ROYAL BOTANIC GARDENS
BATTERSEA PARK
Battersea
Barnes
R I V E R
T H A M E S
Lampton
Hounslow
OLD DEER PARK
Isleworth
Mortlake
Clapham
Polo Ground
Hurlingham House

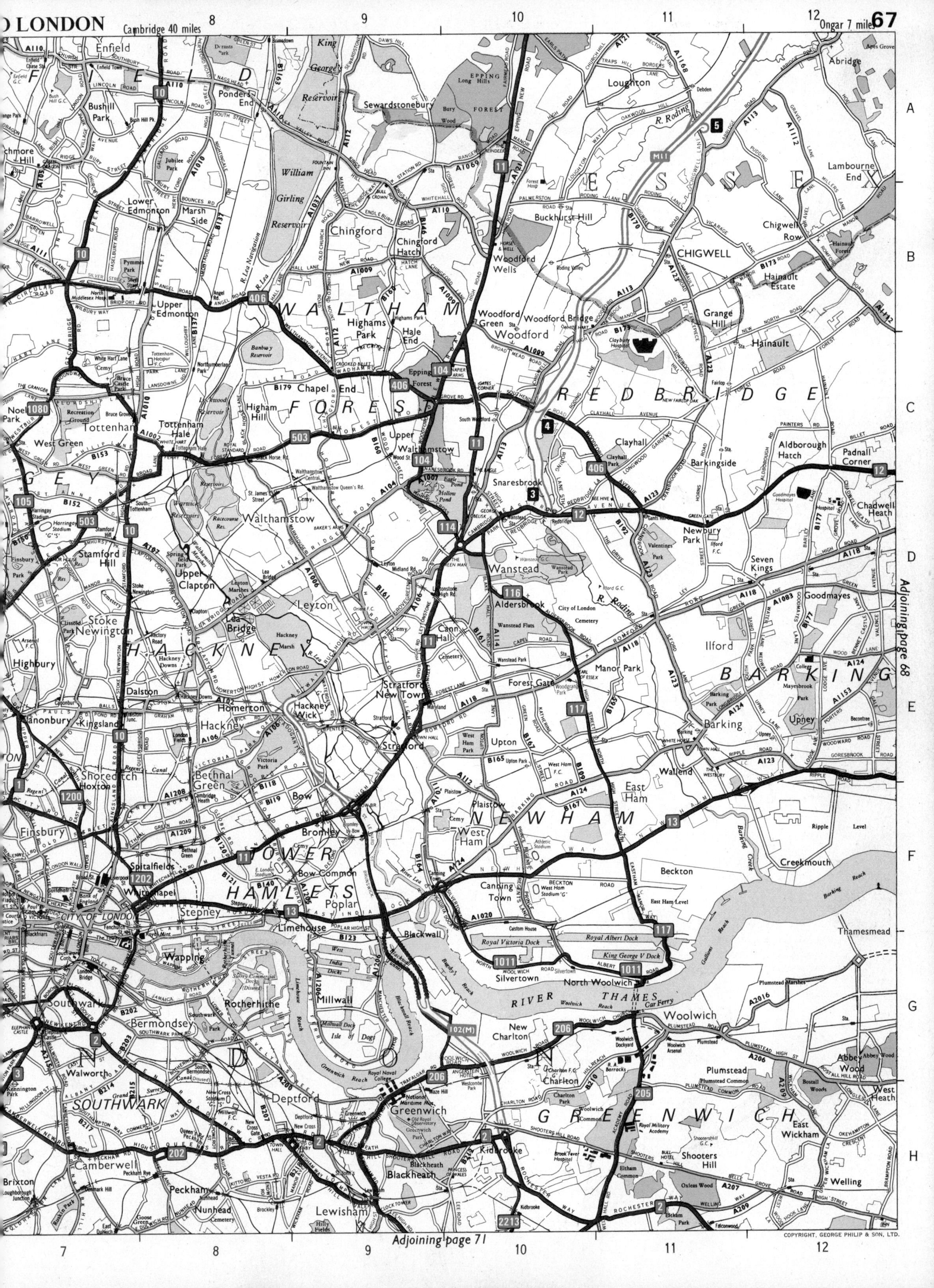

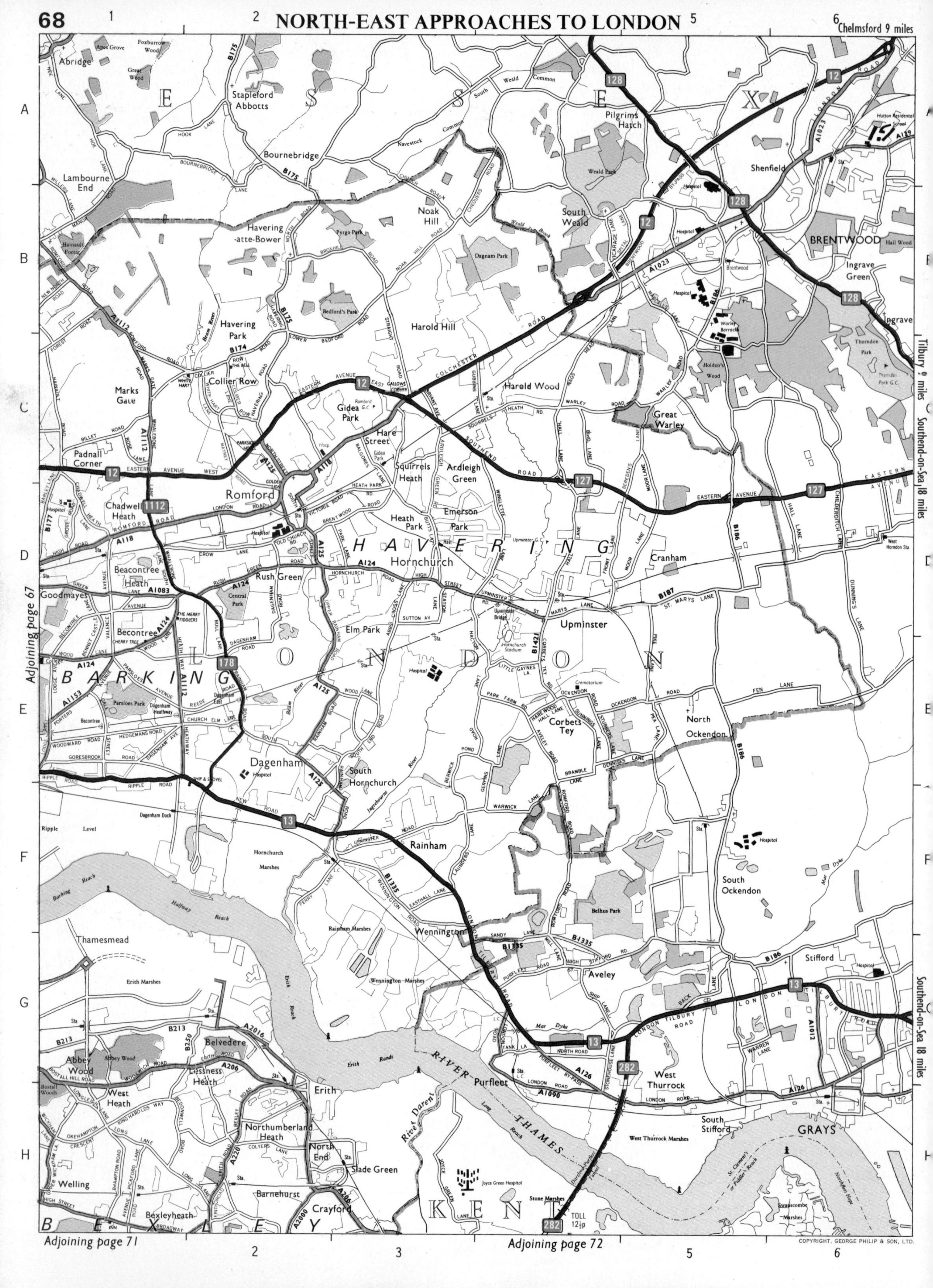

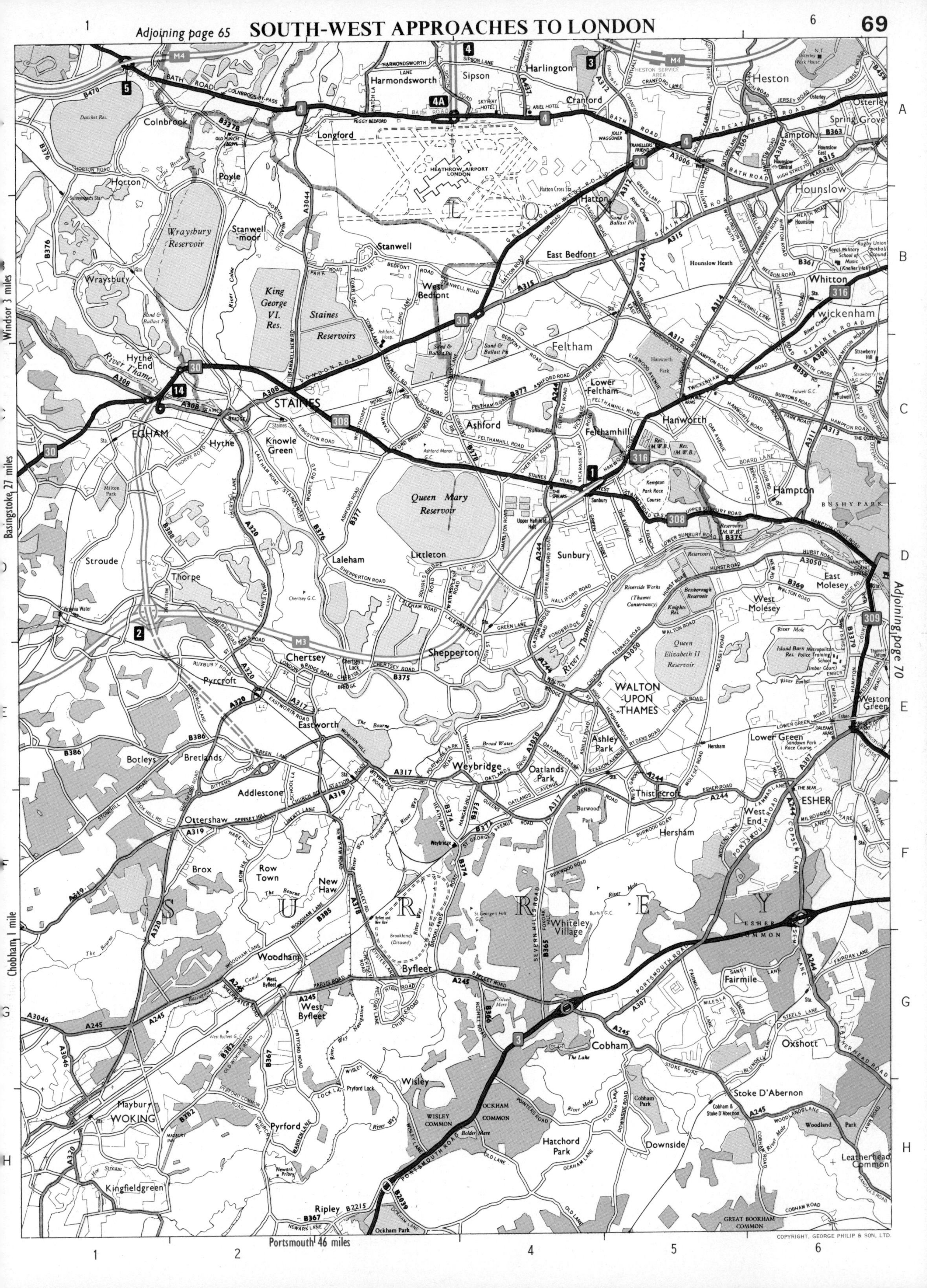
Harmondsworth
Sipson
Harlington
Cranford
Heston
Osterley
Spring Grove
Lampton
Hounslow
Colnbrook
Longford
HEATHROW AIRPORT LONDON
Horton
Poyle
Hatton
Wraysbury Reservoir
Stanwell-moor
Stanwell
East Bedfont
Hounslow Heath
Whitton
Wraysbury
King George VI. Res.
Staines Reservoirs
West Bedfont
Feltham
Twickenham
Hythe End
River Thames
STAINES
Lower Feltham
Ashford
Hanworth
Felthamhill
EGHAM
Hythe
Knowle Green
Queen Mary Reservoir
Sunbury
Hampton
BUSHY PARK
Stroude
Laleham
Littleton
Thorpe
East Molesey
West Molesey
Chertsey
Shepperton
Queen Elizabeth II Reservoir
Pyrcroft
WALTON-UPON-THAMES
Weston Green
Eastworth
Ashley Park
Lower Green
Botleys
Bretlands
Weybridge
Oatlands Park
Addlestone
Thistlecroft
ESHER
Ottershaw
West End
Hersham
Brox
Row Town
New Haw
S U R R E Y
Whiteley Village
ESHER COMMON
Woodham
Byfleet
Fairmile
West Byfleet
Cobham
Oxshott
Wisley
Stoke D'Abernon
Mayberry
WOKING
Pyrford
WISLEY COMMON
OCKHAM COMMON
Hatchord Park
Downside
Woodland
Leatherhead Common
Kingfieldgreen
Ripley
Ockham Park
GREAT BOOKHAM COMMON
Windsor 3 miles
Basingstoke 27 miles
Chobham 1 mile
Portsmouth 46 miles
Adjoining page 70

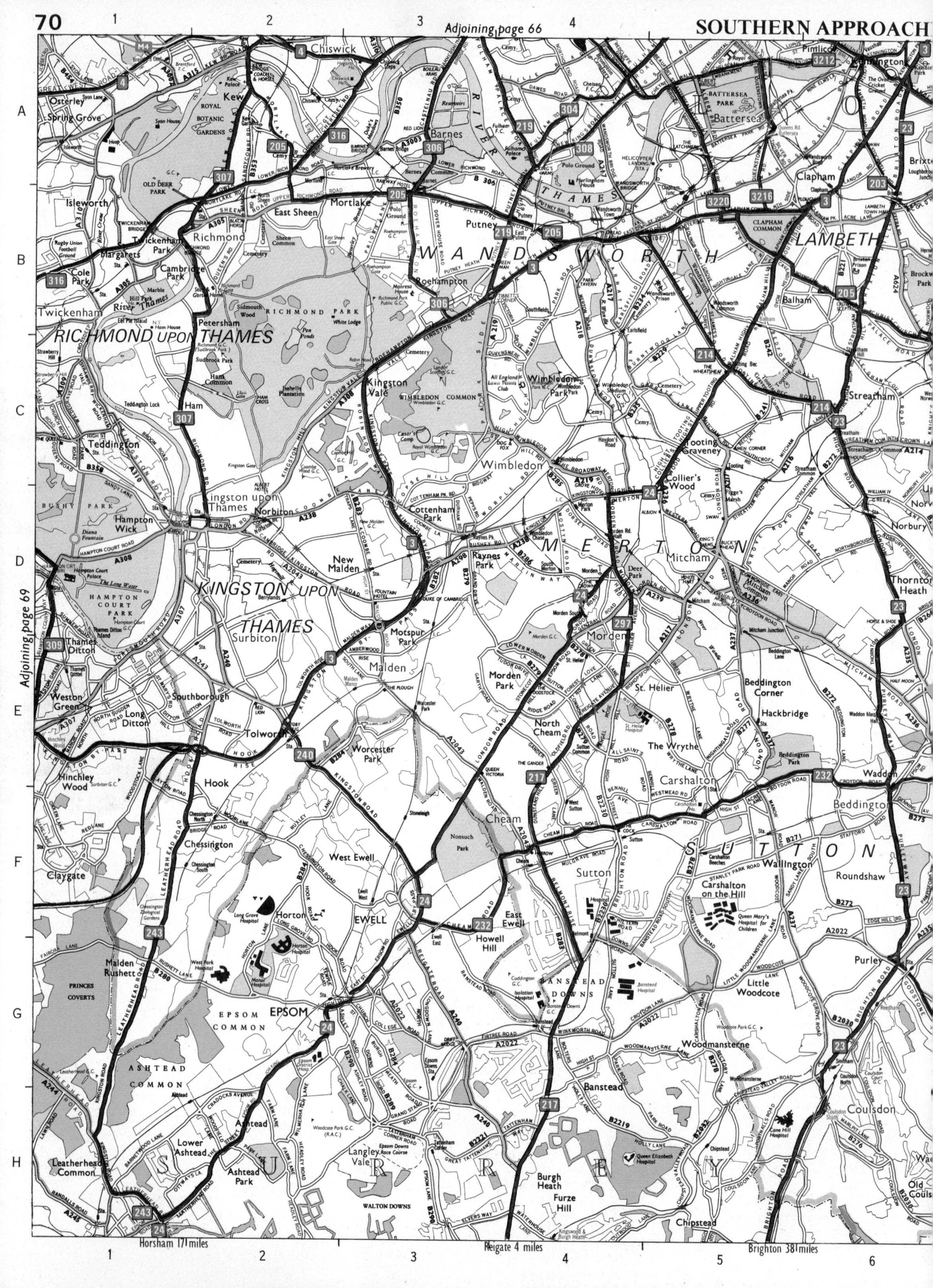

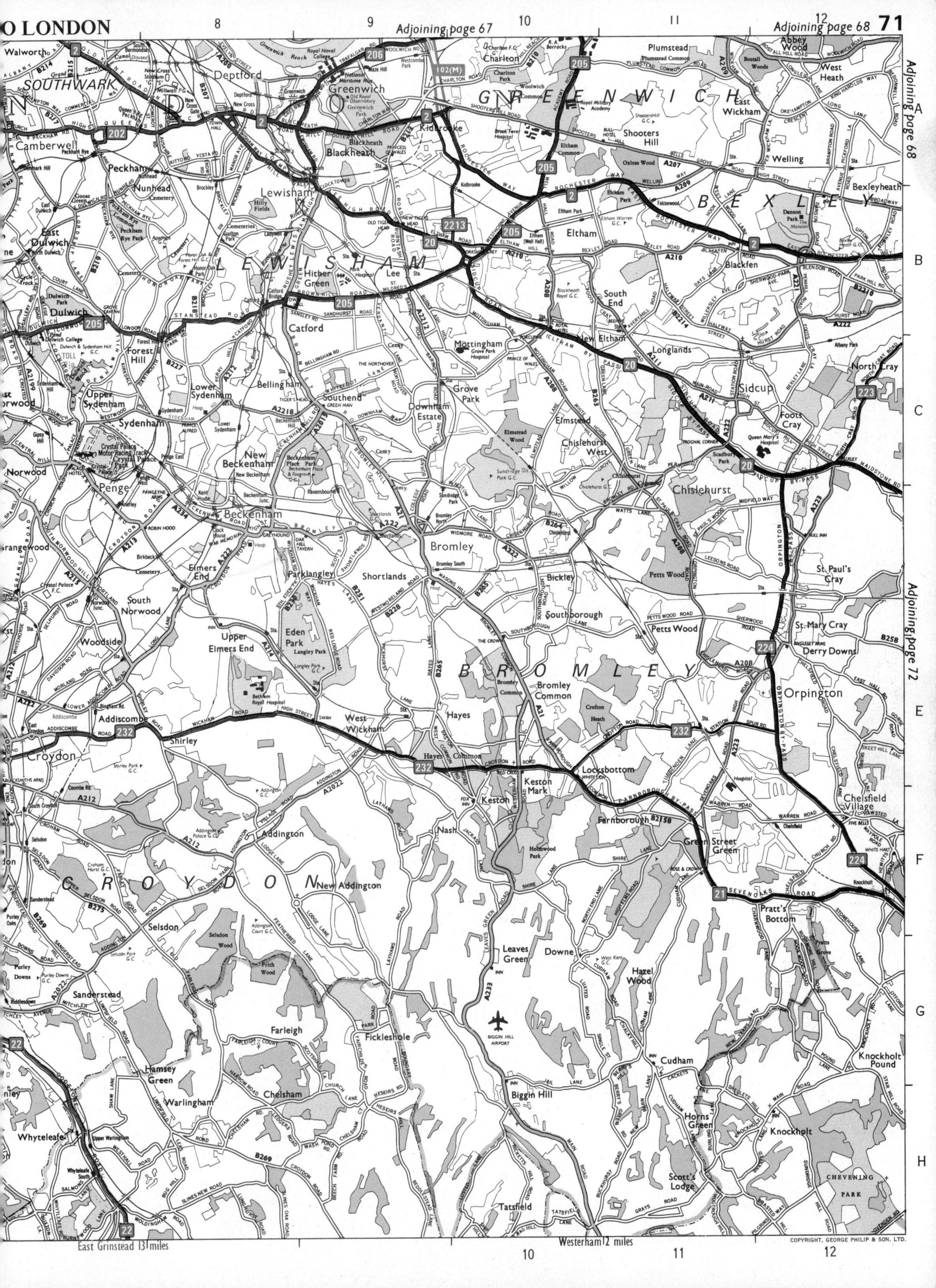
Walworth
SOUTHWARK
Camberwell
Peckham
Nunhead
Deptford
Greenwich
Blackheath
Kidbrooke
Charlton
GREENWICH
Plumstead
Abbey Wood
West Heath
East Wickham
Shooters Hill
Welling
Bexleyheath
BEXLEY
Eltham
Lewisham
LEWISHAM
Hither Green
Lee
Catford
East Dulwich
Dulwich
Forest Hill
Upper Sydenham
Lower Sydenham
Sydenham
Bellingham
Southend
Downham Estate
Grove Park
Mottingham
New Eltham
South End
Blackfen
Longlands
Sidcup
North Cray
Foots Cray
Elmstead
Chislehurst West
Chislehurst
Norwood
Penge
New Beckenham
Beckenham
Bromley
Shortlands
Parklangley
Elmers End
South Norwood
Woodside
Upper Elmers End
Eden Park
Bickley
Petts Wood
Southborough
St. Paul's Cray
St. Mary Cray
Derry Downs
BROMLEY
Bromley Common
Orpington
Hayes
West Wickham
Addiscombe
Shirley
Croydon
Hayes Common
Locksbottom
Keston Mark
Keston
Nash
Farnborough
Chelsfield Village
Green Street Green
Addington
New Addington
CROYDON
Selsdon
Pratt's Bottom
Leaves Green
Downe
Hazel Wood
Sanderstead
Farleigh
Fickleshole
Hamsey Green
Warlingham
Chelsham
Biggin Hill
Cudham
Knockholt Pound
Knockholt
Horns Green
Whyteleafe
Scott's Lodge
Tatsfield
CHEVENING PARK
BIGGIN HILL AIRPORT
Adjoining page 72
East Grinstead 13 miles
Westerham 12 miles

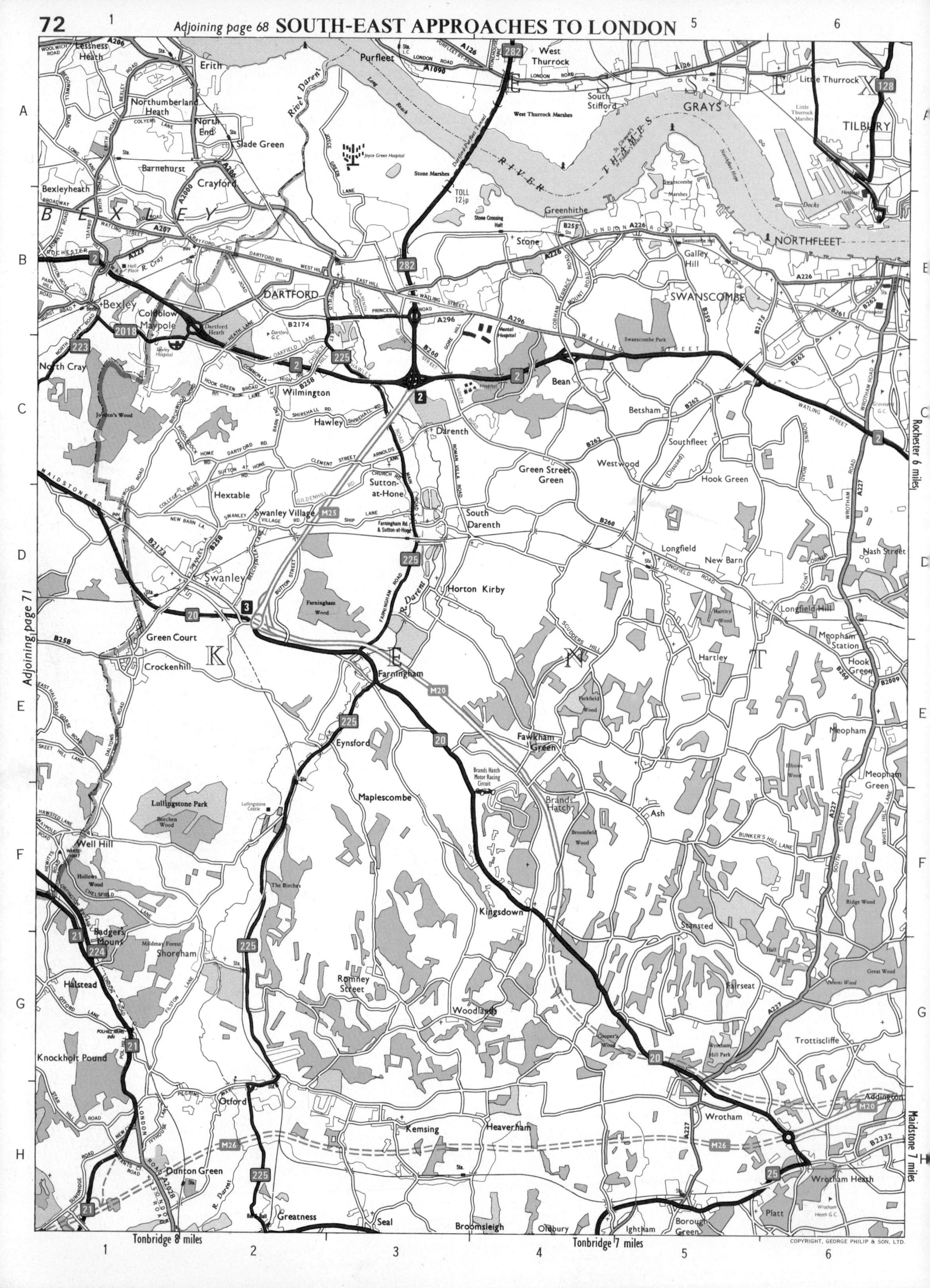
Lessness Heath
Erith
Northumberland Heath
North End
Slade Green
Barnehurst
Crayford
Bexleyheath
BEXLEY
Bexley
Coldblow
Maypole
Dartford Heath
DARTFORD
North Cray
Joyden's Wood
Wilmington
Hawley
Darenth
Hextable
Swanley Village
Sutton-at-Hone
South Darenth
Swanley
Green Court
Crockenhill
Farningham Wood
Farningham
Horton Kirby
Eynsford
Lullingstone Park
Beechen Wood
Maplescombe
Well Hill
Hollows Wood
Badgers Mount
Shoreham
Halstead
Knockholt Pound
Otford
Dunton Green
Greatness
Seal
Kemsing
Heaverham
Broomsleigh
Oldbury
Ightham
Borough Green
Platt
Wrotham Heath
Wrotham
Addington
Trottiscliffe
Fairseat
Stansted
Kingsdown
Woodlands
Romney Street
The Birches
Brands Hatch Motor Racing Circuit
Brands Hatch
Fawkham Green
Ash
Hartley
Hartley Wood
Longfield
New Barn
Longfield Hill
Meopham Station
Hook Green
Meopham
Meopham Green
Nash Street
Westwood
Green Street Green
Betsham
Southfleet
Bean
SWANSCOMBE
Swanscombe Park
Galley Hill
NORTHFLEET
Greenhithe
Stone
Stone Crossing Halt
Stone Marshes
Joyce Green Hospital
Purfleet
West Thurrock
West Thurrock Marshes
South Stifford
GRAYS
Little Thurrock
TILBURY
RIVER THAMES
River Darent
KENT
ESSEX
Rochester 6 miles
Maidstone 7 miles
Tonbridge 8 miles
Tonbridge 7 miles
Adjoining page 71
M25
M20
M26
A2
A20
A225
A282
A296
A226
A227
A2018
A223
TOLL 12½p

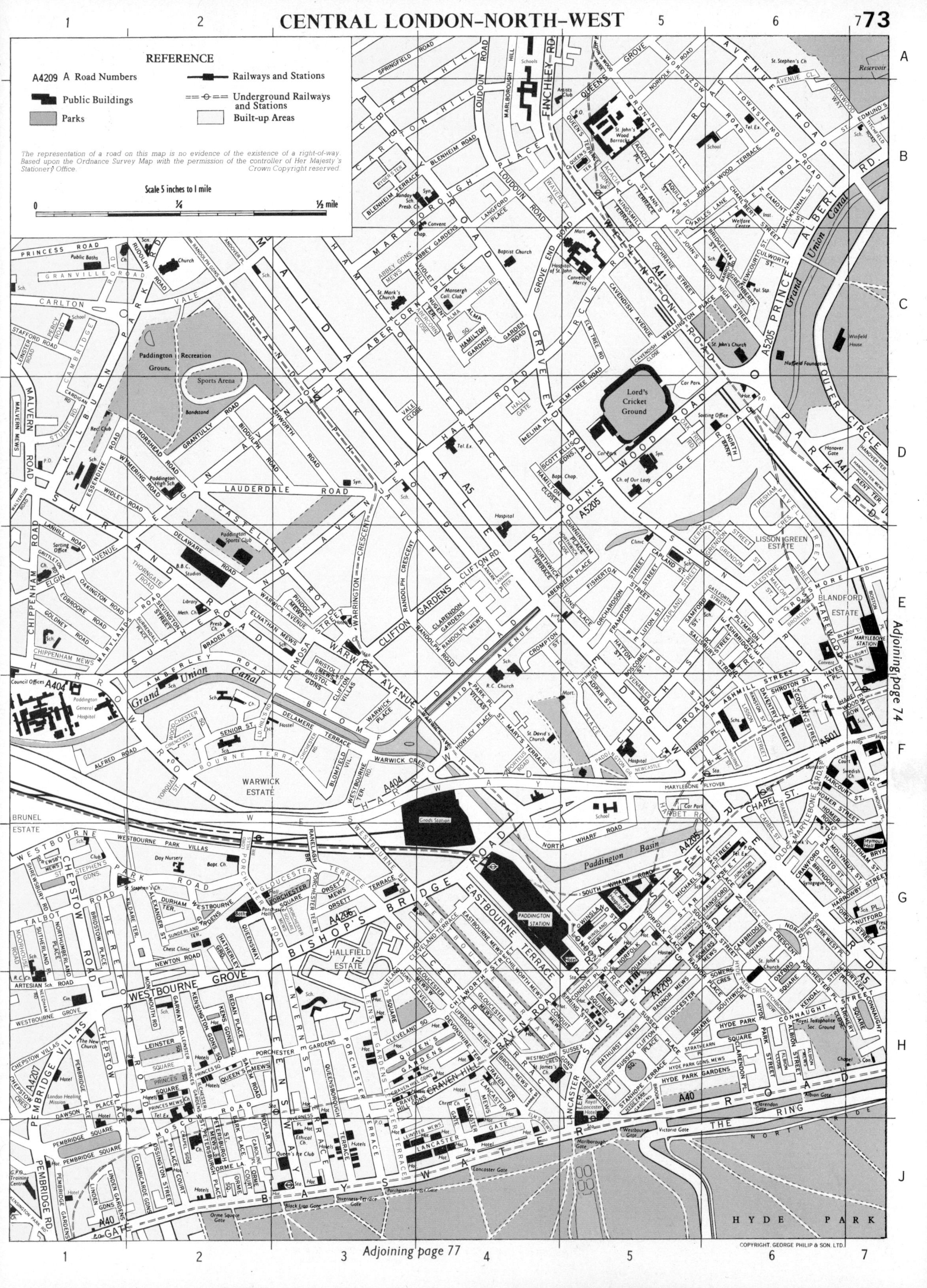

Adjoining page 74

Adjoining page 77

REFERENCE

A4209 A Road Numbers

Public Buildings

Parks

Railways and Stations

Underground Railways and Stations

Built-up Areas

The representation of a road on this map is no evidence of the existence of a right-of-way. Based upon the Ordnance Survey Map with the permission of the controller of Her Majesty's Stationery Office. Crown Copyright reserved.

Scale 5 inches to 1 mile

0   ¼   ½ mile

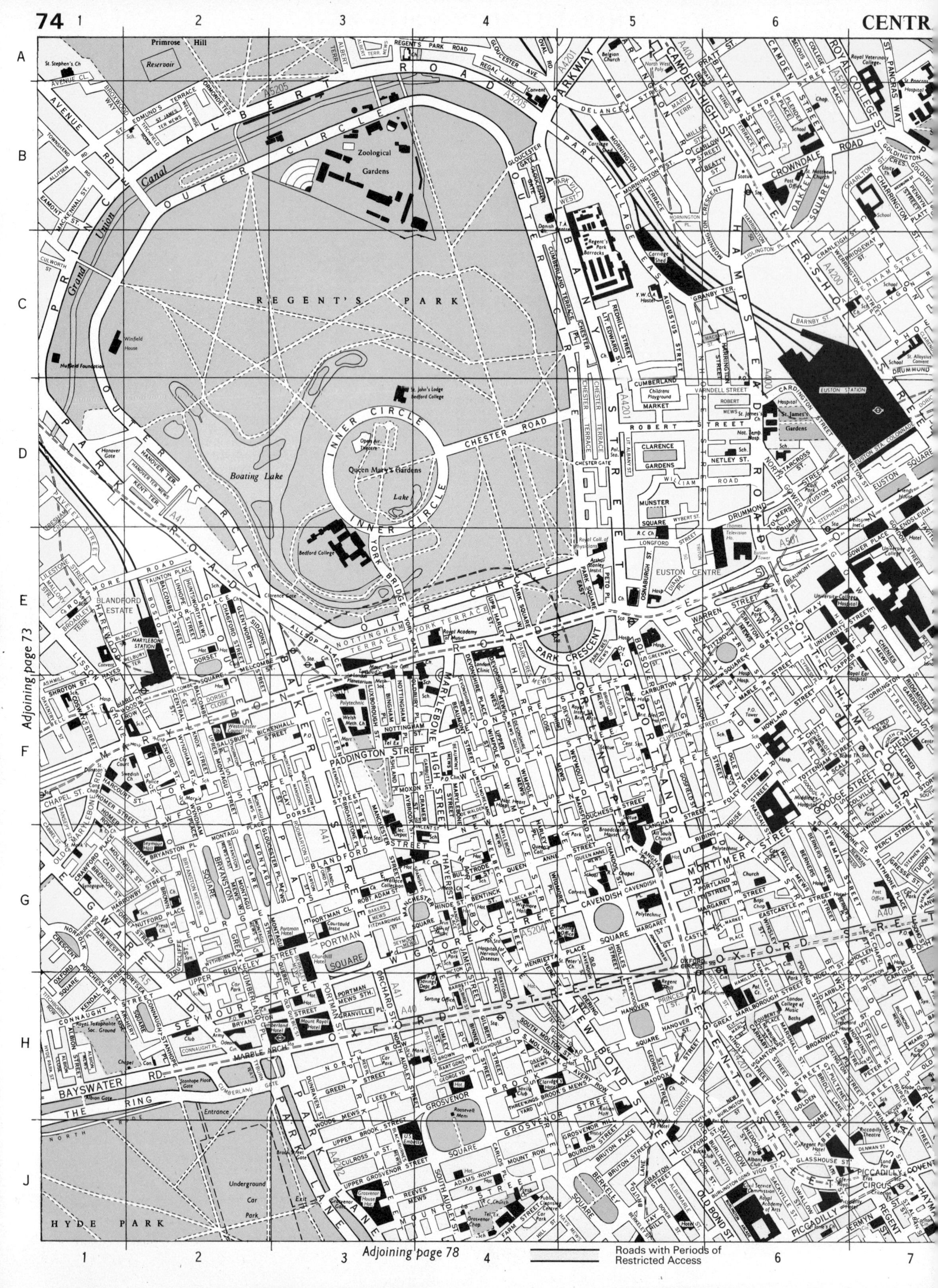

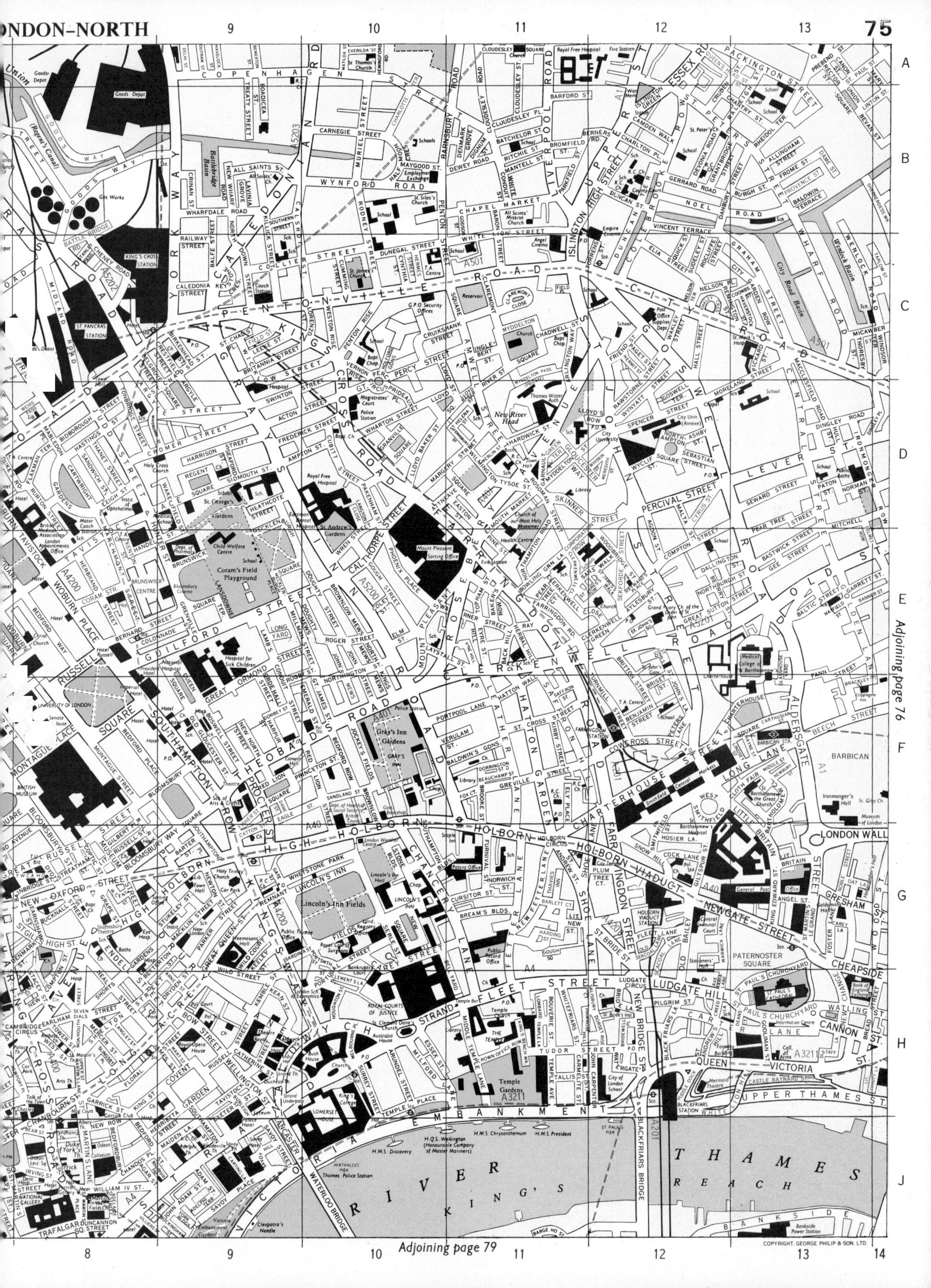
ONDON–NORTH
75
9
10
11
12
13
A
B
C
D
E
F
G
H
J
Adjoining page 76
Adjoining page 79
8
14
COPYRIGHT. GEORGE PHILIP & SON. LTD.
COPENHAGEN STREET
CALEDONIAN ROAD
PENTONVILLE ROAD
KING'S CROSS STATION
ST PANCRAS STATION
Battlebridge Basin
Gas Works
Goods Depot
YORK WAY
EUSTON ROAD
LIVERPOOL ROAD
UPPER STREET
ISLINGTON HIGH STREET
ESSEX ROAD
CITY ROAD
City Road Basin
Wenlock Basin
GOSWELL ROAD
ST JOHN STREET
KING'S CROSS ROAD
GRAY'S INN ROAD
FARRINGDON ROAD
ROSEBERY AVENUE
CLERKENWELL ROAD
Mount Pleasant Sorting Office
New River Head
Coram's Field Playground
GUILFORD STREET
RUSSELL SQUARE
UNIVERSITY OF LONDON
BRITISH MUSEUM
SOUTHAMPTON ROW
THEOBALDS ROAD
Gray's Inn Gardens
HOLBORN
HIGH HOLBORN
HOLBORN VIADUCT
NEW OXFORD STREET
Lincoln's Inn Fields
KINGSWAY
ALDWYCH
STRAND
FLEET STREET
LUDGATE HILL
ST. PAUL'S CATHEDRAL
NEWGATE STREET
CHEAPSIDE
LONDON WALL
BARBICAN
ALDERSGATE
Smithfield Central Markets
CHARTERHOUSE STREET
Temple Gardens
VICTORIA EMBANKMENT
QUEEN VICTORIA ST.
UPPER THAMES ST.
BLACKFRIARS BRIDGE
WATERLOO BRIDGE
RIVER THAMES
KING'S REACH
COVENT GARDEN
CHARING CROSS ROAD
NATIONAL GALLERY
TRAFALGAR SQ.
Cleopatra's Needle
Bankside Power Station
ROYAL COURTS OF JUSTICE
SOMERSET HOUSE

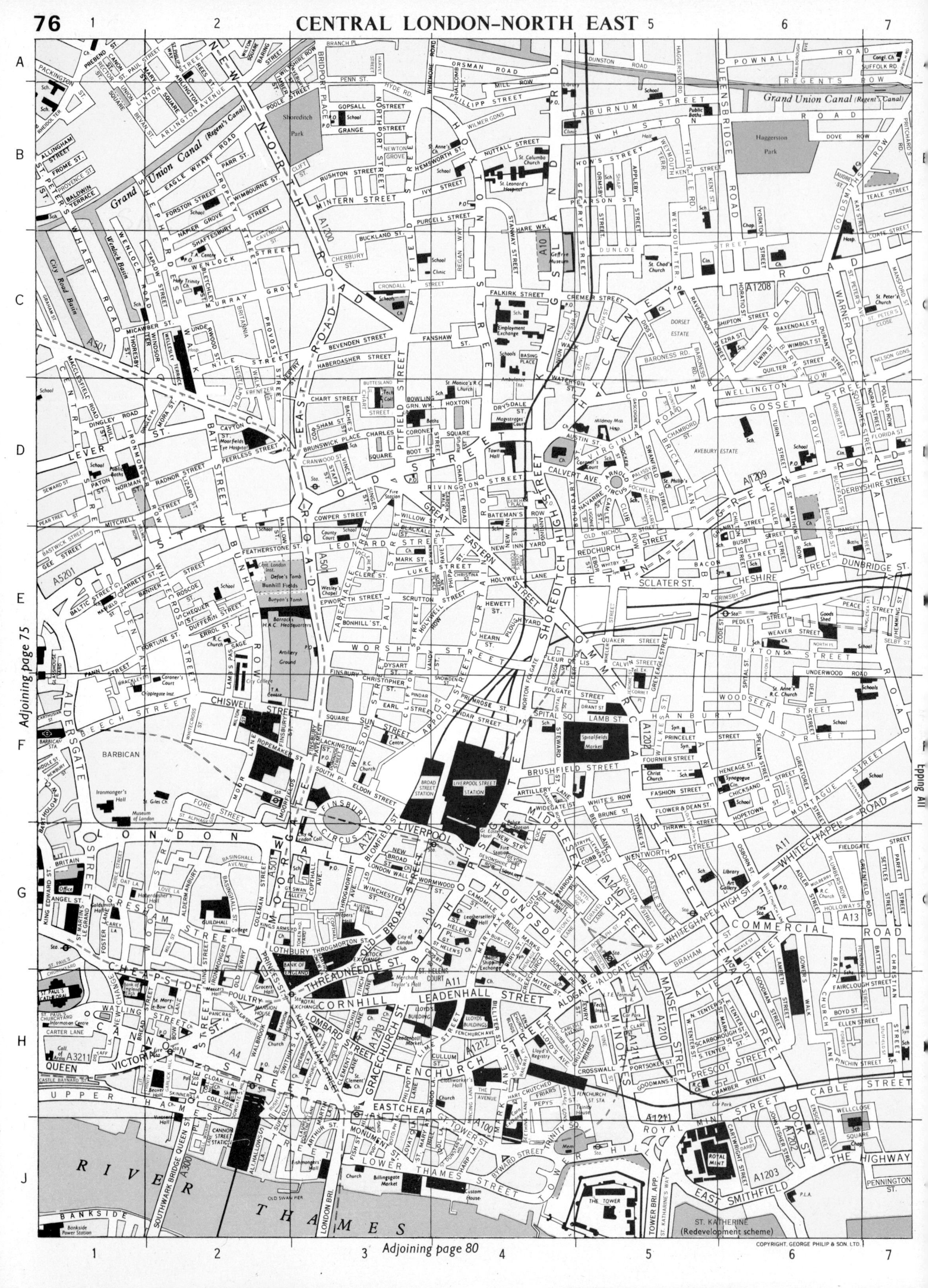

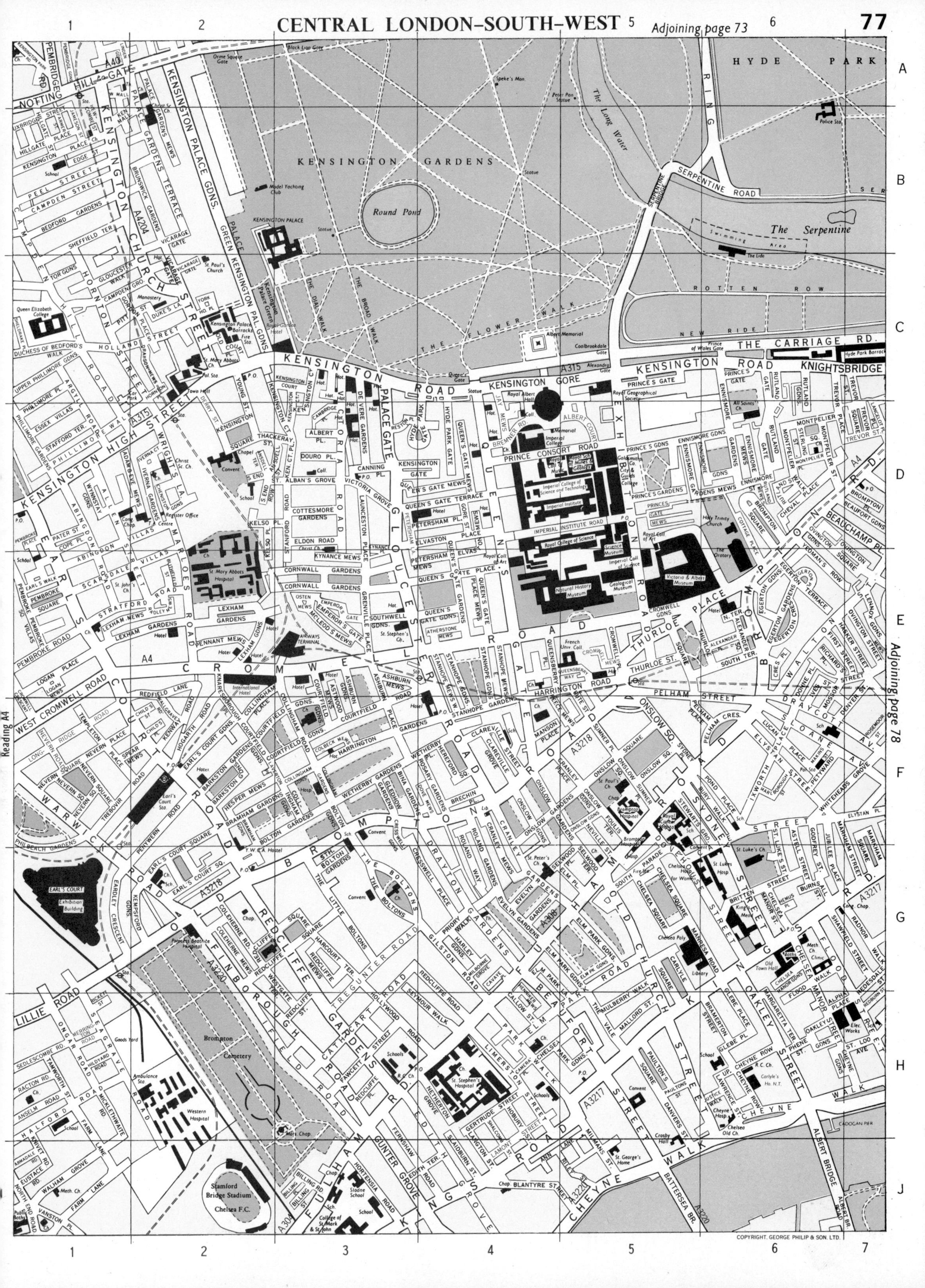
HYDE PARK
KENSINGTON GARDENS
Round Pond
The Long Water
The Serpentine
SERPENTINE ROAD
ROTTEN ROW
NEW RIDE
THE CARRIAGE RD.
THE FLOWER WALK
THE BROAD WALK
THE DIAL WALK
Kensington Palace
Albert Memorial
Royal Albert Hall
KENSINGTON ROAD
KENSINGTON GORE
KNIGHTSBRIDGE
PRINCE CONSORT ROAD
Imperial College of Science and Technology
Imperial Institute
IMPERIAL INSTITUTE ROAD
Royal College of Science
Science Museum
Geological Museum
Natural History Museum
Victoria & Albert Museum
The Oratory
CROMWELL ROAD
KENSINGTON HIGH STREET
KENSINGTON CHURCH STREET
NOTTING HILL GATE
GLOUCESTER ROAD
QUEEN'S GATE
OLD BROMPTON ROAD
FULHAM ROAD
KING'S ROAD
CHEYNE WALK
EARL'S COURT ROAD
WEST CROMWELL ROAD
LILLIE ROAD
REDCLIFFE GARDENS
THE BOLTONS
ONSLOW SQUARE
SYDNEY STREET
OAKLEY STREET
Earl's Court Exhibition Building
Brompton Cemetery
Stamford Bridge Stadium
Chelsea F.C.
St. Stephen's Hospital
Western Hospital
St. Mary Abbots Hospital
Airways Terminal
ALBERT BRIDGE
BATTERSEA BR.
CADOGAN PIER
Reading A4
Adjoining page 78
COPYRIGHT. GEORGE PHILIP & SON LTD.

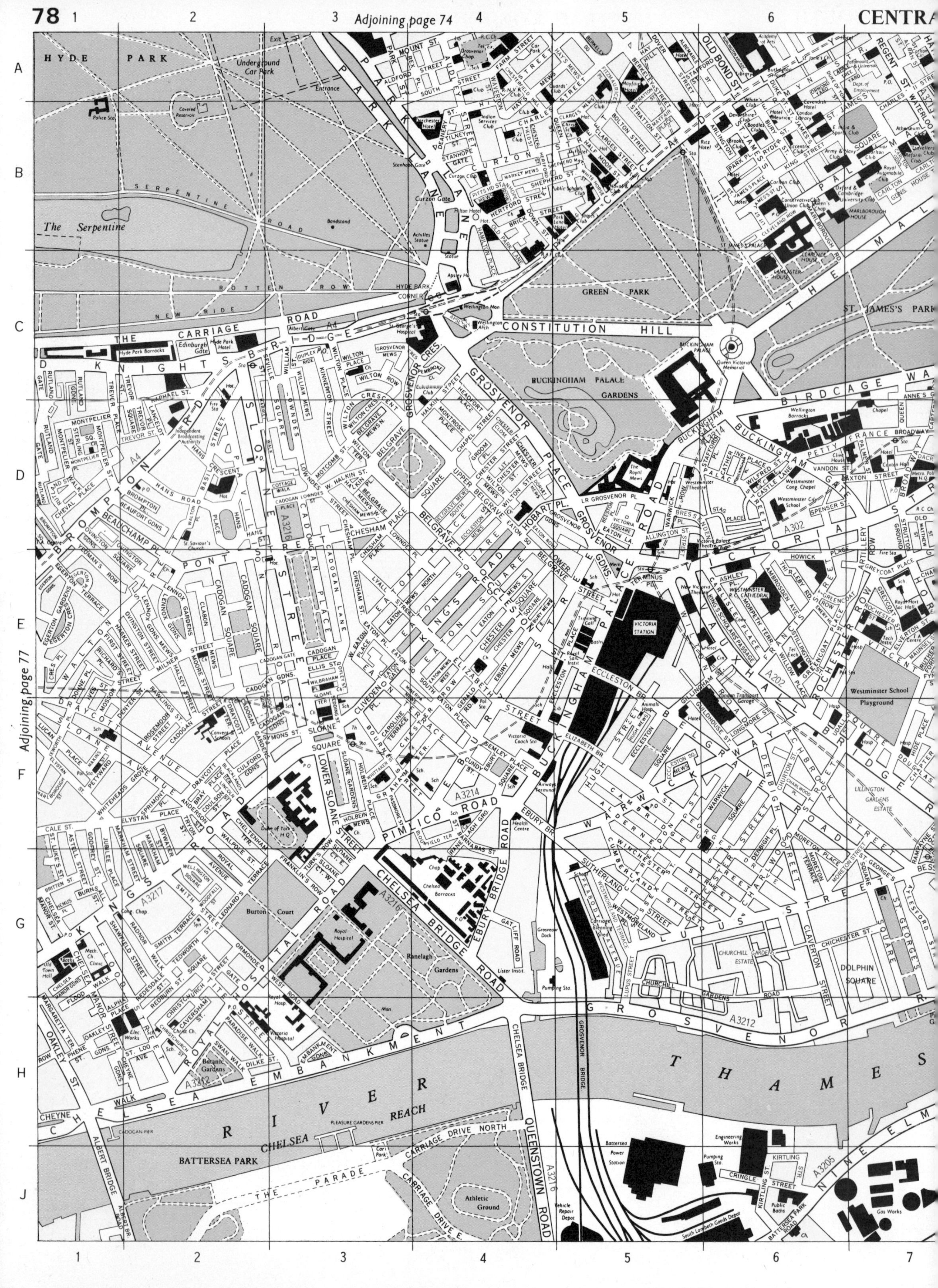

Adjoining page 74
CENTRA
Adjoining page 77
HYDE PARK
The Serpentine
SERPENTINE ROAD
ROTTEN ROW
NEW RIDE
THE CARRIAGE ROAD
KNIGHTSBRIDGE
PARK LANE
CURZON STREET
PICCADILLY
GREEN PARK
CONSTITUTION HILL
BUCKINGHAM PALACE GARDENS
BUCKINGHAM PALACE
Queen Victoria Memorial
ST. JAMES'S PARK
THE MALL
BIRDCAGE WALK
Wellington Barracks
Hyde Park Barracks
HYDE PARK CORNER
Wellington Arch
GROSVENOR PLACE
BELGRAVE SQUARE
EATON SQUARE
SLOANE STREET
SLOANE SQUARE
LOWER SLOANE STREET
BROMPTON ROAD
KING'S ROAD
VICTORIA STATION
VICTORIA STREET
BUCKINGHAM PALACE ROAD
VAUXHALL BRIDGE ROAD
WESTMINSTER R.C. CATHEDRAL
Westminster School Playground
PIMLICO ROAD
CHELSEA BRIDGE ROAD
Burton Court
Royal Hospital
Ranelagh Gardens
Chelsea Barracks
Duke of York's H.Q.
CHURCHILL GARDENS ESTATE
DOLPHIN SQUARE
LILLINGTON GARDENS ESTATE
GROSVENOR ROAD
CHELSEA EMBANKMENT
RIVER THAMES
CHELSEA REACH
CHELSEA BRIDGE
GROSVENOR BRIDGE
ALBERT BRIDGE
QUEENSTOWN ROAD
BATTERSEA PARK
CARRIAGE DRIVE NORTH
THE PARADE
Athletic Ground
Battersea Power Station
NINE ELMS
Gas Works

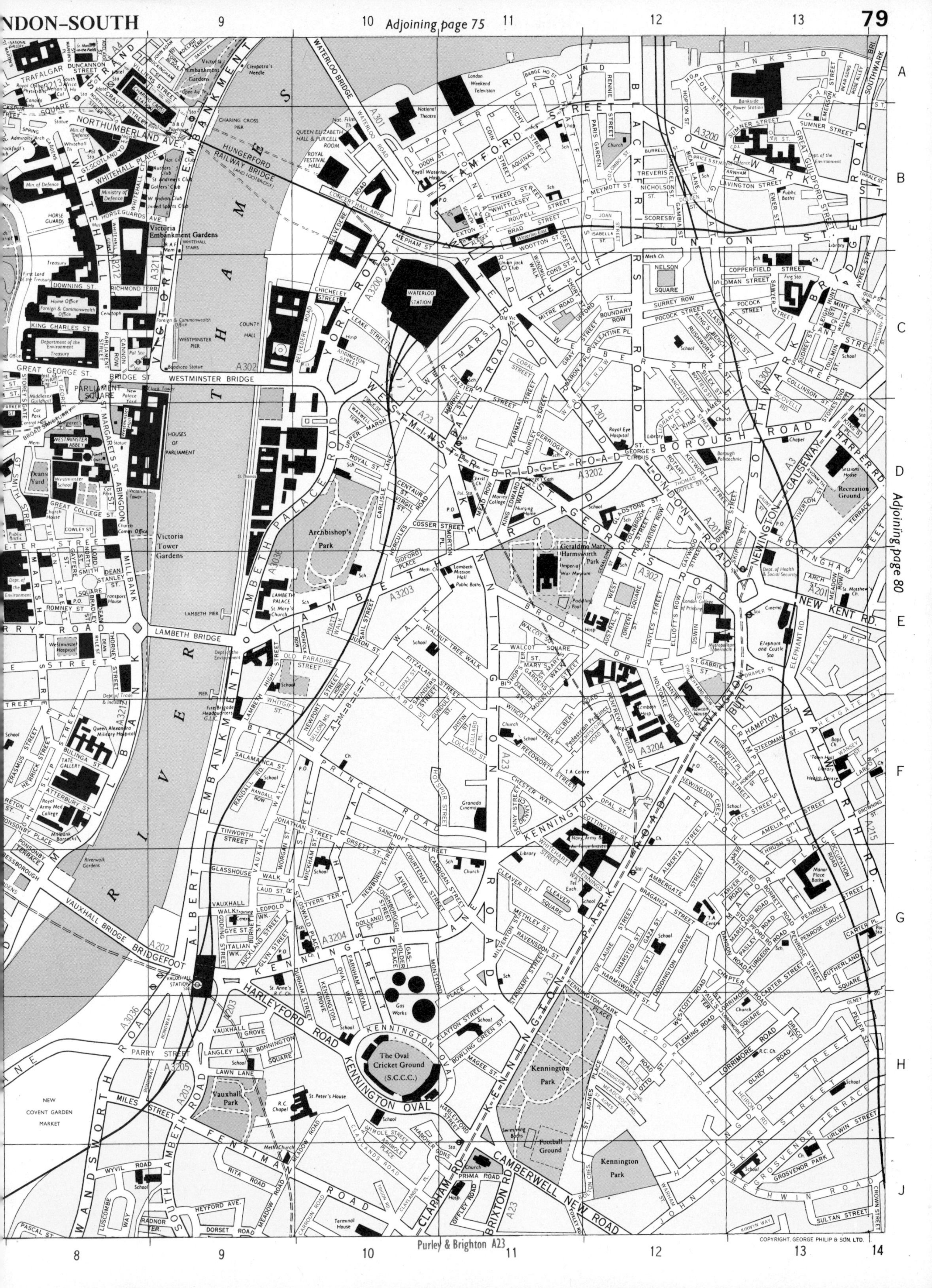

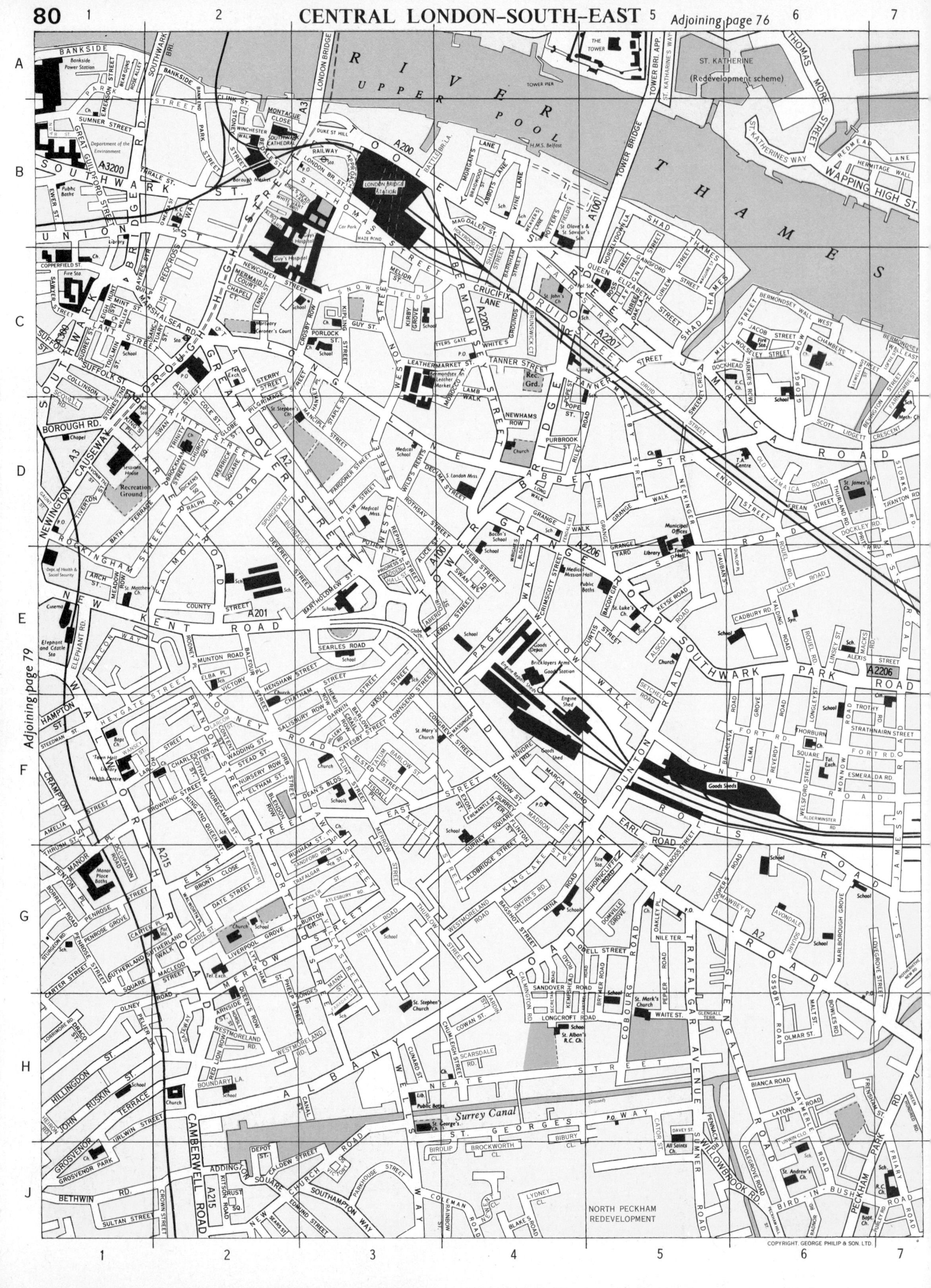
RIVER THAMES
UPPER POOL
THE TOWER
TOWER PIER
H.M.S. Belfast
TOWER BRIDGE
TOWER BRI. APP.
ST. KATHERINE'S WAY
ST. KATHERINE (Redevelopment scheme)
THOMAS MORE STREET
WAPPING HIGH ST.
REDMEAD LANE
HERMITAGE WALL
LONDON BRIDGE
BANKSIDE
Bankside Power Station
SOUTHWARK BRI.
SUMNER STREET
Department of the Environment
SOUTHWARK ST.
CLINK ST.
MONTAGUE CLOSE
DUKE ST. HILL
Southwark Cathedral
Borough Market
TOOLEY STREET
A200
London Bridge Station
ST. THOMAS STREET
Guy's Hospital
NEWCOMEN STREET
MARSHALSEA RD.
BOROUGH HIGH STREET
UNION STREET
GREAT GUILDFORD STREET
A3200
REDCROSS WAY
Mortuary Coroner's Court
SNOWSFIELDS
GUY ST.
CRUCIFIX LANE
A2205
BERMONDSEY STREET
LEATHERMARKET ST.
Bermondsey Leather Market
TANNER STREET
DRUID STREET
A2207
JAMAICA ROAD
SHAD THAMES
QUEEN ELIZABETH STREET
HORSLEYDOWN LA.
MILL STREET
JACOB STREET
BERMONDSEY WALL WEST
BERMONDSEY WALL EAST
DOCKHEAD
PARKERS ROW
SCOTT LIDGETT CRESCENT
LONG LANE
GREAT DOVER STREET
A2
BOROUGH RD.
NEWINGTON CAUSEWAY
A3
Sessions House
Recreation Ground
TRINITY CHURCH SQ.
ROCKINGHAM STREET
ABBEY STR.
GRANGE WALK
GRANGE ROAD
A2206
Municipal Offices
Town Hall
Library
SPA ROAD
NECKINGER
LUCEY ROAD
CADBURY RD.
SOUTHWARK PARK ROAD
NEW KENT ROAD
A201
KENT ROAD
Elephant and Castle Sta.
OLD KENT ROAD
A100
Bricklayers Arms Goods Station
Goods Depot
Engine Shed
Goods Sheds
ROLLS ROAD
LYNTON ROAD
DUNTON ROAD
WALWORTH ROAD
A215
EAST STREET
PORTLAND STREET
ALBANY ROAD
Surrey Canal
NEATE STREET
ST. GEORGE'S WAY
CAMBERWELL ROAD
TRAFALGAR AVENUE
GLENGALL ROAD
COBOURG ROAD
ST. JAMES'S ROAD
ASYLUM ROAD
PECKHAM PARK ROAD
BIRD-IN-BUSH ROAD
SOUTHAMPTON WAY
JOHN RUSKIN STREET
BETHWIN RD.
NORTH PECKHAM REDEVELOPMENT
Adjoining page 79

INDEX TO SECTIONAL MAP OF GREAT BRITAIN

ABBREVIATIONS

Beds. – *Bedfordshire*
Berks. – *Berkshire*
Bri. – *Bridge*
Bucks. – *Buckinghamshire*
Cambs. – *Cambridgeshire*
Cas. – *Castle*
Ches. – *Cheshire*
Cnr. – *Corner*
Co. – *County*
Com. – *Common*
Corn. – *Cornwall*
Cumb. – *Cumbria*
Derby. – *Derbyshire*
Dumf. & Gall. – *Dumfries & Galloway*
Dur. – *Durham*
E. – *East*
E. Sussex – *East Sussex*
Glos. – *Gloucestershire*
Gt. – *Great*
Grn. – *Green*
Hants. – *Hampshire*
Heref. & Worcs. – *Hereford & Worcester*
Hth. – *Heath*
Herts. – *Hertfordshire*
Ho. – *House*
Humber. – *Humberside*
I.o.M. – *Isle of Man*
I.o.W. – *Isle of Wight*
Junc. – *Junction*
L. – *Lake*
Lancs. – *Lancashire*
Leics. – *Leicestershire*
Lincs. – *Lincolnshire*
Lo. – *Lodge*
London – *Greater London*
Manchester – *Greater Manchester*
Mid Glam. – *Mid Glamorgan*
Norf. – *Norfolk*
N. – *North*
N. Yorks. – *North Yorkshire*
Northants. – *Northamptonshire*
Northumb. – *Northumberland*
Notts. – *Nottinghamshire*
Oxon. – *Oxfordshire*
Salop. – *Shropshire*
Som. – *Somerset*
S. – *South*
S. Glam. – *South Glamorgan*
S. Yorks. – *South Yorkshire*
Staffs. – *Staffordshire*
Sta. – *Station*
Suff. – *Suffolk*
Vill. – *Village*
War. – *Warwickshire*
W. – *West*
W. Glam. – *West Glamorgan*
W. Mid. – *West Midlands*
W. Sussex – *West Sussex*
W. Yorks. – *West Yorkshire*
W. Isles. – *Western Isles*
Wilts. – *Wiltshire*

32 Ab Kettleby .... **H 4**
7 Abbas Combe ..... **D 10**
22 Abberley .... **E 1**
19 Abberton, Essex ... **B 10**
22 Abberton, Heref. & Worcs .... **G 3**
45 Abberwick .... **B 9**
18 Abbess Roding ..... **C 6**
6 Abbey .... **E 5**
20 Abbey Cwmhir ..... **E 6**
15 Abbey Dore .... **A 7**
6 Abbey Hill .... **D 6**
31 Abbey Hulton ...... **E 7**
49 Abbey St. Bathans . **C 10**
32 Abbey Town ...... **F 12**
34 Abbey Village ...... **E 5**
38 Abbeylands, I.o.M. . **G 2**
45 Abbeylands, Northumb. ...... **B 10**
34 Abbeystead .... **B 4**
4 Abbots Bickington .. **E 3**
31 Abbots Bromley .... **H 9**
17 Abbots Langley ... **D 11**
22 Abbot's Morton .... **G 4**
25 Abbots Ripton ..... **G 3**
22 Abbot's Salford .... **G 4**
7 Abbotsbury .... **H 9**
4 Abbotsham .... **C 3**
4 Abbotskerswell ..... **J 7**
25 Abbotsley .... **K 3**
8 Abbotswood .... **D 5**
8 Abbots Ann .... **B 5**
21 Abcott .... **E 9**
21 Abdon .... **D 11**
13 Aber, Dyfed .... **B 8**
28 Aber, Gwynedd .... **C 6**
13 Aberarth .... **A 8**
12 Aber-Cych .... **C 6**
20 Aber Gwydol .... **B 3**
28 Aber-Gwynant ..... **H 6**
14 Aber Village .... **B 4**
13 Aberaeron .... **A 8**
14 Aberaman .... **D 3**
20 Aberangell .... **A 4**
57 Aberarder, Highland **G 2**
55 Aberarder, Highland **L 8**
52 Aberargie .... **F 6**
13 Aberavon .... **H 11**
13 Aber-banc .... **C 7**
14 Aberbeeg .... **D 5**
14 Aberbran .... **A 3**
14 Abercanaid .... **D 4**
14 Abercarn .... **E 5**
12 Abercastle .... **D 2**
20 Abercegir .... **B 4**
55 Aberchalder House .. **J 7**
58 Aberchirder .... **B 4**
14 Abercrave .... **C 2**
14 Abercregan .... **E 2**
14 Abercwmboi .... **D 3**
14 Abercynafon .... **C 4**
14 Abercynon .... **E 4**
14 Aberdare .... **D 3**
28 Aberdaron .... **H 1**
59 Aberdeen .... **G 7**
48 Aberdour .... **A 5**
20 Aberdovey .... **C 2**
13 Aberdulais .... **G 11**
20 Aberedw .... **H 6**
12 Abereiddy .... **D 2**
28 Abererch .... **G 3**
14 Aberfan .... **D 4**
52 Aberfeldy .... **B 3**
28 Aberffraw .... **C 3**
20 Aberffrwd .... **E 2**
36 Aberford .... **C 2**
51 Aberfoyle .... **G 12**
14 Abergavenny .... **C 6**
29 Abergele .... **B 9**
13 Abergiar .... **C 8**
13 Abergorlech .... **D 9**
20 Abergwesyn .... **G 4**
13 Abergwili .... **E 8**
14 Abergwynfi .... **E 2**
20 Abergynolwyn ...... **B 2**
20 Aberhosan .... **C 4**
14 Aberkenfig .... **F 2**
49 Aberlady .... **A 7**
53 Aberlemno .... **B 10**
20 Aberllefenni .... **A 3**
20 Abermeurig .... **G 1**
21 Abermule .... **C 7**
13 Abernant, Dyfed ... **E 7**
14 Aber-nant, Mid Glam. **D 3**
53 Abernethy .... **E 7**
53 Abernyte .... **D 7**
12 Aberporth .... **B 6**
28 Abersoch .... **G 3**
14 Abersychan .... **D 6**
14 Aberthin .... **G 3**
14 Abertillery .... **D 5**
14 Abertridwr, Mid Glam. .... **E 4**
29 Abertridwr, Powys .. **H 9**
14 Abertysswg .... **D 5**
52 Aberuthven .... **F 5**
14 Aberyscir .... **A 3**
20 Aberystwyth .... **D 2**
16 Abingdon .... **D 6**
9 Abinger .... **B 12**
9 Abinger Hammer .. **A 12**
48 Abington .... **G 2**
25 Abington Pigotts .... **L 4**
16 Ablington, Glos. .... **C 2**
8 Ablington, Wilts. ... **A 3**
31 Abney .... **B 10**
59 Aboyne .... **H 3**
34 Abram .... **G 5**
56 Abriachan .... **F 1**
18 Abridge .... **D 5**
15 Abson .... **G 10**
23 Abthorpe .... **G 10**
33 Aby .... **B 11**
21 Acaster Malbis ..... **C 4**
36 Acaster Selby ...... **C 3**
4 Accott .... **C 5**
34 Accrington .... **D 6**
62 Achachork .... **D 4**
50 Achadun .... **D 5**
50 Achafolla .... **F 5**
46 Achahoish .... **B 3**
51 Achallader .... **C 10**
46 Achamore Farm .... **E 1**
54 Achanalt .... **D 6**
46 Achanamara .... **A 3**
56 Achandunie .... **C 2**
60 Achany .... **F 6**
55 Achaphubuil .... **M 5**
50 Acharacle .... **A 4**
50 Acharn, Highland ... **C 4**
52 Acharn, Tayside ... **C 2**
61 Acharole .... **C 11**
46 Acharosson .... **B 4**
50 Achateny .... **A 3**
58 Achath .... **F 5**
61 Achavanich .... **C 11**
56 Achavraat .... **E 5**
60 Achavraie .... **F 2**
13 Achddu .... **G 8**
61 Achentoul .... **D 8**
60 Achfary .... **C 4**
60 Achgarve .... **G 1**
60 Achiemore, Kyle of Durness, Highland **A 4**
61 Achiemore, Highland **B 9**
62 A'Chill .... **H 2**
60 Achiltibuie .... **F 2**
61 Achina .... **B 7**
51 Achindarroch ...... **B 7**
55 Achintee, Highland **M 5**
54 Achintee, Highland **F 3**
54 Achintraid .... **F 2**
55 Achlain .... **H 6**
50 Achleck .... **C 1**
46 A'Chleit .... **E 2**
51 Achlian .... **E 8**
55 Achluachrach ...... **L 7**
60 Achlyness .... **B 4**
60 Achmelvich .... **E 2**
52 Achmore, Central .. **D 1**
54 Achmore, Highland . **F 2**
63 Achmore, W. Isles .. **D 4**
51 Achnaba, Strathclyde **D 7**
46 Achnaba, Strathclyde **A 4**
57 Achnabat .... **G 2**
60 Achnacarnin .... **D 2**
55 Achnacarry Ho. .... **L 5**
62 Achnacloich .... **G 5**
61 Achnaclyth .... **D 10**
51 Achnacon .... **B 8**
55 Achnaconeran ..... **H 8**
50 Achnacraig .... **C 2**
50 Achnacroish .... **C 6**
50 Achnadrish .... **B 2**
51 Achnafalnich ...... **E 9**
55 Achnafraschoille .... **L 6**
56 Achnaggaron .... **C 2**
50 Achnaha .... **A 2**
60 Achnahanat .... **G 6**
50 Achnalea .... **A 6**
61 Achnaluachrach .... **F 7**
55 Achnanellan .... **L 5**
60 Achnanerain .... **F 6**
55 Achnangart .... **H 3**
55 Achnasaul .... **K 5**
54 Achnasheen .... **D 5**
56 Achnastank .... **F 8**
50 Achosnich .... **A 2**
50 Achranich .... **C 4**
61 Achreamie .... **A 9**
51 Achriabhach .... **A 8**
60 Achriesgill .... **B 4**
61 Achrimsdale .... **F 9**
61 Achtoty .... **B 7**
25 Achurch .... **G 1**
60 Achuvoldrach ...... **B 6**
61 Achvaich .... **G 7**
57 Achvraid, Highland **G 2**
56 Achvraid, Highland . **F 2**
61 Ackergill .... **B 12**
40 Acklam, Cleveland .. **C 5**
36 Acklam, N. Yorks. .. **A 5**
22 Ackleton .... **B 1**
45 Acklington .... **C 10**
36 Ackton .... **E 2**
36 Ackworth Moor Top **F 2**
26 Acle .... **D 7**
22 Acock's Green ..... **D 5**
11 Acol .... **A 11**
45 Acomb, Northumb. . **F 7**
36 Acomb, N. Yorks. .. **B 4**
15 Aconbury .... **A 8**
34 Acre .... **E 6**
9 Acre Street .... **F 9**
29 Acrefair .... **F 12**
30 Acton, Cheshire .... **E 5**
8 Acton, Dorset ...... **H 1**
18 Acton, London ..... **F 2**
21 Acton, Salop .... **D 8**
27 Acton, Suffolk ..... **L 2**
30 Acton Bridge ...... **C 4**
21 Acton Beauchamp . **G 12**
21 Acton Burnell .... **B 10**
21 Acton Green ..... **G 12**
30 Acton Park .... **E 2**
21 Acton Pigott ..... **B 11**
21 Acton Round ..... **C 11**
21 Acton Scott ...... **C 10**
31 Acton Trussell ..... **H 8**
15 Acton Turville ..... **F 11**
30 Adbaston .... **G 6**
7 Adber .... **D 9**
30 Adderley .... **F 5**
45 Adderstone .... **C 12**
48 Addiewell .... **C 3**
35 Addingham .... **B 9**
17 Addington, Bucks. .. **A 8**
10 Addington, Kent .... **B 5**
18 Addington, London . **G 4**
49 Addinston .... **D 8**
17 Addlestone .... **H 11**
33 Addlethorpe ...... **C 12**
30 Adeney .... **H 5**
20 Adfa .... **B 6**
21 Adforton .... **E 9**
11 Adisham .... **C 11**
16 Adlestrop .... **A 3**
36 Adlingfleet .... **E 6**
31 Adlington, Ches. .... **B 7**
34 Adlington, Lancs. ... **F 5**
21 Admaston, Salop. . **A 11**
31 Admaston, Staffs. .. **H 9**
22 Admington .... **G 5**
17 Adstock .... **A 8**
23 Adstone .... **G 9**
9 Adversane .... **D 12**
56 Advie .... **F 7**
36 Adwick le Street .... **F 3**
36 Adwick upon Dearne **G 3**
4 Adworthy .... **D 6**
58 Adziel **B7**
43 Ae Bridgend ...... **C 10**
43 Ae Village .... **C 10**
4 Affeton Barton ..... **E 6**
58 Affleck, Grampian .. **D 3**
58 Affleck, Grampian .. **E 6**
7 Affpuddle .... **G 11**
55 Affric Lodge .... **G 5**
29 Afon-wen .... **C 10**
5 Afton, Devon .... **J 7**
8 Afton, I.o.W. ...... **G 5**
47 Afton Bridgend ... **H 11**
40 Agglethorpe .... **F 1**
38 Agneash .... **G 2**
63 Aignish .... **D 6**
37 Aike .... **C 8**
64 Aikerness .... **A 2**
64 Aikers .... **E 2**
43 Aiket .... **E 11**
39 Aiketgate .... **A 7**
44 Aikton .... **H 1**
21 Ailey .... **G 9**
24 Ailsworth .... **F 2**
40 Ainderby Steeple .. **F 4**
19 Aingers Green .... **B 11**
34 Ainsdale .... **F 2**
39 Ainstable .... **A 7**
34 Ainsworth .... **F 6**
41 Ainthorpe .... **D 7**
34 Aintree .... **G 3**
42 Aird, Dumf & Gall. . **F 2**
50 Aird, Strathclyde ... **G 5**
63 Aird, W. Isles ...... **C 6**
62 Aird of Sleat .... **H 5**
63 Aird of Tunga ...... **C 6**
63 Aird Uig .... **C 2**
60 Airdachuilinn ...... **C 4**
47 Airdrie .... **C 12**
47 Airdsgreen .... **F 12**
54 Airigh-drishaig ..... **F 1**
36 Airmyn .... **E 5**
52 Airntully .... **D 6**
55 Airor .... **J 1**
52 Airth .... **H 4**
35 Airton .... **A 7**
42 Airyhassen .... **G 4**
33 Aisby, Lincs. ...... **F 7**
32 Aisby, Lincs. ...... **A 6**
39 Aisgill .... **E 10**
5 Aish .... **K 6**
6 Aisholt .... **C 5**
40 Aiskew .... **F 3**
40 Aislaby, N. Yorks. .. **D 4**
41 Aislaby, N. Yorls. .. **G 8**
41 Aislaby, N. Yorks. .. **D 8**
32 Aisthorpe .... **B 6**
64 Aith, Orkney Is. .... **C 4**
64 Aith, Shetland Is. ... **D 7**
64 Aith Hestwall ...... **C 1**
42 Aitkenhead .... **A 4**
56 Aitnoch .... **F 5**
49 Akeld .... **F 12**
49 Akeld Steads ..... **F 12**
23 Akeley .... **H 10**
27 Akenham .... **K 5**
3 Albaston .... **C 11**
21 Alberbury .... **A 9**
12 Albert Town .... **E 3**
10 Albourn .... **F 1**
22 Albrighton, Salop. .. **B 2**
30 Albrighton, Salop. .. **H 4**
27 Alburgh .... **G 6**
27 Alburgh Street ..... **G 5**
18 Albury, Herts. ...... **B 4**
9 Albury, Surrey .... **A 12**
26 Alby Hill .... **B 5**
56 Alcaig .... **D 1**
22 Alcester .... **F 4**
10 Alciston .... **G 4**
6 Alcombe, Som. ..... **B 3**
15 Alcombe, Wilts. ... **G 11**
25 Alconbury .... **H 3**
25 Alconbury Hill ..... **G 3**
25 Alconbury Weston .. **H 3**
47 Aldandulish .... **M 5**
26 Aldborough, Norf. .. **B 5**
40 Aldborough, N. Yorks. **H 4**
16 Aldbourne .... **G 4**
37 Aldbrough, Humber. **C 10**
40 Aldbrough, N. Yorks. **D 2**
17 Aldbury .... **C 10**
52 Aldcharmaig .... **A 3**
34 Aldcliffe .... **A 3**
52 Aldclune .... **A 4**
27 Aldeburgh .... **J 8**
26 Aldeby .... **F 7**
18 Aldenham .... **D 1**
8 Alderbury .... **C 3**
26 Alderford .... **D 4**
15 Alderley .... **E 11**
31 Alderley Edge ..... **B 7**
17 Aldermaston .... **H 7**
17 Aldermaston Wharf . **G 7**
22 Alderminster ...... **G 6**
21 Alder's End ...... **H 11**
8 Alderholt .... **E 3**
9 Aldershot .... **A 10**
16 Alderton, Glos. .... **A 1**
23 Alderton, Northants .... **G 10**
30 Alderton, Salop .... **H 4**
27 Alderton, Suffolk ... **L 6**
15 Alderton, Wilts .... **F 11**
31 Alderwasley ...... **E 11**
40 Aldfield .... **H 3**
30 Aldford .... **D 3**
19 Aldham, Essex ..... **A 9**
27 Aldham, Suffolk .... **L 3**
27 Aldham Street ..... **L 3**
56 Aldie .... **B 3**
9 Aldingbourne ..... **F 10**
38 Aldingham .... **H 5**
22 Aldington .... **H 4**
11 Aldington Corner ... **D 9**
51 Aldochlay .... **H 10**
25 Aldreth .... **H 5**
22 Aldridge .... **B 4**
27 Aldringham .... **J 7**
16 Aldsworth .... **C 3**
58 Aldunie .... **E i**
31 Aldwark, Derby ... **D 10**
36 Aldwark, N. Yorks. . **A 2**
9 Aldwick .... **F 10**
25 Aldwincle .... **G 1**
16 Aldworth .... **F 6**
47 Alexandria .... **A 9**
6 Aley .... **B 5**
4 Alfardisworthy ..... **E 2**
6 Alfington .... **F 5**
9 Alfold .... **C 11**
9 Alfold Crossways .. **C 11**
58 Alford, Grampian ... **F 3**
33 Alford, Lincs. ..... **C 11**
7 Alfold, Somerset .... **C 9**
32 Alfreton .... **E 1**
22 Alfrick .... **G 1**
10 Alfriston .... **H 4**
24 Algarkirk .... **B 4**
7 Alhampton .... **C 9**
63 Aline Lodge .... **F 3**
55 Alisary .... **L 1**
36 Alkborough .... **E 6**
23 Alkerton .... **H 7**
11 Alkham .... **D 11**
30 Alkington .... **F 4**
31 Alkmonton .... **F 10**
27 All Saints, South Elmham .... **G 6**
21 All Stretton .... **C 10**
60 Alladale Lodge ..... **G 5**
5 Allaleigh .... **K 7**
57 Allanaquoich .... **K 7**
56 Allanfearn .... **E 3**
56 Allangrange Ho. .... **E 2**
49 Allanton .... **D 11**
8 Allbrook .... **D 6**
16 All Cannings ...... **H 2**
45 Allendale Town .... **G 7**
39 Allenheads .... **A 10**
18 Allen's Green ...... **B 4**
45 Allensford .... **H 9**
15 Allensmore .... **A 8**
31 Allenton, Derby ... **G 12**
48 Allenton, Strathclyde **D 1**
7 Aller .... **C 7**
43 Allerby .... **H 11**
45 Allerdene .... **C 8**
6 Allerford .... **B 3**
41 Allerston .... **G 9**
36 Allerthorpe .... **B 5**
30 Allerton, Merseyside **B 3**
35 Allerton, W. Yorks. **D 10**
36 Allerton Bywater ... **D 2**
36 Allerton Mauleverer **A 2**
45 Allerwash .... **F 7**
22 Allesley .... **D 6**
31 Allestree .... **F 11**
23 Allexton .... **B 11**
31 Allgreave .... **D 8**
19 Allhallows .... **F 8**
54 Alligin Shuas ...... **D 2**
31 Allimore Green .... **H 7**
32 Allington, Lincs. .... **F 6**
8 Allington, Wilts. .... **B 4**
16 Allington, Wilts. .... **H 2**
38 Allithwaite .... **G 6**
52 Alloa .... **H 4**
43 Allonby .... **G 11**
47 Alloway .... **H 8**
7 Allowenshay .... **E 7**
13 Allt .... **G 9**
55 Alltbeithe, Highland **G 4**
55 Alltneithe, Highland **J 4**
51 Alltchaorunn .... **B 9**
20 Alltmawr .... **H 6**
60 Alltnacaillich ...... **C 5**
57 Allt-na-giubhsaich . **L 8**
60 Allt na h'Airbhe .... **G 3**
60 Allton Dubh .... **F 2**
55 Alltsigh .... **H 8**
13 Alltwalis .... **D 8**
13 Alltwen .... **G 10**
13 Alltyblacca .... **B 8**

7 Allweston E 10
32 Alma Park Estate F 6
21 Almeley G 9
21 Almeley Wooton G 9
7 Almer F 12
36 Almholme F 4
30 Almington G 5
4 Alminstone Cross D 2
52 Almondbank E 5
15 Almondbury F 10
15 Almondsbury F 9
45 Alndyke B 10
36 Alne A 3
56 Alness C 2
45 Alnham B 8
45 Alnmouth B 10
45 Alnwick B 10
27 Alphamstone M 2
27 Alpheton K 2
5 Alphington G 8
31 Alport D 10
30 Alpraham D 4
19 Alresford B 10
22 Alrewas A 5
30 Alsager E 6
30 Alsagers Bank E 6
31 Alsop en le Dale E 10
44 Alston, Cumb. H 5
6 Alston, Devon F 6
16 Alstone, Glos. A 1
6 Alstone, Som. B 6
31 Alstonefield E 9
4 Alswear D 6
61 Altanduin E 8
3 Altarnun B 9
60 Altassmore G 6
46 Altgaltraig B 5
34 Altham D 6
19 Althorne D 9
36 Althorpe F 6
42 Alticry G 4
61 Altnabea E 10
61 Altnabreac Stn. C 9
56 Altnacardich E 1
60 Altnacealgach Hot. F 4
50 Altnacraig E 6
51 Altnafeadh B 9
60 Altnaharra D 6
35 Altofts E 12
32 Alton, Derby D 1
9 Alton, Hants. B 8
31 Alton, Staffs. F 9
16 Alton Barnes H 2
7 Alton Pancras F 10
16 Alton Priors H 2
47 Altonhill E 9
30 Altrincham A 6
55 Altrua K 6
51 Altskeith G 11
56 Alltyre House D 6
52 Alva G 4
30 Alvanley C 4
31 Alvaston G 12
22 Alvechurch E 4
22 Alvecote B 6
8 Alvediston D 1
22 Alveley D 1
4 Alverdiscott C 4
9 Alverstoke F 7
35 Alverthorpe E 11
32 Alverton F 5
16 Alvescot D 4
15 Alveston, Avon E 9
22 Alveston, War. F 6
9 Alverstone G 7
57 Alvie J 4
33 Alvingham A 10
15 Alvington D 9
24 Alwalton F 2
45 Alwinton B 7
35 Alwoodley C 11
53 Alyth B 7
33 Amber Hill E 9
15 Amberley, Glos. D 11
9 Amberley, W. Sussex E 11
31 Ambersgate E 11
45 Amble C 11
22 Amblecote D 2
35 Ambler Thorn D 9
38 Ambleside E 6
12 Ambleston D 3
17 Ambrosden B 7
36 Amcotts F 6
53 Americanmuir D 8
17 Amersham D 10
17 Amersham Com. D 10
45 Amersidelaw C 12
8 Amesbury B 3
63 Amhuinnsuidhe F 2
22 Amington B 6
43 Amisfield Town C 11
28 Amlwch A 4
28 Amlwch Port A 4
13 Ammanford F 9
41 Amotherby H 7
8 Ampfield D 5
48 Ampherlaw D 3
40 Ampleforth G 6
40 Ampleforth Coll. G 6
16 Ampney Crucis D 2
16 Ampney St. Mary D 2
16 Ampney St. Peter D 2
8 Amport B 4
25 Ampthill L 1
27 Ampton H 2
12 Amroth F 5
52 Amulree C 4
62 An Caol C 5
62 An Coroghon H 2
50 Anaheilt A 5
54 Anancaun C 4
33 Ancaster F 7
21 Anchor D 7
49 Ancroft E 12
49 Ancroft Northmoor E 12
49 Ancrum G 9
33 Anderby C 12
7 Anderson F 12
30 Anderton C 5
8 Andover B 5
8 Andover Down B 5
16 Andoversford B 1
38 Andreas F 2
52 Angansk F 6
2 Angarrak F 3
12 Angle G 2
38 Anglers' Hotel D 3
28 Anglesey C 4
9 Angmering F 12
9 Angmering-on-Sea F 12
39 Angram, N. Yorks. E 11
36 Angram, N. Yorks. B 3
52 Anie F 1
56 Ankerville B 4
37 Anlaby D 8
24 Anmer C 8
8 Anna Valley B 5
43 Annan E 12
38 Annaside G 3
54 Annat, Highland D 3
51 Annat, Strathclyde E 7
47 Annathill B 12
47 Annbank G 9
47 Annbank Station G 9
32 Annesley Woodhouse E 2
58 Annfield F 3
45 Annfield Plain H 10
45 Annitsford F 11
21 Annscroft B 10
45 Annstead D 12
7 Ansford C 10
22 Ansley C 6
31 Anslow H 10
31 Anslow Gate H 10
9 Anstey, Hants. B 8
25 Anstey, Herts. M 5
23 Anstey, Leics. A 9
53 Anstruther Easter G 10
53 Anstruther Wester G 10
23 Ansty, War. D 7
10 Ansty, W. Sussex F 2
8 Ansty, Wilts. C 1
9 Anthill Common E 8
43 Anthorn F 12
26 Antingham B 6
3 Antony D 11
4 Anvil Corner E 2
33 Anwick E 8
42 Anwoth F 6
24 Apes Hall F 6
24 Apethorpe F 1
33 Apley C 8
32 Apperknowle B 1
15 Apperley B 11
39 Appersett F 10
50 Appin House C 6
39 Appleby, Cumbria C 9
37 Appleby, Humber. F 7
22 Appleby Magna A 6
22 Appleby Parva A 6
18 Appleby Street D 3
54 Applecross E 1
54 Applecross House E 1
4 Appledore, Devon C 3
6 Appledore, Devon E 4
11 Appledore, Kent E 8
11 Appledore Heath E 8
16 Appleford E 6
8 Appleshaw A 4
38 Applethwaite C 5
30 Appleton, Ches. B 5
40 Appleton, N. Yorks. E 4
16 Appleton, Oxon. D 5
36 Appleton Roebuck C 3
41 Appleton-le-Moors F 7
41 Appleton-le-Street H 7
49 Appletreehall H 8
35 Appletreewick A 9
6 Appley D 4
34 Appley Bridge F 4
9 Apse Heath H 7
18 Apsley End A 1
9 Apuldram F 9
58 Aquhythie F 5
54 Araid D 2
54 Aranarff F 3
59 Arbeadie H 4
53 Arbirlot C 10
17 Arborfield G 8
17 Arborfield Cross G 8
42 Arbrack H 5
53 Arbroath C 11
59 Arbuthnott K 5
56 Archiestown E 8
30 Arclid Green D 6
60 Archadail G 3
46 Ardachearanbeg A 5
50 Ardachoil D 4
46 Ardachuple A 5
55 Ardachvie K 5
50 Ardalanish F 1
51 Ardanaiseig E 8
54 Ardaneaskan F 2
50 Ardanstur F 5
52 Ardargie House F 5
50 Ardarie A 5
54 Ardarroch F 2
46 Ardbeg C 6
60 Ardcharnich G 3
50 Ardchiavaig F 1
51 Ardchonnell F 7
50 Ardchrishnish E 2
52 Ardchullarie More F 1
51 Ardchyle E 12
53 Ardcross G 10
51 Arddarroch H 9
21 Arddleen A 8
18 Ardeley A 3
55 Ardelve G 2
47 Arden A 8
40 Arden Hall F 5
50 Ardencaple Ho. F 5
22 Ardens Grafton G 5
50 Ardentallan Ho. E 5
46 Ardentraive B 5
52 Ardeonaig D 2
51 Ardess H 10
60 Ardessie G 2
50 Ardfern G 5
51 Ardgartan G 10
60 Ardgay G 6
47 Ardgowan B 7
63 Ardhasig G 2
54 Ardheslaig D 2
50 Ardinamar F 5
60 Ardindrean G 3
10 Ardingly E 2
16 Ardington E 5
55 Ardintoul G 2
58 Ardlair E 3
46 Ardlamont House C 5
50 Ardlarach F 5
27 Ardleigh M 3
53 Ardler C 7
16 Ardley A 6
51 Ardlui F 10
46 Ardlussa A 2
51 Ardmaddy D 8
60 Ardmair G 3
46 Ardmaleish C 6
51 Ardmay G 10
46 Ardminish E 2
55 Ardmolich M 1
61 Ardmore, Highland H 7
50 Ardmore, Strathclyde E 5
47 Ardmore, Strathclyde B 8
50 Ardnacross C 3
47 Ardnadam A 7
56 Ardnagrask E 1
55 Ardnamurach K 2
50 Ardnastang A 5
47 Ardneil D 7
51 Ardno G 8
58 Ardo House E 7
52 Ardoch C 6
47 Ardochrig E 11
61 Ardochu F 7
55 Ardochy House J 6
50 Ardow B 2
58 Ardoyne E 4
46 Ardpatrick C 3
46 Ardpatrick House C 3
47 Ardpeaton A 7
46 Ardrishaig A 3
63 Ardroil D 1
56 Ardross Castle B 2
47 Ardrossan E 7
50 Ardshealach A 4
35 Ardsley G 12
35 Ardsley East E 11
50 Ardslignish A 3
52 Ardtalnaig C 2
46 Ardtaraig A 5
50 Ardtoe A 4
52 Ardtrostan E 2
50 Arduaine F 5
56 Ardullie C 1
50 Ardura E 4
62 Ardvasar H 5
50 Ardvergnish E 3
57 Ardverikie L 1
63 Ardvey, Loch Finsbay H 2
63 Ardvey, Loch Stockinish H 2
51 Ardvorlich, Strathclyde F 10
52 Ardvorlich, Tayside E 1
63 Ardvourlie Castle F 3
52 Ardwell, Dumf. & Gall. G 2
42 Ardwell, Strathclyde B 3
22 Areley Kings E 2
9 Arford B 9
52 Argaty G 2
14 Argoed D 5
20 Argoed Mill F 5
63 Aribruach E 6
51 Arichastlich D 10
60 Aridhglas F 1
54 Arinacrinachd D 1
50 Ariogan E 6
55 Arisaig L 1
55 Arisaig House L 1
50 Ariundle A 5
36 Arkendale A 2
25 Arkesden M 6
39 Arkholme H 8
39 Arkle Town E 12
43 Arkleby H 12
44 Arkleton D 2
18 Arkley D 2
36 Arksey F 4
32 Arkwright Town C 2
15 Arle B 12
38 Arlecdon C 3
25 Arlesey L 3
21 Arleston A 12
30 Arley, Cheshire B 5
22 Arley, War. C 6
15 Arlingham C 10
4 Arlington, Devon B 5
10 Arlington, E. Sussex G 4
16 Arlington, Glos. C 2
4 Arlington Beccott B 5
61 Armadale, Highland B 8
48 Armadale, Lothian C 2
62 Armadale Castle H 6
39 Armathwaite A 7
26 Arminghall E 5
22 Armitage A 4
35 Armley D 11
22 Armscote H 6
25 Armston G 2
36 Armthorpe G 4
47 Arnburn A 8
39 Arncliffe H 11
39 Arncliffe Cote H 11
53 Arncroach G 10
8 Arne G 1
23 Arnesby C 9
46 Arnicle F 2
55 Arnisdale H 2
62 Arnish C 5
62 Arnisort C 3
48 Arniston Engine C 6
63 Arnol B 4
37 Arnold, Humber. C 9
32 Arnold, Notts. F 3
52 Arnprior H 1
39 Arnside G 7
50 Aros Mains C 3
38 Arrad Foot G 5
37 Arram C 8
40 Arrathorne F 2
9 Arreton G 7
25 Arrington K 4
51 Arrivain D 10
51 Arrochar G 10
22 Arrow F 4
56 Artafallie E 2
35 Arthington C 11
23 Arthingworth D 11
20 Arthog A 2
58 Arthrath D 7
9 Arundel E 11
51 Aryhoulan A 7
38 Asby C 3
37 Asby cum Fenby G 10
46 Ascog C 6
17 Ascot G 10
16 Ascott-under-Wychwood B 4
40 Asenby H 4
32 Asfordby H 4
32 Asfordby Hill H 4
33 Asgarby, Lincs. D 10
24 Asgarby, Lincs. A 2
11 Ash, Kent B 11
10 Ash, Kent B 5
7 Ash, Somerset D 8
9 Ash, Surrey A 10
4 Ash Bullayne E 6
23 Ash Green D 7
30 Ash Magna F 4
4 Ash Hill D 6
6 Ash Priors C 5
6 Ash Thomas E 3
9 Ash Vale A 10
16 Ashampstead F 6
27 Ashbacking K 5
31 Ashbourne F 10
6 Ashbrittle D 4
5 Ashburton J 6
4 Ashbury, Devon F 4
16 Ashbury, Oxon. F 4
37 Ashby F 7
33 Ashby by Partney D 11
23 Ashby de la Launde E 7
31 Ashby de la Zouch H 12
26 Ashby Dell E 8
23 Ashby Folville A 10
23 Ashby Magna C 9
23 Ashby Parva C 8
33 Ashby Puerorum C 10
23 Ashby St. Ledgers E 9
26 Ashby St. Mary E 6
15 Ashchurch A 12
14 Ashcombe, Avon H 6
6 Ashcombe, Devon H 3
7 Ashcott C 8
47 Ashcraig C 7
17 Ashcroft F 8
25 Ashdon L 7
9 Ashe A 7
19 Asheldham D 9
25 Ashen L 8
17 Ashendon C 8
52 Ashfield, Central G 3
13 Ashfield, Dyfed D 10
27 Ashfield, Suffolk J 5
27 Ashfield Green H 6
31 Ashford, Derby C 10
4 Ashford, Devon C 4
8 Ashford, Hants. E 3
11 Ashford, Kent D 9
17 Ashford, Surrey G 11
21 Ashford Bowdler E 10
21 Ashford Carbonel E 10
16 Ashfrod Hill H 6
47 Ashgill D 12
39 Ashgillside A 10
6 Ashill, Devon E 4
26 Ashill, Norfolk E 2
6 Ashill, Somerset D 6
19 Ashington, Essex E 8
45 Ashington, Northumb. D 10
7 Ashington, Som. D 9
9 Ashington, W. Sussex E 12
49 Ashkirk G 7
8 Ashlett F 6
15 Ashleworth B 11
25 Ashley, Cambs. J 8
30 Ashley, Cheshire B 6
4 Ashley, Devon E 5
15 Ashley, Glos. E 12
8 Ashley, Hants C 5
8 Ashley, Hants G 4
11 Ashley, Kent C 11
23 Ashley, Northants. C 11
30 Ashley, Staffs. F 6
17 Ashley Green D 10
8 Ashley Heath F 3
16 Ashmansworth H 5
4 Ashmansworthy D 2
7 Ashmore D 12
16 Ashmore Green G 6
22 Ashorne F 6
32 Ashover D 1
22 Ashow E 6
21 Ashperton H 11
5 Ashprington K 7
4 Ashreigney E 5
10 Ashtead B 1
30 Ashton, Cheshire C 4
2 Ashton, Cornwall G 3
21 Ashton, Heref. & Worcs. F 10
23 Ashton, Northants. G 11
25 Ashton, Northants. G 2
15 Ashton Common H 12
16 Ashton Keynes E 2
34 Ashton-in-Makerfield G 5
22 Ashton under Hill H 3
35 Ashton under Lyne G 8
34 Ashton-upon-Mersey H 6
15 Ashton Watering G 8
8 Ashurst, Hants. E 5
10 Ashurst, Kent D 4
10 Ashurst, W. Sussex F 1
10 Ashurstwood D 3
4 Ashwater F 3
25 Ashwell, Herts. L 4
23 Ashwell, Leics. A 12
26 Ashwellthorpe F 4
7 Ashwick A 9
24 Ashwicken D 8
49 Ashybank H 8
38 Askam in Furness G 4
36 Askern F 3
7 Askerswell G 9
39 Askham C 7
36 Askham Bryan B 3
36 Askham Richard B 3
36 Asknish H 6
39 Askrigg F 11
35 Askwith B 10
24 Aslackby C 2
26 Aslacton F 4
32 Aslockton F 5
58 Asloun F 3
43 Aspatria G 12
18 Aspenden A 4
23 Aspley Guise H 12
17 Aspley Heath A 10
34 Aspull F 5
36 Asselby D 5
33 Asserby B 12
27 Assington L 2
56 Assynt House C 2
31 Astbury D 7
23 Astcote G 10
21 Asterley B 9
21 Asterton C 9
16 Asthall C 4
16 Asthall Leigh C 4
22 Astley, Heref. & Worcs. E 1
30 Astley, Salop. H 4
22 Astley, War. C 6
21 Astley Abbots C 12
34 Astley Bridge F 6
22 Astley Cross E 2
34 Astley Green G 6
17 Aston, Berks. F 9
30 Aston, Cheshire E 5
30 Aston, Cheshire B 4
29 Aston, Clwyd C 12
31 Aston, Derby B 10
21 Aston, Heref. & Worcs. E 10
21 Aston, Heref. & Worcs. F 10
18 Aston, Herts. B 3
16 Aston, Oxon. D 4
30 Aston, Salop. G 4
21 Aston, Salop A 11
32 Aston, S. Yorks. B 2
30 Aston, Staffs. F 6
31 Aston, Staffs. G 7
22 Aston, W. Midlands C 4
17 Aston Abbotts B 9
16 Aston Blank B 2
21 Aston Botterell D 11
22 Aston Cantlow F 5
17 Aston Clinton C 9
15 Aston Crews B 10
15 Aston Cross A 12
18 Aston End B 3
21 Aston Eyre C 12
22 Aston Fields E 3
23 Aston Flamville C 8
15 Aston Ingham B 10
30 Aston juxta Mondrum D 5
23 Aston le Walls G 8
16 Aston Magna A 3
21 Aston on Clun D 9
21 Aston Pigott B 9
21 Aston Rogers B 9
17 Aston Rowant D 8
17 Aston Sandford C 8
22 Aston Somerville H 4
22 Aston Subedge H 5
16 Aston Tirrold F 6
31 Aston upon Trent G 12
16 Aston Upthorpe E 6

25 Astwick L 3
25 Astwood K 1
22 Astwood Bank F 4
24 Aswarby B 2
33 Aswardby C 10
21 Atcham B 11
27 Athelington H 5
7 Athelney C 7
49 Athelstaneford B 8
4 Atherington, Devon D 5
9 Atherington, W. Sussex F 11
22 Atherstone B6
22 Atherstone on Stour G 5
34 Atherton G 5
55 Athnamulloch G 5
40 Atley Hill E 3
31 Atlow E 10
54 Attadale House F 3
26 Attleborough, Norfolk F 3
23 Attleborough, War. C 7
26 Attlebridge D 4
59 Atton K 1
49 Attonburn G 10
37 Atwick B 9
15 Atworth H 11
32 Aubourn D 6
54 Auchachenna E 7
46 Auchagallon F 4
57 Auchallater K 7
42 Auchalton A 4
57 Auchavan M 7
46 Auchbroad A 3
58 Aucheldy D 6
43 Auchenbainzie B 9
59 Auchenblae J 5
47 Auchenbothie Ho. B 8
43 Auchenbrack B 8
46 Auchenbreck A 5
43 Auchencairn, Dumf. & Gall. C 10
43 Auchencairn, Dumf. & Gall. F 9
47 Auchencarroch A 9
43 Auchencrieff D 10
42 Auchencrosh D 2
49 Auchencrow C 11
48 Auchendinny C 5
47 Auchenfoyle B 8
43 Auchengibbert D 9
48 Auchengray D 3
43 Auchengruith A 9
58 Auchenhairig B 1
48 Auchenheath E 1
42 Auchenmalg F 3
42 Auchensoul B 3
42 Auchentibbert G 2
47 Auchentiber E 8
47 Auchenvennel A 8
43 Auchenvey D 8
57 Auchernack G 6
57 Auchgourish H 5
46 Auchinadrian D 2
58 Auchinderran B 2
51 Auchindrain G 6
54 Auchindrean B 6
58 Auchinhove B 2
58 Auchininna C 4
42 Auchinleck, Dumf. & Gall. D 5
47 Auchinleck, Strathclyde G 10
47 Auchinloch B 11
52 Auchinner F 2
58 Auchintender D 4
59 Auchintoul, Grampian G 4
58 Auchintoul, Grampian F 3
58 Auchiries D 8
58 Auchleven E 4
48 Auchlochan F 1
59 Auchlossan G 3
60 Auchlunachan H 3
59 Auchlunies G 6
51 Auchlyne E 12
58 Auchmacoy D 7
48 Auchmantle E 2
47 Auchmillan F 10
53 Auchmithie C 11
53 Auchmuirbridge G 7
59 Auchmull K 3
51 Auchnacloich Pier D 7
50 Auchnacraig D 4
59 Auchnacree L 2
55 Auchnadaull L 5
52 Auchnafree D 3
56 Auchnagallin F 6
58 Auchnagatt C 7
46 Auchnaha A 4
57 Auchnahannet G 5
56 Auchnahillin F 3
42 Auchnotteroch F 1
59 Aucholzie H 1
51 Auchrioch E 10
57 Auchroisk G 6
59 Auchronie J 2
60 Auchtascailt H 3
52 Auchterarder F 4
55 Auchteraw J 7
53 Auchterderran H 7
53 Auchterhouse C 8
53 Auchtermuchty F 7
54 Auchterneed D 8
57 Auchterteang G 5
53 Auchtertool H 7
51 Auchtertyre, Central E 10
56 Auchtertye, Grampian D 7
55 Auchtertyre, Highland G 2
52 Auchtoo E 1
61 Auckingill B 12
36 Auckley G 4
58 Auckmair E 1
35 Audenshaw G 8
30 Audlem F 5
30 Audley E 6
25 Audley End L 6
58 Auds A 4
36 Aughton, Humber. C 5
34 Aughton, Lancs. G 3
39 Aughton, Lancs. H 8
32 Aughton, S. Yorks. B 2
16 Aughton, Wilts. H 3
53 Auldallan A 8
56 Auldearn D 5
21 Aulden G 10
43 Auldgirth C 10
49 Auldhame A 8
47 Auldhouse D 11
58 Auldtown B 3
58 Auldtown of Carnousie C 4
52 Aulich A 1
32 Ault Hucknall D 2
55 Ault-a-chrinn H 3
60 Aultanrynie D 4
60 Aultbea G 1
54 Aultdearg C 7
56 Aultfearn E 1
54 Aultgowrie E 8
54 Aultgrishan A 1
54 Aultguish Inn C 7
58 Aulthash B 1
61 Aultiphurst A 8
58 Aultmore B 1
57 Aultnagoire G 1
56 Aultnamain Inn B 2
57 Aultnancaber H 5
55 Aultnaslat J 5
58 Aulton E 3
59 Aultonrea H 1
57 Aundorach H 5
6 Aunk F 4
24 Aunsby B 1
15 Aust E 9
17 Austenwood E 10
36 Austerfield H 4
35 Austonley F 9
22 Austrey B 6
39 Austwick H 10
33 Authorpe B 11
33 Authorpe Row C 12
16 Avebury G 2
18 Aveley F 6
15 Avening E 12
52 Avenuehead H 3
32 Averham E 5
5 Aveton Gifford L 6
57 Avielochan H 5
57 Aviemore H 4
46 Avinagillan C 3
16 Avington, Berks. G 5
9 Avington, Hants. C 7
56 Avoch D 3
16 Avon F 1
15 Avon, Co. F 9
23 Avon Dassett G 7
48 Avonbridge B 2
15 Avonmouth F 8
5 Avonwick K 6
8 Awbridge D 5
42 Awhirk F 2
15 Awkley F 9
6 Awliscombe F 5
15 Awre D 10
32 Awsworth F 2
7 Axbridge A 8
9 Axford, Hants. B 7
16 Axford, Wilts. G 3
6 Axminster F 6
6 Axmouth G 6
40 Aycliffe C 3
45 Aydon F 8
15 Aylburton D 9
44 Ayle H 5
6 Aylesbeare G 4
17 Aylesbury C 9
37 Aylesby F 9
4 Aylescott D 5
10 Aylesford B 6
11 Aylsham C 11
23 Aylestone B 9
26 Aylmerton B 5
26 Aylsham C 5
15 Aylton A 9
21 Aymestrey F 9
16 Aynho A 6
18 Ayot St. Lawrence B 2
18 Ayot St. Peter B 2
47 Ayr G 8
39 Aysgarth F 12
6 Ayshford E 4
38 Ayside G 6
23 Ayston B 12
18 Aythorpe Roding B 6
49 Ayton C 11
40 Azerley H 3
5 Babbacombe J 8
30 Babbinswood G 2
7 Babcary C 9
13 Babel C 11
29 Babell C 11
7 Babington A 10
25 Babraham K 6
32 Babworth B 4
63 Back C 6
55 Back of Keppcoh L 1
64 Backaland B 3
64 Backaskaill A 3
38 Backbarrow G 6
35 Blackburn D 3
12 Backe E 6
58 Backfolds B 8
30 Backford C 3
30 Backford Cross C 3
58 Backhill, Grampian D 5
58 Backhill, Grampian F 5
58 Backhill, Grampian D 7
58 Backhill of Clackriach C 7
58 Backhill of Fortree D 7
59 Backhill of Trustach H 4
61 Backies F 8
53 Blackmuir of New Gilston F 9
15 Backwell G 8
45 Backworth F 11
18 Bacon End B 6
26 Baconsthorpe B 4
15 Bacton, Heref. & Worcs. A 7
26 Bacton, Norfolk B 6
27 Bacton, Suffolk J 3
35 Bacup E 7
54 Badachro B 2
60 Badagyle F 2
61 Badanloch Lodge D 8
54 Badavanich D 5
16 Badbury F 3
23 Badby F 9
60 Badcall, Highland G 2
60 Badcall, Highland C 3
60 Badcall, Loch Inchard, Highland B 4
31 Baddeley Green E 8
22 Baddesley Ensor B 6
60 Baddidarach E 2
15 Baddington B 12
56 Baddock D 4
58 Badenyon F 1
7 Badford Peverell G 10
22 Badger B 1
10 Badger's Mount B 4
15 Badgeworth B 12
7 Badgworth A 7
55 Badicaul G 1
27 Badingham H 6
60 Badintagairt F 5
11 Badlesmere C 9
60 Badluchrach G 2
60 Badnabay C 3
57 Badnambiast M 3
56 Badnonan F 5
60 Badrallach G 2
22 Badsey H 4
9 Badshot Lea A 10
36 Badsworth F 2
27 Badwell Ash H 3
33 Bag Enderby C 10
7 Bagber E 11
40 Bagby G 5
16 Bagendon C 1
29 Bagillt C 11
23 Baginton E 7
13 Baglan H 10
30 Bagley G 3
31 Bagnal E 8
16 Bagnor G 5
17 Bagshot, Surrey H 10
16 Bagshot, Wilts. H 4
15 Bagstone F 10
26 Bagthorpe, Norf. B 1
32 Bagthorpe, Notts. E 2
23 Bagworth A 8
15 Bagwy Llydiart B 8
35 Baildon C 10
46 Baile Boidheach B 2
50 Baile Mor F 1
57 Bailebeag H 1
44 Baileyhead E 3
44 Bailliehill D 1
47 Baillieston C 11
58 Bailliesward D 2
39 Bainbridge F 11
58 Bainshole D 4
24 Bainton, Cambs. E 2
37 Bainton, Humberside B 7
44 Bairnkine B 5
18 Baker Street F 6
18 Baker's End B 4
44 Bakethin D 4
31 Bakewell C 10
29 Bala G 8
52 Balado G 6
63 Balallan E 4
56 Balalochan B 1
50 Balarumindubh H 1
57 Balavil J 3
57 Balbeg G 1
52 Balbeggie D 6
58 Balbithan F 5
56 Balblair, Highland E 1
56 Balblair, Highland C 3
43 Balcary G 9
21 Balchedre C 8
58 Belchers B 4
60 Balchladich D 2
56 Balchraggan F 1
60 Balchreick B 3
10 Balcombe E 2
53 Balcurvie G 8
39 Balder Head C 11
40 Baldersby G 4
40 Baldersby St. James G 4
34 Balderstone D 5
30 Balderton D 2
53 Baldinnie F 9
25 Baldock M 3
53 Baldovie D 9
38 Baldrine G 2
11 Baldslow G 7
38 Baldwin G 2
44 Baldwinholme H 2
30 Baldwins Gate F 6
26 Bale B 3
58 Balearn B 8
48 Balerno C 4
59 Balfeith K 5
59 Balfield K 3
64 Balfour C 3
47 Balfron A 10
58 Balgaveny D 4
43 Balgerran E 8
52 Balgonar H 5
58 Balgove D 6
57 Balgowan K 2
62 Balgown A 3
53 Balgray C 9
43 Balgrayhill C 12
42 Balgrochan B 11
54 Balgy D 2
52 Balhaldie G 3
58 Balhalgardy E 5
18 Balham G 3
53 Balharry C 7
64 Baliasta A 8
61 Baligill A 8
56 Balintore, Highland B 4
53 Balintore, Tayside A 7
56 Balintraid C 3
57 Balintuim K 7
52 Balintyre B 2
53 Balkeerie C 8
36 Balkholme D 6
42 Balkissock C 2
30 Ball G 2
16 Ball Hill H 5
38 Ballabeg H 1
38 Ballacannell G 2
38 Ballacarnane Beg G 1
57 Ballachlaggan K 8
59 Ballachrosk H 1
51 Ballachulish Ho. B 7
38 Ballacraine G 1
38 Ballacuberagh G 2
43 Ballaggan B 9
38 Ballajora G 3
38 Ballakaigan H 1
38 Ballaleigh G 1
42 Ballantrae C 2
63 Ballantrushal B 5
19 Ballards Gore E 9
38 Ballasalla, I.o.M. F 2
38 Ballasalla, I.o.M. H 1
59 Ballater H 1
38 Ballaugh G 2
56 Ballchraggan B 3
57 Ballcorah G 7
52 Ballechin B 4
49 Ballencrieff B 7
46 Ballianlay C 5
50 Balliemore E 5
38 Ballig G 1
52 Balikinrain Castle H 1
51 Ballimeanoch F 7
51 Ballimore F 12
56 Ballindalloch F 7
53 Ballindean D 7
27 Ballingdon L 2
17 Ballinger Com. D 10
15 Ballingham A 9
52 Ballingry G 6
56 Ballinlagg F 6
57 Ballinluig, Highland G 6
52 Ballinluig, Tayside B 5
57 Ballintean J 4
52 Ballintuim B 6
42 Ballminnoch E 4
56 Balloan E 2
56 Balloch, Highland E 3
47 Balloch, Strathclyde A 9
59 Ballochan H 3
42 Ballochbroe A 4
42 Ballochdoan D 2
42 Ballochdowan D 2
58 Ballochford D 1
46 Ballochgoy C 6
42 Ballochmorrie C 3
46 Ballochroy D 2
59 Ballogie H 3
9 Balls Cross D 11
10 Ball's Green D 4
50 Ballygown C 2
50 Ballymeanoch H 5
55 Balmacara G 2
43 Balmaclellan D 7
52 Balmacneil B 5
53 Balmacolm F 8
62 Balmacquien A 4
43 Balmae G 7
51 Balmaha H 11
50 Balmaneach D 2
43 Balmangan G 7
58 Balmedie F 7
53 Balmerino E 8
8 Balmerlawn F 5
54 Balmore, Highland F 7
62 Balmore, Skye, Highland D 2
47 Balmore, Strathclyde B 11
52 Balmore, Tayside A 4
56 Balmuchy B 4
53 Balmule H 7
53 Balmullo E 9
56 Balmungie D 3
42 Balmurrie E 3
59 Balnaboth K 1
56 Balnabruaich C 3
56 Balnabual E 3
61 Balnacoil Lodge F 8
54 Balnacra E 3
56 Balnacraig F 1
56 Balnafoich F 2
56 Balnagall B 4
56 Balnageith D 6
59 Balnagowan G 2
52 Balnaguard B 4
56 Balnaguisich C 2
55 Balnain G 8
60 Balnakeil A 5
62 Balnaknock B 3
56 Balnapaling C 4
59 Balquharn L 2
51 Balquhidder E 12
22 Balsall E 6
22 Balsall Common D 6
23 Balscott H 7
25 Balsham K 7
64 Baltasound A 8
30 Balterley E 6
42 Baltersan E 5
32 Balterton E 5
58 Balthangie C 6
7 Baltonsborough C 8
50 Balure C 6
58 Balvack F 4
56 Balvaird D 1
58 Balvenie C 1
50 Balvicar F 5
55 Balvraid, Highland H 2
56 Balvraid, Highland F 4
34 Bamber Bridge E 4
18 Bamber's Green B 6
45 Bamburgh D 12
53 Bamff B7
48 Bamflatt F 3
31 Bamford B 10
39 Bampton, Cumbria C 7
6 Bampton, Devon D 3
16 Bampton, Oxon. D 4
39 Bampton Grange C 7
55 Banavie M 5
23 Banbury H 8
13 Bancffosfelen F 8
59 Banchory, Grampian G 7
59 Banchory, Grampian H 4
13 Bancycapel E 7
12 Banc-y-felin E 6
13 Banc-c-ffordd C 7
53 Bandirran House D 7
58 Banff A 4
28 Bangor C 5
30 Bangor-Is-coed F 3
27 Banham G 4
8 Bank, Hants. E 4
21 Bank, Powys A 8
35 Bank Newton B 8
21 Bank Street F 11
43 Bankend, Dumf. & Gall. E 11
48 Bankend, Strathclyde F 1
47 Bankfoot, Strathclyde B 7
52 Bankfoot, Tayside D 5
47 Bankglen H 11
58 Bankhead, Grampian F 6
59 Bankhead, Grampian G 4
45 Bankhead, Northumb. B 8
47 Bankhead, Strathclyde D 8
48 Bankhead, Strathclyde E 3
47 Banknock B 12
44 Banks, Cumb. F 4
34 Banks, Lancs. E 3
43 Bankshill C 12
26 Banningham C 5
19 Bannister Green B 7
52 Bannockburn H 3
10 Banstead B 1
5 Bantham L 5
47 Banton B 12
15 B anwell H 7
11 Bapchild B 8
50 Barachandroman E 4
47 Barassie F 8
50 Baravullin D 6
56 Barbaraville C 3
31 Barber Booth B 9
47 Barbieston H 9
39 Barbon G 8
50 Barbreck House G 5
4 Barbrook A 6
23 Barby E 9
51 Barcaldine C 7
43 Barcaple F 7
22 Barchesten H 6
47 Barclaugh G 9
43 Barclosh E 9
10 Barcombe G 3
10 Barcombe Cross F 3
40 Barden F 2
35 Barden Scale A 9
42 Bardennoch B 6
64 Bardister C 7
61 Bardnabeinne G 7
33 Bardney C 8
23 Bardon A 8
44 Bardon Mill G 6
47 Bardowie B 10
47 Bardrainney B 8
38 Bardsea H 5
35 Bardsey C 12
27 Bardwell H 2
49 Barelees F 11
21 Barewood G 9
46 Barfad B 4
26 Barford, Norfolk E 4
22 Barford, War. F 6
16 Barford St. John A 5
8 Barford St. Martin C 2
16 Barford St. Michael A 5
11 Barfreston C 11
42 Bargaly E 5
47 Barglas A 8

14 Bargoed D 5
42 Bargrennan D 4
51 Barguillean Farm E 7
25 Barham, Cambs. H 2
11 Barham, Kent C 10
27 Barham, Suffolk K 4
43 Barharrow F 7
24 Barholm D 2
44 Barhough H 5
23 Barkby A 9
23 Barkby Thorpe A 9
32 Barkestone G 5
17 Barkham G 9
18 Barking, London E 5
27 Barking, Suffolk K 4
27 Barking Tye K 4
35 Barkisland E 9
32 Barkston, Lincs. F 6
36 Barkston, N. Yorks. D 3
25 Barkway M 5
42 Barlae F 4
31 Barlaston F 7
43 Barlay D 7
32 Barlborough C 2
36 Barlby D 4
23 Barlestone B 8
25 Barley, Herts. L 5
35 Barley, Lancs. C 7
45 Barley Mow H 11
45 Barleyhill H 8
23 Barleythorpe A 11
19 Barling E 9
32 Barlow, Derby C 1
36 Barlow, N. Yorks. D 4
45 Barlow, Tyne & Wear G 9
36 Barmby Moor B 5
36 Barmby on the Marsh D 5
26 Barmer B 1
49 Barmoor Castle E 12
49 Barmoor Ridge E 12
20 Barmouth A 2
40 Barmpton C 3
37 Barmston A 9
43 Barmurrie D 7
51 Barnacarry H 7
24 Barnack E 2
23 Barnacle D 7
51 Barnaline F 7
39 Barnard Castle C 12
25 Barnardiston K 8
43 Barnbarroch F 9
36 Barnburgh G 3
26 Barnby F 8
36 Barnby Dun F 4
32 Barnby in the Willows E 6
32 Barnby Moor B 4
42 Barncorkrie H 2
18 Barnes F 2
10 Barness Street C 5
18 Barnet D 3
37 Barnetby le Wold F 8
26 Barney B 3
27 Barnham, Suffolk G 2
9 Barnham, W. Sussex F 11
26 Barnham Broom E 4
59 Barnhead L 4
56 Barnhill D 7
42 Barnhills D 1
40 Barningham, Dur. D 1
27 Barningham, Suff. H 3
37 Barnoldby le Beck G 10
35 Barnoldswick C 7
9 Barns Green C 12
16 Barnsley, Glos. D 2
35 Barnsley, S. Yorks. F 12
4 Barnstaple C 4
18 Barnston, Essex B 6
30 Barnston, Merseyside B 1
32 Barnstone G 4
22 Barnt Green E 4
30 Barnton C 5
25 Barnwell All Saints G 2
25 Barnwell St. Andrew G 2
15 Barnwood C 11
21 Barons' Cross G 10
47 Barr, Dumf. & Gall. H 12
43 Barr, Dumf. & Gall. B 9
42 Barr, Strathclyde B 4
58 Barra Castle E 5
42 Barrachan G 4
50 Barrachrail E 5
63 Barraglom D 3
45 Barrasford F 7
50 Barravullin G 5
38 Barregaroow G 2
47 Barrhead D 10
42 Barrhill C 3
25 Barrington, Cambs. K 5
7 Barrington, Som. D 7
2 Barripper F 3
55 Barrisdale J 3
47 Barrmill D 8
61 Barrock A 11
34 Barrow, Lancs. C 6
23 Barrow, Leics. A 12
21 Barrow, Salop. B 12
7 Barrow, Som. C 10
27 Barrow, Suffolk J 1
15 Barrow Gurney G 8
37 Barrow Haven E 8
32 Barrow Hill C 1
32 Barrow-in-Furness H 5
34 Barrow Nook G 3
7 Barrow Street C 11
37 Barrow-upon-Humber E 8
32 Barrow-upon-Soar H 3
31 Barrow-upon-Trent G 12
45 Barrowburn B 7
32 Barrowby G 6
41 Barrowcliff F 10
23 Barrowden B 12
35 Barrowford C 7
30 Barrows Green D 5
51 Barrs D 8
14 Barry, S. Glam. G 4
53 Barry, Tayside D 10
23 Barsby A 10
26 Barsham F 7
22 Barston D 5
21 Bartestree H 11
58 Barthol Chapel D 6
30 Barthomley E 6
34 Bartle Hall D 4
49 Bartlehill E 10
8 Bartley E 4
25 Bartlow L 7
7 Barton, Avon A 7
25 Barton, Cambs. K 5
30 Barton, Cheshire E 3
39 Barton, Cumbria C 7
5 Barton, Devon J 8
16 Barton, Glos. B 2
34 Barton, Lancs. C 4
34 Barton, Lancs. F 2
40 Barton, N. Yorks. D 3
22 Barton, War. G 4
24 Barton Bendish E 8
26 Barton Common C 7
15 Barton End E 11
17 Barton Hartshorn A 7
32 Barton in Fabis G 2
23 Barton-in-the-Beans B 7
25 Barton-in-the-Clay M 2
25 Barton Mills H 8
8 Barton-on-Sea G 4
16 Barton-on-the-Heath A 4
7 Barton St. David C 8
23 Barton Seagrave D 12
8 Barton Stacey B 6
4 Barton Town B 5
37 Barton Waterside E 8
41 Barton-le-Street H 7
36 Barton-le-Willows A 5
31 Barton-under-Needwood H 10
37 Barton-upon-Humber E 8
35 Barugh F 11
63 Barvas B 5
25 Barway H 6
23 Barwell B 8
7 Barwick E 9
36 Barwick in Elmet C 2
30 Baschurch H 3
23 Basecote F 7
31 Basford Green E 8
34 Bashall Eaves C 6
8 Bashley F 4
17 Basildon, Berks F 7
19 Basildon, Essex E 7
9 Basing A 8
9 Basingstoke A 7
31 Baslow C 11
7 Bason Bridge B 7
14 Bassaleg F 6
49 Bassendean E 9
38 Bassenfell B 4
38 Bassenthwaite B 5
38 Bassenthwaite Lake Station B 4
4 Basset's Cross F 4
8 Bassett D 5
22 Bassett's Pole B 5
25 Bassingbourn L 4
32 Bassingfield F 3
32 Bassingham D 6
33 Bassingthorpe G 7
64 Basta B 7
24 Baston D 2
26 Bastwick D 7
18 Batchworth Heath E 1
7 Batcombe, Dorset F 9
7 Batcombe, Som. B 10
30 Bate Heath B 5
15 Bath H 10
15 Bathampton H 11
15 Bathealton D 4
15 Batheaston G 11
15 Bathford H 11
48 Bathgate B 3
32 Bathley D 5
3 Bathpool, Corn. B 10
6 Bathpool, Som. D 6
7 Bathway A 9
35 Batley E 11
16 Batsford A 3
40 Battersby D 6
18 Battersea F 3
27 Battisford K 4
27 Battisford Tye K 3
10 Battle, E. Sussex F 6
14 Battle, Powys A 3
7 Battleborough A 7
21 Battlefield A 10
19 Battlesbridge D 8
17 Battlesden A 10
6 Battleton C 3
8 Battramsley F 5
9 Batt's Corner B 9
58 Bauds of Cullen A 2
17 Baughurst H 7
59 Baulds H 4
16 Baulking E 4
33 Baumber C 9
16 Baunton D 1
8 Baverstock C 2
26 Bawburgh E 5
26 Bawdeswell C 3
7 Bawdrip B 7
27 Bawdsey L 6
32 Bawtry A 4
34 Baxenden E 6
22 Baxterley B 6
9 Baybridge D 7
38 Baycliff H 5
16 Baydon F 4
18 Bayford, Herts. C 3
7 Bayford, Som. C 10
39 Bayles A 9
27 Baylham K 4
16 Baynards' Green A 6
21 Bayston Hill B 10
21 Bayton E 12
15 Beach, Avon G 10
50 Beach, Highland B 5
23 Beachampton H 11
24 Beachamwell E 8
15 Beachley E 9
19 Beacon End A 9
8 Beacon Hill, Dor. G 1
9 Beacon Hill, Surrey B 10
17 Beacon's Bottom E 9
17 Beaconsfield E 10
63 Beacravik H 2
40 Beadlam G 6
45 Beadnell D 12
4 Beaford D 4
45 Beal, Northumb. B 12
36 Beal, N. Yorks. E 3
55 Bealachasan H 3
7 Beaminster F 8
45 Beamish H 10
35 Beamsley B 9
10 Bean A 5
15 Beanacre H 12
45 Beanley A 9
4 Beara Moor D 4
44 Bearbridge G 6
6 Beare F 3
10 Beare Green D 1
45 Bearl G 9
22 Bearley F 5
50 Bearnus C 1
40 Bearpark A 3
47 Bearsden B 10
11 Bearsted C 7
8 Bearwood F 2
6 Beasley B 3
43 Beattock A 11
43 Beattock Summit H 3
18 Beauchamp Roding C 6
32 Beauchief B 1
14 Beaufort C 5
8 Beaulieu F 5
56 Beauly E 1
28 Beaumaris C 5
44 Beaumont, Cumb. G 2
19 Beaumont, Essex A 11
40 Beaumont Hill C 3
22 Beausale E 6
9 Beauworth C 7
4 Beaworthy F 3
19 Beazley End A 7
30 Bebington B 2
45 Bebside E 11
26 Beccles F 7
34 Becconsall E 3
39 Beck Foot F 8
41 Beck Hole E 8
25 Beck Row H 8
38 Beck Side G 5
22 Beckbury B 1
18 Beckenham G 4
43 Beckfoot G 11
16 Beckford A 1
16 Beckhampton G 2
32 Beckingham, Lincs. E 6
32 Beckingham, Notts. A 5
7 Beckington A 11
8 Beckley, Hants. F 4
16 Beckley, Oxon. C 6
11 Beckley, E. Sussex F 7
35 Beckwithshaw B 11
18 Becontree E 5
40 Bedale F 3
40 Bedburn B 1
7 Bedchester D 12
14 Beddau F 4
28 Beddgelert E 5
10 Beddingham G 3
18 Beddington G 3
27 Bedfield J 5
25 Bedford K 2
25 Bedfordshire, Co. K 2
9 Bedhampton E 8
27 Bedingfield H 5
35 Bedlam A 11
45 Bedlington E 10
14 Bedlinog D 4
15 Bedminster G 9
17 Bedmond D 11
31 Bednall H 8
49 Bedrule H 8
49 Bedshiel D 9
21 Bedstone E 9
14 Bedwas E 5
14 Bedwellty D 5
23 Bedworth C 7
23 Beeby A 10
9 Beech, Hants. B 8
31 Beech, Staffs. F 7
17 Beech Hill, Berks. H 8
39 Beech Hill, Cumb. E 7
34 Beech Hill, Manchester F 4
16 Beechingstoke H 2
16 Beedon F 6
16 Beedon Hill F 6
37 Beeford B 9
31 Beeley C 11
37 Beelsby G 9
17 Beenham G 7
2 Beeny B 1
6 Beer, Devon G 6
7 Beer, Somerset C 7
7 Beer Hackett E 9
7 Beercrocombe D 7
5 Beesands M 7
33 Beesby B 11
5 Beeson L 7
25 Beeston, Beds. K 3
30 Beeston, Cheshire D 4
26 Beeston, Norfolk D 2
32 Beeston, Notts. G 3
35 Beeston, W. Yorks. D 11
26 Beeston Regis A 5
43 Beeswing E 10
39 Beetham G 7
26 Beetley D 3
14 Began F 5
16 Begbroke C 5
24 Begdale E 6
12 Begelly F 5
21 Beggar's Bush F 8
21 Beguildy D 7
26 Beighton, Norf. E 7
32 Beighton, S. Yorks. B 2
47 Beith D 8
11 Bekesbourne C 10
26 Belaugh D 6
22 Belbroughton D 3
27 Belchamp Otten L 1
27 Belchamp St. Paul L 1
27 Belchamp Walter L 1
58 Belcherrie D 1
33 Belchford C 10
53 Belfarg G 7
45 Belford C 12
45 Belford Mains C 12
58 Belhelvie F 7
58 Belhinnie E 2
18 Bell Bar C 3
35 Bell Busk B 7
22 Bell Heath D 3
58 Bellabeg F 1
50 Bellanoch H 5
36 Bellasize D 6
35 Belle Vue E 12
33 Belleau B 11
56 Bellehiglash F 7
40 Bellerby F 1
5 Bellever H 5
49 Bellhaven B 9
17 Bellingdon D 10
45 Bellingham E 7
46 Belloch F 2
46 Bellochantuy F 2
10 Bells Yew Green D 5
42 Bellsbank A 5
45 Bellshill, Northumb. C 12
47 Bellshill, Strathclyde C 12
48 Bellspool F 4
48 Bellsquarry C 3
42 Bellymore C 3
56 Belmaduthy D 2
24 Belmesthorpe D 1
34 Belmont, Lancs. F 5
47 Belmont, Strathclyde G 8
64 Belmont, Shetland Is. B 8
47 Belmore A 7
58 Belnacraig F 1
3 Belowda D 7
31 Belper E 11
31 Belper Lane End E 11
45 Belsay E 9
27 Belstead L 4
47 Belston G 9
4 Belstone F 5
4 Belstone Corner F 5
34 Belthorn E 6
11 Beltinge A 10
44 Beltingham G 6
32 Belton, Leics. H 2
23 Belton, Leics. B 11
36 Belton, Humber. F 6
32 Belton, Lincs. F 6
26 Belton, Norfolk E 8
32 Belvoir G 5
9 Bembridge G 8
49 Bemersyde F 8
8 Bemerton C 3
41 Bempton H 12
61 Ben Armine Lodge E 7
63 Ben Casgro D 5
27 Benacre G 8
57 Benalder Lodge L 1
43 Benbruie B 8
48 Bendameer A 5
54 Bendronaig Lodge F 4
24 Benefield F 1
11 Benenden E 7
42 Benfield E 5
27 Benfield Green J 7
45 Benfieldside H 9
43 Bengall D 12
26 Bengate C 6
22 Bengeworth H 4
59 Benholm K 5
36 Beningbrough A 3
18 Benington, Herts. B 3
33 Benington, Lincs. E 11
33 Benington Sea End F 11
28 Benllech B 4
46 Benmore A 6
60 Benmore Lodge F 4
5 Bennacott G 2
46 Bennecarrigan G 4
33 Benniworth B 9
10 Benover C 6
17 Benson E 7
47 Benston H 10
59 Bent K 4
45 Benthall, Northumb. D 12
21 Benthall, Salop. B 12
15 Bentham C 12
59 Benthoul G 5
9 Bentley, Hants. B 9
37 Bentley, Humber. D 8
36 Bentley, S. Yorks. G 3
22 Bentley, War. C 6
22 Bentley Heath D 5
4 Benton B 5
46 Benton Polliwilline H 2
44 Bentpath D 2
24 Bentwick F 4
4 Bentwitchen C 6
9 Bentworth B 8
42 Beoch, Dumf. & Gall. E 2
42 Beoch, Strathclyde B 6
22 Beoley E 4
55 Beoraidberg K 1
9 Bepton D 10
18 Berden A 5
5 Bere Alston J 3
5 Bere Ferrers J 3
7 Bere Regis G 11
2 Berepper G 4
26 Bergh Apton E 6
17 Berinsfield E 7
15 Berkeley D 10
17 Berkhamstead C 10
7 Berkley A 11
16 Berkshire, Co. F 5
22 Berkswell D 6
18 Bermondsey F 3
55 Berners G 2
62 Bernisdale C 3
17 Berrick Salome E 7
61 Berriedale E 10
38 Berrier B 6
21 Berriew B 7
49 Berrington, Northumb. E 12
21 Berrington, Salop. B 10
49 Berringtonlaw E 12
6 Berrow A 6
22 Berrow Green F 1
4 Berry Cross D 3
4 Berry Down Cross B 4
12 Berry Hill, Dyfed C 4
15 Berry Hill, Glos. C 9
5 Berry Pomeroy K 7
58 Berryhillock B 2
4 Berrynarbor A 4
18 Berry's Green H 4
43 Berryscaur B 12
59 Berrysloch H 3
29 Bersham E 12
20 Berthddu H 4
7 Berwick, Dorset G 8
10 Berwick, E. Sussex H 4
16 Berwick Bassett G 2
45 Berwick Hill F 10
8 Berwick St. James B 2
8 Berwick St. John D 1
7 Berwick St. Leonard C 12
49 Berwick-upon-Tweed D 12
29 Berwyn F 11
32 Bescaby G 5
34 Bescar F 3
22 Besford H 3
36 Bessacarr G 4
10 Bessels Green C 4
16 Bessels Leigh D 5
37 Bessingby A 9
26 Bessingham B 4
10 Best Beech Hill E 5
26 Besthorpe, Norf. F 4
32 Besthorpe, Notts. D 5
37 Beswick B 8
10 Betchworth C 1
20 Bethania, Dyfed F 1
28 Bethania, Gwynedd F 6
28 Bethel, Gwynedd C 3
28 Bethel, Gwynedd D 5
29 Bethel, Gwynedd F 9
11 Bethersden D 8
12 Bethesda, Dyfed E 4
28 Bethesda, Gwynedd D 6
13 Bethlehem D 10
18 Bethnal Green F 4
30 Betley E 6
10 Betsham A 5
11 Betteshanger C 11
7 Bettiscombe F 7
30 Bettisfield G 3
30 Betton G 5
14 Bettws F 6
20 Bettws Bledrws G 2
12 Bettws Evan B 6
15 Bettws Newydd D 7
61 Bettyhill B 7
13 Betws F 9
21 Betws Cedewain C 7
28 Betws Garmon D 5
29 Betws Gwerfil Goch F 9
29 Betws-y-coed E 7
29 Betws-yn-Rhos C 8
12 Beulah, Dyfed B 6
20 Beulah, Powys G 5
32 Bevercotes C 4
37 Beverley C 8
15 Beverstone E 11
15 Bevington E 10
38 Bewaldeth B 4
44 Bewcastle F 4
22 Bewdley E 1
35 Bewerley A 10
37 Bewholme B 9
49 Bewlie G 8
10 Bexhill G 6
18 Bexley F 5

18 Bexleyheath **F 5**
24 Bexwell **E 7**
27 Beyton **J 2**
27 Beyton Green **J 2**
16 Bibury **C 2**
17 Bicester **B 7**
22 Bickenhill **D 5**
24 Bicker **B 3**
34 Bickerstaffe **G 3**
30 Bickerton, Ches. **E 4**
45 Bickerton, Northumb. **C 8**
36 Bickerton, N. Yorks. **B 2**
4 Bickingcott **C 6**
4 Bickington, Devon **C 4**
5 Bickington, Devon **H 7**
6 Bickleigh, Devon **E 3**
5 Bickleigh, Devon **J 4**
4 Bickleton **C 4**
30 Bickley Moss **E 4**
19 Bicknacre **D 8**
6 Bicknoller **B 5**
11 Bicknor **B 7**
8 Bickton, Hants. **E 3**
21 Bicton, Heref. & Worc. **F 10**
21 Bicton, Salop **D 8**
21 Bicton, Salop **A 10**
11 Biddenden **D 7**
11 Biddenden Green **D 7**
25 Biddenham **K 1**
15 Biddestone **G 11**
7 Biddisham **A 7**
23 Biddlesden **H 9**
45 Biddlestone **B 8**
31 Biddulph **D 7**
31 Biddulph Moor **D 7**
4 Bideford **C 3**
22 Bidford-on-Avon **G 4**
10 Bidorough **D 4**
6 Bidwell **F 3**
36 Bielby **C 5**
59 Bieldside **G 6**
8 Bierley, I.of Wight **H 6**
35 Bierley, W. Yorks. **D 10**
17 Bierton **C 9**
43 Big Corlae **B 7**
54 Big Sand **B 1**
5 Bigbury **L 5**
5 Bigbury-on-Sea **L 5**
37 Bigby **F 8**
34 Biggar, Lancs. **A 1**
48 Biggar, Strathclyde **F 3**
48 Biggarshiels Mains **E 3**
31 Biggin, Derby **E 11**
31 Biggin, Derby **D 10**
36 Biggin, N. Yorks. **D 3**
18 Biggin Hill **H 4**
25 Biggleswade **L 3**
9 Bighton **C 7**
9 Bignor **E 11**
64 Bigton **F 7**
3 Bilberry **D 7**
32 Bilborough **F 3**
6 Bilbrook **B 4**
36 Bilbrough **C 3**
32 Bilby **B 4**
27 Bildeston **K 3**
3 Billacott **A 9**
19 Billericay **D 7**
32 Billesdon **B 10**
22 Billesley **F 5**
24 Billingborough **B 2**
34 Billinge **G 4**
27 Billingford **G 5**
26 Billingford **C 3**
40 Billingham **C 5**
33 Billinghay **E 8**
36 Billingley **G 2**
9 Billinghurst **C 12**
21 Billingsley **D 12**
17 Billington, Beds. **B 10**
34 Billington, Lancs. **D 6**
24 Billockby **D 7**
40 Billy Row **A 2**
34 Bilsborrow **C 4**
33 Bilsby **C 11**
9 Bilsham **F 11**
11 Bilsington **E 9**
15 Bilson Green **C 9**
32 Bilsthorpe **D 4**
48 Bilston, Lothian **C 5**
22 Bilston, W. Midlands **B 3**
23 Bilstone **B 7**
11 Bilting **C 9**
45 Bilton, Northumb. **B 10**
37 Bilton, Humber. **D 9**
36 Bilton, N. Yorks. **B 3**
23 Bilton, W. Midlands **E 8**
45 Bilton Banks **B 10**
64 Bimbister **C 2**
37 Binbrook **H 10**
7 Bincombe **H 10**
61 Bindal **H 9**
9 Binegar **A 9**
17 Binfield **G 9**
17 Binfield Heath **F 8**
45 Bingfield **F 8**
32 Bingham **F 4**
7 Bingham's Melcombe **F 11**
35 Bingley **C 10**
26 Binham **B 3**
8 Binley **A 6**
48 Binniehill **B 1**
40 Binsoe **G 3**
9 Binstead **G 7**
9 Binsted **B 9**
22 Binton **G 5**
26 Bintree **C 3**
21 Binweston **B 8**
19 Birch, Essex **B 9**
35 Birch, Manchester **F 7**
19 Birch Green **B 9**
31 Birch Vale **B 8**
26 Bircham Newton **B 1**
26 Bircham Tofts **B 1**
18 Birchanger **B 5**
21 Bircher **F 10**
57 Birchfield **G 5**
14 Birchgrove, Cardiff, S. Glam. **F 5**
13 Birchgrove, W. Glam. **G 10**
11 Birchington **A 11**
31 Birchover **D 10**
32 Bircotes **A 3**
22 Bird End **C 4**
25 Birdbrook **L 8**
9 Birdham **F 9**
23 Birdingbury **E 8**
15 Birdlip **C 12**
36 Birdsall **A 6**
22 Birdsgreen **D 1**
7 Birdsmoor Gate **F 7**
47 Birdston **B 11**
35 Birdwell **G 12**
15 Birdwood **B 10**
49 Birgham **E 10**
34 Birkacre **F 4**
40 Birkby **E 3**
34 Birkdale **F 2**
30 Birkenhead **A 2**
58 Birkenhills **C 5**
47 Birkenshaw, Strathclyde **D 12**
35 Birkenshaw, W. Yorks. **D 10**
59 Birkhall **H 1**
49 Birkhill, Borders **E 8**
48 Birkhill, Borders **H 5**
53 Birkhill, Tayside **D 8**
36 Birkin **D 3**
44 Birks **E 6**
43 Birkshaw **C 9**
21 Birley **G 10**
10 Birling, Kent **B 5**
45 Birling, Northumb. **B 10**
22 Birlingham **H 3**
22 Birmingham **D 5**
52 Birnam **C 5**
47 Birnieknowe **G 10**
59 Birse **H 3**
59 Birsemore **H 3**
15 Bournes Green, Gloucestershire **D 12**
22 Bournheath **E 3**
45 Bournmoor **H 11**
22 Bournville **D 4**
16 Bourton, Oxon. **E 3**
7 Bourton, Dorset **C 11**
21 Bourton, Salop. **C 11**
23 Bourton on Dunsmore **E 8**
16 Bourton-on-the-Hill **A 3**
16 Bourton-on-the-Water **A 3**
44 Boustead Hill **G 1**
38 Bouth **G 6**
40 Bouthwaite **H 2**
17 Boveney **F 10**
14 Boverton **G 3**
5 Bovey Tracey **H 7**
17 Bovingdon **D 11**
17 Bovingdon Green **E 9**
18 Bovinger **C 5**
49 Bow, Borders **E 7**
4 Bow, Devon **F 6**
64 Bow, Orkney Is **E 2**
17 Bow Brickhill **A 10**
53 Bow of Fife **F 8**
20 Bow Street **D 2**
39 Bowbank **C 11**
40 Bowburn **A 3**
8 Bowcombe **G 6**
6 Bowd **G 4**
49 Bowden, Borders **F 8**
5 Bowden, Devon **L 7**
15 Bowden Hill **H 12**
39 Bowerdale **E 9**
30 Bowdon **B 6**
44 Bower **E 6**
7 Bower Hinton **D 8**
8 Bowerchalke **D 2**
15 Bowerhill **H 12**
61 Bowermadden **B 11**
31 Bowers **G 7**
19 Bowers Gifford **E 7**
52 Bowershall **H 6**
61 Bowertower **B 11**
39 Bowers **D 12**
34 Bowgreave **C 4**
49 Bowhill **G 7**
43 Bowhouse **E 11**
3 Bowithick **A 9**
34 Bowker's Green **G 3**
38 Bowland Bridge **F 6**
21 Bowley **G 11**
9 Bowlhead Green **B 10**
47 Bowling **B 9**
22 Bowling Green **G 2**
38 Bowmanstead **F 5**
44 Bowness-on-Solway **G 1**
38 Bowness-on-Windermere **E 6**
49 Bowsden **E 12**
61 Bowside Lodge **B 8**
48 Bowtrees **A 2**
15 Box, Glos. **D 11**
15 Box, Wilts. **G 11**
15 Boxbush **C 10**
16 Boxford, Berks. **G 5**
27 Boxford, Suffolk **L 3**
9 Boxgrove **E 10**
10 Boxley **B 6**
4 Box's Shop **F 1**
27 Boxted, Essex **M 3**
27 Boxted, Suffolk **K 1**
27 Boxted Cross **M 3**
25 Boxworth **J 4**
25 Boxworth End **H 5**
11 Boyden Gate **B 11**
31 Boylestone **G 10**
58 Boyndie **A 4**
41 Boynton **H 11**
7 Boys Hill **E 10**
5 Boyton, Cornwall **G 2**
27 Boyton, Suffolk **K 7**
8 Boyton, Wilts. **B 1**
18 Boyton Cross **C 6**
23 Bozeat **F 12**
38 Braaid **H 2**
27 Brabling Green **J 6**
11 Brabourne **D 9**
11 Brabourne Lees **D 9**
61 Brabstermire **A 12**
62 Bracadale **D 3**
24 Braceborough **D 2**
33 Bracebridge Heath **C 7**
33 Braceby **G 7**
35 Bracewell **B 7**
56 Brachla **F 1**
32 Brackenfield **D 1**
38 Brackenthwaite, Cumbria **C 4**
9 Bracklesham **F 9**
55 Brackletter **L 6**
23 Brackley, Northants. **H 9**
46 Brackley, Strathclyde **E 3**
60 Brackloch **E 3**
17 Bracknell **G 9**
52 Braco **F 3**
58 Bracobrae **B 3**
26 Bracon Ash **E 5**
55 Bracora **K 1**
55 Bracorina **K 1**
31 Bradbourne **E 10**
40 Bradbury **B 3**
38 Bradda **H 1**
23 Bradden **G 10**
17 Bradenham **D 9**
16 Bradenstoke **F 1**
17 Bradfield, Berks. **G 7**
6 Bradfield, Devon **E 4**
27 Bradfield, Essex **M 4**
35 Bradfield, S. Yorks. **H 11**
27 Bradfield Combust **J 2**
30 Bradfield Green **D 5**
27 Bradfield Heath **M 4**
27 Bradfield St. Clair **J 2**
27 Bradfield St. George **J 2**
4 Bradford, Devon **E 3**
45 Bradford, Northumb. **D 11**
35 Bradford, W. Yorks. **D 10**
7 Bradford Abbas **E 9**
15 Bradford Leigh **H 11**
4 Bradford Mill **D 7**
15 Bradford-on-Avon **H 11**
6 Bradford-on-Tone **D 5**
9 Brading **G 7**
30 Bradley, Clwyd **E 2**
31 Bradley, Derby. **F 10**
9 Bradley, Hants. **B 7**
22 Bradley, Heref. & Worc. **F 3**
37 Bradley, Humber. **F 10**
39 Bradley, N. Yorks. **G 12**
31 Bradley, Staffs. **H 7**
22 Bradley, W. Midlands **C 3**
30 Bradley Common **F 4**
22 Bradley Green **F 3**
31 Bradley in the Moors **F 9**
32 Bradmore **G 3**
7 Bradney **B 7**
6 Bradninch **F 3**
31 Bradnop **E 8**
7 Bradpole **G 8**
34 Bradshaw **F 6**
5 Bradstone **H 3**
30 Bradwall Green **D 6**
31 Bradwell, Derby. **B 10**
19 Bradwell, Essex **B 8**
26 Bradwell, Suffolk **E 8**
23 Bradwell, Bucks. **H 11**
16 Bradwell Grove **C 3**
19 Bradwell-on-Sea **C 10**
19 Bradwell Waterside **C 10**
4 Bradworthy **E 2**
4 Bradworthy Cross **E 2**
64 Brae **C 7**
60 Brae Doune **G 5**
60 Brae of Achnahaird **E 2**
55 Brae Roy Lodge **K 7**
56 Braeantra **B 1**
57 Braedownie **M 8**
43 Braefoot **A 9**
52 Braegrum **E 5**
58 Braehead, Grampian **F 7**
42 Braehead, Dumf. & Gall. **F 5**
64 Braehead, Orkney Is. **D 3**
48 Braehead, Strathclyde **D 2**
48 Braehead, Strathclyde **F 1**
53 Braehead, Tayside **B 11**
61 Braehungie **D 11**
54 Braeintra **F 2**
60 Braelangwell Lodge (Hotel) **G 6**
57 Braemar **K 7**
61 Braemore, Highland **D 10**
54 Braemore, Highland **B 6**
47 Braeside **B 7**
51 Braeval **G 12**
40 Brafferton, Dur. **C 3**
40 Braverton, N. Yorks. **H 4**
23 Bradfield-on-the Green **F 11**
63 Bragar **B 4**
18 Bragbury End **B 3**
50 Braglenbeg **E 6**
34 Braides **B 3**
49 Braidshawrig **D 8**
48 Braidwood **E 1**
31 Brailsford **F 11**
45 Brainshaugh **C 10**
19 Braintree **B 7**
27 Braiseworth **H 4**
8 Braishfield **D 5**
38 Braithwaite, Cumb. **C 5**
36 Braithwaite, S. Yorks. **F 4**
32 Braithwell **A 3**
10 Bramber **G 1**
32 Bramcote **F 2**
9 Bramdean **C 7**
26 Bramerton **E 6**
18 Bramfield, Herts. **B 3**
27 Bramfield, Suffolk **H 7**
27 Bramford **K 4**
31 Bramhall **B 7**
36 Bramham **C 2**
36 Bramham Crossroads **C 2**
35 Bramhope **C 11**
17 Bramley, Hants. **H 7**
9 Bramley, Surrey **B 11**
32 Bramley, S. Yorks. **A 2**
6 Brampford Speke **F 3**
25 Brampton, Cambs. **H 3**
44 Brampton, Cumb. **G 4**
39 Brampton, Cumb. **C 9**
15 Brampton, Heref. & Worc. **A 7**
32 Brampton, Lincs. **B 6**
36 Brampton, S. Yorks. **G 2**
27 Brampton, Suffolk **G 7**
15 Brampton Abbots **B 9**
23 Brampton Ash **C 11**
21 Brampton Bryan **E 9**
32 Brampton en le Morthen **A 2**
31 Bramshall **G 9**
8 Bramshaw **E 4**
9 Bramshott **C 9**
18 Bran End **A 6**
50 Branault **A 3**
26 Brancaster **A 1**
26 Brancaster Staithe **A 1**
40 Brancepeth **A 2**
56 Branchill **D 6**
15 Brand Green **B 10**
56 Branderburgh **C 8**
37 Brandesburton **B 9**
27 Brandeston **J 5**
4 Brandis Corner **E 3**
26 Brandiston **C 4**
38 Brandingill **C 4**
40 Brandon, Durham **A 3**
32 Brandon, Lincs. **E 6**
45 Brandon, Northumb. **A 8**
27 Brandon, Suffolk **G 1**
23 Brandon, War. **D 7**
24 Brandon Creek **F 7**
26 Brandon Parva **E 4**
40 Brandsby **H 6**
37 Brandy Wharf **G 8**
2 Brane **G 1**
8 Branksome **G 2**
8 Branksome Park **G 2**
8 Bransbury **B 6**
6 Branscombe **G 5**
22 Bransford **G 1**
8 Bransgore **F 3**
22 Branson's Cross **E 4**
32 Branston, Leics. **G 5**
33 Branston, Lincs. **C 7**
31 Branston, Staffs. **H 10**
33 Branston Booths **C 8**
9 Branstone **H 7**
32 Brant Broughton **E 6**
44 Branteth **E 1**
27 Brantham **M 4**
38 Branthwaite, Cumb. **C 3**
38 Branthwaite, Cumb. **B 5**
37 Brantingham **D 7**
45 Branton, Northumb. **A 8**
36 Branton, S. Yorks. **G 4**
44 Branxholme **B 3**
49 Branxton **F 11**
49 Branxtonmoor **F 11**
31 Brassington **E 11**
10 Brasted **C 3**
10 Brasted Chart **C 3**
59 Brathens **H 4**
33 Bratoft **D 11**
32 Brattleby **B 6**
6 Bratton, Somerset **B 3**
8 Bratton, Wilts. **A 1**
5 Bratton Clovelly **G 3**
4 Bratton Fleming **B 5**
7 Bratton Seymour **C 10**
18 Braughing **A 4**
23 Braunston, Leics. **A 11**
23 Braunston, Northants. **E 9**
23 Braunstone **B 9**
4 Braunton **B 4**
12 Brawby, Dyfed **E 2**
41 Brawby, N. Yorks. **G 7**
61 Brawlbin **B 10**
17 Bray **F 10**
3 Bray Shop **B 10**
17 Bray Wick **F 9**
23 Braybrooke **D 11**
4 Brayford **C 6**
36 Brayton **D 4**
3 Brazacott **A 9**
62 Breabost **C 3**
11 Breach **B 7**
18 Breachwood Green **B 2**
63 Breaclete **C 2**
31 Breadsall **F 12**
15 Breadstone **D 10**
54 Breafield **F 8**
2 Breage **G 3**
54 Breakachy **E 8**
15 Bream **D 9**
8 Breamore **D 3**
15 Bream's Eaves **D 9**
6 Brean **A 6**
35 Brearton **A 11**
63 Breasclete **C 3**
32 Breaston **G 2**
13 Brechfa **D 8**
59 Brechin **L 4**
43 Breckonside **A 9**
62 Breckrey **B 4**
14 Brecon **A 4**
35 Bredbury **H 8**
11 Brede **F 7**
21 Bredenbury **G 11**
27 Bredfield **K 6**
11 Bredger **B 7**
11 Bredhurst **B 7**
22 Bredicot **G 3**
15 Bredon **A 12**
22 Bredon's Norton **H 3**
21 Bredwardine **H 9**
32 Breedon on the Hill **H 1**
48 Breich **C 2**
36 Breighton **D 5**
21 Breinton **H 10**
21 Breinton Com. **H 10**
16 Bremhill **G 1**
51 Brenachoille **G 7**
10 Brenchley **D 5**
4 Brendon **A 6**
46 Brenfield **A 3**
63 Brenish **D 1**
45 Brenkley **F 10**
18 Brent **E 2**
27 Brent Eleigh **K 2**
6 Brent Knoll **A 6**
25 Brent Pelham **M 5**
18 Brentford **F 2**
18 Brentwood **E 6**
11 Brenzett **E 8**
22 Brereton **A 4**
30 Brereton Green **D 6**
30 Brereton Heath **D 6**
64 Bressay **E 7**
27 Bressingham **G 4**
64 Bretabister **D 7**
31 Bretby **H 11**
23 Bretford **D 7**
22 Bretforton **H 4**
39 Bretherdale Head **E 8**
34 Bretherton **E 4**
6 Brett **B 4**
27 Brettenham, Suff. **K 3**
27 Brettenhm, Norf. **G 2**
30 Bretton **D 2**
10 Brewer Street **C 2**
22 Brewood **A 2**
56 Briach **D 6**
7 Briantspuddle **G 11**
18 Bricket Wood **D 1**
22 Bricklehampton **H 3**
38 Bride **F 2**
38 Bridekirk **B 4**
12 Bridell **C 5**
5 Bridestowe **G 4**
58 Brideswell **D 3**
5 Bridford **G 7**
11 Bridge, Kent **C 10**
2 Bridge, Cornwall **E 4**
25 Bridge End, Beds. **K 1**
24 Bridge End, Lincs. **B 2**
45 Bridge End, Northumb. **B 9**
40 Bridge Hewick **H 4**
58 Bridge of Alford **F 3**
52 Bridge of Allan **G 3**
56 Bridge of Avon **F 7**
51 Bridge of Awe **E 7**
51 Bridge of Balgie, Perth **C 12**
53 Bridge of Brewlands **A 7**
57 Bridge of Brown **G 7**
52 Bridge of Cally **B 6**
59 Bridge of Canny **H 4**
53 Bridge of Craigisla **B 7**
43 Bridge of Dee **F 8**
56 Bridge of Derrybeg **F 8**
58 Bridge of Don **F 7**
59 Bridge of Dun **L 4**
59 Bridge of Dye **J 4**
52 Bridge of Earn **E 6**
51 Bridge of Ericht **B 12**
59 Bridge of Feugh **H 4**
61 Bridge of Forss **A 10**
59 Bridge of Gairn **H 1**
51 Bridge of Gaur **B 12**
53 Bridge of Lintrathen **B 7**
59 Bridge of Murchalls **H 6**
51 Bridge of Orchy **D 10**
52 Bridge of Tilt **A 4**
64 Bridge of Waith **D 1**
64 Bridge of Walls **D 6**
47 Bridge of Weir **C 9**
4 Bridge Reeve **E 5**
21 Bridge Sollars **H 9**
27 Bridge Street **K 2**

30 Bridge Trafford **C 3**
25 Bridgefoot, Cambs. **L 5**
38 Bridgefoot, Cumb. **B 3**
7 Bridgehampton **D 9**
49 Bridgelands **F 7**
9 Bridgemary **F 7**
3 Bridgend, Corn. **D 8**
38 Bridgend, Cumbria **D 6**
43 Bridgend, Dumf. & Gall. **A 11**
12 Bridgend, Dyfed **B 5**
53 Bridgend, Fife **F 8**
58 Bridgend, Grampian **C 5**
58 Bridgend, Grampian **D 3**
58 Bridgend, Grampian **E 6**
58 Bridgend, Grampian **D 1**
54 Bridgend, Highland **D 7**
48 Bridgend, Lothian **B 3**
14 Bridgend, Mid Glam. **F 2**
50 Bridgend, Strathclyde **H 6**
59 Bridgend, Tayside **K 3**
52 Bridgend, Tayside **E 6**
4 Bridgerule **F 1**
21 Bridges **C 9**
3 Bridgetown, Corn. **A 10**
6 Bridgetown, Som. **C 3**
22 Bridgetown, Staffs. **A 3**
27 Bridgham **G 3**
21 Bridgnorth **C 12**
7 Bridgwater **B 6**
41 Bridlington **H 12**
7 Bridport **G 8**
15 Bridstow **B 9**
35 Brierfield **D 7**
15 Brierley, Glos. **C 9**
21 Brierley, Heref. & Worc. **G 10**
36 Brierley, S. Yorks. **F 2**
22 Brierley Hill **C 3**
40 Brierton **B 5**
14 Briery Hill **C 5**
51 Brig o' Turk **G 12**
37 Brigg **F 8**
59 Briggs of Criggie **J 6**
41 Briggswath **D 9**
38 Brigham, Cumb. **B 3**
37 Brigham, Humber. **B 8**
35 Brighouse **E 10**
8 Brighstone **H 6**
16 Brighthampton **D 5**
31 Brightgate **D 11**
10 Brightling **F 5**
19 Brightlingsea **B 10**
2 Brighton, Corn. **D 6**
10 Brighton, E. Sussex **H 2**
48 Brightons **B 2**
16 Brightwalton **F 5**
17 Brightwell, Oxon. **E 7**
27 Brightwell, Suffolk **L 5**
17 Brightwell Baldwin **E 7**
40 Brignall **D 1**
37 Brigsley **G 10**
39 Brigsteer **F 7**
23 Brigstock **D 12**
17 Brill, Bucks. **C 7**
2 Brill, Cornwall **G 4**
21 Brilley **G 8**
12 Brimaston **D 3**
21 Brimfield **F 10**
32 Brimington **C 1**
15 Brimpsfield **C 12**
16 Brimpton **H 6**
64 Brims **E 1**
15 Brimscombe **D 11**
30 Brimstage **B 2**
57 Brin **G 2**
55 Brinacory **K 1**
36 Brind **D 5**
64 Brindister, Shetland Is. **D 6**
64 Brindister, Shetland Is. **E 7**
34 Brindle **E 5**
31 Brindley Ford **E 7**
22 Brineton **A 2**
23 Bringhurst **C 11**
25 Brington **H 2**
26 Briningham **B 3**
33 Brinkhill **C 10**
25 Brinkley **K 7**
23 Brinklow **D 8**
16 Brinkworth **F 1**
34 Brinscall **E 5**
15 Brinsea **H 7**
32 Brinsley **E 2**
21 Brinsop **H 10**
32 Brinsworth **A 1**
26 Brinton **B 3**
64 Brinyan **B 2**
26 Brisley **C 3**
15 Brislington **G 9**
11 Brissenden Green **D 8**
15 Bristol **G 9**
26 Briston **B 4**
27 Britannia **E 7**
8 Britford **C 3**
29 Brithdir, Gwynedd **H 7**
14 Brithdir, Mid Glam. **D 5**
10 British Legion Village **B 6**
13 Briton Ferry **G 10**
17 Britwell Salome **E 7**
5 Brixham **K 8**
5 Brixton **K 4**
7 Brixton Deverill **B 11**
23 Brixworth **E 10**
16 Brize Norton **C 4**
16 Broad Blunsdon **E 3**
22 Broad Campden **H 5**
8 Broad Chalke **C 2**
6 Broad Clyst **F 3**
25 Broad Green, Beds. **L 1**
19 Broad Green, Essex **B 8**
22 Broad Green, Heref. & Worc. **F 1**
12 Broad Haven **F 2**
21 Broad Heath **F 12**
25 Broad Hill **H 7**
16 Broad Hinton **F 2**
16 Broad Laying **H 5**
22 Broad Marston **G 5**
38 Broad Oak, Cumb. **F 4**
13 Broad Oak, Dyfed **E 9**
11 Broad Oak, E. Sussex **F 7**
15 Broad Oak, Heref. & Worc. **B 8**
36 Broad Oak, N. Yorks. **B 4**
11 Broad Street **B 7**
19 Broad Street Green **C 8**
16 Broad Town **F 2**
35 Broadbottom **H 8**
9 Broadbridge **E 9**
9 Broadbridge Hth. **C 12**
12 Broadfield **G 5**
62 Broadford **F 5**
8 Broadford Bri. **D 12**
48 Broadgairhill **H 5**
44 Broadhaugh **B 3**
61 Broadhaven **C 12**
30 Broadheath **A 6**
7 Broadhembury **F 5**
5 Broadhempston **J 7**
11 Broadland Row **F 7**
13 Broadlay **F 7**
58 Broadley **B 1**
18 Broadley Com. **C 4**
4 Broadmead **D 7**
49 Broadmeadows **F 7**
9 Broadmere **A 7**
12 Broadmoor **F 4**
4 Broadnymet **F 6**
10 Broadoak, E. Sussex **F 5**
11 Broadoak, Kent **B 10**
58 Broadrashes **B 2**
58 Broadsea **E 5**
11 Broadstairs **A 12**
8 Broadstone, Dorset **F 2**
21 Broadstone, Salop. **C 11**
16 Broadtown Lane **F 2**
22 Broadwas **G 1**
18 Broadwater, Herts. **B 2**
23 Birstall, Leics. **A 9**
35 Birstall, W. Yorks. **E 11**
35 Birstwith **A 11**
24 Birthorpe **B 2**
48 Birthwood **F 3**
21 Birtley, Heref. & Worc. **E 9**
45 Birtley, Northumb. **E 7**
45 Birtley, Tyne & Wear **G 11**
15 Birts Street **A 11**
23 Bisbrooke **B 12**
4 Bish Mill **C 6**
17 Bisham **F 9**
22 Bishampton **G 3**
40 Bishop Auckland **B 2**
37 Bishop Burton **C 7**
40 Bishop Middleham **B 3**
40 Bishop Monkton **H 3**
33 Bishop Norton **A 7**
15 Bishop Sutton **H 9**
35 Bishop Thornton **A 10**
36 Bishop Wilton **B 6**
33 Bishopbridge **A 7**
47 Bishopbriggs **B 11**
56 Bishopmill **C 8**
16 Bishops Cannings **H 2**
21 Bishop's Castle **D 8**
7 Bishop's Caundle **E 10**
15 Bishop's Cleeve **B 12**
21 Bishop's Frome **G 12**
18 Bishop's Green **B 6**
6 Bishop's Hull **D 5**
23 Bishop's Itchington **F 7**
6 Bishop's Lydeard **C 5**
4 Bishop's Nymptom **D 6**
30 Bishop's Offley **G 6**
18 Bishop's Stortford **B 5**
9 Bishop's Sutton **C 7**
22 Bishop's Tatchbrook **F 6**
4 Bishop's Tawton **C 4**
9 Bishop's Waltham **D 7**
22 Bishop's Wood **A 2**
11 Bishopsbourne **C 10**
5 Bishopsteignton **H 8**
8 Bishopstoke **D 6**
13 Bishopston **H 9**
17 Bishopstone, Bucks. **C 9**
10 Bishopstone, E. Sussex **H 4**
21 Bishopstone, Heref. & Worcs. **H 9**
8 Bishopstone, Wilts. **C 2**
16 Bishopstone, Wilts. **F 3**
7 Bishopstrow **B 11**
6 Bishopswood **E 6**
15 Bishopsworth **G 9**
36 Bishopthorpe **B 4**
40 Bishopton, Dur. **C 4**
47 Bishopton, Strathclyde **B 9**
15 Bishpool **E 7**
15 Bishton **F 7**
15 Bisley, Glos. **D 12**
17 Bisley, Surrey **H 10**
34 Bispham **C 2**
2 Bissoe **E 5**
8 Bisterne Close **F 4**
33 Bitchfield **G 7**
4 Biteford **D 2**
4 Bittadon **B 4**
5 Bittaford **K 5**
26 Bittering Street **D 2**
21 Bitterley **E 11**
8 Bitterne **E 6**
23 Bitteswell **D 8**
17 Bix **F 8**
64 Bixter **D 7**
23 Blaby **B 9**
16 Black Bourton **D 4**
54 Black Bridge **C 7**
45 Black Callerton **F 10**
42 Black Clauchrie **C 4**
51 Black Corries **B 10**
50 Black Croft **D 6**
4 Black Dog **E 7**
45 Black Heddon **E 9**
51 Black Mount **C 10**
19 Black Notley **B 7**
13 Black Pill **H 9**
4 Black Torrington **E 3**
43 Blackacre **C 11**
49 Blackadder Bank **D 11**
5 Blackawton **L 7**
6 Blackborough **E 4**
24 Blackborough End **D 8**
10 Blackboys **F 4**
31 Blackbrook, Derby. **E 11**
34 Blackbrook, Merseyside **G 4**
30 Blackbrook, Staffs. **F 6**
49 Blackburn, Borders **D 8**
44 Blackburn, Borders **D 3**
58 Blackburn, Grampian **F 6**
34 Blackburn, Lancs. **D 5**
48 Blackburn, Lothian **C 3**
48 Blackburn, Strathclyde **G 2**
43 Blackcraig **D 8**
4 Blackditch Cross **E 6**
54 Blackdog **F 7**
43 Blackdyke **F 12**
35 Blacker Hill **G 12**
8 Blackfield **F 6**
44 Blackford, Cumb. **G 2**
7 Blackford, Som. **A 7**
7 Blackford, Som **D 10**
52 Blackford, Tayside **F 4**
31 Blackfordby **H 11**
8 Blackgang **H 6**
40 Blackhall Colliery **A 5**
45 Blackhall Mill **G 9**
10 Blackham **D 4**
49 Blackhaugh **E 7**
19 Blackheath, Essex **B 10**
27 Blackheath, Suff. **H 7**
9 Blackheath, Surrey **B 11**
22 Blackheath, W. Midlands **D 3**
58 Blackhill, Grampian **B 8**
58 Blackhill, Grampian **C 8**
62 Blackhill, Highland **C 3**
58 Blackhilllock **C 1**
44 Blackhills, Dumf. & Gall. **F 1**
56 Blackhills, Grampian **D 8**
15 Blackhorse **F 10**
48 Blackhopebyre **E 6**
16 Blackland **G 1**
43 Blacklaw **A 11**
35 Blackley **G 7**
52 Blacklunans **A 6**
21 Blackmarstone **H 10**
14 Blackmill **F 3**
9 Blackmoor **C 9**
4 Blackmoor Gate **B 5**
18 Blackmore **D 6**
25 Blackmore End, Essex **M 8**
18 Blackmore End, Hertfordshire **B 2**
48 Blackness **A 3**
9 Blacknest **B 9**
35 Blacko **C 7**
43 Blackpark **C 10**
34 Blackpool **C 2**
44 Blackpool Gate **E 4**
48 Blackridge **C 2**
43 Blackrigg **C 11**
14 Blackrock, Gwent **C 5**
15 Blackrock, Gwent **E 8**
34 Blackrod **F 5**
43 Blackshaw **E 11**
35 Blackshaw Head **D 8**
27 Blacksmith's Cnr. **M 3**
10 Blackstone **F 1**
17 Blackthorn **B 7**
27 Blackthorpe **J 2**
36 Blacktoft **E 6**
59 Blacktop **G 6**
2 Blackwater, Corn. **E 4**
17 Blackwater, Hants. **H 9**
8 Blackwater, I.o.W. **G 6**
6 Blackwater, Som. **E 6**
27 Blackwater, Suff. **H 8**
58 Blackwater Lodge **E 1**
46 Blackwaterfoot **G 4**
31 Blackwell, Derby **C 10**
32 Blackwell, Derby **D 2**
40 Blackwell, Durham **D 3**
6 Blackwell, Som. **D 4**
22 Blackwell, War. **H 6**
43 Blackwood, Dumf. & Gall. **C 10**
14 Blackwood, Gwent **E 5**
47 Blackwood, Strathclyde **E 12**
31 Blackwood Hill **E 8**
30 Blacon **C 2**
42 Bladnoch **F 5**
16 Bladon **C 5**
13 Blaen Celyn **B 7**
14 Blaen Dyryn **A 3**
12 Blaenannerch **B 6**
28 Blaennau-Dolwyddelan **E 6**
28 Blaenau Ffestiniog **F 6**
14 Blaenavon **C 6**
14 Blaenawey **B 6**
12 Blaen-ffos **C 5**
14 Blaengarw **E 2**
14 Blaengavenny **B 6**
14 Blaengwrach **D 2**
14 Blaengwynfi **E 2**
20 Blaenpennal **F 2**
20 Blaenplwyf **E 1**
12 Blaenporth **B 6**
12 Blaenwaun **D 6**
13 Blaen-y-Coed **D 7**
14 Blaerhondda **D 3**
6 Blagdon Hill **D 5**
15 Blagdon **H 8**
55 Blaich **M 4**
50 Blain **A 4**
14 Blaina **D 5**
58 Blair **E 6**
52 Blair Atholl **A 4**
52 Blair Drummond **G 2**
52 Blairadam **H 6**
48 Blairburn **A 3**
58 Blairdaff **F 4**
52 Blairgowrie **C 6**
52 Blairhall **H 5**
52 Blairingone **G 5**
52 Blairlogie **G 3**
60 Blairmore, Highland **B 3**
47 Blairmore, Strathclyde **A 7**
47 Blairnairn **A 8**
57 Blairnamarrow **H 8**
47 Blairquhosh **A 10**
46 Blair's Ferry **B 5**
47 Blairskaith **B 10**
47 Blairvadach **A 7**
15 Blaisdon **C 10**
22 Blakebrook **D 2**
22 Blakedown **D 2**
49 Blakelaw **F 10**
30 Blakemere, Ches. **C 4**
21 Blakemere, Heref. & Worcs **H 9**
15 Blakeney, Glos. **D 10**
26 Blakeney, Norfolk **A 3**
30 Blakenhall, Ches. **E 6**
22 Blakenhall, W. Midlands **B 3**
22 Blakenhall Heath **B 4**
22 Blakeshall **D 2**
23 Blakesley **G 9**
45 Blanchland **H 8**
35 Bland Hill **B 10**
7 Blandford Forum **E 12**
7 Blandford St. Mary **F 12**
47 Blanefield **A 10**
33 Blankney **D 8**
51 Blar a'Chaoruinn **A 8**
50 Blaran **F 6**
51 Blarghour **F 7**
55 Blarmafoldach, Highland **M 5**
51 Blarmachfoldach, Highland **A 8**
60 Blarnaleyoch **G 3**
8 Blashford **E 3**
23 Blaston **C 11**
24 Blatherwycke **F 1**
38 Blawith **F 5**
27 Blaxhall **J 7**
36 Blaxton **G 4**
45 Blaydon **G 10**
7 Bleadon **A 7**
11 Blean **B 10**
33 Bleasby, Lincs. **B 8**
32 Bleasby, Notts. **E 4**
53 Blebocraigs **F 9**
21 Bleddfa **F 7**
16 Bledington **B 3**
17 Bledlow **D 8**
17 Bledlow Ridge **D 9**
4 Blegberry **C 1**
49 Blegbie **C 7**
39 Blencarn **B 9**
43 Blencogo **G 12**
9 Blendworth **E 8**
43 Blennerhasset **G 12**
16 Bletchingdon **B 6**
10 Bletchingley **C 2**
17 Bletchley, Bucks. **A 9**
30 Bletchley, Salop. **G 5**
12 Bletherston **E 4**
25 Bletsoe **J 1**
16 Blewbury **F 6**
26 Blickling **C 5**
32 Blidworth **E 3**
32 Blidworth Bottoms **E 3**
44 Blindburn **B 6**
38 Blindcrake **B 4**
10 Blindley Heath **C 2**
49 Blinkbonny **F 11**
3 Blisland **B 8**
22 Bliss Gate **E 1**
8 Blissford **E 3**
23 Blisworth **G 10**
31 Blithbury **H 9**
31 Blithford **H 9**
43 Blitterlees **F 11**
27 Blo Norton **G 3**
16 Blockley **A 3**
26 Blofield **E 6**
26 Blofield Corner **D 6**
43 Bloomfield, Dumf. & Gall. **D 10**
49 Bloomfield, Borders **G 8**
31 Blore **E 10**
31 Blounts Green **G 9**
16 Bloxham **A 5**
33 Bloxholm **E 8**
22 Bloxwich **B 3**
7 Bloxworth **G 12**
35 Blubberhouses **B 10**
2 Blue Anchor, Corn. **D 6**
6 Blue Anchor, Som. **B 4**
13 Blue Anchor, W. Glam. **G 9**
10 Bluebell Hill **B 6**
60 Blughasary **F 3**
34 Blundellsands **G 2**
26 Blundeston **F 8**
25 Blunham **K 3**
16 Blunsdon St. Andrew **E 2**
22 Bluntington **E 2**
25 Bluntisham **H 5**
3 Blunts **C 10**
37 Blyborough **H 7**
27 Blyford **H 7**
22 Blymhill **A 2**
45 Blyth, Northumb. **E 11**
32 Blyth, Notts. **B 3**
48 Blyth Bridge **E 4**
31 Blyth Marsh **F 8**
27 Blythburgh **H 7**
31 Blythe Bridge **E 4**
31 Blythe Marsh **F 8**
31 Blythebridge **G 9**
36 Blyton **H 6**
53 Boarhills **F 10**
9 Boarhunt **E 7**
16 Boars Hill **D 6**
10 Boarshead **E 4**
17 Boarstall **C 7**
4 Boasley Cross **F 4**
57 Boat of Garten **H 5**
56 Boath **B 1**
11 Bobbing **B 7**
22 Bobbington **C 2**
18 Bobbingworth **C 5**
56 Boblainy **F 1**
19 Bocking **B 7**
19 Bocking Churchstreet **A 7**
3 Boconnoc **D 8**
58 Boddam, Grampian **C 8**
64 Boddam, Shetland Is. **F 7**
7 Bodden **B 10**
28 Bodedern **B 3**
29 Bodelwyddan **C 9**
21 Bodenham, Heref. & Worcs. **G 10**
8 Bodenham, Wilts. **D 3**
21 Bodenham Moor **G 11**
28 Boderwryd **A 3**
29 Bodfari **C 10**
28 Bodffordd **C 4**
26 Bodham Street **B 4**
10 Bodiam **E 6**
23 Bodicote **H 8**
3 Bodieve **B 7**
3 Bodinnick **D 8**
10 Bodle Street Grn. **G 5**
3 Bodmin **C 8**
29 Bodnant **C 7**
26 Bodney **E 1**
28 Bodorgan **C 3**
11 Bodsham Green **D 9**
28 Boduan **F 3**
3 Bodwen **D 7**
56 Bogallan **E 2**
58 Bogbrae **D 8**
49 Bogend, Borders **D 10**
47 Bogend, Strathclyde **F 9**
49 Boghall, Lothian **C 5**
48 Boghall, Lothian **C 3**
47 Boghall, Strathclyde **H 9**
58 Boghead, Grampian **E 7**
47 Boghead, Strathclyde **F 10**
47 Boghead, Strathclyde **E 12**
56 Boghole **D 5**
43 Bogknowe **F 10**
15 Bogmarsh **A 8**
59 Bogmuire, Grampian **K 4**
58 Bogmuir, Grampian **A 1**
58 Bogniebrae **C 3**
9 Bognor Regis **F 11**
58 Bograxie **F 4**
48 Bogsbank **D 4**
48 Bogside **D 1**
58 Bogton **C 4**
43 Bogue **C 7**
2 Bohortha **F 6**
55 Bohuntine **L 7**
3 Bokiddick **C 7**
40 Bolam, Durham **C 2**
45 Bolam, Northumb. **E 9**
5 Bolberry **M 6**
30 Bold Heath **A 4**
45 Boldon Colliery **G 11**
8 Boldre **F 5**
50 Boldron **D 1**
32 Bole **B 5**
31 Bolehill **E 11**
2 Boleigh **G 2**
49 Boleside **F 7**
52 Bolfracks **B 3**
6 Bolham **E 3**
6 Bolham Water **E 5**
2 Bolingey **D 5**
31 Bollington, Ches. **B 8**
30 Bollington, Ches. **B 6**
31 Bollington Cross **C 8**
10 Bolney **F 1**
25 Bolnhurst **J 2**
53 Bolshan **B 11**

32 Bolsover C 2
35 Bolsterstone G 11
15 Bolstone A 8
40 Boltby F 5
17 Bolter End E 9
39 Bolton, Cumbria C 8
34 Bolton, Manchester F 6
36 Bolton, Humber. B 5
49 Bolton, Lothian B 7
45 Bolton, Northumb. B 9
35 Bolton Abbey B 9
35 Bolton Bridge B 9
34 Bolton by Bowland B 6
39 Bolton-le-Sands H 7
38 Bolton Low Houses A 5
36 Bolton-on-Dearne G 2
40 Bolton-on-Swale E 3
36 Bolton Percy C 3
39 Bolton Town End H 7
44 Boltonfellend F 3
3 Bolventor B 9
30 Bomere Heath H 3
60 Bonar Bridge G 6
51 Bonawe Quarries D 7
37 Bonby F 8
12 Boncath C 5
44 Bonchester Bridge B 4
9 Bonchurch H 7
4 Bondleigh E 5
34 Bonds C 4
22 Bonehill B 5
48 Bo'ness A 3
52 Bonhard D 6
47 Bonhill A 9
22 Boningdale B 2
49 Bonjedward G 9
48 Bonkle D 1
48 Bonnington B 4
53 Bonnybank G 8
48 Bonnybridge A 1
58 Bonnykelly B 6
48 Bonnyrigg and Lasswade C 6
47 Bonnyton F 9
31 Bonsall D 11
15 Bont B 7
28 Bont Newydd F 6
28 Bontddu H 6
20 Bont-dolgadfan B 4
20 Bontnewydd, Dyfed F 2
28 Bont-newydd, Gwynedd D 4
20 Bontrhydgaled D 4
29 Bontuchel D 10
14 Bonvilston G 4
13 Bon-y-maen G 10
4 Boode B 4
30 Booley H 4
39 Boon E 8
41 Boosbeck C 7
4 Boot F 1
36 Booth D 5
35 Booth Wood E 9
33 Boothby Graffoe D 7
33 Boothby Pagnell G 7
34 Boothtown G 6
38 Bootle, Cumbria F 4
34 Bootle, Merseyside H 2
52 Boquhan, Central H 2
47 Boquhan, Central A 10
21 Boraston E 11
9 Borden D 9
35 Bordley A 8
9 Bordon C 9
19 Boreham C 7
10 Boreham Street G 5
18 Borhamwood D 2
52 Boreland, Central D 1
43 Boreland, Dumf. & Gall. B 12
43 Boreland of Girthon F 7
62 Boreraig C 1
49 Borewell D 12
61 Borgie House B 7
43 Borgue, Dumf. & Gall. G 7
61 Borgue, Highland E 10
27 Borley L 1
62 Bornaskitaig A 3
43 Borness G 7
10 Borough Green B 5
40 Boroughbridge H 4
30 Borras Head E 2
61 Borrobol Lodge E 8
32 Borrowash G 1
40 Borrowby F 4
38 Borrowdale D 5
59 Borrowfield H 6
20 Borth C 2
44 Borthwickbrae B 2
44 Borthwickshiels B 3
28 Borth-y-gest F 5
62 Borve C 4
63 Borve Lodge G 1
63 Borvemore G 1
39 Borwick H 7
21 Bosbury H 12
3 Boscastle A 8
8 Boscombe, Dorset G 3
8 Boscombe, Wilts. B 3
3 Boscoppa D 7
9 Bosham F 9
12 Bosherston G 3
2 Boskenna G 1
31 Bosley D 7
31 Bossall A 5
59 Bossholes H 6
3 Bossiney A 8
11 Bossingham C 10
6 Bossington A 3
30 Bostock Green C 5
24 Boston A 4
33 Boston Long Hedges E 10
36 Boston Spa C 2
3 Boswinger F 7
2 Botallack F 1
18 Botany Bay D 3
58 Botary Mains C 2
23 Botcheston B 8
27 Botesdale H 3
45 Bothal D 10
32 Bothamsall C 4
43 Bothel H 12
7 Bothenhampton G 8
47 Bothwell D 12
17 Botley, Bucks. D 10
8 Botley, Hants. E 6
16 Botley, Oxon. C 6
17 Botolph Claydon B 8
10 Botolphs G 1
54 Bottacks D 8
37 Bottesford, Humber. F 7
32 Bottesford, Leics. F 5
25 Bottisham J 6
16 Bottlesford H 2
33 Bottom House E 9
34 Bottom O'th'Moor F 5
53 Bottomcraig E 8
35 Bottoms E 8
34 Botton Head A 5
38 Bottongate A 5
4 Bottreaux Mill C 7
3 Botusfleming D 11
28 Botwnnog G 2
10 Bough Beech C 4
21 Boughrood H 7
21 Boughrood Brest H 7
15 Boughspring E 9
24 Boughton, Norfolk E 8
32 Boughton, Notts. C 4
11 Boughton Aluph C 9
23 Boughton E 11
11 Boughton Lees C 9
11 Boughton Malherbe C 7
10 Boughton Monchelsea C 6
11 Boughton Street B 9
41 Boulby C 8
21 Bouldon D 11
45 Boulmer B 11
12 Boulston F 3
58 Boultenstone F 2
32 Boultham C 6
25 Bourn K 4
24 Bourne D 2
25 Bourne End, Beds. L 1
17 Bourne End, Bucks. E 10
17 Bourne End, Herts. D 11
18 Bournebridge D 5
8 Bournemouth G 3
19 Bournes Green, Essex E 9
9 Broadwater, W. Sussex F 12
12 Broadway, Dyfed F 6
12 Broadway, Dyfed F 2
22 Broadway, Heref. & Worc. H 4
6 Broadway, Som. E 6
16 Broadwell, Glos. A 3
16 Broadwell, Oxon D 3
23 Broadwell, War. F 8
45 Broadwell House H 7
15 Broadwell Lane End C 9
7 Broadwey H 10
7 Broadwindsor F 8
4 Broadwood-Kelly E 5
5 Broadwoodwidger G 3
21 Brobury H 9
62 Brochel D 5
9 Brockbridge D 7
45 Brockdam A 9
27 Brockdish G 5
8 Brockenhurst F 4
48 Brocketsbrae E 1
27 Brockford Street J 4
23 Brockhall F 9
10 Brockham C 1
16 Brockhampton, Glos. B 1
15 Brockhampton, Heref. & Worc. A 9
7 Brockhampton Green F 10
35 Brockholes F 10
9 Brockhurst F 7
38 Brcoklebank A 5
37 Brocklesby F 9
15 Brockley H 8
27 Brockley Green K 1
22 Brockton, Salop. B 1
21 Brockton, Salop. B 8
21 Brockton, Salop. C 11
15 Brockweir D 8
9 Brockwood D 7
15 Brockworth C 12
31 Brocton H 8
46 Brodick F 5
58 Brodiesord B 3
36 Brodsworth F 3
62 Brogaig A 4
25 Brogborough L 1
30 Broken Cross, Cheshire C 6
31 Broken Cross, Cheshire C 7
15 Brokenborough E 12
30 Bromborough B 2
27 Brome H 4
27 Brome Street H 5
27 Bromeswell K 6
43 Bromfield, Cumb. G 12
21 Bromfield, Salop. E 10
25 Bromham, Beds. K 1
16 Bromham, Wilts. H 1
18 Bromley G 4
11 Bromley Green D 8
10 Brompton, Kent A 6
41 Brompton, N. Yorks. G 9
40 Brompton, N. Yorks. E 4
21 Brompton Hall C 8
40 Brompton-on-Swale E 2
6 Brompton Ralph C 4
6 Brompton Regis C 3
15 Bromsash B 9
15 Bromsberrow A 10
22 Bromsgrove E 3
30 Bromstead Heath H 6
21 Bromyard G 12
21 Bromyard Downs G 12
28 Bronaber G 6
20 Bronant F 2
12 Brongest C 6
30 Bronington F 4
14 Bronllys A 5
13 Bronwydd Arms E 7
21 Bronydd H 8
12 Brook, Dyfed F 6
8 Brook, Hants. C 5
8 Brook, Hants. E 4
8 Brook, I.o.W. H 5
11 Brook, Kent D 9
9 Brook, Surrey B 12
9 Brook, Surrey B 10
25 Brook End J 2
8 Brook Hill E 4
18 Brook Street, Essex E 6
10 Brook Street, W. Sussex E 2
23 Brooke, Leics. B 12
26 Brooke, Norfolk E 6
15 Brookend D 9
47 Brookfield C 9
31 Brookhouse, Ches. C 8
34 Brookhouse, Lancs. A 4
31 Brookhouse Green D 7
11 Brookland E 8
43 Brooklands D 9
18 Brookmans Park D 2
21 Brooks C 7
17 Brookwood H 10
25 Broom, Beds. L 3
40 Broom, Durham A 3
22 Broom, War. G 4
8 Broom Hill F 2
52 Broom of Dalreoch E 5
49 Broomdykes D 11
22 Broome, Heref. & Worcs. D 3
26 Broome, Norfolk F 6
21 Broome, Salop. D 9
10 Broome Park C 1
30 Broomedge B 5
9 Broomer's Crn. D 12
19 Broomfield, Essex C 7
58 Broomfield, Grampian D 7
11 Broomfield, Kent A 10
11 Broomfield, Kent C 7
6 Broomfield, Som. C 6
48 Broomfield, Strathclyde E 1
36 Broomfleet D 6
17 Broomhall G 10
45 Broomhaugh G 8
45 Broomhill, Northumb. C 10
56 Broomhill, Highland C 3
57 Broomhill Station G 6
26 Broomholm B 6
45 Broomhouse C 11
43 Broomhouses C 12
45 Broomley G 8
15 Brooms Green A 10
15 Broomsberrow Heath A 10
61 Brora F 9
21 Broseley B 12
22 Brotheridge Green H 2
49 Brotherstone F 9
33 Brothertoft F 10
36 Brotherton E 3
45 Brotherwick C 10
41 Brotton C 7
61 Broubster B 10
39 Brough, Cumbria D 10
31 Brough, Derby. B 10
61 Brough, Highland A 11
37 Brough, Humberside D 7
32 Brough, Notts. D 5
64 Brough, Orkney Is. C 2
64 Brough, Whalasay, Shetland Is. C 8
64 Brough, Yell, Shetland Is. C 7
64 Brough, Zetland, Shetland Is. C 7
64 Brough Lodge B 8
39 Brough Sowerby D 10
30 Broughall F 4
23 Broughton, Bucks. H 12
48 Broughton, Borders F 4
25 Broughton, Cambs. G 4
30 Broughton, Clwyd D 2
38 Broughton, Cumb. B 3
8 Broughton, Hants. C 4
37 Broughton, Humber. F 7
34 Broughton, Lancs. D 4
14 Broughton, Mid Glam. G 2
23 Broughton, Northants. E 11
40 Broughton, N. Yorks. E 6
41 Broughton, N. Yorks. H 8
35 Broughton, N. Yorks. B 8
64 Broughton, Orkney Is. A 2
23 Broughton, Oxon H 7
23 Broughton Astley C 8
38 Broughton Beck G 5
15 Broughton Com. H 12
16 Broughton Foggs D 3
15 Broughton Gifford H 12
22 Broughton Hackett G 3
38 Broughton in Funress F 5
38 Broughton Mills F 4
38 Broughton Moor B 3
64 Broughtown B 4
53 Broughty Ferry D 9
44 Browhouses G 1
9 Brown Candover B 7
31 Brown Edge E 7
58 Brownhill, Grampian D 6
30 Brownhill, Salop. H 3
53 Brownhills, Fife F 10
22 Brownhills, W. Midlands B 4
31 Brownlow Heath D 7
59 Brownmuir K 5
45 Brownridge B 11
15 Brown's Hill D 12
23 Brownsover D 8
5 Brownston K 6
45 Brownyside A 9
17 Brox H 11
41 Broxa F 9
18 Broxborune C 4
49 Broxburn, Lothian B 9
48 Broxburn, Lothian B 4
18 Broxted A 6
30 Broxton E 3
21 Broxwood G 9
10 Broyle Side G 3
61 Bruan C 12
57 Bruar Lodge M 4
63 Brue B 4
30 Bruera D 3
16 Bruern Abbey B 4
27 Bruisyard J 6
27 Bruisyard Street J 6
36 Brumby F 6
31 Brund D 9
26 Brundhall E 6
27 Brundish H 5
27 Brundish Street H 6
55 Brunery M 1
45 Brunswick Village F 10
23 Bruntingthorpe C 9
53 Brunton, Fife E 8
45 Brunton, Northumb. A 10
16 Brunton, Wilts. H 3
6 Brushford D 3
4 Brushford Barton E 5
7 Bruton C 10
7 Bryanston F 12
43 Brydekirk E 12
29 Brymbo E 12
7 Brympton E 8
29 Bryn, Clwyd F 12
13 Bryn, Dyfed G 9
34 Bryn, Manchester G 4
13 Bryn, W. Glam H 11
21 Bryn, Salop. D 8
34 Bryn Gates G 5
14 Bryn Golau E 3
28 Bryn-Siencyn D 4
13 Brynamman F 10
12 Bryn-berian C 4
13 Brynbryddan H 11
14 Bryncethin F 2
28 Bryncir F 4
13 Bryn-coch G 10
28 Bryncroes G 2
20 Bryncrug B 2
29 Bryneglwys E 10
29 Brynford C 11
28 Bryngwran B 3
15 Bryngwyn, Gwent C 7
21 Bryngwyn, Powys G 7
12 Bryn-henllan C 4
13 Brynhoffnant B 7
34 Bryning D 3
14 Brynmawr C 5
14 Brynmenyn F 2
13 Brynmill H 10
28 Bryn'refail D 5
14 Brynsadler F 3
29 Bryn-teg E 12
14 Bryn-y-Cae F 3
14 Bryn-y-gwenin C 6
29 Bryn-y-maen C 7
62 Bualintur F 3
23 Bubbenhall E 7
36 Bubwith C 5
48 Buccleuch H 6
42 Buchan D 5
47 Buchanan Castle A 9
51 Buchanan Smithy H 11
58 Buchanhaven C 8
52 Buchanty D 4
52 Buchlyvie H 1
58 Buchts B 7
44 Buckabank H 2
25 Buckden, Cambs. H 3
39 Buckden, N. Yorks. G 11
26 Buckenham E 6
6 Buckerell F 5
5 Buckfast J 6
5 Buckfastleigh J 6
53 Buckhaven G 8
49 Buckholm E 7
18 Buckhurst Hill E 4
58 Buckie A 2
17 Buckingham A 8
17 Buckinghamshire, Co. C 8
17 Buckland, Bucks. C 9
5 Buckland, Devon L 5
16 Buckland, Glos. A 2
25 Buckland, Herts. M 5
11 Buckland, Kent D 11
16 Buckland, Oxon D 4
10 Buckland, Surrey C 1
4 Buckland Brewer D 3
17 Buckland Com. C 10
7 Buckland Dinham A 11
4 Buckland Filleigh E 3
5 Buckland in the Moor H 6
5 Buckland Monachorum J 4
7 Buckland Newton F 10
6 Buckland St. Mary E 6
24 Bucklegate B 4
53 Bucklerheads D 9
8 Bucklers Hard F 5
27 Bucklesham L 5
29 Buckley D 12
30 Bucklow Hill B 6
32 Buckminster H 6
33 Bucknall, Lincs. C 9
31 Bucknall, Staffs. E 7
16 Bucknell, Oxon B 6
21 Bucknell, Salop. E 9
58 Buckpool A 2
4 Buck's Cross D 2
9 Bucks Green C 12
9 Bucks Horn Oak B 9
4 Buck's Mills D 2
7 Buckthorn Weston D 10
21 Buckton, Heref. & Worc. E 9
41 Buckton, Humberside H 11
45 Buckton, Northumb. B 12
25 Buckworth H 2
16 Buclebury G 6
22 Budbrooke F 6
32 Budby C 3
4 Budd's Titson F 1
4 Bude E 1
6 Budlake F 3
45 Budle D 12
6 Budleigh Salterton H 4
2 Budock Water F 5
30 Buerton F 5
23 Bugbrooke F 10
31 Buglawton D 7
3 Bugle D 7
36 Bugthorpe A 5
21 Buildwas B 11
47 Builstonend E 9
20 Builth Road G 6
20 Builth Wells G 6
17 Bulbourne C 10
24 Bulby C 2
32 Bulcote F 4
8 Bulford B 3
30 Bulkeley E 4
23 Bulkington, War. D 7
15 Bulkington, Wilts H 12
4 Bulkworthy E 3
28 Bull Bay A 4
8 Bull Hill F 5
40 Bullamoor F 4
17 Bullbrook G 9
58 Bullers of Buchan D 8
15 Bulley B 11
43 Bullgill H 11
15 Bullinghope A 8
8 Bullington, Hants. B 6
33 Bullington, Lincs. B 8
39 Bullpot Farm G 9
46 Bullwood B 6
27 Bulmer, Essex L 2
41 Bulmer, N. Yorks. H 7
27 Bulmer Tye L 1
18 Bulphan E 6
10 Bulverhythe G 6
58 Bulwark C 7
15 Bulwark Village E 8
32 Bulwell F 3
24 Bulwick F 1
18 Bumble's Green C 4
55 Bunacaimb K 1
55 Bunarkaig L 6
63 Bunaveneadar F 2
30 Bunbury D 4
56 Bunchrew E 2
55 Bundalloch G 3
50 Bunessan E 1
38 Bungalow Station G 2
26 Bungay F 6
57 Bunloit G 1
32 Bunny G 3
54 Buntait F 8
18 Buntingford A 4
26 Bunwell F 4
26 Bunwell Street F 4
31 Burbage, Derby C 9
23 Burbage, Leics. C 8
16 Burbage, Wilts. H 3
17 Burchett's Green F 9
8 Burcombe C 2
22 Burcot, Heref. & Worc. E 3
16 Burcot, Oxon E 6
17 Burcott B 9
36 Burdale A 6
27 Bures M 2
16 Burford, Oxon C 4
21 Burford, Salop. F 11
50 Burg C 1

10 Burgess Hill ... F 2
27 Burgh ... K 5
44 Burgh by Sands ... G 2
26 Burgh Castle ... E 8
10 Burgh Heath ... B 1
33 Burgh le Marsh ... D 12
58 Burgh Muir ... E 5
26 Burgh next Aylsham ... C 5
33 Burgh on Bain ... B 9
26 Burgh St. Margaret ... D 7
26 Burgh St. Peter ... F 8
16 Burghclere ... H 6
56 Burghead ... C 7
17 Burghfield ... G 7
17 Burghfield Com. ... G 7
21 Burghill ... H 10
36 Burghwallis ... F 3
10 Burham ... B 6
9 Buriton ... D 9
30 Burland ... E 5
3 Burlawn ... C 7
17 Burleigh ... G 10
6 Burlescombe ... E 4
7 Burleston ... G 11
8 Burley, Hants. ... F 3
23 Burley, Leics. ... A 12
21 Burley Gate ... H 11
35 Burley in Wharfdale ... C 10
8 Burley Lodge ... E 4
8 Burley Street ... F 3
30 Burleydam ... F 5
21 Burlingjobb ... G 8
10 Burlow ... F 4
30 Burlton ... H 3
11 Burmarsh ... E 9
22 Burmington ... H 6
6 Burn, Devon ... F 3
43 Burn, Dumf. & Gall. ... B 10
36 Burn, N. Yorks. ... D 4
34 Burn Naze ... C 2
52 Burn of Cambus ... G 2
35 Burnage ... H 7
31 Burnaston ... G 11
47 Burnbank ... D 11
47 Burnbrae ... E 12
36 Burnby ... C 6
35 Burncross ... G 12
39 Burneside ... F 7
64 Burness ... A 4
40 Burneston ... G 3
15 Burnett ... H 10
44 Burnfoot, Borders ... A 3
44 Burnfoot, Borders ... B 2
43 Burnfoot, Dumf. & Gall. ... B 10
44 Burnfoot, Dumf. & Gall. ... D 2
45 Burnfoot, Northumb. ... B 8
47 Burnfoot, Strathclyde ... B 11
32 Burngreave ... A 1
17 Burnham, Bucks. ... F 10
37 Burnham, Humberside ... E 8
17 Burnham Beeches ... F 10
26 Burnham Deepdale ... A 1
18 Burnham Green ... B 3
26 Burnham Market ... A 1
26 Burnham Norton ... A 1
26 Burnham Overy ... A 1
26 Burnham Thorpe ... B 2
6 Burnham-on-Sea ... A 6
19 Burnham-on-Crouch ... D 9
58 Burnhaven ... C 8
43 Burnhead, Dumf. & Gall. ... C 10
43 Burnhead, Dumf. & Gall. ... B 9
58 Burnhervie ... F 5
22 Burnhill Green ... B 1
45 Burnhope ... H 10
47 Burnhouse ... D 8
49 Burnhouse Mains ... D 7
41 Burniston ... F 10
35 Burnley ... D 7
49 Burnmouth, Borders ... C 12
43 Burnmouth, Dumf. & Gall. ... A 9
45 Burnopfield ... G 10
59 Burnroot ... H 2
35 Burnsall ... A 9
43 Burnside, Dumf. & Gall. ... C 11
52 Burnside, Fife ... F 6
56 Burnside, Grampian ... F 5
48 Burnside, Lothian ... B 4
64 Burnside, Shetland Is. ... C 6
47 Burnside, Strathclyde ... H 10
53 Burnside, Tayside ... B 9
53 Burnside of Dantrune ... D 9
19 Burnt Heath ... A 10
40 Burnt Houses ... C 2
35 Burnt Yates ... A 11
2 Burnthouse ... F 5
48 Burntisland ... A 5
47 Burnton, Strathclyde ... H 8
42 Burnton, Strathclyde ... A 6
47 Burnton, Strathclyde ... H 10
22 Burntwood ... A 4
9 Burpham, Surrey ... A 11
9 Burpham, W. Sussex ... E 11
45 Burradon, Northumb. ... B 8
45 Burradon, Tyne & Wear ... F 11
64 Burrafirth ... A 8
2 Burras ... F 4
64 Burravoe ... C 7
39 Burrells ... C 9
53 Burrelton ... C 7
4 Burridge, Devon ... C 4
9 Burridge, Hants. ... E 7
40 Burrill ... F 3
36 Burringham ... F 6
15 Burrington, Avon ... H 8
4 Burrington, Devon ... D 5
21 Burrington, Heref. & Worc. ... E 10
25 Borrough Green ... K 7
23 Burrough on the Hill ... A 10
6 Burrow, Devon ... G 4
6 Burrow, Somerset ... B 3
7 Burrow Bridge ... C 7
17 Burrowhill ... H 10
9 Burrows Cross ... A 12
13 Burry ... H 8
13 Burry Port ... G 8
13 Burrygreen ... H 8
34 Burscough ... F 3
34 Burscough Bridge ... F 3
36 Bursea ... D 6
36 Bursea Lane Ends ... D 6
37 Burshill ... B 8
8 Bursledon ... E 6
31 Burslem ... E 7
27 Burstall ... L 4
7 Burstock ... F 7
27 Burston, Norfolk ... G 4
31 Burston, Staffs. ... G 8
10 Burstow ... D 2
37 Burstwick ... D 10
39 Burtersett ... F 11
30 Burton, Cheshire ... D 4
39 Burton, Cumbria ... G 8
7 Burton, Dorest ... G 10
8 Burton, Dorset ... G 3
12 Burton, Dyfed ... F 3
33 Burton, Lincs. ... C 7
30 Burton, Merseyside ... C 2
45 Burton, Northumb. ... D 12
6 Burton, Somerset ... B 5
15 Burton, Wilts. ... F 11
37 Burton Agnes ... A 9
7 Burton Bradstock ... G 8
33 Burton Coggles ... H 7
37 Burton Contable ... C 9
23 Burton Dassett ... G 7
41 Burton Fleming ... H 11
30 Burton Green, Clwyd ... D 2
22 Burton Green, W. Midlands ... E 6
23 Burton Hastings ... C 7
39 Burton in Lonsdale ... H 9
32 Burton Joyce ... F 4
32 Burton Latimer ... E 12
32 Burton Lazars ... H 5
35 Burton Leonard ... A 12
32 Burton on the Wolds ... H 3
31 Burton-on-Trent ... H 10
23 Burton Overy ... B 10
24 Burton Pedwardine ... A 2
37 Burton Pidsea ... D 10
36 Burton Salmon ... D 3
36 Burton upon Stather ... E 6
34 Burtonwood ... H 4
30 Burwardsley ... D 4
21 Burwarton ... D 11
10 Burwash ... F 5
10 Burwash Common ... F 5
10 Burwash Weald ... F 5
25 Burwell, Cambs. ... J 7
33 Burwell, Lincs. ... B 10
28 Burwen ... A 4
64 Burwick ... E 2
25 Bury, Cambs. ... G 4
35 Bury, Manchester ... F 7
6 Bury, Somerset ... C 3
9 Bury, W. Sussex ... E 11
18 Bury Green ... B 4
27 Bury St Edmunds ... J 2
36 Burythorpe ... A 6
47 Busby ... D 10
41 Buscel ... G 9
16 Buscot ... D 3
59 Bush ... L 5
21 Bush Bank ... G 10
27 Bush Green ... G 5
57 Bush ... K 8
22 Bushbury ... B 3
18 Bushey ... D 1
18 Bushey Heath ... E 2
15 Bushley ... A 11
16 Bushton ... F 2
64 Busta ... C 7
45 Buston Barns ... B 10
18 Butcher's Pasture ... B 6
15 Butcombe ... H 8
45 Buteland ... E 7
7 Butleigh ... C 8
7 Butleigh Wootton ... C 8
17 Butler's Cross ... C 9
22 Butlers Marston ... G 6
27 Butley ... K 7
30 Butt Green ... E 5
44 Butterburn ... F 5
36 Buttercrambe ... A 5
40 Butterknowle ... C 1
6 Butterleigh ... E 3
38 Buttermere, Cumb. ... D 4
16 Buttermere, Wilts. ... H 4
30 Butters Green ... E 6
35 Buttershaw ... D 10
52 Butterstone ... C 5
31 Butterton ... E 9
40 Butterwick, Dur. ... B 4
24 Butterwick, Lincs. ... A 5
41 Butterwick, N. Yorks. ... H 10
41 Butterwick, N. Yorks. ... G 7
21 Buttington ... B 8
23 Buttock's Booth ... F 11
22 Buttonoak ... D 1
8 Butt's Green ... C 4
8 Buttsash ... E 6
27 Buxhall ... J 3
49 Buxley ... D 10
10 Buxted ... F 4
31 Buxton, Derby ... C 9
26 Buxton, Norfolk ... C 5
26 Buxton Heath ... C 5
14 Bwlch ... B 5
29 Bwlchgwyn ... E 11
20 Bwlchllan ... F 1
28 Bwlchtocyn ... H 3
29 Bwlch-y-cibau ... H 11
29 Bwlch-y-ddâr ... H 11
13 Bwlchyfadfa ... B 8
20 Bwlch-y-ffridd ... C 6
12 Bwlch-y-groes ... C 6
20 Bwlch-y-sarnau ... E 6
43 Byeloch ... D 11
40 Byers Green ... B 2
23 Byfield ... G 8
17 Byfleet ... H 11
21 Byford ... H 9
25 Bygrave ... L 4
61 Bylbster ... B 11
29 Bylchau ... D 9
30 Byley ... C 6
13 Bynea ... G 9
49 Byrewalls ... E 9
44 Byrness ... C 6
25 Bythorn ... H 2
21 Byton ... F 9
45 Bywell ... G 8
9 Byworth ... D 11
52 Cablea ... C 4
37 Cabourne ... G 9
58 Cabrach ... E 1
54 Cabule Ldoge ... C 5
6 Cadbury ... F 3
4 Cadbury Barton ... D 6
59 Caddam ... K 1
47 Cadder ... B 11
51 Cadderlie ... D 7
17 Caddington ... B 11
49 Caddonfoot ... F 7
10 Cade Street ... F 5
23 Cadeby, Leics. ... B 7
36 Cadeby, S. Yorks. ... G 3
6 Cadeleigh ... E 3
48 Cademuir ... F 5
44 Cadgillhead ... E 2
2 Cadgwith ... H 4
53 Cadham ... G 7
34 Cadishead ... H 6
13 Cadle ... G 9
16 Cadley, Wilts. ... G 3
8 Cadley, Wilts. ... A 4
17 Cadmore End ... E 8
8 Cadnam ... E 5
37 Cadney ... G 8
29 Cadole ... D 11
13 Cadoxton-Juxta-Neath ... G 11
60 Cadubh ... G 3
14 Cae Hopkin ... C 2
28 Caeathraw ... D 4
28 Cae-lwyn-grydd ... C 5
33 Caenby ... A 7
33 Caenby Corner ... A 7
13 Caeo ... C 10
12 Caer Farchell ... D 1
14 Caerau ... E 2
13 Cae'r-bryn ... F 9
28 Caerdeon ... H 6
28 Cae'r-geiliog ... B 3
29 Caergwrle ... D 12
29 Caerhun ... C 7
44 Caerlanrig ... C 2
14 Caerleon ... E 6
12 Caerlleon ... E 6
28 Caernarvon ... D 4
14 Caerphilly ... F 5
20 Caersws ... C 6
13 Caerwedros ... A 7
15 Caerwent ... E 8
29 Caerwys ... C 10
57 Caggan ... H 4
43 Cairn ... C 10
50 Cairnbaan ... H 5
58 Carinbrogie ... E 6
49 Carincross ... C 11
42 Cairnderry ... D 4
51 Carndow ... F 9
58 Cairness ... B 8
48 Cairneyhill ... A 3
42 Cairnfield ... G 5
58 Cairnfield House ... B 2
42 Cairngaan ... H 2
42 Cairngarroch ... G 1
43 Cairnhall ... C 10
58 Cairnhill ... D 4
58 Cairnie, Grampian ... C 2
59 Cairnie, Grampian ... G 5
58 Cairnorrie ... D 6
42 Cairnryan ... E 2
42 Cairnsmore ... E 5
47 Cairntable ... H 9
42 Cairnwhin ... B 3
54 Caiseachan ... D 6
26 Caister-on-Sea ... D 8
37 Caistor ... G 9
26 Caistor St. Edmund ... E 5
45 Caistron ... C 8
49 Caitha Bowland ... E 7
63 Calbost ... E 5
8 Calbourne ... G 6
33 Calceby ... C 11
22 Calchems Corner ... E 6
15 Calcot Farm ... E 11
17 Calcot Row ... G 7
56 Calcots Station ... C 8
11 Calcott ... B 10
38 Caldbeck ... A 6
40 Caldbergh ... G 1
25 Caldecote, Beds. ... L 3
25 Caldecote, Cambs. ... K 4
25 Caldecote, Cambs. ... G 2
23 Caldecott, Leics. ... C 12
25 Caldecott, Northants ... H 1
38 Calder, Cumb. ... E 3
49 Calder, Northumb. ... G 12
38 Calder Bridge ... E 3
35 Calder Grove ... E 11
61 Calder Mains ... B 10
34 Calder Vale ... C 4
47 Calderbank ... C 12
35 Calderbrook ... E 8
48 Caldercruix ... C 1
47 Caldermill ... E 11
47 Calderwood ... D 11
15 Caldicot ... E 8
49 Caldside ... E 9
40 Caldwell ... D 2
30 Caldy ... B 1
13 Caledfwlch ... D 10
13 Calerdhydiau ... B 8
64 Calfsound ... B 3
50 Calgary ... B 1
56 Califer ... D 6
48 California, Central ... B 2
26 California, Norf. ... D 8
27 California, Suff. ... L 5
5 California Cross ... K 6
31 Calke ... H 12
45 Callaly ... B 9
52 Callander ... F 1
63 Callanish ... D 3
51 Callert House ... A 8
2 Callestick ... E 5
62 Calligarry ... H 5
3 Callington ... C 10
15 Callow ... A 8
22 Callow End ... G 2
22 Callow Hill, Heref. & Worcs. ... E 1
22 Callow Hill, Heref. & Worcs. ... F 4
16 Callow Hill, Wilts. ... F 1
17 Callowhill ... G 11
21 Callows Grave ... F 11
8 Calmore ... E 5
16 Calmsden ... C 1
16 Calne ... G 1
32 Calow ... C 1
8 Calshot ... F 6
3 Calstock ... C 11
16 Calstone Wellington ... G 1
26 Calthorpe ... B 5
39 Calthwaite ... A 7
35 Calton, N. Yorks. ... A 8
31 Calton, Staffs. ... E 9
30 Calveley ... D 4
31 Calver ... C 11
21 Calver Hill ... G 9
30 Calverhall ... F 5
6 Calverleigh ... E 3
35 Calverley ... C 10
23 Calverton, Bucks. ... H 11
32 Calverton, Notts. ... E 3
52 Calvine ... A 3
43 Calvo ... F 12
48 Calzeat ... F 4
15 Cam ... D 10
62 Camascross ... G 6
50 Camasine ... A 5
50 Camasnacroise ... B 6
54 Camasterach ... E 1
62 Camastianavaig ... D 4
62 Camasunary ... F 4
56 Camault Muir ... F 1
64 Camb ... B 7
11 Camber ... F 8
17 Camberley ... H 9
18 Camberwell ... F 3
36 Camblesforth ... D 4
53 Cambo, Fife ... F 10
45 Cambo, Northumb. ... D 8
45 Cambois ... E 11
2 Camborne ... F 4
25 Cambridge, Cambs. ... J 5
15 Cambridge, Glos. ... D 10
25 Cambridgeshire Co. ... K 5
52 Cambus ... H 3
59 Cambus o'May ... G 2
52 Cambusbarron ... H 3
52 Cambuskenneth ... H 3
47 Cambuslang ... C 11
61 Cambusmore Lo. ... G 8
54 Cambussorray ... F 7
18 Camden ... E 3
18 Cameley ... H 9
3 Camelford ... A 8
48 Camelon ... A 2
9 Camelsdale ... C 10
56 Camerory ... F 6
7 Camerton, Avon ... A 10
38 Camerton, Cumb. ... B 3
52 Camghouran ... B 1
55 Camisky ... L 5
59 Cammachmore ... H 6
32 Cammeringham ... B 6
56 Campbelltown or Ardersier ... D 3
46 Campbeltown ... G 2
45 Camperdown ... F 11
53 Campmuir ... C 7
25 Camps Green ... L 7
36 Campsall ... F 3
27 Campsey Ash ... K 6
25 Campton ... L 2
44 Camptown ... B 5
12 Camrose ... E 3
52 Camserney ... B 3
61 Camster ... C 11
55 Camus-luinie ... G 3
54 Camusteel ... E 1
52 Camusvrachan ... B 1
8 Canada ... D 4
59 Candacraig ... G 1
58 Candacraig House ... F 1
33 Candlesby ... C 11
59 Candy ... J 5
48 Candyburn ... E 3
17 Cane End ... F 8
19 Canewdon ... D 9
18 Canfield End ... B 6
8 Canford Bottom ... F 2
8 Canford Magna ... F 2
61 Canisbay ... A 12
7 Cann ... D 12
7 Cann Common ... D 12
3 Cannaframe ... B 9
7 Cannards Grave ... B 9
54 Canncih ... F 7
6 Cannington ... B 6
22 Cannock ... A 3
22 Cannock Wood ... A 4
15 Cannop ... C 9
21 Canon Bridge ... H 10
21 Canon Pyon ... G 10
44 Canonbie ... E 2
23 Canons Ashby ... G 9
2 Canonstown ... F 2
11 Canterbury ... B 10
26 Cantley, Norfolk ... E 7
36 Cantley, S. Yorks. ... G 4
14 Canton ... G 5
56 Cantraybruich ... E 3
56 Cantraydoune ... E 3
56 Cantraywood ... E 3
39 Cantsfield ... H 8
19 Canvey ... F 8
33 Canwick ... C 7
2 Canworthy Water ... B 2
55 Caol ... M 5
55 Caonich ... K 4
10 Capel ... D 1
20 Capel-Bangor ... D 2
20 Capel Betws Lleucu ... G 2
28 Capel Carmel ... G 1
28 Capel Curig ... D 6
13 Capel Cynon ... B 7
13 Capel Dewi, Dyfed ... E 8
20 Capel Dewi, Dyfed ... D 2
13 Capel Dewi, Dyfed ... C 8
29 Capel Garmon ... E 7
13 Capel Gwyn ... E 8
13 Capel Gwynfe ... E 10
13 Capel Hendre ... F 9
13 Capel Isaac ... D 9
12 Capel Iwan ... C 6
11 Capel le Ferne ... D 11
14 Capel Llanilterne ... F 4
27 Capel St. Andrew ... K 7
27 Capel St. Mary ... L 4
20 Capel Seion ... D 2
20 Capel Trisant ... E 3
12 Capel Tygwydd ... C 6
28 Capel-côch ... B 4
28 Capel-gwyn ... C 3
13 Capel-lago ... C 9
28 Capel-uchaf ... E 4
29 Capelulo ... C 7
14 Capel-y-ffin ... A 6
30 Capenhurst ... C 2
39 Capenwray ... H 8
45 Capheaton ... E 8
48 Cappercleuch ... G 5
48 Capplegill ... H 4
5 Capton, Devon ... K 7
6 Capton, Somerset ... B 4
52 Caputh ... C 6
33 Car Colston ... F 4
2 Carbis Bay ... F 2
62 Carbost, Skye ... E 3
62 Carbost, Skye ... C 4
60 Carbreck ... B 4
32 Carbrook ... A 1
26 Carbrooke ... E 3
32 Carburton ... C 3
3 Carclaze ... D 7
47 Carcluie ... H 8
36 Carcroft ... F 3
53 Cardenden ... H 7
21 Cardeston ... A 9
14 Cardiff ... G 5
12 Cardigan ... B 5
25 Cardington, Bedfordshire ... K 2
21 Cardington, Salop. ... C 10
3 Cardinham ... C 8
42 Cardorcan ... D 5
56 Cardow ... E 7
48 Cardrona ... F 6
47 Cardross ... B 8
43 Cardurnock ... F 12
24 Careby ... D 1
59 Careston ... L 3
12 Carew ... G 4
12 Carew Cheriton ... G 4
12 Carew Newton ... F 4
44 Carewoodrig ... C 3
15 Carey ... A 9
47 Carfin ... D 12
49 Carfrae ... B 8
43 Cargenbridge ... D 10
52 Cargill ... C 6
44 Cargo ... G 2
3 Cargreen ... C 11
49 Carham ... F 10
6 Carhampton ... B 3

2 Carharrack F 4
52 Carie A 1
8 Carisbrooke G 6
38 Cark G 6
3 Carkeel D 11
2 Carland D 5
44 Carlatton Mill H 4
24 Carlby D 2
35 Carlecotes G 10
2 Carleen G 3
44 Carleton, Cumb. H 3
42 Carleton, Dumf. & Gall. H 5
35 Carleton, N. Yorks. B 8
26 CarletonForehoe E 4
26 Carleton Rode F 4
2 Carlidnack G 5
41 Carlin How C 7
15 Carlingcott H 10
44 Carlisle G 2
48 Carlops D 4
63 Carloway C 3
25 Carlton, Beds. K 1
25 Carlton, Cambs. K 7
40 Carlton, Cleveland C 4
23 Carlton, Leics. B 7
40 Carlton, N. Yorks. E 5
40 Carlton, N. Yorks. F 6
40 Carlton, N. Yorks. G 1
36 Carlton, N. Yorks. E 4
32 Carlton, Notts. F 3
35 Carlton, S. Yorks. F 12
27 Carlton, Suffolk J 7
36 Carlton, W. Yorks. D 1
26 Carlton, Colville F 8
23 Carlton Curlieu B 10
40 Carlton Husthwaite G 5
32 Carlton in Lindrick B 3
40 Carlton Miniott G 4
32 Carlton Scroop F 6
32 Carlton-le-Moorland D 6
32 Carlton-on-Trent D 5
48 Carluke D 1
3 Carlyon Bay D 7
48 Carmacoup G 1
13 Carmarthen E 7
29 Carmel, Clwyd C 11
13 Carmel, Dyfed E 9
28 Carmel, Gwynedd E 4
28 Carmel, Gwynedd B 3
13 Carmel Chapel D 10
38 Carmel Fell F 6
63 Carminish H 1
59 Carmont J 5
47 Carmunnock D 11
47 Carmyle C 11
53 Carmyllie C 10
37 Carnaby A 9
55 Carnach, Highland L 1
55 Carnach, Highland G 4
63 Carnach, W. Isles G 3
57 Carnachuin K 4
57 Carnaquheen K 8
53 Carnbee F 10
52 Carnbo G 5
55 Carndu G 3
47 Carnduff E 11
2 Carne F 6
47 Carnell F 9
14 Carnetown E 4
39 Carnforth H 7
55 Carn-gorm G 3
12 Carnhedryn Uchaf D 2
2 Carnhell Green F 3
63 Carnish D 1
2 Carnkie F 4
20 Carno C 5
55 Carnoch, Highland K 2
54 Carnoch, Highland F 7
54 Carnoch, Highland E 6
52 Carnock H 5
2 Carnon Downs F 5
53 Carnoustie D 10
48 Carnwath E 3
29 Carog E 7
39 Carperby F 12
32 Carr A 2
34 Carr Cross F 3
44 Carr Shield H 6
32 Carr Vale C 2
46 Carradale E 3
63 Carragrich G 3
57 Carrbridge G 5
35 Carrbrook G 8
28 Carreglefn A 3
12 Carregwen C 6
53 Carrick, Fife E 9
51 Carrick, Strathclyde H 9
48 Carriden A 3
34 Carrington, Manchester H 6
33 Carrington, Lincs. E 10
48 Carrington, Lothian C 6
29 Carrog F 10
48 Carron, Central A 2
56 Carron, Grampian E 8
47 Carron Bridge A 12
43 Carronbridge B 9
48 Carronshore A 2
47 Carrot E 10
15 Carrow Hill E 7
43 Carrutherstown D 11
40 Carrville A 3
46 Carsaig, Strathclyde A 2
50 Carsaig, Strathclyde E 3
42 Carscreugh F 3
46 Carse House C 2
42 Carsebuie E 4
42 Carsegown F 5
42 Carseriggan E 4
43 Carsethorn F 10
18 Carshalton G 3
31 Carsington E 11
46 Carskiey H 2
42 Carsluith F 6
42 Carsphairn B 6
48 Carstairs E 2
48 Carstairs Junction E 2
49 Carterhaugh G 7
8 Carter's Clay D 4
16 Carterton C 4
45 Carterway Heads H 8
3 Carthew D 7
40 Carthorpe G 3
45 Cartington C 8
48 Cartland E 1
38 Cartmel G 6
13 Carway F 8
7 Cary Fitzpaine D 9
63 Caryshader D 2
43 Carzield C 10
21 Cascob F 8
51 Cashell H 11
51 Cashlie C 12
8 Cashmoor E 1
16 Cassey Compton C 1
16 Cassington, Oxon C 5
7 Cassington, Som. B 7
40 Cassop Colliery A 4
24 Casswell's Bridge C 3
14 Castell-y-bwch E 6
39 Casterton G 8
26 Castle Acre D 1
23 Castle Ashby F 11
31 Castle Bank H 7
39 Castle Bolton F 12
22 Castle Bromwich C 5
24 Castle Bytham D 1
21 Castle Caereinion B 7
25 Castle Camps L 7
44 Castle Carrock G 4
7 Castle Cary C 10
15 Castle Combe F 11
32 Castle Donnington G 2
43 Castle Douglas E 8
16 Castle Eaton E 2
40 Castle Eden A 4
58 Castle Forbes F 4
21 Castle Frome H 12
17 Castle Green H 10
31 Castle Gresley H 11
49 Castle Heaton E 11
27 Castle Hedingham L 1
10 Castle Hill D 6
41 Castle Howard H 7
53 Castle Huntly D 8
42 Castle Kennedy F 2
12 Castle Morris D 3
44 Castle O'er D 1
21 Castle Pulverbatch B 9
24 Castle Rising C 8
56 Castle Stuart E 3
12 Castlebythe D 4
47 Castlecary B 12
48 Castlecraig, Borders E 4
56 Castlecraig, Highland C 4
43 Castlefairn C 8
36 Castleford E 2
48 Castlehill, Borders F 5
58 Castlehill, Grampian C 5
47 Castlehill, Strathclyde B 9
48 Castlehill, Strathclyde D 1
42 Castlemaddy C 6
12 Castlemartin G 3
43 Castlemilk D 12
15 Castlemorton A 11
45 Castleside H 9
23 Castlethorpe H 11
44 Castleton, Borders D 3
31 Castleton, Derby B 10
35 Castleton, Manchester F 7
14 Castleton, Gwent F 6
41 Castleton, N. Yorks D 7
46 Castleton, Strathclyde A 4
53 Castleton, Tayside C 8
7 Casteltown, Dorset H 7
61 Castletown, Highland A 11
56 Castletown, Highland E 3
38 Castletown, I.o.M. H 1
45 Castletown, Tyne & Wear G 11
35 Castley C 11
26 Caston F 2
24 Castor F 2
43 Castramont E 7
13 Caswell H 9
31 Cat and Fiddle Inn C 8
46 Catacol D 4
15 Catbrain F 9
15 Catbrook D 8
2 Catchall G 2
32 Catcliffe A 2
7 Catcott B 7
7 Catcott Burtle B 7
47 Catcraig F 9
10 Caterham C 2
26 Catfield C 7
64 Catfirth D 7
18 Catford G 4
34 Catforth D 4
14 Cathays F 5
47 Cathcart C 10
14 Cathedine B 5
9 Catherington E 8
7 Catherston Leweston G 7
21 Catherton E 12
49 Cathpair E 7
43 Catlins C 12
57 Catlodge K 2
44 Catlowdy E 3
16 Catmore F 5
34 Caton A 4
5 Cator Court H 5
47 Catrine G 10
15 Cat's Ash E 7
10 Catsfield G 6
22 Catshill E 3
36 Cattal B 2
27 Cattawade M 4
34 Catterall C 4
40 Catterick E 3
40 Catterick Bridge E 3
40 Catterick Camp E 2
39 Catterlen B 7
59 Catterline J 6
36 Catterton C 3
27 Catteshall B 11
23 Catthorpe D 9
7 Cattistock F 9
26 Catton, Norfolk D 5
44 Catton, Northumb. G 6
40 Catton, N. Yorks G 4
37 Catwick C 9
25 Catworth H 2
16 Caulcott B 6
52 Cauldhame H 1
31 Cauldon E 9
44 Cauldside E 3
31 Cauldwell H 11
58 Cauldwells B 5
43 Caulkerbush F 10
7 Caundle Marsh E 10
22 Caunsall D 2
32 Caunton D 5
42 Causeway End F 5
58 Causewayend, Grampian F 7
48 Causewayend, Strathclyde F 3
52 Causewayhead, Central H 3
43 Causewayhead, Cumb. F 12
45 Causey Park Bri. D 10
39 Cautley F 9
27 Cavendish K 1
27 Cavenham H 1
17 Caversfield B 7
17 Caversham G 8
63 Caversta E 5
31 Caverswall F 8
36 Cavil D 5
56 Cawdor E 4
3 Cawsand E 11
26 Cawston C 4
41 Cawthorn F 8
35 Cawthorne F 11
24 Cawthorpe C 2
36 Cawood C 3
40 Cawton G 6
25 Caxton J 4
21 Caynham E 11
32 Caythorpe, Lincs. E 6
32 Caythorpe, Notts. F 4
41 Cayton G 10
61 Ceann-na-coille C 7
29 Cefn-Berain C 9
29 Cefn-Canol G 11
29 Cefn Coch G 10
14 Cefn Cribbwr F 2
14 Cefn Cross F 2
21 Cefn Einion D 8
14 Cefn Fforest D 5
15 Cefn Llaithan B 7
29 Cefn Mawr F 12
14 Cefn Rhigos D 2
29 Cefn-brith E 8
13 Cefn-bryn-brain F 10
14 Cefn-coed-y-cymmer C 3
29 Cefn-ddwysarn F 9
20 Cefngorwydd H 5
29 Cefn-y-bedd E 12
12 Cefn-y-pant D 5
13 Cellan B 9
31 Cellarhead E 8
39 Celleron C 7
28 Cemaes Bay A 3
20 Cemmaes B 4
20 Cemmaes Road B 4
12 Cenarth C 6
53 Ceres F 9
20 Cerist D 5
7 Cerne Abbas F 10
16 Cerney Wick E 2
28 Cerrigceinwen C 4
29 Cerrigydrudion E 9
26 Cess D 7
49 Cessford G 10
28 Ceunant D 5
15 Chaceley A 11
2 Chacewater E 5
17 Chackmore A 8
23 Chacombe H 8
22 Chad Valley D 4
22 Chadbury G 4
35 Chadderton G 7
31 Chaddesden F 12
22 Chaddesley Corbett E 2
16 Chaddleworth F 5
16 Chadlington B 4
23 Chadshunt G 7
32 Chadwell H 5
18 Chadwell St. Mary F 6
22 Chadwick End E 5
7 Chaffcombe E 7
5 Chagford G 6
10 Chailey F 3
24 Chainbridge E 5
10 Chainhurst C 6
8 Chalbury E 2
8 Chalbury Com. E 2
10 Chaldon C 2
7 Chaldon Herring or East Chaldon H 11
8 Chale H 6
8 Chale Green H 6
17 Chalfont St. Giles E 10
17 Chalfont St. Peter E 11
15 Chalford D 12
17 Chalford Com. E 11
17 Chalgrove D 7
10 Chalk A 5
4 Challacombe, Devon B 6
4 Challacombe, Devon D 6
42 Challoch E 5
11 Challock Lees C 8
17 Chalton, Beds. B 11
9 Chalton, Hants. E 8
17 Chalvey F 10
10 Chalvington G 4
48 Champany B 3
20 Chancery E 1
17 Chandler's Cross D 11
8 Chandler's Ford D 6
43 Chanlockfoot B 8
7 Chantry B 10
53 Chapel H 7
7 Chapel Allerton A 7
35 Chapel Allerton C 11
3 Chapel Amble B 7
23 Chapel Brampton E 10
30 Chapel Chorlton F 6
23 Chapel End C 7
22 Chapel Green D 6
36 Chapel Haddlesey D 4
58 Chapel Hill, Grampian D 8
15 Chapel Hill, Gwent D 8
33 Chapel Hill, Lincs. E 9
35 Chapel Hill, N. Yorks. C 12
21 Chapel Lawn E 8
39 Chapel le Dale G 9
49 Chapel Mains E 8
59 Chapel of Barras J 6
58 Chapel of Garioch E 5
42 Chapel Rossan G 2
16 Chapel Row, Berks. G 6
10 Chapel Row, E. Sussex G 5
33 Chapel St. Leonards C 12
38 Chapel Stile E 5
25 Chapeland Way L 8
42 Chapeldonan B 3
31 Chapel-en-le-Frith B 9
47 Chapelhall C 12
43 Chapelhill, Dumf. & Gall. B 11
53 Chapelhill, Tayside E 7
52 Chapelhill, Tayside D 5
48 Chapelhope G 5
44 Chapelknowe F 2
38 Chapels G 5
4 Chapelton, Devon C 5
43 Chapelton, Dumf. & Gall. G 8
59 Chapelton, Grampian J 5
57 Chapelton, Grampian H 5
47 Chapelton, Highland E 11
53 Chapelton, Tayside B 11
57 Chapeltown, Grampian G 8
34 Chapeltown, Lancs. F 6
35 Chapeltown, S. Yorks. G 12
5 Chapmans Well G 2
7 Chapmanslade B 11
18 Chapmore End B 3
19 Chappel A 9
7 Chard E 7
6 Chardstock F 6
44 Chareheads H 6
15 Charfield E 10
11 Charing C 8
8 Charing Cross E 3
11 Charing Heath C 8
22 Charingworth H 5
16 Charlbury B 5
15 Charlcombe H 10
16 Charlcutt G 1
22 Charlecote F 6
4 Charles C 6
43 Charlesfield E 12
53 Charleston C 8
59 Charlestown, Grampian G 7
8 Charlestown, Corn. E 7
7 Charlestown, Dorset H 9
48 Charlestown, Fife A 3
54 Charlestown, Highland B 2
56 Charlestown, Highland E 2
35 Charlestown, W. Yorks. D 8
56 Charlestown of Aberlour E 8
35 Charlesworth H 9
5 Charleton L 6
6 Charlinch B 6
18 Charlton, Herts. A 2
40 Charlton, Cleveland D 6
44 Charlton, Northumb. D 6
16 Charlton, Oxon A 6
9 Charlton, W. Sussex E 10
8 Charlton, Wilts. A 3
8 Charlton, Wilts. D 3
16 Charlton, Wilts. H 2
7 Charlton, Wilts. D 12
16 Charlton, Wilts. E 1
22 Charlton, Heref. & Worc. H 4
16 Charlton Abbots B 1
7 Charlton Adam C 9
7 Charlton Horethorne D 10
16 Charlton Kings B 1
7 Charlton Mackrell C 8
7 Charlton Marshall F 12
45 Charlton Mires A 10
7 Charlton Musgrove C 10
16 Charlton-on-Otmoor C 6
7 Charlton-on-the-Hill F 12
9 Charlwood, Hants. C 8
10 Charlwood, Surrey D 1
7 Charminster G 10
7 Charmouth G 7
17 Charndon B 7
16 Charney Bassett E 5
34 Charnock Richard F 4
27 Charsfield J 5
11 Chart Sutton C 7
17 Charter Alley H 7
49 Charterhouse, Borders F 9
7 Charterhouse, Som. A 8
16 Charterville Allotments C 4
11 Chartham C 9
11 Chartham Hatch B 9
8 Charton A 5
17 Chartridge D 10
23 Charwelton G 8
22 Chase Terrace A 4
22 Chasetown A 4
16 Chastleton A 3
4 Chasty F 2
34 Chatburn C 6
30 Chatcull G 6
10 Chatham B 6
45 Chathill E 12
10 Chattenden A 6
25 Chatteris G 5
27 Chattisham L 4
45 Chatton C 12
17 Chaul End B 11
4 Chawleigh E 6
25 Chawston K 3
9 Chawton B 8
31 Cheadle, Manchester A 7
31 Cheadle, Staffs. F 8
31 Cheadle Hulme B 7
18 Cheam G 2
17 Cheapside G 10
17 Chearsley C 8
31 Chebsey G 7
17 Checkendon F 7
30 Checkley, Cheshire F 6
21 Checkley, Heref. & Worc. H 11
31 Checkley, Staffs. F 9
27 Chedburgh J 1
7 Cheddar A 8
17 Cheddington B 10
31 Cheddleton E 8
6 Cheddon Fitzpaine C 6
26 Chedgrave E 7
7 Chedington F 8
27 Chediston G 7
16 Chedworth C 2
7 Chedzoy B 7
49 Cheeklaw D 10
35 Cheetham Hill G 7
4 Cheglinch B 4
4 Cheldon Barton E 6
31 Chelford C 7
31 Chellaston G 12
25 Chellington K 1
22 Chelmarsh C 1
27 Chelmondiston L 5
31 Chelmorton C 9
19 Chelmsford C 7
18 Chelsea F 3
18 Chelsfield Village G 5
27 Chelsworth K 3
15 Cheltenham, Glos. B 12
14 Cheltenham, Gwent C 5
25 Chelveston H 1
15 Chelvey G 8
15 Chelwood H 9
10 Chelwood Com. E 3
10 Chelwood Gate E 3
21 Cheney Longville D 9
17 Chenies D 11
15 Chepstow E 8
16 Cherhill G 1
15 Cherington, Glos. D 12
22 Cherington, War. H 6
9 Cheriton, Hants. C 7
11 Cheriton, Kent D 11
4 Cheriton, Som. A 6
13 Cheriton, W. Glam. H 8
4 Cheriton Bishop F 6
5 Cheriton Cross G 6
6 CheritonFitzpaine F 2
12 Cheriton or Stackpole Elidor G 3
30 Cherrington H 5
37 Cherry Burton C 7
25 Cherry Hinton K 6
22 Cherry Orchard G 2
52 Cherrybank E 6
49 Cherrytrees F 10
17 Chertsey G 11
7 Cheselbourne F 11
17 Chesham D 10
17 Chesham Bois D 10

30 Cheshire, Co. D 5
18 Cheshunt D 4
22 Cheslyn Hay A 3
18 Chessington H 2
30 Chester D 3
45 Chester Moor H 11
7 Chesterblade B 10
32 Chesterfield C 1
22 Chesterfield B 4
48 Chesterhall F 2
48 Chesterhill C 6
45 Chester-le-Street H 11
44 Chesters, Borders B 5
49 Chesters, Borders G 8
24 Chesterton, Cambs. F 2
16 Chesterton, Oxon B 6
31 Chesterton, Staffs. E 7
23 ChestertonGreen F 7
44 Chesterwood F 6
11 Chestfield B 10
30 Cheswardine G 6
45 Cheswick A 11
45 Cheswick Bldgs. A 11
7 Chetnole E 9
6 Chettiscombe E 3
25 Chettisham G 6
8 Chettle E 1
21 Chetton C 12
30 Chetwynd Aston H 6
30 Chetwynd Park H 6
25 Cheveley J 8
10 Chevening B 4
27 Chevington J 1
45 Chevington Drift C 11
6 Chevithorne E 3
15 Chew Magna H 9
15 Chew Stoke H 9
15 Chewton Keynsham H 9
7 Chewton Mendip A 9
23 Chicheley G 12
9 Chichester F 10
7 Chickerell H 9
7 Chicklade C 12
21 Chickward G 8
9 Chidden D 8
9 Chiddingfold C 11
10 Chiddingly G 4
10 Chiddingstone D 4
10 Chiddingstone Causeway C 4
10 Chiddingstone Hoath D 4
7 Chideock G 7
6 Chidgley C 4
9 Chidham F 9
16 Chieveley G 5
18 Chignall St. James C 6
18 Chignall Smealy C 6
18 Chigwell E 4
18 Chigwell Row E 5
8 Chilbolton B 5
8 Chilcomb C 6
7 Chilcombe G 9
7 Chilcompton A 9
22 Chilcote A 6
7 Child Okeford E 11
30 Childer Thornton B 2
34 Children's Homes E 6
16 Childrey E 5
30 Child's Ercall H 5
22 Childswickham H 4
30 Childwall A 3
18 Childwick Green C 1
7 Chilfrome F 9
9 Chilgrove E 9
11 Chilham C 9
8 Chilhampton C 3
4 Chilla F 3
5 Chillaton H 3
11 Chillenden C 11
8 Chillerton H 6
27 Chillesford K 7
45 Chillingham C 12
5 Chillington, Devon L 7
7 Chillington, Somerset E 7
32 Chillwell G 2
8 Chilmark C 1
16 Chilson B 4
3 Chilsworthy, Corn. B 11
4 Chilsworthy, Devon E 2
7 Chilthorne Domer D 8
17 Chilton, Bucks. C 8
4 Chilton, Devon E 7
16 Chilton, Oxon F 6
40 Chilton, Durham B 3
9 Chilton Candover B 7
7 Chilton Cantelo D 9
16 ChiltonFoliat G 4
40 Chilton Lane B 3
7 Chilton Polden B 7
27 Chilton Street K 1
6 Chilton Trinity B 6
8 Chilworth, Hants. D 5
9 Chilworth, Surrey A 11
16 Chimney D 4
9 Chineham A 8
18 Chingford E 4
31 Chinley B 9
31 Chinley Head B 9
17 Chinnor D 8
30 Chipnall G 6
25 Chippenham, Cambs. H 8
15 Chippenham, Wilts. G 12
17 Chipperfield D 11
25 Chipping, Herts. M 5
34 Chipping, Lancs. C 5
22 Chipping Campden H 5
16 Chipping Norton B 4
15 Chipping Sodbury F 10
23 Chipping Warden G 8
6 Chipstable D 4
10 Chipstead, Kent B 4
10 Chipstead, Surrey B 2
21 Chirbury C 8
29 Chirk F 12
29 Chirk Green F 12
42 Chirmorie D 3
49 Chirnside D 11
49 Chirnsidebridge D 11
16 Chirton H 2
16 Chisbury G 4
7 Chiselborough E 8
16 Chiseldon F 3
17 Chislehampton D 7
18 Chislehurst G 4
11 Chislet B 11
35 Chisley D 9
18 Chiswell Green C 1
18 Chiswick F 2
35 Chisworth H 8
11 Chitcombe F 7
9 Chithurst D 9
25 Chittering H 6
8 Chitterne B 2
4 Chittlehamholt D 5
4 Chittlehampton C 5
15 Chittoe H 12
5 Chivelstone M 6
17 Chobham H 10
49 Choicelee D 10
8 Cholderton B 4
17 Cholesbury C 10
45 Chollerford F 7
45 Chollerton F 7
17 Cholsey E 7
21 Cholstrey F 10
40 Chop Gate E 6
45 Choppington E 10
45 Chopwell G 9
30 Chorley, Cheshire E 4
34 Chorley, Lancs. E 5
21 Chorley, Salop. D 12
22 Chorley, Staffs. A 4
17 Chorleywood E 11
30 Chorlton E 6
35 Chorlton cum Hardy H 7
30 Chorlton Lane E 3
25 Chrishall L 5
24 Christchurch, Cambs. F 6
8 Christchurch, Dorset G 3
15 Christchurch, Gwent E 7
16 Christian Malford F 1
30 Christleton D 3
17 Christmas Com. E 8
7 Christon A 7
45 Christon Bank A 10
5 Christow G 7
9 Christ's Hospital C 12
47 Chryston B 11
5 Chudleigh H 7
5 Chudleigh Knighton H 7
4 Chulmleigh E 6
35 Chunal H 9
34 Church D 6
30 Church Aston H 6
23 Church Brampton E 10
31 Church Broughton G 10
9 Church Crookham A 9
31 Church Eaton H 7
25 Church End, Beds. L 3
19 Church End, Essex A 7
25 Church End, Essex L 7
17 Church End, Hants. H 7
17 Church End, Hertfordshire C 12
37 Church End, Lincs. G 12
18 Church End, London E 3
24 Church End, Norf. E 5
22 Church End, War. C 6
16 Church End, Wilts. F 1
16 Church Enstone B 5
36 Church Fenton C 3
6 Church Green G 5
31 Church Gresley H 11
16 Church Hanborough C 5
30 Church Hill D 5
22 Church Honeybourne H 5
41 Church House E 7
41 Church Houses E 7
8 Church Knowle H 1
32 Church Laneham C 5
23 Church Langton C 10
23 Church Lawford D 8
31 Church Lawton E 7
31 Church Leigh G 9
22 Church Lench G 4
30 Church Minshull D 5
21 Church Preen C 11
21 Church Pulverbatch B 9
21 Church Stoke C 8
23 Church Stowe F 9
10 Church Street, Kent A 6
27 Church Street, Suffolk G 8
21 Church Stretton C 10
39 Church Town F 7
14 Church Village F 4
32 Church Warsop C 3
15 Churcham B 11
15 Churchdown B 12
15 Churchend, Avon E 10
18 Churchend, Essex B 6
19 Churchend, Essex E 10
22 Churchfield C 4
15 Churchill, Avon H 7
4 Churchill, Devon B 5
6 Churchill, Devon F 6
22 Churchill, Heref. & Worc. G 3
16 Churchill, Oxon B4
22 Churchill, Salop. D 2
6 Churchingford E 5
23 Churchover D 8
6 Churchstanton E 5
5 Churchstow L 6
38 Churchtown, Cumb. A 6
4 Churchtown, Dev. F 2
38 Churchtown, I. o. M. G 2
34 Churchtown, Lancs. C 4
34 Churchtown, Merseyside E 3
44 Churnsike Lodge E 5
5 Churston Ferrers K 8
9 Churt B 10
30 Churton E 3
35 Churwell D 11
8 Chute Standen A 5
28 Chwilog F 4
29 Cilcain D 11
13 Cilcennin A 8
13 Cilfrew G 11
14 Ciffnydd E 4
12 Cilgerran C 5
12 Cilgwyn C 4
13 Ciliau Aeron A 8
13 Cilmaengwyn F 10
50 Cilmalieu B 6
20 Cilmery G 5
12 Cilrhedyn D 6
13 Cilsan E 9
29 Ciltalgarth F 8
12 Cilwendeg C 6
13 Cilybebyll F 10
13 Cil-y-cwm C 11
15 Cinderford C 10
12 Cippyn B 5
16 Cirencester D 1
40 Citadilla E 2
28 City Dulas B 4
57 Clach Bharraig J 5
57 Clachaig, Highland H 6
46 Clachaig, Strathclyde A 6
62 Clachan, Highland E 5
50 Clachan, Strathclyde C 6
50 Clachan, Strathclyde F 5
51 Clachan, Strathclyde F 9
46 Clachan, Strathclyde D 3
52 Clachan, Tayside A 3
47 Clachan of Campsie A 11
46 Clachan of Glendaruel A 5
50 Clachan-Seil F 5
46 Clachbreck B 3
59 Clachnabrain L 1
60 Clachtoll D 2
52 Clackavoid A 6
52 Clackmannan H 4
56 Clackmarras D 8
19 Clacton on Sea B 11
47 Cladance E 11
51 Cladich E 8
50 Claggan C 4
62 Claigan C 2
22 Claines F 2
60 Clais Charnach A 4
60 Claisfearn C 3
7 Clandown A 10
9 Clanfield, Hants. D 8
16 Clanfield, Oxon D 4
8 Clanville A 5
46 Claonaig D 4
35 Clap Gate B 12
11 Clap Hill D 9
8 Clapgate, Dorset F 2
13 Clapgate, Herts. A 4
25 Clapham, Beds. K 1
6 Clapham, Devon H 2
18 Clapham, London F 3
39 Clapham, N. Yorks. H 9
9 Clapham, W. Sussex E 12
49 Clappers D 12
38 Clappersgate E 6
16 Clapton, Glos. B 3
7 Clapton, Somerset F 7
7 Clapton, Som. A 10
15 Clapton-in-Gordano G 8
4 Clapworthy D 5
20 Clarach D 2
12 Clarbeston E 4
12 Clarbeston Road E 4
32 Clarborough B 4
27 Clare L 1
43 Clarebrand E 8
43 Clarencefield E 11
49 Clarilaw G 8
49 Clarilawmoor F 8
9 Clarken Green A 7
47 Clarkston D 10
61 Clashcoig G 7
58 Clashindarroch D 2
61 Clashmore G 7
60 Clashnessie D 2
57 Clashnoir G 8
52 Clathy E 5
52 Clathymore E 5
58 Clatt E 3
20 Clatter C 5
8 Clatterford G 6
59 Clattering Bridge J 4
42 Clatteringshawes D 6
6 Clatworthy C 4
34 Claughton, Lancs. A 4
34 Claughton, Lancs. C 4
30 Claughton, Merseyside A 2
6 Clavelshay C 6
22 Claverdon F 5
15 Claverham H 8
25 Clavering M 6
22 Claverley C 2
15 Claverton H 11
14 Clawdd-coch F 4
29 Clawddnewydd E 10
39 Clawthorpe G 8
4 Clawton F 2
37 Claxby, Lincs. H 9
33 Claxby, Lincs. C 11
26 Claxton, Norfolk E 6
36 Claxton, N. Yorks. A 5
23 Clay D 9
27 Clay Common G 8
32 Clay Cross D 1
57 Claybokie K 6
23 Claybrooke Magna C 8
23 Claybrooke Parva C 8
23 Claydon, Oxon G 8
27 Claydon, Suffolk K 4
59 Clayfolds H 6
44 Claygate, Dumf. & Gall. E 2
10 Claygate, Kent D 6
17 Claygate, Surrey H 12
6 Clayhanger, Devon D 4
22 Clayhanger, W. Midlands B 4
6 Clayhidon E 5
11 Clayhill, E. Sussex F 7
8 Clayhill, Hants. E 5
58 Claymires E 7
32 Claypole E 6
31 Clayton, Staffs. F 7
36 Clayton, S. Yorks. G 2
10 Clayton, W. Sussex G 2
35 Clayton, W. Yorks. D 10
34 Clayton Green E 5
35 Clayton West F 11
34 Clayton-le-Moors D 6
34 Clayton-le-Woods E 4
32 Clayworth A 4
45 Cleadon G 12
5 Clearbrook J 4
15 Clearwell D 9
40 Cleasby D 3
64 Cleat E 2
40 Cleatlam C 1
38 Cleator D 3
38 Cleator Moor D 3
35 Cleckheaton E 10
21 Clee St. Margaret D 11
21 Cleedownton D 11
21 Cleehill E 11
21 Cleestanton D 11
37 Cleethorpes F 10
21 Cleeton St. Mary E 11
15 Cleeve, Avon H 8
17 Cleeve, Oxon F 7
16 Cleeve Hill A 1
22 Cleeve Prior G 4
15 Clehonger A 8
50 Cleigh E 6
52 Cleish G 6
48 Cleland D 1
50 Clenamacrie E 6
16 Clench Common H 3
24 Clenchwarton C 7
45 Clennell B 7
22 Clent D 3
21 Cleobury Mortimer E 12
21 Cleobury North D 11
56 Clephanton E 4
47 Clerkland E 9
49 Clerklands G 7
64 Clestran D 1
44 Cleuch Head B 4
43 Cleuchbrae D 11
44 Cleuchfoot E 2
43 Clecuhhead B 9
43 Cleuchheads C 12
43 Cleuchside D 12
16 Clevancy G 2
15 Clevedon G 7
40 Cleveland, Co. C 5
40 Cleveland Tontine Inn E 5
34 Cleveleys C 2
16 Cleverton F 1
14 Clevis G 2
7 Clewer A 8
26 Cley-next-the-Sea A 3
63 Cliasamol F 2
39 Cliburn C 8
9 Cliddesden A 7
50 Cliff A 4
11 Cliff End G 7
10 Cliff Woods A 6
53 Cliffburn C 11
19 Cliffe, Kent F 7
36 Cliffe, N. Yorks. D 4
40 Cliffe, N. Yorks. D 2
4 Clifford, Devon D 2
21 Clifford, Heref. & Worc. H 8
36 Clifford, W. Yorks. C 2
22 Clifford Chambers G 5
15 Clifford's Mesne B 10
11 Cliffsend B 12
15 Clifton, Avon G 9
25 Clifton, Beds. L 3
51 Clifton, Central D 10
39 Clifton, Cumbria C 8
31 Clifton, Derby F 10
22 Clifton, Heref. & Worc. G 2
34 Clifton, Lancs. D 4
48 Clifton, Lothian B 4
35 Cliton, N. Yorks B 10
36 Clifton, N. Yorks. B 4
45 Clifton, Northumb. E 10
32 Clifton, Notts. G 3
16 Clifton, Oxon A 6
36 Clifton, S. Yorks. G 3
22 Clifton Campville A 6
16 Clifton Hampden E 6
23 Clifton Reynes G 12
23 Clifton upon Dunsmore D 8
21 Clifton upon Teme F 12
11 Cliftonville A 12
9 Climping F 11
48 Climpy D 2
7 Clink A 11
35 Clint A 11
26 Clint Green D 3
49 Clintmains F 8
26 Clippesby D 7
24 Clipsham D 1
4 Clipston, Devon F 5
23 Clipston, Northants D 10
32 Clipston, Notts. G 4
32 Clipstone D 3
34 Clitheroe C 6
30 Clive H 4
64 Clivocast B 8
37 Clixby G 8
29 Clocaenog E 10
58 Clochan B 1
13 Clochyrie F 8
30 Clock Face A 4
49 Clockmill D 10
14 Clodock B 6
7 Cloford B 10
13 Cloigyn F 8
58 Clola C 7
25 Clophill L 2
25 Clopton G 2
27 Clopton Green K 1
38 Close Clark H 1
43 Closeburn B 9
43 Closeburnmill B 10
7 Closworth E 9
25 Clothall M 4
40 Clotherholme H 3
30 Clotton D 4
35 Clough F 9
35 Clough Foot E 8
41 Cloughton F 10
41 Cloughton Newlands F 10
64 Clousta D 6
58 Colva, Grampian E 2
59 Clova, Tayside K 1
39 Clove Lodge C 11
4 Clovelly D 2
49 Clovenfords F 7
58 Clovenstone F 5
56 Cloves D 7
51 Clovulin A 7
35 Clow Bridge D 7
32 Clowne C 2
55 Cluanie Inn H 4
55 Cluanie Lodge H 5
21 Cluddley A 11
63 Cluer H 2
21 Clun D 8
56 Clunas E 4
21 Clunbury D 9
56 Clune E 7
55 Clunes K 6
21 Clungunford E 9
58 Clunie, Grampian C 4
52 Clunie, Tayside C 6
21 Clunton D 9
53 Cluny H 7
57 Cluny Castle K 2
15 Clutton, Avon H 9
30 Clutton, Cheshire E 3
29 Clwyd, Co. E 10
14 Clydach, Gwent C 5
13 Clydach, W. Glam. G 10
14 Clydach Vale E 3
47 Clydebank B 10
12 Clydey C 6
16 Clyffe Pypard F 2
47 Clynder A 7
12 Clynderwen E 5
13 Clyne G 11
61 Clynekirkton F 8
61 Clynelish F 8
28 Clynnog-fawr E 4
21 Clyro H 7
6 Clyst Honiton G 3
6 Clyst Hydon F 4
6 Clyst St. George G 3
6 Clyst St. Lawrence F 4
6 Clyst St. Mary G 3
28 Clywt-y-bont D 5
20 Cnwch Coch E 2
58 Coachford C 2
3 Coad's Green B 10
32 Coal Ashton B 1
21 Coalbrookdale B 12
14 Coalbrookvale C 5
48 Coalburn F 1
45 Coalburns G 9
39 Coalcleugh A 10
15 Coaley D 11
59 Coalford G 6
47 Coalhall G 9
19 Coalhill D 7
15 Coalpit Heath F 10
31 Coalpit Hill E 7
21 Coalport B 12
52 Coalsnaughton H 4
53 Coaltown of Balgonie G 8
53 Coaltown of Wemyss H 8
23 Coalville A 8

15 Coalway Lane End . . C 9
7 Coat . . . . D 8
47 Coatbridge . . . . C 12
47 Coatdyke . . . . C 12
16 Coate, Wilts. . . . . H 2
16 Coate, Wilts. . . . . F 3
24 Coates, Cambs. . . . . . F 4
16 Coates, Glos. . . . . D 1
9 Coates, W. Sussex . D 11
40 Coatham . . . . C 6
40 Coatham Mundeville
C 3
43 Coatsgate . . . . A 11
4 Cobbaton . . . . C 5
15 Coberley . . . . C 12
10 Cobham, Kent . . . . . A 5
17 Cobham, Surrey . . . H 11
51 Cobleland . . . . H 12
21 Cobnash . . . . F 10
58 Coburty . . . . A 7
57 Cock Bridge . . . . H 8
19 Cock Clarks . . . . D 8
21 Cock Gate . . . . F 10
40 Cockayne . . . . E 6
25 Cockayne Hatley . . . K 4
49 Cockburnspath . . . . B 10
49 Cockenzie and
Port Seton . . . . B 7
34 Cockerham . . . . B 3
38 Cockermouth . . . . . . B 4
18 Cockernhoe Green . . B 1
40 Cockfield, Durham . . C 2
27 Cockfield, Suffolk . . K 2
9 Cocking . . . . D 10
5 Cockington . . . . J 8
7 Cocklake . . . . A 8
45 Cocklaw . . . . F 7
49 Cocklawfoot . . . . . . G 11
49 Cockles . . . . B 8
26 Cockley Clet . . . . E 1
58 Cockmuir . . . . D 4
17 Cockpole Green . . . . F 9
30 Cockshutt . . . . G 3
26 Cockthorpe . . . . A 3
6 Cockwood . . . . H 3
15 Cockyard . . . . A 7
3 Codda . . . . B 9
27 Coddenham . . . . K 4
30 Coddington, Ches. . . E 3
21 Coddington, Heref. &
Worc. . . . . H 12
32 Coddington, Notts. . . E 5
8 Codford St. Mary . . . B 1
8 Codford St. Peter . . . B 1
18 Codicote . . . . B 2
9 Codmore Hill . . . . . D 12
32 Codnor . . . . E 1
15 Codrington . . . . F 10
22 Codsall . . . . B 2
22 Codsall Wood . . . . . . B 2
14 Coed Ely . . . . F 4
15 Coed Morgan . . . . . . C 7
28 Coed Ystumgwern . . H 5
28 Coedana . . . . B 4
14 Coedkernew . . . . F 6
29 Coedpoeth . . . . E 12
21 Coedway . . . . A 9
13 Coed-y-bryn . . . . C 7
15 Coed-y-fedw . . . . C 7
14 Coed-yr-ynys . . . . B 5
14 Coelbren . . . . C 2
5 Coffinswell . . . . J 8
6 Cofton . . . . H 3
22 Cofton Hacket . . . . . . E 3
14 Cogan . . . . G 5
23 Cogenhoe . . . . F 11
19 Coggeshall . . . . B 8
19 Coggeshall Hamlet . . B 8
57 Coignafearn Lo. . . . . . H 2
57 Coignafeuinternich . H 3
57 Coignascallan . . . . . . H 3
59 Coilacreich . . . . H 1
57 Coilintuie . . . . J 6
61 Coillaig . . . . E 7
55 Coille Mhorgil . . . . . . J 5
62 Coillore . . . . D 3
55 Coiltry . . . . J 7
57 Coire Bhachdaidh
Lodge . . . . M 1
14 Coity . . . . F 3
60 Colaboll . . . . F 6
2 Colan . . . . D 6
6 Colaton Raleigh . . . . G 4
62 Colbost . . . . C 1
40 Colburn . . . . E 2
8 Colbury . . . . E 5
39 Colby, Cumbria . . . . C 9
38 Colby, I.o.M. . . . . H 1
26 Colby, Norfolk . . . . . B 5
19 Colchester . . . . A 10
14 Colcot . . . . G 4
16 Cold Ash . . . . G 6
23 Cold Ashby . . . . D 10
15 Cold Ashton . . . . . . G 10
12 Cold Blow . . . . F 5
23 Cold Brayfield . . . . G 12
33 Cold Hanworth . . . . . B 7
30 Cold Hatton . . . . H 5
45 Cold Hesleden . . . . H 12
35 Cold Hiendly . . . . . . F 12
23 Cold Higham . . . . . G 10
40 Cold Kirby . . . . G 5
3 Cold Northcott . . . . . A 9
19 Cold Norton . . . . D 8
23 Cold Overton . . . . . A 11
39 Coldbeck . . . . E 9
60 Coldbackie . . . . B 6
10 Coldean . . . . G 2
5 Coldeast . . . . H 7
8 Colden Common . . . D 6
27 Coldfair Green . . . . . . J 7
24 Coldham . . . . E 5
15 Coldharbour, Glos. . D 8
10 Coldharbour, Kent . . C 4
58 Coldhome . . . . C 3
49 Coldingham . . . . C 11
52 Coldrain . . . . G 6
11 Coldred . . . . C 11
4 Coldridge . . . . E 6
49 Coldstream . . . . E 11
9 Coldwaltham . . . . . D 11
58 Coldwells . . . . D 8
58 Coldwells Croft . . . . . E 3
7 Cole . . . . C 10
18 Cole Green . . . . C 3
6 Cole Henley . . . . A 6
21 Colebatch . . . . D 8
6 Colebrook . . . . F 3
4 Colebrooke . . . . F 6
56 Coleburn . . . . D 8
37 Coleby, Humber. . . . E 7
33 Coleby, Lincs. . . . . . . D 7
4 Coleford, Devon . . . . F 6
15 Coleford, Glos. . . . . . C 9
7 Coleford, Som. . . . . . A 10
31 Colehill . . . . F 2
10 Coleman's Hatch . . . E 3
30 Colemere . . . . G 3
9 Colemore . . . . C 8
32 Coleorton . . . . H 1
15 Colerne . . . . G 11
16 Colesbourne . . . . C 1
25 Colesden . . . . K 2
17 Coleshill, Bucks. . . . E 10
16 Coleshill, Oxon . . . . . E 3
22 Coleshill, War. . . . . . C 5
6 Colestocks . . . . F 4
10 Colgate . . . . E 1
47 Colgrain . . . . A 8
53 Colinsburhg . . . . G 9
48 Colinton . . . . C 5
46 Colintraive . . . . B 5
26 Colkirk . . . . C 2
63 Coll . . . . C 6
53 Collace . . . . D 7
64 Collafirth . . . . C 7
2 Collamoor Head . . . . B 2
5 Collaton . . . . L 4
5 Collaton St. Mary . . . K 7
47 Collenan . . . . F 8
53 Collesie . . . . F 7
4 Colleton Mills . . . . . . D 5
18 Collier Row . . . . E 5
10 Collier Street . . . . . . C 6
18 Collier's End . . . . B 4
58 Collieston . . . . E 8
43 Collin . . . . D 11
8 Collingbourne Ducis
A 4
8 Collingbourne
Kingston . . . . A 4
35 Collingham . . . . C 12
21 Collington . . . . F 12
23 Collingtree . . . . G 11
34 Collins Green . . . . . . H 4
53 Colliston . . . . C 10
6 Colliton . . . . F 4
59 Collmuir . . . . G 3
58 Collynie . . . . D 6
24 Collyweston . . . . E 1
42 Colmonell . . . . C 3
25 Colmworth . . . . J 2
16 Coln Rogers . . . . C 2
16 Coln St. Aldwyn . . . . D 2
16 Coln St. Dennis . . . . C 2
57 Colnabaichin . . . . H 8
17 Colnbrook . . . . F 11
25 Colne, Cambs. . . . . . H 5
35 Colne, Lancs. . . . . C 7
27 Colne Engaine . . . . . M 2
26 Colney . . . . E 5
18 Colney Heath . . . . . . C 2
18 Colney Street . . . . . . D 2
45 Colpitts Grange . . . . G 8
58 Colpy . . . . D 4
48 Colquhar . . . . E 6
4 Colscott . . . . D 2
40 Colsterdale . . . . G 2
32 Colsterworth . . . . H 6
32 Colston Bassett . . . . . G 4
56 Coltfield . . . . C 7
26 Coltishall . . . . D 6
38 Colton, Cumbria . . . G 5
26 Colton, Norfolk . . . . D 4
36 Colton, N. Yorks. . . . C 3
31 Colton, Staffs. . . . . . . H 9
35 Colton, W. Yorks. . D 12
21 Colva . . . . G 7
22 Colwall Green . . . . . . H 1
22 Colwall Stone . . . . . . H 1
45 Colwell . . . . E 8
31 Colwich . . . . H 8
14 Colwinston . . . . G 3
38 Colwith . . . . E 5
9 Colworth . . . . F 10
29 Colwyn Bay . . . . B 8
6 Colyford . . . . G 6
6 Colyton . . . . G 6
44 Comb . . . . D 6
16 Combe, Berks. . . . . . H 5
21 Combe, Heref. &
Worc. . . . . F 9
16 Combe, Oxon . . . . . . C 5
9 Combe Common . . B 10
21 Combe Moor . . . . F 9
6 Combe Florey . . . . . . C 5
4 Combe Martin . . . . . A 5
6 Combe Raleigh . . . . . F 5
6 Combe St. Nicholas . E 6
5 Combebow . . . . G 4
5 Combeinteignhead . . J 8
30 Comberbach . . . . C 5
25 Comberton, Cambs. . K 5
21 Comberton, Heref. &
Worc. . . . . F 10
6 Combpyne . . . . G 6
31 Combridge . . . . F 9
22 Combrook . . . . G 6
31 Combs, Derby . . . . . . B 9
27 Combs, Suffolk . . . . . K 3
6 Combwich . . . . B 6
59 Comers . . . . G 4
20 Comin Capel Betws . G 2
20 Comins-coch Dyfed . D 2
20 Comins-coch Powys . B 4
58 Comisty . . . . C 3
14 Common Coed-y-paen
D 6
32 Common Side . . . . . . C 1
41 Commondale . . . . D 7
3 Common Moor . . . . . C 9
31 Commonside . . . . . . F 11
31 Compstall . . . . A 8
43 Compstonend . . . . F 7
16 Compton, Berks. . . . . F 6
5 Compton, Devon . . . . J 7
8 Compton, Hants. . . . C 6
9 Compton, Surrey . . A 11
9 Compton, W. Sussex
E 9
8 Compton, Wilts. . . . . A 3
7 Compton Abbas . . D 12
16 Compton Abdale . . . C 2
16 Compton Bassett . . . G 1
16 Compton Beauchamp
E 4
7 Compton Bishop . . . A 7
8 Compton
Chamberlayne . . . . C 2
15 Compton Dando . . . . H 9
7 Compton Dundon . . . C 8
15 Compton Greenfield
F 9
7 Compton Martin . . . A 8
7 Compton Pauncefoot
D 10
7 Compton Valence . . G 9
52 Comrie, Fife . . . . H 5
52 Comrie, Tayside . . . . E 3
51 Conaglen House . . . . A 7
46 Conchra . . . . A 5
34 Conder Green . . . . . . B 3
16 Condicote . . . . A 3
47 Condorrat . . . . B 12
21 Condover . . . . B 10
27 Coney Weston . . . . . G 3
9 Coneyhurst Com. . . D 12
41 Coneysthorpe . . . . . . H 7
35 Coneythorpe . . . . . . A 12
58 Confunderland . . . . . F 3
3 Congdon's Shop . . . B 10
43 Congeith . . . . E 9
23 Congerstone . . . . B 7
24 Congham . . . . C 8
31 Congleton . . . . D 7
28 Congl-y-wal . . . . F 6
15 Congresbury . . . . H 7
56 Conicavel . . . . D 5
33 Coningsby . . . . D 9
25 Conington, Cambs. . . J 4
25 Conington, Cambs. . G 3
36 Conisbrough . . . . G 3
37 Conisholme . . . . H 11
38 Coniston, Cumbria . . E 5
37 Coniston, Humber. . D 9
35 Coniston Cold . . . . . . B 7
39 Conistone . . . . H 12
29 Connah's Quay . . . . C 12
50 Connel . . . . D 6
47 Connel Park . . . . . . H 11
47 Connelbush . . . . H 12
2 Connor Downs . . . . . F 3
56 Cononbridge . . . . D 1
35 Cononley . . . . B 8
53 Cononsyth . . . . C 10
31 Consall . . . . E 8
45 Consett . . . . H 9
40 Constable Burton . . . F 2
2 Constantine . . . . G 4
2 Constantine Bay . . . . B 6
54 Contin . . . . D 8
56 Contullich . . . . C 2
49 Conundrum . . . . D 12
59 Conveth Mains . . . . . K 5
56 Convinth . . . . F 1
29 Conwy . . . . B 7
11 Conyer . . . . B 8
27 Conyer's Green . . . . H 2
10 Cooden . . . . G 6
4 Cookbury . . . . E 3
17 Cookham . . . . F 10
17 Cookham Dean . . . . . F 9
17 Cookham Rise . . . . . . F 9
22 Cookhill . . . . F 4
22 Cookley, Heref. &
Worc. . . . . D 2
27 Cookley, Suffolk . . . H 6
17 Cookley Green . . . . . E 8
59 Cookney . . . . H 6
10 Cooksbridge . . . . G 3
18 Cooksmill Green . . . C 6
9 Coolham . . . . D 12
10 Cooling, Kent . . . . . . A 6
19 Cooling, Kent . . . . . . F 7
10 Cooling Street . . . . . . A 6
2 Coombe, Cornwall . . D 6
4 Coombe, Cornwall . . E 1
6 Coombe, Devon . . . . D 4
8 Coombe, Wilts. . . . . . A 3
8 Coombe Bissett . . . . C 3
15 Coombe Down . . . . H 11
15 Coombe Hay . . . . . . H 10
15 Coombe Hill . . . . . . B 12
7 Coombe Keynes . . . H 11
10 Coombes . . . . G 1
12 Coombs . . . . F 4
56 Cooperhill . . . . D 6
10 Cooper's Corner . . . . C 4
10 Cooper's Green . . . . . F 4
18 Coopersale Com. . . . D 5
9 Cootham . . . . E 12
27 Copdock . . . . L 4
19 Copford Green . . . . . B 9
64 Copister . . . . C 7
25 Cople . . . . K 2
40 Copley . . . . C 1
36 Copmanthorpe . . . . . B 3
2 Coppathorne . . . . A 2
31 Coppenhall . . . . H 7
2 Copperhouse . . . . F 3
25 Coppingford . . . . G 3
7 Coppleridge . . . . . . D 11
4 Copplestone . . . . F 6
34 Coppull . . . . F 4
34 Coppull Moor . . . . . . F 4
10 Copsale . . . . F 1
34 Copster Green . . . . . D 5
22 Copt Heath . . . . D 5
40 Copt Hewick . . . . H 4
23 Copt Oak . . . . A 8
10 Copthorne . . . . D 2
26 Copy's Green . . . . B 2
8 Copythorne . . . . E 5
45 Corbridge . . . . G 8
23 Corby . . . . C 12
33 Corby Glen . . . . H 7
21 Coreley . . . . E 11
17 Cores End . . . . E 10
6 Corfe . . . . D 6
8 Corfe Castle . . . . H 1
8 Corfe Mullen . . . . F 1
21 Corfton . . . . D 10
57 Corgariff . . . . J 8
9 Corhampton . . . . D 7
10 Cork's Pond . . . . D 5
22 Corley . . . . D 6
22 Corley Ash . . . . C 6
22 Corley Moor . . . . D 6
48 Cormiston . . . . F 3
51 Cormonachan . . . . . . H 9
53 Cormuir . . . . A 8
57 Corndavon Lodge . . . J 8
40 Cornforth . . . . B 3
58 Cornhill . . . . B 3
49 Cornhill-on-Tweed
E 11
45 Cornhills . . . . E 8
35 Cornholme . . . . D 8
25 Cornish Hall End . . . L 8
40 Cornsay . . . . A 2
40 Cornsay Colliery . . . A 2
56 Corntown, Mid Glam.
G 3
56 Corntown, Highland
D 1
59 Corntulloch . . . . H 2
3 Cornwall, County . . . C 8
16 Cornwell . . . . A 4
5 Cornwood . . . . K 5
5 Cornworthy . . . . K 7
55 Corpach . . . . M 5
26 Corpusty . . . . C 4
51 Corran, Highland . . . A 7
55 Corran, Highland . . . J 2
46 Corranbuie . . . . C 3
38 Corrany . . . . G 2
55 Corribeg . . . . L 4
46 Corrie . . . . E 5
43 Corrie Common . . . C 12
46 Corriecravie . . . . G 4
54 Corriefeol . . . . E 6
55 Corriegour . . . . K 6
54 Corriemoillie . . . . C 7
60 Corriemulzie Lo . . . . G 4
57 Corrievorrie . . . . G 3
54 Corrieviuc . . . . E 6
55 Corrimony . . . . G 7
19 Corringham, Essex . . F 7
32 Corringham, Lincs. . A 6
20 Corris . . . . B 3
51 Corrour Shooting
Lodge . . . . A 11
51 Corrow . . . . G 9
62 Corry . . . . F 6
56 Corry of Ardnagrask
E 1
46 Corrygills . . . . F 5
55 Corryhully . . . . L 3
60 Corrykinloch . . . . E 5
52 Corrymuckloch . . . . . D 4
50 Corrynachenchy . . . . C 4
49 Corsbie . . . . E 8
7 Corscombe . . . . F 8
58 Corse, Grampian . . . D 3
58 Corse, Grampian . . . B 7
59 Corse House . . . . G 3
58 Corse of Kinnoir . . . . C 3
59 Corsebauld . . . . J 5
58 Corsehill . . . . B 7
42 Corsemalzie . . . . F 4
15 Corhsam . . . . G 11
59 Corsindae . . . . G 4
7 Corsley . . . . B 11
7 Corsley Heath . . . . . B 11
47 Corsliehill . . . . C 9
43 Corsock . . . . D 8
15 Corston, Avon . . . . H 10
15 Corston, Wilts. . . . . F 12
48 Corstorphine . . . . B 5
59 Cortachy Castle . . . . . L 1
26 Corton, Suffolk . . . . . F 8
8 Corton, Wilts. . . . . . . B 1
7 Corton Denham . . . . D 9
51 Coruanan Lodge . . . . A 8
29 Corwen . . . . F 10
7 Coryates . . . . H 9
5 Coryton, Devon . . . . G 3
19 Coryton, Essex . . . . . F 7
23 Cosby . . . . C 9
22 Coseley . . . . C 3
23 Cosgrove . . . . H 11
9 Cosham . . . . F 8
12 Cosheston . . . . G 3
52 Coshieville . . . . B 3
32 Cossall . . . . F 2
23 Cossington . . . . A 9
64 Costa . . . . B 2
26 Costessey . . . . D 5
32 Costock . . . . H 3
32 Coston, Leics. . . . . . . H 6
26 Coston, Norfolk . . . . E 4
44 Cote . . . . C 1
30 Cotebrook . . . . D 4
44 Cotehill . . . . H 3
31 Cotes, Cumbria . . . . . F 7
31 Cotes, Staffs. . . . . G 7
23 Cotesbach . . . . D 8
32 Cotgrave . . . . G 3
58 Cothall . . . . F 6
32 Cotham . . . . E 5
6 Cothelstone . . . . C 5
39 Cotherstone . . . . . . C 12
49 Cothill, Borders . . . D 10
16 Cothill, Oxon . . . . . . D 6
6 Cotleigh . . . . F 5
32 Cotmanhay . . . . F 2
25 Coton, Cambs. . . . . . . J 5
23 Coton, Northants. . E 10
31 Coton, Staffs. . . . . . . H 7
31 Coton, Staffs. . . . . . . G 8
31 Coton Clanford . . . . H 7
31 Coton in the Clay . . G 10
22 Coton in the Elms . . A 6
5 Cott . . . . K 6
34 Cottam, Lancs. . . . . . D 4
32 Cottam, Notts. . . . . . B 5
56 Cottartown . . . . F 6
25 Cottenham . . . . H 5
39 Cotterdale . . . . F 10
18 Cottered . . . . A 3
24 Cotterstock . . . . F 1
23 Cottesbrooke . . . . . E 10
23 Cottesmore . . . . A 12
6 Botteylands . . . . E 3
37 Cottingham,
Humberside . . . . . . D 8
23 Cottingham,
Northants. . . . . . . C 11
35 Cottingley . . . . C 9
17 Cottisford . . . . A 7
27 Cotton . . . . J 4
25 Cotton End . . . . L 2
58 Cot-town, Grampian
E 2
58 Cot-town, Grampian
D 6
31 Cotwalton . . . . G 8
58 Cotwells . . . . B 5
3 Couchsmill . . . . D 8
15 Coughton, Heref. &
Worc. . . . . B 9
22 Coughton, War. . . . . . F 4
46 Coulaghailtro . . . . . . C 2
54 Coulags . . . . E 3
54 Couldoran . . . . E 2
54 Coulin Lodge . . . . . . D 4
59 Coull . . . . G 3
47 Coulport . . . . A 7
18 Coulsdon . . . . H 3
8 Coulston . . . . A 1
48 Coulter . . . . F 3
40 Coulton . . . . H 6
21 Cound . . . . B 11
40 Coundon, Durham . . . B 3
22 Coundon, W. Midlands
D 6
40 Coundon Grange . . . B 2
39 Countersett . . . . F 11
23 Countesthorpe . . . . . C 9
8 Countess . . . . B 3
6 Countess Wear . . . . . G 3
4 Countisbury . . . . A 6
53 Coupar Angus . . . . . . C 7
49 Coupland . . . . F 12
6 Couple Cross . . . . B 3
46 Cour . . . . E 3
43 Courance . . . . C 11
17 Court Corner . . . . H 7
13 Court Henry . . . . E 9
55 Courteachan . . . . K 1
23 Courteenhall . . . . . . G 11
19 Courtsend . . . . E 10
6 Courtway . . . . C 5
48 Cousland . . . . C 6
10 Cousleywood . . . . E 5
46 Coustonn . . . . B 6
6 Cove, Devon . . . . D 3
9 Cove, Hampshire . . A 10
54 Cove, Highland . . . . . A 2
47 Cove, Strathclyde . . . A 7
59 Cove Bay . . . . G 7
27 Covehithe . . . . G 8
22 Coven . . . . A 3
25 Coveney . . . . G 6
37 Covenham St.
Bartholomew . . . H 11
37 Covenham St. Mary
H 11
23 Coventry . . . . D 7
2 Coverack . . . . H 5
40 Coverham . . . . F 1
25 Covington . . . . H 2
22 Cow Honeybourne . . H 5
39 Cowan Bridge . . . . . . G 8
10 Cowbeech . . . . G 5
24 Cowbit . . . . D 4
14 Cowbridge, S. Glam.
G 3
6 Cowbridge, Som. . . . B 3
10 Cowden, Kent . . . . . . D 3
45 Cowden, Northumb. E 7
52 Cowdenbeath . . . . . . H 6
48 Cowdenburn . . . . D 5
8 Cowes . . . . F 6
40 Cowesby . . . . F 5
10 Cowfold . . . . F 1
52 Cowie, Central . . . . . H 3
59 Cowie, Grampian . . . J 6
45 Cowpen . . . . E 11
40 Cowpen Bewley . . . . C 5
31 Cowers Lane . . . . . . E 11
6 Cowley, Devon . . . . . G 3
15 Cowley, Glos. . . . . . C 12
18 Cowley, London . . . . F 1

16 Cowley, Oxon D 6
40 Cowling, N. Yorks. F 3
35 Cowling, N. Yorks. C 8
25 Cowlinge K 8
9 Cowplain E 8
39 Cowshill A 10
52 Cowstrandburn H 5
36 Cowthorpe B 2
17 Cox Green F 9
30 Coxbank F 5
31 Coxbench F 12
10 Coxheath C 6
11 Coxhill C 11
40 Coxhoe B 3
7 Coxley B 8
18 Coxtie Green D 5
40 Coxwold G 5
14 Coychurch F 3
47 Coylton G 9
57 Coylumbridge H 5
59 Coynach G 2
58 Coynachie D 2
14 Coytrahen F 2
54 Cozae Lodge F 6
22 Crabbs Cross F 4
10 Crabtree F 1
61 Crackaig F 9
39 Crackenthorpe C 9
2 Crackington B 2
2 Crackington Haven B 2
22 Crackley E 6
22 Crackley Bank A 1
39 Crackpot E 12
35 Cracoe A 8
6 Craddock E 4
22 Cradley G 1
22 Cradley Heath D 3
14 Cradoc A 3
3 Crafthole D 10
45 Cragend C 9
35 Cragg E 8
57 Craggan, Highland G 6
60 Craggan, Highland G 4
51 Craggan, Strathclyde H 10
56 Craggiemore F 3
45 Craghead H 10
58 Craibstone, Grampian F 6
58 Craibstone, Grampian B 2
53 Craichie B 10
43 Craig, Dumf. & Gall. D 7
43 Craig, Dumf. & Gall. E 8
54 Craig, Highland E 4
42 Craig, Strathcylde A 5
46 Craig Lodge B 5
14 Craig Penllyn F 3
13 Craig Trebanos G 10
52 Craiganour Lodge A 1
55 Craigard J 7
55 Craigbeg L 8
42 Craigcaffie E 2
13 Craig-cefn-parc G 10
58 Craigdam E 6
43 Craigdarrcoh, Dumf. & Gall. C 8
43 Craigdarroch, Strathclyde A 7
42 Craigdews D 6
54 Craigdhu F 8
58 Craigearn F 5
56 Craigellachie E 8
42 Craigencallie D 6
42 Craigencross E 1
48 Craigend, Strathclyde F 1
52 Craigend, Tayside E 6
47 Craigendoran A 8
42 Craigengillan A 5
42 Craigenrae C 4
47 Craigens G 10
59 Craiggiecat H 6
56 Craighead, Grampian F 8
48 Craighead, Strathclyde G 2
58 Craigie, Grampian F 6
47 Craigie, Strathclyde F 9
52 Craigie, Tayside C 6
43 Craigieburn A 11
48 Craiglockhart B 5
42 Craimalloch B 5
58 Craigmaud B 6
46 Craigmore C 6
59 Craigmoston K 4
30 Craignant G 1
42 Craigneil C 2
43 Craigneston C 8
47 Craigneuk D 12
50 Craignure D 4
59 Craigo L 4
52 Craigow F 6
53 Craigrothie F 8
53 Craigs G 7
59 Craigton, Grampian G 6
54 Craigton, Highland F 3
56 Craigton, Highland E 2
47 Craigton, Strathclyde D 10
53 Craigton, Tayside C 10
53 Craigton, Tayside B 8
61 Craigtown B 9
13 Craig-y-Duke G 10
14 Craig-y-nos C 2
44 Craik B 2
53 Crail F 11
49 Crailing G 9
49 Crailinghall G 9
36 Craiselound G 5
48 Craimalt G 5
36 Crambe A 5
45 Cramlington E 11
48 Cramond B 5
48 Cramond Bridge B 4
55 Cranachan L 7
30 Cranage C 6
31 Cranberry G 7
58 Cranbog F 7
8 Cranborne E 2
17 Cranbourne G 10
10 Cranbrook D 6
10 Cranbrook Com. D 6
35 Crane Moor G 11
25 Cranfield L 1
18 Cranford F 1
23 Cranford St. Andrew D 12
23 Cranford St. John D 12
15 Cranham, Glos. C 12
18 Cranham, London E 6
34 Crank G 4
9 Cranleigh B 12
8 Cranmore G 5
58 Cranna B 4
58 Crannach B 2
50 Crannich C 2
23 Cranoe C 11
27 Cransford J 6
49 Cranshaws C 9
38 Cranstal F 2
37 Cranswick B 8
2 Crantock D 5
33 Cranwell E 7
26 Cranwich F 1
26 Cranworth E 3
42 Cranyard H 2
5 Crapstone J 4
51 Crarae H 7
60 Crask Inn E 6
54 Crask of Aigas E 8
54 Craskie F 7
59 Craskins G 3
45 Craster A 10
27 Cratfield H 6
59 Crathes H 5
57 Crathie K 1
40 Crathorne D 5
21 Craven Arms D 10
45 Crawcrook G 9
48 Crawford G 2
48 Crawfordjohn G 2
43 Crawfordton B 9
47 Crawick H 12
8 Crawley, Hants. C 6
16 Crawley, Oxon C 4
10 Crawley, W. Sussex D 1
10 Crawley Down D 2
39 Crawleyside A 12
35 Crawshaw Booth E 7
59 Crawton J 6
39 Cray, N. Yorks. G 11
14 Cray, Powys B 2
18 Crayford F 5
40 Crayke H 6
19 Crays Hill E 7
17 Cray's Pond F 7
17 Crazies Hill F 9
50 Creach Bheinn Lodge E 4
4 Creacombe D 7
51 Creag a' Phuill G 8
51 Creagan C 7
46 Creagan Beag A 3
51 Creaguaineach Lo. A 10
23 Creaton E 10
44 Creca F 1
21 Credenhill H 10
4 Crediton F 7
42 Creebank D 4
42 Creebridge E 5
6 Creech Heathfield D 6
6 Creech St. Michael D 6
2 Creed E 6
18 Creekmouth F 5
42 Creeside C 4
27 Creeting St. Mary J 4
24 Creeton D 1
42 Creetown F 6
21 Cregerina G 7
51 Creggans G 8
38 Cregneish H 1
38 Creg-ny-Baa G 2
53 Creich E 8
14 Creigiau F 4
54 Crelevan F 7
3 Cremyll D 11
21 Cressage B 11
12 Cresselly F 4
17 Cressex E 9
19 Cressing B 8
12 Cresswell, Dyfed F 4
45 Cresswell, Northumb. D 11
31 Cresswell, Staffs. F 8
32 Creswell C 2
27 Cretingham J 5
46 Cretshengan C 2
21 Crew Green A 8
30 Crewe, Cheshire E 3
30 Crewe, Cheshire E 6
7 Crewkerne E 7
51 Crainlarich E 11
13 Cribyn B 8
28 Criccieth F 4
32 Crich, Derby E 12
15 Crick, Gwent E 8
23 Crick, Northants. E 9
20 Crickadarn H 6
7 Cricket Malherbie E 7
7 Cricket St. Thomas E 7
30 Crickheath H 2
14 Crickhowell B 5
16 Cricklade E 2
36 Cridling Stubbs E 3
52 Crieff E 3
21 Criggian A 8
35 Crigglestone E 11
58 Crimond B 8
58 Crimonmogate B 8
24 Crimplesham E 7
54 Crinaglack F 8
50 Crinan H 5
26 Cringleford E 3
12 Crinow F 5
8 Cripplestyle E 3
10 Cripp's Corner F 6
38 Croasdale C 3
7 Crock Street E 7
10 Crockenhill A 4
5 Crockernwell G 6
7 Crockerton B 11
43 Crocket or Ninemile Bar D 9
36 Crockey Hill B 4
10 Crockham Hill C 3
10 Crockhurst Street D 5
19 Crockleford Hth. A 10
21 Crockmeole A 9
14 Croes-Hywel C 6
14 Croeserw E 2
12 Croes-goch D 2
13 Croes-Ian C 7
28 Croesor F 6
14 Croes-y-ceilog E 6
13 Croesyceiliog E 7
14 Croes-y-mwyalch E 6
12 Croft, Dyfed C 5
23 Croft, Leics. C 8
34 Croft, Merseyside H 5
33 Croft, Lincs. D 12
40 Croft, N. Yorks. D 3
47 Croftamie A 9
47 Crofthead E 12
52 Croftmill C 3
57 Croftmore H 5
57 Crofthaven H 5
35 Crofton, W. Yorks. E 12
16 Crofton, Wilts. H 4
43 Crofts D 8
58 Crofts of Belnagoak C 6
58 Crofts of Haddo D 6
58 Crofts of Hillbrae C 3
58 Crofts of Meikle Ardo D 6
58 Crofts of Savoch B 8
58 Crofts of Shanquhar D 3
13 Crofty G 8
50 Croggan E 4
44 Croglin H 4
43 Crogo D 8
60 Croick G 5
63 Croir C 2
56 Cromarty C 3
54 Cromasag D 4
58 Cromblet D 5
57 Cromdale G 6
28 Cromer, Herts. A 3
26 Cromer, Norfolk A 5
31 Cromford E 11
15 Cromhall E 10
15 Cromhall Com. E 10
63 Cromore E 5
57 Cromra K 1
32 Cromwell D 5
47 Cronan E 10
47 Cronberry G 11
9 Crondall A 9
38 Cronk-y-Voddy G 2
30 Cronton A 4
39 Crook, Cumbria F 7
40 Crook, Durham B 2
56 Crook of Alves D 7
52 Crook of Devon G 5
34 Crooke F 4
47 Crookedholm F 9
48 Crookedstane H 2
32 Crookes B 1
16 Crookham, Berks. H 6
49 Crookham, Northumb. F 11
9 Crookham Village A 9
49 Crookham Westfield F 11
48 Crookhaugh G 4
49 Crookhouse G 10
39 Crooklands G 8
47 Crookston C 10
49 Crookston North Mains D 7
22 Croome Court H 2
23 Cropredy G 8
23 Cropston A 9
22 Cropthorne H 3
41 Cropton F 8
32 Cropwell Bishop G 4
32 Cropwell Butler F 4
47 Crosbie D 7
43 Crosby, Cumb. H 11
38 Crosby, I.o.M. G 2
36 Crosby, Humber. F 6
34 Crosby, Merseyside G 2
40 Crosby Court F 4
39 Crosby Garrett D 9
39 Crosby Ravensworth D 8
43 Crosby Villa H 11
7 Croscombe B 9
7 Cross A 7
15 Cross Ash B 7
10 Cross-at-Hand C 6
20 Cross Foxes A 3
35 Cross Gates D 12
27 Cross Green K 2
15 Cross Hands, Avon F 9
13 Cross Hnads, Dyfed F 9
12 Cross Hands, Dyfed F 4
35 Cross Hills C 9
21 Cross Houses B 11
10 Cross in Hand F 4
13 Cross Inn, Dyfed A 7
13 Cross Inn, Dyfed A 9
13 Cross Inn, Dyfed D 11
14 Cross Inn, Mid Glam F 4
10 Cross Keys, Kent C 4
15 Cross Keys, Wilts. G 11
2 Cross Lanes, Corn. G 4
30 Cross Lanes, Clwyd F 2
7 Cross Lanes, Dorest F 11
36 Cross Lanes, N. Yorks. A 3
63 Cross North Dell A 6
14 Cross Oak B 4
58 Cross of Jackson D 5
31 Cross o'th Hands F 11
27 Cross Street H 5
46 Crossaig D 3
63 Crossbost D 5
43 Crosscanonby H 11
48 Crossleuch G 5
26 Crossdale Street B 5
34 Crossens E 3
48 Crossford, Fife A 3
48 Crossford, Strathclyde E 1
24 Crossgate C 3
48 Crossgatehall C 6
52 Crossgates, Fife H 6
40 Crossgates, N. Yorks. H 2
20 Crossgates, Powys F 6
39 Crossgill, Cumb. A 9
34 Crossgill, Lancs. A 4
5 Crossgreen, Devon G 3
21 Crossgreen, Salop A 10
49 Crosshall E 10
12 Crosshands, Dyfed E 5
47 Crosshands, Strathclyde F 9
52 Crosshill, Fife G 6
42 Crosshill, Strathcylde A 4
47 Crosshill, Strathclyde G 9
47 Crosshouse F 9
44 Crossings E 3
14 Crosskeys E 5
61 Crosskirk A 10
38 Crosslands F 6
30 Crosslanes H 2
48 Crosslee G 6
47 Crosslees D 10
43 Crossmichael E 8
34 Crossmor C 3
10 Crosspost F 1
59 Crossroads, Grampian H 5
47 Crossroads, Strathclyde F 9
35 Crossroads, W. Yorks. C 9
64 Cross-voe-sand C 6
15 Crossway, Heref. & Worc. A 9
15 Crossway, Gwent B 8
20 Crossway, Powys G 6
22 Crossway Green E 2
7 Crossways G 11
12 Crosswell C 5
20 Crosswood E 2
34 Croston E 4
26 Crostwick D 6
10 Crouch C 5
7 Crouch Hill E 10
8 Croucheston D 2
16 Croughton A 6
58 Crovie A 5
8 Crow F 3
35 Crow Edge G 10
15 Crow Hill B 9
2 Crowan F 4
10 Crowborough E 4
20 Crowborough Town E 4
6 Crowcombe C 5
35 Crowden G 9
17 Crowell D 8
23 Crowfield, Northants. H 9
27 Crowfield, Suffolk J 5
10 Crowhurst, E. Sussex G 6
10 Crowhurst, Surrey C 3
10 Crowhurst Lane End C 3
24 Crowland D 3
2 Crowlas F 2
22 Crowle, Heref. & Worc. G 3
36 Crowle, Humber. F 5
63 Crowlista D 1
17 Crowmarsh Gifford E 7
2 Crown Town G 3
5 Crownhill K 4
26 Crownthorpe E 4
42 Crows F 4
2 Crows-an-wra G 1
17 Crowthorne H 9
30 Crowton C 4
22 Croxall A 5
37 Croxby G 9
40 Croxdale B 3
31 Croxden F 9
17 Croxley Green E 11
25 Croxton, Cambs. J 3
37 Croxton, Humber. F 8
27 Croxton, Norfolk G 2
30 Croxton, Staffs. G 6
32 Croxton Kerrial G 5
56 Croy, Highland E 4
47 Croy, Strathclyde B 12
4 Croyde B 3
4 Croyde Bay B 3
25 Croydon, Cambs. K 4
18 Croydon, London G 3
57 Crubenmore Lo. K 2
58 Cruden Bay D 8
30 Crudington H 5
16 Crudwell E 1
21 Crug E 1
2 Crugmeer B 6
13 Crugybar C 10
54 Cruive F 8
63 Crulivig D 3
14 Crumlin D 5
3 Crumplehorn E 9
12 Crundale, Dyfed E 3
11 Crundale, Kent C 9
44 Crurie D 1
6 Cruwys Morchard E 2
16 Crux Easton H 5
13 Crwbin F 8
17 Cryers Hill D 9
12 Crymmych D 5
13 Crynant F 11
54 Cuaig D 1
23 Cubbington E 7
2 Cubert D 5
17 Cublington B 9
10 Cuckfield F 2
7 Cucklington D 10
32 Cuckney C 3
17 Cuddesdon D 7
17 Cuddington, Bucks. C 8
30 Cuddington, Ches. C 4
30 Cuddington Heath F 3
34 Cuddy Hill C 4
18 Cudham H 4
5 Cudlipptown H 4
7 Cudworth, Som. E 7
36 Cudworth, S. Yorks. F 2
12 Cuffern E 2
18 Cuffley D 3
63 Cuiashader A 6
54 Culaneilan D 4
56 Culbo D 2
56 Culbokie D 2
56 Culburnie E 1
56 Culcabock E 2
56 Culcairn C 2
56 Culcharry E 4
34 Culcheth H 5
56 Culcraggie C 2
52 Culdees F 4
58 Culdrain D 3
54 Culduie F 1
27 Culford H 1
39 Culgaith B 8
16 Culham E 6
46 Culinlongart H 2
60 Culkien D 2
60 Culkein Drumbeg D 3
15 Culkerton E 12
57 Cullachie G 5
58 Cullen A 3
45 Cullercoats F 12
59 Cullerlie G 5
56 Cullicudden C 2
54 Culligran F 7
35 Cullingworth D 9
50 Cullipool F 5
64 Cullivoe B 8
52 Culloch E 3
55 Cullochy J 7
56 Culloden House E 3
6 Cullompton E 4
6 Culm Davy E 5
61 Culmaily G 8
42 Culmalzie F 5
21 Culmington D 10
6 Culmstock E 4
60 Culnacraig F 2
43 Culnaightrie F 8
62 Culnakncok B 4
42 Culquhirk F 5
60 Culrain G 6
48 Culross A 3
47 Culroy H 8
42 Culscadden G 5
59 Culsh H 1
42 Culshabbin F 4
64 Culswick D 6
58 Cultercullen E 7
42 Cults, Dumf. & Gall. G 5
58 Cults, Grampian D 3
59 Cults, Grampian G 6
52 Cultybraggan E 3
10 Culverstone Green B 5
33 Culverthorpe F 7
23 Culworth G 9
56 Culzie Lodge C 1
47 Cumberhead F 12
49 Cumberland Bower D 12
47 Cumbernauld B 12
33 Cumberworth C 12
38 Cumbria, Co. C 6
58 Cuminestown C 5
49 Cumledge D 10
44 Cummersdale H 2
43 Cummertrees E 12
56 Cummingstown C 7
47 Cumnock G 10
16 Cumnor D 5
44 Cumrew H 4
43 Cumrue C 11
43 Cumstone C 12
44 Cumwhinton H 3
44 Cumwhitton H 3
40 Cundall H 4
47 Cunninghamhead E 8
64 Cunnister B 7
53 Cupar F 8
53 Cupar Muir F 8
8 Cupernnam D 5
31 Curbar C 11
16 Curbridge, Oxon C 4
9 Curdbridge, Hants. E 7

22 Curdworth C 5
54 Curin D 7
6 Curland E 6
42 Currarie B 2
16 Curridge G 6
48 Currie C 4
7 Curry Mallet D 7
7 Curry Rivel D 7
10 Curtisden Green D 6
2 Cury G 4
58 Cushnie B 5
6 Cushuish C 5
21 Cusop H 8
64 Cusvie B 3
42 Cutcloy H 5
6 Cutcombe B 3
61 Cuthill, Highland H 8
48 Cuthill, Lothian B 6
22 Cutnall Green E 2
16 Cutsdean A 2
31 Cutthorpe C 11
17 Cuxham E 7
10 Cuxton A 6
37 Cuxwold G 9
29 Cwm, Clwyd C 10
14 Cwm, Gwent D 5
20 Cwm-Cewydd A 4
12 Cwm Cych C 6
13 Cwm-Duad D 7
14 Cwm Ffrwd Oer D 6
20 Cwm Irfon G 4
13 Cwm-Mawr F 8
12 Cwm-Morgan D 6
29 Cwm-Penmachno E 7
14 Cwmaman D 3
13 Cwmann B 9
13 Cwmavon H 11
12 Cwm-bach, Dyfed D 6
14 Cwm-bach, Mid. Glam. D 4
20 Cwm-bach, Powys G 6
21 Cwm-bach, Powys H 7
20 Cwmbelan D 5
14 Cwmbran E 6
20 Cwmbrwyno D 3
14 Cwmcarn E 5
15 Cwmcarvan D 8
12 Cwmcoy C 6
14 Cwmdare D 3
13 Cwm-du, Dyfed D 9
14 Cwm-du, Powys B 5
14 Cwmfelin, Mid Glam. D 4
14 Cwmfelin, Mid Glam. E 2
12 Cwmfelin Boeth E 5
14 Cwmfelin-fach E 5
12 Cwmfelin-Mynach E 6
13 Cwm-ffrwd E 7
14 Cwmgiedd C 1
13 Cwmgors F 10
13 Cwmgwili F 9
13 Cwmifor D 10
13 Cwmisfael E 8
20 Cwmlline B 4
13 Cwmllyfri F 7
13 Cwmllynfell F 10
12 Cwmmiles E 5
14 Cwm-parc E 3
13 Cwm-pengraig C 7
14 Cwm-rhos B 5
13 Cwmsychpant B 8
14 Cwmtillery D 5
14 Cwmwysg A 2
13 Cwm-y-glo F 9
13 Cwmyoy B 6
20 Cwmystwyth E 3
20 Cwrt B 2
13 Cwrt-newydd B 8
13 Cwrt-y-Cadno C 10
14 Cwrt-y-defaid F 1
14 Cwrt-y-gollen C 6
28 Cwym-y-glo D 5
29 Cyffilliog D 10
14 Cymmer, Mid Glam. E 3
14 Cymmer, W. Glam. E 2
14 Cyncoed F 5
13 Cynghordy, Dyfed C 11
13 Cynghordy, W. Glam. G 10
13 Cynheidre F 8
14 Cynonville E 2
29 Cynwyd F 10
13 Cynwyl Elfed D 7
35 Dacre Banks A 10
23 Dadford H 10
23 Dadlington B 7
13 Dafen G 8
18 Dagenham F 5
16 Daglingworth D 1
17 Dagnall C 10
51 Dail D 8
42 Dailly B 3
57 Dail-na-mine Lo. M 3
53 Dairsie or Osnaburgh E 9
34 Daisy Hill G 5
51 Dalavich F 7
43 Dalbeattie E 9
63 Dalbeg B 3
47 Dalblair G 11
59 Dalbog K 3
38 Dalby H 1
61 Dalchalm F 9
51 Dalchenna G 8
52 Dalchonzie E 2
60 Dalchork F 6
55 Dalchreichart H 7
52 Dalchruin E 2
54 Dalchuirn F 3
56 Dalcross Station E 3
33 Dalderby D 9
32 Dale, Derby F 2
12 Dale, Dyfed F 2
64 Dale, Shetland Is. D 6
39 Dale Head D 7
41 Dalehouse C 8
50 Dalelia A 5
57 Dalestie H 7
43 Dalfibble C 11
47 Dalfram G 11
47 Dalgarven E 8
48 Dalgetty Bay A 4
47 Dalgig H 10
52 Dalginross E 3
52 Dalguise B 5
61 Dalhalvaig B 9
25 Dalham J 8
46 Dalinlongart A 6
48 Dalkeith C 6
52 Dall B 1
56 Dallas D 7
47 Dalleagles H 10
27 Dallinghoo K 5
10 Dallington, E. Sussex F 5
23 Dallington, Northants. F 10
39 Dalmain Dacre C 7
43 Dalmakerran B 8
51 Dalmally E 9
42 Dalmellington A 6
48 Dalmeny B 4
48 Dalmeny Rows B 4
60 Dalmichy F 6
57 Dalmigavie H 3
57 Dalmigavie Lodge G 3
56 Dalmore, Highland C 2
56 Dalmore, Highland B 1
63 Dalmore, W. Isles B 3
47 Dalmuir B 10
56 Dalmunach E 8
50 Dalnabreck A 4
57 Dalnacardoch Lo. M 3
52 Dalnacarn A 5
57 Dalnahaitnach H 4
61 Dalnamain G 7
57 Dalnaspidal M 2
61 Dalnawillan Lo. C 10
57 Dalness B 9
61 Dalnessie E 7
52 Daloist A 3
52 Dalqueich G 6
42 Dalquhairn B 4
61 Dalreavoch F 7
52 Dalriach A 2
43 Dalry, Dumf. & Gall. C 7
47 Dalry, Strathclyde D 8
47 Dalrymple H 8
48 Dalserf D 1
44 Dalston H 2
43 Dalswinton C 10
43 Dalton, Dumf. & Gall. D 12
34 Dalton, Lancs. F 4
45 Dalton, Northumb. F 9
45 Dalton, Northumb. G 7
40 Dalton, N. Yorks. G 4
40 Dalton, N. Yorks. D 1
32 Dalton, S. Yorks. A 2
40 Dalton Piercy B 5
38 Dalton-in-Furness H 5
45 Dalton-le-Dale H 12
40 Dalton-on-Tees D 3
46 Daltot A 3
42 Dalvadie F 2
52 Dalveich E 1
47 Dalvennan H 9
61 Dalvina Lodge C 7
42 Dalwhat B 8
57 Dalwhinnie L 2
6 Dalwood F 6
8 Damerham D 3
26 Damgate E 7
42 Damnaglaur H 2
48 Damside D 4
11 Danaway borden B 7
19 Danbury C 8
41 Danby D 7
40 Danby Wiske E 3
56 Dandaleith E 8
48 Danderhall B 6
18 Dane End B 3
23 DaneHills B 9
31 Danebridge D 8
10 Danehill E 3
34 Dangerous Corner F 4
40 Dan's Corner A 1
49 Danskine C 8
22 Danzey Green E 5
14 Daren—felen C 5
10 Darenth A 4
30 Daresbury B 4
36 Darfield G 2
11 Dargate B 9
45 Dargues D 7
3 Darite C 9
22 Darlaston C 3
35 Darley A 10
31 Darley Bridge D 11
22 Darlingscott H 6
40 Darlington D 3
30 Darliston G 4
32 Darlton C 5
32 Darnall A 1
56 Darnaway Castle D 5
47 Darnconner G 10
43 Darngarroch E 7
49 Darnick F 8
20 Darowen B 4
58 Darra C 5
4 Darracott, Corn D 1
4 Darracott, Devon B 3
45 Darras Hall F 9
36 Darrington E 3
27 Darsham H 7
10 Dartford A 4
5 Dartington J 6
5 Dartmeet H 5
5 Dartmouth K 7
35 Darton F 11
47 Darvel F 10
34 Darwen E 6
17 Datchet F 10
18 Datchworth B 3
18 Datchworth Green B 3
34 Daubill F 6
16 Dauntsey F 1
16 Dauntsey Green F 1
16 Dauntsey Lock F 1
30 Davenham C 5
23 Daventry F 9
20 David's Well E 6
48 Davidson's Mains B 5
56 Davidston C 3
3 Davidstow A 8
44 Davington C 1
58 Daviot, Grampian E 5
6 Daviot, Highland F 3
17 Davis Street G 9
58 Davoch of Grange C 2
35 Daw Cross B 11
10 Dawesgreen C 1
21 Dawley B 12
21 Dawley Bank B 12
21 Dawley Magna B 12
5 Dawlish H 8
7 Dawlish Wake E 7
6 Dawlish Warren H 3
29 Dawn C 8
19 Daws Heath E 8
3 Daw's House A 10
24 Dawsmere C 5
38 Dawthwaitehead C 6
16 Daylesford B 3
44 Deadwater C 4
47 Deadwaters E 12
11 Deal C 12
38 Dean, Cumb C 3
4 Dean, Devon B 4
4 Dean, Devon B 5
5 Dean, Devon J 6
8 Dean, Dorset D 1
9 Dean, Hants D 7
7 Dean, Somerset B 10
5 Dean Prior J 6
31 Dean Row B 7
10 Dean Street C 6
44 Deanburnhaugh B 2
9 Deane A 7
60 Deanich Lodge H 5
8 Deanland D 2
38 Deanscales C 3
23 Deanshanger Hill H 11
52 Deanston G 2
38 Dearham B 3
27 Debach K 5
25 Debden, Essex M 7
18 Debden Estate D 4
25 Debden Green M 7
27 Debenham J 5
48 Dechmont B 3
16 Deddington A 6
27 Dedham M 4
59 Deebank H 4
59 Deecastle H 2
23 Deene C 12
24 Deenethorpe F 1
17 Deepcut H 10
24 Deeping Gate E 3
24 Deeping St. James E 3
24 Deeping St. Nicholas D 3
58 Deerhill B 2
15 Deerhurst A 11
64 Deerness D 3
22 Defford H 3
14 Defynnog B 2
29 Deganwy B 7
40 Deighton, N. Yorks. E 4
35 Deighton, W. Yorks. E10
36 Deighton C 4
28 Deiniolen D 5
3 Delabole A 8
30 Delamere C 4
42 Delamford B 4
56 Delchirach F 7
58 Delfrigs E 7
57 Dell Lodge H 6
56 Delliefure F 6
57 Delnabo H 7
57 Delnadamph Lo J 8
57 Delnamer M 7
48 Deloraineshiel H 6
35 Delph F 8
45 Delves H 9
24 Dembleby B 1
36 Denaby G 3
36 Denaby Main G 3
43 Denbie Mains D 11
29 Denbigh D10
5 Denbury J 7
32 Denby F 1
35 Denby Dale F 11
16 Denchworth E 5
58 Denend D 3
25 Denford H 1
19 Dengie D 9
17 Denham, Bucks E 11
27 Denham, Suffolk H 5
27 Denham, Suffolk J 1
53 Denhead, Fife F 9
58 Denhead, Grampian B 7
58 Denhead, Grampian E 7
49 Denholm G 8
35 Denholme D 9
9 Denmead E 8
27 Dennington H 6
48 Denny A 1
10 Denny Bottom D 4
8 Denny Lodge E 5
48 Dennyloanhead A 1
35 Denshaw F 8
59 Denside H 5
27 Denston K 1
31 Denstone F 9
39 Dent F 9
39 Dent Station F 10
25 Denton, Cambs G 2
40 Denton, Durham C 2
10 Denton, E. Sussex H 3
11 Denton, Kent C 11
32 Denton, Lincs G 6
35 Denton, Manchester H 8
27 Denton, Norfolk G 6
35 Denton, N. Yorks B 10
23 Denton, Northants F 11
17 Denton, Oxon D 7
24 Denver E 7
45 Denwick B 10
45 Denwick Lane End A 10
26 Deopham E 3
26 Deopham Green F 3
4 Deptford, Devon D 5
4 Deptford, Devon D 1
18 Deptford, London F 4
8 Deptford, Wilts B 2
31 Derby G 11
38 Derbyhaven H 1
32 Derbyshire, Co D11
52 Derculich B 4
42 Dergoals F 3
14 Deri D 5
20 Deri—Odwyn F 2
52 Derry E 1
15 Derry Hill G 12
50 Derryguaig D 2
11 Derringstone C 10
31 Derrington H 7
36 Derrythorpe F 6
24 Dersingham C 8
50 Dervaig B 2
29 Derwen E 10
13 Derwlwyn C 9
23 Desborough D 11
23 Desford B 8
45 Detchant B 12
11 Detling B 7
29 Deuddwr H 11
15 Devauden D 8
59 Devenick G 7
20 Devil's Bridge E 3
16 Devizes H 1
4 Devon, County F 5
48 Devonburn E 1
3 Devonport D 11
52 Devonside G 4
2 Devoran F 5
48 Dewar D 6
7 Dewlish F 11
15 Dewsall Court A 8
35 Dewsbury E 11
38 Dhoon G 2
38 Dhoor F 2
38 Dhowin F 2
9 Dial Post D 12
8 Dibden E 5
8 Dibden Purlieu E 5
27 Dickleburgh G 4
16 Didbrook A 2
16 Didcot E 6
25 Diddington J 3
21 Diddlebury D 10
15 Didley A 7
9 Didling D 10
15 Didmarton F 11
35 Didsbury H 7
5 Didworthy J 5
60 Diebidale Lodge H 5
33 Digby E 8
62 Digg A 4
35 Diggle F 9
34 Digmoor G 4
18 Digswell Water B 3
13 Dihewid A 8
47 Dikeneuk D 11
26 Dilham C 6
31 Dilhorne F 8
48 Dillarburn E 1
25 Dillington J 2
45 Dilston G 8
7 Dilton Marsh A 11
21 Dilwyn G 9
48 Dinanrig H 1
12 Dinas, Dyfed D 6
12 Dinas, Dyfed C 4
28 Dinas, Gwynedd G 3
20 Dinas Mawddwy A 4
14 Dinas Powis G 5
13 Dinasbach C 11
7 Dinder B 9
15 Dinedor A 8
15 Dinedor Cross A 8
15 Dingestow C 7
30 Dingle B 2
49 Dingleton F 8
23 Dingley C 11
56 Dingwall D 1
44 Dinlabyre D 4
44 Dinley C 3
59 Dinnet H 2
43 Dinning C 9
45 Dinnington, Northumb F 10
7 Dinnington, Som. E 7
28 Dinorwic D 5
40 Dinsdale Station D 4
17 Dinton, Bucks C 8
8 Dinton, Wilts C 2
42 Dinvin F 1
43 Dinwoodie Mains C 11
43 Dinwoodiegreen C 11
4 Dinworthy D 2
46 Dippen F 3
9 Dippenhall A 9
46 Dippin G 5
58 Dipple, Grampian B 1
42 Dipple, Strathclyde A 3
5 Diptford K 6
45 Dipton H 9
49 Dirleton A 8
21 Discoed F 8
32 Diseworth H 2
40 Dishforth H 4
31 Disley B 8
27 Diss G 4
20 Disserth G 6
38 Distington C 2
8 Ditchampton C 2
7 Ditcheat C 9
26 Ditchingham F 6
10 Ditchling F 2
15 Ditteridge G 11
5 Dittisham K 7
30 Ditton, Cheshire B 3
10 Ditton, Kent B 6
25 DittonGreen J 8
21 Ditton Priors D 11
57 Divach G 1
13 Divlyn C 11
16 Dixton, Glos A 1
15 Dixton, Gwent C 8
35 Dobcross F 8
3 Dobwalls C 9
5 Doccombe G 6
56 Dochfour House F 2
56 Dochgarroch F 2
26 Docking B 1
21 Docklow G 11
38 Dockray C 6
44 Dodburn B 3
18 Doddinghurst D 6
24 Doddington, Cambs. F 5
11 Doddington, Kent B 8
32 Doddington, Lincs. C 6
49 Doddington, Northumb F 12
21 Doddington, Salop. E 11
6 Doddiscombsleigh H 2
22 Dodford, Heref. and Worc E 3
23 Dodford, Northants. F 9
15 Dodington, Avon F 10
6 Dodington, Som B 5
30 Dodleston D 2
35 Dodworth G 11
32 Doe Lea D 2
6 DogVillage G 3
33 Dogdyke E 9
9 Dogmersfield A 9
20 Dolanog A 6
14 Dolau, Mid. Glam F 3
21 Dolau, Powys F 7
28 Dolbenmaen F 4
20 Dolfach E 5
20 Dol-ffanog A 3
20 Dol-for, Powys B4
20 Dol-for, Powys D 6
29 Dolgarrog C 7
28 Dolgellau H 6
13 Dolgerdd B 7
21 Dol-goch B 2
13 Dol-gran D 8
21 Dolhelfa E 5
61 Doll F 8
52 Dollar G 4
52 Dollarbeg G 4
21 Dolley Green F 8
21 Dolleycanney G 7
34 Dolphinholme B 4
48 Dolphinton E 4
4 Dolton E 4
29 Dolwen, Clwyd C 8
20 Dolwen, Powys B 5
29 Dolwyd B 7
29 Dolwyddelan E 7
20 Dol-y-bont D 2
20 Dolypandy D 2
36 Doncaster G 4
8 Donhead St. Andrew D 1
7 Donhead St. Mary D 12
52 Donibristle H 6
6 Doniford B 4
24 Donington, Lincs B 3
22 Donington, Salop B 2
33 Donington on Bain B 9
24 Donington South Ing B 3
22 Donisthorpe A 6
17 Donkey Town H 10
44 Donkleywood D 6
16 Donnington, Berks. G 6
16 Donnington, Glos A 3
15 Donnington, Heref. and Worc. A 10
21 Donnington, Salop. B 11
21 Donnington, Salop. A 12
9 Donnington, W. Sussex F 10
21 Donnington Wood A 12
7 Donyatt E 7
47 Doonbank H 9
47 Doonfoot G 8
47 Doonholm H 8
57 Dorback Lodge H 6
7 Dorchester, Dorset G 10
17 Dorchester, Oxon E 7
22 Dordon B 6
31 Dore B 11
56 Dores F 2
32 Dorket Head E 3

10 Dorking C 1
10 Dormans Land D 3
40 Dormanstown C 6
21 Dormington H 11
17 Dorney F 10
55 Dornie G 3
61 Dornoch G 8
44 Dornock F 1
61 Dorrery B 10
22 Dorridge E 5
33 Dorrington, Lincs E 8
21 Dorrington, Salop. B 10
7 Dorset, County F 10
22 Dorsington G 5
21 Dorstone H 8
17 Dorton C 7
55 Dorusduain G 3
54 Dosmuckeran D 6
22 Dosthill B 6
7 Dottery B 6
3 Doublebois C 9
15 Doughton E 12
38 Douglas, I.o.M. H 2
48 Douglas, Strathclyde F 1
53 Douglas & Angus D 9
28 Douglas Hill D 5
48 Douglas Water F 2
48 Douglas West F 1
53 Douglastown B 9
46 Dougrie F 4
7 Doulting B 10
64 Dounby C 1
52 Doune, Central G 2
55 Doune, Highland J 1
42 Dounepark B 3
59 Douneside G 2
60 Dounie G 6
58 Dounie Park B 4
47 Doura F 9
5 Dousland J 4
31 Dove Holes B 9
38 Dovenby B 3
11 Dover D 12
27 Dovercourt M 6
22 Doverdale F 2
31 Doveridge G 9
52 Dowally B 5
34 Dowbridge D 3
16 Dowdeswell B 1
42 Dowhill A 3
14 Dowlais D 4
4 Dowland E 4
16 Down Ampney D 2
15 Down Hatherley B 11
4 Down St. Mary E 6
5 Down Thomas L 4
56 Downan, Grampian F 7
42 Downan, Strathclyde C 2
3 Downderry D 10
18 Downe H 4
15 Downend, Avon G 9
16 Downend, Berks G 6
9 Downend, I.o.W. G 7
53 Downfield D 8
3 Downgate B 10
25 Downham, Cambs. G 6
19 Downham, Essex D 7
34 Downham, Lancs C 6
49 Downham, Northumb. F 11
24 Downham Market E 7
7 Downhead, Som D 9
7 Downhead, Som B 10
52 Downhill D 6
34 Downholland Cross F 2
40 Downholme E 1
59 Downies H 7
17 Downley E 9
7 Downside, Som A 10
7 Downside, Som B 9
15 Downside, Avon H 8
17 Downside, Surrey H 12
8 Downton, Hants G 4
8 Downton, Wilts D 3
21 Donton on the Rock E 9
24 Dowsby C 2
45 Doxford A 10
15 Doynton G 10
14 Draethen F 5
48 Draffan E 1
9 Dragons Green D 12
5 Drakeland Corner K 4
47 Drakemyre D 8
22 Drake's Broughton G 4
22 Drakes Cross D 4
3 Drakewalls C 11
42 Dranigower E 3
23 Draughton, Northants D 11
35 Draughton, N.Yorks. B 9
36 Drax D 5
16 Draycot Foliat F 3
23 Draycote E 8
32 Draycott, Derby G 2
16 Draycott, Glos A 3
7 Draycott, Som A 8
31 Draycott in the Clay G 10
31 Draycott in the Moors F 8
4 Drayford E 6
9 Drayton, Hants E 8
23 Drayton, Leics C 11
24 Drayton, Lincs B 4
26 Drayton, Norfolk D 5
16 Drayton, Oxon E 6
23 Drayton, Oxon H 8
22 Drayton, Salop E 3
7 Drayton, Som D 7
22 Drayton Bassett B 5
17 Drayton Beauchamp C 10
17 Drayton Parslow A 9
17 Drayton St. Leonard D 7
35 Drebley A 9
12 Dreenhill F 3
13 Dre-fach, Dyfed B 8
13 Drefach, Dyfed C 7
13 Drefach, Dyfed F 8
47 Dreghorn F 8
11 Drellingore N 11
49 Drem A 8
5 Drewsteignton G 6
33 Driby C 11
16 Driffield, Glos D 2
37 Driffield, Humber. A 8
38 Drigg E 3
35 Drighlington D 11
51 Drimfern F 8
58 Drimmies E 5
50 Drimnin B 3
50 Drimnin House B 3
7 Drimpton F 7
55 Drimsallie L 3
51 Drimsynie G 9
27 Drinkstone J 3
27 Drinkstone Green J 3
51 Drishaig F 8
48 Drochil E 4
31 Drointon G 9
22 Droitwich F 2
52 Dron F 6
32 Dronfield B 1
31 Dronfield Woodhouse B 11
47 Drongan G 9
53 Dronley D 8
14 Drope G 4
9 Droxford D 7
29 Druid F 9
55 Druidhall B 9
59 Druidsdale J 6
12 Druidston E 2
46 Druim A 2
55 Druimarbin M 5
51 Druimavuic C 7
54 Druimdhu D 5
46 Druimdrishaig B 2
54 Druimindarroch F 8
46 Druimyeon More D 2
58 Drum, Grampian C 6
56 Drum, Highland D 2
46 Drum, Strathclyde B 4
52 Drum, Tayside G 5
60 Drumbeg D 3
58 Drumblade D 3
58 Drumblair House C 4
42 Drumbreddan G 2
42 Drumbuie, Dumf. & Gall. C 6
55 Drumbuie, Highland G 2
44 Drumburgh G 1
43 Drumburn E 10
47 Drumchapel B 10
56 Drumchardine E 1
47 Drumclog E 11
43 Drumcoltran E 9
56 Drumcroy F 1
43 Drumcruilton A 9
58 Drumdaig F 3
56 Drumdyre D 2
59 Drumeldrie G 9
48 Drumelzier F 4
62 Drumfearn G 6
47 Drumfork G 10
57 Drumgask K 2
53 Drumgley B 9
56 Drumguish, Highland F 6
57 Drumguish, Highland J 4
59 Drumhead, Grampian H 4
58 Drumhead, Grampian F 7
42 Drumjohn B 6
43 Drumlanrig Castle B 9
59 Drumlasie G 4
46 Drumlemble G 2
58 Drumligair F 6
59 Drumlithie J 5
42 Drummoddie G 5
56 Drummond C 2
42 Drummore H 2
57 Drumnadrochit G 1
59 Drumnagair K 4
58 Drumnagorrach B 3
58 Drumnahoy F 4
42 Drumpail E 3
43 Drumpark D 9
42 Drumrae G 5
43 Drumrash D 7
60 Drumrunie Lodge F 3
58 Drums E 7
47 Drumshang H 7
43 Drumstinchall F 9
59 Drumtochty Castle J 4
62 Drumuie D 4
57 Drumuillie G 5
52 Drumvaich G 2
42 Drumwalt F 4
58 Drumwhindle D 7
43 Drumwhirn D 8
29 Drury D 12
32 Dry Doddington F 6
25 Dry Drayton J 5
19 Dry Street E 7
39 Drybeck D 9
58 Drybridge Grampian A 2
47 Drybridge Strathclyde F 8
15 Drybrook C 9
49 Dryburgh F 8
43 Dryfesdale Gate C 11
48 Dryhope G 5
47 Drymen A 9
58 Drymuir C 6
62 Drynoch E 3
60 Duag Bridge G 4
58 Dubford, Grampian C 5
58 Dubford, Grampian A 5
58 Dubiton C 4
60 Duchally E 5
43 Duchrae C 7
8 Duck Street A 5
30 Duckington E 4
16 Ducklington C 4
32 Duckmanton C 2
25 Duck's Cross K 2
25 Duddenhoe End L 6
48 Duddingston B 6
24 Duddington E 1
10 Duddleswell E 3
49 Duddo E 12
38 Duddon D 4
38 Duddon Bridge F 4
30 Dudleston F 2
30 Dudleston Heath F 2
45 Dudley, Northants. F 10
22 Dudley, W.Midlands C 3
12 Dudwells E 3
31 Duffield F 11
14 Duffryn E 2
58 Dufftown D 1
56 Duffus C 7
39 Dufton C 9
41 Duggleby H 9
62 Duisdalemore G 6
55 Duisky M 4
14 Dukestown C 5
35 Dukinfield G 8
56 Dularich F 1
26 Dulas A 4
58 Dulax F 1
7 Dulcote B 9
6 Dulford F 4
52 Dull B 3
47 Dullatur B 12
25 Dullingham J 7
57 Dulnain Bridge G 5
25 Duloe, Beds. J 3
3 Duloe, Cornwall D 9
56 Dulsie E 5
6 Dulverton C 3
18 Dulwich G 3
47 Dumbarton B 9
16 Dumbleton A 1
43 Dumcrieff A 11
58 Dumeath D 2
43 Dumfries D 10
47 Dumgoyne A 10
9 Dummer B 7
59 Dun L 4
63 Dun Carloway C 3
57 Dunachtonmore J 4
56 Dunain House E 2
52 Dunalastair A 2
46 Dunan, Strathclyde B 6
52 Dunan, Tayside D 2
51 Dunan, Tayside B 11
62 Dunan, Skye E 5
51 Dunans H 7
49 Dunbar B 9
61 Dunbeath D 11
52 Dunblane G 3
53 Dunbog E 7
6 Dunboll B 6
8 Dunbridge C 5
61 Duncansby Head A 12
58 Duncanston, Grampian E 3
56 Duncanston, Highland D 2
6 Dunchideock G 2
23 Dunchurch E 8
23 Duncote G 10
43 Duncow C 10
51 Duncraggan G 12
54 Duncraig Castle F 2
52 Duncrievie F 6
9 Duncton D 11
53 Dundee D 9
7 Dundon C 8
53 Dundonald, Fife H 7
47 Dundonald, Strathclyde F 8
60 Dundonnell Hotel H 2
60 Dundonnell House H 3
43 Dundraw G 12
55 Dundreggan H 7
43 Dundrennan G 8
15 Dundry H 8
52 Dunduff H 6
59 Dunecht G 5
48 Dunfermline A 4
35 Dunford Bridge G 10
7 Dunge A 12
32 Dunham C 5
30 Dunham Town B 6
30 Dunham-on-the-Hill C 3
22 Dunhampton E 2
33 Dunholme B 7
52 Dunie D 4
53 Dunino F 10
48 Dunipace A 1
52 Dunira E 2
52 Dunkeld C 5
15 Dunkerton H 10
6 Dunkeswell E 5
11 Dunkirk B 9
10 Dunk's Green C 5
59 Dunlappie K 3
22 Dunley E 1
56 Dunlichity Lodge F 2
47 Dunlop D 9
57 Dunmaglass Lodge G 2
3 Dunmere C 7
52 Dunmore, Central H 4
46 Dunmore, Strathclyde C 3
11 Dunn Street B 7
61 Dunnet A 11
53 Dunnichen B 10
53 Dunninald B 11
52 Dunning F 5
37 Dunnington, Humberside B 9
36 Dunnington, N. Yorks. B 4
22 Dunnington, War G 4
35 Dunnockshaw D 7
59 Dunnottar Mains J 6
58 Dunnydeer E 4
50 Dunollie D 6
46 Dunoon B 6
53 Dunotter G 9
42 Dunragit F 2
46 Dunrostan A 2
49 Duns D 10
16 Duns Tew A 5
24 Dunsby C 2
43 Dunscore C 9
36 Dunscroft F 4
40 Dunsdale C 6
17 Dunsden Green F 8
9 Dunsfold B 11
5 Dunsford G 7
53 Dunshelt F 7
58 Dunshillock C 7
41 Dunsley D 8
17 Dunsmore D 9
34 Dunsop Bridge B 5
17 Dunstable B 11
50 Dunstaffnage Fm D 6
31 Dunstall H 10
6 Dunster B 3
33 Dunston, Lincs D 8
26 Dunston, Norfolk E 5
45 Dunston, Northumb. A 10
31 Dunston, Staffs H 8
45 Dunston, Tyne & Wear G 10
5 Dunstone H 6
36 Dunsville F 4
37 Dunswell D 8
48 Dunsyre E 3
44 Dunterley E 6
5 Dunterton H 2
16 Duntisbourne Abbots C 1
16 Duntisbourne Rouse D 1
7 Duntish F 10
47 Duntocher B 9
25 Dunton, Beds L 3
17 Dunton, Bucks B 9
26 Dunton, Norfolk C 2
23 Dunton Bassett C 9
10 Dunton Green B 4
18 Dunton Wayletts E 6
62 Duntulm A 3
47 Dunure H 7
47 Dunure Mains H 7
13 Dunvant H 9
62 Dunvegan C 2
27 Dunwich H 8
52 Dupplin Castle E 5
44 Durdar H 2
40 Durham A 3
43 Durisdeer A 10
43 Durisdeermill A 9
6 Durleigh C 6
16 Durley, Wilts H 3
8 Durley, Hants D 6
9 Durley Street D 7
60 Durnamuck G 2
60 Durness A 5
58 Durno E 5
9 Durrington, W.Sussex F 12
8 Durrington, Wilts. B 3
15 Dursley D 10
6 Durston C 6
7 Durweston E 11
64 Dury D 7
23 Duston F 10
57 Duthil G 5
21 Dutlas E 7
18 Duton Hill A 6
3 Dutson A 10
30 Dutton B 4
25 Duxford L 6
28 Dwygyfylchi C 7
26 Dwyran D 4
58 Dyce F 6
45 Dye House G 7
13 Dyfatty G 8
12 Dyfed, Co D 6
12 Dyffryn, Dyfed E 6
12 Dyffryn, Dyfed C 3
14 Dyffryn, Mid. Glam. F 4
14 Dyffryn, S. Glam G 4
14 Dyffryn, W. Glam E 2
28 Dyffryn-Ardudwy H 5
14 Dyffryn Cellwen C 2
20 Dyffryn-castell D 3
4 Dyke, Devon D 2
24 Dyke, Lincs C 2
56 Dyke, Grampian D 5
49 Dykegatehead D 11
52 Dykehead, Central G 1
48 Dykehead, Strathclyde C 2
59 Dykehead, Tayside L 1
59 Dykelands K 5
53 Dykends A 7
58 Dykeside C 5
50 Dylife C 4
11 Dymchurch E 9
15 Dymock A 10
15 Dyrham G 10
53 Dysart H 8
29 Dyserth B 10
35 Eachwick F 9
45 Eagland Hill C 3
32 Eagle D 6
40 Eaglescliffe Junc D 4
38 Eaglesfield, Cumb B 3
44 Eaglesfield, Dumf. & Gall. F 1
47 Eaglesham D 10
24 Eaglethorpe F 2
38 Eairy H 1
23 Eakley Lanes G 11
32 Eakring D 4
36 Ealand F 6
18 Ealing F 2
39 Eamont Bridge B 7
35 Earby C 8
34 Earcroft E 6
21 Eardington C 12
21 Eardisland F 9
21 Eardisley G 8
21 Eardiston, Heref. & Worc. F 12
30 Eardiston, Salop H 2
25 Earith H 5
23 Earl Shilton B 8
27 Earl Soham J 5
31 Earl Sterndale C 9
27 Earl Stonham J 4
49 Earle G 12
17 Earley G 8
26 Earlham E 5
62 Earlish B 3
23 Earls Barton F 12
19 Earls Colne A 8
22 Earl's Croome H 2
27 Earl's Green J 3
22 Earlsdon D 6
53 Earlsferry G 9
58 Earlsford D 6
49 Earlston, Borders F 8
47 Earlston, Strathclyde F 9
22 Earlswood E 5
15 Earlswood Com. E 8
9 Earnley F 9
47 Earnockmuir D 11
45 Earsdon, Northumb. D 10
45 Earsdon, Tyne & Wear F 11
26 Earsham F 6
36 Earswick A 4
9 Eartham E 10
38 Earystane H 1
40 Easby, N. Yorks. D 6
40 Easby, N. Yorks. E 2
50 Easdale F 5
9 Easebourne D 10
23 Easenhall D 8
9 Eashing B 11
17 Easington, Bucks. C 8
41 Easington, Cleveland C 7
40 Easington, Dur. A 4
37 Easington, Humberside E 11
45 Easington, Northumb. C 12
17 Easington, Oxon. D 7
40 Easington Colliery A 4
45 Easington Grange B 12
45 Easington Lane H 12
40 Easingwold H 5
11 Easole Street C 11
53 Eassie & Nevay C 8
14 East Aberthaw H 4
16 East Adderbury A 6
5 East Allington L 6
45 East Ancroft A 11
4 East Anstey C 7
9 East Ashling E 9
58 East Auchronie F 6
41 East Ayton G 10
14 East Bank D 5
33 East Barkwith B 9
10 East Barming C 6
41 East Barnby D 8
18 East Barnet D 3
49 East Barns B 9
26 East Barsham B 2
26 East Beckham B 5
18 East Bedfont F 1
27 East Bergholt M 4
26 East Bilney D 3
49 East Blanerne D 11
10 East Blatchington H 4
7 East Bloxworth G 12
45 East Boldon G 11
8 East Boldre F 5
45 East Bolton A 9
47 East Brackenridge E 11
26 East Bradenham E 2
7 East Brent A 7
27 East Bridge J 7
32 East Bridgford F 4
45 East Brunton F 10
4 East Buckland C 5
6 East Budleigh H 4
64 East Burra E 7
64 East Burrafirth D 7
7 East Burton G 11
40 East Butsfield A 1
36 East Butterwick G 6
59 East Cairnbeg K 5
48 East Calder C 4
26 East Carleton E 5
23 East Carlton C 11
16 East Challow E 5
7 East Chelborough F 9

10 East Chiltington ....G 3
7 East Chinnock ......E 8
8 East Chisenbury ....A 3
9 East Clandon .....A 12
17 East Claydon ....B 8
15 East Clevedon ......G 7
7 East Coker ....E 9
6 East Combe ....C 5
7 East Compton ......B 9
36 East Cottingwith ....C 5
8 East Cowes ....F 6
36 East Cowick ....E 4
40 East Cowton ....E 3
45 East Cramlington ..E 11
7 East Cranmore ....B 10
8 East Creech ....H 1
57 East Croachy ....G 2
46 East Darlochan .....G 2
8 East Dean, Hants ...C 4
9 East Dean, W. Sussex E 10
26 East Dereham ......D 3
45 East Ditchburn .....A 9
4 East Down ....B 5
32 East Drayton ....C 5
15 East Dundry ....H 9
45 East Edington ......E 10
15 East End, Avon ....G 8
8 East End, Dorset....F 2
16 East End, Hants. ...H 5
9 East End, Hants. ....D 8
8 East End, Hants. ....F 5
18 East End, Herts ....A 4
37 East End, Humber. D 10
11 East End, Kent .....E 7
26 East End, Norfolk ..D 8
16 East End, Oxon .....C 5
8 East Erlestoke ......A 1
10 East Farleigh ....C 6
23 East Farndon .....D 10
6 East Ferry ....G 6
45 East Fleetham ....D 12
53 East Flisk ....E 8
49 East Fortune ....A 8
36 East Garforth ......D 2
16 East Garston ....F 5
16 East Ginge ....E 5
49 East Gordon ....E 9
16 East Grafton ....H 4
8 East Grimstead .....C 4
10 East Grinstead .....D 3
11 East Guldeford .....F 8
23 East Haddon ......E 10
16 East Hagbourne ....E 6
37 East Halton ....E 9
37 East Halton Skitter .E 9
18 East Ham ....F 4
16 East Hanney ....E 5
19 East Hanningfield ..D 7
36 East Hardwick ......E 2
27 East Harling ....G 3
40 East Harlsey ....E 4
8 East Harnham ......C 3
7 East Harptree ......A 9
45 East Hartford .....E 11
9 East Harting ....D 9
7 East Hatch ....C 12
25 East Hatley ....K 4
52 East Haugh ....B 4
40 East Hauxwell ....F 2
53 East Haven ....D 10
24 East Heckington ....A 3
40 East Hedleyhope ...A 2
16 East Hendred ....E 5
41 East Heslerton .....G 9
10 East Hoathly ....F 4
7 East Horrington ....B 9
9 East Horsley ......A 12
45 East Horton ....C 11
7 East Huntspill ......B 7
17 East Hyde ....B 12
4 East Ilkerton ....A 6
16 East Ilsley ....F 6
33 East Keal ....D 11
16 East Kennett ....G 2
35 East Keswick ......C 12
47 East Kilbride ......D 11
58 East Kinharrachie ..D 7
33 East Kirby ....D 10
41 East Knapton ....G 9
7 East Knighton ....H 11
4 East Knowstone ....D 7
7 East Knoyle ....C 12
7 East Lambrook .....D 7
11 East Langdon .....C 12
23 East Langton .....C 10
61 East Langwell ....F 7
9 East Lavant ....E 10
40 East Layton ....D 2
32 East Leake ....H 3
4 East Leigh ....E 6
49 East Learmouth ....F 11
26 East Lexham ....D 2
45 East Lilburn ....A 8
49 East Linton ....B 8
9 East Liss ....C 9
47 East Lockhead .....D 8
3 East Looe ....D 9
36 East Lound ....G 6
9 East Lovington E10
7 East Lulworth ....H 12
41 East Lutton ....H 9
7 East Lydford ......C 9
59 East Mains ....H 4
10 East Malling ....B 6
9 East Marden ....E 9
32 East Markham ......C 5
35 East Marton ....B 8
9 East Meon ....D 8
6 East Mere ....E 3
19 East Mersea ......C 10
17 East Molesey .....G 12
7 East Mordon ......G 12
43 East Morton, Dumf. & Gall. ....B 9
35 East Morton, W. Yorks. ....C 9
42 East Muntloch .....H 2
41 East Ness ....G 7
23 East Norton ....B 11
6 East Nynehead .....D 5
9 East Oakley ....A 7
5 East Ogwell ....J 7
7 East Orchard .....D 11
49 East Ord ....D 12
5 East Panson ....G 2
10 East Peckham ......C 5
12 East Pennar ....G 3
7 East Pennard ....C 9
52 East Plean ....H 3
26 East Poringland .....E 6
5 East Portlemouth ...M 6
5 East Prawle ....M 6
9 East Preston ....F 12
6 East Quantoxhead ..B 5
45 East Rainton .....H 11
37 East Ravendale ...G 10
26 East Raynham ......C 2
32 East Retford ....B 4
35 East Rigton ....C 12
40 East Rounton ......E 4
26 East Rudham ....C 1
26 East Runton ....A 5
26 East Ruston ....C 6
49 East Saltoun ....C 7
44 East Scales ....F 1
16 East Shefford ....G 5
45 East Sleekburn ....E 11
26 East Somerton .....D 8
36 East Stockwith .....H 6
7 East Stoke, Dorset H 12
32 East Stoke, Notts....E 5
7 East Stour ....D 11
11 East Stourmouth ..B 11
4 East Stowford ......C 5
8 East Stratton ....B 7
11 East Studdal ......C 11
10 East Sussex, Co .....F 5
3 East Taphouse ......C 9
19 East Tilbury ....F 7
43 East Tinwald ......C 11
9 East Tistead ....C 8
33 East Torrington .....B 8
59 East Town ....J 5
26 East Tuddenham ....D 4
8 East Tytherley ......C 4
16 East Tytherton .....G 1
4 East Village ....E 7
24 East Walton ....D 8
24 East Warlington ....E 6
5 East Week ....G 5
8 East Wellow ....D 5
53 East Wemyss ....G 8
48 East Whitburn ......C 2
19 East Wick ....D 10
12 East Williamston ....F 4
24 East Winch ....D 8
9 East Wittering ......F 9
40 East Witton ....G 2
45 East Woodburn ....D 7
16 East Woodhay .....H 5
9 East Worldham .....B 9
26 East Wretham ......F 2
4 East Youlstone .....D 1
10 Eastbourne ....H 5
37 Eastburn ....B 7
18 Eastbury, Herts .....E 1
16 Eastbury, Berks .....F 4
11 Eastchurch ....A 8
15 Eastcombe ....D 12
18 Eastcote, London ...E 1
23 Eastcote, Northants G 10
22 Eastcote, W. Midlands D 5
4 Eastcott, Devon ....D 1
8 Eastcott, Wilts .....A 2
16 Eastcourt, Wilts. ....H 3
16 Eastcourt, Wilts. ....E 1
10 Eastdean ....H 4
19 Eastend ....E 9
56 Easter Ardross .....B 2
58 Easter Aucharnie ...D 4
57 Easter Aviemore ....H 4
56 Easter Balcroy .....E 4
57 Easter Balmoral ....K 8
57 Easter Boleskine ...G 1
56 Easter Brae ....C 2
15 Easter Compton ....F 9
54 Easter Crochail .....F 8
56 Easter Culbo ....D 2
59 Easter Davoch .....G 2
55 Easter Drummond ..H 8
52 Easter Dullater .....F 1
43 Easter Earshaig ...A 11
61 Easter Fearn ....H 7
44 Easter Fodderlee ...B 4
56 Easter Galcantray ..E 4
22 Easter Green ....D 6
48 Easter Happrew .....E 4
48 Easter Howgate .....C 5
49 Easter Howlaws ...E 10
56 Easter Kinkell ......D 1
49 Easter Langlee ......F 8
53 Easter Lednathie ...A 8
56 Easter Milton ......D 5
56 Easter Moniack .....E 1
56 Easter Muckovie ....E 3
59 Easter Ord ....G 6
64 Easter Quarff ......E 7
58 Easter Silverford ...A 5
64 Easter Skeld ....D 6
54 Easter Slumbay .....F 3
49 Easter Softlaw .....F 10
48 Easter Stanhope ....F 4
59 Easter Tillygarmond H 4
59 Easter Tulloch .....K 5
56 Easterfield ....E 3
9 Eastergate ....F 11
47 Easterhouse, Strathclyde ......C 11
48 Easterhouse, Strathclyde ......D 3
8 Easterton ....A 2
58 Eastertown, Grampian D 1
48 Eastertown, Strathclyde ......F 2
48 Eastertown, Strathclyde ......E 3
48 Eastertown, Strathclyde ......G 1
7 Eastertown, Som. ...A 7
58 Eastertown of Auchleuchries ....D 8
59 Eastfield, Grampian H 1
41 Eastfield, N. Yorks G 10
48 Eastfield, Strathclyde C 2
48 Eastfield, Strathclyde E 2
45 Eastfield Hall .....B 10
49 Eastfield of Lempitlaw F 10
39 Eastgate, Dur. ....A 11
26 Eastgate, Norfolk ...C 4
30 Eastham ....B 2
17 Easthampstead .....G 9
17 Eastheath ....G 9
4 East-the-Water .....C 3
21 Easthope ....C 11
19 Easthorpe, Essex ...B 9
32 Easthorpe, Notts. ...E 4
48 Easthouses ....C 6
4 Eastington, Devon ..E 6
15 Eastington, Glos. ..D 11
16 Eastington, Glos ...C 2
16 Eastleach Martin ...D 3
16 Eastleach Turville ..D 3
4 Eastleigh, Devon ...C 4
8 Eastleigh, Hants ...D 6
11 Eastling ....B 8
45 Eastnook ....D 8
15 Eastnor ....A 10
36 Eastoft ....E 6
9 Eastoke ....F 8
25 Easton, Cambs ......H 2
44 Easton, Cumb. ......G 1
44 Easton, Cumb. ......F 3
5 Easton, Devon ......G 6
7 Easton, Dorset .....H 7
8 Easton, Hants. .....C 6
8 Easton, I.o.W. ......G 5
32 Easton, Leics. ......G 6
26 Easton, Norfolk ....D 4
7 Easton, Somerset ...A 8
27 Easton, Suffolk .....J 6
15 Easton, Wilts. .....G 12
15 Easton Grey ......E 12
15 Easton-in-Gordano G 8
23 Easton Maudit .....F 12
24 Easton-on-the-Hill .E 1
16 Easton Royal ......H 3
24 Eastrea ....F 4
44 Eastriggs ....F 1
36 Eastrington ....D 5
11 Eastry ....C 11
33 Eastville ....E 11
32 Eastwell ....G 5
18 Eastwick ....C 4
19 Eastwood, Essex ....E 8
32 Eastwood, Notts ....F 2
23 Eathorpe ....E 7
30 Eaton, Cheshire ....D 4
31 Eaton, Cheshire ....D 7
32 Eaton, Leics ....B 4
32 Eaton, Leics ....G 5
26 Eaton, Norfolk .....E 5
16 Eaton, Oxon. ......D 5
21 Eaton, Salop ....C 9
21 Eaton, Salop. .....C 10
21 Eaton Bishop .....H 10
17 Eaton Bray ....B 10
21 Eaton Constantine .B 11
17 Eaton Green ......B 10
16 Eaton Hastings .....D 4
25 Eaton Socon ....J 3
30 Eaton upon Tern ...H 5
41 Ebberston ....G 9
8 Ebbesbourne Wake .D 2
14 Ebbw Vale ....C 5
45 Ebchester ....G 9
15 Ebdon ....H 7
6 Ebford ....G 3
15 Ebley ....D 11
22 Ebrington ....H 5
5 Ebsworthy Town ....G 4
16 Ecchinswell ....H 6
49 Ecclaw ....C 10
43 Ecclefechan D12
49 Eccles, Borders ....E 10
10 Eccles, Kent ....B 6
34 Eccles, Manchester .G 6
21 Eccles Green ....H 9
26 Eccles Road ....F 3
49 Eccles Tofts ....E 10
32 Ecclesall ....B 1
35 Ecclesfield ....H 12
59 Ecclesgreig ....L 5
31 Eccleshall ....G 7
35 Eccleshill ....D 10
48 Ecclesmachan ......B 3
30 Eccleston, Ches. ....D 3
34 Eccleston, Lancs. ...E 4
34 Eccleston, Merseyside H 4
34 Eccleston Green ....E 4
35 Eccup ....C 11
59 Echt ....G 5
49 Eckford ....G 9
22 Eckington ....H 3
23 Ecton ....F 11
31 Edale ....B 9
10 Edburton ....G 1
43 Edderside ....G 11
61 Edderton ....H 7
16 Eddington, Berks. ..G 4
11 Eddington, Kent ..A 10
4 Eddistone ....D 1
48 Eddleston ....E 5
47 Eddlewood ....D 12
49 Eden Hall ....F 10
10 Edenbridge ....C 3
35 Edenfield ....E 7
39 Edenhall ....B 8
24 Edenham ....C 2
31 Edensor ....C 11
51 Edentaggart ......H 10
36 Edenthorpe ....F 4
44 Edentown ....G 2
28 Edern ....F 2
7 Edgarley ....C 8
22 Edgbaston ....D 4
17 Edgcott, Bucks. .....B 8
6 Edgcott, Som. ......B 2
21 Edge ....B 9
15 Edge End ....C 9
30 Edge Green, Ches. ..E 3
27 Edge Green, Norf. ..G 3
30 Edge Hill ....A 2
30 Edgebottom ....H 4
26 Edgefield ....B 4
26 Edgefield Green ....B 6
30 Edgemond ....H 6
44 Edgerston ....B 5
44 Edges Green ....F 5
35 Edgeside ....E 7
15 Edgeworth ....D 12
4 Edgeworthy ....E 7
30 Edgmond Marsh ....H 6
21 Edgton ....D 9
18 Edgware ....E 2
34 Edgworth ....E 6
52 Edinample ....E 1
62 Edinbain ....C 3
48 Edinburgh ....B 5
52 Edinchip ....E 1
22 Edingale ....A 6
32 Edingley ....E 4
26 Edingthorpe ....B 6
49 Edington, Borders .D 11
7 Edington, Som. ......B 7
8 Edington, Wilts. ....A 1
7 Edington Burtle ....B 7
7 Edingworth ....A 7
58 Edintore ....C 2
23 Edith Weston .....B 12
6 Edithmead ....A 6
17 Edlesborough .....B 10
45 Edlingham ....B 9
33 Edlington ....C 9
8 Edmondsham ....E 2
45 Edmondsley ......H 10
32 Edmondthorpe .....H 6
64 Edmonstone ....C 3
18 Edmonton ....E 3
45 Edmundbyers ......H 8
49 Ednam ....F 10
51 Edra ....F 11
49 Edrom ....D 11
30 Edstaston ....G 4
22 Edstone ....F 5
21 Edvin Loach ......G 12
32 Edwalton ....G 3
27 Edwardstone ....L 2
13 Edwinsford ....D 9
32 Edwinstowe ....D 3
25 Edworth ....L 3
21 Edwyn Ralph .....G 12
59 Edzell ....K 3
14 Efail Isaf ....F 4
29 Efail-Parcy ....C 11
13 Efail-fâch ....G 11
28 Efailnewydd ....G 3
29 Efail-rhyd ....H 11
12 Efailwen ....D 5
29 Efenechtyd ....E 10
9 Effingham ....A 12
64 Effirth ....D 6
4 Efford ....F 8
11 Egerton, Kent ......C 8
34 Egerton, Manchester F 6
5 Egg Buckland ......K 4
17 Eggington ....B 10
40 Egglescliffe ....D 4
39 Eggleston ....C 12
17 Egham ....G 11
23 Egleton ....A 12
45 Eglingham ....A 9
3 Egloshayle ....C 7
3 Egloskerry ....A 9
14 Eglwys-Brewis .....G 3
29 Eglwysbach ....C 7
20 Eglwysfach ....C 3
12 Eglwyswrw ....C 5
32 Egmanton ....C 4
38 Egremont, Cumb ...D 3
30 Egremont, Merseyside ....A 2
41 Egton ....D 8
41 Egton Bridge ....E 8
17 Egypt ....F 10
19 Eight Ash Green ...A 9
50 Eignaig ....C 5
57 Eil ....H 4
55 Eilanreach ....H 2
49 Eildon ....F 8
60 Eilean Darach ....H 3
56 Eileanach Lodge ....C 1
63 Eishken ....F 4
20 Elan Village ....F 5
15 Elberton ....E 9
5 Elburton ....K 4
52 Elcho ....E 6
16 Elcombe ....F 2
24 Eldernell ....F 4
15 Eldersfield ....A 11
40 Eldon ....B 3
42 Eldrick ....C 4
34 Eldroth ....A 6
35 Eldwick ....C 10
20 Elerch ....D 2
59 Elfhill ....J 5
45 Elford, Northumb. .D 12
22 Elford, Staffs ......A 5
56 Elgin ....C 8
62 Elgol ....G 4
11 Elham ....D 10
53 Elie ....G 9
45 Elilaw ....B 8
8 Eling ....E 5
62 Elishader ....B 4
45 Elishaw ....D 7
32 Elkesley ....C 4
16 Elkstone ....C 1
57 Ellan ....G 5
35 Elland ....E 10
46 Ellary ....B 2
31 Ellastone ....F 9
34 Ellel ....B 4
49 Ellemford ....C 10
31 Ellenhall ....G 7
9 Ellen's Green .....C 12
40 Ellerbeck ....E 4
41 Ellerby ....D 8
30 Ellerdine Heath ....H 5
6 Ellerhayes ....F 3
51 Elleric ....C 7
37 Ellerker ....D 7
36 Ellerton, Humber. ..C 5
40 Ellerton, N. Yorks. ..E 3
30 Ellerton, Salop .....H 6
17 Ellesborough ....C 9
30 Ellesmere ....G 2
30 Ellesmere Port .....C 3
8 Ellingham, Hants ...E 3
26 Ellingham, Norf. ....F 6
45 Ellingham, Northumb. E 12
40 Ellingstring ....G 2
25 Ellington, Cambs. ...H 3
45 Ellington, Northumb. D 11
9 Ellisfield ....B 8
23 Ellistown ....A 8
58 Ellon ....D 7
38 Ellonby ....B 6
37 Elloughton ....D 7
15 Ellwood ....C 9
24 Elm ....E 6
18 Elm Park ....E 5
22 Elmbridge ....E 2
25 Elmdon, Essex ......L 6
22 Elmdon, W. Midlands ......D 5
22 Elmdon Heath .....D 5
18 Elmers End ....G 4
23 Elmesthorpe ....C 8
9 Elmfield ....G 7
22 Elmhurst ....A 5
22 Elmley Castle ......H 3
22 Elmley Lovett ......E 2
15 Elmore ....C 11
15 Elmore Back ......C 10
4 Elmscott ....D 1
27 Elmsett ....K 3
19 Elmstead Market ..B 10
11 Elmstone ....B 11
15 Elmstone Hardwicke B 12
37 Elmswell, Humber. .A 7
27 Elmswell, Suffolk ...J 3
32 Elmton ....C 2
60 Elphin ....F 3
48 Elphinstone ....B 6
59 Elrick ....G 6
42 Elrig ....G 4
51 Elrigbeag ....F 8
45 Elsdon ....D 7
35 Elsecar ....G 12
18 Elsenham ....A 5
16 Elsfield ....C 6
37 Elsham ....F 8
26 Elsing ....D 4
35 Elslack ....B 8
30 Elson ....G 2
48 Elsrickle ....E 3
9 Elstead ....B 10
9 Elsted ....D 9
32 Elston, Notts. ......E 5
8 Elston, Wilts ....B 2
4 Elstone ....D 5
37 Elstonwick ....D 10
25 Elstow ....K 2
18 Elstree ....D 2
34 Elswick ....C 3
25 Elsworth ....J 4
38 Elterwater ....E 5
18 Eltham ....F 4
25 Eltisley ....J 4
24 Elton, Cambs. ......F 2
30 Elton, Cheshire .....C 3
40 Elton, Cleveland ....C 4
31 Elton, Derby ......D 10
15 Elton, Glos. ....C 10
21 Elton, Heref. & Worc. ....E 10
32 Elton, Notts. ....F 5
48 Elvanfoot ....H 2
31 Elvaston ....G 12
27 Elveden ....G 1
11 Elvington, Kent ...C 11
36 Elvington, N. Yorks B 5
49 Elwartlaw ....E 10
40 Elwick, Cleveland ..B 5
45 Elwick, Northumb. B 12

30 Elworth D 6
6 Elworthy C 4
25 Ely, Cambs. G 6
14 Ely, S. Glam. G 5
23 Emberton G 12
44 Emblehope D 6
38 Embleton, Cumb B 4
40 Embleton, Dur B 4
45 Embleton, Northumb. A 10
61 Embo G 8
35 Embsay B 8
8 Emery Down E 4
35 Emley F 11
35 Emley Moor F 11
17 Emmbrook G 8
17 Emmington D 8
24 Emneth E 6
24 Emneth Hungate E 6
23 Empingham A 12
9 Empshott C 9
9 Emsworth E 9
63 Enaclete D 2
16 Enborne G 5
16 Enborne Row H 5
21 Enchmarsh C 10
7 Encombe H 12
23 Enderby B 8
39 Endmoor G 7
31 Endon E 7
31 Endon Bank E 8
18 Enfield D 3
8 Enford A 3
15 Engine Common F 10
17 Englefield G 7
17 Englefield Green G 10
15 English Bicknor C 9
30 English Frankton G 3
15 Englishcombe H 10
8 Enham Alamein A 5
6 Enmore C 6
38 Ennerdale Bridge D 3
43 Enoch B 9
52 Enochdu A 5
50 Ensay C 1
8 Ensbury F 2
21 Ensdon A 9
4 Ensis C 4
16 Enstone B 5
43 Enterkinfoot A 9
40 Enterpen E 5
22 Enville C 2
50 Eorabus E 1
63 Eoropie A 6
15 Epney C 11
32 Epperstone E 4
18 Epping D 4
18 Epping Green C 3
18 Epping Green C 4
18 Epping Upland C 4
40 Eppleby D 2
10 Epsom B 1
23 Epwell H 7
36 Epworth G 5
29 Erbistock F 12
55 Erbusaig G 1
54 Erchless Castle E 8
22 Erdington C 5
51 Eredine G 7
60 Eriboll B 5
48 Ericstane H 3
10 Eridge Green E 4
46 Erines B 4
25 Eriswell G 8
18 Erith F 5
33 Ermine C 7
5 Ermington K 5
26 Erpingham B 5
55 Errocht L 5
57 Errogie G 1
53 Errol E 7
42 Ervie E 1
27 Erwarton M 5
20 Erwood H 6
40 Eryholme D 3
29 Eryrys D 11
46 Escart C 3
40 Escomb B 2
36 Escrick C 4
13 Esgair D 7
20 Esgairgeiliog B 3
13 Esgerdawe C 9
40 Esh A 2
40 Esh Winning A 2
17 Esher H 12
45 Eshott C 10
35 Eshton B 8
54 Eskadale F 8
48 Eskbank C 6
38 Eskdale Green E 4
44 Eskdalemuir C 1
37 Eskham G 11
34 Esprick D 3
24 Essendine D 1
18 Essendon C 3
19 Essex, Co C 7
56 Essich F 2
22 Essington B 3
40 Eston C 6
49 Etal E 11
16 Etchilhampton H 2
10 Etchingham E 6
11 Etchinghill, Kent D 10
31 Etchinghill, Staffs H 8
17 Eton F 10
17 Eton Wick F 10
57 Etteridge K 3
22 Ettington G 6
24 Etton, Cambs. E 2
37 Etton, Humberside C 7
48 Ettrick H 5
48 Ettrickbridge End G 6
31 Etwall G 11
27 Euston G 2
24 Euximoor Drove F 6
34 Euxton E 4
14 Evanstown E 3
56 Evanton C 2
33 Evedon E 8
61 Evelix G 7
21 Evenjobb F 8
17 Evenley A 7
16 Evenlode A 3
40 Evenwood C 2
40 Evenwood Gate C 2
64 Everbay C 4
7 Evercreech B 9
23 Everdon F 9
36 Everingham C 6
8 Everleigh A 3
41 Everley F 10
25 Evershot M 1
7 Evershot F 9
17 Eversley H 8
17 Eversley Cross H 9
37 Everthorpe D 7
25 Everton, Beds K 3
8 Everton, Hants G 4
30 Everton, Merseyside A 2
32 Everton, Notts A 4
44 Evertown E 2
21 Evesbatch H 12
22 Evesham H 4
23 Evington B 10
35 Ewden Village G 11
10 Ewell B 1
11 Ewell Minnis D 11
17 Ewelme E 7
16 Ewen D 1
14 Ewenny G 2
33 Ewerby E 8
44 Eweslees C 2
11 Ewhurst, E.Sussex F 7
9 Ewhurst, Surrey B 12
9 Ewhurst Green B 12
29 Ewloe D 12
4 Eworthy F 3
9 Ewshot A 9
15 Ewyas Harold B 7
4 Exbourne F 5
8 Exbury F 6
6 Exebridge D 3
40 Exelby F 3
6 Exeter G 3
6 Exford B 2
22 Exhall G 4
17 Exlade Street F 7
6 Exminster G 3
6 Exmouth H 4
64 Exnaboe F 7
25 Exning J 7
6 Exton, Devon H 3
9 Exton, Hants D 7
23 Exton, Leics. A 12
6 Exton, Somerset C 3
6 Exwick G 3
31 Eyam C 10
23 Eydon G 9
24 Eye, Cambs. E 3
21 Eye, Heref. & Worc. F 10
27 Eye, Suffolk H 4
49 Eyemouth C 12
25 Eyeworth L 4
11 Eyhorne Street C 7
27 Eyke K 6
25 Eynesbury J 3
10 Eynsford B 4
16 Eynsham C 5
7 Eype G 8
62 Eyre C 3
11 Eythorne C 11
29 Eyton, Clwyd F 12
21 Eyton, Heref. & Worc. F 10
21 Eyton, Salop D 9
30 Eyton, Salop H 3
21 Eyton upon the Weald Moors A 12
16 Faccombe H 5
40 Faceby E 5
28 Fachwen D 5
35 Facit E 7
30 Faddiley E 4
55 Faddoch G 3
41 Fadmoor F 7
31 Fagginton G 11
13 Fagwyr G 10
47 Fail F 9
15 Failand G 8
47 Failford G 9
35 Failsworth G 8
54 Fain B 5
6 Fair Oak, Devon D 4
8 Fair Oak, Hants. D 6
17 Fair Oak Green H 7
20 Fairbourne A 2
36 Fairburn D 2
22 Fairfield, Heref. & Worc. H 4
22 Fairfield, Heref. & Worc. E 3
16 Fairford D 3
43 Fairgirth F 9
47 Fairlie D 7
11 Fairlight G 7
11 Fairlight Cove G 7
6 Fairmile F 4
48 Fairmilehead C 5
49 Fairnilee F 7
30 Fairoak G 6
10 Fairseat B 5
19 Fairstead, Essex B 7
26 Fairstead, Norfolk C 6
10 Fairwarp E 3
4 Fairy Cross D 3
26 Fakenham C 2
49 Fala C 7
49 Falahill D 6
41 Falcon Inn E 10
33 Faldingworth B 8
15 Falfield E 10
27 Falkenham L 6
48 Falkirk A 2
53 Falkland F 7
44 Falla B 5
32 Fallgate D 1
52 Fallin H 3
45 Fallowfield F 7
49 Fallsidehill E 9
10 Falmer G 2
2 Falmouth F 5
44 Falnash B 2
41 Falsgrave F 10
44 Falstone D 5
60 Fanagmore C 3
40 Fangdale Beck F 6
36 Fangfoss B 5
50 Fanmore C 2
54 Fannich Lodge C 6
49 Fans E 9
17 Far Bletchley A 9
23 Far Cotton F 11
38 Far Sawrey F 6
24 Farcet F 3
21 Farden E 11
9 Fareham F 7
22 Farewell A 4
33 Farforth B 10
44 Farglow F 5
16 Faringdon E 4
34 Farington E 4
44 Farlam G 4
15 Farleigh, Avon G 8
10 Farleigh, Surrey B 3
7 Farleigh Hungerford A 11
9 Farleigh Wallop A 8
15 Farleigh Wick H 11
33 Farlesthorpe C 11
39 Farleton G 8
15 Farley, Avon G 7
31 Farley, Cheshire F 9
21 Farley, Salop B 9
8 Farley, Wiltshire C 4
9 Farley Green B 12
17 Farley Hill H 8
15 Farleys End C 11
40 Farlington H 6
21 Farlow D 11
29 Farm Yard D 7
15 Farmborough H 10
16 Farmcote A 2
13 Farmers C 10
43 Farmersfield C 9
16 Farmington C 2
16 Farmoor C 5
58 Farmtown C 3
16 Farnborough, Berks. F 5
9 Farnborough, Hants. A 10
18 Farnborough, London G 4
23 Farnborough, War. G 8
17 Farnborough Green H 9
9 Farncombe B 11
30 Farndon, Clwyd E 3
32 Farndon, Notts E 5
53 Farnell B 11
8 Farnham, Dorset E 1
18 Farnham, Essex A 5
35 Farnham, N.Yorks A 12
27 Farnham, Suffolk J 7
9 Farnham, Surrey B 9
17 Farnham Com F 10
18 Farnham Green A 5
17 Farnham Royal F 10
35 Farnhill C 9
6 Farningdon G 4
10 Farningham A 4
35 Farnley, N.Yorks B 11
35 Farnley, W.Yorks D 11
35 Farnley Tyas F 10
30 Farnworth, Ches. B 4
34 Farnworth, Manchester G 6
56 Farr, Highland F 2
57 Farr, Highland J 4
61 Farr, Highland B 7
56 Farr House F 2
9 Farringdon C 8
7 Farrington Gurney A 9
35 Farsley D 10
23 Farthinghoe H 8
11 Farthingloe D 11
23 Farthingstone G 9
35 Fartown E 10
6 Farway G 5
54 Fasag D 3
50 Faskadale A 2
55 Fasnakyle G 7
59 Fasque K 4
55 Fassfern L 4
45 Fatfield H 11
58 Fattahead B 4
44 Faugh G 3
48 Fauldhouse C 2
44 Fauldie F 2
19 Faulkbourne B 8
7 Faulkland A 10
30 Faulsgreen G 4
11 Faversham B 9
56 Favillar F 8
45 Fawdon B 8
31 Fawfieldhead D 9
10 Fawkham Green B 5
16 Fawler B 5
16 Fawley, Berks F 5
17 Fawley, Bucks E 8
8 Fawley, Hants F 6
15 Fawley Chapel A 9
49 Fawside E 9
36 Faxfleet E 6
3 Faygate E 1
22 Fazeley B 5
40 Fearby G 2
56 Fearn B 4
60 Fearn Lodge H 6
52 Fearnan C 2
54 Fearnbeg D 1
30 Fearnhead A 5
54 Fearnmore D 1
22 Featherstone, Staffs. B 3
36 Featherstone, W. Yorks. E 2
44 Featherwood C 6
22 Feckenham F 4
56 Feddan D 5
19 Feering B 8
39 Feetham E 12
10 Felbridge D 3
26 Felbrigg B 5
10 Felcourt D 3
17 Felden D 11
5 Feldownhead H 2
21 Felhampton D 10
12 Felin-Wnda B 6
20 Felindre, Dyfed G 1
13 Felindre, Dyfed D 10
13 Felindre, Dyfed G 9
13 Felindre, Dyfed E 9
21 Felindre, Powys D 7
14 Felindre, Powys B 5
13 Felinfach, Dyfed A 8
14 Felin-fach, Powys A 4
13 Felinfoel G 8
13 Felin-gwm Isaf E 8
13 Felin-gwm Uchaf E 8
40 Felixkirk G 5
27 Felixstowe M 6
27 Felixstoweferry L 6
49 Felkington E 12
45 Felling G 11
38 Fellside B 5
25 Felmersham J 1
26 Felmingham C 6
9 Felpham F 11
27 Felsham J 2
19 Felstead B 7
18 Feltham G 1
26 Felthorpe D 5
21 Felton, Heref. & Worc. G 11
45 Felton, Northumb. C 10
15 Felton, Somerset H 8
21 Felton Butler A 9
24 Feltwell F 8
25 Fen Drayton H 4
22 Fen End E 6
35 Fenay Bridge F 10
35 Fence C 7
45 Fence Houses H 11
33 Fendike Corner D 11
56 Fendom B 4
24 Fengate F 3
45 Fenham B 12
45 Fenhamhill B 12
34 Feniscowles E 5
6 Feniton F 4
31 Fenny Bentley E 10
23 Fenny Compton G 7
23 Fenny Drayton B 7
17 Fenny Stratford A 10
45 Fenrother D 10
25 Fenstanton H 4
25 Fenton, Cambs. G 4
32 Fenton, Lincs C 6
32 Fenton, Notts E 6
31 Fenton, Staffs F 7
49 Fenton Barns A 8
49 Fenton Town F 12
49 Fentonhill F 12
45 Fenwick, Northumb. F 9
45 Fenwick, Northumb. B 12
36 Fenwick, N. Yorks E 4
47 Fenwick, Strathclyde E 9
46 Feochaig H 3
2 Feock F 5
62 Ferindonald G 6
62 Feriniquarrie C 1
50 Ferlochan D 6
59 Fern L 2
55 Fern Villa G 3
14 Ferndale E 3
8 Ferndown F 2
49 Ferneyhill F 10
16 Fernham E 4
10 Fernhill D 2
22 Fernhill Heath F 2
9 Fernhurst C 10
53 Fernie F 8
62 Fernilea E 3
31 Fernilee B 8
21 Ferny Common G 9
35 Ferrensby A 12
9 Ferring F 12
25 Ferry Hill G 5
36 Ferrybridge E 3
53 Ferryden B 12
40 Ferryhill, Durham B 3
59 Ferryhill, Grampian G 7
40 Ferryhill Station B 3
13 Ferryside F 7
61 Ferrytown H 7
27 Fersfield G 4
55 Fersit L 7
57 Feshiebridge J 4
17 Fetcham H 12
58 Fetterangus C 7
59 Fettercairn K 4
35 Fewston B 10
13 Ffairfach E 9
20 Ffair-rhôs F 3
13 Ffaid-y-Brenin C 9
14 Ffawyddog B 5
28 Ffestiniog F 6
29 Ffordd-las, Gwynedd C 7
21 Fforddlas, Powys H 7
13 Fforest G 9
13 Fforest fach G 9
13 Fforest Goch G 10
13 Ffostrasol B 7
13 Ffos-y-ffin A 8
29 Ffrith E 12
13 Ffynnon Gynydd H7
13 Ffynnon-ddrain E 7
29 Ffynnongroew B 10
60 Fiag Bridge E 5
60 Fiag Lodge D 5
50 Fidden G 1
15 Fiddington, Glos A 12
6 Fiddington, Som B 5
7 Fiddleford E 11
18 Fiddlers Hamlet D 5
44 Fiddleton C 2
31 Field G 9
38 Field Broughton G 6
26 Field Dalling B 3
23 Field Head A 8
47 Fieldhead D 11
53 Fife, County G 7
58 Fife of Keith C 2
7 Fifehead Magdalen D 11
7 Fifehead Neville E 11
7 Fifehead St. Quinton E 11
17 Fifield, Berks F 10
16 Fifield, Glos. B 3
8 Fifield, Wilts A 3
8 Fifield Bavant D 2
8 Figheldean A 3
40 Fighting Cocks D 4
26 Filby D 8
41 Filey G 11
23 Filgrave G 12
16 Filkins D 3
4 Filleigh, Devon E 6
4 Filleigh, Devon C 5
32 Fillingham B 6
22 Fillongley C 6
15 Filton F 9
37 Fimber A 7
59 Finavon L 2
24 Fincham E 8
17 Finchampstead H 9
50 Fincharn G 6
9 Finchdean E 9
25 Finchingfield M 8
18 Finchley E 3
53 Fincraigs E 8
31 Findern G 11
56 Findhorn C 6
57 Findhorn Bridge G 4
58 Findochty A 2
59 Findon, Grampian H 7
9 Findon, W.Sussex E 12
56 Findon Mains D 2
59 Findrack House G 3
23 Finedon E 12
27 Fingal Street H 5
58 Fingask, Grampian E 5
52 Fingask, Tayside E 6
22 Fingerpost E 1
17 Fingest E 8
40 Finghall F 2
44 Fingland, Cumb G 1
47 Fingland, Dumf. & Gall. H 12
11 Finglesham C 12
19 Fingringhoe B 10
55 Finiskaig K 2
52 Finlarig D 1
17 Finmere A 7
51 Finnart B 12
43 Finniegill B 12
27 Finningham H 3
36 Finningley G 4
58 Finnygaud B 3
63 Finsbay H 2
18 Finsbury F 3
22 Finstall E 3
38 Finsthwaite F 6
16 Finstock C 4
64 Finstown C 2
43 Fintloch D 7
47 Fintry, Central A 11
58 Fintry, Grampian B 5
53 Fintry, Tayside D 9
50 Fionnphort F 1
40 Fir Tree B 2
32 Firbeck A 3
41 Firby, N.Yorks H 7
40 Firby, N.Yorks G 3
33 Firsby D 11
60 First Coast G 1
36 Fishlake F 4
43 Fishbeck C 11
9 Fishbourne, I. o. W. G 7
9 Fishbourne, W.Sussex F 10
40 Fishburn B 4
52 Fishcross H 4
58 Fisherford D 4
8 Fisher's Pond D 6
9 Fisherstreet C 11
56 Fisherton, Highland E 3
47 Fisherton, Strathclyde H 7
8 Fisherton de la Mere B 2
12 Fishguard C 3
15 Fishponds G 9
35 Fishpool, Manchester F 7

32 Fishpool, Notts ..... E 3
24 Fishtoft .... A 5
33 Fishtoft Drive ..... E 10
53 Fishtown of Usan .. B 12
49 Fishwick .... D 11
62 Fiskavaig .... E 2
33 Fiskerton, Lincs .... C 7
32 Fiskerton, Notts .... E 4
37 Fitling .... D 10
24 Fitten End .... D 5
8 Fittleton .... A 3
9 Fittleworth .... D 11
30 Fitz .... H 3
6 Fitzhead .... C 5
36 Fitzwilliam .... F 2
50 Fiunary .... C 3
15 Five Acres .... C 9
10 Five Ashes .... F 4
34 Five Lane Ends ..... B 4
3 Five Lanes .... B 9
10 Five Oak Green .... D 5
9 Five Oaks .... C 12
63 Five Penny Borve ... A 5
63 Five Penny Ness .... A 6
13 Five Roads .... F 8
30 Fivecrosses .... C 4
7 Fivehead .... D 7
19 Flack's Green ...... B 7
17 Flackwell Heath .... E 9
22 Fladbury .... G 3
64 Fladdabister .... E 7
31 Flagg .... C 10
41 Flamborough .... H 2
17 Flamstead .... C 11
9 Flansham .... F 11
35 Flappit Spring ...... C 9
35 Flasby .... B 8
31 Flash .... C 8
17 Flaunden .... D 11
32 Flawborough .... F 5
36 Flawith .... A 3
15 Flax Bourton .... G 8
35 Flaxby .... A 12
15 Flaxley .... C 10
6 Flaxpool .... C 5
36 Flaxton .... A 4
23 Fleckney .... C 10
23 Flecknoe .... F 8
7 Fleet, Dorset .... H 9
9 Fleet, Hants .... A 9
9 Fleet, Hants .... F 8
24 Fleet, Lincs .... C 5
33 Fleet Hargate ..... H 11
45 Fleetham .... E 12
34 Fleetwood .... B 2
14 Flemingston .... G 3
47 Flemington, Strathclyde ...... C 11
47 Flemington, Strathclyde ..... E 12
27 Flempton .... H 1
38 Fletchertown .... A 4
10 Fletching .... F 3
4 Flexbury .... E 1
9 Flexford .... A 10
38 Flimby .... B 3
10 Flimwell .... E 6
19 Flint .... C 11
29 Flint Mountain .... C 11
32 Flintham .... F 5
37 Flinton .... D 10
24 Flitcham .... C 8
25 Flitton .... L 2
4 Flitton Barton ...... C 6
25 Flitwick .... M 1
36 Flixborough .... F 6
34 Flixton, Manchester . H 6
41 Flixton, N.Yorks .. G 10
27 Flixton, Suffolk ..... G 6
35 Flockton .... F 11
35 Flockton Green .... F 11
49 Flodden .... F 11
63 Flodabay .... H 2
62 Flodigarry Hotel .... A 4
24 Flood's Ferry .... F 5
38 Flookburgh .... H 6
26 Flordon .... F 5
23 Flore .... F 9
45 Flotterton .... C 8
35 Flouch Inn .... G 10
27 Flowton .... K 4
2 Flushing, Cornwall .. F 5
58 Flushing, Grampian C 8
6 Fluxton .... G 4
22 Flyford Flavell ..... G 3
19 Fobbing .... E 7
56 Fochabers .... B 1
14 Fochriw .... D 4
36 Fockerby .... E 6
56 Fodderty .... D 1
7 Foddington .... C 9
20 Foel .... A 5
13 Foelgastell .... E 9
53 Foffarty .... C 9
36 Foggathorpe .... C 5
49 Fogo .... D 10
49 Fogorig .... E 10
60 Foindle .... C 3
53 Folda .... A 7
31 Fole .... F 9
23 Foleshill .... D 7
7 Folke .... E 10
11 Folkestone .... E 11
24 Folkingham .... B 2
10 Folkington .... H 4
24 Folksworth .... F 2
41 Folkton .... G 10
58 Folla Rule .... D 5
35 Follifoot .... B 12
4 Folly Gate .... F 4
9 Folly Hill .... A 9
14 Fonmon .... G 4
8 Fonthill Bishop ..... C 1
7 Fonthill Gifford ... C 12
7 Fontmell Magna ... E 12
9 Fontwell .... E 10
31 Foolow .... C 10
18 Foots Cray .... G 5
58 Forbestown .... F 1
6 Forches Corner ..... D 5
17 Ford, Bucks .... C 8
5 Ford, Devon .... L 7
4 Ford, Devon .... D 3
16 Ford, Glos. .... A 2
49 Ford, Northumb. ... F 12
21 Ford, Salop .... A 9
6 Ford, Somerset ..... C 4
31 Ford, Staffs .... E 9
50 Ford, Strathclyde ... G 6
9 Ford, W.. Sussex ... F 11
15 Ford, Wilts .... G 11
6 Ford Barton .... D 3
19 Ford End .... B 7
6 Ford Street .... D 5
10 Fordcombe .... D 4
52 Fordel .... F 6
52 Fordell .... H 6
21 Forden .... B 8
25 Fordham, Cambridgeshire .. H 7
19 Fordham, Essex .... A 9
24 Fordham, Norfolk .. E 7
22 Fordhouses .... B 3
8 Fordingbridge ...... E 3
41 Fordon .... H 10
59 Fordoun .... K 5
19 Fordstreet .... A 9
16 Fordwells .... C 4
11 Fordwich .... B 10
58 Fordyce .... A 3
31 Forebridge .... H 8
9 Forest Green ...... B 12
39 Forest Hall .... E 8
44 Forest Head .... G 4
17 Forest Hill .... C 7
51 Forest Lo., Highland .... C 10
57 Forest Lo., Highland .... H 6
52 Forest Lo., Tayside . A 4
52 Forest Mill .... H 4
10 Forest Row .... D 3
32 Forest Town .... D 3
45 Forestburn Gate .... C 9
56 Foresterseat .... D 7
9 Forestside .... E 9
53 Forfar .... B 9
52 Forgandenny .... E 6
14 Forge Hammer ..... E 6
14 Forge Side .... D 6
58 Forgie .... B 1
58 Forgieside .... B 1
58 Forglen House ...... B 4
34 Formby .... F 2
26 Forncett End .... F 4
26 Forncett St. Mary ... F 4
26 Forncett St. Peter ... F 5
52 Forneth .... C 6
27 Fornham All Saints .. J 1
27 Fornham St. Martin . H 2
56 Forres .... D 6
48 Forrestfield .... C 1
31 Forsbrook .... F 8
61 Forse .... D 11
61 Forse House ...... D 11
61 Forsinain .... C 9
61 Forsinard .... C 9
61 Forsinard Station ... C 8
7 Forston .... G 10
55 Fort Augustus ...... J 7
56 Fort George .... D 3
55 Fort William .... M 5
47 Fortacres .... F 9
52 Forteviot .... E 5
48 Forth .... D 2
15 Forthampton ...... A 11
52 Fortingall .... B 2
8 Forton, Hants ...... B 6
34 Forton, Lancs ...... B 4
21 Forton, Salop ...... A 9
7 Forton, Somerset ... E 7
30 Forton, Staffs ...... H 6
58 Fortrie .... C 4
56 Fortrose .... D 3
7 Fortuneswell .... H 7
17 Forty Green .... E 10
25 Forty Feet Bridge ... G 4
27 Forward Green ...... J 4
16 Fosbury .... H 4
24 Fosdyke .... B 4
24 Fosdyke Bridge ..... B 4
52 Foss .... A 3
16 Fossebridge .... C 2
18 Foster Street .... C 5
36 Fosterhouses .... F 4
31 Foston, Derby .... G 10
32 Foston, Lincs .... F 6
36 Foston, N.Yorks .... A 5
37 Foston on the Wolds B 8
33 Fotherby .... A 10
24 Fotheringhay .... F 2
64 Foubister .... D 3
10 Foul Mile .... F 5
49 Foulden, Borders .. D 11
26 Foulden, Norfolk ... E 1
56 Foulis Castle .... C 1
35 Foulridge .... C 7
26 Foulsham .... C 3
58 Fountainbleau, Grampian .... D 8
58 Fountainbleau, Grampian .... E 7
49 Fountainhall .... D 7
27 Four Ashes .... H 3
28 Four Crosses, Gwynedd F 3
29 Four Crosses, Powys H 12
20 Four Crosses, Powys B 6
22 Four Crosses, Staffs. A 3
10 Four Elms .... C 3
6 Four Forks .... C 6
34 Four Gate .... F 5
34 Four Gates .... D 5
30 Four Lane Ends, Ches. D 4
39 Four Lane Ends, Cumbria .... F 8
34 Four Lane Ends, Lancashire .... B 4
34 Four Lane Ends, Lancashire .... C 2
36 Four Lane Ends, N. Yorks .... B 4
2 Four Lanes .... F 4
9 Four Marks .... C 8
28 Four Mile Bridge ... B 2
11 Four Oaks, E. Sussex .... F 7
15 Four Oaks, Glos .. B 10
22 Four Oaks, W. Midlands ..... D 6
22 Four Oaks, W.Midlands .... B 4
13 Four Roads, Dyfed .. F 8
38 Four Roads, I.o.M. . H 1
10 Four Throws .... E 6
30 Fourlanes End ..... D 6
45 Fourlaws .... E 7
45 Fourstones .... F 7
8 Fovant .... C 2
58 Foveran .... E 7
3 Fowey .... D 8
58 Fowlershill .... F 7
10 Fowlhall .... C 6
53 Fowlis .... D 8
52 Fowlis Wester ...... E 4
25 Fowlmere .... L 5
15 Fownhope .... A 9
9 Fox Corner .... A 11
17 Fox Lane .... H 9
7 Foxcote .... A 10
38 Foxdale .... H 1
27 Foxearth .... L 1
38 Foxfield .... G 5
16 Foxham .... F 1
3 Foxhole .... D 7
41 Foxholes .... H 10
10 Foxhunt Green ..... F 4
26 Foxley, Norfolk ..... C 3
15 Foxley, Wilts ...... F 12
31 Foxt .... E 9
25 Foxton, Cambs ..... K 5
40 Foxton, Durham .... C 4
23 Foxton, Leics ..... C 10
39 Foxup .... G 11
30 Foxwist Green ...... C 5
21 Foxwood .... E 11
15 Foy .... A 9
57 Foyers .... G 1
7 Foys .... E 9
2 Fraddam .... F 3
2 Fraddon .... D 6
22 Fradley .... A 5
31 Fradswell .... G 8
37 Fraisthorpe .... A 9
10 Framfield .... F 4
26 Framingham Earl ... E 6
26 Framingham Pigot .. E 6
27 Framlingham .... J 6
7 Frampton, Dorset .. G 9
24 Frampton, Lincs .... B 4
15 Frampton Cotterell .. F 9
15 Frampton Mansell . D 12
15 Frampton on Severn D 10
24 Frampton West End B 4
27 Framsden .... J 5
40 Framwellgate Moor . A 3
22 Franche .... D 2
30 Frandley .... B 5
30 Frankby .... B 1
22 Frankley .... D 3
21 Frank's Bridge ..... G 7
23 Frankton .... E 7
20 Frankwell, Powys ... C 5
21 Frankwell, Salop .. A 10
10 Frant .... E 5
58 Fraserburgh .... A 7
19 Frating .... B 10
19 Frating Green ..... B 10
3 Freathy .... D 11
32 Frecheville .... B 1
25 Freckenham .... H 8
34 Freckleton .... D 3
32 Freeby .... H 5
16 Freeland .... C 5
26 Freethorpe .... E 7
26 Freethorpe Com. ... E 7
24 Freiston .... A 5
4 Fremington, Devon . C 4
40 Fremington, N.Yorks E 1
15 Frenchay .... F 9
5 Frenchbeer .... G 5
51 Frenich, Central ... G 11
52 Frenich, Tayside .... A 3
9 Frensham .... B 9
61 Fresgoe .... A 9
34 Freshfield .... F 2
8 Freshwater .... G 5
12 Freshwater East .... G 4
27 Fressingfield .... H 5
61 Freswick .... A 12
15 Fretherne .... C 10
26 Frettenham .... D 5
53 Freuchie .... F 7
12 Freystrop Cross ..... F 3
7 Friar Waddon ..... H 10
52 Friarton .... E 6
24 Friday Bridge ...... E 6
10 Friday Street .... H 5
36 Fridaythorpe .... A 6
18 Friern Barnet .... E 3
33 Friesthorpe .... B 8
32 Frieston .... E 6
17 Frieth .... E 9
16 Frilford .... D 5
16 Frilsham .... G 6
17 Frimley .... H 9
17 Frimley Green .... H 10
10 Frindsbury .... A 6
24 Fring .... B 8
17 Fringford .... A 7
11 Frinsted .... B 7
19 Frinton .... B 12
53 Friockheim .... B 10
20 Friog .... A 2
32 Frisby on the Wreake H 4
33 Friskney .... E 11
10 Friston, E.Sussex ... H 4
27 Friston, Suffolk ..... J 7
32 Fritchley .... E 1
33 Frith Bank .... E 10
21 Frith Common .... E 12
8 Fritham .... E 4
4 Frithelstock .... D 3
4 Frithelstock Stone .. D 3
17 Frithsden .... C 11
33 Frithville .... E 10
11 Frittenden .... D 7
26 Fritton, Norfolk ..... F 5
26 Fritton, Norfolk ..... E 7
16 Fritwell .... A 6
38 Frizington .... D 3
15 Frocester .... D 11
21 Frochas .... B 7
21 Frodesley .... B 10
37 Frodingham .... F 7
30 Frodsham .... B 4
49 Frogden .... G 10
31 Froggatt .... C 11
31 Froghall .... E 9
15 Frogland Cross ..... F 9
5 Frogmore, Devon ... L 6
17 Frogmore, Hants ... H 9
23 Frolesworth .... C 8
7 Frome .... B 11
7 Frome St.Quintin ... F 9
21 Fromes Hill .... H 12
13 Fron, Dyfed ...... D 11
28 Fron, Gwynedd ..... E 4
28 Fron, Gwynedd ..... F 3
21 Fron, Powys .... B 8
20 Fron, Powys .... F 6
29 Fron Isaf .... F 12
29 Froncysyllte .... F 12
29 Fron-deg .... E 12
29 Frongoch .... F 8
28 Fron-oleu .... G 6
39 Frosterley .... A 12
64 Frotoft .... B 2
16 Froxfield .... G 4
9 Froxfield Green .... D 8
9 Froyle .... B 9
18 Fryerning .... D 6
41 Fryton .... H 7
32 Fulbeck .... E 6
25 Fulbourn .... K 6
16 Fulbrook .... C 4
36 Fulford, N.Yorks ... B 4
6 Fulford, Somerset ... C 5
31 Fulford, Staffs ...... F 8
18 Fulham .... F 2
10 Fulking .... G 1
36 Full Sutton .... B 5
4 Fullaford .... B 6
47 Fullarton .... F 8
19 Fuller Street .... B 7
30 Fuller's Moor .... E 4
8 Fullerton .... B 5
33 Fulletby .... C 10
47 Fullwood .... D 9
17 Fulmer .... F 10
26 Fulmodestone ...... B 3
33 Fulnetby .... B 8
37 Fulstow .... G 11
34 Fulwood, Lancs .... D 4
6 Fulwood, Som ...... D 5
9 Funtington .... E 9
9 Funtley .... E 7
52 Funtullich .... D 2
64 Funzie .... B 8
6 Furley .... F 6
54 Furnace, Highland .. C 3
51 Furnace, Strathclyde G 7
22 Furnace End .... C 6
10 Furner's Green ..... E 3
36 Furness .... E 5
31 Furness Vale .... B 8
18 Furneux Pelham .... A 4
17 Furze Platt .... F 9
7 Furzebrook .... H 12
4 Furzehill .... B 6
6 Fyfett .... E 6
18 Fyfield, Essex ...... C 6
16 Fyfield, Glos. ...... D 3
8 Fyfield, Hants ...... A 4
16 Fyfield, Oxon ...... D 5
16 Fyfield, Wilts ...... G 2
41 Fyling Thorpe ...... E 9
58 Fyvie .... D 5
47 Gabroc Hill .... D 9
23 Gaddesby .... A 10
47 Gadgirth .... G 9
14 Gaer .... B 5
28 Gaerwen .... C 4
16 Gagingwell .... B 5
57 Gaick Lodge .... L 3
47 Gailes .... F 8
22 Gailey .... A 3
40 Gainford .... C 2
32 Gainsborough, Lincs. A 5
27 Gainsborough, Suff. . L 5
25 Gainsford End ...... L 8
43 Gairloch, Dumf. & Gall. .... D 11
59 Gairloch, Grampian G 5
54 Gairloch, Highland . B 2
55 Gairlochy .... L 6
52 Gairney Bank .... G 6
57 Gairnshiel Lodge .... J 8
39 Gaisgill .... E 8
44 Gaitsgill .... H 2
48 Galalaw .... E 3
49 Galashiels .... F 7
23 Galby .... B 10
42 Galdenoch .... E 3
49 Galewood .... F 12
34 Galgate .... B 4
7 Galhampton .... C 9
43 Gallaberry .... C 10
50 Gallanach .... E 5
50 Gallanachmore ..... E 5
53 Gallatown .... H 7
50 Gallchoille .... H 5
22 Galley Common .... C 6
19 Galleyend .... D 7
19 Galleywood .... D 7
51 Gallin .... C 12
53 Gallowfauld .... C 9
22 Gallows Green, Heref. & Worc. .... F 3
31 Gallows Green, Staffs. F 9
55 Galltair .... G 2
5 Galmpton, Devon .. K 7
5 Galmpton, Devon .. M 6
40 Galphay .... H 3
47 Galston .... F 10
62 Galtrigill .... C 1
43 Galtway .... G 8
39 Gamblesby .... A 8
25 Gamlingay .... K 3
4 Gammaton Moor ... D 4
40 Gammersgill .... G 1
58 Gamrie .... A 5
32 Gamston, Notts ..... C 4
32 Gamston, Notts ..... F 3
15 Ganarew .... C 8
50 Ganavan .... D 6
28 Ganllwyd .... H 6
59 Gannachy .... K 3
52 Gannochy .... E 6
30 Gannow Hill .... G 2
37 Ganstead .... D 9
41 Ganthorpe .... H 7
41 Ganton .... G 10
50 Gaodhail .... D 3
54 Garbat .... C 8
51 Garbhallt .... H 7
27 Garboldisham ...... G 3
57 Garbole .... G 3
29 Garden City .... C 12
58 Gardenstown ...... A 5
64 Garderhouse .... D 6
37 Gardham .... C 7
7 Gare Hill .... B 11
51 Garelochhead ...... H 9
16 Garford .... E 5
36 Garforth .... D 2
35 Gargrave .... B 8
52 Gargunnock .... H 2
63 Garinin .... C 3
28 Garizim .... C 6
42 Garlieston .... G 5
11 Garlinge Green ..... C 9
59 Garlogie .... G 5
58 Garmond .... B 5
50 Garmony .... D 4
58 Garmouth .... A 1
28 Garn .... G 2
28 Garn-Dolbenmaen .. F 4
13 Garnant .... F 10
14 Garndiffaith .... D 6
39 Garnett Bridge ..... E 7
47 Garnkirk .... C 11
14 Garnlydan .... C 5
13 Garnswllt .... F 9
14 Garn-yr-erw .... C 5
63 Garrabost .... D 6
57 Garragie .... H 1
2 Garras .... G 4
28 Garreg .... F 5
52 Garrick .... F 3
39 Garrigill .... A 9
40 Garriston .... F 2
43 Garroch .... C 7
42 Garrochtrie .... H 2
62 Garros .... B 4
52 Garrow .... C 3
47 Garryhorn .... H 8
39 Garsdale Head .... F 10
16 Garsdon .... E 1
31 Garshall Green ..... G 8
17 Garsington .... D 7
34 Garstang .... C 4
30 Garston .... B 3
34 Garswood .... G 4
51 Gartachoil .... H 12
47 Gartcosh .... C 11
29 Garth, Clwyd. ..... F 11
38 Garth, I.o.M. ...... H 2
14 Garth, Mid.Glam. ... E 2
20 Garth, Powys ...... G 5
52 Garth House .... B 2
14 Garth Place .... E 5
47 Garthamlock ...... C 11
14 Garthbrengy .... A 4
59 Garthdee .... G 7
21 Garthmyl .... C 7
36 Garthorpe, Humber. E 6
32 Garthorpe, Leics ... H 5
58 Gartly .... D 3
51 Gartmore .... H 12

46 Gartnagrenach **C 3**
47 Gartness **A 10**
47 Gartocharn **A 9**
37 Garton **D 10**
37 Garton-on-the-Wolds **A 7**
61 Gartymore **E 9**
48 Garvald, Borders **D 6**
49 Garvald, Lothian **B 8**
57 Garvamore **K 1**
55 Garvan **M 3**
50 Garvard **H 1**
54 Garve **D 8**
26 Garvestone **E 3**
47 Garvock, Strathclyde **B 7**
59 Garvock, Tayside **K 5**
15 Garway **B 8**
63 Garynahine **D 3**
58 Gash of Philorth **A 7**
55 Gaskan **M 2**
7 Gaspar **C 11**
42 Gass **A 5**
43 Gasstown **D 10**
47 Gasswater **G 11**
15 Gastard **G 12**
27 Gasthorpe **G 3**
8 Gatcombe **H 6**
36 Gate Helmsley **B 5**
30 Gateacre **A 3**
39 Gatebeck **G 8**
36 Gateforth **D 3**
47 Gatehead **F 9**
44 Gatehouse, Northumb. **D 6**
52 Gatehouse, Tayside **B 4**
43 Gatehouse of Fleet **F 7**
43 Gatelawbridge **B 10**
26 Gateley **C 3**
40 Gatenby **F 3**
38 Gatesgarth **D 4**
49 Gateshaw **G 10**
45 Gateshead **G 10**
30 Gatesheath **D 3**
52 Gateside, Fife **F 6**
56 Gateside, Grampian **D 7**
47 Gateside, Strathclyde **D 8**
47 Gateside, Strathclyde **B 8**
53 Gateside, Tayside **C 9**
43 Gateslack **A 10**
34 Gathurst **F 4**
31 Gatley **A 7**
10 Gatton **C 3**
49 Gattonside **F 8**
20 Gaufron **F 5**
53 Gauldry **E 8**
24 Gaultree **E 6**
8 Gaunt's Common **F 2**
33 Gautby **C 9**
49 Gavinton **D 10**
58 Gawanhill **A 8**
35 Gawber **F 11**
17 Gawcott **A 8**
38 Gawthwaite **G 5**
23 Gaydon **G 7**
23 Gayhurst **G 11**
39 Gayle **F 11**
40 Gayles **D 1**
30 Gayton, Merseyside **B 1**
24 Gayton, Norfolk **D 8**
23 Gayton, Northants. **G 10**
31 Gayton, Staffs **G 8**
33 Gayton le Marsh **B 11**
33 Gayton le Wold **B 9**
24 Gayton Thorpe **D 8**
24 Gaywood **C 7**
25 Gazeley **J 8**
62 Geary **B 2**
56 Geddes House **D 4**
27 Gedding **J 2**
23 Geddington **D 12**
62 Gedintailor **E 4**
24 Gedney **C 5**
24 Gedney Broadgate **C 5**
24 Gedney Drove End **C 6**
24 Gedney Dyke **C 5**
24 Gedney Hill **D 4**
35 Gee Cross **H 8**
60 Geisgeil **C 3**
26 Geldeston **F 7**
29 Gell **C 8**
14 Gelli **E 3**
14 Gellideg **D 3**
14 Gelligaer **E 5**
28 Gellilydan **F 6**
13 Gellinudd **G 10**
29 Gellioedd **F 8**
52 Gellyburn **C 6**
43 Gelston **F 8**
37 Gembling **A 9**
42 Genoch Square **F 2**
22 Gentleshaw **A 4**
63 Geocrab **H 2**
17 George Green **F 11**
4 George Nympton **D 6**
44 Georgefield **D 1**
4 Georgeham **B 3**
43 Georgetown, Dumf. & Gall. **D 10**
14 Georgetown, Gwent **C 5**
47 Georgetown, Strathclyde **C 9**
61 Georgmas Junction Station **B 11**
64 Georth **C 2**
28 Gerlan **C 6**
4 Germansweek **F 3**
2 Germoe **G 3**
2 Gerrans **F 6**
43 Gerranton **E 8**
17 Gerrards Cross **E 11**
63 Geshader **D 2**
27 Gestingthorpe **L 1**
21 Geuffordd **A 7**
43 Gibbshill **D 8**
33 Gibraltar **D 12**
15 Giddeahall **G 11**
18 Gidea Park **E 5**
5 Gidleigh **G 5**
49 Gifford **C 8**
53 Giffordtown **F 7**
35 Giggleswick **A 7**
36 Gilberdyke **D 6**
43 Gilchristland **B 10**
49 Gilchriston **C 7**
43 Gilcrux **H 12**
35 Gildersome **D 11**
32 Gildingwells **B 3**
40 Gilesgate Moor **A 3**
14 Gileston **H 3**
14 Gilfach **D 5**
14 Gilfach Goch **E 3**
13 Gilfachrheda **A 7**
41 Gillamoor **F 7**
43 Gillenbie **C 12**
43 Gillesbie **B 12**
42 Gillespie **F 3**
40 Gilling East **G 6**
40 Gilling West **E 2**
7 Gillingham, Dorset **D 11**
11 Gillingham, Kent **A 7**
26 Gillingham, Norfolk **F 7**
61 Gillock **B 11**
31 Gillow Heath **D 7**
43 Gillroanie **G 8**
61 Gills **A 12**
10 Gill's Green **E 6**
48 Gilmanscleuch **G 6**
48 Gilmerton, Lothian **C 5**
52 Gilmerton, Tayside **E 4**
39 Gilmonby **D 12**
23 Gilmorton **C 9**
44 Gilsland **F 5**
44 Gilsland Spa **F 5**
49 Gilston **D 7**
14 Gilwern **C 6**
26 Gimingham **B 6**
27 Gipping **J 4**
33 Gipsey Bridge **E 10**
47 Girdle Toll **E 8**
64 Girlsta **D 7**
40 Girsby **D 4**
25 Girtford **K 3**
47 Girthill **E 7**
43 Girthon **F 7**
25 Girton, Cambs **J 5**
32 Girton, Notts **D 5**
42 Girvan **B 3**
42 Girvan Mains **B 3**
35 Gisburn **B 7**
63 Gisla **D 2**
26 Gisleham **F 8**
27 Gislingham **H 4**
27 Gissing **G 4**
6 Gittisham **F 5**
10 Givons Grove **C 1**
52 Glack **D 5**
56 Glackbea **F 1**
56 Glackossian **F 2**
11 Gladdish **C 7**
21 Gladestry **G 8**
48 Gladhouse **D 6**
49 Gladsmuir **B 7**
31 Gladwin's Mark **D 11**
13 Glais **G 10**
41 Glaisdale **E 8**
43 Glaisters **D 8**
53 Glamis **B 8**
13 Glan Duar **C 8**
28 Glan-Dwyfach **F 4**
28 Glanaber **E 6**
13 Glanamman **F 10**
26 Glandford **B 3**
14 Glandwr **D 5**
12 Glan-dwr **D 5**
20 Glandyfi **C 3**
14 Glangrwyney **C 5**
14 Glanllynfi **E 2**
21 Glan-miwl **C 7**
12 Glanryd **C 5**
12 Glan-ryd, Dyfed **D 5**
14 Glan-ryd, Powys **C 1**
45 Glanton **B 9**
45 Glanton Pike **B 9**
7 Glanvilles Wootton **E 10**
29 Glan-y-don **B 11**
20 Glan-y-nant **D 5**
29 Glanyrafon **F 9**
28 Glan-y-Wern **G 5**
24 Glapthorn **F 1**
32 Glapwell **D 2**
57 Glas-allt Shiel **L 8**
21 Glasbury **H 7**
56 Glaschoil **F 6**
38 Glascoe **F 2**
29 Glascoed **C 9**
58 Glascoforest **F 5**
22 Glascote **B 6**
21 Glascwm **G 7**
51 Glasdrum **C 7**
29 Glasfryn **E 8**
47 Glasgow **C 10**
62 Glashvin **A 4**
28 Glasinfryn **C 5**
59 Glaslaw **J 6**
55 Glasnacardoch, Highland **L 1**
55 Glasnacardoch, Highland **K 1**
62 Glasnakille **G 5**
20 Glaspwll **C 3**
54 Glassburn **F 7**
42 Glasserton **H 5**
47 Glassford **E 12**
15 Glasshouse Hill **B 10**
35 Glasshouses **A 10**
53 Glasslie **G 7**
42 Glassoch **E 4**
44 Glasson, Cumb **G 1**
34 Glasson, Lancs **B 3**
39 Glassonby **A 8**
53 Glasterlaw **B 10**
23 Glaston **B 12**
7 Glastonbury **B 8**
47 Glastron **H 8**
25 Glatton **G 2**
34 Glazebury **G 5**
21 Glazely **D 12**
32 Gleadless Townend **B 1**
38 Gleaston **H 5**
46 Glecknabae **C 5**
43 Gledpark **F 7**
42 Gledsnest **B 3**
46 Glemanuilt **H 1**
27 Glemsford **K 1**
42 Glen, Dumf. & Gall. **F 6**
43 Glen, Dumf. & Gall. **D 9**
58 Glen, Grampian **D 2**
52 Glen, Tayside **E 6**
38 Glen Auldyn **G 2**
58 Glen Barry **B 3**
62 Glen Bernisdale **C 3**
50 Glen Borrodale **A 3**
57 Glen Clunie Lodge **L 7**
58 Glen Dronoch **C 4**
48 Glen House **F 6**
38 Glen Mona **G 2**
55 Glen Nevis House **M 5**
23 Glen Parva **B 9**
59 Glen Tanar House **H 2**
63 Glen Tolsta **B 6**
48 Glen Village **B 2**
38 Glen Vine **G 2**
55 Glenancross **K 1**
50 Glenaros House **C 3**
46 Glenbarr **F 2**
57 Glenbeg, Grampian **G 6**
50 Glenbeg, Highland **A 3**
59 Glenbervie **J 5**
47 Glenboig **C 12**
51 Glenbranter **H 8**
48 Glenbreck **G 3**
55 Glenbrein Lodge **H 8**
62 Glenbrittle House **F 3**
58 Glenbuchat Lodge **F 1**
47 Glenbuck **F 12**
47 Glenburn **C 9**
59 Glencally **L 1**
60 Glencalvie Lodge **G 5**
60 Glencanisp Lodge **E 3**
43 Glencaple **E 10**
54 Glencarron Lodge **E 4**
53 Glencarse **E 7**
60 Glencassley Castle **F 5**
46 Glencloy **F 5**
51 Glencoe **B 8**
57 Glenconglass **G 7**
52 Glencraig **H 6**
50 Glencripesdale **B 4**
58 Glencuie **F 2**
59 Glendavan House **G 2**
49 Glendearg, Borders **F 8**
44 Glendearg, Dumf. & Gall. **C 1**
52 Glendevon **G 5**
55 Glendoe Lodge **H 8**
55 Glendoebeg **J 8**
53 Glendoik **E 7**
57 Glendoll Lodge **M 8**
53 Glenduckie **E 7**
59 Glendye Lodge **J 4**
52 Gleneagles Hotel **F 4**
55 Gleneig **H 2**
56 Glenerney **E 6**
51 Glenfalloch Farm **F 10**
52 Glenfarg **F 6**
59 Glenfenzie **G 1**
56 Glenferness House **E 5**
58 Glenfiddich Lodge **D 1**
23 Glenfield **B 9**
47 Glenfinart House **A 7**
55 Glenfinnan **L 3**
55 Glenfintaig Lodge **L 6**
52 Glenfoot **F 6**
55 Glenforslan **M 1**
51 Glenfyne Lodge **F 9**
43 Glengap **F 7**
47 Glengarnock **D 8**
52 Glengoulandie **B 3**
62 Glengrasco **D 4**
51 Glengyle **F 11**
42 Glengyre **E 1**
43 Glenhead, Dumf. & Gall **F 8**
52 Glenhead, Tayside **G 4**
53 Glenhead Farm **A 7**
48 Glenhighton **F 4**
42 Glenhoise **E 5**
43 Glenholm **D 12**
43 Glenhoul **C 7**
50 Glenhurich **A 5**
48 Glenkerry **H 5**
43 Glenkiln **D 9**
58 Glenkindie **F 2**
48 Glenkirk **F 3**
56 Glenlatterach **D 7**
43 Glenlee **D 7**
57 Glenlia **H 1**
43 Glenlochar **E 8**
57 Glenlochsie **M 6**
46 Glenloig **F 4**
42 Glenluce **F 3**
54 Glenmarksie **D 7**
46 Glenmassan **A 6**
38 Glenmaye **G 1**
54 Glenmeanne **D 7**
43 Glenmidge **C 9**
38 Glenmooar **G 2**
50 Glenmore, Highland **A 3**
62 Glenmore, Highland **D 4**
50 Glenmore, Strathclyde **F 6**
57 Glenmore Lodge **H 5**
50 Glenmorven Cott. **B 3**
42 Glenmuck **A 6**
48 Glenochar **H 2**
59 Glenquiech **L 2**
48 Glenrath **F 5**
38 Glenridding **D 6**
46 Glenrisdell **D 4**
60 Glenrossal **F 5**
53 Glenrothes **G 7**
42 Glenruther **D 4**
50 Glensanda **C 5**
59 Glensaugh **J 4**
52 Glenshee **D 5**
43 Glenshimmeroch **C 7**
57 Glenshirra Lodge **K 1**
47 Glenside, Strathclyde **D 7**
63 Glenside, W.Isles **E 5**
51 Glensluain **H 8**
46 Glenstriven **B 6**
55 Glensulaig **L 4**
48 Glentaggart **G 1**
33 Glentham **A 7**
48 Glentress, Borders **E 5**
48 Glentress, Borders **E 6**
57 Glentromie Lodge **K 3**
42 Glentrool Village **D 4**
38 Glentruan **F 2**
57 Glentruim House **K 2**
32 Glentworth **A 6**
56 Glenurquhart **C 3**
43 Glenwhargen **A 8**
42 Glenwhilly **D 3**
48 Glespin **G 1**
64 Gletness **D 7**
15 Glewstone **B 9**
24 Glinton **E 3**
59 Glithno **H 6**
23 Glooston **C 11**
35 Glossop **H 9**
45 Gloster Hill **C 10**
15 Gloucester **C 11**
15 Gloucestershire, Co. **D 10**
64 Gloup **A 7**
2 Gloweth **E 5**
35 Glusburn **C 8**
61 Glutt Lodge **D 9**
2 Gluvian **C 6**
16 Glympton **B 5**
29 Glyn **D 7**
12 Glyn-Arthen **B 6**
29 Glyn Ceiriog **F 11**
20 Glynbrochan **D 5**
14 Glyncoch **E 4**
14 Glyncorrwg **D 2**
10 Glynde **G 3**
10 Glyndebourne **G 3**
29 Glyndyfrdwy **F 10**
28 Glynllifon Park **E 4**
14 Glynneath **D 2**
14 Glyntaff **E 4**
13 Glynteg **C 7**
31 Gnosall **H 7**
31 Gnosall Heath **H 7**
23 Goadby **B 11**
32 Goadby Marwood **H 5**
11 Goat Lees **C 9**
16 Goatacre **F 1**
7 Goathill **E 10**
41 Goathland **E 8**
6 Goathurst **C 6**
10 Goathurst Com **C 4**
60 Gobernuisgach Lo. **C 5**
30 Gobowen **G 2**
9 Godalming **B 11**
11 Goddard's Green **E 7**
10 Godden Green **C 4**
6 Godford Cross **F 5**
25 Godmanchester **H 3**
7 Godmanston **F 10**
11 Godmersham **C 9**
7 Godney **B 8**
2 Godolphin Cross **F 3**
13 Godre'r-graig **F 11**
8 Godshill, Hants **E 3**
9 Godshill, I.o.W. **H 7**
10 Godstone **C 2**
8 Godwinscroft **F 3**
14 Goetre **D 6**
18 Goff's Oak **D 3**
48 Gogar **B 4**
20 Gogfnan **D 2**
28 Golan **F 5**
3 Golant **D 8**
3 Golberdon **C 10**
34 Golborne **G 5**
35 Golcar **E 9**
24 Gold Hill, Cambs **F 6**
7 Gold Hill, Dorset **E 11**
15 Goldcliff **F 7**
16 Golden Balls **D 6**
10 Golden Cross **G 4**
10 Golden Green **C 5**
13 Golden Grove **E 9**
12 Golden Hill, Dyfed **G 3**
8 Golden Hill, Hants. **F 4**
9 Golden Pot **B 8**
15 Golden Valley **B 12**
31 Goldenhill **E 7**
18 Golders Green **E 3**
19 Goldhanger **C 9**
21 Golding **B 11**
25 Goldington **K 2**
41 Goldsborough, N.Yorks. **D 8**
36 Goldsborough, N.Yorks **B 2**
2 Goldsithney **G 3**
30 Goldstone **G 6**
36 Goldthorpe **G 3**
4 Goldworthy **D 3**
56 Gollanfield **D 4**
40 Gollinglith Foot **G 2**
6 Golsoncott **B 4**
61 Golspie **G 8**
61 Golval **B 9**
8 Gomeldon **C 3**
35 Gomersal **E 10**
50 Gometra House **C 1**
9 Gomshall **A 12**
32 Gonalston **E 4**
64 Gonfirth **D 7**
18 Good Easter **C 6**
26 Gooderstone **E 1**
43 Goodhope **B 11**
4 Goodleigh **C 5**
36 Goodmanham **C 6**
11 Goodnestone, Kent **C 11**
11 Goodnestone, Kent **B 9**
15 Goodrich **B 9**
5 Goodrington **K 8**
12 Goodwick **C 3**
8 Goodworth Clatford **B 5**
23 Goodyers End **D 7**
36 Goole **E 5**
36 Goole Fields **E 5**
2 Goonbell **E 4**
2 Goonhavern **D 5**
10 Goose Green **C 5**
59 Goosecruives **J 5**
4 Gooseham **D 1**
43 Goosehill **A 8**
5 Goosewell **K 4**
16 Goosey **E 4**
34 Goosnargh **C 4**
30 Goostrey **C 6**
22 Gorcott Hill **E 4**
28 Gorddinog **C 6**
49 Gordon **E 9**
61 Gordonbush **F 8**
58 Gordonstown, Grampian **D 5**
58 Gordonstown, Grampian **B 3**
48 Gorebridge **C 6**
24 Gorefield **D 5**
17 Goring **F 7**
9 Goring-by-Sea **F 12**
17 Goring Heath **F 7**
26 Gorleston on Sea **E 8**
22 Gornalwood **C 3**
3 Gorran Churchtown **E 7**
3 Gorran Haven **E 7**
44 Gorrenberry **C 3**
20 Gors **E 2**
16 Gorse Hill **E 3**
29 Gorsedd **C 10**
13 Gorseinon **G 9**
64 Gorseness **C 2**
31 Gorseybank **E 11**
13 Gorsgoch **B 8**
13 Gorslas **F 9**
15 Gorsley **B 10**
54 Gorstan **D 7**
55 Gorstanvorran **M 2**
30 Gorstella **D 2**
15 Gorsty Common **A 8**
35 Gorton **G 7**
27 Gosbeck **K 5**
24 Gosberton **B 3**
24 Gosberton Clough **C 3**
27 Gosfield **M 1**
21 Gosford **F 10**
49 Gosford House **B 7**
38 Gosforth, Cumb **E 3**
45 Gosforth, Tyne & Wear **F 10**
18 Gosmore **A 2**
9 Gosport **F 7**
64 Gossabrough **C 8**
45 Goswick **B 12**
32 Gotham **G 3**
16 Gotherington **A 1**
10 Goudhurst **D 6**
33 Goulceby **B 9**
47 Gourock **B 7**
58 Gourdas **C 5**
59 Gourdon **K 6**
47 Govan **C 10**
32 Goverton **E 4**
5 Goveton **L 6**
14 Govilon **C 6**
36 Gowdall **E 4**
56 Gower **D 1**
13 Gowerton **G 9**
52 Gowkhall **H 5**
36 Gowthorpe **B 5**
37 Goxhill, Humber. **E 9**
37 Goxhill, Humber. **C 9**
37 Goxhill Haven **E 9**
13 Goytre **H 11**
43 Gracefield **C 9**
49 Graden **F 10**
9 Graffham **D 10**
25 Grafham, Cambs **H 3**
9 Grafham, Surrey **B 11**
15 Grafton, Heref.& Worc **A 8**
21 Grafton, Heref.& Worc **F 11**
16 Grafton, Oxon **D 4**
30 Grafton, Salop **H 3**
36 Grafton, N.Yorks **A 2**

22 Grafton Flyford .... **G 3**
23 Grafton Regis .... **G 11**
23 Grafton Underwood **D 12**
11 Grafty Green .... **C 7**
29 Graianrhyd .... **E 11**
29 Graig .... **C 7**
29 Graig-fechan .... **E 10**
48 Graigmillar .... **B 6**
19 Grain .... **F 9**
37 Grainsby .... **G 10**
37 Grainthorpe .... **G 11**
2 Grampound .... **E 6**
2 Grampound Road .. **E 6**
17 Granborough .... **B 8**
32 Granby .... **G 5**
23 Grandborough .... **E 8**
52 Grandtully .... **B 4**
34 Grane .... **E 6**
38 Grange, Cumb. .... **C 5**
53 Grange, Fife .... **F 10**
30 Grange, Merseyside **B 1**
40 Grange, N. Yorks. ... **F 6**
47 Grange, Strathclyde . **F 9**
53 Grange, Tayside .... **E 7**
58 Grange Crossroads .. **B 2**
7 Grange Gate .... **H 12**
56 Grange Hall .... **D 6**
35 Grange Moor .... **E 11**
53 Grange of Lindores . **E 7**
45 Grange Villa .... **H 10**
48 Grangehall .... **E 2**
31 Grangemill .... **D 11**
48 Grangemouth .... **A 2**
38 Grange-over-Sands . **G 6**
48 Grangepans .... **A 3**
40 Grangetown, Cleveland .... **C 6**
14 Grangetown, S. Glam. .... **G 5**
57 Granish .... **H 5**
37 Gransmoor .... **A 9**
12 Granston .... **D 2**
25 Grantchester .... **K 5**
32 Grantham .... **G 6**
58 Grantlodge .... **F 5**
48 Granton, Dumf. & Gall. .... **H 3**
48 Granton, Lothian ... **B 5**
57 Granton-on-Spey ... **G 6**
21 Grantsfield .... **F 10**
49 Grantshouse .... **C 10**
30 Grappenhall .... **B 5**
37 Grasby .... **G 8**
38 Grasmere .... **D 6**
35 Grasscroft .... **G 8**
30 Grassendale .... **B 3**
39 Grassholme .... **C 11**
35 Grassington .... **A 9**
45 Grasslees .... **C 8**
32 Grassmoor .... **D 1**
32 Grassthorpe .... **C 5**
8 Grateley .... **B 4**
31 Gratwich .... **G 9**
25 Graveley, Cambs. ... **J 4**
18 Graveley, Herts. .... **A 2**
22 Gravelly Hill .... **C 5**
11 Graveney .... **B 9**
10 Gravesend .... **A 5**
63 Gravir .... **E 5**
37 Grayingham .... **G 7**
39 Grayrigg .... **E 8**
18 Grays .... **F 6**
9 Grayshott .... **C 10**
9 Grayswood .... **C 10**
40 Graythorp .... **B 5**
17 Grazeley .... **G 8**
36 Greasbrough .... **H 2**
30 Greasby .... **B 1**
32 Greasley .... **E 2**
25 Great Abington .... **K 6**
25 Great Addington ... **H 1**
22 Great Alne .... **F 5**
34 Great Altcar .... **F 2**
18 Great Amwell .... **C 4**
39 Great Asby .... **D 9**
27 Great Ashfield .... **H 3**
40 Great Ayton .... **D 6**
19 Great Baddow .... **C 7**
15 Great Badminton .. **F 11**
25 Great Bardfield .... **M 8**
25 Great Barford .... **K 2**
22 Great Barr .... **C 4**
16 Great Barrington ... **C 3**
30 Great Barrow .... **C 3**
27 Great Barton .... **J 2**
41 Great Barugh .... **G 7**
45 Great Bavington .... **E 8**
27 Great Bealings .... **K 5**
16 Great Bedwyn .... **H 4**
19 Great Bentley .... **B 11**
23 Great Billing .... **F 11**
26 Great Bircham .... **B 1**
27 Great Blakenham ... **K 4**
39 Great Blencow .... **B 7**
30 Great Bolas .... **H 5**
9 Great Bookham ... **A 12**
17 Great Bourton .... **H 8**
23 Great Bowden .... **C 11**
25 Great Bradley .... **K 8**
19 Great Braxted .... **G 8**
27 Great Bricett .... **K 3**
17 Great Brickhill ... **A 10**
31 Great Bridgeford ... **G 7**
23 Great Brington .... **F 10**
19 Great Bromley ... **A 10**
30 Great Budworth .... **B 5**
40 Great Burdon .... **B 5**
19 Great Burstead .... **E 7**
40 Great Busby .... **E 5**
18 Great Canfield .... **B 6**
23 Great Carlton .... **B 11**
24 Great Casterton .... **E 1**
15 Great Chalfield ... **H 11**
11 Great Chart .... **D 8**
18 Great Chatwell .... **A 1**
25 Great Chesterfield .. **L 6**
8 Great Cheverall .... **A 1**
25 Great Chishill .... **L 5**
19 Great Clacton .... **B 11**
38 Great Clifton .... **B 3**
37 Great Coate .... **F 10**
22 Great Comberton ... **H 3**
44 Great Corby .... **H 3**
27 Great Cornard .... **L 2**
37 Great Cowden .... **C 10**
16 Great Coxwell .... **E 4**
40 Great Crakehall .... **F 3**
23 Great Cransley ... **D 11**
26 Great Cressingham . **E 1**
34 Great Crosby .... **G 2**
31 Great Cubley .... **F 10**
23 Great Dalby .... **A 10**
23 Gt. Doddington .... **F 12**
6 Great Dorweeke .... **F 3**
15 Great Doward .... **C 9**
25 Great Dunham .... **D 2**
18 Great Dunmow .... **B 6**
8 Great Durnford .... **B 3**
18 Great Easton, Essex **A 6**
23 Great Easton, Leics. **C 11**
34 Great Eccleston .... **C 3**
41 Great Edstone .... **G 7**
26 Great Ellingham .... **F 3**
7 Great Elm .... **A 10**
25 Great Eversden .... **K 5**
40 Great Fencote .... **F 3**
27 Great Finborough ... **J 3**
26 Great Fransham ... **D 2**
17 Great Gaddesden .. **C 11**
25 Great Gidding .... **G 2**
36 Great Givendale .... **B 6**
27 Great Glenham .... **J 6**
23 Great Glen .... **B 10**
32 Great Gonerby .... **F 6**
15 Great Graig .... **B 7**
25 Great Gransden .... **K 4**
26 Great Green, Norf. .. **F 6**
27 Great Green, Suff. .. **K 2**
41 Great Habton .... **G 8**
24 Great Hale .... **A 2**
18 Great Hallingbury .. **B 5**
21 Great Hanwood ... **B 10**
23 Great Harrowden .. **E 12**
34 Great Harwood .... **D 6**
17 Great Haseley .... **D 7**
37 Great Hatfield .... **C 9**
31 Great Haywood .... **H 8**
23 Great Heath .... **D 7**
36 Great Heck .... **E 4**
27 Great Henny .... **L 2**
15 Great Hinton .... **H 12**
26 Great Hockham .... **F 2**
19 Great Holland .... **B 12**
27 Great Horkesley ... **M 3**
25 Great Hormead .... **M 5**
35 Great Horton .... **D 10**
17 Great Horwood .... **A 8**
23 Great Houghton, Northants .... **F 11**
36 Great Houghton, S. Yorks. .... **F 2**
31 Great Hucklow .... **B 10**
37 Great Kelk .... **A 8**
17 Great Kimble .... **D 9**
17 Great Kingshill .... **D 9**
40 Great Langton .... **F 3**
19 Great Leighs .... **B 7**
37 Great Limber .... **F 9**
23 Great Linford .... **H 12**
27 Great Livermere ... **H 2**
31 Great Longstone .. **C 10**
45 Great Lumley .... **H 11**
22 Great Malvern .... **G 2**
27 Great Maplestead .. **M 1**
34 Great Marton .... **D 2**
26 Great Massingham .. **C 1**
26 Great Melton .... **E 4**
17 Great Milton .... **D 7**
17 Great Missenden .. **D 10**
34 Great Mitton .... **C 6**
11 Great Mongeham .. **C 12**
34 Great Moss .... **G 4**
39 Great Musgrave ... **D 10**
30 Great Ness .... **H 3**
19 Great Oakley, Essex **A 11**
23 Great Oakley, Northants .... **D 12**
18 Great Offley .... **A 1**
39 Great Ormside .... **C 9**
44 Great Orton .... **H 2**
36 Great Ouseburn .... **A 2**
23 Great Oxendon .... **D 10**
18 Great Oxney Grn. .. **C 6**
26 Great Palgrave .... **D 1**
18 Great Parndon .... **C 4**
25 Great Paxton .... **J 3**
34 Great Plumpton .... **D 3**
26 Great Plumstead ... **D 6**
32 Great Ponton .... **G 6**
36 Great Preston .... **D 2**
25 Great Raveley .... **G 4**
16 Great Rissington ... **B 3**
16 Great Rollright .... **A 4**
12 Great Rudbaxton ... **E 3**
26 Great Ryburgh .... **C 3**
45 Great Ryle .... **B 8**
19 Great Saling .... **A 7**
39 Great Salkeld .... **B 8**
25 Great Sampford .... **L 7**
30 Great Sankey .... **A 4**
30 Great Saughall .... **C 2**
27 Great Saxham .... **J 1**
16 Great Shefford .... **G 5**
25 Great Shelford .... **K 6**
40 Great Smeaton .... **E 4**
26 Great Snoring .... **B 2**
16 Great Somerford .... **F 1**
30 Great Soudley .... **G 6**
40 Great Stainton .... **C 3**
19 Great Stambridge ... **E 9**
25 Great Staughton .... **J 2**
33 Great Steeping .... **D 11**
11 Great Stonar .... **B 12**
39 Great Strickland .... **C 8**
25 Great Stukeley .... **H 3**
33 Great Sturton .... **C 9**
30 Gt. Sutton, Ches. ... **C 2**
21 Gt. Sutton, Salop. . **D 10**
45 Great Swinburne .... **E 7**
19 Great Tarpots .... **E 7**
16 Great Tew .... **A 5**
19 Great Tey .... **A 9**
25 Great Thurlow .... **K 8**
4 Great Torrington ... **D 4**
45 Great Tosson .... **C 8**
19 Great Totham .... **C 8**
38 Great Urswick .... **H 5**
19 Great Wakering .... **E 9**
27 Great Waldingfield .. **L 2**
26 Great Walsingham .. **B 2**
19 Great Waltham .... **C 7**
18 Great Warley .... **E 6**
16 Great Washbourne . **A 1**
27 Great Welnetham ... **J 2**
27 Great Wenham .... **L 4**
45 Great Whittington .. **F 8**
19 Great Whigborough . **B 9**
25 Great Wilbraham ... **J 6**
8 Great Wishford .... **C 2**
15 Great Witcombe ... **C 12**
22 Great Witley .... **E 1**
16 Great Wolford .... **A 3**
23 Great Woolstone .. **H 12**
25 Great Wratting .... **K 8**
18 Great Wymondley .. **A 2**
22 Great Wyrley .... **A 3**
30 Great Wytheford ... **H 4**
26 Great Yarmouth .... **E 8**
27 Great Yeldham .... **L 1**
18 Greater London, Co. **F 3**
35 Greater Manchester, Co. .... **G 7**
24 Greatford .... **D 2**
31 Greatgate .... **F 9**
40 Greatham, Cleveland **B 5**
9 Greatham, Hants. .. **C 9**
9 Greatham, W. Sussex **E 11**
11 Greatstone-on-Sea .. **F 9**
23 Greatworth .... **H 9**
25 Green End .... **K 2**
36 Green Hammerton . **A 2**
7 Green Ore .... **A 9**
10 Green Street Green . **A 5**
19 Green Tye .... **B 4**
34 Greenbank .... **B 4**
43 Greenbeck .... **C 11**
48 Greenburn .... **C 2**
38 Greendale .... **E 4**
7 Greendown .... **A 9**
45 Greendykes .... **C 12**
49 Greenend .... **G 8**
25 Greenfield, Beds. .. **M 2**
29 Greenfield, Clwyd . **B 11**
55 Greenfield, Highland **J 6**
35 Greenfield, Manchester .... **G 8**
17 Greenfield, Oxon. .. **E 8**
18 Greenford .... **F 1**
48 Greengairs .... **B 1**
44 Greengate Well .... **F 5**
34 Greenhalgh .... **D 3**
16 Greenham, Berks. .. **H 6**
6 Greenham, Som. ... **D 4**
44 Greenhaugh .... **D 6**
43 Greenhead, Dunf. & Gal. .... **C 10**
44 Greenhead, Northumb. .... **F 5**
47 Greenhead, Strathclyde .... **E 9**
48 Greenhill, Central .. **B 1**
11 Greenhill, Kent ... **A 10**
47 Greenhills .... **D 8**
10 Greenhithe .... **A 5**
47 Greenholm .... **F 10**
39 Greenholme .... **E 8**
49 Greenhouse .... **G 8**
35 Greenhow Hill .... **A 9**
64 Greenigo .... **D 2**
49 Greenknowe .... **E 9**
61 Greenland .... **A 11**
17 Greenlands .... **F 8**
49 Greenlaw, Borders .. **E 9**
58 Greenlaw, Grampian **B 4**
49 Greenlaw Walls ... **E 12**
43 Greenlea, Dumf. & Gal. .... **D 11**
47 Greenlea, Dumf. & Gal. .... **A 7**
52 Greenloaning .... **F 3**
34 Greenmount .... **F 6**
47 Greenock .... **B 8**
38 Greenodd .... **G 5**
48 Greenrig .... **E 1**
43 Greenrow .... **F 11**
23 Greens Norton .... **G 10**
32 Greenscares .... **F 3**
48 Greenshields .... **E 3**
45 Greenside .... **G 9**
45 Greensidehill .... **A 8**
58 Greenskairs .... **A 5**
19 Greenstead Green .. **A 8**
18 Greensted Green ... **D 5**
64 Greenwall .... **C 3**
12 Greenway, Dyfed ... **D 4**
14 Greenway, S. Glam. **G 4**
18 Greenwich .... **F 4**
16 Greet .... **A 1**
21 Greete .... **E 11**
23 Greetham, Leics. .. **A 12**
33 Greetham, Lincs. .. **C 10**
35 Greetland .... **E 9**
7 Greinton .... **C 7**
23 Grendon, N'thants . **F 12**
22 Grendon, War. .... **B 6**
22 Grendon Common .. **B 6**
21 Grendon Green ... **G 11**
17 Grendon Underwood **B 8**
42 Grennan .... **E 3**
5 Grenofen .... **J 4**
35 Grenoside .... **H 11**
30 Gresford .... **E 2**
26 Gresham .... **B 5**
62 Greshornish .... **C 3**
63 Gress .... **C 6**
26 Gressenhall .... **D 3**
26 Gressenhall Grn. ... **D 3**
39 Gressingham .... **H 8**
30 Grestey Green .... **E 6**
40 Greta Bridge .... **D 1**
44 Gretna .... **F 2**
44 Gretna Green .... **F 1**
16 Gretton, Glos. .... **A 1**
23 Gretton, N'thants .. **C 12**
21 Gretton, Salop. .... **C 10**
40 Grewelthorpe .... **G 2**
58 Grey Stone .... **E 6**
40 Greygarth .... **H 2**
13 Greynor .... **F 9**
48 Greyrigg, Central ... **B 2**
43 Greyrigg, Dumf. & Gall. .... **C 11**
38 Greysouthen .... **B 3**
39 Greystoke, Cumb. .. **B 7**
53 Greystoke, Tayside **C 10**
43 Greystone .... **D 10**
9 Greywell .... **A 8**
4 Gribbleford Bridge .. **F 4**
36 Gribthorpe .... **D 5**
50 Gribun .... **D 2**
5 Gridley Corner .... **G 2**
23 Griff .... **C 7**
14 Griffithstown .... **D 6**
39 Grigghall .... **F 7**
64 Grimbister .... **C 2**
34 Grimeford Village .. **F 5**
36 Grimethorpe .... **F 2**
22 Grimley .... **F 2**
47 Grimmet .... **H 8**
33 Grimoldby .... **A 11**
34 Grimsargh .... **D 5**
37 Grimsby .... **F 10**
23 Grimscote .... **G 10**
4 Grimscott .... **E 1**
63 Grimshader .... **D 5**
24 Grimsthorpe .... **C 2**
37 Grimston, Humber. **D 10**
32 Grimston, Leics. .... **H 4**
24 Grimston, Norfolk .. **C 8**
7 Grimstone .... **G 9**
5 Grinacombe Moor .. **G 3**
41 Grindale .... **H 11**
22 Grindle .... **B 1**
31 Grindleford .... **B 11**
34 Grindleton .... **C 6**
30 Grindley Brook .... **F 4**
31 Grindlow .... **B 10**
40 Grindon, Cleveland . **C 4**
44 Grindon, Northumb. **F 6**
49 Grindon, Northumb. **E 11**
31 Grindon, Staffs. .... **E 9**
44 Grindon Hill .... **F 6**
49 Grindonrigg .... **E 11**
32 Gringley on the Hill **A 4**
44 Grinsdale .... **G 2**
30 Grinshill .... **H 4**
40 Grinton .... **E 1**
41 Gristhorpe .... **G 11**
26 Griston .... **E 2**
16 Grittenham .... **F 1**
15 Grittleton .... **F 11**
38 Grizebeck .... **G 5**
38 Grizedale .... **F 6**
64 Grobister .... **C 4**
23 Groby .... **A 8**
29 Groes, Clwyd .... **D 9**
13 Groes, W. Glam. .. **H 11**
14 Groesfaen .... **F 4**
28 Groesffordd .... **F 2**
29 Groesffordd .... **C 7**
29 Groesffordd Marli .. **C 9**
21 Groesllwyd .... **A 7**
28 Groeslon, Gwynedd . **C 3**
28 Groeslon, Gwynedd . **E 4**
46 Grogport .... **E 3**
29 Gronant .... **B 10**
10 Groombridge .... **D 4**
63 Grosebay .... **H 2**
15 Grosmont, Gwent ... **B 7**
41 Grosmont, N. Yorks. **E 8**
27 Groton .... **L 2**
7 Grove, Dorset .... **H 7**
16 Grove, Oxon. .... **E 5**
32 Grove, Notts. .... **B 4**
13 Grovesend .... **G 9**
54 Grudie .... **D 7**
60 Gruids .... **F 6**
60 Gruinard House .... **G 1**
62 Grula .... **E 3**
50 Gruline House .... **D 3**
2 Grumbla .... **G 1**
27 Grundisburgh .... **K 5**
64 Grundsound .... **E 7**
64 Gruting .... **D 6**
64 Grutness .... **F 7**
28 Grwedog .... **B 3**
51 Gualachulain .... **C 8**
60 Gualin House .... **B 4**
53 Guard Bridge .... **E 9**
22 Guarlford .... **H 2**
52 Guay .... **B 5**
43 Gubhill .... **B 10**
11 Guestling Green .... **G 7**
11 Guestling Icklesham **F 7**
26 Guestwick .... **C 3**
34 Guide .... **E 6**
45 Guide Post .... **E 10**
25 Guilden Morden .... **L 4**
30 Guilden Sutton .... **C 3**
9 Guildford .... **A 11**
53 Guildtown .... **D 6**
23 Guilsborough .... **E 10**
21 Guilsfield .... **A 8**
11 Guilton .... **B 11**
47 Guiltreehill .... **H 8**
4 Guineaford .... **B 4**
55 Guisachan House ... **G 7**
40 Guisborough .... **D 6**
35 Guiseley .... **C 10**
26 Guist .... **C 3**
16 Guiting Power .... **B 2**
64 Gulberwick .... **E 7**
49 Gullane .... **A 7**
2 Gulval .... **F 2**
5 Gulworthy .... **H 3**
12 Gumfreston .... **G 4**
23 Gumley .... **C 10**
2 Gummow's Shop ... **D 6**
36 Gunby, Humber. ... **D 5**
32 Gunby, Lincs. .... **H 6**
9 Gundleton .... **C 7**
4 Gunn .... **C 5**
39 Gunnerside .... **E 11**
45 Gunnerton .... **F 7**
45 Gunnerton Fell .... **E 7**
36 Gunness .... **F 6**
3 Gunnislake .... **C 11**
64 Gunnista .... **D 7**
36 Gunthorpe, Humber. **G 6**
26 Gunthorpe, Norf. ... **B 3**
32 Gunthorpe, Notts. .. **F 4**
8 Gunville .... **G 6**
6 Gupworthy .... **C 3**
8 Gurnard .... **F 6**
7 Gurney Slade .... **A 9**
14 Gurnos .... **C 1**
8 Gussage All Saints .. **E 2**
8 Gussage St. Andrew . **E 1**
8 Gussage St. Michael . **E 1**
11 Guston .... **D 11**
64 Gutcher .... **B 8**
53 Guthrie .... **B 10**
24 Guy's Head .... **C 6**
7 Guy's Marsh .... **D 11**
24 Guyhirn .... **E 5**
45 Guyzance .... **C 10**
14 Gwaelod-y-garth .... **F 4**
29 Gwaenysgor .... **B 10**
28 Gwalchmai .... **C 3**
12 Gwastad .... **D 4**
13 Gwaun-cae-Gurwen **F 10**
12 Gwbert-on-Sea .... **B 5**
2 Gweek .... **G 4**
15 Gwehelog Com. .... **D 7**
20 Gwenddwr .... **H 6**
2 Gwennap .... **F 4**
14 Gwent, Co. .... **D 6**
2 Gwenter .... **H 4**
29 Gwernaffield .... **D 11**
21 Gwernaffel .... **E 8**
15 Gwernesney .... **D 7**
13 Gwernogle .... **D 8**
29 Gwernymynydd ... **D 11**
14 Gwern-y-Steeple ... **G 4**
30 Gwersyllt .... **E 2**
29 Gwespyr .... **B 10**
2 Gwinear .... **F 3**
2 Gwithian .... **F 3**
29 Gwddelwern .... **F 10**
13 Gwyddgrug .... **C 8**
29 Gwynfryn .... **E 11**
28 Gwynedd, Co. .... **E 5**
20 Gwystre .... **F 6**
29 Gwytherin .... **D 8**
29 Gyfelia .... **F 12**
29 Gyffin .... **C 7**
29 Gyffylliog .... **D 10**
21 Habberley .... **B 9**
63 Habost, W. Isles .... **E 4**
63 Habost, W. Isles .... **A 6**
37 Habrough .... **F 9**
24 Hacconby .... **C 2**
24 Haceby .... **B 1**
27 Hacheston .... **J 6**
32 Hackenthorpe .... **B 1**
18 Hacketts .... **C 3**
26 Hackford .... **E 3**
40 Hackforth .... **F 3**
64 Hackland .... **C 2**
63 Hacklete .... **C 2**
23 Hackleton .... **G 11**
41 Hackness .... **F 10**
18 Hackney .... **E 4**
33 Hackthorn .... **B 7**
39 Hackthorpe .... **C 7**
18 Hacton .... **E 5**
49 Hadden .... **F 10**
17 Haddenham, Bucks. . **C 8**
25 Haddenham, Cambs. **H 6**
49 Haddington, Lothian **B 8**
32 Haddington, Lincs. . **D 6**
26 Haddiscoe .... **F 7**
58 Haddoch .... **C 3**

24 Haddon ....F 2
35 Hade Edge ......G 10
22 Hademore ....A 5
35 Hadfield ....G 9
18 Hadham Cross ...B 4
18 Hadham Ford ....B 4
19 Hadleigh, Essex ..E 8
27 Hadleigh, Suffolk ..L 3
21 Hadley ....A 12
31 Hadley End ......H 10
18 Hadley Wood ....D 3
10 Hadlow ....C 5
10 Hadlow Down ....F 4
30 Hadnall ....H 4
25 Hadstock ....L 7
45 Hadwin's Close ..B 10
22 Hadzor ....F 3
11 Haffenden Quarter .D 7
20 Hafod ....G 1
29 Hafod-Dinbych ...E 8
20 Hafod-Peris .....F 1
35 Haggate ....D 7
44 Haggbeck ....F 3
45 Haggerston .....B 11
21 Hagley, Heref. & Worcs. ....H 11
22 Hagley, Heref. & Worcs. ....D 3
33 Hagworthingham ..C 10
34 Haigh, Manchester ..F 5
35 Haigh, S. Yorks. ..F 11
35 Haigh Moor .....E 11
34 Haighton Green ..D 4
25 Hail Weston .....J 3
38 Haile ....D 3
18 Hailey, Herts. ...C 4
16 Hailey, Oxon. ...C 4
10 Hailsham ....G 5
18 Hainault ....E 4
26 Hainford ....D 5
33 Hainton ....B 9
37 Haisthorpe .....A 9
32 Halam ....E 4
52 Halbeath ....H 6
6 Halberton ......E 3
61 Halcro ....B 11
30 Hale, Cheshire ...B 3
30 Hale, Manchester ..B 6
8 Hale, Hants. ....D 3
9 Hale, Surrey ....A 10
30 Hale Clift ......B 3
10 Hale Street .....C 5
30 Halebarns ......B 6
26 Hales, Norfolk ...F 7
30 Hales, Staffs. ...G 6
30 Halesowen ......D 3
27 Halesworth .....H 7
30 Halewood ....B 3
22 Halfrod, War. ...H 6
21 Halford, Salop. ..D 10
12 Halfpenny Furze ..F 6
22 Halfpenny Green ..C 2
16 Halfway, Berks. ..G 5
13 Halfway, Dyfed ..D 11
13 Halfway, Dyfed ..D 10
3 Halfway House, Cornwall ....C 8
6 Halfway House, Devon ....G 4
21 Halfway House, Salop. ....A 9
42 Halfway House, Dumf. & Gall. ...E 4
11 Halfway Houses ..A 8
35 Halifax ....E 9
47 Halket ....D 9
61 Halkirk ....B 10
29 Halkyn ....C 11
47 Hall ....D 9
38 Hall Dunnerdale ..F 5
22 Hall Green .....D 5
47 Hall of Carnduff ..E 11
21 Hall of the Forest ..D 7
38 Hall Waberthwaite ..F 3
10 Halland ....F 4
23 Hallaton ....B 11
7 Hallatrow ....A 10
44 Hallbankgate ...G 4
15 Hallen ....F 8
32 Hallfield Gate ...D 1
49 Halliburton ....D 9
62 Hallin ....B 2
10 Halling ....B 6
33 Hallington, Lincs. ..B 10
45 Hallington, Northumb. ...E 8
34 Halliwell ....F 6
32 Halloughton ....E 4
22 Hallow ....F 2
44 Hallrule ....B 4
49 Halls ....B 9
18 Hall's Green ....A 3
5 Hallsands ......M 7
43 Hallscaur ......B 8

24 Halltoft End ....A 5
49 Halltree ....D 7
3 Hallworthy ......A 9
48 Hallyne ....E 5
30 Halmer End .....E 6
15 Halmore ....D 10
48 Halmyre Mains ..D 4
9 Halnaker ....E 10
34 Halsall ....F 2
23 Halse, Northants. ..H 9
6 Halse, Somerset ..C 5
2 Halsetown ......F 2
37 Halsham ....D 10
8 Halsinger ....B 4
27 Halstead, Essex ..M 1
10 Halstead, Kent ..B 4
23 Halstead, Leics. ..B 11
7 Halstock ....E 8
38 Haltcliff Bridge ..B 6
33 Haltham ....D 9
17 Halton, Bucks. ...C 9
30 Halton, Cheshire ..B 4
29 Halton, Clwyd ...F 12
34 Halton, Lancs. ...A 4
45 Halton, Northumb. ..F 8
35 Halton East .....B 9
39 Halton, Gill .....G 11
33 Halton Holegate ..D 11
44 Halton Lea Gate ..G 5
35 Halton Moor ....D 12
34 Halton Park ....A 4
11 Halton Shields ..F 8
35 Halton West .....B 7
44 Haltwhistle .....C 5
26 Halvergate ......E 7
5 Halwell ....K 6
4 Halwill ....F 3
4 Halwill Junction ..F 3
6 Ham, Devon .....F 6
15 Ham, Glos. ......D 10
11 Ham, Kent ......C 12
18 Ham, London ....G 2
16 Ham, Wilts. .....H 4
15 Ham Green, Avon ..G 8
22 Ham Green, Heref. & Worcs. ..F 4
11 Ham Green, Kent ..A 7
10 Ham Hill ....B 6
11 Ham Street, Kent ..E 8
7 Ham Street, Som. ..C 9
8 Hamble ....E 6
17 Hambledon .....E 8
8 Hambledon, Hants. ..E 8
9 Hambledon, Surrey ..B 11
34 Hambleton, Lancs. ..C 3
36 Hambleton, N. Yorks. ..D 3
7 Hambridge ......D 7
9 Hambrook ....E 9
33 Hameringham ...C 10
25 Hamerton ....G 2
47 Hamilton ....D 12
9 Hammer ....C 10
9 Hammerpot .....F 11
18 Hammersmith ...F 2
22 Hammerwich ....A 4
7 Hammoon ....E 11
64 Hamnavoe, W. Burra ..E 7
64 Hamnavoe, Yell ..C 7
64 Hamnavoe, Zetland .C 6
64 Hamnavoe, Zetland ..C 7
10 Hampden ....H 5
17 Hampden Row ...D 9
16 Hampnett ....C 2
36 Hampole ....F 3
8 Hampreston .....F 2
8 Hampshire, Co. ..C 6
18 Hampstead ......E 3
16 Hampstead Norris ..F 6
35 Hampsthwaite ...A 11
22 Hampton, Heref. & Worcs. ....H 4
18 Hampton, London ..G 1
22 Hampton, Salop. ..D 1
15 Hampton Bishop ..A 9
30 Hampton Heath ..E 4
22 Hampton in Arden ..D 5
22 Hampton Lovett ..F 2
22 Hampton Lucy ...F 6
22 Hampton on the Hill ..F 6
16 Hampton Poyle ..C 6
31 Hamstall Ridware ..H 9
8 Hamstead, I. o. W. ..G 5
22 Hamstead, W. Midlands ......C 4
16 Hamstead Marshall .H 5
40 Hamsteels ......A 2
40 Hamsterley, Dur. ..B 1
45 Hamsterley, Dur. ..G 9
8 Hamworthy .....G 1
31 Hanbury, Staffs. ..G 10

22 Hanbury, Heref. & Worcs. ....F 3
30 Handbridge .....D 3
10 Handcross ......E 2
31 Handforth ......B 7
30 Handley, Cheshire ..D 3
8 Handley, Dorset ..D 2
22 Handsacre ......A 4
22 Handsworth .....C 4
17 Handy Cross, Bucks. ..E 9
4 Handy Cross, Devon ..C 3
31 Hanford ....F 7
8 Hanging Langford ..B 2
43 Hangingshaw, Dumf. & Gall. ...C 11
48 Hangingshaw, Strathclyde .....E 2
30 Hankelow ....F 5
16 Hankerton ......E 1
10 Hankham ....G 5
31 Hanley ....E 7
22 Hanley Castle ...H 2
21 Hanley Childe ...F 12
22 Hanley Swan ....H 2
21 Hanley William ..F 12
35 Hanlith ....A 8
30 Hanmer ....F 3
9 Hannington, Hants. .A 7
23 Hannington, Northants. ...E 11
16 Hannington, Wilts. ..E 3
16 Hannginton Wick ..E 3
23 Hanslope ....G 11
24 Hanthorpe ......C 2
18 Hanwell, London ..F 2
23 Hanwell, Oxon. ..H 8
18 Hanworth, Lond. ..G 1
26 Hanworth, Norf. ..B 5
48 Happendon ......F 1
26 Happisburgh ....B 7
26 Happisburgh Com. ..C 7
30 Hapsford ....C 3
34 Hapton, Lancs. ..D 6
26 Hapton, Norfolk ..F 5
10 Harberton ......K 6
5 Harbertonford ...K 6
11 Harbledown .....B 10
22 Harborne ....F 3
23 Harborough Magna .D 8
45 Harbottle ....C 7
5 Harbourneford ...J 6
23 Harbury ....F 7
32 Harby, Leics. ....G 5
32 Harby, Notts. ...F 5
6 Harcombe, Devon .H 2
6 Harcombe, Devon .G 5
2 Harcourt ....F 5
35 Harden ....C 9
15 Hardenhuish ....G 12
43 Hardgate, Dumf. & Gall. ....E 9
59 Hardgate, Grampian ..G 5
43 Hardgrove ......D 11
9 Hardham ....D 11
34 Hardhorn ....C 2
26 Hardingham .....E 3
31 Hardings Wood ..E 7
32 Hardingstone ...F 11
7 Hardington .....A 10
7 Hardington Mandeville ......E 8
7 Hardington Marsh ..E 8
4 Hardisworthy ...D 4
8 Hardley ....F 6
26 Hardley Street ...E 7
32 Hardmonsworth ..F 1
39 Hardrow ....F 11
32 Hardstoft ....D 2
7 Hardway ....C 10
17 Hardwick, Bucks. ..B 9
25 Hardwick, Cambs. ..J 5
32 Hardwick, Lincs. ..C 6
26 Hardwick, Norf. ..F 5
23 Hardwick, Northants. ..E 11
16 Hardwick, Oxon. ..D 5
17 Hardwick, Oxon. ..A 7
32 Hardwick Grange ..C 4
15 Hardwicke, Glos. ..B 12
15 Hardwicke, Glos. ..C 11
21 Hardwicke, Heref. & Worcs. ....H 8
19 Hardy's Green ...B 9
9 Hare & Hounds Inn .F 6
19 Hare Green .....A 10
17 Hare Hatch .....F 9
18 Hare Street, Essex ..L 2
18 Hare Street, Herts. ..A 4
10 Harebeating .....G 5
33 Hareby ....D 10
34 Hareden ....B 5

18 Harefield ....E 1
17 Harefield Moor ..E 11
33 Harehills ....D 11
45 Harehope ....A 9
49 Harelaw, Borders ..G 8
48 Harelaw, Strathclyde ..E 2
47 Harelaw, Strathclyde ..D 9
59 Haremuir ....K 5
39 Haresceugh .....A 8
15 Harescombe ....C 11
15 Haresfield ......C 11
48 Hareshaw ....C 1
35 Harewood ....C 12
15 Harewood End ...B 8
36 Harewood Estate ..F 3
4 Harford, Devon ..F 7
5 Harford, Devon ..K 5
26 Hargate ....F 4
31 Hargatewall .....C 9
30 Hargrave, Ches. ..D 3
25 Hargrave, Northants. ..H 1
27 Hargrave Green ..J 1
3 Haringey ....E 3
44 Harker ....G 2
27 Harkstead ......M 5
22 Harlaston ......A 5
31 Harlaw House ...E 5
32 Harlaxton ......G 6
29 Harle Syke .....D 7
28 Harlech ....G 5
21 Harlescott ......A 10
18 Harlesden ......F 2
26 Harleston, Norf. ..G 5
27 Harleston, Suffolk ..J 3
23 Harlestone .....F 10
21 Harley ....B 11
48 Harleyholm .....F 2
25 Harlington, Beds. ..M 1
18 Harlington, Lond. ..F 1
36 Harlington, S. Yorks. ..G 3
62 Harlosh ....D 2
18 Harlow ....C 5
18 Harlow Hill .....F 9
36 Harlthorpe ......C 5
25 Harlton ....K 5
8 Harman's Cross ..H 1
40 Harmby ....F 2
18 Harmer Green ...B 3
31 Harmerhill ......H 3
33 Harmston ......D 7
16 Harnhill ....D 2
31 Harold Hill .....E 5
12 Haroldston West ..E 2
64 Haroldswick ....A 8
17 Harome ....G 6
17 Harpenden .....C 12
49 Harper Ridge ...E 11
49 Harpertoun .....E 10
6 Harpford ....G 4
37 Harpham ....A 8
21 Harpley, Heref. & Worcs. ....F 12
26 Harpley, Norfolk ..C 1
32 Harpole ....F 10
31 Harpsden ......F 8
32 Harpswell ......A 6
31 Harpur Hill .....C 9
35 Harpurhey ......G 7
64 Harra ....B 7
44 Harraby ....H 3
4 Harracott ....C 4
52 Harrapool ......F 6
52 Harrietfield ....D 5
49 Harrietsfield ...G 9
48 Harrietsham ....C 7
38 Harrington, Cumb. ..C 2
33 Harrington, Lincs. .C 10
23 Harrington, Northants. ..D 11
23 Harringworth ...B 12
23 Harriseahead ...E 7
35 Harrogate ......B 12
23 Harrold ....F 12
18 Harrow ....E 2
27 Harrow Street ...L 3
18 Harrow Weald ..E 2
3 Harrowbarrow ..C 11
3 Harrowbridge ...B 9
40 Harrowgate Village .C 3
25 Harston, Cambs. ..K 5
32 Harston, Leics. ..G 5
36 Harswell ....C 6
44 Hart Law ....C 10
45 Hartburn ....D 9
2 Hartest ....K 1
7 Hartfoot Lane ...F 11
25 Hartford, Cambs. ..H 4
30 Hartford, Ches. ..C 5
19 Hartford End ...B 7

17 Hartfordbridge ..H 8
30 Harthill, Cheshire ..E 4
32 Harthill, S. Yorks. ..B 2
48 Harthill, Strathclyde ..C 2
31 Hartington ......D 9
4 Hartland ....D 1
22 Hartlebury .....E 2
40 Hartlepool ......B 5
39 Hartley, Cumbria .D 10
10 Hartley, Kent ...A 5
10 Hartley, Kent ...E 6
45 Hartley, Northumb. ..E 11
10 Hartley Green ...A 5
17 Hartley Wespall ..H 8
17 Hartley Wintney ..H 8
11 Hartlip ....B 7
36 Harton, N. Yorks. ..A 5
21 Harton, Salop ...D 10
45 Harton, Tyne & Wear ....G 12
15 Hartpury ....B 11
35 Hartshead ......E 10
23 Hartshill ....C 7
31 Hartshorne .....H 11
48 Hartside ....F 2
38 Hartsop ....D 6
17 Hartwell, Bucks. ..C 9
23 Hartwell, Northants. ..G 11
35 Hartwith ....A 11
48 Hartwood ......C 1
49 Hartwoodburn ..G 7
49 Hartwoodmyres ..G 7
10 Harvel ....B 5
22 Harvington .....G 4
22 Harvington Cross ..G 4
16 Harwell ....E 6
27 Harwich ....M 6
39 Harwood, Dur. ..B 10
34 Harwood, Manchester ......F 6
45 Harwood, Northumb. ..D 8
41 Harwood Dale ...F 9
32 Harworth ....A 3
9 Hascombe ......B 11
23 Haselbech ......D 10
7 Haselbury Plucknett ..E 8
22 Haseley ....E 6
22 Haselor ....F 5
15 Hasfield ....B 11
12 Hasguard ....F 2
12 Hasguard Cross ..F 2
34 Haskayne ......F 2
27 Hasketon ......K 5
32 Hasland ....C 1
9 Haslemere ......C 10
34 Haslingden .....E 6
25 Haslingfield ....K 5
30 Haslington .....E 6
30 Hassall ....D 6
30 Hassall Green ...D 6
11 Hassell Street ...C 9
49 Hassendean ....G 8
26 Hassingham .....E 6
49 Hassington .....E 10
10 Hassocks ....F 2
31 Hassop ....C 10
61 Hastigrow ......B 11
11 Hastingleigh ...D 9
11 Hastings ....G 7
18 Hastingwood ...C 5
17 Hastoe ....C 10
40 Haswell ....A 4
40 Haswell Plough ..A 4
48 Haswellsykes ...E 5
9 Hatch ....A 8
6 Hatch Beauchamp ..D 6
18 Hatch End ......E 1
30 Hatch Green ....D 6
46 Hatchednize ....E 10
8 Hatchet Gate ...F 5
37 Hatcliffe ....G 10
21 Hatfield, Heref. & Worcs. ....F 11
22 Hatfield, Heref. & Worcs. ....G 2
18 Hatfield, Herts. ..C 2
36 Hatfield, S. Yorks. ..F 4
18 Hatfield Broad Oak ..B 5
18 Hatfield Heath ..B 5
19 Hatfield Peverel ..C 8
36 Hatfield Woodhouse ..F 5
16 Hatford ....E 4
8 Hatherden .....A 5
4 Hatherleigh ....E 4
32 Hathern ....H 2
16 Hatherop ....D 3

31 Hathersage .....B 10
35 Hathershaw .....G 8
30 Hatherton, Ches. ..E 5
22 Hatherton, Staffs. ..A 3
25 Hatley St. George ..K 4
3 Hatt ....C 11
9 Hattingley ......B 8
30 Hatton, Cheshire ..B 4
31 Hatton, Derby ...G 10
58 Hatton, Grampian ..D 8
33 Hatton, Lincs. ...C 9
18 Hatton, London ..F 1
21 Hatton, Salop. ..C 10
22 Hatton, War. ....E 6
58 Hatton Fintray ..E 8
30 Hatton Heath ...D 3
58 Hattoncrook ....E 6
34 Haultwick ......B 3
50 Haunn ....C 1
22 Haunton ....A 6
45 Hauxley ....C 11
25 Hauxton ....K 5
35 Haugh, Manchester .F 8
47 Haugh, Strathclyde ..G 10
49 Haugh Head ....G 12
58 Haugh of Glass ..D 2
43 Haugh of Urr ...F 9
33 Haugham ....B 10
47 Haughhead ......B 11
27 Haughley ....J 3
22 Haughley Green ..J 3
58 Haughs of Clinterty .C 10
45 Haughterslaw ...A 9
32 Haughton, Notts. ..C 5
21 Haughton, Salop. .A 11
21 Haughton, Salop. .C 12
30 Haughton, Salop. ..G 2
31 Haughton, Staffs. ..H 2
45 Haughton Castle ..F 7
35 Haughton Green ..H 8
30 Haughton Moss ..E 4
9 Havant ....F 8
21 Haven ....G 9
37 Haven Side .....E 10
9 Haven Street ...G 7
36 Havercroft .....F 2
12 Haverfordwest ..C 3
25 Haverhill ....L 8
38 Haverigg ......G 4
18 Havering ....E 5
18 Havering-atte-Bower ..D 6
18 Havering's Grove .D 6
23 Haversham .....H 11
38 Haverthwaite ...G 6
40 Haverton Hill ...C 5
29 Hawarden ......D 12
19 Hawbush Green ..B 8
13 Hawen ....B 7
39 Hawes ....F 11
22 Hawford ....F 2
44 Hawick ....B 3
31 Hawk Green ....B 8
7 Hawkchurch ....F 7
27 Hawkedon ......K 1
10 Hawkenbury ....D 5
9 Hawkeridge ....A 11
22 Hawkes End ....D 6
15 Hawkesbury ....F 10
15 Hawkesbury Upton ..F 11
45 Hawkhill ....B 10
10 Hawkhurst .....E 6
9 Hawkley ....C 8
9 Hawkridge .....C 2
34 Hawkshaw Lane ..F 6
38 Hawkshead .....E 6
38 Hawkshead Hill ..E 6
18 Hawksland .....C 4
39 Hawkswick .....H 12
32 Hawksworth, Notts. .E 5
35 Hawksworth, W. Yorks. ......C 10
18 Hawkwell ......C 4
10 Hawley ....A 4
17 Hawley ....H 9
16 Hawling ....B 2
40 Hawnby ....F 5
35 Haworth ....D 9
27 Hawstead ......J 1
40 Hawthorn, Dur. ..B 7
15 Hawthorn, Wilts. .G 11
44 Hawthornside ...G 6
24 Hawthorpe .....C 2
32 Hawton ....E 5
36 Haxby ....A 4
36 Haxey ....G 5
10 Haxted ....D 3
21 Hay-on-Wye ....H 8
18 Hay Street .....A 4
12 Haycastle ......D 2
12 Haycastle Cross ..D 3
34 Haydock ....G 4

7 Haydon, Dorset ... E 10
45 Haydon, Northumb. . F 7
45 Haydon Bridge ..... G 7
16 Haydon Wick ...... E 2
3 Haye .... C 10
18 Hayes, Kent .... G 4
18 Hayes, London ..... F 1
31 Hayfield, Derby .... B 9
53 Hayfield, Fife ...... H 7
47 Hayhill .... H 9
2 Hayle .... F 3
9 Hayling Island ..... F 8
49 Haymount .... F 9
6 Hayne .... F 2
25 Haynes .... L 2
25 Haynes West End ... L 2
10 Haysden .... D 4
53 Hayshead .... C 11
43 Hayton, Cumb. .... G 11
44 Hayton, Cumb. ..... G 3
59 Hayton, Grampian .. G 7
36 Hayton, Humber. ... C 6
32 Hayton, Notts. .... B 4
21 Hayton's Bent .... D 10
5 Haytor Vale .... H 6
10 Hayward's Heath ... F 2
32 Haywood Oaks .... E 3
31 Hazel Grove .... B 8
48 Hazelbank .... E 1
7 Hazelbury Bryan .. E 11
17 Hazeley .... H 8
22 Hazelslade .... A 4
53 Hazelton Walls ..... E 8
31 Hazelwood .... F 11
17 Hazlemere .... E 10
45 Hazlerigg .... F 10
16 Hazleton .... B 2
45 Hazon .... C 10
24 Heacham .... B 8
8 Headbourne Worthy C 6
21 Headbrook .... G 8
11 Headcorn .... D 7
16 Headington .... C 6
40 Headlam .... C 2
22 Headless Cross ..... F 4
9 Headley, Hants. .... C 9
16 Headley, Hants. .... H 6
10 Headley, Surrey .... C 1
9 Headley Down .... B 10
32 Headon .... C 5
47 Heads .... E 12
44 Heads Nook .... G 3
32 Heage .... E 1
39 Healaugh, N. Yorks. E 12
36 Healaugh, N. Yorks. B 3
31 Heald Green .... B 7
4 Heale, Devon ...... A 5
7 Heale, Somerset ... B 10
35 Healey, Lancs. ..... E 7
45 Healey, Nothumb. .. G 8
40 Healey, N. Yorks. .. G 2
45 Healey Cote .... C 9
45 Healeyfield .... H 9
37 Healing .... F 10
2 Heamor .... G 2
32 Heanor .... F 2
4 Heanton Punchardon B 4
32 Heapham .... A 6
48 Hearthstane .... G 4
4 Heasley Mill .... C 6
62 Heast .... F 6
32 Heath .... C 2
17 Heath and Reach .. A 10
4 Heath Cross .... F 7
17 Heath End, Berks. .. H 7
9 Heath End, Surrey . A 10
22 Heath End, W. Midlands ...... B 4
22 Heath Hayes .... A 4
22 Heath Hill .... A 1
7 Heath House .... B 7
6 Heath Pault Cross ... C 3
22 Heath Town .... B 3
31 Heathcote .... D 10
23 Heather .... A 7
62 Heatherfield .... D 4
52 Heatheryhaugh ..... B 6
43 Heathfield, Cumb. . G 12
5 Heathfield, Devon .. H 7
10 Heathfield, East Sussex ...... F 4
6 Heathfield, Som. ... D 5
47 Heathfield, Strathclyde ...... C 8
43 Heathhall .... D 10
22 Heathton .... C 2
30 Heatley .... A 5
34 Heaton, Lancs. ..... A 3
35 Heaton, Manchester H 7
31 Heaton, Staffs. ..... D 8
35 Heaton, W. Yorks. D 10
34 Heaton's Bridge .... F 3
10 Heaverham .... B 4
31 Heaviley .... A 7
6 Heavitree .... G 3
45 Hebburn .... G 11
35 Hebden .... A 9
35 Hebden Bridge ..... D 8
30 Hebden Green ..... D 5
12 Hebron, Dyfed ..... D 5
45 Hebron, Northumb. D 10
43 Heck .... D 11
17 Heckfield .... H 8
27 Heckfield Green .... H 5
24 Heckington .... A 2
48 Hecklebirnie .... F 2
35 Heckmondwike .... E 10
16 Heddington .... G 1
16 Heddington Wick ... G 1
4 Heddon .... C 5
45 Heddon on the Wall . F 9
26 Hedenham .... F 6
5 Hedge Cross .... G 4
8 Hedge End .... E 6
17 Hedgerley .... E 10
6 Hedging .... C 6
45 Hedley on the Hill .. G 9
22 Hednesford .... A 3
37 Hedon .... D 9
17 Hedsor .... E 10
21 Hedgon Hill .... G 11
45 Heiferlaw Bank ... A 10
40 Heighington, Dur. .. C 3
33 Heighington, Lincs. . C 7
56 Heights of Brae .... D 1
54 Heights of Kinlochewe C 4
60 Heilam .... B 5
49 Heiton .... F 9
6 Hele, Devon .... F 3
4 Hele, Devon .... A 4
5 Hele, Devon .... G 2
6 Hele, Somerset ..... D 5
4 Hele Lane .... E 7
47 Helensburgh .... A 8
47 Helentongate .... F 9
2 Helford .... G 5
2 Helford Passage .... G 5
26 Helhoughton .... C 2
25 Helions Bumpstead . L 7
3 Helland .... C 8
3 Hellandbridge ...... C 8
26 Hellesdon .... D 5
23 Hellidon .... F 8
35 Hellifield .... B 7
10 Helling .... G 4
26 Hellington .... E 6
45 Helm .... C 10
23 Helmdon .... H 9
27 Helmingham .... J 5
40 Helmington Row ... B 2
61 Helmsdale .... E 10
34 Helmshore .... E 6
40 Helmsley .... G 6
40 Helperby .... H 5
41 Helperthorpe ...... H 9
24 Helpringham .... B 2
24 Helpston .... E 2
30 Helsby .... C 3
2 Helston .... G 4
3 Helstone .... B 8
39 Helton .... C 7
39 Helwith Bridge .... H 10
17 Hemel Hempstead . D 11
36 Hemingbrough ..... D 4
33 Hemingby .... C 9
36 Hemongfield .... G 2
25 Hemingford Abbots H 4
25 Hemingford Grey ... H 4
27 Hemingstone .... K 5
32 Hemington, Leics. .. G 2
25 Hemington, Northants. .... G 2
7 Hemington, Som. .. A 10
27 Hemley .... L 6
40 Hemlington .... D 5
22 Hempholme .... B 8
26 Hempnall .... F 5
26 Hempnall Green .... F 5
25 Hempstead, Essex .. L 7
10 Hempstead, Kent ... B 6
26 Hempstead, Norf. ... B 4
15 Hempsted .... C 11
26 Hempton, Norfolk .. C 2
16 Hempton, Oxon. ... A 5
26 Hemsby .... D 8
32 Hemswell .... A 6
36 Hemsworth .... F 2
6 Hemyock .... E 5
15 Henbury, Avon ..... F 9
31 Henbury, Ches. .... C 7
4 Henderbarrow Corner F 3
18 Hendon, London ... E 2
45 Hendon, Tyne & Wear .... G 12
15 Hendre .... C 8
14 Hendreforgan ...... E 3
12 Hendre-wen .... D 3
13 Hendy .... G 9
28 Heneglwys .... C 4
12 Hen-feddau .... D 6
15 Henfield, Avon ... F 10
10 Henfield, W. Sussex . F 1
11 Hengherst .... D 8
14 Hengoed, Mid Glam. E 5
21 Hengoed, Powys ... G 8
30 Hengoed, Salop. ... G 2
27 Hengrave .... H 1
18 Henham .... A 5
45 Henhill .... E 12
21 Heniarth .... B 7
6 Henlade .... D 6
45 Henlaw .... C 11
7 Henley, Dorset ... F 10
21 Henley, Salop. .... D 10
7 Henley, Somerset ... C 8
27 Henley, Suffolk .... K 5
9 Henley, W. Sussex . D 10
22 Henley-in-Arden ... E 5
17 Henley-on-Thames . F 8
10 Henley Street ...... A 5
29 Henllan, Clwyd ..... C 9
13 Henllan, Dyfed ..... C 7
12 Henllan Amgoed ... E 5
14 Henllys .... E 6
25 Henlow .... L 3
5 Hennock .... H 7
27 Henny Street .... L 2
29 Henryd .... C 7
12 Henry's Moat ..... D 4
34 Hensall .... E 4
44 Henshaw .... G 6
38 Hensingham .... D 2
27 Heanstead .... G 8
7 Henstridge .... D 10
7 Henstridge Ash ... D 10
7 Henstridge Bowden D 10
17 Henton, Oxon. ..... D 8
7 Henton, Som. ...... B 8
7 Henstridge Marsh . D 11
22 Henwick .... G 2
3 Henwood .... B 9
64 Heogan .... D 7
14 Heol Senni .... B 3
13 Heol-las .... G 10
14 Heol-y-Cyw .... F 3
45 Hepburn .... A 9
45 Hepple .... C 8
45 Hepple Whitefield .. C 8
45 Hepscott .... E 10
35 Hepstonstall .... D 8
27 Hepworth, Suff. .... H 3
35 Hepworth, W. Yorks. F 10
12 Herbrandston ...... F 2
21 Hereford .... H 10
22 Hereford & Worcester, Co. .... F 2
48 Heriot .... D 6
49 Heriot Station ..... D 7
49 Hermiston .... G 8
16 Hermitage, Berks. .. G 6
44 Hermitage, Borders . C 3
7 Hermitage, Dorset . F 10
44 Hermitage, Dumf. & Gall. .... E 9
9 Hermitage, W. Sussex F 9
13 Hermon, Dyfed ... D 10
12 Hermon, Dyfed .... D 5
28 Hermon, Gwynedd .. C 3
11 Herne .... B 10
11 Herne Bay .... A 10
4 Herner .... C 5
11 Hernhill .... B 9
3 Herodsfoot .... D 9
11 Heronden .... C 11
18 Herongate .... E 6
42 Heronsford .... C 2
17 Heronsgate .... E 11
2 Herriard .... B 8
26 Herringfleet .... F 8
25 Herring's Green .... L 2
25 Herringswell ...... H 8
45 Herrington .... H 11
11 Hersden .... B 10
17 Hersham .... H 12
10 Herstmonceux ..... G 5
8 Herston, Dorset ... H 2
64 Herston, Orkney Is. . E 2
18 Hertford .... C 3
18 Hertford Heath .... C 3
18 Hertfordshire, Co. .. B 2
18 Hertingfordbury .... C 3
38 Hesket Newmarket . A 6
34 Hesketh Bank ...... E 3
34 Hesketh Lane ...... C 5
34 Heskin Green ...... F 4
40 Hesleden .... A 4
44 Hesleyside .... E 6
36 Heslington .... B 4
36 Hessay .... B 3
3 Hessenford .... D 10
27 Hessett .... J 2
47 Hessilhead .... D 9
37 Hessle .... E 8
34 Hest Bank .... A 3
18 Heston .... F 1
30 Heswall .... B 1
17 Hethe .... A 7
26 Hethersett .... E 5
44 Hethersgill .... F 3
49 Hethpool .... G 11
40 Hett .... B 3
35 Hetton .... A 8
45 Hetton Downs .... H 11
45 Hetton Law ...... C 11
45 Hetton Steads ..... B 11
45 Hetton-le-Hole ... H 11
45 Heugh .... F 9
58 Heugh-head .... F 1
27 Heveningham ...... H 6
10 Hever .... D 4
39 Heversham .... G 7
26 Hevingham .... C 5
15 Hewelsfield .... D 9
15 Hewish, Avon ..... H 7
7 Hewish, Somerset ... E 7
36 Heworth .... B 4
45 Hexham .... G 7
49 Hexpath .... E 9
10 Hextable .... A 4
5 Hexworthy .... H 5
19 Heybridge, Essex ... C 8
18 Heybridge, Essex ... D 6
19 Heydridge Basin .... C 8
5 Heybrook Bay ...... L 4
25 Heydon, Cambs. .... L 5
26 Heydon, Norfolk ... C 4
33 Heydour .... F 7
34 Heysham .... A 3
35 Heyshaw .... A 10
9 Heyshott .... D 10
8 Heytesbury .... B 1
16 Heythrop .... A 4
35 Heywood Manchester .... F 7
7 Heywood, Wilts. .. A 12
37 Hibaldstow .... G 7
36 Hickleton .... G 3
26 Hickling, Norfolk ... C 7
32 Hickling, Notts. .... G 4
26 Hickling Green ..... C 7
22 Hidcote Boyce ..... H 5
36 High Ackworth ..... E 2
45 High Angerton ..... E 9
39 High Bankhill ...... A 8
18 High Beach .... D 4
39 High Bentham ..... H 9
4 High Bickington .... D 5
39 High Birkwith .... G 10
47 High Blantyre .... D 11
48 High Bonnybridge .. B 1
43 High Borgue .... F 7
47 High Boydston ..... E 7
35 High Bradley .... B 9
4 High Bray .... C 6
10 High Brooms .... D 5
4 High Bullen .... D 4
40 High Burton .... G 2
45 High Buston ...... B 10
45 High Callerton .... F 10
36 High Catton .... B 5
45 High Church ...... E 10
47 High Cleughearn .. E 11
16 High Cogges .... C 5
40 High Conniscliffe ... D 3
49 High Cross, Borders E 8
9 High Cross, Hants. .. C 8
18 High Cross, Herts. .. B 4
47 High Cross, Strathclyde .... E 9
31 High Cross Bank .. H 11
47 High Duncryne .... A 9
18 High Easter .... B 6
42 High Eldrig .... E 3
40 High Ellington ..... G 2
40 High Entercommon . E 4
21 High Ercall .... A 11
40 High Etherley ...... B 2
19 High Garrett .... A 7
47 High Glengarth .... D 8
40 High Grange .... B 2
40 High Grantley ...... H 3
22 High Green, Heref. & Worcs. .. H 2
26 High Green, Norf. .. E 4
35 High Green, S. Yorks. G 12
11 High Halden .... D 8
10 High Halstow ...... A 6
7 High Ham .... C 8
38 High Harrington .... C 3
40 High Haswell ...... A 4
30 High Hatton .... H 5
41 High Hawsker ..... D 9
39 High Hesket .... A 7
40 High Hesleden ..... A 5
35 High Hoyland .... F 11
37 High Hursley ...... D 7
10 High Hurstwood .... E 4
41 High Hutton .... H 8
38 High Ireby .... B 5
40 High Kilburn ...... G 5
31 High Lane, Manchester .... B 8
21 High Lane, Heref. & Worcs. . F 12
18 High Laver .... C 5
30 High Legh .... B 5
40 High Leven .... D 5
15 High Littleton ..... H 9
38 High Lorton .... C 4
41 High Marishes ...... G 8
32 High Marnham ..... C 5
36 High Melton .... G 3
45 High Mickley ...... G 9
42 High Mindork ...... F 4
41 High Mowthorpe ... H 9
38 High Newton ...... G 6
45 High Newton by-the-Sea .... E 12
38 High Nibthwaite .... F 5
30 High Offley .... H 6
18 High Ongar .... D 5
22 High Onn .... A 2
42 High Pennyvenie ... A 6
18 High Roding .... B 6
38 High Row .... B 6
34 High Salter .... A 5
39 High Shaw .... F 11
40 High Skelding ..... H 2
45 High Spen .... G 9
40 High Stoop .... A 1
3 High Street, Corn. .. D 7
27 High Street, Suff. ... K 7
27 High Street, Suff. ... K 2
27 High Street Green .. K 3
40 High Throston ..... B 5
33 High Toynton .... C 10
45 High Trewhitt ...... B 8
48 High Valleyfield ... A 3
45 High Warden ...... F 7
38 High Wray .... E 6
18 High Wych .... C 5
17 High Wycombe .... E 9
32 Higham, Derby ..... D 1
10 Higham, Kent ...... A 6
35 Higham, Lancs. .... D 7
25 Higham, Suffolk .... J 8
27 Higham, Suffolk .... L 3
45 Higham Dykes ..... E 9
25 Higham Ferrers .... H 1
25 Higham Gobion .... M 2
23 Higham on the Hill .. C 7
10 Higham Wood ...... C 5
4 Highampton .... E 4
55 Highbridge, Highland .... L 6
6 Highbridge, Som. ... B 6
10 Highbrook .... E 2
35 Highburton .... F 10
7 Highbury .... A 10
44 Highchesters ...... B 3
16 Highclere .... H 5
8 Highcliffe .... G 4
7 Higher Alham ..... B 10
7 Higher Ansty ..... F 11
6 Higher Ashton ..... H 2
34 Higher Ballam ..... D 2
2 Higher Boscaswell .. F 1
6 Higher Combe ...... C 3
30 Higher Heath ...... G 4
29 Higher Kinnerton . D 12
7 Higher Nyland .... D 10
34 Higher Penwortham D 4
2 Higher Town .... C 2
30 Higher Walton, Ches. B 4
34 Higher Walton, Lancs. D 5
7 Higher Whatcombe F 11
30 Higher Whitley ..... B 5
30 Higher Wych .... F 3
4 Highfield, Devon ... F 6
32 Highfield, S. Yorks. . B 1
47 Highfield, Strathclyde .... D 8
45 Highfield, Tyne & Wear .... G 9
25 Highfields, Cambs. .. J 5
49 Highfields, Northumb. D 12
18 Highgate, London .. E 3
36 Highgate, N. Yorks. . E 4
44 Highgreen Manor ... D 6
40 Highlands, Dur. .... C 2
58 Highlands, Grampian F 6
32 Highlane .... B 1
15 Highleadon .... B 11
9 Highleigh .... F 9
22 Highley .... D 1
17 Highmoor Cross .... F 8
15 Highmoor Hill ..... E 8
15 Highnam Green ... B 11
4 Highridge .... D 6
11 Highsted .... B 8
27 Highstreet Green ... M 1
27 Hightae .... D 11
31 Hightown, Ches. .... D 7
43 Hightown, Dumf. & Gall. .... C 11
34 Hightown, Merseyside .... G 2
43 Hightown of Craigs D 11
2 Highway, Corn. ..... E 4
16 Highway, Wilts. .... G 2
5 Highweek .... J 7
16 Highworth .... E 3
26 Hilborough .... E 1
32 Hilcote .... D 2
16 Hilcott .... H 2
10 Hilden Park .... C 4
10 Hildenborough ..... C 4
25 Hildersham .... K 6
31 Hilderstone .... G 8
37 Hilderthorpe ...... A 9
7 Hilfield .... F 9
24 Hilgay .... F 7
15 Hill, Avon .... E 9
4 Hill, Devon .... E 9
22 Hill, W. Midlands ... B 5
9 Hill Brow .... D 9
41 Hill Cottages ...... E 7
34 Hill Dale .... F 4
33 Hill Dyke .... E 10
39 Hill End, Dur. .... B 12
52 Hill End, Fife ...... H 5
15 Hill Gate .... B 8
9 Hill Head, Hants. ... F 7
45 Hill Head, Northumb. F 7
38 Hill Millom .... G 4
12 Hill Mountain ..... F 3
52 Hill of Beath ...... H 6
56 Hill of Fearn ...... B 4
58 Hill of Maud Crofts . B 2
31 Hill Ridware ...... H 9
25 Hill Row .... H 5
8 Hill Top, Hants .... F 5
35 Hill Top, W. Yorks. F 12
8 Hill View .... F 1
36 Hillam .... D 3
39 Hillbeck .... D 10
38 Hillberry .... G 2
11 Hillborough ...... A 10
8 Hillbourne .... G 2
58 Hillbrae .... E 5
8 Hillbutts .... F 1
53 Hillcairnie .... E 8
6 Hillcommon .... D 5
48 Hillend, Fife ...... A 4
48 Hillend, Strathclyde . E 3
15 Hillersland .... C 9
17 Hillesden .... A 8
15 Hillesley .... E 11
6 Hillfarance .... D 5
5 Hillhead, Devon ... K 8
43 Hillhead, Dumf. & Gall. .... B 8
58 Hillhead, Grampian . E 5
45 Hillhead, Northumb. B 9
47 Hillhead, Strathclyde F 10
47 Hillhead, Strathclyde G 9
48 Hillhead, Strathclyde E 3
58 Hillhead of Auchentumb .... B 7
58 Hillhead of Cocklaw C 8
49 Hillhouse .... D 7
22 Hilliard's Cross .... A 5
18 Hillingdon .... F 1
24 Hillington .... C 8
23 Hillmorton .... E 8
59 Hillockhead, Grampian .... G 1
58 Hillockhead, Grampian .... F 2

9 Hillpound **D 7**
43 Hillside, Dumf. & Gall. **C 12**
59 Hillside, Grampian **H 7**
64 Hillside, Shetlands **C 7**
59 Hillside, Tayside **L 4**
8 Hillstreet **D 5**
64 Hillswick **C 6**
9 Hillway **G 8**
64 Hillwell **F 7**
16 Hilmarton **G 1**
15 Hilperton **H 12**
15 Hilperton Marsh **H 11**
9 Hilsea **F 8**
37 Hilston **D 10**
25 Hilton **J 4**
49 Hilton, Borders **D 11**
40 Hilton, Cleveland **D 5**
39 Hilton, Cumbria **C 9**
31 Hilton, Derby **G 11**
7 Hilton, Dorset **F 11**
40 Hilton, Durham **C 2**
58 Hilton, Grampian **D 7**
22 Hilton, Salop **C 1**
56 Hilton of Cadboll **B 4**
22 Himbleton **F 3**
22 Himley **C 2**
39 Hincaster **G 7**
16 Hinchwick **A 2**
23 Hinckley **C 7**
27 Hinderclay **H 3**
41 Hinderwell **D 8**
30 Hindford **G 2**
9 Hindhead **C 10**
34 Hindley, Manchester **G 5**
45 Hindley, Northumb. **G 8**
34 Hindley Green **G 5**
22 Hindlip **F 2**
26 Hindolveston **C 3**
7 Hindon **C 12**
26 Hindringham **B 3**
26 Hingham **E 3**
30 Hinstock **H 5**
27 Hintlesham **L 4**
15 Hinton, Avon **G 10**
8 Hinton, Hants. **G 4**
21 Hinton, Heref. & Worcs. **H 9**
23 Hinton, Northants. **G 8**
21 Hinton, Salop. **B 9**
9 Hinton Ampner **C 7**
7 Hinton Blewett **A 9**
15 Hinton Charterhouse **H 11**
22 Hinton Green **H 4**
23 Hinton-in-the-Hedge **H 9**
9 Hinton Marsh **C 7**
8 Hinton Martell **E 2**
22 Hinton on the Green **H 4**
16 Hinton Parva **F 3**
7 Hinton St. George **E 7**
7 Hinton St. Mary **E 11**
16 Hinton Waldrist **D 5**
21 Hints, Salop. **E 11**
22 Hints, Staffs. **B 5**
23 Hinwick **F 12**
11 Hinxhill **D 9**
25 Hinxton **L 6**
25 Hinxworth **L 3**
35 Hipperholme **E 10**
40 Hipswell **E 2**
12 Hiraeth **E 5**
59 Hirn **G 5**
29 Hirnant, Powys **H 10**
20 Hirnant, Powys **E 4**
45 Hirst **D 11**
36 Hirst Courtney **E 4**
29 Hirwaen **D 10**
14 Hirwaun **D 3**
4 Hiscott **C 4**
25 Histon **J 5**
27 Hitcham **K 3**
43 Hitchill **E 12**
18 Hitchin **A 2**
18 Hither Green **F 4**
4 Hittisleigh Cross **F 6**
36 Hive **D 6**
31 Hixon **H 8**
11 Hoaden **B 11**
15 Hoaldalbert **B 7**
31 Hoar Cross **H 10**
15 Hoarwithy **A 8**
11 Hoath **B 10**
21 Hobarris **E 8**
64 Hobbister **D 2**
18 Hobbs Cross **D 5**
44 Hobkirk **B 4**
45 Hobson **G 10**
32 Hoby **H 4**
26 Hockering **D 4**
32 Hockerton **E 4**
19 Hockley **E 8**
22 Hockley Heath **E 5**
17 Hockliffe **A 10**
25 Hockwold cum Wilton **G 8**
6 Hockworthy **D 4**
18 Hoddesdon **C 4**
34 Hoddlesden **E 6**
43 Hoddomcross **D 12**
12 Hodgeston **G 4**
30 Hodnet **G 5**
10 Hodsoll Street **B 5**
16 Hodson **F 3**
32 Hodthorpe **C 3**
9 Hoe, Hampshire **D 7**
26 Hoe, Norfolk **D 3**
9 Hoe Gate **E 8**
39 Hoff **C 9**
17 Hoggeston **B 9**
34 Hoghton **E 5**
31 Hognaston **E 11**
33 Hogsthorpe **C 12**
24 Holbeach **C 5**
24 Holbeach Bank **C 5**
24 Holbeach Clough **C 4**
24 Holbeach Drove **D 4**
24 Holbeach Hurn **C 5**
24 Holbeach St. Johns **D 4**
24 Holbeach St. Marks **C 5**
24 Holbeach St. Matthew **B 5**
32 Holbeck, Notts. **C 3**
35 Holbeck, W. Yorks. **D 11**
22 Holberrow Green **F 4**
5 Holbeton **L 5**
31 Holbrook, Derby **F 12**
27 Holbrook, Suffolk **L 5**
8 Holbury **F 6**
45 Holburn **B 11**
5 Holcombe, Devon **H 8**
34 Holcombe, Manchester **E 6**
7 Holcombe, Som. **A 10**
34 Holcombe Brook **F 6**
6 Holcombe Rogus **D 4**
23 Holcot **E 11**
34 Holden **B 6**
23 Holdenby **E 10**
8 Holdenhurst **G 3**
21 Holdgate **C 11**
33 Holdingham **E 7**
7 Holditch **F 7**
49 Holefield **F 10**
47 Holehouse, Strathclyde **H 9**
47 Holehouse, Strathclyde **D 8**
15 Hole-in-the-Wall **A 9**
43 Holestane **B 9**
6 Holford **B 5**
38 Holker **G 6**
26 Holkham **A 2**
4 Hollacombe **F 2**
64 Holland, Papa Westray Orkney Is. **A 3**
64 Holland, Stronsay, Orkney, Is. **C 4**
33 Holland Fen **E 9**
19 Holland-on-Sea **B 11**
64 Hollandstoun **A 4**
44 Hollee **F 1**
27 Hollesley **L 6**
11 Hollingbourne **C 7**
10 Hollingrove **F 6**
31 Hollington, Derby **F 10**
10 Hollington, E. Sussex **G 6**
31 Hollington, Staffs. **F 9**
35 Hollingworth **G 8**
35 Hollins **F 7**
30 Hollins Green **A 5**
34 Hollins Lane **B 4**
31 Hollinsclough **D 9**
4 Hollocombe **E 5**
22 Hollow Court **F 3**
31 Hollow Meadows **A 11**
31 Holloway **E 11**
23 Hollowell **E 10**
44 Hollows **E 2**
30 Holly Bush, Clwyd **F 3**
14 Holly Bush, Gwent **D 5**
24 Holly End **E 6**
22 Holly Green **H 2**
15 Hollybush, Heref. & Worcs. **A 10**
47 Hollybush, Strathclyde **H 9**
37 Hollym **E 11**
22 Hollywood **D 4**
44 Holm, Dumf. & Gall. **C 1**
63 Holm, W. Isles **D 5**
43 Holm St. Cuthbert **G 12**
4 Holmacott **C 4**
35 Holmbridge **F 10**
9 Holmbury St. Mary **B 12**
3 Holmbush **D 7**
31 Holmcroft **H 8**
25 Holme, Cambs. **G 3**
39 Holme, Cumbria **G 7**
37 Holme, Humber. **F 7**
40 Holme, N. Yorks. **G 4**
32 Holme, Notts. **D 5**
35 Holme, W. Yorks. **F 9**
35 Holme Chapel **D 7**
26 Holme Hale **E 2**
15 Holme Lacy **A 9**
21 Holme Marsh **G 9**
24 Holme next the Sea **A 8**
37 Holme on the Wolds **C 7**
32 Holme Pierrepont **F 3**
36 Holm upon Spalding Moor **C 6**
21 Holmer **H 10**
17 Holmer Green **D 10**
30 Holmes Chapel **C 6**
31 Holmesfield **B 11**
34 Holmeswood **E 3**
32 Holmewood **D 2**
35 Holmfirth **F 10**
43 Holmfoot **B 9**
47 Holmhead **G 10**
62 Holmisdal **C 1**
37 Holmpton **E 11**
38 Holmrook **E 3**
45 Holmside **H 10**
44 Holmwrangle **H 4**
5 Holne **J 6**
4 Holsworthy **F 2**
4 Holsworthy Beacon **E 2**
30 Holt, Clwyd **E 3**
8 Holt, Dorset **F 2**
26 Holt, Norfolk **B 4**
15 Holt, Wilts. **H 11**
22 Holts, Heref. & Worcs. **F 2**
9 Holt End, Hants. **B 8**
22 Holt End, Heref. & Worcs. **E 4**
22 Holt Heath **F 2**
8 Holt Wood **E 2**
36 Holtby **B 4**
33 Holton, Lincs. **B 8**
17 Holton, Oxon. **G 7**
7 Holton, Som. **D 10**
27 Holton, Suffolk **H 7**
8 Holton Heath **G 1**
37 Holton le Clay **G 10**
37 Holton le Moor **G 8**
27 Holton St. Mary **L 4**
10 Holtye **D 3**
7 Holwell, Dorset **E 10**
18 Holwell, Herts. **A 2**
32 Holwell, Leics. **H 5**
16 Holwell, Oxon. **C 3**
29 Holwick **C 11**
7 Holworth **H 11**
22 Holy Cross **D 3**
45 Holy Island **B 12**
9 Holybourne **B 9**
28 Holyhead **B 2**
31 Holymoorside **C 11**
17 Holyport **F 10**
45 Holystone **C 8**
47 Holytown **C 12**
25 Holywell, Cambs. **H 4**
29 Holywell, Clwyd **C 11**
2 Holywell, Corn. **D 5**
44 Holywell, Cumb. **E 3**
7 Holywell, Dorset **F 9**
45 Holywell, Northumb. **F 11**
35 Holywell Green **E 9**
6 Holywell Lake **D 5**
25 Holywell Row **H 8**
43 Holywood **C 10**
15 Hom Green **B 9**
49 Homebank **E 10**
49 Homebyres **E 9**
21 Homer **B 11**
27 Homersfield **G 6**
8 Homington **D 3**
11 Honey Hill **B 10**
16 Honey Street **H 2**
27 Honey Tye **L 2**
12 Honeyborough **F 2**
4 Honeychurch **F 5**
22 Honiley **E 6**
26 Honing **C 6**
26 Honingham **D 4**
32 Honington, Lincs. **F 6**
27 Honington, Suff. **H 2**
22 Honington, War. **H 6**
6 Honiton **F 5**
35 Honley **F 10**
10 Hoo **A 6**
22 Hoobrook **E 2**
35 Hood Green **G 11**
5 Hooe, Devon **K 4**
10 Hooe, E. Sussex **G 6**
10 Hooe Common **G 6**
12 Hook, Dyfed **F 3**
9 Hook, Hants. **A 8**
36 Hook, Humber. **E 5**
18 Hook, London **G 2**
16 Hook, Wilts. **F 2**
10 Hook Green, Kent **A 5**
10 Hook Green, Kent **D 5**
16 Hook Norton **A 4**
7 Hooke **F 9**
30 Hookgate **G 6**
4 Hookway **F 7**
10 Hookwood **D 2**
30 Hoole **C 3**
10 Hooley **B 2**
30 Hooton **B 2**
32 Hooton Levitt **A 2**
36 Hooton Pagnell **F 3**
36 Hooton Roberts **G 3**
64 Hoove **D 7**
24 Hop Pole **D 3**
31 Hope, Derby **B 10**
5 Hope, Devon **M 5**
29 Hope, Clwyd **D 12**
60 Hope, Highland **B 5**
21 Hope, Powys **B 8**
21 Hope, Salop. **B 9**
21 Hope Bagot **E 11**
21 Hope Bowdler **C 10**
15 Hope Mansell **B 9**
21 Hope under Dinmore **G 10**
56 Hopeman **C 7**
21 Hopesay **D 9**
36 Hopperton **B 2**
31 Hopton, Derby **E 11**
30 Hopton, Salop. **G 4**
31 Hopton, Staffs. **H 8**
26 Hopton, Suffolk **E 8**
27 Hopton, Suffolk **G 3**
21 Hopton Cangeford **D 11**
21 Hopton Castle **E 9**
21 Hopton Wafers **E 11**
21 Hoptonheath **E 9**
22 Hopwas **B 5**
22 Hopwood **E 4**
10 Horam **F 4**
24 Horbling **B 2**
35 Horbury **E 11**
40 Horden **A 5**
21 Horderley **D 9**
8 Hordle **F 4**
30 Hordley **G 2**
5 Hordon **H 4**
13 Horeb, Dyfed **C 7**
13 Horeb, Dyfed **D 8**
15 Horfield **F 9**
27 Horham **H 5**
19 Horkesley Heath **A 9**
37 Horkstow **E 7**
23 Horley, Oxon. **H 7**
10 Horley, Surrey **D 2**
7 Hornblotton Grn. **C 9**
39 Hornby, Lancs. **H 8**
40 Hornby, N. Yorks. **F 2**
40 Hornby, N. Yorks. **E 4**
33 Horncastle **C 9**
18 Hornchurch **E 5**
49 Horncliffe **D 11**
49 Horndean, Borders **D 11**
9 Horndean, Hants. **E 8**
18 Horndon on the Hill **F 6**
10 Horne **D 2**
6 Horner **B 3**
26 Horning **D 6**
23 Horninghold **B 11**
31 Horninglow **H 10**
25 Horningsea **J 6**
7 Horningsham **B 11**
26 Horningtoft **C 2**
3 Horningtops **D 9**
4 Horns Cross, Devon **D 3**
11 Horns Cross, E. Sussex **F 7**
44 Hornsby **H 3**
37 Hornsea **B 9**
37 Hornsea Bridge **B 9**
18 Hornsey **E 3**
23 Hornton **H 7**
5 Horrabridge **J 4**
27 Horringer **J 1**
9 Horringford **H 7**
48 Horsburgh **E 6**
31 Horse Bridge **E 8**
8 Horsebridge **C 5**
22 Horsebrook **A 2**
15 Horsecastle **H 7**
21 Horsehay **B 12**
25 Horseheath **K 7**
39 Horsehouse **G 12**
17 Horsell **H 10**
30 Horseman's Grn. **F 3**
17 Horsenden **D 9**
26 Horsey **C 8**
26 Horsford **D 5**
35 Horsforth **C 11**
22 Horsham, Heref. & Worcs. **F 1**
10 Horsham, W. Sussex **E 1**
26 Horsham St. Faith **D 5**
33 Horsington, Lincs. **C 9**
7 Horsington, Som. **D 10**
32 Horsley, Derby **F 1**
15 Horsley, Glos. **E 11**
45 Horsley, Northumb. **C 7**
45 Horsley, Northumb. **F 9**
19 Horsley Cross **A 11**
32 Horsley Woodhouse **F 1**
19 Horsleycross St. **A 11**
49 Horsleyhill **G 8**
10 Horsmonden **D 6**
17 Horspath **D 7**
26 Horstead **D 5**
10 Horsted Keynes **E 3**
15 Horton, Avon **F 10**
17 Horton, Bucks. **B 10**
17 Horton, Bucks. **F 11**
8 Horton, Dorset **E 2**
35 Horton, Lancs. **B 7**
23 Horton, Northants. **G 11**
6 Horton, Somerset **E 6**
31 Horton, Staffs. **D 8**
16 Horton, Wilts. **H 2**
13 Horton, W. Glam. **H 8**
7 Horton Cross **E 7**
30 Horton Green **E 3**
8 Horton Heath **D 6**
39 Horton in Ribblesdale **H 10**
10 Horton Kirby **A 4**
34 Horwich **F 5**
4 Horwood **C 4**
44 Hoscote **B 2**
32 Hose **G 5**
49 Hoselaw **F 10**
38 Hoses **F 5**
64 Hoswick **E 7**
37 Hotham **D 7**
11 Hothfield **D 8**
32 Hoton **H 3**
44 Hott **D 6**
64 Houbie **B 8**
30 Hough **E 6**
30 Hough Green **B 3**
32 Hough-on-the-Hill **F 6**
32 Hougham **F 6**
25 Houghton, Cambs. **H 4**
44 Houghton, Cumb. **G 2**
12 Houghton, Dyfed **F 3**
8 Houghton, Hants. **C 5**
9 Houghton, W. Sussex **E 11**
25 Houghton Conquest **L 2**
30 Houghton Green **A 5**
17 Houghton Regis **B 11**
45 Houghton-le-Spring **H 11**
23 Houghton on the Hill **B 10**
41 Houlsyke **D 7**
8 Hound **E 6**
17 Hound Green **H 8**
49 Houndridge **F 10**
49 Houndslow **E 9**
6 Houndsmoor **D 5**
49 Houndwood **C 11**
8 Hounsdown **E 5**
18 Hounslow **F 2**
64 Housay **C 8**
59 House of Glenmuick **H 1**
58 Housieside **E 6**
47 Houston **C 9**
61 Houstry **D 10**
10 Hove **H 2**
32 Hoveringham **E 4**
26 Hoveton **D 6**
41 Hovingham **H 7**
44 How **G 3**
16 How Caple **A 9**
10 How Green **C 4**
38 How Head **E 6**
35 Howbrook **G 11**
35 Howburn **F 10**
49 Howden, Borders **G 9**
36 Howden, Humber. **D 5**
35 Howden Clough **D 11**
40 Hoden-le-Wear **B 2**
39 Howe, Cumbria **F 7**
61 Howe, Highland **B 12**
26 Howe, Norfolk **E 6**
19 Howe Green **D 7**
58 Howe of Teucher **C 5**
19 Howe Street, Essex **B 7**
25 Howe Street, Essex **M 8**
33 Howell **F 8**
43 Howes **E 12**
20 Howey **F 6**
48 Howford **F 6**
48 Howgate, Lothian **D 5**
48 Howgate, Strathclyde **F 2**
45 Howick **A 10**
30 Howle **H 5**
15 Howle Hill **B 9**
25 Howlett End **M 7**
6 Howley **E 6**
49 Howliston **D 7**
49 Hownam **G 10**
49 Hownam Mains **G 10**
44 Howpasley **B 2**
37 Howsham, Humber. **G 8**
36 Howsham, N. Yorks. **A 5**
49 Howtel **F 11**
64 Howth **D 2**
15 Howton **A 7**
39 Howtown **C 7**
47 Howwood **C 9**
64 Hoxa **E 2**
27 Hoxne **G 5**
30 Hoylake **A 1**
35 Hoylake Nether **G 12**
35 Hoylake Swaine **G 11**
12 Hubberston **F 2**
24 Hubbert's Bridge **A 4**
36 Huby, N. Yorks. **A 3**
35 Huby, N. Yorks. **B 11**
15 Hucclecote **C 12**
11 Hucking **B 7**
32 Hucknall **E 3**
35 Huddersfield **E 10**
22 Huddington **F 3**
40 Hudswell **E 2**
36 Huggate **B 6**
2 Hugh Town **D 2**
17 Hughenden Valley **D 9**
21 Hughley **C 11**
4 Huish, Devon **E 4**
16 Huish, Wilts. **H 2**
6 Huish Barton **B 4**
6 Huish Champflower **C 4**
7 Huish Episcopi **D 8**
17 Hulcott **B 9**
31 Hulland **F 11**
15 Hullavington **F 12**
19 Hullbridge **D 8**
31 Hulme End **D 9**
31 Hulme Walfield **D 7**
34 Hulton Lane Ends **G 6**
27 Hulver Street **G 8**
8 Hulverstone **H 5**
21 Humber Court **G 11**
37 Humberside, Co. **C 7**
37 Humberston **G 10**
23 Humberstone **B 10**
49 Humbie **C 7**
37 Humbleton, Humber. **D 10**
49 Humbleton, Northumb. **G 12**
49 Hume **E 9**
47 Humeston **H 7**
45 Humshaugh **F 7**
61 Huna **A 12**
34 Huncoat **D 6**
23 Huncote **B 8**
49 Hundalee **G 9**
39 Hunderthwaite **C 12**
33 Hundleby **D 11**
12 Hundleton **G 3**
25 Hundon **K 8**
9 Hundred Acres **E 7**
34 Hundred End **E 3**
21 Hundred House **G 7**
23 Hungarton **A 10**
34 Hunger Hill **F 5**
16 Hungerford, Berks. **G 4**
8 Hungerford, Hants. **E 3**
16 Hungerford Newton **G 5**
32 Hungerton **G 6**
23 Hungladder **A 3**
63 Hunisish **F 1**
41 Hunmanby **G 11**
23 Hunningham **E 7**
8 Hunny Hill **G 6**
18 Hunsdon **C 4**
36 Hunsingore **B 2**
35 Hunslett Carr **D 11**
39 Hunsonby **B 8**
61 Hunspow **A 11**

24 Hunstanton .... **B 8**
45 Hunstanworth ...... **H 8**
27 Hunston, Suffolk ... **H 3**
9 Hunston, W. Sussex **F 10**
15 Hunstrete .... **H 9**
35 Hunsworth .... **D 10**
12 Hunt End .... **F 4**
41 Hunt Ho .... **E 7**
47 Hunter's Quay ...... **B 7**
49 Huntershall .... **F 10**
47 Hunterston Works .. **D 7**
44 Huntford .... **B 5**
59 Hunthill Lodge ..... **K 2**
25 Huntingdon, Cambs. **H 3**
22 Huntingdon, Staffs. . **A 3**
27 Huntingfield .... **H 6**
21 Huntington, Heref. & Worcs. .. **G 8**
21 Huntington, Heref. & Worcs. . **H 10**
36 Huntington, N. Yorks. **B 4**
52 Huntingtower Haugh **E 5**
15 Huntley, Glos. .... **B 10**
31 Huntley, Staffs ...... **F 8**
58 Huntly .... **D 3**
49 Huntlywood .... **E 9**
10 Hunton, Kent ...... **C 6**
40 Hunton, N. Yorks. .. **F 2**
17 Hunton Bridge .... **D 11**
30 Hunt's Cross .... **B 3**
6 Huntscott .... **B 3**
6 Huntsham .... **D 3**
6 Huntspill .... **B 6**
7 Huntworth .... **C 7**
40 Huntwick .... **B 2**
26 Hunworth .... **B 4**
7 Hurcott .... **E 7**
8 Hurdcott .... **C 3**
17 Hurley, Berks. ...... **F 9**
22 Hurley, War. .... **C 9**
47 Hurlford .... **F 9**
64 Hurliness .... **E 1**
8 Hurn .... **F 3**
31 Hursdfield .... **C 8**
8 Hursley .... **D 6**
17 Hurst, Berks. .... **G 9**
35 Hurst, Manchester .. **G 8**
40 Hurst, N. Yorks. .... **E 1**
7 Hurst, Somerset .... **D 8**
10 Hurst Green, E. Sussex .... **E 6**
34 Hurst Green, Lancs. . **C 6**
10 Hurst Green, Surrey **C 3**
10 Hurst Wickham ..... **F 2**
8 Hurstbourne Priors . **A 6**
8 Hurstbourne Tarrant **A 5**
21 Hurstley .... **G 9**
10 Hurstpierpoint ...... **F 2**
21 Hurstway Com. ...... **G 8**
9 Hurtmore .... **B 11**
40 Hurworth .... **D 3**
39 Hury .... **C 11**
62 Husabost Piers ..... **C 1**
23 Husbands Bosworth **D 10**
25 Husborne Crawley .. **L 1**
40 Husthwaite .... **H 5**
32 Huthwaite .... **D 2**
49 Hutlertown .... **G 7**
33 Huttoft .... **C 12**
15 Hutton, Avon ...... **H 7**
49 Hutton, Borders .. **D 11**
39 Hutton, Cumb. ...... **C 7**
18 Hutton, Essex ...... **D 6**
37 Hutton, Humber. ... **B 8**
34 Hutton, Lancs. ..... **D 4**
41 Hutton Buscel ...... **G 9**
40 Hutton Conyers .... **H 3**
39 Hutton End .... **A 7**
40 Hutton Hang .... **F 2**
40 Hutton Henry ...... **B 4**
39 Hutton-in-the-Forest **B 7**
39 Hutton John .... **C 7**
41 Hutton-le-Hole .... **F 7**
40 Hutton Lowcross ... **D 6**
40 Hutton Magna ..... **D 2**
38 Hutton Roof, Cumb. **B 6**
39 Hutton Roof, Cumbria **G 8**
40 Hutton Rudby ...... **E 5**
40 Hutton Sessay ...... **H 5**
36 Hutton Wandesley .. **B 3**
4 Huxford .... **D 6**
6 Huxham .... **F 3**
30 Huxley .... **D 4**
64 Huxter .... **D 7**
30 Huyton .... **A 3**
38 Hycemoor .... **F 3**
15 Hyde, Glos. .... **D 12**
35 Hyde, Manchester .. **H 8**
17 Hyde Heath ...... **D 10**
31 Hyde Lea .... **H 7**
9 Hydestile .... **B 11**
38 Hydro .... **F 2**
48 Hyndford .... **E 2**
21 Hyssington .... **C 8**
8 Hythe, Hants. ...... **E 5**
11 Hythe, Kent .... **E 10**
7 Hythe, Somerset .... **A 8**
17 Hythe End .... **G 11**
58 Hythie .... **C 7**
58 Ianstown .... **A 2**
7 Ibberton .... **E 11**
31 Ible .... **D 11**
8 Ibsley .... **E 3**
23 Ibstock .... **A 7**
17 Ibstone .... **E 8**
8 Ibthorpe .... **A 5**
9 Ibworth .... **A 7**
15 Icelton .... **H 7**
26 Ickburgh .... **F 1**
18 Ickenham .... **E 1**
17 Ickford .... **C 7**
11 Ickham .... **B 11**
18 Ickleford .... **A 2**
25 Ickleton .... **L 6**
27 Icklingham .... **H 1**
25 Ickwell Green ...... **L 3**
16 Icomb .... **B 3**
16 Idbury .... **B 3**
4 Iddesleigh .... **E 4**
6 Ide .... **G 2**
10 Ide Hill .... **C 4**
5 Ideford .... **H 8**
11 Iden .... **F 8**
10 Iden Green, Kent .. **D 6**
11 Iden Green, Kent ... **E 7**
35 Idle .... **C 10**
22 Idlicote .... **H 6**
58 Idoch .... **C 5**
13 Idole .... **E 7**
42 Idridgehay .... **E 11**
62 Idrigil .... **B 3**
16 Idstone .... **F 4**
53 Idvies .... **B 10**
17 Ifield .... **D 1**
9 Ifold .... **C 11**
10 Iford .... **G 3**
15 Ifton .... **E 8**
30 Ifton Heath .... **G 2**
30 Ightfield .... **F 5**
10 Ightham .... **B 5**
27 Iken .... **K 7**
31 Ilam .... **E 10**
7 Ilchester .... **D 8**
49 Ilderton .... **G 12**
18 Ilford .... **E 4**
4 Ilfracombe .... **A 4**
32 Ilkeston .... **F 2**
27 Ilketshall St. Andrew **G 6**
27 Ilketshall St. Margaret **G 2**
35 Ilkley .... **B 9**
35 Illingworth .... **D 9**
22 Illey .... **D 3**
2 Illogan .... **E 4**
2 Illogan Highway .... **E 4**
23 Illston on the Hill . **B 10**
17 Ilmer .... **D 8**
22 Ilmington .... **H 5**
7 Ilminster .... **E 7**
5 Ilsington .... **H 6**
15 Ilston .... **H 9**
40 Ilton, N. Yorks. .... **G 2**
7 Ilton, Somerset ..... **D 7**
46 Imachar .... **E 4**
37 Immingham .... **F 9**
37 Immingham Dock ... **E 9**
25 Impington .... **J 5**
55 Inbhireala or Strathossian Ho. **M 8**
30 Ince .... **C 3**
34 Ince Blundell .... **G 2**
34 Ince-in-Makerfield . **G 5**
59 Inch .... **K 4**
54 Inchbae Lodge ..... **C 8**
59 Inchbare .... **L 3**
47 Inchbean .... **F 9**
58 Inchberry .... **B 1**
53 Incheoch .... **B 7**
60 Inchina .... **G 2**
47 Inchinnan .... **B 9**
60 Inchkinloch .... **C 6**
55 Inchlaggan .... **J 5**
56 Inchlumpie .... **B 1**
59 Inchnabobart ...... **J 1**
55 Inchnacardoch (Hotel) **H 7**
60 Inchnadamph ...... **E 4**
57 Inchrory .... **J 7**
53 Inchture .... **D 7**
54 Inchvuilt .... **F 6**
52 Inchyra .... **E 6**
2 Indian Queens ..... **D 6**
4 Indicott .... **B 4**
18 Ingatestone .... **D 6**
35 Ingbirchworth ..... **G 10**
31 Ingestre .... **H 8**
32 Ingham, Lincs. ..... **B 6**
26 Ingham, Norfolk .... **C 7**
27 Ingham, Suffolk .... **H 2**
24 Ingleborough, Norfolk **D 6**
39 Ingleborough, N. Yorks. .... **H 10**
31 Ingleby .... **G 12**
40 Ingleby Arncliffe ... **E 5**
40 Ingleby Cross ...... **E 5**
40 Ingleby Greenhow .. **E 6**
15 Inglesbatch .... **H 10**
16 Inglesham .... **D 3**
40 Ingleton, Durham .. **C 2**
39 Ingleton, N. Yorks. . **H 9**
34 Inglewhite .... **C 4**
45 Ingoe .... **F 8**
33 Ingoldmells .... **C 12**
33 Ingoldsby .... **G 7**
24 Ingoldsthorpe ..... **B 8**
45 Ingram .... **A 8**
18 Ingrave .... **E 6**
35 Ingrow .... **C 9**
39 Ings .... **E 7**
15 Ingst .... **E 9**
26 Ingworth .... **C 5**
51 Inistrynich .... **E 8**
38 Injebreck .... **G 2**
22 Inkberrow .... **F 4**
16 Inkpen .... **H 4**
61 Inkstack .... **A 11**
46 Inellan .... **B 6**
48 Innerleithen .... **F 6**
53 Innerleven .... **G 8**
42 Innermessan .... **E 2**
42 Innerwell Fishery ... **G 6**
49 Innerwick, Lothian **B 10**
52 Innerwick, Tayside .. **B 1**
51 Innis Chonain ..... **E 8**
51 Innischoarach ..... **D 12**
58 Insch .... **E 4**
58 Inschtammack ...... **C 2**
57 Insh .... **J 4**
57 Insh House .... **J 4**
51 Inshaig .... **B 7**
60 Inshore .... **A 4**
34 Inskip .... **C 3**
4 Instow .... **C 3**
35 Intake Gate .... **C 10**
57 Inver, Grampian .... **K 8**
56 Inver, Highland ..... **B 4**
52 Inver, Tayside ...... **C 5**
54 Inver Alligin .... **D 2**
55 Inver Mallie .... **K 5**
55 Inverailort .... **L 1**
58 Inverllochy .... **A 8**
60 Inveran .... **G 6**
51 Inverary .... **G 8**
53 Inverarity .... **C 9**
51 Inverarnan .... **F 10**
54 Inverasdale .... **A 2**
54 Inverbain .... **D 2**
51 Inverbeg Hotel .... **H 10**
59 Inverbervie .... **K 6**
58 Inverboyndie .... **A 4**
60 Inverbroom .... **H 3**
57 Invercauld House ... **K 7**
46 Inverhcaolain ...... **B 6**
46 Inverchapel .... **A 6**
51 Invercharnan .... **C 8**
54 Inverchoran .... **E 6**
54 Invercreran .... **C 7**
57 Inverdruie .... **H 5**
58 Inverebrie .... **D 7**
57 Inveredrie .... **M 7**
57 Invereshie House .... **J 4**
48 Inveresk .... **B 6**
51 Inveresragan .... **D 7**
54 Inverewe House .... **B 2**
57 Inverey .... **K 6**
57 Inverfarigaig .... **G 1**
55 Invergarry .... **J 7**
52 Invergeldie .... **D 2**
55 Invergloy .... **L 6**
56 Invergordon .... **C 3**
53 Invergowrie .... **D 8**
55 Inverguseran .... **J 1**
52 Inverhadden .... **A 2**
58 Inverharroch .... **D 1**
51 Inverherive .... **E 10**
55 Inverie .... **J 1**
51 Inverinan .... **F 7**
55 Inverinate .... **G 3**
53 Inverkeilor .... **B 11**
48 Inverkeithing ...... **A 4**
58 Inverkeithny .... **C 4**
47 Inverkip .... **B 7**
60 Inverkirkaig .... **E 2**
60 Inverlael .... **H 3**
60 Inverlael Lodge .... **H 3**
55 Inverlair .... **L 7**
51 Inverlochlarig ..... **F 11**
51 Inverlochy .... **E 9**
59 Invermark Lodge .... **J 2**
55 Invermoriston ...... **H 8**
58 Invernan House ..... **F 1**
61 Invernaver .... **B 7**
56 Inverness .... **E 2**
58 Invernetie .... **C 8**
51 Invernoaden .... **H 8**
51 Inveroran Hotel ... **C 10**
60 Inverpolly Lodge ... **E 2**
58 Inverquhomery ..... **C 8**
55 Inverroy .... **L 6**
50 Inversanda .... **B 7**
55 Invershiel .... **H 3**
60 Invershin .... **G 6**
60 Invershin Station ... **G 6**
55 Inverskilavulin ..... **L 5**
51 Inversnaid Hotel .. **G 10**
58 Inverugie, Grampian **C 8**
56 Inverugie, Grampian **C 7**
51 Inveruglas .... **G 10**
57 Inveruglass .... **J 4**
58 Inverurie .... **E 5**
52 Invervar .... **B 2**
59 Invery House ...... **H 4**
58 Inverythan .... **C 5**
4 Inwardleigh .... **F 4**
19 Inworth .... **B 8**
9 Iping .... **D 10**
5 Ipplepen .... **J 7**
18 Ippollits .... **A 2**
17 Ipsden .... **F 7**
31 Ipstones .... **E 8**
27 Ipswich .... **L 5**
30 Irby .... **B 1**
33 Irby in the Marsh .. **D 11**
37 Irby Upon Humber . **G 9**
23 Irchester .... **E 12**
39 Ireby .... **H 9**
38 Ireleth .... **G 5**
39 Ireshopeburn ..... **A 11**
55 Irine .... **L 1**
34 Irlam .... **H 6**
33 Irnham .... **G 7**
15 Iron Acton .... **F 10**
21 Iron Bridge .... **B 12**
22 Iron Cross .... **G 4**
43 Ironmacannie ...... **D 7**
32 Ironville .... **E 2**
26 Irstead .... **C 7**
23 Irthlingborough ... **E 12**
44 Irthington .... **G 3**
41 Irton .... **G 10**
47 Irvine .... **E 8**
44 Irvington .... **F 1**
61 Isauld .... **A 9**
64 Isbister, Orkney .... **C 2**
64 Isbister, Zetland .... **B 7**
64 Isbister, Zetland .... **C 8**
10 Isfield .... **F 3**
23 Isham .... **E 12**
50 Ishriff .... **D 4**
7 Isle Abbots .... **D 7**
7 Isle Brewers .... **D 7**
18 Isle of Dogs .... **F 4**
42 Isle of Whithorn .... **H 6**
25 Isleham .... **H 7**
62 Isleornsay .... **G 6**
43 Islesteps .... **D 10**
18 Isleworth .... **F 2**
32 Isley Walton .... **H 2**
18 Islington .... **E 3**
25 Islip, Northants. .... **G 1**
16 Islip, Oxon. .... **C 6**
63 Islivig .... **D 1**
8 Itchen .... **E 6**
9 Itchen Abbas .... **C 7**
9 Itchen Stoke .... **C 7**
9 Itchingfield ...... **C 12**
15 Itchington .... **F 10**
26 Itteringham .... **C 4**
15 Itton Common ..... **E 8**
38 Ivegill .... **A 6**
17 Ivelet .... **E 11**
17 Iver .... **F 11**
17 Iver Heath .... **F 11**
45 Iveston .... **H 9**
17 Ivinghoe .... **B 10**
17 Ivinghoe Aston .... **B 10**
21 Ivington .... **G 10**
21 Ivington Green .... **G 10**
10 Ivy Hatch .... **C 5**
5 Ivybridge .... **K 5**
11 Ivychurch .... **E 9**
11 Iwade .... **A 7**
7 Iwerne Courtney or Shroton .... **E 12**
7 Iwerne Minster .... **E 12**
27 Ixworth .... **H 2**
27 Ixworth Thorpe .... **H 2**
35 Jack Hill .... **B 10**
32 Jacksdale .... **E 2**
58 Jackstown .... **D 5**
47 Jackton .... **D 10**
2 Jacobstow .... **B 2**
4 Jacobstowe .... **F 5**
9 Jacobswell .... **A 11**
12 Jameston .... **G 4**
44 Jamestown, Dumf. & Gall. .... **C 1**
54 Jamestown, Highland **D 8**
47 Jamestown, Strathclyde ...... **A 9**
61 Janetstown .... **D 11**
45 Jarrow .... **F 11**
10 Jarvis Brook .... **E 4**
19 Jasper's Green ..... **A 7**
48 Jawcraig .... **B 1**
19 Jaywick Sands .... **C 11**
17 Jealott's Hill ...... **G 9**
40 Jeater Houses ...... **F 4**
49 Jedburgh .... **G 9**
12 Jeffreston .... **F 4**
56 Jemimaville .... **C 3**
13 Jersey Marine .... **H 10**
59 Jessiefield .... **G 6**
10 Jevington .... **H 4**
17 Jockey End ...... **C 11**
30 Jodrell Bank .... **C 6**
35 John O'Gaunts .... **D 12**
61 John o'Groats .... **A 12**
38 Johnby .... **B 6**
10 John's Cross .... **F 6**
59 Johnshaven .... **K 6**
12 Johnston .... **F 3**
44 Johnstone, Dumf. & Gall. .... **C 1**
47 Johnstone, Strathclyde ...... **C 9**
43 Johnstonebridge .. **B 11**
29 Johnstown, Clwyd . **F 12**
13 Johnstown, Dyfed ... **E 7**
20 Joppa, Dyfed .... **F 1**
48 Joppa, Lothian ..... **B 6**
17 Jordans .... **E 10**
12 Jordanston .... **D 3**
19 Jordons .... **E 8**
35 Jump .... **G 12**
8 Jumpers Green ..... **G 3**
48 Juniper Green ..... **B 5**
38 Jurby East .... **F 2**
38 Jurby West .... **F 2**
44 Justicetown .... **G 2**
39 Kaber .... **D 10**
58 Kaecloch .... **C 4**
48 Kaimes .... **C 5**
49 Kalemouth .... **G 9**
54 Kalnakill .... **D 1**
46 Kames, Strathclyde . **B 5**
50 Kames, Strathclyde . **F 5**
47 Kames, Strathclyde **G 11**
36 Keadby .... **F 6**
33 Keal Cotes .... **D 10**
34 Kearsley .... **G 6**
39 Kearstwick .... **G 8**
39 Kearton .... **E 12**
60 Kearvaig .... **A 4**
39 Keasden .... **H 9**
33 Keddington ...... **A 10**
25 Kedington .... **K 8**
31 Kedleston .... **F 11**
49 Kedslie .... **E 8**
37 Keelby .... **F 9**
25 Keeley Green ...... **L 1**
45 Keepershield ...... **F 7**
12 Keeston .... **E 3**
15 Keevil .... **H 12**
32 Kegworth .... **G 2**
2 Kehelland .... **F 3**
58 Keig .... **F 3**
35 Keighley .... **C 9**
51 Keil .... **B 7**
52 Keilarsbrae .... **H 4**
58 Keilhill .... **B 5**
46 Keillmore .... **A 2**
52 Keillour .... **E 5**
7 Keinton Mandeville . **C 9**
52 Keir House .... **G 3**
43 Keir Mill .... **B 9**
24 Keisby .... **C 1**
61 Keiss .... **B 12**
58 Keith .... **C 2**
58 Keithen .... **C 5**
35 Kelbrook .... **C 8**
33 Kelby .... **F 7**
39 Keld, Cumbria ..... **D 8**
39 Keld, N. Yorks. .... **E 11**
41 Keldholme .... **F 7**
41 Keldy Castle ...... **F 8**
36 Kelfield .... **C 4**
32 Kelham .... **E 5**
43 Kelhead .... **E 12**
50 Kellan .... **C 3**
56 Kellas, Grampian .. **D 7**
53 Kellas, Tayside .... **D 9**
5 Kellaton .... **M 7**
16 Kellaways .... **G 1**
39 Kelleth .... **E 9**
26 Kelling .... **A 4**
36 Kellingley .... **E 3**
36 Kellington .... **E 3**
40 Kelloe .... **B 4**
49 Kelloe Mains ..... **D 11**
5 Kelly .... **H 3**
3 Kelly Bray .... **C 10**
23 Kelmarsh .... **D 10**
16 Kelmscot .... **D 3**
27 Kelsale .... **J 7**
30 Kelsall .... **C 4**
30 Kelsall Hill .... **C 4**
25 Kelshall .... **L 4**
43 Kelsick .... **F 12**
49 Kelso .... **F 10**
31 Kelstedge .... **D 11**
33 Kelstern .... **A 9**
29 Kelsterton .... **C 12**
15 Kelston .... **H 10**
43 Kelton .... **D 10**
43 Kelton Hill .... **F 8**
52 Kelty .... **H 6**
19 Kelvedon .... **B 8**
18 Kelvedon Hatch .... **D 6**
2 Kelynack .... **G 1**
53 Kemback .... **F 9**
22 Kemberton .... **B 1**
16 Kemble .... **D 1**
22 Kemerton .... **H 3**
15 Kemeys Commander **D 7**
58 Kemnay .... **F 5**
10 Kemp Town .... **H 2**
60 Kempie .... **B 5**
15 Kempley .... **A 10**
22 Kempsey .... **G 2**
16 Kempsford .... **D 3**
9 Kempshott .... **A 7**
25 Kempston .... **K 1**
25 Kempston Hardwick **L 1**
25 Kempston West End **K 1**
21 Kempton .... **D 9**
10 Kemsing .... **B 4**
11 Kemsley .... **A 8**
11 Kenardington ...... **E 8**
21 Kenchester Sugwas **H 10**
16 Kencot .... **D 4**
39 Kendal .... **F 7**
15 Kenderchurch ..... **A 7**
14 Kenfig .... **F 1**
14 Kenfig Hill .... **F 2**
22 Kenilworth .... **E 6**
51 Kenknock .... **D 11**
21 Kenley .... **B 11**
54 Kenmore, Highland . **D 1**
51 Kenmore, Strathclyde **G 8**
52 Kenmore, Tayside .. **C 3**
15 Kenn, Avon .... **G 7**
6 Kenn, Devon ...... **H 3**
63 Kennacley .... **G 3**
46 Kennacraig .... **C 3**
3 Kennards House .. **A 10**
44 Kennedy's Corner .. **E 1**
2 Kenneggy Downs .. **G 3**
4 Kennerleigh .... **E 7**
52 Kennet .... **H 4**
43 Kenneth Bank ..... **E 10**
25 Kennett .... **H 8**
6 Kennford .... **G 3**
27 Kenninghall .... **G 3**
11 Kennington, Kent .. **D 9**
18 Kennington, London **F 3**
16 Kennington, Oxon. . **D 6**
53 Kennoway .... **G 8**
47 Kennox .... **E 8**
25 Kennyhill .... **G 8**
36 Kennythorpe ...... **A 6**
62 Kensaleyre .... **C 3**
18 Kensington .... **F 3**
17 Kensworth .... **B 11**
17 Kensworth Com. .. **B 11**
11 Kentl County ...... **C 8**
10 Kent Street .... **C 5**
51 Kentallen .... **B 7**
15 Kentchurch .... **B 7**
25 Kentford .... **J 8**
6 Kentisbeare .... **E 4**
4 Kentisbury .... **B 5**

4 Kentisburyford B 5
39 Kentmere E 7
6 Kenton, Devon H 3
18 Kenton, London E 2
27 Kenton, Suffolk J 5
45 Kenton Bank Foot F 10
50 Kentra A 4
38 Kents Bank H 6
15 Kent's Green B 10
8 Kent's Oak D 5
45 Kentstone B 11
30 Kenwick G 3
2 Kenwyn E 5
60 Keoldale A 5
63 Keose E 5
55 Keppcoh G 3
46 Keprigan H 2
40 Kepwick F 5
49 Kerchesters F 10
23 Keresley D 7
15 Kerne Bridge B 9
48 Kerrcleuch H 5
31 Kerridge C 8
2 Kerris G 2
54 Kerrowwood F 7
21 Kerry C 7
46 Kerrylamont D 6
15 Kerry's Gate A 7
54 Kerrysdale B 2
46 Kerrytonlia D 6
32 Kersall D 4
6 Kersbrooke H 4
4 Kerscott C 5
47 Kerse D 8
27 Kersey L 3
63 Kershader E 4
44 Kershopefoot E 3
49 Kersmains F 9
22 Kersoe H 3
6 Kerswell F 4
22 Kerswell Green G 2
27 Kesgrave L 5
38 Keskadale C 4
27 Kessingland G 8
27 Kessingland Beach G 8
2 Kestle Mill D 5
18 Keston G 4
38 Keswick, Cumb. C 5
26 Keswick, Norfolk B 6
26 Keswick, Norfolk E 5
21 Ketley A 12
49 Kettelshiel D 9
23 Kettering D 12
26 Ketteringham E 5
53 Kettins C 7
27 Kettlebaston K 3
53 Kettlebridge F 8
22 Kettlebrook B 6
27 Kettlebrugh J 5
53 Kettlehill F 8
41 Kettleness D 8
31 Kettleshulme B 8
35 Kettlesing B 11
35 Kettlesing Bottom A 11
26 Kettlestone B 3
32 Kettlethorpe C 6
64 Kettletoft B 4
39 Kettlewell H 11
24 Ketton E 1
18 Kew F 2
14 Kewstoke H 6
35 Kexbrough F 11
32 Kexby, Lincs. B 5
36 Kexby, N. Yorks. B 5
31 Key Green D 7
11 Key Street B 7
23 Keyham B 10
8 Keyhaven G 5
37 Keyingham E 10
10 Keymer F 2
15 Keynsham G 9
33 Key's Toft D 12
25 Keysoe J 2
25 Keysoe Roe J 2
25 Keyston H 1
45 Kibblesworth G 10
23 Kibworth Beauchamp C 10
23 Kibworth Harcourt C 10
18 Kidbrooke F 4
22 Kiddemore Green A 2
22 Kidderminster D 2
16 Kiddington B 5
16 Kidlington C 6
17 Kidmore End F 8
30 Kidnal E 3
58 Kidrummy F 2
31 Kidsgrove E 7
39 Kidstones G 11
13 Kidwelly F 7
50 Kiel Crofts D 6
44 Kielder D 4
52 Kilbagie H 4
47 Kilbarchan C 9
62 Kilbeg H 6
46 Kilberry C 2
47 Kilbirnie D 8
50 Kilbride E 6
62 Kilbride, Highland F 5
50 Kilbride, Strathclyde E 6
32 Kilburn, Derby F 1
40 Kilburn, N. Yorks. G 5
59 Kilburn, Tayside K 1
23 Kilby C 9
48 Kilcadzow D 2
50 Kilchattan, Strathclyde H 1
46 Kilchattan, Strathclyde D 6
46 Kilchenzie G 2
50 Kilcheran D 5
50 Kilchoan, Highland A 2
55 Kilchoan, Highland K 2
50 Kilchoan, Strathclyde F 5
51 Kilchrenan E 7
53 Kilconquhar G 9
15 Kilcot B 10
56 Kilcoy E 1
47 Kilcreggan A 7
40 Kildale D 6
46 Kildalloig G 4
46 Kildavanan C 5
56 Kildermorie Lodge B 1
46 Kildonan, Arran G 5
61 Kildonan, Highland E 9
61 Kildonan Lodge E 9
42 Kildrochat House F 2
35 Kildwick C 9
46 Kilfinan B 4
55 Kilfinnan K 6
29 Kilford D 10
12 Kilgetty F 5
37 Kilham, Humber. A 8
49 Kilham, Northumb. F 11
42 Kilkerran A 4
4 Kilkhampton E 1
32 Killamarsh B 2
13 Killay H 9
50 Killbeg C 3
46 Killchianaig A 1
46 Killean E 2
47 Killearn A 10
46 Killellan H 2
56 Killen D 2
40 Killerby C 2
42 Killern F 6
51 Killichonan B 12
50 Killichronan C 3
55 Killiechanate L 6
52 Killiecrankie A 4
57 Killiehuntly K 4
50 Killiemor D 2
55 Killilan G 3
61 Killimster B 12
52 Killin D 1
57 Killin Lodge J 1
35 Killinghall A 11
39 Killington F 8
49 Killochyett E 7
50 Killunaig E 2
50 Killundine C 3
43 Killyleoch C 9
47 Kilmacolm B 8
50 Kilmahumaig H 5
62 Kilmaluag A 4
53 Kilmany E 8
62 Kilmarie F 5
47 Kilmarnock F 9
53 Kilmaron Castle E 8
50 Kilmartin H 5
47 Kilmaurs E 9
50 Kilmelford F 6
7 Kilmersdon A 10
9 Kilmeston D 7
46 Kilmichael G 2
50 Kilmichael Glassary H 6
46 Kilmichael of Inverlussa A 3
6 Kilmington, Devon F 6
7 Kilmington, Wilts. C 11
7 Kilmington Street C 11
56 Kilmorack E 1
62 Kilmore, Highland G 6
50 Kilmore, Strathclyde E 6
46 Kilmory, Arran G 4
55 Kilmory, Highland A 3
46 Kilmory, Strathclyde B 2
61 Kilmote F 9
62 Kilmuir, Highland A 3
62 Kilmuir, Highland C 2
56 Kilmuir, Highland B 3
56 Kilmuir, Highland E 2
46 Kilmun A 6
17 Kiln Green F 9
44 Kiln Hill F 4
45 Kiln Pit Hill H 8
10 Kilndown E 6
43 Kilness D 10
47 Kilnford F 8
36 Kilnhurst G 2
50 Kilninian C 1
50 Kilninver E 5
37 Kilnsea F 11
39 Kilnsey H 12
37 Kilnwick B 7
36 Kilnwick Percy B 6
50 Kiloran H 1
46 Kilpatrick G 4
15 Kilpeck A 7
61 Kilphedir E 9
36 Kilpin D 5
36 Kilpin Pike D 5
53 Kilrenny G 10
23 Kilsby E 9
53 Kilspindie E 7
47 Kilsyth B 12
41 Kilton, Cleveland C 7
6 Kilton, Somerset B 5
62 Kilvaxter A 3
6 Kilve B 5
32 Kilvington F 5
47 Kilwinning E 8
26 Kimberley, Norf. E 4
32 Kimberley, Notts. F 2
17 Kimble Wick C 9
45 Kimblesworth H 11
25 Kimbolton, Cambs. H 2
21 Kimbolton, Heref. & Worcs. F 10
23 Kimcote C 9
7 Kimmeridge H 12
49 Kimmerston F 12
8 Kimpton, Hants. A 4
18 Kimpton, Herts. B 2
61 Kinbrace D 8
55 Kinbreack K 4
52 Kinbuck G 3
47 Kincaidston G 8
53 Kincaple E 9
52 Kincardine, Fife H 4
60 Kincardine, Highland G 6
59 Kincardine O'Neil G 3
52 Kinclaven C 6
59 Kincorth G 7
56 Kincorth House D 6
57 Kincraig J 4
52 Kindallachan B 5
56 Kindrummond F 2
46 Kinerarach D 2
16 Kineton, Glos. B 2
23 Kineton, War. G 7
52 Kinfauns E 6
15 King Stanley D 11
50 Kingairloch Ho. B 6
46 Kingarth D 6
15 Kincoed D 7
33 Kingerby A 7
4 Kingford D 5
16 Kingham B 3
50 Kingharair C 2
43 Kingholm Quay D 10
48 Kinghorn A 5
53 Kinglassie G 7
58 Kingoodie, Grampian E 6
53 Kingoodie, Tayside D 8
21 King's Acre H 10
31 Kings Bromley H 9
15 Kings Caple A 9
24 King's Cliffe F 1
22 King's Coughton F 4
22 Kings Heath D 4
17 Kings Langley D 11
24 King's Lynn D 7
39 King's Meaburn C 8
48 Kings Muir E 5
23 King's Norton, Leics. B 10
22 King's Norton, W. Midlands D 4
4 Kings Nympton D 6
21 King's Pyon G 10
25 Kings Ripton H 4
8 Kings Samborne C 5
7 King's Stag E 10
16 King's Sutton A 6
18 King's Walden B 2
11 Kings Wood C 7
8 Kings Worth C 6
3 Kingsand E 11
53 Kingsbarns F 10
5 Kingsbridge, Devon L 6
6 Kingsbridge, Som. C 3
62 Kingsburgh C 3
18 Kingsbury, London E 2
22 Kingsbury, War. C 6
7 Kingsbury Episcopi D 8
16 Kingsclere H 6
15 Kingscote E 11
4 Kingscott D 4
46 Kingscross G 5
7 Kingsdon D 8
11 Kingsdown C 12
52 Kingseat H 6
17 Kinsey C 4
10 Kingsfold D 1
59 Kingsford, Grampian G 6
22 Kingsford, Heref & Worcs. D 2
47 Kingsford, Strathclyde E 9
27 Kingshall Street J 2
4 Kingsheanton B 4
52 Kingshouse E 1
51 Kinghouse Hotel B 10
5 Kingskerswell J 7
53 Kingskettle F 8
28 Kingsland, Gwynedd B 2
21 Kingsland, Heref. & Worcs. F 10
30 Kingsley, Ches. C 4
9 Kingsley, Hants. B 9
31 Kingsley, Staffs F 8
9 Kingsley Green C 10
31 Kingsley Holt F 9
53 Kingsmuir B 9
11 Kingsnorth D 9
22 Kingstanding C 4
5 Kingsteignton H 7
15 Kingsthorne A 8
23 Kingsthorpe F 11
25 Kingston, Cambs. K 4
5 Kingston, Devon L 5
7 Kingston, Dorset E 11
8 Kingston, Dorset H 1
58 Kingston, Grampian A 1
8 Kingston, Hants. F 3
8 Kingston, I.o.W. H 6
11 Kingston, Kent C 10
49 Kingston, Lothian A 8
9 Kingston, W. Sussex F 12
16 Kingston Bagpuize D 5
17 Kingston Blount D 8
10 Kingston by Sea H 1
7 Kingston Deverill C 11
16 Kingston Lisle E 4
10 Kingston near Lewes G 3
32 Kingston on Soar G 2
7 Kingston Russell G 9
6 Kingston St Mary C 6
15 Kingston Seymour H 7
37 Kingston upon Hull D 8
18 Kingston upon Thames G 2
18 Kingston Vale G 2
15 Kingstone, Heref. & Worcs. A 7
7 Kingstone, Som. E 7
31 Kingstone, Staffs. G 9
44 Kingstown G 2
5 Kingswear K 7
22 Kingswinford C 2
15 Kingswood, Avon G 9
17 Kingswood, Bucks. B 8
15 Kingswood, Glos. E 10
21 Kingswood, Powys B 8
10 Kingswood, Surrey B 1
22 Kingswood, War. E 5
21 Kingswood Com. G 8
21 Kington, Heref. & Worcs. G 8
22 Kington, Heref. & Worcs. G 3
15 Kington Langley G 12
7 Kington Magna D 11
15 Kington St. Michael F 12
57 Kingussie J 3
7 Kingweston C 8
43 Kinharvie E 10
52 Kinkell Bridge E 4
58 Kinknockie, Grampian C 7
58 Kinknockie, Grampian E 7
44 Kinkry Hill E 3
22 Kinlet D 1
53 Kinloch, Fife F 7
62 Kinloch, Highland F 6
60 Kinloch, Highland D 4
52 Kinloch, Tayside C 6
53 Kinloch, Tayside C 7
62 Kinloch Castle H 3
55 Kinloch Hourn J 3
57 Kinloch Laggan K 1
60 Kinloch Lodge B 6
52 Kinloch Rannoch A 2
50 Kinlochan A 5
51 Kinlochard G 11
55 Kinlochbeoraid L 2
60 Kinlochbervie B 3
55 Kinlocheil L 4
51 Kinlochetive C 8
54 Kinlochewe D 4
51 Kinlochleven A 9
55 Kinlochmoidart M 1
55 Kinlochmorar K 2
51 Kinlochmore A 9
55 Kinlochnanuagh L 1
50 Kinlochspelve E 4
55 Kinloid L 1
56 Kinloss D 6
29 Kinmel Bay B 9
58 Kinmuck F 6
58 Kinnadie C 7
54 Kinnahaird D 8
59 Kinnaid Castle L 4
53 Kinnaird D 7
59 Kinneff K 6
43 Kinnelhead B 11
53 Kinnell B 10
30 Kinnerley H 2
21 Kinnersley, Heref. & Worcs. G 9
22 Kinnersley, Heref. & Worcs. H 2
21 Kinnerton F 8
52 Kinnesswood G 6
40 Kinninvie C 1
53 Kinnordy B 8
32 Kinoulton G 4
57 Kinrara J 4
52 Kinross G 6
53 Kinrossie D 7
21 Kinsham F 9
36 Kinsley F 2
8 Kinson F 2
56 Kinsteary Lodge D 5
63 Kintaravay E 3
16 Kintbury G 5
56 Kintessack D 6
52 Kintillo E 6
59 Kintocher G 3
21 Kinton, Heref. & Worcs. E 9
30 Kinton, Salop. H 2
58 Kintore F 5
50 Kintra F 1
56 Kintrae C 7
50 Kintraw G 5
50 Kinuachdrach H 4
57 Kinveachy H 5
22 Kinver D 2
36 Kippax D 2
52 Kippen H 1
43 Kippford or Scaur F 9
10 Kipping's Cross D 5
64 Kirbister D 2
38 Kirby H 2
26 Kirby Bedon E 6
32 Kirby Bellars H 4
26 Kirby Cane F 7
19 Kirby Cross B 12
41 Kirby Grindalythe H 9
40 Kirby Hill, N. Yorks. E 2
40 Kirby Hill, N. Yorks. H 4
40 Kirby Knowle F 5
19 Kirby le Soken B 12
41 Kirby Misperton G 8
23 Kirby Muxloe B 8
35 Kirby Overblow B 12
26 Kirby Row F 7
40 Kirby Sigston F 4
36 Kirby Underdale A 6
40 Kirby Wiske G 4
9 Kirdford C 11
63 Kirivick C 3
61 Kirk B 11
36 Kirk Bramwith F 4
35 Kirk Deighton B 12
37 Kirk Ella D 8
32 Kirk Hallam F 2
36 Kirk Hammerton B 3
31 Kirk Ireton E 11
31 Kirk Langley F 11
40 Kirk Merrington B 3
38 Kirk Michael G 1
48 Kirk of Shotts C 1
36 Kirk Sandall F 4
36 Kirk Smeaton E 3
49 Kirk Yetholm G 11
64 Kirkabister E 7
43 Kirkandrews G 7
44 Kirkandrews upon Eden G 2
44 Kirkbampton G 1
43 Kirkbank C 11
43 Kirkbean F 10
64 Kirkbrae A 2
44 Kirkbride, Cumb. G 1
43 Kirkbride, Dumf. & Gall. C 9
53 Kirkbuddo C 9
48 Kirkburn, Borders F 5
37 Kirkburn, Humber. B 7
35 Kirkburton F 10
34 Kirkby, Merseyside G 3
33 Kirkby, Lincs. A 8
40 Kirkby, N. Yorks. E 5
40 Kirkby Fleetham F 3
33 Kirkby Green D 8
32 Kirkby in Ashfield E 2
24 Kirkby le Thorpe A 2
39 Kirkby Lonsdale G 8
35 Kirkby Malham A 7
23 Kirkby Mallory B 8
40 Kirkby Malzeard H 2
41 Kirkby Mills G 7
33 Kirkby on Bain D 9
39 Kirkby Stephen D 10
39 Kirkby Thore C 9
24 Kirkby Underwood C 2
36 Kirkby Wharf C 3
41 Kirkbymoorside F 7
53 Kirkcaldy H 7
44 Kirkcambeck F 4
43 Kirkcarswell G 8
42 Kirkcolm E 1
47 Kirkconnel H 12
43 Kirkconnell, Dumf. & Gall. E 10
43 Kirkconnell, Dumf. & Gall. F 7
42 Kirkcowan E 4
43 Kirkcudbright F 8
30 Kirkdale A 2
42 Kirkdale House F 6
49 Kirkdean E 4
48 Kirkfieldbank E 1
43 Kirkgunzeon E 9
34 Kirkham, Lancs. D 3
36 Kirkham, N. Yorks. A 5
35 Kirkhamgate E 11
45 Kirkharle E 8
45 Kirkheaton, Nothumb. E 8
35 Kirkheaton, W. Yorks. E 10
56 Kirkhill, Highland E 1
48 Kirkhill, Lothian C 5
59 Kirkhill, Tayside L 4
58 Kirkhill of Kennethmont E 3
48 Kirkhope G 6
48 Kirkhouse F 6
62 Kirkibost, Highland F 5
63 Kirkibost, W. Isles C 3
53 Kirkinch C 8
42 Kirkinner F 5
47 Kirkintilloch B 11
39 Kirkland, Cumb. B 9
38 Kirkland, Cumb. C 3
43 Kirkland, Dumf. & Gall. C 9
43 Kirkland, Dumf. & Gall. C 11
47 Kirkland, Dumf. & Gall. H 12
42 Kirkland, Dumf. & Gall. G 5
43 Kirkland Guards G 12
43 Kirkland of Gelston F 8
40 Kirkleatham C 6
40 Kirklevington D 4
26 Kirkley F 8
45 Kirkley March E 9
31 Kirkleyditch B 7
32 Kirklington, Notts. D 4
40 Kirklington, N. Yorks. G 3
44 Kirklinton F 3
48 Kirkliston B 4
42 Kirkmaiden H 2
42 Kirkmichael, Strathclyde A 4
52 Kirkmichael, Tayside A 6
47 Kirkmuirhill E 12
48 Kirknewton, Lothian C 4
49 Kirknewton, Northumb. F 11
58 Kirkney D 3
39 Kirkoswald, Cumb. A 8
42 Kirkoswald, Strathclyde A 3
43 KirkpatrickDurham D 8
44 Kirkpatrick-Fleming F 1

38 Kirksanton **G 4**
33 Kirkstead **D 9**
44 Kirkstile, Dumf. & Gall. **D 2**
58 Kirkstile, Grampian **D 3**
58 Kirkston of Culsalmond **D 4**
61 Kirkstyle **A 12**
44 Kirkton, Borders **B 4**
43 Kirkton, Dumf. & Gall. **C 10**
53 Kirkton, Fife **E 8**
58 Kirkton, Grampian **C 6**
58 Kirkton, Grampian **E 4**
58 Kirkton, Grampian **F 6**
58 Kirkton, Grampian **F 4**
58 Kirkton, Grampian **C 4**
56 Kirkton, Highland **F 2**
56 Kirkton, Highland **C 3**
54 Kirkton, Highland **F 3**
48 Kirkton, Strathclyde **G 2**
53 Kirkton, Tayside **C 9**
59 Kirkton, Tayside **J 2**
48 Kirkton Manor **D 5**
53 Kirkton of Airlie **B 8**
53 Kirkton of Auchterhouse **C 8**
56 Kirkton of Barevan **E 4**
53 Kirkton of Collace **D 7**
53 Kirkton of Craig **B 11**
59 Kirkton of Durris **H 5**
58 Kirkton of Glenbuchat **F 1**
53 Kirkton of Glenisla **A 7**
53 Kirkton of Kingoldrum **B 8**
53 Kirkton of Largo **G 9**
52 Kirkton of Lethendy **C 6**
58 Kirkton of Logie Buchan **E 7**
59 Kirkton of Menmuir **L 3**
53 Kirkton of Monikie **C 10**
58 Kirkton of Oyne **E 4**
59 Kirkton of Skene **G 5**
53 Kirkton of Strathmartine **D 8**
53 Kirkton of Tealing **C 9**
53 Kirktonbarns **D 9**
58 Kirktown **B 8**
58 Kirktown of Alvah **B 4**
58 Kirktown of Auchterless **C 5**
58 Kirktown of Bourtie **E 5**
58 Kirktown of Deskford **B 2**
59 Kirktown of Fetteresso **J 6**
58 Kirktown of Mortlach **D 1**
58 Kirktown of Rayne **E 4**
58 Kirktown of Slains **E 8**
64 Kirkwall **D 2**
45 Kirkwhelpington **E 8**
37 Kirmington **F 9**
33 Kirmond le Mire **A 9**
47 Kirn **B 7**
43 Kirncleuch **B 12**
53 Kirriemuir **B 8**
26 Kirstead Green **F 6**
44 Kirtlebridge **F 1**
44 Kirtleton **E 1**
25 Kirtling **J 8**
25 Kirtling Green **K 8**
16 Kirtlington **B 6**
61 Kirtomy **B 7**
56 Kirton, Highland **D 3**
24 Kirton, Lincs. **B 4**
32 Kirton, Notts. **C 4**
27 Kirton, Suffolk **L 6**
24 Kirton End **B 4**
24 Kirton Holme **A 4**
37 Kirton in Lindsey **G 7**
23 Kislingbury **F 10**
23 Kites Hardwick **E 8**
6 Kittisford **D 4**
13 Kittle **H 9**
31 Kitts Moss **B 7**
59 Kittybrewster **G 7**
9 Kitwood **C 8**
4 Kiverley **D 4**
15 Kivernoll **A 8**
32 Kiveton Park **B 2**
60 Klibreck **D 6**
60 Klibreck Lodge **D 6**
32 Knaith **B 5**
32 Knaith Park **B 5**
7 Knap Corner **D 11**
17 Knaphill **H 10**
6 Knapp, Somerset **D 6**
53 Knapp, Tayside **D 7**
58 Knaps of Auchlee **C 8**
26 Knapton, Norfolk **B 6**
36 Knapton, N. Yorks. **B 3**
21 Knapton Green **G 10**
25 Knapwell **J 4**
35 Knaresborough **A 12**
44 Knarsdale **H 5**
40 Knayton **F 4**
18 Knebworth **B 3**
36 Knedlington **D 5**
32 Kneesall **D 4**
25 Kneesworth **L 4**
32 Kneeton **F 4**
13 Knelston **H 8**
27 Knettishall **G 3**
4 Knightacott **B 5**
23 Knightcote **G 7**
5 Knighton, Devon **L 4**
7 Knighton, Dorset **E 9**
23 Knighton, Leics. **B 9**
21 Knighton, Powys **E 8**
30 Knighton, Staffs. **F 6**
30 Knighton, Staffs. **G 6**
16 Knighton, Wilts. **G 4**
22 Knightsforld Bridge **G 1**
21 Knill **F 8**
32 Knipton **G 5**
45 Knitsley **H 9**
31 Kniveton **E 10**
39 Knock, Cumbria **B 9**
58 Knock, Grampian **B 3**
62 Knock, Highland **G 6**
50 Knock, Strathclyde **D 3**
63 Knock, W. Isles **D 6**
60 Knockan **F 3**
56 Knockando **E 7**
57 Knockandhu **G 8**
60 Knockanrock **F 3**
61 Knockarthur **F 7**
56 Knockbain **D 2**
62 Knockbreck **B 2**
43 Knockbrex **G 7**
61 Knockdee **B 11**
42 Knockdolian Cas. **C 2**
42 Knockdon **B 5**
47 Knockendon **D 7**
47 Knockenjig **H 12**
46 Knockenkelly **G 5**
47 Knockentiber **E 9**
58 Knockespock Ho. **E 3**
42 Knockgardner **A 4**
42 Knockglass **F 1**
10 Knockholt **B 3**
10 Knockholt Pound **B 4**
55 Knockie Lodge **H 8**
30 Knockin **H 2**
47 Knockinlaw **E 9**
42 Knocklaugh **B 3**
43 Knocklearn **D 8**
42 Knocknain **E 1**
46 Knockrome **B 1**
53 Knockshannoch **A 7**
38 Knocksharry **G 1**
42 Knocksheen **C 6**
43 Knockvennie **D 8**
42 Knockycoid **D 3**
27 Knodishall **J 7**
7 Knole **D 8**
15 Knole Park **F 9**
30 Knolls Green **B 6**
30 Knolton **F 2**
8 Knook **B 1**
23 Knossington **A 11**
34 Knott End-on-Sea **B 2**
25 Knotting **J 1**
25 Knotting Green **J 1**
36 Knottingley **E 3**
39 Knotts **C 7**
30 Knotty Ash **A 3**
17 Knotty Green **E 10**
42 Knowe **D 4**
43 Knowhead, Dumf. & Gall. **C 7**
58 Knowhead, Grampian **F 2**
45 Knowesgate **D 8**
47 Knoweside **H 7**
49 Knowetownhead **G 8**
27 Knowl Green **L 1**
17 Knowl Hill **F 9**
15 Knowle, Avon **G 9**
6 Knowle, Devon **H 4**
4 Knowle, Devon **F 6**
4 Knowle, Devon **B 4**
7 Knowle, Somerset **B 7**
22 Knowle, W. Midlands **D 5**
34 Knowle Green **C 5**
8 Knowlton, Dorset **E 2**
11 Knowlton, Kent **C 11**
58 Knowsie **B 8**
34 Knowsley **H 3**
4 Knowstone **D 7**
10 Knox Brdige **D 6**
21 Knucklas **E 8**
30 Knutsford **B 6**
31 Knypersley **E 7**
2 Kuggar **H 4**
55 Kyle of Lochalsh **G 1**
55 Kyleakin **G 1**
55 Kylechorky Lodge **G 8**
61 Kyleoag **G 7**
55 Kylerhea **G 2**
63 Kyles Scalpay **G 3**
63 Kyles Stockinish **H 2**
55 Kylesbeg **M 1**
55 Kylesknoydart **K 2**
60 Kylesku **D 3**
55 Kylesmorar **K 2**
60 Kylestrome **D 4**
57 Kyllachy House **G 3**
15 Kymin **C 8**
15 Kynaston **B 8**
21 Kynnersley **A 12**
21 Kyre Park **F 11**
63 Labost **B 4**
37 Laceby **F 10**
17 Lacey Green **D 9**
30 Lach Dennis **C 5**
63 Lackalee **H 2**
40 Lackenby **C 6**
27 Lackford **H 1**
15 Lacock **G 12**
23 Ladbroke **F 7**
10 Laddingford **C 6**
33 Lade Bank **E 11**
2 Ladcok **E 6**
53 Ladybank, Fife **F 8**
42 Ladybank, Strathclyde **A 3**
3 Ladycross **A 10**
49 Ladyflat **D 10**
49 Ladykirk **E 11**
58 Ladyleys **E 6**
58 Ladysford **B 6**
43 Lag **C 9**
50 Lagalochan **F 6**
46 Lagg, Strathclyde **B 1**
47 Lagg, Strathclyde **H 7**
46 Lagg, Strathclyde **G 4**
52 Laggan, Central **F 1**
58 Laggan, Grampian **D 1**
55 Laggan, Highland **K 7**
57 Laggan, Highland **K 2**
42 Laggan, Strathclyde **C 2**
42 Laggan, Strathclyde **C 3**
42 Lagganmullan **F 6**
50 Lagganulva **C 2**
60 Laid **B 5**
60 Laide **G 1**
47 Laigh Braidley **E 10**
47 Laigh Brocklar **G 10**
47 Laigh Cleughearn **D 11**
47 Laigh Fenwick **E 9**
47 Laigh Smithstone **E 8**
47 Laighmuir **E 9**
47 Laighstonehall **D 12**
43 Laight **B 9**
19 Laindon **E 7**
57 Laintachan **H 6**
54 Lair **E 4**
60 Lairg **F 6**
60 Lairg Muir **F 6**
60 Lairg Station **F 6**
51 Lairigmor **A 8**
35 Laisterdyke **D 10**
39 Laithes **B 7**
8 Lake **B 3**
56 Lake of Moy **D 6**
38 Lake Side **F 6**
25 Lakenheath **G 8**
24 Lakes End **F 6**
17 Laleham **G 11**
14 Laleston **F 2**
48 Lamancha **D 5**
27 Lamarsh **L 2**
26 Lamas **C 5**
27 Lamb Corner **M 3**
64 Lambaness **B 4**
49 Lambden **E 10**
10 Lamberhurst **D 5**
10 Lamberhurst Quarter **D 5**
18 Lambeth **F 3**
32 Lambley, Notts. **F 3**
44 Lambley, Northumb. **G 5**
16 Lambourn **F 4**
18 Lambourne End **D 5**
10 Lambs Green **D 1**
12 Lambston **E 3**
3 Lamellion **C 9**
5 Lamerton **H 3**
45 Lamesley **G 10**
42 Lamford **B 6**
56 Lamington, Highland **B 3**
48 Lamington, Strathclyde **F 3**
46 Lamlash **F 5**
42 Lamloch **B 6**
38 Lamonby **B 6**
2 Lamorna **G 2**
2 Lamorran **E 6**
13 Lampeter **B 9**
12 Lampeter Velfrey **F 5**
12 Lamphey **G 4**
38 Lamplugh **C 3**
23 Lamport **E 11**
7 Lamyatt **C 10**
4 Lana, Devon **F 2**
4 Lana, Devon **E 2**
48 Lanark **E 2**
34 Lancashire, Co. **E 5**
34 Lancaster **A 4**
45 Lanchester **H 10**
6 Landacre **C 2**
25 Lanbeach **J 6**
4 Landcross **D 3**
59 Landerberry **G 5**
2 Landewednack **H 4**
8 Landford **D 4**
8 Landford Manor **D 4**
13 Landimore **H 8**
4 Landkey **C 5**
13 Landlore **G 10**
3 Landrake, Corn. **D 10**
6 Landrake, Devon **D 3**
12 Landshipping **F 4**
3 Landulph **D 11**
22 Landywood **B 3**
2 Lane **D 5**
17 Lane End, Bucks. **E 9**
38 Lane End, Cumb. **F 3**
9 Lane End, Hants. **D 7**
9 Lane End, Hants. **G 8**
10 Lane End, Kent **A 4**
40 Lane Ends **B 2**
31 Lane Head, Derby **C 10**
40 Lane Head, Dur. **D 1**
34 Lane Head, Manchester **G 5**
3 Laneast **A 9**
32 Laneham **C 5**
44 Lanehad **D 6**
35 Laneshaw Bridge **C 8**
32 Langar **G 4**
47 Langbank **B 8**
35 Langbar **B 9**
44 Langburnshiels **C 4**
35 Langcliffe **A 7**
41 Langdale End **F 9**
61 Langdale Lodge **C 7**
2 Langdon, Corn. **B 2**
3 Langdon, Corn. **A 10**
15 Langdon, Heref. & Worc. **A 11**
39 Langdon Beck **B 11**
19 Langdon Hills **E 7**
53 Langdyke **G 8**
19 Langenhoe **B 10**
25 Langford, Beds. **L 3**
6 Langford, Devon **F 4**
19 Langford, Essex **C 8**
32 Langford, Notts. **D 5**
16 Langford, Oxon **D 3**
6 Langford Budville **D 4**
25 Langford End **K 3**
27 Langham, Essex **M 3**
23 Langham, Leics. **A 11**
26 Langham, Norf. **B 3**
27 Langham, Suffolk **H 3**
34 Langho **D 6**
44 Langholm, Dumf. & Gall. **E 2**
48 Langholm, Strathclyde **F 3**
47 Langlands **D 11**
49 Langleeford **G 12**
17 Langley, Berks. **F 11**
31 Langley, Ches. **C 8**
8 Langley, Hants. **F 6**
18 Langley, Herts. **B 2**
11 Langley, Kent **C 7**
44 Langley, Northumb. **G 6**
6 Langley, Som. **C 4**
22 Langley, War. **F 5**
9 Langley, W. Sussex **C 9**
15 Langley Burrell **G 12**
10 Langley Green **D 1**
11 Langley Heath **C 7**
25 Langley Lower Green **M 5**
32 Langley Mill **E 2**
40 Langley Moor **A 3**
40 Langley Park **A 2**
26 Langley Street **E 7**
25 Langley Upper Green **M 5**
10 Langney **H 5**
32 Langold **B 3**
3 Langore **A 10**
7 Langport **D 7**
33 Langrick **E 9**
15 Langridge **G 10**
4 Langridge Ford **D 4**
43 Langrigg **G 12**
9 Langrish **D 8**
33 Langriville **E 10**
35 Langsett **G 10**
49 Langshaw **E 8**
47 Langside, Strathclyde **D 8**
52 Langside, Tayside **F 3**
64 Langskaill **A 2**
9 Langstone **F 8**
40 Langthorne, N. Yorks. **F 3**
40 Langthorpe, N. Yorks. **H 4**
39 Langthwaite **E 12**
41 Langtoft, Humberside **H 10**
24 Langtoft, Lincs. **D 2**
40 Langton, Dur. **C 2**
33 Langton, Lincs. **C 9**
33 Langton, Lincs. **C 11**
41 Langton, N. Yorks. **H 8**
33 Langton by Wragby **C 8**
10 Langton Green **D 4**
7 Langton Herring **H 9**
8 Langton Matravers **H 2**
4 Langtree **D 3**
39 Langwathby **B 8**
60 Langwell **G 5**
61 Langwell Hotel **E 10**
33 Langworth **C 8**
3 Lanivet **C 7**
3 Lank **B 8**
3 Lanlivery **D 8**
2 Lanner **F 4**
3 Lanreath **D 9**
52 Lanrick Castle **G 2**
3 Lansallos **E 9**
15 Lansdown, Avon **G 10**
16 Lansdown, Glos. **B 3**
3 Lanteglos Highway **D 8**
49 Lanton, Borders **G 9**
49 Lanton, Northumb. **F 11**
4 Lapford **E 6**
22 Lapley **A 2**
22 Lapworth **E 5**
50 Larachbeg **C 4**
48 Larbert **A 1**
43 Larbreck **D 9**
58 Largie **D 4**
46 Largiemore **A 4**
53 Largo Ward **F 9**
47 Largs **C 7**
46 Largymore **G 5**
10 Larkfield, Kent **B 6**
47 Larkfield, Strathclyde **B 7**
47 Larkhall **D 12**
8 Larkhill **B 3**
26 Larling **F 3**
51 Laroch **B 8**
44 Larriston **D 4**
39 Lartington **C 12**
59 Lary **G 1**
9 Lasham **B 8**
40 Laskill **F 6**
15 Lassington **B 11**
52 Lassodie **H 6**
41 Lastingham **F 7**
19 Latchingdon & Shoreham **D 8**
3 Latchley **B 11**
17 Latchmore Green **H 7**
34 Lately Common **G 5**
23 Lathbury **H 11**
61 Latheron **D 11**
53 Lathockar **F 9**
53 Lathones **F 9**
17 Latimer **D 10**
38 Latterhead **C 4**
15 Latteridge **F 10**
7 Lattiford **D 10**
16 Latton **E 2**
58 Lauchintilly **F 5**
50 Laudale House **B 5**
49 Lauder **E 8**
12 Laugharne **F 6**
32 Laughterton **C 5**
10 Laughton, E. Sussex **G 4**
36 Laughton, Humber. **G 6**
23 Laughton, Leics. **C 10**
32 Laughton en le Morthen **A 2**
4 Launcells **E 1**
3 Launceston **A 10**
7 Launcherley **B 9**
17 Launton **B 7**
38 Laurel Bank **G 1**
59 Laurencekirk **K 5**
48 Laurieston, Central **A 2**
43 Laurieston, Dumf. & Gall. **E 7**
23 Lavendon **G 12**
27 Lavenham **K 2**
43 Laverhay **B 12**
14 Lavernock **G 5**
8 Laverstock **C 3**
8 Laverstoke **A 6**
16 Laverton, Glos. **A 2**
40 Laverton, N. Yorks. **H 2**
7 Laverton, Som. **A 11**
30 Lavister **D 2**
48 Law **D 1**
52 Lawers, Tayside **C 2**
52 Lawers, Tayside **E 3**
27 Lawford **M 4**
3 Lawhitton **A 10**
39 Lawkland **H 10**
21 Lawley **B 12**
31 Lawnhead **H 7**
12 Lawrenny **F 4**
27 Lawshall **K 2**
21 Lawton **F 10**
63 Laxay **E 4**
63 Laxdale **C 5**
38 Laxey **G 2**
27 Laxfield **H 6**
64 Laxfirth **D 7**
60 Laxford Bridge **C 4**
64 Laxo **C 7**
64 Laxobigging **C 7**
36 Laxton, Humber. **E 6**
24 Laxton, Northants. **F 1**
32 Laxton, Notts. **D 4**
35 Laycock **C 9**
19 Layer Breton **B 9**
19 Layer-de-la-Haye **B 9**
19 Layer Marney **B 9**
27 Layham **L 3**
16 Layland's Green **G 5**
7 Laymore **F 7**
21 Laysters Pole **F 11**
36 Laytham **C 5**
40 Lazenby **C 6**
39 Lazonby **A 8**
31 Lea, Derby **D 11**
15 Lea, Heref. & Worc. **B 10**
32 Lea, Lincs. **B 5**
21 Lea, Shropshire **B 9**
21 Lea, Shropshire **C 9**
15 Lea, Wilts. **F 12**
22 Lea Marston **C 5**
34 Lea Town **D 4**
39 Lea Yeat **F 10**
32 Leabrooke **E 1**
55 Leacachan **G 3**
56 Leachkin **E 2**
48 Leadburn **D 5**
18 Leaden Roding **C 6**
33 Leadenham **E 7**
49 Leaderfoot **F 8**
39 Leadgate, Cumb. **A 9**
45 Leadgate, Dur. **H 9**
45 Leadgate, Tyne & wear **G 9**
48 Leadhills **H 2**
16 Leafield **C 4**
17 Leagrave **B 11**
40 Leake **F 4**
33 Leake Common Side **E 11**
33 Leake Hurn's End **E 11**
41 Lealholm **D 8**
62 Leatt **B 4**
23 Leamington **E 7**
23 Leamington Hastings **E 8**
22 Leamonsley **A 4**
45 Leamside **H 11**
51 Leanach **H 7**
55 Leanachan **L 6**
56 Leanaig **D 1**
46 Leargybreck **B 1**
39 Leasgill **G 7**
33 Leasingham **E 7**
40 Leasingthorne **B 3**
17 Leatherhead **H 12**
35 Leathley **B 11**
43 Leaths **E 8**
30 Leaton **H 3**
11 Leaveland **C 8**
36 Leavening **A 5**
18 Leaves Green **H 4**
18 Leavesden Green **D 1**
45 Leazes **G 10**
41 Lebberston **G 10**
16 Lechlade **D 3**
39 Leck **G 9**
8 Leckford **B 5**
61 Leckfurin **B 7**
16 Leckhampstead, Berks. **G 5**

23 Leckhampstead, Bucks. H 10
16 Leckhampstead Street F 5
16 Leckhampstead Thicket F 5
15 Leckhampton B 12
54 Leckie C 5
60 Leckmelm G 3
55 Leckroy K 7
14 Leckwith G 5
37 Leconfield C 8
50 Ledaig D 6
17 Ledburn B 10
15 Ledbury A 10
51 Ledcharrie E 12
21 Ledgemoor G 9
54 Ledgowan D 5
21 Ledicot F 9
60 Ledmore F 4
61 Lednagullin B 8
30 Ledsham, Ches. C 2
36 Ledsham, W. Yorks. D 2
36 Ledston D 2
16 Ledwell A 5
50 Lee, Strathclyde E 1
4 Lee, Devon A 4
8 Lee, Hampshire D 5
34 Lee, Lancashire B 4
30 Lee, Shropshire G 3
30 Lee Brockenhurst G 4
17 Lee Clump D 10
30 Lee Green D 5
5 Lee Mill Bridge K 5
5 Lee Mill Estate K 5
5 Lee Moor J 4
9 Lee-on-the-Solent F 7
21 Leebotwood C 10
38 Leece H 5
11 Leeds, Kent C 7
35 Leeds, W. Yorks. D 11
2 Leedstown F 3
31 Leek E 8
22 Leek Wootton E 6
40 Leeming F 3
40 Leeming Bar F 3
31 Lees, Derby F 11
35 Lees, Manchester G 8
44 Lees Hill F 4
29 Leeswood D 12
30 Leftwich Green C 5
33 Legbourne B 10
49 Legerwood E 8
33 Legsby B 8
23 Leicester B 9
23 Leicestershire, Co. B 9
23 Leicester For. East. B 8
7 Leigh, Dorset E 9
15 Leigh, Glos. B 11
10 Leigh, Kent C 4
34 Leigh, Manchester G 5
21 Leigh, Shropshire B 9
10 Leigh, Surrey C 1
16 Leigh, Wiltshire E 2
22 Leigh, Heref. & Worc. G 1
19 Leigh Beck F 8
15 Leigh Delamere F 12
11 Leigh Green E 8
19 Leigh-on-Sea E 8
9 Leigh Park E 8
22 Leigh Sinton G 1
7 Leigh upon Mendip B 10
6 Leighland Chapel C 4
15 Leighterton E 11
40 Leighton, N. Yorks. G 2
21 Leighton, Powys B 8
21 Leighton, Salop B 11
7 Leighton, Som. B 10
25 Leighton Bromswold H 2
17 Leighton Buzzard B 10
59 Leightonhill L 4
15 Leighwoods G 9
21 Leinthall Earls F 10
21 Leinthall Starkes E 10
21 Leintwardine E 9
23 Leire C 8
60 Leirinmore A 5
54 Leishmore F 8
27 Leiston J 7
53 Leitfie C 7
48 Leith B 5
49 Leitholm E 10
2 Lelant F 3
37 Lelley D 10
22 Lem Hill E 1
56 Lemlair D 1
45 Lemmington Hall B 9
49 Lempitlaw F 10
63 Lemreway F 5
18 Lemsford C 2
58 Lenabo C 8
22 Lenchwick G 4
42 Lendalfoot C 2
51 Lendrick G 12
11 Lenham C 7
11 Lenham Heath C 8
49 Lennel E 11
42 Lennies F 5
47 Lennoxtown B 11
17 Lent Rise F 10
24 Lenton C 1
26 Lenwade D 4
47 Lenzie B 11
58 Leochel-Cushnie F 3
21 Leominster F 10
15 Leonard Stanley D 11
8 Lepe F 6
62 Lephin C 1
51 Lephinchapel H 7
51 Lephinmore H 7
36 Leppington A 5
35 Lepton F 10
50 Lerags E 6
3 Lerryn D 8
64 Lerwick E 7
45 Lesbury B 10
53 Leslie, Fife G 7
58 Leslie, Grampian E 3
48 Lesmahagow E 1
2 Lesnewth B 2
26 Lessingham C 7
44 Lessonhall H 1
42 Leswalt E 1
18 Letchmore Heath D 2
25 Letchworth M 3
16 Letcombe Bassett F 5
16 Letcombe Regis E 5
53 Letham, Fife F 8
53 Letham, Tayside B 10
52 Letham, Tayside E 6
53 Letham Grange C 11
56 Lethen House D 5
57 Lethendryveole H 5
58 Lethenty D 5
27 Letheringham J 6
26 Letheringsett B 4
5 Lettaford G 6
64 Lettan A 4
54 Letterewe C 3
55 Letterfearn G 3
55 Letterfinlay K 6
55 Lettermorar K 1
50 Lettermore C 2
60 Letters H 3
48 Lettershaws G 2
12 Letterston D 3
57 Lettoch, Highland H 6
56 Lettoch, Highland F 6
21 Letton, Heref. & Worc. E 9
21 Letton, Heref. & Worc. H 9
18 Letty Green C 3
32 Letwell B 3
53 Leuchars E 9
56 Leuchars House C 8
63 Leurbost D 5
22 Levedale A 3
37 Leven, Humberside C 8
53 Leven, Fife G 8
46 Levencorroch G 5
39 Levens G 7
35 Levenshulme H 7
64 Levenwick F 7
63 Leverburgh H 1
24 Leverington D 5
16 Leverton, Berks. G 4
33 Leverton, Lincs. E 11
33 Leverton Outgate E 11
27 Levington L 5
41 Levisham F 8
16 Lew D 4
3 Lewannick B 9
5 Lewdown G 3
10 Lewes G 3
12 Leweston E 3
18 Lewisham G 3
57 Lewiston G 1
14 Lewistown E 3
17 Lewknor D 8
4 Leworthy B 5
63 Lews Castle D 5
11 Lewson Street B 8
5 Lewtrenchard G 3
3 Ley, Cornwall C 9
58 Ley, Grampian F 3
10 Leybourne B 5
40 Leyburn F 1
30 Leycett E 6
18 Leygreen B 2
17 Leyhill Com. D 10
34 Leyland E 4
58 Leylodge F 5
58 Leys B 7
56 Leys Castle F 2
53 Leys of Cossans B 8
58 Leys of Dummuies D 3
11 Leysdown-on-Sea A 9
53 Leysmill B 10
18 Leyton E 4
18 Leytonstone E 4
3 Lezant B 10
54 Liatrie F 6
14 Libanus B 3
48 Liberton, Lothian B 5
48 Libberton, Strathclyde E 3
22 Lichfield A 5
22 Lickey E 3
22 Lickey End E 3
9 Lickfold D 10
50 Liddesdale B 5
16 Liddington F 3
25 Lidgate J 8
25 Lidlington L 1
16 Lidstone B 4
55 Lienassie G 3
53 Liff D 8
5 Lifton G 3
5 Liftondown G 2
23 Lighthorne G 7
17 Lightwater H 10
31 Lightwood F 7
23 Lilbourne D 9
49 Lilburn Hill G 12
45 Lilburn Tower A 8
22 Lilleshall A 1
16 Lilley, Berks. F 5
18 Lilley, Herts. A 1
49 Lilliesleaf G 8
23 Lillingstone Dayrell H 10
23 Lillingstone Lovell H 10
7 Lillington, Dorest E 9
23 Lillington, War. E 7
8 Lilliput G 2
6 Lilstock B 5
47 Lilybank B 8
34 Limbrick F 5
35 Limefield F 7
47 Limekilnburn D 12
48 Limekilns A 3
48 Limerigg B 1
8 Limestone H 6
44 Limestone Brae H 6
7 Limington D 8
26 Limpenhoe E 7
15 Limpley Stoke H 11
10 Limpsfield C 3
32 Linby E 3
9 Linchmere C 10
43 Lincluden D 10
33 Lincoln C 7
33 Lincolnshire, Co. D 8
22 Lincomb E 2
62 Lincro B 3
38 Lindal in Furness H 5
38 Lindale G 6
49 Lindean F 7
10 Lindfield E 2
9 Lindford C 9
53 Lindifferon E 8
35 Lindley E 10
35 Lindley Green B 11
53 Lindores E 7
21 Lindridge E 12
18 Lindsell A 6
27 Lindsey L 3
38 Linefoot B 3
19 Linford, Essex F 7
8 Linford, Hants. E 3
38 Lingague H 1
41 Lingdale D 7
21 Lingen F 9
10 Lingfield D 3
10 Lingfield Com. D 3
30 Lingley Green A 4
26 Lingwood E 7
44 Linhope, Borders C 2
45 Linhope, N'thumb. A 8
16 Linkenholt H 5
3 Linkinhorne B 10
64 Linklater E 2
53 Linktown H 7
21 Linley Green G 12
48 Linlithgow B 3
48 Linlithgow Bridge B 3
60 Linneraineach F 3
12 Linney G 2
43 Linns D 11
63 Linshader D 3
45 Linshiels B 7
60 Linsidemore G 6
17 Linslade B 10
27 Linstead Parva G 6
44 Linstock G 3
49 Linthaugh F 12
22 Linthurst E 3
35 Linthwaite F 9
49 Lintlaw D 11
58 Lintmill A 3
49 Linton, Borders G 10
25 Linton, Cambs. K 7
22 Linton, Derby A 6
15 Linton, Heref. & Worc. B 9
10 Linton, Kent C 6
35 Linton, N. Yorks. A 8
35 Linton, W. Yorks. B 12
36 Linton-on-Ouse A 3
8 Linwood, Hants. E 3
33 Linwood, Lincs. B 8
47 Linwood, Strathclyde C 9
29 Lioc C 10
63 Lionel A 6
9 Liphook C 9
6 Liscombe C 2
3 Liskeard C 9
9 Liss C 9
9 Liss Forest C 9
37 Lisset A 9
33 Lissington B 8
14 Lisvane F 5
15 Liswerry F 7
26 Litcham D 2
23 Litchborough G 9
8 Litchfield A 6
34 Litherland G 2
25 Litlington, Camb. L 4
10 Litlington, E. Sussex H 4
25 Little Abington K 6
25 Little Addington H 1
22 Little Alne F 5
18 Little Amwell C 3
60 Little Assynt E 3
22 Little Aston B 4
8 Little Atherfield H 6
64 Little Ayre E 1
40 Little Ayton D 6
19 Little Baddow C 7
15 Little Badminton F 11
52 Little Ballinluig B 4
44 Little Bampton G 1
25 Little Bardfield M 8
25 Little Barford J 3
26 Little Barningham B 4
16 Little Barrington C 3
30 Little Barrow C 3
41 Little Barugh G 8
45 Little Bavington E 8
27 Little Bealings K 5
16 Little Bedwyn G 4
42 Little Bennane C 2
19 Little Bentley A 11
18 Little Berkhampsted C 3
23 Little Billing F 11
15 Little Birch A 8
27 Little Blakenham K 4
39 Little Blencow B 7
9 Little Bookham A 12
23 Little Bowden C 11
25 Little Bradley K 8
21 Little Brampton D 9
19 Little Braxted B 8
59 Little Brechin L 3
7 Little Bredy G 9
17 Little Brickhill A 10
23 Little Brington F 10
19 Little Bromley A 10
30 Little Budworth D 5
18 Little Burstead E 6
24 Little Bytham D 1
42 Little Cairnbrock E 1
33 Little Carlton, Lincs. B 11
32 Little Carlton, Notts. D 5
24 Little Casterton E 1
33 Little Cawthorpe B 10
17 Little Chalfont D 11
11 Little Chart D 8
7 Little Cheney G 9
25 Little Chesterford L 6
8 Little Cheverell A 2
25 Little Chishill L 5
19 Little Clacton B 11
38 Little Clifton B 3
58 Little Colp C 5
22 Little Comberton H 3
16 Little Compton A 4
27 Little Cornard L 2
21 Little Cowarne G 11
16 Little Coxwell E 4
40 Little Crakehall F 3
26 Little Cressingham E 2
34 Little Crosby G 2
23 Little Dalby A 11
58 Little Dens C 8
15 Little Dewchurch A 8
37 Little Driffield A 8
26 Little Dunham D 2
52 Little Dunkeld C 5
18 Little Dunmow B 6
18 Little Easton B 6
31 Little Eaton F 12
26 Little Ellingham E 3
7 Little Elm B 10
18 Little End D 5
25 Little Eversden K 5
27 Little Fakenham H 2
16 Little Faringdon D 3
40 Little Fencote F 3
36 Little Fenton D 3
26 Little Fransham D 2
17 Little Gaddesden C 11
15 Little Garway B 8
25 Little Gidding G 2
27 Little Glemham J 6
25 Little Gransden K 4
7 Little Green A 10
33 Little Grimsby A 10
60 Little Gruinard G 1
18 Little Hadham B 4
24 Little Hale B 2
18 Little Hallingbury B 5
17 Little Hampden D 9
23 Little Harrowden E 12
17 Little Haseley D 7
37 Little Hatfield C 9
12 Little Haven F 2
22 Little Hay B 5
31 Little Hayfield A 9
31 Little Haywood H 8
21 Little Hereford F 11
27 Little Horkesley M 2
18 Little Hormead A 4
10 Little Horsted F 3
35 Little Horton D 10
17 Little Horwood A 9
23 Little Houghton F 11
31 Little Hucklow B 10
34 Little Hulton G 6
17 Little Hungerford G 8
23 Little Irchester E 12
37 Little Kelk A 8
17 Little Kimble C 9
17 Little Kingshill D 10
38 Little Langdale E 5
8 Little Langford C 2
58 Little Ledikin E 4
30 Little Leigh C 5
19 Little Leighs B 7
34 Little Lever F 6
23 Little Linford H 11
10 Little Londond, E. Sussex F 4
8 Little London, Hants. A 5
17 Little London, Hants. H 7
24 Little London, Lincs. C 5
35 Little London, W. Yorks. C 10
31 Little Longstone C 10
58 Little Lynturk F 3
22 Little Malvern H 1
27 Little Maplestead M 1
15 Little Marcle A 10
17 Little Marlow E 9
26 Little Massingham C 1
26 Little Melton E 5
12 Little Milford F 3
14 Little Mill D 6
17 Little Milton D 7
17 Little Missenden D 10
30 Little Ness H 3
30 Little Neston C 2
12 Little Newcastle D 3
40 Little Newsham C 1
19 Little Oakley, Essex A 12
23 Little Oakley, Northants. D 12
44 Little Orton G 2
36 Little Ouseburn A 2
25 Little Paxton J 3
2 Little Petherick B 6
42 Little Pinmore C 3
26 Little Plumstead D 6
32 Little Ponton G 6
4 Little Potheridge E 4
25 Little Raveley G 4
35 Little Ribson B 12
16 Little Rissington B 3
26 Little Ryburgh C 3
45 Little Ryle B 8
39 Little Salkeld B 8
8 Little Samborne C 5
25 Little Sampford M 7
17 Little Sandhurst H 9
30 Little Saughall C 2
27 Little Saxham J 1
54 Little Scatwell D 7
25 Little Shelford K 5
4 Little Silver, Devon F 7
6 Little Silver, Devon E 3
36 Little Smeaton E 3
26 Little Snoring B 2
15 Little Sodbury F 10
16 Little Somerford F 1
40 Little Stainton C 4
30 Little Stanney C 3
25 Little Staughton J 2
33 Little Steeping D 11
27 Little Stonham J 4
23 Little Stretton, Leics. B 10
21 Little Stretton, Shropshire C 10
39 Little Strickland C 8
25 Little Stukeley H 3
45 Little Swinburne E 8
49 Little Swinton E 11
16 Little Tew A 5
25 Little Thetford H 6
25 Little Thurlow K 8
18 Little Thurrock F 6
42 Little Torhouse F 5
4 Little Torrington D 4
45 Little Tosson C 8
19 Little Totham C 9
38 Little Town C 5
56 Little Urchany E 4
38 Little Urswick H 5
19 Little Wakering E 9
27 Little Waldingfield L 2
26 Little Walsingham B 2
19 Little Waltham C 7
18 Little Warley E 6
37 Little Weighton D 7
27 Little Welnetham J 2
21 Little Wenlock B 12
27 Little Whittingham Green H 6
45 Little Whittington F 8
25 Little Wilbraham J 6
8 Little Wishford B 2
22 Little Witley F 1
16 Little Wittenham E 6
16 Little Wolford A 3
23 Little Woolstone H 12
25 Little Wymington J 1
18 Little Wymondley A 2
22 Little Wyrley B 4
27 Little Yeldam L 1
64 Little-ayre C 6
41 Littlebeck E 9
35 Littleborough, Manchester F 8
32 Littleborough, Notts. B 5
11 Littlebourne B 10
25 Littlebury L 6
34 Littledale A 4
15 Littledean C 10
61 Littleferry G 8
4 Littleham, Devon D 3
6 Littleham, Devon H 4
9 Littlehampton F 11
5 Littlehempston J 7
45 Littlehoughton A 10
59 Littlemill, Grampian H 1
56 Littlemill, Highland E 5
45 Littlemill, Northumb. A 10
47 Littlemill, Strathclyde H 9
16 Littlemore D 6
31 Littleover G 11
25 Littleport G 7
25 Littleport Bridge G 7
11 Littlestone-on-Sea F 9
40 Littlethorpe H 3
30 Littleton, Ches. D 3
43 Littleton, Dumf. & Gall. F 7
8 Littleton, Hants. C 6
7 Littleton, Som. C 8
9 Littleton, Surrey A 11
17 Littleton, Surrey G 11
53 Littleton, Tayside D 7
15 Littleton Drew F 11
8 Littleton Panell A 2
15 Littleton upon Severn E 9
40 Littletown A 4
17 Littlewick Green F 9
15 Littleworth, Glos. D 11
16 Littleworth, Oxon D 4
22 Littleworth, Heref. & Worc. G 2
22 Littleworth, Staffs. A 4
31 Littleworth, Staffs. H 8
10 Littleworth, W. Sussex F 1
31 Litton, Derby C 10
39 Litton, N. Yorks. H 11
7 Litton, Som. A 9
30 Liverpool A 2
35 Liversedge E 10

41 Liverton, Cleveland **D 7**
5 Liverton, Devon **H 7**
48 Livingston **C 3**
48 Livingston Station **C 3**
29 Lixwm **C 11**
2 Lizard **H 4**
28 Llaingoch **B 2**
20 Llaithddu **D 6**
20 Llan **B 4**
14 Llan-Rumney **F 5**
28 Llanaber **H 5**
28 Llanaelhaearn **F 3**
20 Llanafan **E 2**
20 Llanafan-fawr **G 5**
20 Llanafan-fechan **G 5**
28 Llanallgo **B 4**
29 Llanarmon Dyffryn Ceiriog **G 10**
29 Llanarmon-yn-Ial **E 11**
13 Llanarth, Dyfed **A 7**
15 Llanarth, Gwent **C 7**
13 Llanarthney **E 8**
29 Llanasa **B 10**
28 Llanbabo **B 3**
20 Llanbadarn Fawr **D 2**
20 Llanbadarn Fynyda **E 6**
21 Llanbadarn-y-garreg **G 7**
15 Llanbadoc **D 7**
28 Llanbadrig **A 3**
15 Llanbeder **E 7**
28 Llanbedr, Gwynedd **H 5**
14 Llanbedr, Powys **B 6**
21 Llanbedr, Powys **H 7**
29 Llanbedr-Dyffryn-Clwyd **D 10**
28 Llanbedr-goch **B 4**
28 Llanbedrog **G 3**
29 Llanbedr-y-cennin **C 7**
28 Llanberis **D 5**
14 Llanbethery **G 4**
20 Llanbister **E 6**
14 Llanblethian **G 3**
12 Llanboidy **E 5**
14 Llanbradach **E 5**
56 Llanbryde **D 8**
20 Llanbrynmair **B 5**
14 Llancadle **G 4**
14 Llancaiach **E 4**
14 Llancarfan **G 4**
15 Llancayo **D 7**
15 Llancloudy **B 8**
21 Llancoch **E 7**
14 Llandaff **F 5**
28 Llandanwg **G 5**
13 Llandarcy **G 10**
12 Llandawke **F 6**
28 Llanddaniel Fab **C 4**
13 Llanddarog **E 8**
28 Llanddeiniol **E 1**
28 Llanddeiniolen **D 5**
29 Llandderfel **F 9**
13 Llanddeusant, Dyfed **E 11**
28 Llanddeusant, Gwynedd **B 3**
14 Llanddew **A 4**
13 Llanddewi **H 8**
20 Llanddewi-Brefi **G 2**
15 Llanddewi Rhydderch **C 7**
12 Llanddewi Velfrey **E 5**
20 Llanddewi'r Cwm **G 6**
13 Llanddoget **D 7**
28 Llanddona **B 5**
12 Llanddowror **F 6**
29 Llanddulas **B 8**
28 Llanddyfnan **B 4**
14 Llandefaelog Fach **A 4**
14 Llandefaelog ter-graig **A 4**
14 Llandefalle **A 4**
28 Llandegai **C 5**
28 Llandegfan **C 5**
15 Llandegfedd **E 7**
29 Llandegla **E 11**
21 Llandegley **F 7**
13 Llandeilo **E 9**
20 Llandeilo Graban **H 6**
14 Llandeilo'r Fan **A 2**
12 Llandeloy **D 2**
15 Llandenny **D 7**
15 Llandevenny **F 7**
12 Llandewi Velfrey **E 5**
20 Llandewi Ystradenny **E 6**
12 Llandilo **D 4**
15 Llandinabo **A 8**
20 Llandinam **D 6**
12 Llandissilio **E 5**
15 Llandogo **D 8**
14 Llandough, S. Glam. **G 5**
14 Llandough, S. Glam. **G 3**
13 Llandovery **D 11**
14 Llandow **G 3**
20 Llandre, Dyfed **D 2**
13 Llandre, Dyfed **C 10**
29 Llandrillo **F 9**
29 Llandrillo-yn-Rhos. **B 7**
20 Llandrindod Wells **F 6**
21 Llandrinio **A 8**
29 Llandudno **B 7**
29 Llandudno Junc. **B 7**
28 Llandwrog **E 4**
13 Llandybie **E 9**
13 Llandyfaelog **F 7**
13 Llandyfan **E 9**
14 Llandyfodwg **F 3**
13 Llandyfriog **C 7**
28 Llandyfrydog **B 4**
12 Llandygwydd **C 6**
29 Llandyrnog **D 10**
29 Llandysilio **H 12**
21 Llandyssil **C 7**
13 Llandyssul **C 7**
14 Llanedeyrn **F 5**
20 Llaneglwys **H 6**
20 Llanegryn **B 2**
13 Llanegwad **E 8**
28 Llaneilian **A 4**
29 Llanelian-y-Rhos **C 8**
29 Llanelidan **E 10**
14 Llanelieu **A 5**
14 Llanellen **C 6**
13 Llanelli, Dyfed **G 8**
14 Llanelli, Gwent **C 5**
28 Llanelltyd **H 6**
20 Llanelwedd **G 6**
28 Llanenddwyn **H 5**
28 Llanengan **G 2**
28 Llanerchymedd **B 4**
20 Llanerfyl **A 6**
28 Llanfachraeth **B 3**
29 Llanfachreth **H 7**
28 Llanfaelog **C 3**
28 Llanfaelrhys **G 2**
15 Llanfaenor **C 7**
28 Llanfaes, Gwynedd **C 5**
14 Llanfaes, Powys **B 4**
28 Llanfaethlu **B 3**
28 Llanfalgan **D 4**
28 Llanfair **G 5**
20 Llanfair-Caereinion **B 6**
20 Llanfair-Clydogau **G 2**
29 Llanfair Dyffryn Clwyd **E 10**
12 Llanfair Nant-Gwyn **C 5**
29 Llanfair Talhaiarn **C 8**
21 Llandfair Waterdine **E 8**
28 Llanfairfechan **C 6**
28 Llanfair-P.G. **C 5**
28 Llanfair-y-Cwmmwd **D 4**
28 Llanfairynghornwy **A 3**
28 Llanfair-yn-Neubwll **C 2**
12 Llanfallteg **E 5**
12 Llanfallteg West **E 5**
20 Llanfaredd **G 6**
20 Llanfarian **E 2**
29 Llanfechain **H 11**
28 Llanfechell **A 3**
20 Llanfendigaid **B 1**
29 Llanferres **D 11**
28 Llanfflewyn **A 3**
28 Llanfigael **B 3**
20 Llanfihangel **A 6**
14 Llanfihangel Crucorney **B 6**
29 Llanfihangel Glyn Myfyr **E 9**
14 Llanfihangel Llantarnam **E 6**
14 Llanfihangel Nant Bran **A 3**
21 Llanfihangel Rhydithon **F 7**
15 Llanfihangel Rogiet **F 8**
14 Llanfihangel Tal-y-llyn **A 4**
13 Llanfihangel ar-arth **C 8**
21 Llanfihangel-nant-Melan **G 7**
13 Llanfihangel-uwch-Gwili **E 8**
20 Llanfihangel-y-Creuddyn **E 2**
28 Llanfihangel yn Nhowyn **C 3**
20 Llanfihangel-y-Pennant **B 2**
28 Llanfihangel-y-pennant **F 5**
28 Llanfihangel-y-traethau **G 5**
14 Llanfilo **A 4**
14 Llanfoist **C 6**
29 Llanfor **G 8**
14 Llanfrechfa **E 6**
28 Llanfrothen **F 5**
14 Llanfrynach **B 4**
29 Llanfwrog, Clwyd **D 10**
28 Llanfwrog, Gwynedd **B 2**
29 Llanfyllin **H 10**
29 Llanfynydd, Clwyd **E 12**
13 Llanfynydd, Dyfed **D 9**
12 Llanfyrnach **D 6**
20 Llangadfan **A 6**
13 Llangadog, Dyfed **D 10**
13 Llangadog, Dyfed **F 7**
29 Llangadwaladr, Clwyd **G 11**
28 Llangadwaladr, Gwynedd **C 3**
28 Llangaffo **C 4**
13 Llangain **E 7**
20 Llangammarch Wells **H 5**
14 Llangan **G 3**
15 Llangarron **B 8**
14 Llangasty-Tal-y-llyn **B 5**
13 Llangathen **E 9**
15 Llangattock **C 5**
15 Llangattock Lingoed **B 7**
14 Llangattock nigh Usk **C 6**
15 Llangattock Vibon-Avel **C 8**
29 Llangedwyn **H 11**
28 Llangefni **C 4**
14 Llangeinor **F 2**
28 Llangeinwen **D 4**
20 Llangeitho **F 2**
13 Llangeler **C 7**
20 Llangelynin **B 1**
13 Llangendeirne **F 8**
13 Llangennech **G 9**
13 Llangennith **H 7**
14 Llangenny **C 6**
29 Llangernyw **C 8**
28 Llangian **G 2**
13 Llangiwg **F 10**
13 Llangloffan **D 3**
12 Llanglydwen **D 5**
28 Llangoed **B 5**
12 Llangoedmor **B 5**
29 Llangollen **F 11**
12 Llangolman **D 5**
14 Llangorse **B 4**
15 Llangoven **D 8**
29 Llangower **G 8**
12 Llangranog **B 6**
28 Llangristiolus **C 4**
15 Llangrove **B 8**
15 Llangua **B 7**
21 Llangunllo **E 7**
13 Llangunnor **E 8**
20 Llangurig **D 5**
29 Llangwm, Clwyd **F 9**
12 Llangwm, Dyfed **F 3**
15 Llangwm, Gwent **D 7**
15 Llangwm-isaf **D 7**
28 Llangwnnadl **G 2**
29 Llangwyfan **D 10**
28 Llangwyfanisaf **C 3**
28 langwyllog **B 4**
28 Llangwyryfon **E 2**
20 Llangybi, Dyfed **G 2**
15 Llangybi, Gwent **E 7**
28 Llangybi, Gwynedd **F 4**
13 Llangyfelach **G 10**
20 Llangynfelyn **C 2**
29 Llangynhafal **D 10**
14 Llangynidr **B 5**
12 Llangynin **E 6**
13 Llangynllo **C 7**
13 Llangynog, Dyfed **E 7**
29 Llangynog, Powys **H 9**
14 Llangynwyd **E 2**
14 Lanhamlach **B 4**
14 Llanharan **F 3**
14 Llanharry **F 3**
15 Llanhennock **E 7**
14 Llanhilleth **D 5**
20 Llanidloes **D 5**
28 Llaniestyn **G 2**
21 Llanigan **H 7**
20 Llanilar **E 2**
14 Llanilid **F 3**
14 Llanilterne **F 4**
15 Llanishen, Gwent **D 8**
14 Llanishen, S. Glam. **F 5**
13 Llandllawddog **D 8**
28 Llanllechid **C 5**
20 Llanllugan **B 6**
21 Llanllwchaiarn **C 7**
13 Llanllwch **E 7**
28 Llanllyfni **E 4**
15 Llanllywel **D 7**
13 Llanmadoc **H 8**
14 Llanmaes **G 3**
15 Llanmartin **E 7**
21 Llanmerewig **C 7**
14 Llanmihangel **G 3**
12 Llanmiloe **F 6**
13 Llanmorlais **G 8**
29 Llannefydd **C 9**
13 Llannon **F 9**
28 Llannor **F 3**
20 Llanon **F 1**
13 Llanpumsaint **D 7**
12 Llanreithan **D 2**
29 Llanrhaeadr **D 10**
29 Llanrhaeadr-ym-Mochnant **H 10**
13 Llanrhidian **H 8**
29 Llanrhos **B 7**
28 Llanrhyddlad **A 3**
20 Llanrhystyd **E 1**
12 Llanrian **D 2**
28 Llanrug **D 5**
29 Llanrwst **D 7**
12 Llansadurnen **F 6**
13 Llansadwrn, Dyfed **D 10**
28 Llansadwrn, Gwynedd **C 5**
13 Llan-saint **F 7**
13 Llansamlet **G 10**
29 Llansannan **D 8**
14 Llansannor **G 3**
14 Llansantffraed **B 5**
20 Llansantffraed Cwmdeuddwr **F 5**
20 Llansantffraed-in-Elvel **G 6**
20 Llansantffraid **F 1**
29 Llansantffraid Glan Conway **C 7**
29 Llansantffraid-ym-Mechain **H 11**
13 Llansawel **C 9**
29 Llansilin **G 11**
15 Llansoy **D 7**
14 Llanspyddid **B 3**
12 Llanstadwell **F 3**
13 Llanstephan **F 7**
12 Llanteg **F 5**
15 Llanthony **B 6**
15 Llantilio Crossenny **C 7**
15 Llantilio Pertholey **C 6**
12 Llantood **C 5**
15 Llantrisant, Gwent **E 7**
14 Llantrisant, Mid Glam. **F 4**
14 Llantrithyd **G 4**
14 Llantwit Fardre **F 4**
14 Llantwit-Major **G 3**
29 Llanuwchllyn **G 8**
15 Llanvaches **E 7**
15 Llanvair Discoed **E 8**
15 Llanvapley **C 7**
15 Llanvetherine **C 7**
14 Llanveynoe **A 6**
15 Llanvihangel Gobion **C 7**
14 Llanvihangel Pontymoel **D 6**
15 Llanvihangel Ystern-Llewern **C 7**
15 Llanwarne **B 8**
29 Llanwddyn **H 9**
14 Llanwenarth **C 6**
13 Llanwenog **B 8**
15 Llanwern **E 7**
12 Llanwinio **D 6**
12 Llanwnda, Dyfed **C 3**
28 Llanwnda, Gwynedd **D 4**
13 Llanwnen **B 8**
20 Llanwnog **C 6**
13 Llanwrda **D 10**
20 Llanwrin **B 3**
20 Llanwrthwl **F 5**
20 Llanwrtyd **H 4**
20 Llanwrtyd Wells **H 4**
20 Llanwyddelan **B 6**
30 Llanyblodwel **H 1**
13 Llanybri **F 7**
13 Llanybyther **C 8**
12 Llanycefn **E 4**
12 Llanychaer Birdge **C 3**
29 Llanymawddwy **H 8**
30 Llanymynech **H 1**
28 Llanynghenedl **B 3**
29 Llanynys **D 10**
30 Llan-y-pwll **E 2**
20 Llanyre **F 6**
28 Llanystumdwy **F 4**
14 Llanywern **A 4**
12 Llawhaden **E 4**
30 Llawnt **G 1**
20 Llawr-y-glyn **C 5**
30 Llay **E 2**
14 Llechfaen **A 4**
12 Llechryd, Dyfed **C 5**
14 Llechryd, Mid Glam. **C 4**
29 Llechrydau **G 11**
13 Llethrid **H 8**
20 Lledrod **E 2**
13 Llidiad-Nenog **C 9**
28 Llidairdau, Gwynedd **G 1**
29 Llidiardau, Gwynedd **F 8**
29 Llidiart-y-parc **F 10**
28 Llithfaen **F 3**
29 Llong **D 12**
21 Llowes **H 7**
20 Llundain-fach **G 1**
14 Llwydcoed **D 3**
13 Llwyn-Celyn **A 8**
13 Llwyn Dafydd **B 7**
21 Llwynderw, Powys **B 7**
20 Llwynderw, Powys **D 5**
12 Llwyn-drain **D 6**
20 Llwyngwril **A 2**
13 Llwyn-hendy **G 9**
29 Llwyn-mawr **G 11**
14 Llwyn-on **C 3**
20 Llwyn-y-groes **G 2**
14 Llwyn-y-pia **E 3**
30 Llynclys **H 1**
28 Llynfaes **B 3**
20 Llysdinam **F 6**
29 Llysfaen **C 8**
14 Llyswen **A 4**
14 Llysworney **G 3**
12 Llys-y-fran **E 4**
14 Llywel **A 2**
20 Llywernog **D 3**
49 Loanend **D 12**
48 Loanhead, Lothian **C 5**
47 Loanhead, Strathclyde **D 9**
48 Loanhead, Strathclyde **F 3**
58 Loanhead of Fedderate **C 6**
47 Loans **F 3**
45 Loansdean **E 10**
4 Lobb **B 3**
61 Loch Choire Lodge **D 7**
42 LochHead **G 4**
60 Loch Loyal Lo. **C 6**
55 Lochailort **L 2**
50 Lochaline **C 4**
42 Lohans **F 2**
43 Locharbriggs **D 10**
43 Locharwoods **E 11**
60 Lochassynt Lodge **D 3**
51 Lochawe **E 8**
50 Lochbuie **E 3**
57 Lochcallater **L 7**
54 Lochcarron **F 3**
61 Lochdhu Lodge **C 9**
51 Lochdochart Ho. **E 11**
50 Lochdonhead **D 5**
54 Lochdrum **B 6**
46 Lochead, Strathclyde **B 3**
46 Lochead, Strathclyde **A 5**
52 Lochearnhead **E 1**
53 Lochee **D 8**
43 Lochend, Dumf. & Gall. **F 9**
52 Lochend, Fife **H 6**
56 Lochend, Highland **F 2**
61 Lochend, Highland **A 11**
43 Locherben **B 10**
43 Lochfoot **D 9**
50 Lochgair **H 6**
57 Lochgarthside **H 1**
47 Lochgate **F 11**
53 Lochgelly **H 7**
46 Lochgilphead **A 4**
51 Lochgoilhead **G 9**
56 Loch-hill **C 8**
47 Lochhill **H 11**
56 Lochindorb Lo. **F 5**
47 Lochingirrcoh **H 11**
60 Lochinver **E 3**
48 Lochlycock **F 2**
43 Lochmaben **C 11**
60 Lochmore Lodge **D 4**
52 Lochore **G 6**
46 Lochranza **D 4**
47 Lochridge **E 9**
58 Lochs Crofts **B 1**
59 Lochside, Grampian **L 5**
56 Lochside, Highland **D 4**
61 Lochside, Highland **D 8**
60 Lochstack Lodge **C 4**
61 Lochstrathy **C 8**
59 Lochton **H 5**
59 Lochton of Leys **H 4**
53 Lochty, Fife **F 10**
59 Lochty, Tayside **L 3**
50 Lochuisge **B 5**
43 Lochurr **C 8**
47 Lochwinnoch **C 8**
43 Lochwood **B 11**
55 Lochy Brdige **M 5**
44 Lock Hills **H 3**
3 Lockengate **D 7**
43 Lockerbie **C 12**
16 Lockeridge **G 3**
8 Lockerley **C 4**
15 Locking **H 7**
16 Lockinge **E 5**
37 Lockington, Humber. **B 7**
32 Lockington, Leics. **G 2**
30 Lockleywood **G 5**
8 Lock's Heath **E 6**
4 Lockshill **E 4**
41 Lockton **F 8**
23 Loddington, Leics. **B 11**
23 Loddington, Northants. **D 11**
5 Loddiswell **L 6**
26 Loddon **F 6**
25 Lode **J 6**
7 Loders **G 8**
9 Lodsworth **D 10**
40 Lofthouse, N. Yorks. **H 1**
35 Lofthouse, W. Yorks. **E 12**
41 Loftus **C 7**
47 Logan **G 10**
42 Logan Mains **G 2**
30 Loggerheads **G 6**
53 Logie, Fife **E 7**
53 Logie, Fife **E 9**
56 Logie Hill **B 3**
58 Logie Newton **D 4**
59 Logie Pert **L 4**
52 Logiealmond Lo. **D 4**
52 Logierait **B 5**
12 Login **E 5**
25 Lolworth **J 5**
54 Lonbain **D 1**
36 Londesborough **C 6**
18 London **F 3**
3 London Apprentice **E 7**
18 London Colney **D 2**
40 Londonderry **F 3**
33 Londonthorpe **F 7**
54 Londubh **B 2**
60 Lone **C 4**
15 Long Ashton **G 9**
32 Long Bennington **F 5**
7 Long Bredy **G 9**
23 Long Buckby **E 9**
7 Long Burton **E 10**
32 Long Clawson **G 4**
8 Long Common **E 6**
31 Long Compton, Staffordshire **H 7**
16 Long Compton, Warwickshire **A 4**
17 Long Crendon **C 8**
8 Long Crichel **E 1**
17 Long Ditton **G 12**
36 Long Drax **D 5**
32 Long Duckmanton **C 2**
32 Long Eaton **G 2**
30 Long Green **C 3**
16 Long Hanborough **C 5**
48 Long Hermiston **B 4**
23 Long Itchington **F 7**
23 Long Lawford **D 8**
7 Long Load **D 8**
17 Long Marston, Herts. **C 9**
36 Long Marston, N. Yorks. **B 3**
39 Long Marton **C 9**
22 Long Marston **G 5**
27 Long Melford **K 2**
15 Long Newnton **E 12**
40 Long Newton **D 4**
35 Long Preston **A 7**
37 Long Riston **C 9**
36 Long Sandall **F 4**
25 Long Stanton All Sainsts **J 5**
25 Long Stanton St. Michael **J 5**
26 Long Stratton **F 5**
23 Long Street **G 11**
9 Long Sutton, Hants. **A 9**
24 Long Sutton, Lincs. **C 5**
7 Long Sutton, Som. **D 8**
21 Long Waste **A 11**
32 Long Whatton **H 2**
41 Long Whins **G 11**
16 Long Wittenham **E 6**

47 Longbar D 8
45 Longbenton F 11
16 Longborough A 3
22 Longbridge, War. F 6
22 Longbridge, W. Midlands D 3
7 Longbridge Deverill B 11
54 Longbridgemuir E 11
44 Longbyre F 5
42 Longcastle G 5
31 Longcliffe E 10
16 Longcot E 4
49 Longcroft, Borders D 8
48 Longcroft, Central A 1
17 Longcross H 10
21 Longden B 10
22 Longdon A 4
22 Longdon Green A 4
21 Longdon upon Tern A 11
6 Longdown G 2
2 Longdowns F 4
45 Longdyke B 10
10 Longfield A 5
10 Longfield Hill A 5
31 Longford, Derby F 10
15 Longford, Glos. B 11
18 Longford, London F 1
30 Longford, Salop G 5
23 Longford, W. Midlands D 7
53 Longforgan D 8
49 Longformacus D 9
45 Longframlington C 9
8 Longham, Dorset F 2
26 Longham, Norf. D 2
58 Longhill B 7
45 Longhirst D 10
15 Longhope B 10
45 Longhorsley D 9
45 Longhoughton B 10
38 Longlands B 5
16 Longlane, Berks. G 6
31 Longlane, Derby F 11
15 Longlevens B 11
22 Longley Green G 1
58 Longmanhill A 5
9 Longmoor Camp C 9
56 Longmorn D 8
49 Longnewton G 8
15 Longney C 11
49 Longniddry B 7
31 Longnor D 9
21 Longnot B 10
8 Longparish B 6
34 Longridge, Lancs. D 5
48 Longridge, Lothian C 2
48 Longriggend B 1
31 Longsdon E 8
58 Longside C 8
30 Longslow G 5
8 Longstock B 5
3 Longstone B 7
25 Longstowe K 4
24 Longthorpe F 3
34 Longton, Lancs. E 4
31 Longton, Staffs F 7
44 Longtown, Cumb. F 2
14 Longtown, Heref. & Worc. A 6
21 Longville in the Dale C 11
15 Longwell Green G 10
17 Longwick D 8
45 Longwitton D 9
21 Longwood B 11
16 Longworth D 5
49 Longyester C 8
62 Lonmore D 2
10 Loose C 6
17 Loosley Row D 9
58 Lootcherbrae B 3
8 Lopcombe Corner C 4
7 Lopen E 8
30 Loppington G 3
45 Lorbottle B 8
45 Lorbottle Hall B 8
9 Lordington E 9
44 Lordsgate F 3
43 Lorg B 7
32 Loscoe E 2
56 Lossiemouth C 8
30 Lostock Gralam C 5
30 Lostock Green C 5
34 Lostock Junction F 5
3 Lostwithiel D 8
61 Lothbeg F 9
35 Lothersdale C 8
61 Lothmore F 9
7 Lottisham C 9
17 Loadwater E 10
32 Loughborough H 3
13 Loughor G 9
23 Loughton, Bucks. H 11
18 Loughton, Essex D 4
21 Loughton, Salop D 11
24 Lound, Lincs. D 2
32 Lound, Notts. B 4
26 Lound, Suffolk E 8
31 Lount H 12
33 Louth B 10
35 Love Clough D 7
9 Lovedean E 8
4 Loveacott C 4
8 Lover D 4
36 Loversall G 4
18 Loves Green C 6
40 Lovesome Hill E 4
12 Loveston F 4
7 Lovington C 9
42 Low Ardwell G 2
43 Low Barlay F 7
35 Low Bradfield H 11
35 Low Bradley B 9
38 Low Braithwaite A 6
45 Low Brunton F 7
36 Low Burnham G 5
40 Low Burton G 3
45 Low Buston B 10
36 Low Catton B 5
40 Low Coniscliffe D 3
42 Low Craighead A 3
44 Low Cranecleugh D 5
44 Low Crosby G 3
41 Low Dalby F 8
40 Low Dinsdale D 4
36 Low Eggborough E 3
40 Low Etherley B 2
44 Low Geltbridge G 4
47 Low Grange H 8
22 Low Habberley D 2
7 Low Ham C 8
45 Low Hedgeley A 9
39 Low Hesket A 7
45 Low Hesleyhurst C 9
41 Low Hutton H 8
42 Low Knockbrex E 5
31 Low Leighton B 8
38 Low Lorton C 4
42 Low Malzie F 4
41 Low Marishes G 8
32 Low Marnham C 5
41 Low Mill F 7
34 Low Moor C 6
45 Low Moorsley H 11
45 Low Newton-by-the-Sea A 10
44 Low Row, Cumb. G 4
38 Low Row, Cumb. B 6
39 Low Row, N. Yorks. E 12
42 Low Salchrie E 1
37 Low Santon F 7
47 Low Shawsburn D 12
26 Low Street C 6
26 Low Thurlton E 7
48 Low Torry A 3
45 Low Town C 9
47 Low Waters D 12
40 Low Worsall D 4
38 Low Wray E 6
39 Lowbridge House E 7
38 Lowca C 2
32 Lowdham F 4
30 Lowe G 4
6 Lower Aisholt C 5
7 Lower Ansty F 11
6 Lower Ashton H 2
17 Lower Assendon F 8
63 Lower Bayble D 6
10 Lower Beeding E 1
39 Lower Bentham H 9
7 Lower Bockhampton G 10
23 Lower Boddington G 8
2 Lower Boscaswell F 1
9 Lower Bourne B 10
22 Lower Brailes H 6
62 Lower Breakish F 6
22 Lower Broadheath F 2
15 Lower Bullingham A 8
25 Lower Caldecote K 3
15 Lower Cam D 10
14 Lower Chapel A 4
8 Lower Chicksgrove C 1
8 Lower Chute A 4
10 Lower Cokeham H 1
31 Lower Crossings B 9
35 Lower Cumberworth F 11
14 Lower Cwm-twrch C 1
34 Lower Darwen E 6
25 Lower Dean H 2
54 Lower Diabaig D 2
10 Lower Dicker G 4
21 Lower Dinchope D 10
61 Lower Dounreay A 9
21 Lower Down D 9
2 Lower Drift G 2
36 Lower Dunsforth A 2
8 Lower Everleigh A 3
15 Lower Failand G 8
9 Lower Farringdon C 8
38 Lower Foxdale G 1
12 Lower Freystrop F 3
9 Lower Froyle B 9
60 Lower Gledfield G 6
10 Lower Green, Kent D 5
26 Lower Green, Norf. B 3
27 Lower Hacheston J 6
62 Lower Halistra B 2
11 Lower Halstow A 7
11 Lower Hardres C 10
56 Lower Hempriggs C 7
21 Lower Hergest G 8
16 Lower Heyford B 6
10 Lower Higham A 6
30 Lower Hordley G 3
10 Lower Horsebridge G 4
51 Lower Kinchrackine E 8
7 Lower Kingcombe F 9
10 Lower Kingswood C 1
30 Lower Kinnerton D 2
15 Lower Langford H 8
53 Lower Largo G 9
31 Lower Leigh G 8
57 Lower Lenie G 1
20 Lower Llanfadog F 5
4 Lower Loxhore B 5
15 Lower Lydbrook C 9
21 Lower Lye F 9
14 Lower Machen E 5
15 Lower Maes-coed A 7
19 Lower Mayland D 9
62 Lower Milovaig C 1
22 Lower Moor G 3
18 Lower Nazeing C 4
52 Lower Oakfield H 6
62 Lower Ollach D 4
14 Lower Penarth G 5
22 Lower Penn C 2
8 Lower Pennington G 5
30 Lower Peover C 6
35 Lower Place F 8
22 Lower Quinton G 5
21 Lower Rochford F 11
34 Lower Salter A 5
16 Lower Seagry F 1
63 Lower Shader A 5
25 Lower Shelton L 1
17 Lower Shiplake F 8
23 Lower Shuckburgh F 8
16 Lower Slaughter B 3
15 Lower Stanton St. Quintin F 12
11 Lower Stoke A 7
26 Lower Street B 6
22 Lower Strensham H 3
17 Lower Sundon A 11
8 Lower Swanwick E 6
16 Lower Swell B 3
62 Lower Tote B 4
12 Lower Town C 3
23 Lower Tysoe H 7
9 Lower Upham D 7
6 Lower Vexford C 5
34 Lower Walton H 5
7 LowerWaterston G 10
7 Lower Weare A 7
21 Lower Welson G 8
30 Lower Whitley B 5
9 Lower Wield B 8
17 Lower Winchendon C 8
17 Lower Woodend E 9
8 Lower Woodford C 3
22 Lower Wyche H 1
23 Lowesby A 10
26 Lowestoft F 8
26 Lowestoft End F 8
38 Loweswater C 4
10 Lowfield Heath D 2
34 Logwill, Lancs. A 5
39 Lowgill, Cumbria E 8
25 Lowick, Northants. G 1
45 Lowick, Northumb. B 11
38 Lowick Green G 5
14 Lowlands E 6
22 Lowsonford E 5
39 Lowther C 8
37 Lowthorpe A 8
34 Lowton, Manchester G 5
6 Lowton, Som. D 5
34 Lowton Common G 5
6 Loxbeare E 3
9 Loxhill B 11
4 Loxhore B 5
22 Loxley G 6
7 Loxton A 7
9 Loxwood C 11
60 Lubachoinnich G 5
60 Lubcroy F 4
23 Lubenham C 10
51 Lubnaclach A 11
54 Lubriach B 7
6 Luccombe B 3
9 Luccombe Village H 7
45 Lucker D 11
3 Luckett B 11
15 Luckington F 11
53 Lucklawhill E 9
6 Luckwell Bridge B 2
21 Lucton F 10
37 Ludborough H 10
12 Ludchurch F 5
35 Luddenden E 9
35 Luddenden Foot E 9
10 Luddesdown B 5
36 Luddington, Humberside E 6
22 Luddington, War. G 5
25 Luddington in the Brook G 2
21 Ludford E 10
33 Ludford Magna A 9
33 Ludford Parva A 9
17 Ludgershall B 7
8 Ludgershall A 4
2 Ludgvan F 2
26 Ludham D 7
21 Ludlow E 10
7 Ludwell D 12
40 Ludworth A 4
4 Luffincott F 2
47 Lugar G 10
49 Lugate E 7
49 Luggate Burn B 8
47 Luggiebank B 12
47 Lugton D 9
21 Lugwardine H 11
62 Luib E 5
51 Luib Hotel E 12
51 Luibeilt A 9
21 Lulham H 9
22 Lullington, Derby A 6
7 Lullington, Som. A 11
22 Lulsey G 1
15 Lulsgate Bottom H 8
35 Lumb E 9
35 Lumbutts E 8
36 Lumby D 3
47 Lumloch B 11
59 Lumphanan G 3
52 Lumphinnans H 6
49 Lumsdaine B 11
58 Lumsden E 2
53 Lunan B 11
53 Lunanhead B 9
52 Luncarty D 6
37 Lund, Humberside B 7
36 Lund, N. Yorks. D 4
51 Lundavra A 8
58 Lunderton C 8
55 Lundie, Highland H 5
53 Lundie, Tayside D 8
53 Lundin Links G 9
50 Lungar (Hotel) G 5
64 Lunna C 7
64 Lunning C 7
13 Lunnon H 9
10 Lunsford B 6
10 Lunsford's Cross G 6
34 Lunt G 2
21 Luntley G 9
6 Luppitt F 5
35 Lupsett E 11
39 Lupton G 8
9 Lurgashall C 10
56 Lurgmore F 1
33 Lusby C 10
51 Luss H 10
62 Lusta C 2
5 Lustleigh H 6
21 Luston F 10
59 Luthermuir K 4
53 Luthrie E 8
17 Luton, Beds. B 12
5 Luton, Devon H 8
10 Luton, Kent A 6
23 Lutterworth D 9
5 Lutton, Devon K 5
24 Lutton, Lincs. C 5
25 Lutton, Northants. G 2
6 Luxborough B 3
3 Luxulyan D 7
61 Lybster D 11
21 Lydbury North D 9
11 Lydd F 9
11 Lydd-on-Sea F 9
11 Lydden D 11
23 Lyddington B 12
17 Lyde Green H 8
6 Lydeard St. Lawrence C 4
5 Lydford G 4
35 Lydgate E 8
21 Lydham C 9
16 Lydiard Millicent F 2
34 Lydiate G 2
7 Lydlinch E 10
15 Lydney D 9
12 Lydstep G 4
22 Lye D 3
15 Lye Cross H 8
17 Lye Green, Bucks. D 10
10 Lye Green, E Sussex E 4
16 Lyford E 5
47 Lylestone, Strathclyde E 8
49 Lylestone, Borders D 8
11 Lymbridge Green D 10
7 Lyme Regis G 7
11 Lyminge D 10
8 Lymington F 4
9 Lyminster F 11
30 Lymm B 5
8 Lymore G 4
11 Lympne E 10
6 Lympsham A 6
6 Lympstone H 3
57 Lynaberack K 3
57 Lynachlaggan J 4
6 Lynch B 3
26 Lynch Green E 4
57 Lynchat J 3
8 Lyndhurst E 4
23 Lyndon B 12
48 Lyne, Borders E 5
17 Lyne, Surrey G 11
15 Lyne Down A 9
57 Lyne of Gorthleck H 1
58 Lyne of Skene F 5
30 Lyneal G 3
62 Lynedale House C 3
16 Lyneham, Oxon B 4
16 Lyneham, Wilts. F 1
44 Lyneholmeford F 4
57 Lynmore G 6
45 Lynemouth D 11
64 Lyness E 1
26 Lyng, Norfolk D 4
7 Lyng, Somerset C 7
4 Lynmouth A 6
11 Lynsted B 8
4 Lynton A 6
7 Lyon's Gate F 10
21 Lyonshall G 9
8 Lytchett Matravers G 1
8 Lytchett Minster G 1
61 Lyth B 11
34 Lytham D 3
34 Lytham St Anne's D 2
41 Lythe D 8
64 Lythes E 3
63 Maaruig F 3
2 Mabe Burnthouse F 5
43 Mabie D 10
33 Mablethorpe B 12
48 Macbiehill D 4
31 Macclesfield C 7
31 Macclesfield For. C 8
58 Macduff A 4
52 Machany F 4
14 Machen E 5
46 Machrihanish G 1
50 Machrins H 1
20 Machynlleth B 3
31 Mackworth F 11
49 Macmerry B 7
52 Madderty E 4
48 Maddiston B 2
9 Madehurst E 11
21 Madeley, Salop B 12
30 Madeley, Staffs. F 6
30 Madeley Heath F 6
25 Madingley J 5
21 Madley H 9
22 Madresfield G 2
2 Madron F 2
28 Maenaddwyn B 4
12 Maenclochog D 4
14 Maendy G 3
28 Maentwrog F 6
13 Maen-y-groes A 7
30 Maer F 6
29 Maerdy, Clwyd F 9
13 Maerdy, Dyfed D 10
15 Maerdy, Gwent B 7
14 Maerdy, Mid Glam. D 3
30 Maesbrook Green H 2
30 Maesbury H 2
30 Maesbury Marsh H 2
12 Maesgwynne E 5
29 Maeshafn D 11
13 Maesllyn C 7
20 Maesmynis H 6
14 Maesteg E 2
13 Maestir B 9
13 Maestwynog C 10
13 Maes-y-bont E 9
13 Maesycrugiau C 8
14 Maes-y-cwmmer E 5
13 Maesymeillion B 7
18 Magdalen Laver C 5
58 Maggieknockater C 1
10 Magham Down G 5
34 Maghull G 3
15 Magor F 7
7 Maiden Bradley B 11
45 Maiden Law H 10
7 Maiden Newton F 9
12 Maiden Wells G 3
5 Maidencombe J 8
48 Maidencots G 2
17 Maidenhead F 10
39 Maidenhill B 7
42 Maidens A 3
17 Maiden's Green G 9
33 Maidenwell B 10
23 Maidford G 9
17 Maid's Moreton A 8
10 Maidstone C 6
23 Maidwell D 10
64 Mail E 7
14 Maindee E 6
61 Mains, Highland F 8
47 Mains, Strathclyde D 11
52 Mains, Tayside B 6
42 Mains of Airies E 1
59 Mainsof Allardice K 6
59 Mains of Altries H 6
58 Mains of Annochie C 7
53 Mains of Ardestie D 10
58 Mains of Arnage D 7
58 Mains of Auchindachy C 2
58 Mains of Auchmedden A 6
53 Mains of Balgavies B 10
53 Mains of Ballindarg B 9
59 Mains of Balnakettle K 4
58 Mains of Birness D 7
56 Mains of Bunachton F 2
58 Mains of Cairnborrow D 2
58 Mains of Cardno A 7
58 Mains of Crichie C 7
56 Mains of Dalvey F 7
59 Mains of Drum G 5
58 Mains of Drummuir C 2
56 Mains of Drynie E 2
58 Mains of Edingight B 3
58 Mains of Esslemont E 7
59 Mains of Glenfarquhar J 5
59 Mains of Haulkerton K 5
58 Mains of Inkhorn D 7
58 Mains of Keithfield D 6
58 Mains of Kirkhall F 6
58 Mains of Logie B 8
59 Mains of Melgund L 3
56 Mains of Newhall C 3
43 Mains of Terregles D 10
59 Mains of Thornton K 4
52 Mains of Throsk H 3
56 Mains of Tore D 2
58 Mains of Towie C 5
53 Mains of Usan B 12
40 Mainsforth B 3
43 Mainsriddle F 10
21 Mainstone D 8
15 Maisemore B 11
5 Malborough M 6
18 Malden Rushett H 2
19 Maldon C 8
35 Malham A 8
55 Mallaig K 1
55 Mallaigvaig K 1
48 Malleny Mills C 4
52 Malling G 1
28 Malltraeth C 3
20 Mallwyd A 4
15 Malmesbury F 12
4 Malmsmead A 7
30 Malpas, Chershire E 3
2 Malpas, Corn. E 5
14 Malpas, Gwent E 6
51 Malt Land F 8
40 Maltby, Cleveland D 5
32 Maltby, S. Yorks. A 3
33 Maltby le Marsh B 11
11 Maltman's Hill D 8
41 Malton H 8
22 Malvern Link G 1
22 Malvern Wells H 1
21 Mamble E 12
14 Mamhilad D 6
2 Manaccan G 5
21 Manafon B 7
5 Manaton H 6

33 Manby **B 11**
22 Mancetter **C 6**
35 Manchester **G 7**
29 Mancot **D 12**
24 Manea **F 6**
42 Maneight **A 6**
40 Manfield **D 2**
64 Mangaster **C 7**
63 Mangersta **D 1**
44 Mangertton **D 3**
15 Mangotsfield **G 10**
12 Manian Fawr **B 5**
63 Manish **H 2**
30 Manley **C 4**
14 Manmoel **D 5**
16 Manningford Bohune **H 2**
16 Manningford Bruce **H 2**
35 Manningham **D 10**
10 Mannings Heath **E 1**
8 Mannington **F 2**
27 Manningtree **M 4**
59 Mannofield **G 6**
12 Manorbier **G 4**
12 Manorbier Newton **G 4**
49 Manorhill **F 9**
12 Manorowen **C 3**
43 Mansefield **B 9**
13 Manselfield **H 9**
21 Mansell Gamage **H 9**
21 Mansell Lacy **H 9**
39 Mansergh **G 8**
47 Mansfield, Strathclyde **H 11**
32 Mansfield, Notts. **D 3**
32 Mansfield Woodhouse **D 3**
38 Mansriggs **G 5**
7 Manston, Dorset **E 11**
11 Manston, Kent **B 12**
8 Manswood **E 2**
37 Manton, Humber. **G 7**
23 Manton, Leics. **B 12**
24 Manthorpe, Lincs. **D 2**
32 Manthorpe, Lincs. **F 6**
16 Manton, Wilts. **G 3**
18 Manuden **A 5**
50 Maolachy **F 6**
7 Maperton **D 10**
17 Maple Cross **E 11**
32 Maplebeck **D 4**
17 Mapledurham **F 7**
9 Mapledurwell **A 8**
10 Maplehurst **F 1**
10 Maplescombe **B 4**
31 Mapleton **E 10**
32 Mapperley **F 2**
32 Mapperley Park **F 3**
7 Mapperton, Dorset **F 12**
7 Mapperton, Dorset **F 8**
22 Mappleborough Green **E 4**
37 Mappleton **C 10**
35 Mapplewell **F 12**
7 Mappowder **F 10**
57 Mar Lodge **K 7**
2 Marazion **G 2**
30 Marbury **F 4**
24 March, Cambs. **F 5**
48 March, Strathclyde **H 3**
16 Marcham **D 5**
30 Marchamley **G 4**
43 Marchbankwood **B 11**
47 Marchburn **H 11**
31 Marchington **G 9**
31 Marchington Woodlands **G 9**
30 Marchwiel **E 2**
8 Marchwood **E 5**
14 Marcross **G 3**
21 Marden, Heref. & Worc. **H 10**
10 Marden, Kent **D 6**
16 Marden, Wilts. **H 2**
10 Marden Beech **D 6**
10 Marden Thorn **D 6**
14 Mardy **C 6**
7 Mare Green **D 7**
17 Marefield, Bucks. **E 9**
23 Marefield, Leics. **A 11**
33 Mareham le Fen **D 10**
33 Mareham on the Hill **C 10**
32 Marehey **E 1**
10 Maresfield **F 3**
37 Marfleet **D 9**
30 Marford **E 2**
13 Margam **H 11**
7 Margaret Marsh **D 11**
18 Margaret Roding **C 6**
18 Margaretting **D 6**
11 Margate **A 12**
46 Margnaheglish **F 5**
24 Marham **D 8**
4 Marhamchurch **F 1**
24 Marholm **E 2**
28 Marianglas **B 4**
4 Mariansleigh **D 6**
59 Marionburgh **G 5**
62 Marishader **B 4**
63 Mariveg **E 5**
43 Marjoriebanks **C 11**
43 Mark, Dumf. & Gall. **F 7**
42 Mark, Strathclyde **D 2**
7 Mark, Somerset **A 7**
7 Mark Causeway **B 7**
10 Mark Cross **E 5**
10 Markbeech **D 4**
33 Markby **B 12**
23 Market Bosworth **B 7**
23 Market Deeping **E 2**
30 Market Drayton **G 5**
23 Market Harborough **C 10**
8 Market Lavington **A 2**
23 Market Overton **A 12**
33 Market Rasen **A 8**
33 Market Stainton **B 9**
26 Market Street **C 6**
36 Market Weighton **C 6**
27 Market Weston **G 3**
23 Markfield **A 8**
14 Markham **D 5**
32 Markham Moor **C 4**
53 Markinch **G 8**
35 Markington **A 10**
49 Markle **B 8**
19 Marks Tey **B 9**
15 Marksbury **H 10**
17 Markyate **C 11**
43 Marlage **D 1**
16 Marlborough **G 3**
21 Marlbrook, Heref. & Worc. **G 10**
22 Marlbrook, Heref. & Worc. **E 3**
22 Marlcliff **G 4**
5 Marldon **J 7**
27 Marlesford **J 6**
30 Marley Green **F 4**
45 Marley Hill **G 10**
8 Marley Mount **F 4**
49 Marleyknowe **F 12**
26 Marlingford **E 4**
12 Marloes **F 1**
17 Marlow, Bucks. **E 9**
21 Marlow, Heref. & Worc. **E 9**
17 Marlow Bottom **E 9**
10 Marlpit Hill **C 3**
7 Marnhull **D 11**
58 Marnoch **C 3**
31 Marple **A 8**
36 Marr **G 3**
61 Marrel **E 9**
40 Marrick **E 1**
12 Marros **F 5**
45 Marsden, Tyne & Wear **G 12**
35 Marsden, W. Yorks. **F 9**
39 Marsett **F 11**
6 Marsh, Devon **E 6**
6 Marsh, Somerset **C 4**
16 Marsh Baldon **D 6**
16 Marsh Benham **G 5**
37 Marsh Chapel **G 11**
17 Marsh Gibbon **B 7**
6 Marsh Green, Devon **G 4**
10 Marsh Green, Kent **D 3**
21 Marsh Green, Shropshire **A 11**
6 Marsh Street **B 3**
18 Marshall's Heath **B 2**
26 Marsham **C 5**
34 Marshaw **B 5**
11 Marshborough **B 11**
21 Marshbrook **C 10**
15 Marshfield, Avon **G 11**
14 Marshfield, Gwent **F 6**
2 Marshgate **B 2**
32 Marshland **B 1**
34 Marshside **E 2**
7 Marshwood **F 7**
40 Marske **E 1**
40 Marske-by-the-Sea **C 6**
30 Marston, Ches. **C 5**
21 Marston, Heref. & Worc. **G 9**
32 Marston, Lincs. **F 6**
16 Marston, Oxon **C 6**
22 Marston, Staffs. **A 2**
31 Marston, Staffs. **G 8**
22 Marston, War. **C 5**
16 Marston, Wilts. **H 1**
22 Marston Green **D 5**
7 Marston Magna **D 9**
16 Marston Meysey **D 2**
31 Marston Montgomery **F 10**
25 Marston Moretaine **L 1**
31 Marston on Dove **G 11**
23 Marston St. Lawrence **H 8**
21 Marston Stannett **G 11**
23 Marston Trussell **D 10**
15 Marstow **B 9**
17 Marsworth **C 10**
16 Marten **H 4**
30 Marthall **C 6**
26 Martham **D 8**
8 Martin, Hants. **D 2**
11 Martin, Kent **C 12**
33 Martin, Lincs. **D 8**
8 Martin Drove End **D 2**
22 Martin Hussingtree **F 2**
4 Martinhoe **A 5**
4 Martinhoe Cross **A 6**
30 Martinscroft **A 5**
44 Martinshouse **B 3**
7 Martinstown **G 10**
27 Martlesham **K 6**
12 Martletwy **F 4**
22 Martley **F 1**
7 Martock **D 8**
31 Marton, Ches. **C 7**
40 Marton, Cleveland **D 5**
37 Marton, Humber. **C 9**
32 Marton, Lincs. **B 5**
41 Marton, N. Yorks. **G 7**
36 Marton, N. Yorks. **A 2**
21 Marton, Salop **B 8**
23 Marton, War. **E 7**
40 Marton le Moor **H 4**
40 Marton-in-the-Forest **H 6**
8 Martyr Worthy **C 6**
17 Martyr's Green **H 11**
43 Marwhirn **B 8**
64 Marwick **C 1**
4 Marwood **B 4**
4 Marwood Middle **B 4**
5 Mary Tavy **H 4**
54 Marybank **D 8**
56 Maryburgh **D 1**
59 Maryculter **G 6**
49 Marygold **C 10**
58 Maryhill, Grampian **C 6**
47 Maryhill, Strathclyde **B 10**
59 Marykirk **L 4**
56 Marypark **F 7**
38 Maryport, Cumb. **B 3**
42 Maryport, Dumf. & Gall. **H 2**
53 Maryton, Tayside **B 8**
53 Maryton, Tayside **B 11**
59 Marywell, Grampian **H 3**
59 Marywell, Grampian **G 7**
53 Marywell, Tayside **C 11**
40 Masham **G 2**
45 Mason **F 10**
32 Mastin Moor **C 2**
59 Mastrick **G 6**
18 Matching **C 5**
18 Matching Green **C 5**
18 Matching Tye **C 5**
45 Matfen **F 8**
10 Matfield **D 5**
15 Mathern **E 8**
22 Mathon **H 1**
12 Mathry **D 2**
26 Matlask **B 5**
31 Matlock **D 11**
31 Matlock Bath **D 11**
15 Matson **C 11**
38 Matterdale End **C 6**
32 Mattersey **A 4**
32 Mattersey Thorpe **A 4**
17 Mattingley **H 8**
26 Mattishall **D 4**
26 Mattishall Burgh **D 4**
53 Mattocks **C 9**
47 Mauchline **G 10**
58 Maud **C 7**
13 Maudsland **D 7**
16 Maugersbury **B 3**
38 Maughold **G 3**
54 Mauld **F 8**
25 Maulden **L 2**
39 Maulds Meaburn **D 8**
40 Maunby **F 4**
21 Maund Bryan **G 11**
6 Maundown **C 4**
26 Mautby **D 8**
22 Mavesyn Ridware **A 4**
33 Mavis Enderby **D 10**
56 Maviston **D 5**
22 Maw Green **B 4**
43 Mawbray **G 11**
52 Mawcarse **G 6**
34 Mawdesley **F 4**
14 Mawdlam **F 1**
2 Mawgan **G 4**
2 Mawla **E 4**
2 Mawnan **G 5**
2 Mawnan Smith **G 5**
24 Maxey **E 2**
22 Maxstroke **C 6**
49 Maxton, Borders **F 8**
11 Maxton, Kent **D 11**
49 Maxwellheugh **F 10**
42 Maxwellston **B 4**
43 Maxwellstown **D 10**
5 Maxworthy **G 1**
31 May Bank **E 7**
13 Mayals **H 9**
47 Maybole **H 8**
17 Maybury **H 11**
10 Mayfield, E. Sussex **E 5**
31 Mayfield, Staffs. **F 10**
17 Mayford **H 10**
19 Mayland **D 9**
10 Maynard's Green **F 5**
15 Maypole, Gwent **C 8**
2 Maypole, Is. of Scilly **D 2**
26 Maypole Green **F 7**
64 Maywick **E 7**
4 Mead **D 1**
15 Meadgate **H 10**
47 Meadowfoot **E 11**
21 Meadowtown **B 8**
39 Meal Bank **F 8**
37 Meals **G 11**
38 Mealsgate **A 4**
35 Mearbeck **A 7**
7 Meare **B 8**
6 Meare Green **D 6**
47 Mearns **D 10**
23 Mears Ashby **E 11**
23 Measham **A 7**
10 Meath Green **D 2**
39 Meathop **G 7**
63 Meavag **G 3**
5 Meavy **J 4**
23 Medbourne **C 11**
45 Medburn **F 9**
4 Meddon **D 2**
17 Medmenham **F 9**
45 Medomsley **H 9**
9 Medstead **B 8**
22 Meer End **E 6**
31 Meerbrook **D 8**
33 Meers Bridge **B 12**
25 Meesden **M 5**
4 Meeth **E 4**
44 Megdale **C 1**
48 Meggethead **G 4**
12 Meidrim **E 6**
21 Meifod **A 7**
53 Meigle **C 7**
43 Meikle Barncleugh **D 10**
43 Meikle Beoch **D 9**
47 Meikle Carco **H 12**
47 Meikle Earnock **D 12**
59 Meikle Fiddes **J 5**
52 Meikle Forter **A 6**
61 Meikle Gluich **H 7**
46 Meikle Grenach **C 6**
47 Meikle Hareshaw **E 11**
47 Meikle Ittington **E 7**
56 Meikle Kildrummie **D 4**
49 Meikle Pinkerton **B 9**
59 Meikle Strath **K 4**
58 Meikle Tarty **E 7**
58 Meikle Wartle **D 5**
43 Meikleholm **C 11**
47 Meiklelaught **E 7**
52 Meikleour **C 6**
58 Meikleton **C 3**
28 Meillteyrn **G 2**
43 Meinbank **D 12**
13 Meinciau **F 8**
31 Meirheath **F 8**
63 Melbost **D 6**
63 Melbost Borve **A 5**
25 Melbourn **L 5**
31 Melbourne, Derby **H 12**
36 Melbourne, Humberside **C 5**
48 Melbourne, Strathclyde **E 4**
7 Melbury Abbas **D 12**
7 Melbury Bubb **F 9**
7 Melbury Osmond **E 9**
7 Melbury Sampford **F 9**
64 Melby **D 6**
25 Melchbourne **J 1**
7 Melcombe Regis **H 10**
5 Meldon, Devon **G 4**
45 Meldon, N'thumb. **E 9**
25 Meldreth **L 5**
58 Meldrum House **E 6**
50 Melfort **F 5**
55 Melgarve **K 8**
29 Meliden **B 10**
14 Melin Court **D 2**
20 Melin-byrhedin **C 4**
29 Melin-y-coed **D 7**
20 Melin-y-grug **B 6**
29 Melin-y-wig **E 9**
39 Melkinthorpe **C 8**
44 Melkridge **G 5**
15 Melksham **H 12**
54 Mellanguan **A 2**
46 Melldalloch **B 4**
39 Melling, Lancs. **H 8**
34 Melling, Merseyside **G 3**
34 Melling Mount **G 3**
27 Mellis **H 4**
60 Mellon Charles **G 1**
60 Mellon Udrigle **G 1**
31 Mellor, Manchester **A 8**
34 Mellor, Lancs. **D 5**
34 Mellor Brook **D 5**
7 Mells **A 10**
39 Melmerby, Cumb. **B 8**
40 Melmerby, N. Yorks. **G 4**
40 Melmerby, N. Yorks. **G 1**
7 Melplash **F 8**
49 Melrose **F 8**
64 Melsetter **E 1**
40 Melsonby **D 2**
35 Meltham **F 9**
35 Meltham Mills **F 10**
37 Melton, Humber. **D 7**
27 Melton, Suffolk **K 6**
26 Melton Constable **B 3**
32 Melton Mowbray **H 5**
37 Melton Ross **F 8**
36 Meltonby **B 6**
54 Melvaig **A 1**
21 Melverley **A 9**
61 Melvich **B 8**
6 Membury **F 6**
58 Memsie **A 7**
59 Memus **L 2**
3 Menabilly **E 8**
28 Menai Bridge **C 5**
27 Mendham **G 6**
27 Mendlesham **J 4**
27 Mendlesham Green **J 4**
3 Menheniot **C 10**
43 Mennock **A 9**
35 Menston **C 10**
52 Menstrie **G 3**
36 Menthorpe **D 5**
17 Mentmore **B 10**
55 Meoble **L 2**
21 Meole Brace **A 10**
9 Meonstroke **D 7**
10 Meopham **B 5**
10 MeophamGreen **B 5**
10 Meopham Station **A 5**
25 Mepal **G 5**
25 Meppershall **L 2**
21 Merbach **H 8**
30 Mere, Cheshire **B 6**
7 Mere, Wilts. **C 11**
34 Mere Brow **E 3**
35 Mere Clough **D 7**
22 Mere End **E 6**
11 Meresborough **B 7**
34 Mereside **D 2**
30 Meretown **H 6**
10 Mereworth **C 5**
59 Mergie **H 5**
22 Meriden **D 6**
62 Merkadale **E 3**
43 Merkland **D 8**
60 Merkland Lodge **D 5**
12 Merlin's Bridge **F 3**
30 Merrington **H 3**
12 Merrion **G 3**
7 Merriot **E 8**
5 Merrivale **H 4**
9 Merrow **A 11**
44 Merrylaw **C 2**
3 Merrymeet **C 10**
34 Merseyside, Co. **H 3**
11 Mersham **D 9**
10 Merstham **C 2**
9 Merston **F 10**
8 Merstone **H 6**
2 Merther **E 6**
13 Merthyr **E 7**
14 Merthyr Cynog **A 3**
14 Merthyr Mawr **F 2**
14 Merthyr Tydfil **D 4**
14 Merthyr Vale **D 4**
4 Merton, Devon **E 4**
18 Merton, London **G 3**
26 Merton, Norfolk **F 2**
17 Merton, Oxon **B 7**
44 Mervinslaw **B 5**
4 Meshaw **D 6**
19 Messing **B 9**
37 Messingham **G 7**
27 Metfield **G 6**
33 Metheringham **D 8**
53 Methil **G 8**
28 Methlem **G 1**
35 Methley **D 12**
58 Methlick **D 6**
52 Methven **E 5**
24 Methwold **F 8**
24 Methwold Hythe **F 8**
26 Mettingham **F 6**
26 Metton **B 5**
3 Mevagissey **E 7**
36 Mexborough **G 3**
61 Mey **A 12**
16 Meysey Hampton **D 2**
63 Miavaig **C 2**
58 Michael Muir **D 6**
15 Michaelchurch **B 8**
14 Michaelchurch Escley **A 6**
21 Michaelchurch-on-Arrow **G 8**
14 Michaelston-le-Pit **G 5**
14 Michaelston-super-Ely **G 4**
14 Michaelstone-y-Vedw **F 6**
3 Michaelstow **B 8**
8 Michelmersh **C 5**
27 Mickfield **J 4**
30 Mickle Trafford **C 3**
36 Micklebring **H 3**
41 Mickleby **D 8**
36 Micklefield **D 2**
10 Mickleham **C 1**
31 Mickleover **G 11**
44 Micklethwaite **H 1**
39 Mickleton, Dur. **C 12**
22 Mickleton, Glos. **H 5**
35 Mickletown **D 12**
40 Mickley **G 3**
45 Mickley Square **G 9**
58 Mid Ardlaw **A 7**
59 Mid Beltie **G 4**
59 Mid Cairncross **J 2**
48 Mid Calder **C 3**
61 Mid Clyth **D 11**
58 Mid Cowbog **B 6**
54 Mid Crochail **F 7**
58 Mid Culsh **C 6**
47 Mid Drumloch **D 11**
14 Mid Glamorgan, Co. **E 4**
48 Mid Hartwood **C 3**
43 Mid Laggan **D 8**
9 Mid Lavant **E 10**
54 Mid Mains **F 8**
46 Mid Sannox **E 5**
54 Mid Strom **F 2**
46 Mid Thundergay **E 4**
64 Mid Yell **B 7**
64 Midbea **A 2**
17 Middle Assendon **F 8**
16 Middle Aston **A 6**
16 Middle Barton **B 5**
15 Middle Bridge **G 8**
7 Middle Chinnock **E 8**
59 Middle Drums **L 3**
58 Middle Essie **B 8**
32 Middle Handley **B 1**
17 Middle Claydon **B 8**
22 Middle Littleton **G 4**
12 Middle Mill **D 2**
49 Middle Ord **D 12**
33 Middle Rasen **A 8**
52 Middle Rigg **F 5**
15 Middle Street **D 11**
23 Middle Tysoe **H 7**
8 Middle Wallop **B 4**
8 Middle Winterslow **C 4**
8 Middle Woodford **C 3**
43 Middlebie **D 12**
57 Middlebridge **M 4**
49 Middlefield **D 10**
43 Middlegill **A 11**
40 Middleham **F 2**
21 Middlehope **D 10**
7 Middlemarsh **E 10**
58 Middlemuir **C 6**
58 Middlemuir House **E 7**
40 Middlesbrough **C 5**
39 Middleshaw, Cumb. **F 8**
43 Middleshaw, Dumf. & Gall. **D 12**
44 Middlesknowes **B 6**
40 Middlesmoor **H 1**
40 Middlestone **B 3**
40 Middlestone Moor **B 3**
35 Middlestown **E 11**
49 Middlethird **E 9**
15 Middleton, Avon **G 8**

31 Middleton, Derby . E 11
31 Middleton, Derby . D 10
27 Middleton, Essex . . . L 2
58 Middleton, Grampian . . . . E 6
35 Middleton, Manchester . . . . F 7
8 Middleton, Hants. . . B 6
21 Middleton, Heref. & Worc. . . E 11
34 Middleton, Lancs. . . A 3
48 Middleton, Lothian . D 6
24 Middleton, Norf. . . . D 8
41 Middleton, N. Yorks. . . . . G 8
35 Middleton, N. Yorks. . . . . B 10
25 Middleton, Northants. . . . . . . C 11
45 Middleton, Northumberland . . E 9
45 Middleton, Northumb. . . . . . . B 12
21 Middleton, Salop . . E 11
30 Middleton, Salop . . . G 2
47 Middleton, Strathclyde . . . . E 8
27 Middleton, Suffolk . . H 7
52 Middleton, Tayside . . F 6
52 Middleton, Tayside . . B 6
22 Middleton, War . . . B 5
13 Middleton, W. Glam. H 7
35 Middleton, W. Yorks. . . . . D 11
23 Middleton Cheney . . H 8
31 Middleton Green . . . G 8
49 Middleton Hall . . . . G 12
39 Middleton in Teesdale . . . . C 11
58 Middleton of Rora . . C 8
9 Middleton-on-Sea . F 11
21 Middleton on the Hill . . . . F 11
37 Middleton-on-the Wolds . . . . B 7
40 Middleton One Row . . . . D 4
21 Middleton Priors . . C 11
40 Middleton Quernhow . . . . G 3
40 Middleton St. George D 4
21 Middleton Scriven . D 12
16 Middleton Stoney . . . B 6
40 Middleton Tyas . . . . . E 3
21 Middletown . . . . A 8
30 Middlewich . . . . D 6
27 Middlewood Green . . J 4
47 Middleyard . . . . F 10
7 Middlezoy . . . . C 7
40 Middridge . . . . C 3
60 Midfield . . . . A 6
15 Midford . . . . H 10
34 Midge Hall . . . . E 4
44 Midgeholme . . . . G 5
35 Midgeley . . . . F 11
16 Midgham . . . . G 6
35 Midgley . . . . D 9
35 Midhopestones . . . . G 11
9 Midhurst . . . . D 10
49 Midlem . . . . G 8
48 Midlock . . . . G 2
7 Midssomer Norton A 10
60 Midtown . . . . B 6
54 Midtown Brae . . . . . . A 2
59 Midtown of Barras . . J 6
58 Midtown of Buchromb . . . . C 1
33 Midville . . . . E 11
43 Miefield . . . . F 7
61 Migdale . . . . G 7
59 Migvie . . . . G 2
7 Milborne Port . . . . . D 10
7 Milborne St. Andrew F 11
7 Milborne Wick . . . . D 10
45 Milbourne . . . . E 9
50 Milbuie . . . . H 1
39 Milburn . . . . B 9
15 Milbury Heath . . . . E 10
40 Milby . . . . H 4
16 Milcombe . . . . A 5
27 Milden . . . . K 3
25 Mildenhall, Suff. . . . H 8
16 Mildenhall, Wilts. . . G 3
16 Mile Elm . . . . G 1
19 Mile End, Essex . . . . A 9
26 Mile End, Suffolk . . . F 6
21 Milebrook . . . . E 8
26 Mileham . . . . D 2
15 Miles End . . . . C 9
30 Miles Green . . . . E 6
21 Miles Hope . . . . F 11
52 Milesmark . . . . H 5
49 Milfield . . . . F 12
31 Milford, Derby . . . . F 12
4 Milford, Devon . . . . . D 1
31 Milford, Staffs. . . . . . H 8
9 Milford, Surrey . . . . B 11
8 Milford, Wilts. . . . . . C 3
12 Milford Haven . . . . . . F 4
8 Milford on Sea . . . . . G 4
47 Milhall . . . . D 10
15 Milkwall . . . . C 9
8 Milkwell . . . . D 1
35 Mill Bank . . . . E 9
31 Mill Brow . . . . A 8
27 Mill Common . . . . . . G 7
17 Mill End, Bucks. . . . . F 9
25 Mill End, Cambs. . . . G 4
17 Mill End, Herts. . . . E 11
25 Mill End, Herts. . . . . M 4
18 Mill Green, Essex . . . D 6
27 Mill Green, Suffolk . L 3
18 Mill Hill . . . . E 2
39 Mill Houses . . . . H 8
9 Mill Lane . . . . A 9
58 Mill of Ardo, Grampian . . . . E 7
58 Mill of Ardo, Grampian . . . . D 6
58 Mill of Carden . . . . . . E 4
58 Mill of Culfork . . . . . . F 2
59 Mill of Gellan . . . . . . G 3
59 Mill of Mondynes . . . J 5
59 Mill of Monquich . . . H 6
58 Mill of Muiresk . . . . . C 4
58 Mill of Pot . . . . C 5
59 Mill of Uras . . . . J 6
26 Mill Street . . . . D 3
38 Millbeck . . . . C 5
64 Millbounds . . . . B 3
58 Millbreck . . . . C 7
58 Millbrex . . . . C 6
9 Millbridge . . . . B 10
25 Millbrook, Beds. . . . . . L 1
3 Millbrook, Corn. . . D 11
4 Millbrook, Devon . . . C 6
8 Millbrook, Hants. . . . . E 5
47 Millburn . . . . F 9
5 Millcombe . . . . L 7
11 Millcorner . . . . F 7
31 Milldale . . . . E 10
59 Millden Lodge . . . . . . J 3
53 Milldens . . . . B 10
48 Millerhill . . . . B 6
31 Miller's Dale . . . . . . C 10
31 Millers Green . . . . . E 11
59 Millfield . . . . H 2
30 Millgreen . . . . G 5
21 Millhalf . . . . H 8
6 Millhayes . . . . E 5
49 Millheugh, Borders . G 9
47 Millheugh, Strathclyde D 12
39 Millholme . . . . F 8
38 Millhouse, Cumb. . . . B 6
35 Millhouse, S. Yorks. G 11
46 Millhouse, Strathclyde B 4
43 Millhousebridge . . . C 11
32 Millhouses . . . . B 1
43 Milliganton . . . . C 10
47 Millikenpark . . . . C 9
36 Millington . . . . B 6
49 Millknowe . . . . C 9
31 Millmeece . . . . G 7
38 Millom . . . . G 4
3 Millpool . . . . C 8
49 Millport . . . . D 6
43 Millquarter . . . . C 7
31 Millthorpe . . . . C 11
39 Millthrop . . . . F 9
59 Milltimber . . . . G 6
53 Millton . . . . C 8
57 Millton of Auchriachan . . . . . H 7
58 Milltown, Grampian . F 2
58 Milltown, Grampian . F 7
59 Milltown, Grampian G 4
58 Milltown, Grampian C 3
32 Milltown, Derby . . . . D 1
4 Milltown, Devon . . . . B 4
54 Milltown, Highland . D 7
59 Milltown, Tayside . . K 5
52 Milltown of Aberdalgie . . . . E 5
58 Milltown of Auchindown . . . . . D 1
59 Milltown of Campfield . . . . . . G 4
58 Milltown of Craigston . . . . B 5
56 Milltown of Edinvillie . . . . F 8
58 Milltown of Minnes . E 7
58 Milltown of Towie . . . F 2
47 Millwell . . . . D 11
53 Milnacraig . . . . B 7
52 Milnathort . . . . G 6
43 Milne . . . . B 12
47 Milngavie . . . . B 10
43 Milnmark . . . . C 7
35 Milnrow . . . . F 8
39 Milnthorpe . . . . G 7
21 Milson . . . . E 11
11 Milstead . . . . B 7
8 Milston . . . . B 3
14 Milton, Avon . . . . H 6
25 Milton, Cambs. . . . . . J 6
51 Milton, Central . . . . G 12
44 Milton, Cumb. . . . . . G 4
31 Milton, Derby . . . . . G 11
43 Milton, Dumf. & Gall. . . . . C 9
43 Milton, Dumf. & Gall. . . . . D 9
42 Milton, Dumf. & Gall. . . . . F 3
12 Milton, Dyfed . . . . . . G 4
58 Milton, Grampian . . . E 1
58 Milton, Grampian . . . A 3
9 Milton, Hants. . . . . . . F 8
61 Milton, Highland . . C 12
57 Milton, Highland . . . H 5
57 Milton, Highland . . . G 1
56 Milton, Highland . . . D 2
56 Milton, Highland . . . E 1
56 Milton, Highland . . . B 3
54 Milton, Highland . . . E 1
16 Milton, Oxon . . . . E 6
16 Milton, Oxon . . . . . . A 5
7 Milton, Som. . . . . D 8
42 Milton, Strathclyde . B 4
42 Milton, Strathclyde . A 3
47 Milton, Strathclyde . B 9
59 Milton, Tayside . . . . . J 2
52 Milton, Tayside . . . . A 6
7 Milton Abbas . . . . . . F 11
5 Milton Abbot . . . . H 3
48 Milton Bridge . . . . . . C 5
25 Milton Bryna . . . . M 1
7 Milton Clevedon . . . C 10
58 Milton Coldwells . . . D 7
4 Milton Damerel . . . . E 3
16 Milton End . . . . D 2
25 Milton Ernest . . . . . . K 1
30 Milton Green . . . . . . D 3
16 Milton Hill . . . . E 6
23 Milton Keynes . . . . H 12
16 Milton Lilbourne . . . H 3
23 Milton Malsor . . . . . G 10
58 Milton of Ardlethen D 6
59 Milton of Auchinhove . . . . . . G 3
53 Milton of Balgonie . . G 8
56 Milton of Braicklaich . . . . D 3
47 Milton of Campsie . B 11
58 Milton of Cushnie . . . F 3
59 Milton of Dillavaird . J 5
56 Milton of Farr . . . . . . F 2
58 Milton of Fishrie . . . B 5
58 Milton of Lesmore . . E 2
59 Milton of Logie . . . . G 2
59 Milton of Murtle . . . . G 6
58 Milton of Noth . . . . . E 2
46 Milton of Smerby . . . G 2
59 Milton of Tullich . . . H 1
7 Milton on Stour . . . C 11
11 Milton Regis . . . . B 7
16 Milton under Wychwood . . . . B 4
5 Miltoncombe . . . . J 4
56 Miltonduff . . . . D 7
42 Miltonise . . . . D 3
6 Milverton . . . . D 4
31 Milwich . . . . G 8
51 Minard . . . . H 7
15 Minchinhampton . . D 12
49 Mindrum . . . . F 11
49 Mindrummill . . . . . . F 11
6 Minehead . . . . B 3
29 Minera . . . . E 12
16 Minety . . . . E 1
28 Minffordd . . . . F 5
50 Mingarrypark . . . . . . A 4
33 Miningsby . . . . D 10
3 Minions . . . . C 9
47 Minishant . . . . H 8
57 Minmore . . . . G 7
42 Minnigaff . . . . E 5
58 Minnonie . . . . B 5
38 Minorca . . . . G 2
44 Minsca . . . . E 1
36 Minskip . . . . A 2
8 Minstead . . . . E 4
11 Minster, Kent . . . . . B 11
11 Minster, Kent . . . . . . A 8
16 Minster Lovell . . . . . . C 4
45 Minsteracres . . . . . . G 8
21 Minsterley . . . . B 9
15 Minsterworth . . . . . C 11
7 Minterne Magna . . . F 10
33 Minting . . . . C 9
58 Mintlaw . . . . C 7
49 Minto . . . . G 8
43 Minto Cott . . . . F 7
21 Minton . . . . C 9
12 Minwear . . . . F 4
22 Minworth . . . . C 5
64 Mirbister . . . . C 1
38 Mirehouse . . . . D 2
61 Mireland . . . . B 12
35 Mirfield . . . . E 10
15 Miserden . . . . C 12
14 Miskin, Mid Glam. . . F 4
14 Miskin, Mid Glam. . . D 4
36 Misson . . . . H 5
36 Misterton, Notts. . . . H 5
7 Misterton, Som. . . . . E 8
23 Misterton, War. . . . . D 9
27 Mistley . . . . M 4
18 Mitcham . . . . G 3
15 Mitcheldean . . . . B 9
8 Mitcheldever . . . . B 6
15 Mitchel Troy . . . . C 8
2 Mitchell . . . . D 6
15 Mitcheltroy Com. . . . C 8
45 Mitford . . . . D 10
2 Mithian . . . . E 4
22 Mitton . . . . A 2
17 Mixbury . . . . A 7
31 Mixon . . . . D 9
53 Moanzie . . . . E 8
44 Moat Common . . . . . F 3
30 Mobberley . . . . B 6
21 Moccas . . . . H 9
29 Mochdre, Clwyd . . . . B 7
20 Mochdre, Powys . . . . D 6
42 Mochrum . . . . G 4
10 Mockbeggar, Kent . . C 6
10 Mockbeggar, Kent . . A 6
38 Mockerkin . . . . C 3
5 Modbury . . . . K 5
31 Moddershall . . . . G 8
61 Modsarie . . . . B 7
29 Moelfre, Clwyd . . . G 11
28 Moelfre, Gwynedd . . B 4
43 Moffat . . . . A 11
25 Moggerhanger . . . . . . K 2
60 Moin House . . . . B 6
22 Moira . . . . A 6
11 Molash . . . . C 9
62 Mol-chlach . . . . G 4
29 Mold . . . . D 11
35 Moldgreen . . . . F 10
18 Molehill Green . . . . . A 5
37 Molescroft . . . . C 8
45 Molesden . . . . E 9
25 Molesworth . . . . H 2
4 Molland . . . . C 7
4 Molland Cross . . . . . . C 6
30 Mollington, Ches. . . . C 2
23 Mollington, Oxon . . G 8
47 Mollinsburn . . . . B 12
19 Molting Green . . . . . . B 9
13 Monachty . . . . A 8
51 Monachylemore . . . F 11
46 Monamore Bridge . . . F 5
21 Monaughty . . . . F 8
59 Monboddo House . . . J 5
51 Monevechadan . . . . . G 9
27 Moneyden . . . . J 5
52 Moneydie . . . . D 5
43 Moniaive . . . . C 8
53 Monifieth . . . . D 9
53 Monikie . . . . C 9
53 Monimail . . . . F 8
12 Monington . . . . C 5
35 Monk Bretton . . . . . F 12
36 Monk Fryston . . . . . . D 3
17 Monk Sherborne . . . . . H 7
27 Monk Soham . . . . J 5
45 Monk-Wearmouth . G 12
21 Monkhide . . . . H 11
21 Monkhopton . . . . . . C 11
21 Monkland . . . . G 10
4 Monkleigh . . . . D 3
14 Monknash . . . . G 3
4 Monkokehampton . . E 5
45 Monkridge . . . . D 7
27 Monks Eleigh . . . . . . K 3
10 Monk's Gate . . . . E 1
31 Monks' Heath . . . . . . C 7
23 Monks Kirby . . . . D 8
17 Monks Risborough . D 9
58 Monkshill . . . . D 5
6 Monksilver . . . . C 4
22 Monkspath Street . . . D 5
15 Monkswood . . . . D 7
6 Monkton, Devon . . . . F 5
12 Monkton, Dyfed . . . . G 3
11 Monkton, Kent . . . . B 11
6 Monkton, Som. . . . . . C 6
47 Monkton, Strathclyde . . . . G 8
15 Monkton Coombe . H 11
7 Monkton Deverill . B 11
15 Monkton Farleigh . H 11
6 Monkton Heathfield . . . . D 6
8 Monkton Up Wimborne . . . . E 2
7 Monkton Wyld . . . . . F 7
47 Monktonhill . . . . F 8
9 Monkwood . . . . C 8
15 Monmouth . . . . C 8
15 Monmouth Cap . . . . . B 7
21 Monnington on Wye . . . . H 9
53 Monorgan . . . . D 8
42 Monreith . . . . G 4
42 Monreith Mains . . . . G 4
7 Montacute . . . . E 8
58 Montcoffer House . . B 4
21 Mountford . . . . A 9
21 Montford Bridge . . . A 9
58 Montgarrie . . . . F 3
21 Montgomery . . . . C 8
47 Montgreenan . . . . E 8
53 Montrave . . . . F 8
59 Montrose . . . . L 5
8 Monxton . . . . B 5
31 Monyash . . . . D 10
58 Monymusk . . . . F 4
52 Monzie, Tayside . . . . E 4
57 Monzie, Tayside . . . . M 5
47 Moodiesburn . . . . . . B 11
35 Moat Allerton . . . . C 11
8 Moor Crichel . . . . E 2
36 Moor Ends . . . . F 5
36 Moor Monkton . . . . . B 3
56 Moor of Granary . . . D 6
38 Moor Row . . . . D 3
11 Moor Street . . . . B 7
33 Moorby . . . . D 10
8 Moordown . . . . G 3
30 Moore . . . . B 4
15 Moorend . . . . D 10
8 Moorgreen . . . . E 6
31 Moorhall . . . . C 11
21 Moorhampton . . . . . . H 9
44 Moorhouse, Cumb. . G 2
32 Moorhouse, Notts. . . D 5
7 Moorlinch . . . . C 7
41 Moorsholm . . . . D 7
5 Moorshop . . . . H 4
35 Moorside, Manchester . . . . F 8
33 Moorside, Lincs. . . . . D 9
8 Moortown, Hants. . . . F 3
8 Moortown, I. o. W. . H 6
37 Moortown, Lincs. . . . G 8
55 Morar . . . . K 1
24 Morborne . . . . F 2
4 Morchard Bishop . . . E 6
23 Morcott . . . . B 12
30 Morda . . . . G 2
7 Morden, Dorest . . . G 12
18 Morden, London . . . G 2
15 Mordiford . . . . A 9
49 Mordington Mains . . . . D 12
40 Mordon . . . . C 3
21 More . . . . C 9
6 Morebath . . . . D 3
49 Morebattle . . . . G 10
34 Morecambe . . . . A 3
7 Morecombelake . . . . G 7
60 Morefield . . . . G 3
39 Moreland . . . . C 8
5 Moreleigh . . . . K 6
52 Morenish . . . . D 1
38 Moresby . . . . C 2
8 Morestead . . . . D 6
7 Moreton, Dorest . . G 11
18 Moreton, Essex . . . . . C 5
30 Moreton, Merseyside A 1
17 Moreton, Oxon . . . . . D 8
16 Moreton-in-Marsh . . A 3
21 Moreton Jeffries . . G 11
22 Moreton Morrell . . . . F 6
21 Moreton on Lugg . . H 10
23 Moreton Pinkney . . . G 9
30 Moreton Say . . . . . . G 5
15 Moreton Valence . . C 11
5 Moretonhampstead . G 6
13 Morfa . . . . F 9
28 Morfa Bychan . . . . . . F 5
14 Morfa Glas . . . . D 2
28 Morfa-Nefyn . . . . F 2
8 Morgan's Vale . . . . . D 4
32 Morley, Derby . . . . . . F 1
40 Morley, Dur. . . . . B 2
35 Morley, W. Yorks. . D 11
31 Morley Green . . . . . . B 7
26 Morley St. Botolph . . E 4
26 Morning Thorpe . . . . F 5
48 Morningside, Lothian . . . . B 5
48 Morningside, Strathclyde . . . . D 1
45 Morpeth . . . . D 10
31 Morrey . . . . H 10
43 Morrington . . . . C 9
25 Morris Green . . . . . . M 8
42 Morriston, Strathclyde . . . . A 3
13 Morriston, W. Glam. . . . . G 10
26 Morston . . . . A 3
4 Mortehoe . . . . B 3
32 Morthen . . . . A 2
17 Mortimer Com. . . . . . H 7
17 Mortimer West End . H 7
21 Mortimer's Cross . . . F 9
18 Mortlake . . . . F 2
15 Morton, Avon . . . . . . E 9
44 Morton, Cumb. . . . . . . H 2
32 Morton, Derby . . . . . D 1
24 Morton, Lincs. . . . . . C 2
32 Morton, Lincs. . . . . . A 5
26 Morton, Norf. . . . . . . D 4
32 Morton, Notts. . . . . . E 4
30 Morton, Salop . . . . . . H 2
22 Morton Bagot . . . . F 4
40 Morton-on-Swale . . . F 3
40 Morton Tinmouth . . . C 2
2 Morvah . . . . F 1
3 Morval . . . . D 9
55 Morvich . . . . G 3
61 Morvich Lodge . . . . . F 8
21 Morville . . . . C 12
4 Morwenstow . . . . D 1
32 Mosborough . . . . B 2
44 Moscow, Cumb. . . . . . F 4
47 Moscow, Strathclyde E 9
38 Mosedale . . . . B 6
35 Moselden Height . . . . F 9
22 Moseley, Heref. & Worc. . . . . F 2
22 Moseley, W. Midlands D 4
29 Moss, Clywd . . . . . . E 12
50 Moss, Highland . . . . A 4
36 Moss, S. Yorks. . . . . . F 4
34 Moss Bank . . . . G 4
17 Moss End . . . . G 9
56 Moss of Barmuckity . . . . . . D 8
58 Mossat . . . . F 2
64 Mossbank . . . . C 7
44 Mossburnford . . . . . . A 5
43 Mossdale . . . . D 7
47 Mossend . . . . C 12
38 Mosser . . . . C 4
47 Mossgiel . . . . F 9
49 Mosshouses . . . . E 8
43 Mosslands . . . . B 11
31 Mossley, Ches. . . . . . D 7
35 Mossley, Manchester G 8
30 Mossley Hill . . . . B 3
44 Mosspeeble . . . . D 2
56 Moss-side . . . . D 4
58 Mosstodloch . . . . B 1
7 Mosterton . . . . F 8
29 Mostyn . . . . B 11
7 Motcombe . . . . D 11
5 Mothecombe . . . . L 5
47 Motherwell . . . . D 12
18 Mottingham . . . . G 4
8 Mottisfont . . . . C 5
8 Mottistone . . . . H 5
35 Mottram . . . . H 8
30 Mouldsworth . . . . . . C 4
52 Moulin . . . . A 4
52 Moulinearn . . . . B 4
17 Moulsford . . . . F 7
23 Moulsoe . . . . H 12
30 Moulton, Ches. . . . . . C 5
24 Moulton, Lincs. . . . . . C 4
26 Moulton, Norf. . . . . . E 7
40 Moulton, N. Yorks. . E 3
23 Moulton, Northants . . . . E 11
14 Moulton, S. Glam. . . G 4
25 Moulton, Suffolk . . . . J 8
24 Moulton Chapel . . . . D 4
25 Moulton St. Michael . F 5
24 Moulton Seas End . . . C 4
57 Moulzie . . . . L 8
44 Mounces . . . . D 5
58 Mounie Castle . . . . . . E 5
3 Mount . . . . C 8
2 Mount Ambrose . . . . E 4
27 Mount Bures . . . . . . M 2
2 Mount Hawke . . . . . . E 4
48 Mount Lothian . . . . . D 5
49 Mount Pleasant, Borders . . . . D 10

31 Mount Pleasant, Derbyshire E 11
29 Mount Pleasant, Clywd C 11
14 Mount Pleasant, Mid Glam. D 4
8 Mount Pleasant, Hampshire F 4
17 Mount Pleasant, Hampshire H 7
22 Mount Pleasant, Heref. & Worc. F 3
27 Mount Pleasant, Suffolk G 8
8 Mount Sorrel D 2
35 Mount Tabor D 9
45 Mountain B 8
14 Mountain Ash D 4
48 Mountain Cross E 4
12 Mountain Water E 3
48 Mountbenger G 6
58 Mountblairy B 4
10 Mountfield F 6
56 Mountgerald D 1
2 Mountjoy D 6
18 Mountnessing D 6
15 Mounton E 8
58 Mountsolie B 7
23 Mountsorrel A 9
2 Mousehole G 2
43 Mouswald D 11
31 Mow Cop D 7
49 Mowhaugh G 10
23 Mowsley C 10
59 Mowtie H 6
55 Moy, Highland L 5
55 Moy, Highland L 8
56 Moy, Highland F 3
56 Moy Hall F 3
56 Moy House D 6
55 Moy Lodge L 8
56 Moybeg F 3
55 Moyle H 3
8 Moyles Court E 3
12 Moylgrove C 5
46 Muasdale E 2
15 Much Birch A 8
21 Much Cowarne H 11
15 Much Dewchurch A 8
18 Much Hadham B 4
34 Much Hoole E 3
15 Much Marcle A 10
21 Much Wenlock B 11
59 Muchalls H 6
7 Muchelney D 8
3 Muchlarnick D 9
54 Muchrachd F 6
56 Muckernich D 2
42 Muckfoot C 3
19 Mucking F 7
7 Muckleford G 9
30 Mucklestone F 6
30 Muckleton H 4
58 Muckletown E 3
22 Muckley Corner B 4
33 Muckton B 10
60 Mudale D 6
4 Muddiford B 4
10 Muddles Green G 4
8 Mudeford G 3
7 Mudford D 9
7 Mudgley B 8
47 Mugdock B 10
62 Mugeary D 4
31 Mugginton F 11
45 Muggleswick H 9
61 Muie F 7
57 Muir K 6
54 Muir of Fairburn D 8
58 Muir of Fowlis F 3
56 Muir of Ord E 1
58 Muirden B 4
48 Muirfoot D 2
53 Muirhead, Fife E 9
53 Muirhead, Fife G 7
59 Muirhead, Grampian L 5
47 Muirhead, Strathclyde B 11
53 Muirhead, Tayside D 8
48 Muirhouses, Lothian A 3
47 Muirhouses, Strathclyde D 11
47 Muirkirk G 11
47 Muirmill A 12
53 Muirsdrum C 10
55 Muirshearlich L 5
47 Muirshield D 10
59 Muirskie H 6
58 Muirtack, Grampian C 5
58 Muirtack, Tayside D 7
56 Muirton, Highland C 3
59 Muirton, Tayside L 4
52 Muirton, Tayside E 6
54 Muirton Mains D 8
52 Muirton of Ardblair C 6
52 Muirtown F 4
58 Muiryfold C 5
43 Muiryhill A 9
39 Muker E 11
26 Mulbarton E 5
58 Mulben C 1
41 Mulgrave D 8
2 Mullion H 4
55 Mullochbuie L 1
13 Mumbles H 9
33 Mumby C 12
21 Munderfield Row G 12
21 Munderfield Stocks G 12
26 Mundesley B 6
26 Mundford F 1
26 Mundham F 6
19 Mundon Hill D 8
55 Munerigie J 6
60 Mungasdale G 2
38 Mungrisdale B 6
56 Munlochy D 2
47 Munnoch E 7
21 Munsley H 12
21 Munslow D 10
21 Munslow Aston D 10
5 Murchington G 6
17 Murcott C 7
61 Murkle A 11
55 Murlaggan, Highland K 4
55 Murlaggan, Highland L 7
48 Murrayfield, Lothian B 5
52 Murrayfield, Tayside D 5
43 Murraythwaite D 12
24 Murrow E 5
17 Mursley A 9
59 Murthil L 2
52 Murthly C 6
52 Murthly Castle C 5
39 Murton, Cumbria C 9
45 Murton, Dur. H 12
49 Murton, Northumb. E 12
36 Murton, N. Yorks. B 4
40 Murton Grange F 5
6 Musbury G 6
41 Muscoates G 7
48 Musselburgh B 6
32 Muston, Leics. F 5
41 Muston, N. Yorks. G 11
22 Mustow Green E 2
43 Mutehill G 7
27 Mutford G 8
52 Muthill E 4
6 Mutterton F 4
21 Muxton A 12
61 Mybster B 11
13 Myddfai D 11
30 Myddle H 3
13 Mydroilyn B 8
2 Mylor Bridge F 5
12 Mynachlog-ddu D 5
21 Myndtown C 9
20 Mynydd-bach, Dyfed E 8
15 Mynydd-bach, Gwent E 8
13 Mynyddygarreg F 7
28 Myntho G 3
58 Myre of Bedlam C 6
59 Myrebird G 5
9 Mytchett A 10
35 Mytholmroyd E 9
34 Mythop D 2
40 Myton-on-Swale H 4
36 Naburn C 4
11 Nackington C 10
27 Nacton L 5
37 Nafferton A 8
15 Nailbridge C 9
15 Nailsea G 8
23 Nailstone A 7
15 Nailsworth D 11
56 Nairn D 4
10 Nalderswood D 1
2 Nancegollan F 3
2 Nancledra F 2
9 Nanhurst B 11
29 Nannerch C 11
32 Nanpantan H 2
3 Nanpean D 7
3 Nanstallon C 7
28 Nant Peris D 5
14 Nant-ddu C 3
13 Nanteris A 7
13 Nantgaredig E 8
14 Nantgarw F 4
20 Nant-glâs F 5
29 Nantglyn D 9
20 Nantgwyn E 5
28 Nantlle E 4
30 Nantmawr H 1
20 Nantmel F 6
28 Nantmor F 5
30 Nantwich E 5
13 Nantybai C 11
14 Nant-y-Bwch C 5
14 Nant-y-cafn D 2
14 Nant-y-derry D 6
13 Nant-y-ffin D 9
14 Nantyffyllon E 2
14 Nantyglo C 5
21 Nant-y-Meichiaid A 7
14 Nant-y-moel E 3
28 Nant-y-pandy C 6
17 Naphill D 9
35 Nappa B 7
23 Napton on the Hill F 8
12 Narberth E 4
23 Narborough, Leics. B 8
24 Narborough, Norf. D 8
3 Narkurs D 10
50 Narrachan F 6
28 Nasareth E 4
23 Naseby D 10
17 Nash, Bucks. A 8
21 Nash, Heref. & Worc. F 8
15 Nash, Gwent F 7
21 Nash, Salop E 11
24 Nassington F 2
18 Nasty B 4
4 Natcott D 2
39 Nateby, Cumbria D 10
34 Nateby, Lancs. C 3
39 Natland F 7
27 Naughton K 3
16 Naunton, Glos. B 2
22 Naunton, Heref. & Worc. H 2
22 Naunton, Beauchamp G 3
54 Naust B 2
33 Navenby D 7
18 Navestock D 5
18 Navestock Side D 5
61 Navidale E 10
41 Nawton G 7
27 Nayland M 3
19 Naze Park B 12
18 Nazeing C 4
8 Neacroft F 3
64 Neap D 7
31 Near Cotton E 9
38 Near Sawrey F 6
40 Neasham D 4
13 Neath G 11
13 Neath Abbey G 10
31 Neather Heage E 12
26 Neatishead C 6
20 Nebo, Dyfed F 1
28 Nebo, Gwynedd A 4
28 Nebo, Gwynedd E 4
29 Nebo, Gwynedd E 7
26 Necton E 2
60 Nedd D 3
27 Nedging K 3
27 Nedging Tye K 3
27 Needham G 5
27 Needham Market K 4
25 Needingworth H 4
31 Needlewood H 10
21 Neen Savage H 10
21 Neen Sollars E 12
21 Neenton D 11
28 Nefyn F 3
23 Neithrop H 8
21 Nelly Andrews Green A 8
35 Nelson, Lancs. C 7
14 Nelson, Mid Glam. E 4
45 Nelson Village E 10
48 Nemphlar E 1
15 Nempnett Thrubwell H 8
39 Nenthall A 10
39 Nenthead A 10
49 Nenthorn F 9
29 Nercwys D 11
47 Nerston D 11
35 Nesfield B 9
49 Nesbit F 12
30 Ness C 2
30 Nesscliffe H 3
30 Neston, Ches. B 2
15 Neston, Wilts. G 11
31 Nether Alderley C 7
49 Nether Blainslie E 8
31 Nether Booth B 10
49 Nether Brotherstone D 7
32 Nether Broughton H 4
39 Nether Burrow H 8
44 Nether Cassock C 1
7 Nether Cerne F 10
59 Nether Contlaw G 6
43 Nether Craigenputtock C 9
58 Nether Crimond E 6
48 Nether Dalgliesh H 5
58 Nether Dallachy A 1
6 Nether Exe F 3
48 Nether Fingland H 2
58 Nether Glasslaw B 6
43 Nether Gribton D 10
53 Nether Handwick C 8
36 Nether Haugh G 2
23 Nether Hayford F 10
44 Nether Hindhope B 6
48 Nether Howcleugh H 3
39 Nether Kellet H 7
58 Nether Kinmundy C 8
47 Nether Kirkton D 9
32 Nether Langwith C 3
58 Nether Leask D 8
47 Nether Newton E 10
31 Nether Padley B 11
58 Nether Park B 7
59 Nether Pitforthie J 6
36 Nether Poppleton B 3
40 Nether Silton F 5
6 Nether Stowey B 5
59 Nether Thaneston K 4
53 Nether Urquhart F 7
8 Nether Wallop B 5
22 Nether Whitacre C 6
48 Nether Whitecleuch G 1
16 Nether Worton A 5
8 Netheravon A 3
58 Netherbrae B 5
48 Netherburn E 1
7 Netherbury F 8
44 Netherby, Cumb. F 2
35 Netherby, N. Yorks. C 11
4 Nethercott B 4
15 Netherend D 9
10 Netherfield F 6
8 Netherhampton C 3
49 Netherhowden D 7
43 Netherlaw G 8
59 Netherley H 6
43 Nethermill, Dumf. & Gall. C 11
58 Nethermill, Grampian D 8
43 Nethermiln A 11
58 Nethermuir C 7
47 Netherplace D 10
22 Netherseal A 6
16 Netherstreet H 1
43 Netherthird, Dumf. & Gall. F 8
47 Netherthird, Strathclyde G 10
35 Netherthong F 10
45 Netherwitton D 9
47 Netherwood F 11
47 Netherton, Central A 10
5 Netherton, Devon J 8
6 Netherton, Hants. H 5
22 Netherton, Heref. & Worc. H 3
34 Netherton, Merseyside G 2
45 Netherton, Northumb. B 8
48 Netherton, Strathclyde G 2
47 Netherton, Strathclyde D 12
59 Netherton, Tayside L 3
52 Netherton, Tayside B 6
22 Netherton, W. Midlands C 3
35 Netherton, W. Yorks. F 10
35 Netherton, W. Yorks. F 11
64 Nethertown, Highland F 2
38 Nethertown, Cumb. D 2
57 Nethy Bridge G 6
8 Netley E 6
8 Netley Marsh E 5
17 Nettlebed E 8
7 Nettlebridge A 10
7 Nettlecombe, Dorset G 8
9 Nettlecombe, I.o.W. H 7
6 Nettlecombe, Som. C 4
17 Nettleden C 11
33 Nettleham C 7
10 Nettlestead C 6
10 Nettlestead Green C 5
9 Nettlestone G 8
45 Nettlesworth H 10
37 Nettleton, Lincs. G 9
15 Nettleton, Wilts. F 11
5 Netton, Devon L 4
8 Netton, Wilts. B 3
14 Neuadd, Powys C 4
20 Neuadd, Powys B 6
20 Neuadd-ddu E 5
19 Nevendon E 7
12 Nevern C 4
43 New Abbey E 10
58 New Aberdour A 6
18 New Addington H 4
9 New Alresford C 7
53 New Alyth B 7
32 New Annesley E 2
10 New Ash Green B 5
18 New Barnet D 3
49 New Belses G 8
45 New Berwick A 9
23 New Bilton E 8
33 New Bolingbroke D 10
23 New Bradwell H 11
32 New Brampton C 1
40 New Brancepeth A 2
43 New Bridge, Dumf. & Gall. D 10
36 New Bridge, Humberside E 4
29 New Brighton, Clwyd D 11
30 New Brighton, Merseyside A 2
32 New Brinsley E 2
26 New Buckenham F 4
58 New Byth B 6
26 New Catton E 5
10 New Chapel D 2
32 New Clipstone D 3
26 New Costessey D 5
43 New Cowper G 12
20 New Cross E 2
47 New Cumnock H 11
58 New Deer C 6
45 New Delaval E 11
17 New Denham F 11
2 New Downs E 4
23 New Duston F 10
36 New Earswick B 4
36 New Edlington G 3
56 New Elgin D 8
37 New Ellerby C 9
22 New End F 4
30 New Ferry B 2
36 New Fryston D 2
43 New Galloway D 7
2 New Grimsby D 2
45 New Haggerston B 11
45 New Hartley E 11
12 New Hedges G 5
45 New Herrington H 11
35 New Hey F 8
16 New Hinksey D 6
26 New Holkham B 2
37 New Holland E 8
38 New Hotel E 5
45 New Horton Grange E 10
32 New Houghton, Derbyshire D 2
26 New Houghton, Norfolk C 1
39 New Houses H 10
39 New Hutton F 8
10 New Hythe B 6
13 New Inn, Dyfed C 8
15 New Inn, Gwent D 8
39 New Inn, N. Yorks. H 10
21 New Invention E 8
54 New Kelso E 3
58 New Kendal E 6
45 New Lambton H 11
48 New Lanark E 2
34 New Lane F 3
33 New Leake D 11
58 New Leeds B 7
34 New Longdon E 4
42 New Luce E 3
49 New Mains, Lothian A 8
48 New Mains, Strathclyde F 1
59 New Mains of Ury J 6
18 New Malden G 2
40 New Marske C 6
30 New Marton G 2
59 New Mill, Grampian J 5
35 New Mill, W. Yorks. F 10
16 New Mill, Wilts. H 3
2 New Mills, Corn. D 6
31 New Mills, Derby B 8
20 New Mills, Powys B 6
8 New Milton F 4
27 New Mistley M 4
12 New Moat D 4
47 New Monkland C 12
45 New Mousen C 12
58 New Pitsligo B 6
2 New Polzeath B 6
47 New Prestwick G 8
13 New Quay A 7
21 New Radnor F 7
39 New Rent B 7
11 New Romney F 9
36 New Rossington G 4
20 New Row E 3
8 New Sarum C 3
52 New Sauchie H 4
52 New Scone E 6
50 New Selma D 6
63 New Shawbost B 4
45 New Shoreston D 12
47 New Stevenston C 12
8 New Swanage H 2
63 New Tolsta B 6
17 New Town, Berks. G 7
8 New Town, Dorset D 2
7 New Town, Dorset D 11
10 New Town, E. Sussex F 3
49 New Town, Lothian B 7
17 New Town, Hants. H 7
16 New Town, Wilts. G 4
14 New Tredegar D 5
48 New Trows F 1
32 New Tupton D 1
63 New Valley C 5
37 New Waltham G 10
25 New Wimpole K 4
49 New Winton B 7
16 New Yatt C 5
33 New York, Lincs. E 9
45 New York, Tyne & Wear F 11
64 Newark A 4
24 Newark, Cambs. E 3
32 Newark, Notts. E 5
48 Newarthill C 1
48 Newbattle C 6
39 Newbiggin, Cumb. B 7
44 Newbiggin, Cumbria H 4
38 Newbiggin, Cumbria H 5
39 Newbiggin, Cumbria B 8
39 Newbiggin, Dur. B 11
45 Newbiggin, Dur. H 9
45 Newbiggin, Northumb. G 8
39 Newbiggin, N. Yorks. F 11
39 Newbiggin, N. Yorks. G 12
45 Newbiggin-by-the Sea D 11
39 Newbiggin on Lune E 9
49 Newbigging, Borders D 8
48 Newbigging, Strathclyde E 3
59 Newbigging, Tayside K 1
32 Newbold, Derby C 1
32 Newbold, Leics. H 1
23 Newbold on Avon D 8
22 Newbold on Stour G 6
22 Newbold Pacey F 6
23 Newbold Verdon B 8
24 Newborough, Cambs. E 3
28 Newborough, Gwynedd D 4
31 Newborough, Staffordshire H 10
23 Newbottle, Northants H 8
45 Newbottle, Tyne & Wear H 11
27 Newbourn L 6
29 Newbridge, Clwyd F 12
2 Newbridge, Corn. F 1
3 Newbridge, Corn. C 10
12 Newbridge, Dyfed D 3
14 Newbridge, Gwent E 5
15 Newbridge, Gwent E 7
8 Newbridge, Hants. E 4
8 Newbridge, I.o.W. G 6
48 Newbridge, Lothian B 4
20 Newbridge on Wye F 6
45 Newbrough F 7
48 Newburgh, Borders G 6
53 Newburgh, Fife E 7
58 Newburgh, Grampian B 7
58 Newburgh, Grampian E 7
40 Newburgh Priory G 5
49 Newburn, Northumb. E 11
45 Newburn, Tyne & Wear G 10

16 Newbury ....G 5
39 Newby, Cumbria ....C 8
40 Newby, N. Yorks...D 5
41 Newby, N. Yorks. ...F 10
39 Newby, N. Yorks...H 9
38 Newby Bridge ......G 6
44 Newby East ....G 3
44 Newby West ....H 2
40 Newby Wiske ....F 4
15 Newcastle, Gwent ...C 7
21 Newcastle, Salop ...D 8
12 Newcastle Emlyn ...C 6
31 Newcastle-under-Lyme ....F 7
45 Newcastle upon Tyne ...F 10
44 Newcastleton ......D 3
12 Newchapel, Dyfed ..C 6
31 Newchapel, Staffs. .E 7
13 Newchurch, Dyfed ..E 7
15 Newchurch, Gwent ..E 8
9 Newchurch, I.o.W. ..H 7
11 Newchurch, Kent ...E 9
35 Newchurch, Lancs. .C 7
35 Newchurch, Lancs. .E 7
21 Newchurch, Powys ..G 7
31 Newchurch, Staffs. ..H 10
6 Newcott ....E 6
10 Newdigate ....D 1
17 Newell Green ....G 9
11 Newenden ,,,,,, F 7
15 Newent ....B 10
15 Newerne ....D 9
43 Newfield, Dumf. & Gall. ..E 12
43 Newfield, Dumf. & Gall. ....E 9
40 Newfield, Dur. ....B 2
45 Newfield, Dur. ...H 10
56 Newfield, Highland .B 3
9 Newfound ....A 7
12 Newglae ....E 2
26 Newgate ....A 3
18 Newgate Street ....C 3
64 Newgord ....A 8
48 Newhall, Borders ...F 6
30 Newhall, Ches. ....F 5
31 Newhall, Derby ...H 11
56 Newhallpoint ....C 3
18 Newham, London ...F 4
45 Newham, Northumb. .E 12
45 Newham Hall ..D 12
10 Newhaven ....H 3
31 Newhaven House ..D 10
41 Newholm ....D 8
48 Newhouse ....C 1
45 Newhouses ....E 8
10 Newick ....F 3
11 Newingreen ......D 10
11 Newington, Kent ...B 7
11 Newington, Kent ..D 10
32 Newington, Notts. ..A 4
17 Newington, Oxen ...D 7
21 Newington, Salop ..D 9
59 Newkirk ....G 2
15 Newland, Glos. ....C 9
22 Newland, Heref. & Worc. ..G 2
37 Newland, Humber. ..D 8
36 Newland, N. Yorks. .E 5
6 Newland, Som. .....B 2
53 Newlandhead ......C 9
44 Newlands, Borders ..D 3
43 Newlands, Dumf. & Gall. ..C 10
56 Newlands, Grampian E 8
45 Newlands, Northumb. ......G 9
47 Newlands, Strathclyde .....G 8
47 Newlands, Strathclyde ....D 11
61 Newlands of Geise .A 10
2 Newlyn ....G 2
2 Newlyn East ....D 5
58 Newmachar ....F 6
48 Newmains ....D 1
25 Newmarket, Suff. ..J 7
63 Newmarket, W. Isles .....C 5
44 Newmill, Borders ..B 3
2 Newmill, Corn. ....F 2
58 Newmill, Grampian .B 2
59 Newmill of Inshewan ......L 2
35 Newmillerdam ....F 12
48 Newmills, Fife .....A 3
15 Newmills, Gwent ...D 8
56 Newmills, Highland .C 2
48 Newmills, Lothian ..C 4
58 Newmills of Boyne .B 3
52 Newmiln ....D 6
47 Newmilns ....F 10

15 Newnham, Glos. ...C 10
9 Newnham, Hants. ..A 8
25 Newnham, Herts. ..L 3
11 Newnham, Kent ...B 8
23 Newnham, Northants ...F 9
21 Newnham Bridge ..E 11
53 Newpark ....F 9
4 Newport, Devon ...C 4
12 Newport, Dyfed ...C 4
25 Newport, Essex ....M 6
15 Newport, Glos. ....E 10
14 Newport, Gwent ...F 6
61 Newport, Highland ...E 10
36 Newport, Humber. ..D 6
8 Newport, I.o.W. ...G 6
26 Newport, Norfolk ..D 8
30 Newport, Salop ....H 6
53 Newport-on-Tay ...D 9
23 Newport Pagnell ..H 12
9 Newpound Com. ..C 11
1 Newquay ....D 5
52 Newrow ....H 4
35 Newsam Green ...D 12
40 Newseat ....D 4
34 Newsham, Lancs. ..D 4
40 Newsham, N. Yorks. D 1
40 Newsham, N. Yorks. .....G 4
36 Newsholme, Humberside ....D 5
35 Newsholme, Lancs. .B 7
35 Newsholme, W. Yorks. ....C 9
49 Newstead, Borders .F 8
45 Newstead, Northumb. ....E 12
32 Newstead, Notts. ..E 2
36 Newthorpe ....D 3
40 Newton, Borders ..G 8
25 Newton, Cambs. ..K 5
30 Newton, Ches. ....C 3
30 Newton, Ches. ....C 4
30 Newton, Ches. ....D 4
35 Newton, Ches. ....G 8
40 Newton, Cleveland .D 6
38 Newton, Cumbria ..H 5
32 Newton, Derby ....D 2
7 Newton, Dorset ....F 11
43 Newton, Dumf. & Gall. ..B 12
58 Newton, Grampian ..C 8
56 Newton, Grampian ..C 7
15 Newton, Heref. & Worc. ..A 7
21 Newton, Heref. & Worc. ..G 10
61 Newton, Highland .C 12
56 Newton, Highland ..E 3
56 Newton, Highland ..C 3
56 Newton, Highland ..E 1
60 Newton, Highland ..D 4
34 Newton, Lancs. ...D 2
34 Newton, Lancs. ...D 3
39 Newton, Lancs. ...H 8
34 Newton, Lancs. ...B 6
24 Newton, Lincs. ...B 1
48 Newton, Lothian ..B 4
14 Newton, Mid Glam. .G 2
24 Newton, Norfolk ..D 5
26 Newton, Norfolk ..D 1
41 Newton, N. Yorks. .H 9
23 Newton, Northants. .....D 12
45 Newton, Northumb. .B 8
45 Newton, Northumb. .G 8
32 Newton, Notts. ....F 4
6 Newton, Som. .....B 5
31 Newton, Staffs. ...H 9
47 Newton, Strathclyde .....C 11
48 Newton, Strathclyde F 2
27 Newton, Suffolk ..L 2
52 Newton, Tayside ..D 4
58 Newton, War. .....D 8
13 Newton, W. Glam. ..H 9
36 Newton, W. Yorks. .D 2
8 Newton, Wilts. ....D 4
5 Newton Abbot ....J 7
44 Newton Arlosh ...F 12
40 Newton Aycliffe ...C 3
40 Newton Bewley ....C 5
23 Newton Blossomville ...G 12
25 Newton Bromswold .J 1
23 Newton Burgoland ..A 7
33 Newton by Toft ...B 7
5 Newton Ferrers ....L 4
26 Newton Flotman ..F 5
23 Newton Harcourt ..B 9
58 Newton House .....E 4
34 Newton-le-Willows, Lancashire ....H 4

40 Newton-le-Willows, N. Yorkshire ......F 2
36 Newton Kyme ....C 2
17 Newton Longville ..A 9
47 Newton Mearns ...D 10
40 Newton Morrell ...D 3
12 Newton Mulgrave ..D 8
12 Newton Mountain ...F 3
50 Newton of Ardtoe ..A 4
52 Newton of Balcanquhal ......F 6
53 Newton of Falkland .F 7
58 Newton of Murcar ..F 7
60 Newton of Ochtow ..G 5
52 Newton of Pitcairns .F 5
36 Newton-on-Ouse ...A 3
41 Newton-on-Rawcliffe ...F 8
45 Newton-on-the-Moor ...C 10
32 Newton on Trent ..C 5
6 Newton Poppleford .G 4
17 Newton Purcell ...A 7
22 Newton Regis .....A 6
39 Newton Reigny ....B 7
49 Newton St. Boswells .F 8
4 Newton St. Cyres ..F 7
26 Newton St. Faith ..D 5
15 Newton St. Loe ...H 10
4 Newton St. Petrock .E 3
31 Newton Solney ...H 11
8 Newton Stacey ....B 6
42 Newton Stewart ...E 5
8 Newton Toney .....B 4
4 Newton Tracey ....C 4
47 Newton upon Ayr ..G 8
36 Newton upon Derwent ......B 5
9 Newton Valence ...C 8
43 Newtonairds ......D 9
58 Newtongarry Croft .D 3
48 Newtongrange ....C 6
59 Newtonmill ......L 3
57 Newtonmore ......J 3
31 Newtown, Ches. ...B 8
30 Newtown, Ches. ...E 5
2 Newtown, Corn. ...G 4
44 Newtown, Cumb. ..G 2
44 Newtown, Cumb. ..G 3
39 Newtown, Cumbria .C 7
4 Newtown, Devon ..C 6
8 Newtown, Dorset ..G 2
15 Newtown, Glos. ...A 12
15 Newtown, Glos. ...D 10
56 Newtown, Grampian ....C 7
8 Newtown, Hants. ..D 4
9 Newtown, Hants. ..D 7
8 Newtown, Hants. ..E 4
8 Newtown, Hants. ..E 7
16 Newtown, Hants. ..H 6
21 Newtown, Heref. & Worc. ..G 10
21 Newtown, Heref. & Worc. ..H 11
55 Newtown, Highland ......J 7
38 Newtown, I.o.M. ..H 2
8 Newtown, I.o.W. ..G 5
34 Newtown, Lancs. ..E 4
45 Newtown, Northumb. ......A 8
45 Newtown, Northumb. ......C 8
49 Newtown, Northumb. ......F 12
20 Newtown, Powys ..C 6
30 Newtown, Salop ...G 3
31 Newtown, Staffs. ..D 7
31 Newtown, Staffs. ..D 9
7 Newtown, Wilts. ..C 12
23 Newtown Linfold ..A 8
48 Newtown of Covington ......E 3
58 Newtown of Melrose ......A 5
53 Newtyle ....C 8
12 Neyland ....F 3
8 Nibley ....F 10
6 Nicholashayne ....E 5
13 Nicholaston ......H 8
44 Nickie's Hill ......F 4
35 Nidd ....A 11
59 Nigg, Grampian ...G 7
59 Nigg, Highland ...C 4
56 Nigg Station .....B 4
18 Nightcott ....D 2
18 Nine Ashes ....D 6
48 Nine Mile Burn ...D 4
26 Ninebanks ....H 6
8 Ninfield ....G 6
8 Ningwood ....G 5
49 Nisbet ....B 7
43 Nithside ....D 10

8 Niton ....H 6
30 No Man's Heath, Cheshire ......E 4
22 No Man's Heath, Warwickshire ...A 6
2 No Man's Land, Cornwall ......C 6
4 No Man's Land, Devon ....E 7
18 Noak Hill ....E 5
48 Noblehall ....E 4
48 Noblehouse ......D 5
35 Nobold ....A 10
23 Nobottle ....F 10
33 Nocton ....D 8
16 Noke ....C 6
12 Nolton ....E 2
12 Nolton Haven ....E 2
30 Noneley ....G 3
11 Nonington ......C 11
39 Nook ....G 8
30 Norbury, Ches. ...E 4
31 Norbury, Derby ...F 9
21 Norbury, Salop ...C 9
30 Norbury, Staffs. ...H 6
24 Nordelph ....E 7
35 Norden ....F 7
8 Norden Heath .....H 1
21 Nordley ....C 12
16 Nore Marsh ......F 2
26 Norfolk, Co. .....D 4
30 Norham ....E 11
30 Norley ....C 4
8 Norley Wood .....F 5
24 Norman Cross ....F 3
36 Normanby, Humber. E 6
33 Normanby, Lincs. ..A 7
41 Normanby, N. Yorks. G 7
37 Normanby le Wold ..H 9
9 Normandy ......A 10
10 Norman's Bay ....G 6
6 Norman's Green ...F 4
8 Normansland .....D 4
31 Normanton, Derbyshire ....G 11
32 Normanton, Leics. .F 5
32 Normanton, Lincs. ..F 6
32 Normanton, Notts. ..E 4
36 Normanton, W. Yorks. ......E 2
23 Normanton le Heath ....A 7
32 Normanton on Soar ....H 2
32 Normanton on the Wolds ....G 3
32 Normanton on Trent ....C 5
34 Normoss ....C 2
9 Norney ....B 10
15 Norrington Com. ..H 12
31 Norris Hill ......H 11
56 North Anston .....B 2
34 North Ashton ....G 4
16 North Aston .....A 6
58 North Atrochie ...D 7
8 North Baddesley ..D 5
51 North Ballachulish .B 8
7 North Barrow ....C 9
26 North Barsham ...B 2
19 North Benfleet ...E 7
9 North Bersted ....F 10
49 North Berwick ....A 8
9 North Boarhunt ...E 7
5 North Bovey .....G 6
47 North Brackenridge ......E 12
7 North Bradley ....A 12
5 North Brentor ....H 4
7 North Brewham ...C 10
4 North Buckland ..B 4
26 North Burlingham .D 7
7 North Cadbury ...D 9
32 North Carlton, Lincolnshire ....B 6
32 North Carlton, Notts. ....B 3
46 North Carrine ....H 2
36 North Cave ......D 6
16 North Cerney ....C 1
9 North Chapel ....C 11
8 North Charford ...D 3
45 North Charlton ...A 10
7 North Cheriton ...D 10
7 North Chideock ..G 8
36 North Cliffe .....C 6
31 North Clifton ....C 5
37 North Coates ....G 11
33 North Cockerington ....A 10
7 North Coker .....E 9
32 North Collingham .D 5
10 North Common ...F 3
14 North Cornelly ...F 2

50 North Corry ......B 5
58 North Cottown ...F 5
26 North Cove ......F 8
43 North Cowshaw ..C 11
40 North Cowton ....E 3
44 North Craigs .....E 1
23 North Crawley ...H 12
18 North Cray ......G 5
26 North Creake ....B 2
7 North Curry .....D 7
37 North Dalton ....B 7
3 North Darley ....B 10
35 North Deighton ..B 12
47 North Drumboy ..D 10
36 North Duffield ...C 5
33 North Elkington ..A 10
26 North Elmham ...C 3
36 North Elmsall ...F 3
15 North End, Avon .G 11
15 North End, Avon ..H 7
17 North End, Bucks. .A 9
17 North End, Bucks. .E 8
7 North End, Dorset .D 11
18 North End, Essex ..B 6
9 North End, Hants. .F 8
16 North End, Hants. .H 5
37 North End, Humberside ....D 10
24 North End, Lincs. .B 3
34 North End, Merseyside ......G 2
45 North End, Northumb. .....C 9
6 North End, Som. ..D 6
9 North End, W. Sussex ...E 12
54 North Erradale ...B 1
4 North Esworthy ..D 2
19 North Fambridge ..D 8
46 North Feorline ...F 4
37 North Ferriby ....E 7
37 North Frodingham .B 8
63 North Galson .....A 5
64 North Gluss .....C 7
8 North Gorley ....E 3
58 North Gorrachie ..B 5
26 North Green .....F 5
44 North Greenhill ...F 4
41 North Grimston ...H 8
10 North Halling ....B 6
47 North Halls ......F 11
9 North Hayling ....F 9
45 North Hazelrigg ..C 12
9 North Heath .....D 12
3 North Hill ......B 9
16 North Hinksey ...D 6
10 North Holmwood ..C 1
47 North Hourat ....D 8
5 North Huish .....K 6
32 North Hykeham ..D 6
12 North Johnston ...F 3
37 North Kelsey .....G 8
56 North Kessock ...E 2
37 North Killingholme .E 9
40 North Kilvington ..G 4
23 North Kilworth ...D 9
58 North Kinmundy ..F 6
58 North Kirkton ....C 8
33 North Kyme .....C 8
10 North Lancing ...G 1
40 North Lees ......H 3
23 North Luffenham ..B 12
16 North Leigh .....C 5
32 North Leverton with Habblesthorpe ..B 5
22 North Littleton ...G 8
27 North Lopham ...G 3
45 North Lyham ....C 12
9 North Marden ...D 9
17 North Marston ...B 8
48 North Middleton, Lothian ....C 6
49 North Middleton, Northumb. ....G 12
4 North Molton ...C 6
58 North Monkshill ..C 5
41 North Moor .....H 12
16 North Moreton ...C 6
9 North Mundham ..F 10
32 North Muskham ..D 5
37 North Newbald ...C 7
23 North Newington ..H 7
16 North Newton ...H 2
6 North Newton ...C 6
15 North Nibley ....E 10
9 North Oakley ....A 7
18 North Ockendon ..E 6
40 North Ormesby ...C 5
33 North Ormsby ...A 10
40 North Otterington .F 5
37 North Owersby ...H 8
7 North Perrott ....E 8
6 North Petherton ..C 6
3 North Petherwin ..A 10

26 North Pickenham ..E 1
22 North Piddle .....G 3
7 North Poorton ...F 8
6 North Quarme ...C 3
48 North Queensferry .A 4
4 North Radworthy ..C 6
33 North Rauceby ...F 7
35 North Rigton ....B 11
31 North Rode .....D 7
24 North Runcton ...D 7
64 North Sandwick ..B 8
38 North Scale ......H 4
32 North Scarle .....D 6
45 N. Seaton Colliery .D 11
63 North Shawbost ..B 4
50 North Shian .....C 6
45 North Shields ....F 11
19 North Shoebury ..E 9
34 North Shore .....D 2
48 North Shortcleugh .H 2
38 North Side, Cumb. .B 2
24 North Side, Cambs. .E 4
41 North Skelton ...C 5
37 North Somercotes .G 12
40 North Stainley ...G 3
37 North Stainmore .D 10
15 North Stoke, Avon ...G 10
17 North Stoke, Oxon ..F 7
9 North Stoke, W. Sussex ....E 11
17 North Street, Berks. ...G 7
8 North Street, Hants. .C 8
45 North Sunderland .D 12
4 North Tamerton ..F 2
4 North Tawton ...F 5
37 North Thoresby ..G 10
8 North Tidworth ...A 4
45 North Togston ...C 10
63 North Tolsta .....B 6
26 North Tuddenham .D 3
45 North Walbottle ..F 10
26 North Walsham ..C 6
9 North Waltham ...B 7
9 North Warnborough ....A 8
59 North Water Bri...L 4
61 North Watten ...B 11
18 North Weald Bassett ....D 5
32 North Wheatley ..B 5
15 North Wick ......H 9
5 North Whilborough .J 7
33 North Willingham ..A 8
32 North Wingfield ..D 1
32 North Witham ...H 6
7 North Wootton, Dorset ....E 10
24 North Wootton, Norfolk ....C 7
7 North Wootton, Somerset ......B 9
15 North Wraxall ...G 11
16 North Wroughton ..F 3
45 North Yardhope ..C 7
40 North Yorkshire, Co. ....F 5
40 Northallerton ....F 4
4 Northam, Devon ..C 3
8 Northam, Hants. ..E 6
23 Northampton ....F 11
23 Northamptonshire, County ......E 11
18 Northaw ....D 3
24 Northborough Peakirk ......E 3
11 Northbourne ....C 12
8 Northbrook ......B 6
17 Northchurch ....C 10
5 Northcott ......G 2
23 Northend ......C 11
49 Northfield, Borders ....C 11
59 Northfield, Grampian ....G 6
22 Northfield, W. Midlands ...D 4
10 Northfleet ......A 5
11 Northiam ......D 5
25 Northill ....K 3
9 Northington ....B 7
33 Northlands .....E 10
16 Northleach .....C 2
6 Northleigh .....G 5
4 Northlew ......F 4
16 Northmoor ......D 5
6 Northmoor Green or Moorland ....C 6
53 Northmuir ......B 10
9 Northney ......F 9
18 Northolt ....E 1
29 Northop ......C 11

29 Northophall .... **C 12**
24 Northorpe, Lincs. ... **B 3**
24 Northorpe, Lincs. ... **D 2**
37 Northorpe, Lincs. ... **G 7**
7 Northover, Som. .... **B 8**
7 Northover, Som. .... **D 8**
35 Northowram ...... **D 10**
8 Northport .... **G 1**
26 Northrepps .... **B 5**
63 Northton .... **H 1**
64 Northtown .... **D 3**
45 Northumberland, County .... **D 8**
15 Northway, Glos. ... **A 12**
6 Northway, Som. .... **C 5**
30 Northwich .... **C 5**
15 Northwick .... **F 9**
24 Northwold .... **F 8**
8 Northwood, I.o.W. . **G 6**
18 Northwood, Lond. .. **E 1**
30 Northwood, Salop .. **G 3**
25 Northwood End .... **L 2**
15 Northwood Green . **C 10**
30 Northwood, Ches. .. **B 4**
40 Norton, Cleveland .. **C 5**
15 Norton, Glos. ..... **B 11**
15 Norton, Gwent ..... **B 7**
22 Norton, Heref. & Worc. .... **G 2**
22 Norton, Heref. & Worc. .... **G 4**
8 Norton, I.o.W. ..... **G 5**
41 Norton, N. Yorks. .. **H 8**
23 Norton, Northants. .. **F 9**
32 Norton, Notts. ..... **C 3**
21 Norton, Powys ..... **F 8**
21 Norton, Salop ..... **A 11**
22 Norton, Salop ..... **B 1**
21 Norton, Salop ..... **D 10**
36 Norton, S. Yorks. ... **F 3**
27 Norton, Suffolk .... **J 3**
15 Norton, Wilts. ..... **F 12**
8 Norton Bavant ..... **B 1**
31 Norton Bridge ..... **G 7**
22 Norton Canes ..... **A 4**
21 Norton Canon ..... **H 9**
32 Norton Disney ..... **D 6**
22 Norton East .... **A 4**
7 Norton Ferris ..... **C 11**
6 Norton Fitzwarren .. **D 5**
8 Norton Green ...... **G 5**
15 Norton Hawkfield .. **H 9**
18 Norton Heath ...... **D 6**
30 Norton in Hales ..... **F 5**
31 Norton in the Moors .... **E 7**
23 Norton Juxta Twycross .... **A 7**
40 Norton-le-Clay ..... **H 4**
22 Norton Lindsey ..... **F 6**
15 Norton Malreward .. **H 9**
7 Norton St. Philip .. **A 11**
7 Norton sub Hamdon **E 8**
26 Norton Subcourse ... **F 7**
32 Norton Woodseats .. **B 1**
32 Norwell .... **D 5**
32 Norwell Woodhouse **D 5**
26 Norwich .... **E 5**
64 Norwick .... **A 8**
32 Norwood .... **B 2**
10 Norwood Hill ...... **D 1**
23 Noseley .... **B 10**
5 Noss Mayo .... **L 4**
40 Nosterfield .... **G 3**
55 Nostie .... **G 2**
16 Notgrove .... **B 2**
14 Nottage .... **F 1**
32 Nottingham .... **F 3**
32 Nottinghamshire, County .... **D 4**
35 Notton, W. Yorks. . **F 12**
15 Notton, Wilts. ..... **G 12**
19 Nounsley .... **C 8**
22 Noutard's Green .... **E 2**
56 Novar House ...... **C 2**
21 Nox .... **A 9**
17 Nuffield .... **E 7**
57 Nuide .... **K 3**
36 Nun Monkton ...... **A 3**
36 Nunburnholme ..... **B 6**
32 Nuncargate .... **E 2**
23 Nuneaton .... **C 7**
16 Nuneham Courtenay **D 6**
49 Nunlands .... **D 12**
38 Nunnery Howe .... **H 2**
7 Nunney .... **B 10**
41 Nunnington .... **G 7**
45 Nunnykirk .... **D 9**
37 Nunsthorpe .... **F 10**
40 Nunthorpe .... **D 5**
8 Nunton .... **C 3**
40 Nunwick .... **H 3**
43 Nunwood .... **D 10**
8 Nursling .... **D 5**
9 Nutbourne .... **F 9**
9 Nutbourne .... **D 12**
10 Nutfield .... **C 2**
32 Nuthall .... **F 2**
25 Nuthampstead ..... **M 5**
10 Nuthurst .... **E 1**
10 Nutley, E. Sussex ... **E 3**
9 Nutley, Hants. ...... **B 7**
36 Nutwell .... **G 4**
9 Nyetimber .... **F 10**
9 Nyewood .... **D 9**
4 Nymet Rowland .... **E 6**
4 Nymet Tracey ...... **F 6**
15 Nympsfield .... **D 11**
6 Nynehead .... **D 5**
7 Nythe .... **C 7**
9 Nyton .... **E 10**
11 Oad Street .... **B 7**
23 Oadby .... **B 9**
31 Oakamoor .... **F 9**
48 Oakbank .... **C 4**
14 Oakdale .... **D 5**
6 Oake .... **D 5**
22 Oaken .... **B 2**
34 Oakenclough ...... **B 4**
21 Oakengates .... **A 12**
29 Oakenholt .... **C 12**
40 Oakenshaw, Dur. ... **A 2**
35 Oakenshaw, W. Yorks. **D 10**
14 Oakfield, Gwent .... **E 6**
8 Oakfield, Hants. .... **C 5**
6 Oakford, Devon .... **D 3**
13 Oakford, Dyfed .... **A 8**
6 Oakfordbridge ..... **D 3**
31 Oakgrove .... **C 8**
23 Oakham .... **A 12**
9 Oakhanger .... **C 9**
7 Oakhill .... **B 9**
25 Oakington .... **J 5**
29 Oaklands .... **D 7**
15 Oakle Street ...... **C 10**
25 Oakley, Beds. ...... **K 1**
17 Oakley, Bucks. ..... **C 7**
8 Oakley, Dorset ..... **F 2**
52 Oakley, Fife .... **H 5**
9 Oakley, Hants. ..... **A 7**
27 Oakley, Suffolk .... **H 5**
17 Oakley Green ..... **F 10**
20 Oakleypark .... **D 5**
15 Oakridge Lynch ... **D 12**
16 Oaksey .... **E 1**
22 Oakthorpe .... **A 6**
40 Oaktree Hill .... **E 4**
45 Oakwood, Northumb. **F 8**
49 Oakwood, Borders .. **G 7**
9 Oakwoodhill ...... **B 12**
35 Oakworth .... **C 9**
11 Oar .... **B 9**
16 Oare, Berks. .... **G 6**
6 Oare, Som. .... **B 2**
16 Oare, Wilts. .... **H 3**
6 Oareford .... **B 2**
33 Oasby .... **F 7**
59 Oathlaw .... **M 2**
55 Oban, Highland .... **K 2**
50 Oban, Strathclyde .. **E 6**
58 Obliston .... **B 1**
7 Oborne .... **D 10**
56 Obsdale .... **C 2**
30 Occlestone Green .. **D 5**
27 Occold .... **H 5**
52 Ochil Hills Hosp. .... **F 6**
47 Ochiltree .... **G 10**
52 Ochtermuthill ...... **E 3**
42 Ochtrelure .... **F 2**
32 Ockbrook .... **G 2**
17 Ockham .... **H 11**
50 Ockle .... **A 3**
21 Ocle Pychard ..... **H 11**
9 Ocley .... **B 12**
41 Octon .... **H 10**
7 Odcombe .... **E 8**
15 Odd Down .... **H 10**
39 Oddendale .... **D 8**
22 Oddingley .... **F 3**
16 Oddington, Glos. ... **B 3**
16 Oddington, Oxon ... **C 6**
25 Odell .... **J 1**
64 Odie .... **B 4**
9 Odiham .... **A 9**
8 Odstock .... **C 3**
23 Odstone .... **A 7**
23 Offchurch .... **F 7**
22 Offenham .... **G 4**
45 Offerton .... **G 11**
10 Offham, E. Sussex .. **G 3**
10 Offham, Kent ...... **B 5**
25 Offord Cluny ...... **J 3**
25 Offord D'Arcy ..... **J 3**
27 Offton .... **K 4**
6 Offwell .... **F 5**
16 Ogbourne Maizey .. **G 3**
16 Ogbourne St. Andrew **G 3**
16 Ogbourne St. George **G 3**
45 Ogle .... **E 9**
14 Ogmore .... **G 2**
14 Ogmore-by-Sea .... **G 2**
14 Ogmore Vale ...... **E 3**
7 Okeford Fitzpaine . **E 11**
4 Okehampton .... **F 5**
59 Old Aberdeen ..... **G 7**
9 Old Alredford ..... **C 7**
53 Old Balkello ...... **C 8**
45 Old Berwick ...... **A 9**
52 Old Blair .... **A 4**
33 Old Bolingbroke .. **D 10**
35 Old Bramhope .... **C 11**
31 Old Brampton .... **C 11**
43 Old Bridge of Urr .. **E 8**
26 Old Buckenham .... **F 4**
16 Old Burghclere .... **H 6**
40 Old Byland .... **G 6**
37 Old Clee .... **F 10**
6 Old Cleeve .... **B 4**
43 Old Clouden ...... **D 9**
29 Old Colwyn .... **B 8**
43 Old Craighouse ... **C 12**
42 Old Dailly .... **B 3**
32 Old Dalby .... **H 4**
58 Old Deer .... **C 7**
60 Old Drumrunie Lo. .. **F 3**
49 Old Dryburn ...... **E 12**
36 Old Edlington ..... **G 3**
40 Old Eldon .... **B 3**
37 Old Ellerby .... **C 9**
24 Old Fletton .... **F 3**
36 Old Goole .... **E 5**
44 Old Graitney ...... **F 2**
37 Old Hall .... **E 10**
19 Old Heath .... **B 10**
10 Old Heathfield .... **F 5**
25 Old Hurst .... **H 4**
39 Old Hutton .... **F 8**
2 Old Kea .... **E 5**
47 Old Kilpatrick ..... **B 9**
18 Old Knebworth .... **B 2**
26 Old Lakenham ..... **E 5**
38 Old Laxey .... **G 2**
33 Old Leake .... **E 11**
45 Old Lyham ...... **C 12**
41 Old Malton .... **H 8**
36 Old Micklefield .... **D 2**
8 Old Milton .... **G 4**
22 Old Milverton ..... **E 6**
47 Old Monkland .... **C 12**
19 Old Montsale .... **D 10**
45 Old Mousen ..... **C 12**
8 Old Netley .... **E 6**
27 Old Newton .... **J 4**
43 Old Orchardton .... **F 9**
48 Old Philpstoun .... **B 3**
40 Old Quarrington ... **A 3**
32 Old Radford .... **F 3**
21 Old Radnor .... **F 8**
58 Old Rattray .... **B 8**
58 Old Rayne .... **E 4**
11 Old Romney .... **E 9**
52 Old Scone .... **D 6**
36 Old Snydale .... **E 2**
15 Old Sodbury ...... **F 10**
33 Old Somerby ...... **G 7**
23 Old Stratford .... **H 11**
30 Old Swan .... **A 3**
39 Old Tebay .... **E 8**
40 Old Thirsk .... **G 4**
39 Old Town, Cumb. .. **A 7**
39 Old Town, Cumbria . **G 8**
2 Old Town, Is. of Scilly .... **D 2**
45 Old Town, Northumb. .... **D 7**
35 Old Trafford ...... **G 7**
32 Old Tupton .... **D 1**
25 Old Warden ...... **L 2**
25 Old Weston ...... **H 2**
17 Old Windsor ..... **G 10**
11 Old Wives Lees .... **C 9**
17 Old Woking ...... **H 11**
60 Oldany .... **D 3**
22 Oldberrow .... **F 5**
4 Oldborough .... **E 6**
21 Oldbury, Salop .. **C 12**
22 Oldbury, War. ..... **C 6**
22 Oldbury, W. Midlands **C 3**
15 Oldbury on the Hill **E 11**
15 Oldbury-upon-Severn **E 9**
14 Oldcastle, Gwent ... **B 6**
14 Oldbury, Mid Glam. . **F 2**
32 Oldcotes .... **A 3**
22 Oldfield, Heref. & Worc. .... **F 2**
35 Oldfield, W. Yorks. . **C 8**
7 Oldford .... **A 11**
35 Oldham .... **G 8**
49 Oldhamstocks ..... **B 10**
15 Oldland .... **G 10**
58 Oldmeldrum ...... **E 6**
58 Oldnoth .... **D 3**
21 Oldpark .... **A 12**
60 Oldshore Beg ...... **B 3**
60 Oldshore More ..... **B 3**
40 Oldstead .... **G 5**
58 Oldtown of Ord .... **B 4**
14 Oldway .... **H 9**
4 Oldways End .... **D 7**
58 Oldwhat .... **C 6**
48 Oliver .... **G 4**
8 Oliver's Battery .... **C 6**
64 Ollaberry .... **C 7**
30 Ollerton, Ches. ..... **C 6**
32 Ollerton, Notts. .... **C 4**
30 Ollerton, Salop .... **H 5**
20 Olmarch .... **G 2**
23 Olney .... **G 12**
22 Olton .... **D 5**
15 Olveston .... **F 9**
22 Ombersley .... **F 2**
32 Ompton .... **D 4**
38 Onchan .... **H 2**
31 Onecote .... **E 9**
15 Onen .... **C 7**
18 Ongar .... **D 5**
24 Onger Hill .... **C 7**
21 Onibury .... **D 10**
51 Onich .... **A 7**
14 Onllwyn .... **C 2**
30 Onneley .... **F 6**
9 Onslow Village .... **A 11**
47 Onthank .... **E 9**
35 Openshaw .... **G 7**
32 Openwoodgate ..... **E 1**
54 Opinan, Highland ... **C 1**
60 Opinan, Highland .. **G 1**
49 Orange Lane ..... **E 10**
62 Orbost .... **D 2**
33 Orby .... **C 12**
46 Orcadia .... **C 6**
4 Orchard Hill .... **C 3**
6 Orchard Portman ... **D 6**
8 Orcheston .... **B 2**
15 Orcop .... **B 8**
15 Orcop Hill .... **A 8**
62 Ord .... **G 5**
58 Ordens .... **B 4**
58 Ordhead .... **F 4**
59 Ordie .... **G 2**
58 Ordiequish .... **B 1**
32 Ordsall .... **B 4**
11 Ore .... **G 7**
30 Orford, Cheshire ... **A 5**
21 Oreton, Salop .... **D 12**
27 Orford, Suffolk .... **K 7**
8 Organ Ford .... **G 1**
64 Orgill .... **D 1**
22 Orgreave .... **A 5**
64 Orkney, Co. .... **C 2**
11 Orlestone .... **E 8**
21 Orleton, Heref. & Worc. .... **F 10**
21 Orleton, Heref. & Worc. .... **F 12**
23 Orlingbury .... **E 12**
40 Ormesby .... **C 5**
26 Ormesby St. Margaret **D 8**
26 Ormesby St. Michael **D 8**
60 Ormiscaig .... **G 1**
49 Ormiston .... **B 7**
38 Ormely Hall .... **F 2**
50 Ormsaigbeg .... **A 2**
50 Ormsaigmore ...... **A 2**
46 Ormsary House .... **B 2**
34 Ormskirk .... **F 3**
63 Orosay .... **F 5**
64 Orphir .... **D 2**
18 Orpington .... **G 5**
34 Orrell, Merseyside .. **G 2**
34 Orrell, Manchester . **G 4**
34 Orrell Post .... **G 4**
53 Orrock .... **H 7**
43 Orroland .... **G 8**
18 Orsett .... **F 6**
18 Orsett Heath ...... **F 6**
22 Orslow .... **A 2**
32 Orston .... **F 5**
38 Orthwaite .... **B 5**
39 Orton, Cumbria ... **D 8**
23 Orton, Northants. . **D 11**
24 Orton Longueville .. **F 3**
22 Orton on the Hill ... **B 6**
58 Orton Station ...... **B 1**
24 Orton Waterville .... **F 3**
25 Orwell .... **K 5**
34 Osbaldeston ...... **D 5**
36 Osbaldwick .... **B 4**
23 Osbaston .... **B 7**
24 Osbournby .... **B 2**
30 Oscroft .... **D 4**
62 Osdale .... **D 3**
62 Ose .... **D 2**
32 Osgathorpe .... **H 2**
33 Osgodby, Lincs. .... **A 8**
36 Osgodby, N. Yorks. . **D 4**
41 Osgodby, N. Yorks. **G 10**
62 Oskaig .... **D 5**
50 Oskamuil .... **D 2**
31 Osmaston .... **F 10**
7 Osmington .... **H 10**
7 Osmington Mills .. **H 10**
35 Osmondthorpe .... **D 12**
40 Osmotherley ...... **E 5**
11 Ospringe .... **B 8**
35 Ossett .... **E 11**
32 Ossington .... **D 5**
19 Ostend .... **D 9**
40 Oswaldkirk .... **G 6**
34 Oswaldtwistle ..... **D 6**
30 Oswestry .... **G 2**
10 Otford .... **B 4**
11 Otham .... **C 7**
7 Othery .... **C 7**
27 Otley, Suffolk ...... **K 5**
35 Otley, W. Yorks. .. **C 10**
46 Otter Ferry .... **A 4**
8 Otterbourne .... **D 6**
45 Otterburn, Northumb. **D 7**
35 Otterburn, N. Yorks. **A 7**
45 Otterburn Camp .... **C 7**
2 Otterham .... **B 2**
6 Otterhampton ..... **B 6**
17 Ottershaw .... **H 11**
64 Otterswick .... **B 7**
6 Otterton .... **H 4**
6 Ottery St. Mary .... **G 5**
11 Ottinge .... **D 10**
37 Ottingham .... **E 10**
39 Oughtershaw ..... **G 11**
43 Oughterside ..... **H 12**
35 Oughtibridge ..... **H 11**
40 Oulston .... **H 6**
44 Oulton, Cumb. ..... **H 1**
26 Oulton, Norfolk .... **C 4**
31 Oulton, Staffs. ..... **G 7**
26 Oulton, Suffolk .... **F 8**
35 Oulton, W. Yorks. . **D 12**
26 Oulton Broad ...... **F 8**
26 Oulton Street ...... **C 5**
25 Oundle .... **G 1**
39 Ousby .... **B 8**
61 Ousdale .... **E 10**
25 Ousden .... **J 8**
36 Ousefleet .... **E 6**
45 Ouston, Dur. ...... **H 10**
45 Ouston, Northumb. . **F 9**
44 Ouston, Northumb. . **H 6**
38 Out Gate .... **E 6**
37 Out Newton ...... **E 11**
34 Out Rawcliffe ..... **C 3**
45 Outchester ...... **C 12**
64 Outertown .... **D 1**
39 Outhgill .... **E 10**
35 Outlane .... **E 9**
24 Outwell .... **E 6**
8 Outwick .... **D 3**
10 Outwood, Surrey ... **D 2**
35 Outwood, W. Yorks. **E 12**
35 Ovenden .... **D 9**
49 Ovenscloss .... **F 7**
25 Over, Cambs. ...... **H 5**
30 Over, Cheshire ..... **D 5**
15 Over, Glos. .... **F 9**
43 Over Cleuchbrae .. **B 11**
7 Over Compton ..... **E 9**
48 Over Dalgleish .... **H 5**
31 Over Haddon ..... **D 10**
43 Over Hazlefield .... **G 8**
39 Over Kellet .... **H 7**
16 Over Kiddlington .. **B 5**
16 Over Norton ...... **A 4**
40 Over Silton .... **F 5**
6 Over Stowey ...... **B 5**
7 Over Stratton ..... **E 8**
30 Over Tabley .... **B 6**
8 Over Wallop ...... **B 4**
22 Over Whitacre ..... **C 6**
49 Over Whitton .... **G 10**
32 Over Woodhouse ... **C 2**
64 Overbister .... **B 4**
22 Overbury .... **H 3**
58 Overhall .... **C 5**
58 Overhill .... **D 4**
7 Overleigh .... **C 8**
22 Overley Green ..... **F 4**
30 Overpool .... **C 3**
22 Overseal .... **A 6**
58 Overside .... **B 8**
11 Oversland .... **B 9**
23 Overstone .... **E 11**
26 Overstrand .... **B 5**
23 Overthorpe .... **H 8**
30 Overton, Ches. ..... **C 4**
30 Overton, Clwyd .... **F 2**
43 Overton, Dumf. & Gall. .... **E 10**
58 Overton, Grampian . **F 6**
8 Overton, Hants. .... **A 6**
34 Overton, Lancs. .... **A 3**
36 Overton, N. Yorks. . **B 3**
21 Overton, Salop .... **E 10**
47 Overton, Strathclyde **D 8**
48 Overton, Strathclyde **D 1**
13 Overton, W. Glam. . **H 8**
29 Overton Bridge .... **F 12**
30 Overton Green ..... **D 6**
58 Overtown, Grampian **D 7**
48 Overtown, Strathclyde **D 1**
39 Overtown, Lancs. ... **H 8**
16 Overtown, Wilts. .... **F 3**
58 Overtown of Memsie **B 7**
26 Overy Staithe ...... **A 1**
17 Oving, Bucks. ...... **B 8**
9 Oving, W. Sussex .. **F 10**
10 Ovingdean .... **H 2**
45 Ovingham .... **G 9**
40 Ovington, Durham .. **D 2**
27 Ovington, Essex .... **L 1**
9 Ovington, Hants. ... **C 7**
26 Ovington, Norfolk .. **E 2**
45 Ovington, Northumb. **G 9**
8 Ower .... **D 5**
7 Owermoigne ..... **H 11**
31 Owler Bar .... **B 11**
32 Owlerton .... **A 1**
17 Owlswick .... **C 8**
33 Owmby, Lincs. ..... **A 7**
37 Owmby, Lincs. ..... **G 8**
8 Owslebury .... **D 6**
23 Owston, Leics. .... **A 11**
36 Owston, S. Yorks. ... **F 3**
36 Owston Ferry ...... **G 6**
37 Owstwick .... **D 10**
32 Owthorpe .... **G 4**
24 Oxborough .... **E 8**
38 Oxen Park .... **F 5**
39 Oxenholme .... **F 8**
35 Oxenhope .... **D 9**
49 Oxenrig .... **E 11**
16 Oxenton .... **A 1**
16 Oxenwood .... **H 4**
16 Oxford .... **D 6**
4 Oxford Cross ...... **B 3**
16 Oxfordshire, Co. .... **C 5**
18 Oxhey .... **D 1**
22 Oxhill .... **G 6**
22 Oxley .... **B 2**
19 Oxley Green .... **C 9**
49 Oxnam .... **G 9**
17 Oxshott .... **H 12**
35 Oxspring .... **G 11**
10 Oxted .... **C 3**
49 Oxton, Borders .... **D 7**
32 Oxton, Notts. ...... **E 3**
36 Oxton, N. Yorks. ... **C 3**
13 Oxwich .... **H 8**
13 Oxwich Green ..... **H 8**
60 Oykel Bridge ...... **G 5**
58 Oyne .... **E 4**
13 Oystermouth ...... **H 9**
7 Packers Hill ...... **E 10**
23 Packington .... **A 7**
22 Packington Park .... **D 5**
53 Padanaram .... **B 9**
17 Padbury .... **A 8**
18 Paddington .... **F 3**
11 Paddlesworth .... **D 10**
10 Paddock Wood ..... **D 5**
56 Paddockhaugh ..... **D 8**
44 Paddockhole ...... **E 1**
30 Paddolgreen ...... **G 4**
35 Padfield .... **G 9**
30 Padgate .... **A 5**
35 Padiham .... **D 7**
29 Padog .... **E 8**
35 Padside .... **A 10**
2 Padstow .... **B 6**
17 Padworth .... **G 7**
40 Page Bank .... **B 3**
9 Pagham .... **F 10**
19 Paglesham .... **E 9**
63 Paible .... **G 1**

5 Paignton **K 8**
23 Pailton **D 8**
21 Painscastle **H 7**
45 Painshawfield **G 9**
15 Painswick **C 12**
11 Painter's Forstal **B 8**
47 Paisley **C 9**
58 Paithnick **B 2**
26 Pakefield **F 8**
27 Pakenham **J 2**
29 Pale **G 9**
10 Palehouse Com. **F 4**
8 Palestine **B 4**
17 Paley Street **G 9**
42 Palgowan **C 5**
27 Palgrave **G 4**
11 Palmarsh **E 10**
18 Palmers Green **E 3**
43 Palnackie **F 9**
42 Palnure **E 5**
32 Palterton **C 2**
17 Pamber End **H 7**
17 Pamber Green **H 7**
17 Pamber Heath **H 7**
8 Pamphill **F 1**
25 Pampisford **K 6**
7 Panborough **B 8**
53 Panbride **D 10**
4 Pancrasweek **E 2**
29 Pandy, Clwyd **G 11**
15 Pandy, Gwent **B 7**
20 Pandy, Gwynedd **B 2**
20 Pandy, Powys **B 5**
29 Pandy Tudor **D 8**
19 Panfield **A 7**
17 Pangbourne **F 7**
43 Panlands **C 11**
35 Pannal **B 11**
59 Pannancih **H 1**
30 Pant **H 1**
20 Pant Mawr **D 4**
28 Pant-glas, Gwynedd **E 4**
21 Pantglas, Salop **C 8**
13 Pantgwyn, Dyfed **D 9**
12 Pantgwyn, Dyfed **B 6**
13 Pant-lasau **G 10**
33 Panton **B 9**
20 Pant-perthog **B 3**
20 Pant-y-dwr **E 5**
21 Pant-y-ffrid **B 7**
13 Pantyffynnon **F 9**
14 Pantygasseg **D 5**
15 Pant y Goitre **C 7**
12 Pantymenyn **D 5**
29 Pantymwyn **D 11**
14 Pant-yr-awel **E 3**
26 Panxworth **D 6**
38 Papcastle **B 3**
49 Papple **B 8**
32 Papplewick **E 3**
25 Papworth Everard **J 4**
25 Papworth St. Agnes **J 4**
3 Par **D 8**
7 Parbrook **C 9**
29 Parc **G 8**
12 Parc-llyn **B 6**
38 Pardshaw **C 3**
27 Parham **J 6**
43 Park, Dumf. & Gall. **B 10**
59 Park, Grampian **G 5**
50 Park, Strathclyde **C 6**
17 Park Corner, Berks. **F 9**
10 Park Corner, E. Sussex **D 4**
17 Park Corner, Oxon **E 8**
40 Park End, Cleveland **C 5**
45 Park End, Northumb. **E 7**
9 Park Gate **E 7**
44 Park Nook **F 4**
58 Parkdargue **C 4**
38 Parkend, Cumb. **A 5**
15 Parkend, Glos. **D 9**
27 Parkeston **M 5**
3 Parkfield **C 10**
30 Parkgate, Ches. **B 1**
43 Parkgate, Dumf. & Gall. **C 11**
10 Parkgate, Surrey **D 1**
48 Parkgatestone **F 4**
4 Parkham **D 3**
4 Parkham Ash **D 2**
56 Parkhead **F 8**
58 Parkhill House **F 6**
15 Parkhouse **D 8**
8 Parkhurst **G 6**
13 Parkmill **H 9**
59 Parkneuk **K 5**
30 Parkside **E 3**
8 Parkstone **G 2**
8 Parley Cross **F 2**
4 Parracombe **B 5**
30 Parrah Green **F 6**
12 Parrog **C 4**
24 Parson Drove **E 5**
19 Parson's Heath **A 10**
47 Partick **C 10**
34 Partington **H 6**
33 Partney **C 11**
38 Parton, Cumb. **C 2**
43 Parton, Dumf. & Gall. **E 8**
15 Parton, Glos. **B 12**
10 Partridge Green **F 1**
31 Parwich **E 10**
23 Passenham **H 11**
9 Passfield **C 9**
26 Paston Street **B 6**
4 Patchacott **F 3**
10 Patcham **G 2**
9 Patching **E 12**
4 Patchole **B 5**
15 Patchway **F 9**
35 Pateley Bridge **A 10**
19 Paternoster Heath **B 9**
52 Path of Condie **F 5**
7 Pathe **C 7**
53 Pathead, Fife **H 8**
48 Pathead, Lothian **C 6**
47 Pathhead **H 11**
52 Pathstruie **F 5**
47 Patna **H 9**
16 Patney **H 2**
38 Patrick **G 1**
40 Patrick Brompton **F 2**
34 Patricroft **G 6**
37 Patrington **E 10**
11 Patrixbourne **C 10**
38 Patterdale **D 6**
44 Pattieshill **F 3**
22 Pattingham **B 2**
23 Pattishall **G 10**
19 Pattiswick Green **B 8**
2 Paul **G 2**
23 Paulerspury **G 10**
37 Paull **E 9**
7 Paulton **A 10**
45 Pauperhaugh **C 9**
25 Pavenham **K 1**
6 Pawlett **B 6**
49 Pawston **F 11**
22 Paxford **H 5**
49 Paxton **D 12**
6 Payhembury **F 4**
35 Paythorne **B 7**
10 Peacehaven **H 3**
22 Peachley **F 2**
31 Peak Dale **C 9**
31 Peak Forest **B 9**
58 Peaknowe **B 4**
55 Peanmeanach **L 1**
59 Pearsie **L 1**
10 Pearsons Green **D 6**
10 Pease Pottage **E 1**
7 Peasedown St. John **A 10**
16 Peasemore **F 5**
27 Peasenhall **H 7**
9 Peaslake **B 12**
34 Peasley Cross **H 4**
11 Peasmarsh **F 7**
49 Peaston Bank **C 7**
53 Peat Inn **F 9**
58 Peathill **A 7**
23 Peatling Magna **C 9**
23 Peatling Parva **C 9**
21 Peaton **D 10**
27 Pebmarsh **M 2**
22 Pebworth **G 5**
35 Peckett Well **D 8**
30 Peckforton **E 4**
18 Peckham **F 3**
23 Peckleton **B 8**
44 Pedderhill **F 3**
17 Pedlinge **E 10**
22 Pedmore **D 3**
7 Pedwell **C 8**
48 Peebles **E 5**
38 Peel **G 1**
9 Peel Common **F 7**
25 Pegsdon **M 2**
45 Pegswood **D 10**
62 Peinaha **B 4**
62 Peinchorran **E 4**
62 Peinlick **B 3**
62 Peinmore **C 4**
12 Pelcomb Cross **E 3**
19 Peldon **B 9**
22 Pelsall **B 4**
45 Pelton **H 10**
45 Pelton Fell **H 10**
43 Pelutho **G 12**
3 Pelynt **D 9**
13 Pemberton, Dyfed **G 8**
34 Pemberton, Manchester **G 4**
13 Pembrey **G 7**
21 Pembridge **G 9**
12 Pembroke **G 3**
12 Pembroke Dock **G 3**
10 Pembury **D 5**
13 Pen Rhiwfawr **F 10**
13 Pen-Sarn **E 7**
15 Penalt **C 8**
12 Penally **G 5**
15 Penalt **A 9**
3 Penare **F 7**
14 Penarth **G 5**
20 Pen-bont-rhyd-y-beddau **D 2**
12 Penbryn **B 6**
13 Pencader **C 8**
13 Pen-cae **A 7**
28 Pencaenewydd **F 3**
28 Pencarnisiog **C 3**
13 Pencarreg **C 8**
14 Pencelli **B 4**
13 Penclawdd **G 9**
15 Pencoed, Heref. & Worc. **B 8**
14 Pencoed, Mid Glam. **F 3**
21 Pencombe **G 11**
15 Pencraig, Heref. & Worc. **B 9**
29 Pencraig, Powys **G 9**
2 Pendeen **F 1**
14 Penderyn **C 3**
12 Pendine **F 6**
34 Pendlebury **G 6**
34 Pendleton, Lancs. **C 6**
35 Pendleton, Manchester **G 7**
15 Pendock **A 11**
3 Pendoggett **B 7**
7 Pendomer **E 8**
14 Pendoylan **G 4**
14 Pendre **F 2**
20 Penegoes **B 3**
12 Penfeidir **D 2**
13 Pen-ffordd, Dyfed **C 8**
12 Pen-ffordd, Dyfed **E 4**
14 Pengam **D 5**
18 Penge **G 3**
3 Pengelly **A 8**
14 Pengenffordd **A 5**
3 Pengover Green **C 10**
14 Pen-groes oped **D 6**
2 Penhale **H 4**
2 Penhalurick **F 4**
16 Penhill **E 2**
15 Penhow **E 7**
10 Penhurst **F 6**
20 Peniarth **B 2**
48 Penicuik **C 5**
13 Peniel **E 8**
62 Penifiler **D 4**
46 Peninver **G 4**
28 Penisar-waum **D 5**
35 Penistone **G 11**
30 Penketh **A 4**
42 Penkill **B 3**
42 Penkiln **G 6**
22 Penkridge **A 3**
30 Penley **F 3**
13 Penllergaer **G 9**
28 Pen-llyn, Gwynedd **B 3**
14 Penllyn, S. Glam. **G 3**
29 Penmachno **E 7**
13 Penmaen **H 8**
28 Penmaenen **C 6**
28 Penmaenmawr **C 6**
28 Penmaenpool **H 6**
29 Penmaenrhos **B 8**
14 Penmark **G 4**
28 Penmon **B 6**
50 Penmore Mill **B 1**
28 Penmorfa **F 5**
28 Penmynydd **C 4**
17 Penn **E 10**
17 Penn Street **E 10**
20 Pennal **B 3**
58 Pennan **A 6**
29 Pennant, Clwyd **G 9**
13 Pennant, Dyfed **A 8**
29 Pennant, Gwynedd **D 7**
20 Pennant, Powys **C 4**
29 Pennant-Melangell **H 9**
13 Pennard **H 9**
21 Pennerley **C 9**
38 Pennington, Cumb. **G 5**
8 Pennington, Hants. **G 4**
14 Pennorth **B 4**
15 Pennsylvania Vil. **E 8**
38 Penny Bridge **G 5**
24 Penny Hill **C 5**
50 Pennyghael **E 3**
47 Pennyglen **H 7**
50 Pennygown **C 3**
4 Pennymoor **E 7**
45 Pennywell **G 11**
12 Penparc, Dyfed **B 5**
12 Penparc, Dyfed **D 2**
20 Penparcau **D 2**
14 Penpelleni **D 6**
3 Penpillick **D 8**
3 Penpoint **B 8**
2 Penpol **F 5**
43 Penpont, Dumf. & Gall. **B 9**
14 Penpont, Powys **A 3**
12 Penrherber **C 6**
12 Penrhiw **C 6**
14 Penrhiwceiber **E 4**
13 Penrhiw-goch **E 9**
13 Pen-rhiw-llan **C 7**
13 Penrhiwpal **B 7**
15 Penrhos, Gwent **C 7**
28 Penrhos, Gwynedd **G 3**
14 Penrhos, Powys **C 1**
28 Penrhos,garnedd **C 5**
28 Penrhyn **A 3**
29 Penrhyn Bay **B 7**
20 Penrhyn-coch **D 2**
28 Penrhyndeudraeth **F 5**
29 Penrhynside **B 7**
13 Penrice **H 8**
12 Penrieth **C 6**
39 Penrith **B 7**
2 Penrose **C 6**
38 Penruddock **B 6**
2 Penryn **F 5**
29 Pensarn **B 9**
22 Pensax **E 1**
30 Pensby **B 1**
7 Penselwood **C 10**
15 Pensford **H 9**
45 Penshaw **H 11**
10 Penshurst **D 4**
3 Pensilva **C 10**
49 Penston **B 7**
3 Pentewan **E 7**
28 Pentir **D 5**
2 Pentire **D 5**
2 Pentireg **B 6**
12 Pentlepoir **F 5**
27 Pentlow **L 1**
24 Pentney **D 8**
8 Penton Mewsey **A 5**
28 Pentraeth **B 5**
29 Pentre, Clwyd **D 10**
29 Pentre, Clwyd **F 12**
14 Pentre, Mid Glam. **E 3**
21 Pentre, Powys **B 8**
21 Pentre, Powys **C 8**
20 Pentre, Powys **D 6**
21 Pentre, Salop **A 9**
29 Pentre Bagillt **C 11**
28 Pentre Berw **C 4**
20 Pentre Dolau-Honddu **H 5**
13 Pentre Gwenlais **E 9**
28 Pentre Gwyffryn **G 5**
29 Pentre Halkyn **C 11**
29 Pentre-Isaf **C 8**
14 Pentre Meyrick **G 3**
29 Pentre-bach, Clwyd **G 10**
13 Pentrebach, Dyfed **B 9**
14 Pentrebâch, Mid Glam. **D 4**
14 Pentre-bach, Powys **A 2**
13 Pentrebach, W. Glam. **F 9**
21 Pentrebeirdd **A 7**
29 Pentre-bont **E 7**
13 Pentre-cagal **C 7**
29 Pentre-celyn **E 10**
13 Pentre-cwrt **C 7**
29 Pentre-dwfr **F 11**
13 Pentre-dwr **G 10**
13 Pentrefelin, Dyfed **E 9**
28 Pentrefelin, Gwynedd **A 4**
29 Pentrefoelas **E 8**
12 Pentre-galar **D 5**
13 Pentregat **B 7**
20 Pentre-llwyn-llwyd **G 5**
14 Pentre-poeth **F 6**
13 Pentre'r-felin, Dyfed **B 9**
28 Pentre'r felin, Gwynedd **F 5**
14 Pentrer-felin, Powys **A 3**
29 Pentre-tafarn-y-fedw **D 7**
13 Pentre-ty-gwyn **C 11**
29 Pentre-uchaf **C 10**
32 Pentrich **E 1**
8 Pentridge **D 2**
15 Pen-twyn, Gwent **C 8**
14 Pentwyn, Mid Glam. **D 4**
14 Pentyrch **F 4**
14 Penuchadre **G 2**
20 Penuwch **F 2**
3 Penwithick Stents **D 7**
16 Penwood **H 5**
14 Penwylit **C 2**
13 Pen-y-banc, Dyfed **E 9**
13 Pen-y-banc, Dyfed **F 9**
21 Penybont, Powys **F 7**
29 Pen-y-bont, Clwyd **H 11**
29 Pen-y-bont-fawr **H 10**
12 Pen-y-bryn **C 5**
29 Pen-y-cae, Clwyd **F 12**
14 Peb-y-cae, Powys **C 2**
15 Pen-y-cae-mawr **E 7**
15 Pen-y-clwdd **D 7**
14 Pen-y-coedcae **F 4**
12 Pen-y-cwm **E 2**
14 Pen-y-fai **F 2**
29 Penyffordd **D 12**
29 Pen-y-garnedd **H 10**
14 Pen-y-graig **E 3**
13 Pen-y-groes, Dyfed **F 9**
12 Penygroes, Dyfed **C 5**
28 Penygroes, Gwynedd **E 4**
14 Pen-y-groes, S. Glam. **F 5**
28 Pen-y-groeslon **G 2**
28 Pen-y-Gwyrd **E 6**
14 Penyrheol **E 5**
14 Pen-yr-Heolgerrig **D 4**
14 Penyrynys **B 2**
28 Penysarn **A 4**
29 Pen-y-stryt **E 11**
14 Penywaun **D 3**
2 Penzance **G 2**
22 Peopleton **G 3**
30 Peover Heath **C 6**
30 Peover Superior **C 6**
9 Peper Harow **B 10**
30 Peplow **H 5**
17 Peppard Common **F 8**
45 Peppermoor **B 10**
47 Perceton **E 8**
59 Percie **H 3**
58 Percyhorner **A 7**
45 Perkinsville **H 10**
32 Perlethorpe **C 4**
2 Perranarworthal **F 5**
2 Perranporth **D 5**
2 Perranuthnoe **G 3**
2 Perranwell **F 5**
2 Perranwell Station **F 5**
2 Perranzabuloe **D 5**
25 Perry **J 2**
22 Perry Barr **C 4**
18 Perry Green **B 4**
10 Perry Street **A 5**
22 Pershore **G 3**
59 Pert **L 4**
25 Pertenhall **J 2**
52 Perth **E 6**
22 Perton **B 2**
7 Pertwood **C 12**
5 Peter Tavy **H 4**
24 Peterborough **F 3**
54 Peterburn **B 1**
21 Peterchurch **H 9**
59 Petercutter **G 6**
58 Peterhead **C 8**
40 Peterlee **A 4**
18 Peter's Green **B 2**
4 Peters Marland **E 3**
9 Petersfield **D 9**
14 Peterstone Wentlooge **F 6**
14 Peterston-super-Ely **G 4**
15 Peterstow **B 9**
4 Petrockstow **E 4**
11 Pett **G 7**
27 Pettaugh **J 5**
53 Petterden **C 9**
48 Pettinain **E 2**
27 Pettistree **K 6**
6 Petton, Devon **D 4**
30 Petton, Salop **G 3**
18 Petts Wood **G 4**
58 Petty **D 5**
48 Pettycur **A 5**
58 Pettymuck **E 6**
9 Petworth **D 11**
10 Pevensey **H 5**
10 Pevensey Bay **H 5**
16 Pewsey **H 3**
17 Pheasants **E 9**
17 Pheasant's Hill **E 9**
4 Philham **D 1**
49 Philiphaugh **G 7**
2 Phillack **F 3**
2 Philleigh **F 6**
48 Phil-stoun **B 3**
15 Phocle Green **B 9**
17 Phoenix Green **H 8**
57 Phoines **K 3**
38 Phurt **F 2**
38 Pica **C 3**
17 Piccott's End **C 11**
36 Pickburn **F 3**
41 Pickering **G 8**
8 Picket Piece **A 5**
8 Picket Post **E 3**
40 Pickhill **G 4**
21 Picklescott **B 10**
53 Pickletillem **E 9**
30 Pickmere **C 5**
6 Pickney **C 5**
4 Pickwell, Devon **B 3**
23 Pickwell, Leics. **A 11**
24 Pickworth, Lincs. **B 1**
24 Pickworth, Leics. **D 1**
30 Picton, Cheshire **C 3**
40 Picton, N. Yorks. **D 4**
10 Piddinghoe **H 3**
17 Piddington, Bucks. **E 9**
23 Piddington, Northants. **G 11**
17 Piddington, Oxon **B 7**
7 Piddlehinton **F 10**
7 Piddletrenhide **F 10**
25 Pidley **H 4**
40 Piercebridge **D 2**
62 Pierowall **A 2**
45 Pigdon **D 9**
31 Pikehall **D 10**
18 Pilgrims Hatch **D 6**
32 Pilham **A 6**
15 Pill **G 8**
3 Pillaton **C 10**
22 Pillerton Hersey **G 6**
22 Pillerton Priors **G 6**
21 Pilleth **F 8**
8 Pilley, Hants. **F 5**
35 Pilley, S. Yorks. **G 12**
14 Pillgwenlly **F 6**
4 Pillhead **C 3**
34 Pilling **B 3**
34 Pilling Lane **B 3**
15 Pillowell **D 9**
7 Pillwell **D 11**
44 Pilmuir, Borders **B 3**
59 Pilmuir, Grampian **H 5**
31 Pilsbury **D 9**
7 Pilsdon **F 7**
31 Pilsley, Derby **C 11**
32 Pilsley, Derby **D 2**
25 Pilton, Northants. **G 1**
23 Pilton, Leics. **B 12**
7 Pilton, Somerset **B 9**
13 Pilton Green **H 8**
7 Pimperne **E 12**
24 Pinchbeck **C 3**
24 Pinchbeck Bars **C 3**
24 Pinchbeck West **C 3**
42 Pinclanty **C 3**
34 Pinfold **F 3**
6 Pinhoe **G 3**
17 Pinkneys Green **F 9**
22 Pinley Green **E 5**
42 Pinminnoch **B 3**
42 Pinmoee **B 3**
42 Pinmore Mains **C 3**
6 Pinn **G 4**
18 Pinner **E 1**
22 Pinvin **G 3**
42 Pinwherry **C 3**
32 Pinxton **E 2**
21 Pipe and Lyde **H 10**
30 Pipe Gate **F 6**
22 Pipehill **A 4**
56 Piperhill **E 4**
3 Pipers Pool **A 9**
23 Pipewell **D 11**
4 Pippacott **B 4**
14 Pipton **A 5**
17 Pirbright **H 10**
49 Pirnie **G 9**
46 Pirnmill **E 4**
22 Pirton, Heref. & Worc. **G 2**
18 Pirton, Herts. **A 2**
17 Pishill **E 8**
28 Pistyll **F 3**
52 Pitagowan **A 3**
58 Pitblae **A 7**
53 Pitcairlie Farm **F 7**
52 Pitcairn **B 4**
52 Pitcairngreen **D 5**
58 Pitcaple **E 5**
53 Pitcarity **A 8**
17 Pitch Green **D 8**
9 Pitch Place **A 11**
15 Pitchcombe **D 11**
17 Pitchcott **B 8**
21 Pitchford **B 10**
7 Pitcombe **C 10**
53 Pitcorthie **F 10**
49 Pitcox **B 9**
59 Pitdrichie **J 5**

58 Pitfichie F 4
53 Pitfour Castle E 7
53 Pitkevy G 7
53 Pitlessie F 8
52 Pitlochry A 4
58 Pitmachie E 4
57 Pitmain J 3
58 Pitmedden E 6
6 Pitminster D 5
53 Pitmuies B 10
58 Pitmunie F 4
7 Pitney C 8
53 Pitroddie E 7
53 Pitscottie F 9
19 Pitsea E 7
23 Pitsford E 11
17 Pitstone C 10
17 Pitstone Green C 10
59 Pittarrow K 5
56 Pittendreich D 7
61 Pittenraill F 7
53 Pittenweem G 10
40 Pittington A 3
58 Pittodrie E 4
8 Pitton C 4
10 Pittswood C 5
58 Pittulie A 7
40 Pity Me, Durham A 3
45 Pity Me, Northumb. E 7
27 Pixey Green H 5
10 Pixham C 1
21 Pixley H 12
58 Plaidy B 5
12 Plain Dealings E 4
48 Plains C 1
6 Plainsfield C 5
21 Plaish C 10
9 Plaistow C 11
10 Plaistow Street D 3
8 Plaitford D 4
20 Plas Llysyn C 5
29 Plas Newydd F 11
44 Plashetts D 5
16 Plastow Green H 6
29 Plas-yn-Cefn C 9
10 Platt B 5
34 Platt Bridge G 5
45 Plawsworth H 11
10 Plaxtol C 5
17 Play Hatch F 8
11 Playden F 8
27 Playford K 5
2 Playing Place E 5
15 Playley Green A 10
21 Plealey B 9
52 Plean H 3
53 Pleasance F 7
34 Pleasington E 5
32 Pleasley D 2
44 Plenmeller G 5
18 Pleshey B 6
45 Plessey Checks E 10
54 Plockton F 2
21 Ploughfield H 9
49 Ploughlands E 10
21 Plowden D 9
21 Ploxgreen B 9
11 Pluckley D 8
11 Pluckley Thorne D 8
43 Plumbland H 12
30 Plumley C 6
10 Plumpton G 2
39 Plumpton Foot A 7
10 Plumpton Green F 2
39 Plumpton Head B 7
39 Plumpton Wall B 7
26 Plumstead B 4
32 Plumtree G 3
32 Plungar B 5
7 Plush F 10
13 Plwmp B 7
5 Plymouth K 4
5 Plympton K 4
5 Plympton St. Maurice K 3
5 Plymstock K 4
6 Plymtree F 4
40 Pockley G 6
36 Pocklington B 6
24 Pode Hole C 3
7 Podimore D 9
23 Podington F 12
30 Podmore G 6
24 Pointon B 2
8 Pokesdown G 3
42 Polbae D 4
60 Polbain F 2
3 Polbathic D 10
48 Polbeth C 3
43 Poldean B 11
58 Poldullie Bridge F 1
35 Pole Moor E 9
25 Polebrook G 2
10 Polegate G 5
30 Polelane Ends B 5
22 Polesworth B 6
60 Polglass F 2
3 Polgooth E 7
9 Poling F 11
9 Poling Corner E 11
3 Polkerris D 8
60 Polla B 5
36 Pollington E 4
50 Polloch A 5
47 Pollockshaws C 10
47 Pollokshields C 10
43 Polmaddie C 7
54 Polmaily F 8
3 Polmassick E 7
47 Polmont B 2
48 Polmoody H 4
47 Polnessan H 9
55 Polnish L 1
9 Polperro E 9
3 Polruan E 8
7 Polsham B 8
43 Polskeoch A 8
27 Polstead L 3
6 Poltimore G 3
48 Polton C 5
49 Polwarth D 10
3 Polyphant B 9
3 Polzeath B 6
24 Pondersbridge F 4
9 Pondtail A 9
2 Ponsanooth F 5
5 Ponsworthy H 6
13 Pont-Antwn F 8
29 Pont Cyfyngf D 7
14 Pont Ebbw F 6
13 Pont Henry F 8
12 Pont Hirwaun C 6
20 Pont-Llogel A 6
28 Pont Pen-y-benglog D 6
20 Pont-Robert A 6
13 Pont Yates F 8
13 Pontamman F 9
14 Pont ar Hydfer B 2
13 Pontardawe G 10
13 Pontardulais G 9
13 Pontargothi E 8
13 Pont-ar-llechau E 10
13 Pont-ar-Sais D 8
29 Pontblyddyn D 12
14 Pontbren Llwyd D 3
36 Pontefract E 2
45 Ponteland F 10
20 Ponterwyd D 3
27 Pontesbury B 9
21 Pontesford B 9
29 Pontfadog F 11
12 Pontfaen, Dyfed D 4
14 Pont-faen, Powys A 3
13 Pontgarreg B 7
14 Pont-hir E 6
14 Pont-llan-fraith E 5
13 Pontlliw G 9
14 Pontlottyn D 4
28 Pont-lyfni E 4
14 Pontneddfechan D 2
14 Pontnewydd E 6
20 Pontrhydfendigaid F 3
13 Pont-rhyd-y-fen G 11
20 Pont-rhyd-y-groes E 3
14 Pontrhydyrun E 6
15 Pontrilas B 7
28 Pont-rug D 4
10 Ponts Green F 5
13 Pontshaen B 8
15 Pontshill B 9
14 Pontsticill C 4
13 Pont-tywely C 7
13 Pontyberem F 8
29 Pont-y-bodkin D 12
29 Pont y Clogwyn E 8
14 Pontyclun F 4
14 Pontycymer E 2
12 Pontyglazier C 5
14 Pont-y-gwaith E 3
29 Ponty-y-pant E 7
14 Pontypool D 6
14 Pontypool Road D 6
14 Pontypridd E 4
12 Pont-yr-hafod D 3
21 Pont-ysgawrhyd A 7
14 Pont-y-waun E 5
8 Pooksgreen E 5
2 Pool, Cornwall E 4
21 Pool Heref. & Worc. H 10
35 Pool, W. Yorks C 11
34 Pool Hay F 2
21 Pool Head G 11
52 Pool of Muckhart G 5
21 Pool Quay A 8
27 Pool Street L 1
8 Poole G 2
30 Poole Green E 5
16 Poole Keynes E 1
31 Poolend D 8
54 Poolewe B 2
39 Pooley Bridge C 7
15 Poolhill A 10
32 Poolsbrook C 2
38 Poortown G 1
10 Pootings C 3
17 Popeswood G 9
9 Popham B 7
18 Poplar F 4
8 Porchfield G 6
54 Porin D 7
2 Porkellis F 4
6 Porlock B 2
6 Porlock Weir B 2
53 Port Allen E 7
50 Port Appin C 6
46 Port Bannatyne C 6
44 Port Carlisle G 1
40 Port Clarence C 5
28 Port Dinorwic C 5
46 Port Driseach B 5
58 Port Elphinstone F 5
38 Port Erin H 1
58 Port Erroll D 8
13 Port Eynon H 8
47 Port Glasgow B 8
54 Port Henderson B 1
3 Port Isaac B 7
46 Port Lamont B 6
42 Port Logan H 2
41 Port Mulgrave C 8
52 Port of Menteith G 1
63 Port of Ness A 6
3 Port Quin B 7
50 Port Ramsay C 6
38 Port St. Mary H 1
51 Port Sonachan E 7
30 Port Sunlight B 2
13 Port Talbot H 10
13 Port Tennant H 10
42 Port William G 4
46 Portachoillan D 3
46 Port an Eilein B 5
46 Portavadie B 5
15 Portbury G 8
9 Portchester F 7
47 Portencross D 7
7 Portesham H 9
58 Portessie A 2
38 Port e Vullen G 3
12 Portfield Gate E 3
5 Portgate G 3
58 Portgordon A 1
61 Portgower E 9
14 Porth E 4
2 Porth Mellin H 4
2 Porth Navas G 5
2 Porthallow, Corn. D 9
2 Porthallow, Corn G 5
14 Porthcawl G 1
2 Porthcothan Bay C 6
2 Porthcurno G 1
28 Porthdafarch B 2
12 Porthgain D 2
2 Porthilly B 6
14 Porthkerry H 4
2 Porthleven G 3
28 Porthmadog F 5
2 Porthmeor F 2
11 Portholland F 7
2 Porthoustock G 5
2 Porthowann E 4
3 Porthpean D 7
13 Porth-y-rhyd, Dyfed E 8
13 Porth-y-rhyd, Dyfed C 10
51 Portincaple H 9
36 Portington D 6
51 Portinnisherrich F 7
38 Portinscale C 5
15 Portishead G 8
58 Portknockie A 2
59 Portlethen H 7
2 Portloe F 6
61 Portmahomack H 9
28 Portmeirion F 5
3 Portmellon E 7
8 Portmore F 5
62 Port na Long F 3
63 Portnaguiran C 6
55 Portnaluchaig K 1
60 Portnancon B 5
51 Portnellan, Central E 11
51 Portnellan, Central F 11
35 Portnocroish C 6
48 Portobello B 6
8 Porton B 3
42 Portpatrick F 1
2 Portreath E 4
62 Portree D 4
47 Portrye D 7
2 Portscatho F 6
9 Portsea F 8
61 Portskerra A 8
15 Portskewett E 8
10 Portslade, Surrey G 1
10 Portslade, Surrey G 2
42 Portslogan F 1
9 Portsmouth, Hants F 8
35 Portsmouth, W.Yorks E 7
58 Portsoy A 3
8 Portswood E 6
50 Portuairk A 2
63 Portvoller C 6
63 Portway, Heref. & Worc. A 8
22 Portway, War. E 4
3 Portwrinkle D 10
42 Portyerrock H 5
2 Postbridge H 5
17 Postcombe D 8
11 Postling D 10
27 Postlingford K 1
26 Postwick E 6
59 Potarch H 3
47 Poteath D 7
44 Potholm D 2
17 Potsgrove A 10
24 Pott Row C 8
31 Pott Shrigley B 8
17 Potten End C 11
41 Potter Brompton G 10
26 Potter Heigham D 7
18 Potter Street C 5
33 Potterhanworth D 7
33 Potterhanworth Booths C 8
16 Potterne H 1
16 Potterne Wick H 1
18 Potters Bar D 3
22 Potters Cross D 2
23 Potterspury H 11
40 Potto E 5
25 Potton K 3
4 Poughill, Corn E 1
4 Poughill, Devon E 7
16 Poulshot H 1
30 Poulton, Ches. D 3
16 Poulton, Glos. D 2
34 Poulton-Le-Fylde C 2
14 Pound F 1
22 Pound Bank E 1
10 Pound Green, E.Sussex F 4
8 Pound Green, I.o.W. G 5
10 Pound Hill D 2
41 Poundland, Dumf. & Gall. C 9
42 Poundland, Strathclyde C 3
17 Poundon B 7
10 Poundsbridge D 4
5 Poundsgate J 6
5 Poundstock A 2
53 Pourie D 9
45 Powburn A 9
6 Powderham H 3
7 Powerstock G 8
43 Powfoot E 12
53 Powgavie E 7
22 Powick G 2
4 Powler's Piece D 2
52 Powmill G 5
20 Powys, Co E 6
7 Poxwell H 11
17 Poyle F 11
10 Poynings G 1
7 Poyntington D 10
31 Poynton B 8
30 Poynton Green H 4
27 Poys Street H 6
12 Poyston Cross E 3
27 Poystreet Green J 3
2 Praa Sands G 3
62 Prabost C 3
18 Pratt's Bottom H 5
11 Pratt'sHeath H 7
2 Praze F 3
2 Praze-an-Beeble F 3
2 Predannack Manor Farm H 4
30 Prees G 4
34 Preesall B 2
34 Preesall Park C 2
12 Prendergast E 3
45 Prendwick B 8
13 Pren-gwyn C 7
28 Prenteg F 5
30 Prenton B 2
30 Prescot A 3
30 Prescott H 3
49 Pressen F 11
30 Pressgreen G 4
29 Prestatyn B 10
31 Prestbury, Ches. C 7
15 Prestbury, Glos. B 12
21 Presteigne F 8
21 Presthope C 11
7 Prestleigh B 9
49 Preston, Borders D 10
5 Preston, Devon H 7
7 Preston, Dorset H 10
10 Preston, E. Sussex G 2
27 Preston, Essex K 2
15 Preston, Glos A 10
16 Preston, Glos D 2
18 Preston, Herts A 2
37 Preston, Humber. D 9
11 Preston, Kent B 9
11 Preston, Kent B 11
34 Preston, Lancs D 4
45 Preston, Northumb. E 12
48 Preston, Lothian B 6
49 Preston, Lothian B 8
16 Preston, Wilts F 1
22 Preston Bagot E 5
17 Preston Bissett A 7
6 Preston Bowyer D 5
30 Preston Brockhurst H 4
30 Preston Brook B 4
9 Preston Candover B 7
23 Preston Capes G 9
17 Preston Crowmarsh E 7
3 Preston Gubbals H 4
22 Preston on Stour G 5
30 Preston on the Hill B 4
21 Preston on Wye H 9
7 Preston Plucknett E 8
21 Preston upon the Weald Moors A 12
21 Preston Wynne H 11
43 Prestonmill F 10
48 Prestonpans B 6
40 Preston-under-Scar F 1
35 Prestwich G 7
47 Prestwick, Northumb. F 10
47 Prestwick, Strathclyde G 8
17 Prestwood D 9
14 Price Town E 3
25 Prickwillow G 7
7 Priddy A 8
39 Priest Hulton H 7
44 Priesthaugh C 3
47 Priesthill C 10
47 Priestland F 10
21 Priestweston C 8
23 Primethorpe C 8
24 Primrose Hill, Cambs. F 5
32 Primrose Hill, Notts. D 2
49 Primrosehill, Borders D 10
17 Primrosehill, Herts D 11
49 Primsidemill G 10
12 Princes Gate F 5
17 Princes Risborough D 9
23 Princethorpe E 7
5 Princetown, Devon H 5
14 Princetown, Mid Glam. C 4
49 Printonan E 10
29 Prion D 10
21 Priors Frame H 11
23 Priors Hardwick G 8
23 Priors Marston F 8
21 Priorslee A 12
21 Priory Wood H 8
15 Priston H 10
19 Prittlewell E 8
9 Privett C 8
4 Prixford B 4
2 Probus E 6
43 Prospect G 12
58 Protstonhill A 6
45 Prudhoe G 9
51 Ptarmigan Lodge G 10
51 Pubil C 11
15 Publow H 9
18 Puckeridge B 4
7 Puckington D 7
15 Pucklechurch G 10
8 Pucknall D 5
30 Puddington, Ches. C 2
4 Puddington, Devon E7
26 Puddledock F 4
7 Puddletown G 10
21 Pudlestone F 11
35 Pudsey D 11
9 Pulborough D 12
30 Puleston H 6
30 Pulford D 2
7 Pulham E 10
27 Pulham Market G 5
27 Pulham St. Margaret G 5
25 Pulloxhill M 2
48 Pumpherston B 3
43 Pumplaburn B 12
13 Pumpsaint C 10
12 Puncheston D 3
7 Puncknoll G 9
19 Punnett's Town F 5
9 Purbrook E 8
44 Purdomstone E 1
8 Purewell G 3
18 Purfleet F 5
7 Puriton B 7
19 Purleigh D 8
17 Purley, Berks F 7
18 Purley, London H 3
25 Purls Bridge G 6
7 Purse Caundle D 10
21 Purslow D 9
36 Purston Jaglin E 2
7 Purtington E 7
15 Purton, Glos D 10
16 Purton, Wilts E 2
16 Purton Stoke E 2
49 Purvishaugh E 8
23 Pury End H 10
16 Pusey D 4
4 Putford D 2
15 Putley A 9
18 Putney F 2
4 Putsborough B 3
17 Puttenham, Bucks. C 9
9 Puttenham,Surrey A 10
15 Puxton H 7
13 Pwll G 8
12 Pwllcrochan G 3
28 Pwlldefaid H 1
14 Pwllgloyw A 3
28 Pwllheli G 3
15 Pwll-Meyric E 8
12 Pwlltrap E 6
13 Pwll-y-glaw H 11
29 Pydew B 7
32 Pye Bridge E 2
15 Pye Corner, Gwent F 7
18 Pye Corner, Herts C 4
22 Pye Green A 3
10 Pyecombe G 2
8 Pyle, I.o.W. H 6
14 Pyle, Mid Glam. F 2
7 Pylle B 9
25 Pymore G 6
17 Pyrford H 11
14 Pyrgad C 4
17 Pyrton E 8
23 Pytchley E 12
4 Pyworthy F 2
21 Quabbs D 7
24 Quadring B 3
17 Quainton B 8
8 Quarley B 4
31 Quarndon, Derby F 11
23 Quarndon, Leics. A 9
47 Quarrier's Homes C 8
24 Quarrington A 2
40 Quarrington Hill A 4
22 Quarry Bank C 3
30 Quarrybank D 4
58 Quarryburn A 6
56 Quarryhill B 3
56 Quarrywood C 7
47 Quarter D 12
6 Quartley D 3
22 Quat C 1
22 Quatford C 1
40 Quebec A 2
15 Quedgeley C 11
25 Queen Adelaide G 7
15 Queen Charlton H 9
4 Queen Dart D 7
7 Queen Oak C 11
10 Queen Street D 6
11 Queensborough A 8
7 Queens Camel D 9
30 Queens Head G 2
30 Queen's Park E 2
35 Queensbury D 9
29 Queensferry, Clwyd C 12
48 Queensferry, Lothian B 4
34 Queenstown D 2
47 Queenzieburn B 11
16 Quemerford G 1
64 Quendale F 7
25 Quendon M 6
23 Queniborough A 10
16 Quenington D 2
34 Quernmore A 4
3 Quethiock C 10
27 Quidenham G 3
8 Quidhampton, Hants. A 6

8 Quidhampton, Wilts. C 3
58 Quilquox D 6
38 Quine's Hill H 2
50 Quinish House B 2
23 Quinton G 11
2 Quintrel Downs D 5
49 Quixwood C 10
4 Quoditch F 3
52 Quoig E 3
48 Quothquan E 3
64 Quoys D 7
62 Rassay House (Hotel) D 5
4 Rabscott C 6
30 Raby B 2
4 Rackenford D 7
9 Rackham E 11
26 Rackheath Com. D 6
43 Racks D 11
64 Rackwick, Orkney D 1
64 Rackwick, Orkney A 2
31 Radbourne G 11
34 Radcliffe, Manchester F 6
45 Radcliffe, Northumb. C 11
32 Radcliffe on Soar G 2
32 Radcliffe on Trent F 4
17 Radclive A 7
16 Radcot D 4
56 Raddery House D 3
23 Radford Semele F 7
7 Radpole H 10
18 Radlett D 2
16 Radley D 6
17 Radnage D 8
7 Radstock A 10
23 Radstone H 9
23 Radway G 7
30 Radway Green E 6
25 Radwell J 1
25 Radwinter L 7
14 Radyr F 5
48 Raecleugh H 3
63 Raerinish D 5
60 Raffin D 2
56 Rafford D 6
32 Ragdale H 4
53 Ragfield F 10
15 Raglan D 7
32 Ragnall C 5
34 Rainford G 4
18 Rainham, Essex F 5
11 Rainham, Kent B 7
11 Rainham Mark A 7
30 Rainhill A 4
30 Rainhill Stoops A 4
31 Rainow C 8
40 Rainton H 4
32 Rainworth D 3
39 Raisbeck D 9
44 Raise H 5
36 Raisthorpe A 6
53 Rait D 7
33 Raithby, Lincs. C 10
33 Raithby, Lincs. B 10
9 Rake C 9
11 Ram Lane C 8
62 Ramasaig D 1
3 Rame, Corn. E 11
2 Rame, Corn. F 4
7 Rampisham F 9
34 Rampside A 1
25 Rampton, Cambs. H 5
32 Rampton, Notts. B 5
35 Ramsbottom E 7
16 Ramsbury G 4
61 Ramscraigs D 10
9 Ramsdean D 8
17 Ramsdell H 7
16 Ramsden C 4
19 Ramsden Bellhouse E 7
19 Ramsden Heath D 7
25 Ramsay, Cambs. G 4
27 Ramsey, Essex M 5
38 Ramsey, I.O.M. G 2
19 Ramsay Island C 9
25 Ramsay St. Mary's G 4
48 Ramseycleuch H 5
11 Ramsgate B 12
26 Ramsgate Street B 4
40 Ramsgill H 1
45 Ramshaw H 8
44 Ramshope C 6
31 Ramshorn F 9
5 Ramsley G 5
9 Ramsnest Com. C 11
32 Ranby B 4
33 Rand B 8
15 Randwick D 11
47 Ranfurly C 9
31 Rangemore H 10
15 Rangeworthy F 10
47 Rankinston H 9
9 Ranmore Com. A 12
34 Rann E 6
38 Rannerdale C 4
51 Rannoch Station B 11
55 Ranochan L 2
6 Ranscombe B 3
32 Ranskill A 4
31 Ranton H 7
26 Ranworth D 7
64 Rapness B 3
55 Rarsaidh H 2
43 Rascarre G 9
58 Rashiereive E 7
40 Raskelf H 5
14 Rassau C 5
35 Rastrick E 10
55 Ratagan H 3
23 Ratby B 8
23 Ratcliffe Culey B 7
23 Ratcliffe on the Wreake A 9
58 Rathen B 7
53 Rathillet E 8
35 Rathmell A 7
48 Ratho B 4
48 Ratho Station B 4
58 Rathven A 2
23 Ratley G 7
21 Ratlinghope C 9
61 Rattar A 11
5 Rattery K 6
27 Rattlesden J 3
53 Rattray C 7
38 Raughton Head A 6
25 Raunds H 1
49 Ravelaw D 11
36 Ravenfield H 3
38 Ravenglass F 3
26 Raveningham F 7
41 Ravenscar E 10
38 Ravensdale G 2
25 Ravensden K 2
32 Ravenshead E 3
30 Ravensmoor E 5
23 Ravensthorpe, Northants. E 10
35 Ravensthorpe, W. Yorks. E 10
23 Ravenstone, Bucks. G 11
23 Ravenstone, Leics. A 7
39 Ravenstonedale E 9
48 Ravenstruther E 2
40 Ravensworth D 2
41 Raw E 9
49 Rawburn D 9
36 Rawcliffe, Humber. E 5
36 Rawcliffe, N. Yorks. B 4
36 Rawcliffe Bridge E 5
35 Rawdon C 11
36 Rawmarsh G 2
19 Rawreth E 8
6 Rawridge F 5
47 Raws E 9
35 Rawtenstall E 7
47 Rawyards C 12
58 Raxton D 6
27 Raydon L 3
19 Rayleigh E 8
7 Raymond's Hill F 7
19 Rayne B 7
25 Reach J 7
34 Read D 6
17 Reading G 8
11 Reading Street E 8
39 Reagill C 8
61 Rearquhar G 7
23 Rearsby A 10
61 Reaster A 11
45 Reaveley A 8
64 Reawick D 6
61 Reay B 9
11 Reculver A 11
6 Red Ball E 4
44 Red Dial H 1
22 Red Hill G 2
5 Red Post J 7
34 Red Rock F 5
12 Red Roses F 5
45 Red Row C 10
31 Red Street E 7
28 Red Wharf B 5
12 Redberth G 4
17 Redbourn C 12
37 Redbourne G 7
18 Redbridge E 4
30 Redbrook, Clwyd F 4
15 Redbrook, Gwent C 8
11 Redbrook Street D 8
56 Redburn, Highland E 5
56 Redburn, Highland C 1
44 Redburn, Northumb. G 6
40 Redcar C 8
56 Redcastle, Highland E 1
53 Redcastle, Tayside B 11
15 Redcliffe Bay G 7
47 Redcraig G 9
49 Redden F 10
48 Redding B 2
48 Reddingmuirhead B 2
35 Reddish H 8
22 Redditch E 4
47 Reddochbraes F 12
27 Redenhall G 6
44 Redesdale Camp C 6
45 Redesmouth E 7
53 Redford, Tayside C 10
59 Redford, Tayside K 5
48 Redfordgreen H 6
52 Redgorton D 6
27 Redgrave G 3
59 Redheugh L 2
15 Redhill, Avon H 8
58 Redhill, Grampian D 4
59 Redhill, Grampian G 5
10 Redhill, Surrey C 2
46 Redhouse C 3
27 Redisham G 7
15 Redland, Avon G 9
64 Redland, Orkney C 2
27 Redlingfield H 5
8 Redlynch, Dorset D 4
7 Redlynch, Som. C 10
39 Redmain B 4
15 Redmarley D'Abitot A 10
40 Redmarshall C 4
32 Redmile G 5
40 Redmire F 1
3 Redmoor D 8
59 Redmyre K 5
30 Rednal G 2
49 Redpath F 8
54 Redpoint C 1
2 Redruth E 4
48 Redscarhead E 5
15 Redwick, Avon F 8
15 Redwick, Gwent F 7
40 Redworth C 3
25 Reed L 5
26 Reedham E 7
36 Reedness E 6
49 Reedy Loch D 11
63 Reef C 2
33 Reepham, Lincs. C 7
26 Reepham, Norf. C 4
40 Reeth E 1
38 Regaby F 2
56 Rehaurie E 5
61 Reidhbreac G 7
60 Reiff E 2
10 Reigate C 1
41 Reighton H 11
41 Reighton Gap G 11
58 Reisque E 6
61 Reiss B 12
2 Rejerrah D 5
2 Releath F 4
43 Relief D 12
2 Relubbus F 3
56 Relugas E 5
17 Remenham F 8
17 Remenham Hill F 9
52 Remony C 3
32 Rempstone H 3
16 Rendcomb C 1
27 Rendham J 6
47 Renfrew C 10
25 Renhold K 2
32 Renishaw B 2
45 Rennington A 10
47 Renton B 9
39 Renwick A 8
26 Repps D 7
31 Repton G 11
55 Reraig G 2
53 Rescobie B 10
50 Resipol A 4
56 Resolis C 2
14 Resolven D 2
55 Resourie M 2
49 Reston C 11
2 Retew D 6
19 Rettendon D 7
19 Rettendon Place D 7
2 Retyn D 6
50 Reudle C 1
33 Revesby D 10
8 Rew Street G 6
6 Rewe F 3
27 Reydon G 8
26 Reymerston E 3
12 Reynalton F 4
13 Reynoldston H 8
3 Rezare B 10
15 Rhadyr D 7
13 Rhandir-mwyn C 11
20 Rhayader F 5
60 Rhegreanoch E 3
56 Rheindown E 1
50 Rhemore C 3
29 Rhewl, Clwyd D 10
29 Rhewl, Clwyd F 11
60 Rhicarn E 2
60 Rhiconich B 4
56 Rhicullen C 3
60 Rhidorroch G 3
60 Rhidorroch Old Lodge G 4
28 Rhid-y-sarn F 6
61 Rhifail C 7
14 Rhigos D 3
60 Rhimichie B 4
56 Rhinduie E 1
60 Rhiroy G 3
28 Rhiw G 2
28 Rhiwbryfdir F 6
14 Rhiwderyn F 6
29 Rhiwlas, Clwd G 11
28 Rhiwlas, Gwynedd D 5
29 Rhiwlas, Gwynedd F 8
6 Rhode C 6
11 Rhodes Minnis D 10
32 Rhodesia B 3
12 Rhodiad D 1
14 Rhoose H 4
13 Rhos, Dyfed C 7
13 Rhos, W. Glam. G 10
13 Rhos Amman F 10
12 Rhos-Hill C 5
28 Rhoscolyn C 2
12 Rhoscrowther G 3
29 Rhosesmor C 11
12 Rhosfach D 5
28 Rhos-fawr B 4
28 Rhosgadfan D 4
28 Rhosgoch, Gwynedd A 3
21 Rhos goch, Powys H 7
28 Rhos-lan F 4
20 Rhoslefain B 1
29 Rhosllanerchrugog F 12
13 Rhosmaen E 9
28 Rhos-meirch B 4
28 Rhosneigr C 3
29 Rhos-on-Sea B 8
13 Rhossili H 7
12 Rhosson D 1
28 Rhostryfan D 4
30 Rhostyllen E 2
28 Rhosybol A 4
28 Rhos-y-gwaliau G 9
28 Rhos-y-llan F 2
46 Rhu, Strathclyde C 3
47 Rhu, Strathclyde A 7
54 Rhu Noa C 4
29 Rhualt C 10
46 Rhubodach B 5
30 Rhuddall Heath D 4
29 Rhuddlan B 9
4 Rhude Cross E 1
21 Rhulen G 7
46 Rhunahaorine E 2
28 Rhyd, Gwynedd F 6
20 Rhyd, Powys B 5
28 Rhyd-Ddu E 5
13 Rhyd-Lewis B 7
29 Rhyd-Lydan E 8
13 Rhydargaeau D 8
14 Rhydberry A 3
13 Rhydcymerau C 9
22 Rhydd H 2
13 Rhydding G 10
13 Rhyddlan C 8
29 Rhyd-leos G 11
28 Rhydlios G 1
20 Rhydlydan C 6
13 Rhydlydan C 6
13 Rhydowen C 8
20 Rhydrosser F 1
21 Rhydspence H 8
29 Rhydtalog E 11
28 Rhydwyn A 3
29 Rhyd-y-croesau G 11
28 Rhydyelafdy G 3
14 Rhydyfelin E 4
20 Rhyd-y-felin D 2
13 Rhyd-y-fro F 10
21 Rhyd-y-groes B 8
29 Rhydymain H 7
14 Rhyd-y-meirch D 6
29 Rhydymwyn D 11
20 Rhyd-yr-onmen B 2
20 Rhyfud F 2
29 Rhyl B 9
14 Rhymney D 4
53 Rhynd, Fife E 9
52 Rhynd, Tayside E 6
58 Rhynie E 2
22 Ribble E 1
39 Ribblehead G 10
34 Ribbleton D 4
34 Ribby D 3
34 Ribchester D 5
60 Ribigill B 6
37 Riby F 9
37 Riby Cross Roads F 9
36 Riccall C 4
47 Riccarton F 9
44 Riccarton Junction C 4
21 Richards Castle E 10
17 Richings Park F 11
18 Richmond, London F 2
40 Richmond, N. Yorks. E 2
54 Rickarton H 5
31 Rickerscote H 7
27 Rickinghall Inferior H 3
27 Rickinghall Superior H 3
25 Rickling M 6
18 Rickling Green A 5
17 Rickmansworth E 11
44 Riddings, Cumb. E 3
32 Riddings, Derby E 2
4 Riddlecombe E 5
35 Riddlesden C 9
8 Ridge, Dorset G 1
8 Ridge, Hants. D 5
18 Ridge, Herts. D 2
8 Ridge, Wilts. C 1
10 Ridge Green C 2
22 Ridge Lane C 6
20 Ridgebourne F 6
15 Ridgehill H 8
32 Ridgeway B 1
21 Ridgeway Cross H 12
25 Ridgewell L 8
10 Ridgewood F 3
25 Ridgemont L 1
45 Riding Mill G 8
10 Ridley, Kent B 5
44 Ridley, Northumb. G 6
30 Ridley Green E 4
23 Ridlington, Leics. B 11
26 Ridlington, Norf. B 6
45 Ridsdale E 7
52 Riechip B 5
52 Riemore B 5
60 Rienachait D 2
40 Rievaulx G 6
55 Rifern K 2
47 Rigfoot D 9
44 Rigg F 1
47 Riggend B 12
47 Righead F 10
56 Righoul E 4
39 Rigmaden Park G 8
43 Rigsby C 11
48 Rigside F 2
22 Rileyhill A 5
3 Rilla Mill B 10
41 Rillington H 8
35 Rimington C 7
7 Rimpton D 9
61 Rimsdale C 7
37 Rimswell D 10
12 Rinaston D 3
43 Ringford F 8
31 Ringinglow B 11
26 Ringland D 4
10 Ringles Cross F 3
10 Ringmer G 3
5 Ringmore, Devon J 8
5 Ringmore, Devon L 5
56 Ringorm E 8
24 Ring's End E 5
27 Ringsfield G 7
27 Ringsfield Corner G 7
17 Ringshall, Bucks. C 10
27 Ringshall, Suffolk K 3
27 Ringshall Stocks K 4
24 Ringstead, Norf. B 8
25 Ringstead, Northants. H 1
8 Ringwood F 3
11 Ringwould C 12
58 Ringmore F 2
64 Rinnigill E 2
2 Rinsey G 3
10 Ripe G 4
32 Ripley, Derby E 1
8 Ripley, Hants. F 3
35 Ripley, N. Yorks. A 11
17 Ripley, Surrey H 11
37 Riplingham D 7
40 Ripon H 3
24 Rippingale C 2
22 Ripple, Heref. & Worcs. H 2
11 Ripple, Kent C 12
35 Ripponden E 9
21 Risbury G 11
37 Risby, Humberside F 7
27 Risby, Suffolk J 1
14 Risca E 6
37 Rise C 9
24 Risegate C 3
33 Riseholme C 7
25 Riseley, Beds. J 1
17 Riseley, Berks. H 8
27 Rishangles H 4
34 Rishton D 6
35 Rishworth E 9
32 Risley G 2
40 Risplith H 3
60 Rispond A 5
16 Rivar H 4
19 Rivenhall End B 8
25 River Bank H 6
10 Riverhead B 4
4 Riverton C 5
34 Rivington F 5
4 Roachill D 7
23 Roade G 11
44 Roadhead F 4
48 Roadmeetings D 1
61 Roadside, Highland B 11
47 Roadside, Strathclyde H 10
59 Roadside of Catterline J 6
59 Roadside of Kinneff K 6
6 Roadwater B 4
62 Roag D 2
42 Roan of Craigoch A 4
44 Roansgreen E 3
14 Roath F 5
43 Roberthill D 12
44 Roberton, Borders B 3
48 Roberton, Strathclyde F 2
10 Robertsbridge F 6
35 Roberttown E 10
12 Robeston Cross F 2
12 Robeston Wathen E 4
35 Robin Hood D 11
31 Robin Hood Inn C 11
41 Robin Hood's Bay E 9
4 Roborough D 4
30 Roby A 3
34 Roby Mill F 4
31 Rocester F 9
12 Roch E 2
12 Roch Gate E 2
35 Rochdale F 7
3 Roche D 7
10 Rochester, Kent A 6
44 Rochester, Northumb. C 6
10 Rochford E 8
2 Rock, Cornwall B 6
45 Rock, Northumb. A 10
22 Rock, Heref. & Worcs. E 1
9 Rock, W. Sussex E 12
30 Rock Ferry B 2
22 Rock Hill E 3
6 Rockbeare G 4
44 Rockcliffe, Cumb. G 2
43 Rockcliffe, Dumf. & Gall. F 9
15 Rockfield, Gwent C 8
61 Rockfield, Highland H 9
8 Rockford E 3
15 Rockhampton E 9
26 Rockheath D 6
23 Rockingham C 12
26 Rockland All Saints F 3
26 Rockland St. Mary E 6
26 Rockland St. Peter F 3
16 Rockley G 3
17 Rockwell End E 9
6 Rockwell Green D 5
15 Rodborough D 11
16 Rodbourne, Wilts. F 2
15 Rodbourne, Wilts. F 12
16 Rodbourne Cheney E 2
21 Rodd F 8
49 Roddam G 12
49 Roddam Rigg G 12
7 Rodden H 9
7 Rode A 11
30 Rode Heath D 6
31 Rodeheath C 7
63 Rodel H 1
21 Roden A 11
6 Rodhuish B 4
21 Rodington A 11
15 Rodley C 10
15 Rodmarton D 12
10 Rodmell G 3
11 Rodmersham B 8
7 Rodney Stoke A 8
31 Rodsley F 10

6 Rodway B 6
7 Rodwell H 7
35 Roecliffe A 12
18 Roehampton G 2
64 Roesound C 7
10 Roffey E 1
61 Rogart F 7
9 Rogate D 9
14 Rogerstone E 6
47 Rogerton D 11
15 Rogiet E 8
26 Rollesby D 7
23 Rolleston, Leics. B 10
32 Rolleston, Notts. E 5
31 Rolleston, Staffs. G 10
37 Rolston C 10
11 Rolvenden E 7
11 Rolvenden Layne E 7
39 Romaldkirk C 12
26 Roman Hill F 8
40 Romanby F 4
48 Romannobridge E 4
4 Romansleigh D 6
62 Romesdal C 3
18 Romford E 5
31 Romiley A 8
8 Romsey D 5
22 Romsley, Salop. D 1
22 Romsley, Salop. D 3
38 Ronague H 1
41 Rookdale H 9
39 Rookhope A 11
8 Rookley H 6
7 Rooks Bridge A 7
6 Rook's Nest C 4
37 Roos D 10
48 Rootpark D 2
9 Ropley C 8
9 Ropley Dean C 7
33 Ropsley G 7
58 Rora C 8
58 Rorandle F 4
21 Rorrington B 8
2 Rose D 5
4 Rose Ash D 7
10 Rose Hill F 3
10 Roseacre, Kent C 6
34 Roseacre, Lancs. C 3
48 Rosebank D 1
45 Rosebrough C 12
12 Rosebush D 4
2 Rosecare B 2
41 Rosedale Abbey F 7
45 Roseden A 8
60 Rosehall F 5
58 Rosehearty A 7
30 Rosehill G 5
56 Roseisle C 7
12 Rosemarket F 3
56 Rosemarkie D 3
6 Rosemary Lane E 5
47 Rosemount, Strathclyde F 8
53 Rosemount, Tayside C 7
2 Rosenannon C 6
2 Rosewarne F 3
48 Rosewell C 5
40 Roseworth C 4
2 Roseworthy F 3
39 Rosgill D 8
55 Roshven L 1
62 Roskhill D 2
38 Rosley A 6
48 Roslin C 5
31 Rosliston H 11
47 Rosneath A 7
43 Ross, Dumf. & Gall. G 7
45 Ross, Northumb. B 12
15 Ross-on-Wye B 9
30 Rossett D 2
52 Rossie Ochill F 6
36 Rossington G 4
56 Rosskeen C 2
47 Rossland B 9
61 Roster C 11
30 Rostherne B 6
38 Rosthwaite D 5
31 Roston F 10
2 Rosudgeon G 3
48 Rosyth A 4
45 Rothbury C 9
23 Rotherby A 10
10 Rotherfield E 4
17 Rotherfield Greys F 8
17 Rotherfield Peppard F 8
32 Rotherham A 2
23 Rothersthorpe F 10
17 Rotherwick H 8
56 Rothes E 8
46 Rothesay C 6
58 Rothiebrisbane D 5
58 Rothienorman D 5
64 Rothiesholm C 4
45 Rothill B 9
23 Rothley A 9
58 Rothmaise D 4
37 Rothwell, Lincs. G 9
23 Rothwell, Northants. D 11
35 Rothwell, W. Yorks. D 12
35 Rothwell Haigh D 12
37 Rotsea B 8
59 Rottal K 1
10 Rottingdean H 3
38 Rottington D 2
43 Roucan D 11
8 Roud H 6
31 Rough Close F 8
11 Rough Common B 10
31 Rough Hay H 10
26 Rougham C 1
27 Rougham Green J 2
55 Roughburn L 7
35 Roughlee C 7
22 Roughley B 5
44 Roughsike E 3
33 Roughton, Lincs. D 9
26 Roughton, Norf. B 5
22 Roughton, Salop. C 1
47 Roughwood D 8
17 Round Oak H 7
7 Roundham E 7
35 Roundhay C 12
43 Roundstonefoot A 12
9 Roundstreet Com. C 12
16 Roundway H 1
22 Rous Lench G 4
6 Rousdon G 6
47 Routdaneburn D 7
37 Routh C 8
61 Rovie Lodge F 7
3 Row, Cornwall B 8
39 Row, Cumbria F 7
44 Rowanburn E 2
51 Rowardennan Hotel H 10
31 Rowarth A 8
16 Rowde H 1
15 Rowden Down G 12
29 Ro-wen C 7
44 Rowfoot G 5
19 Rowhedge B 10
9 Rowhook C 12
22 Rowington E 5
31 Rowland C 10
9 Rowland's Castle E 9
45 Rowland's Gill G 10
9 Rowledge B 9
37 Rowley, Humber. D 7
21 Rowley, Salop. B 8
22 Rowley Regis C 3
15 Rowlstone B 7
9 Rowly B 11
22 Rowney Green E 4
8 Rownhams D 5
17 Rowsham B 9
31 Rowsley D 11
33 Rowston E 8
30 Rowton, Ches. D 3
30 Rowton, Salop. H 5
49 Roxburgh F 9
49 Roxburgh Newtown F 9
37 Roxby, Humber. E 7
41 Roxby, N. Yorks. D 7
25 Roxton K 3
18 Roxwell C 6
34 Royal Oak G 3
55 Roybridge L 6
18 Roydon, Essex C 4
27 Roydon, Norfolk G 4
24 Roydon, Norfolk C 8
25 Royston, Herts. L 5
35 Royston, S. Yorks. F 12
35 Royton F 8
29 Ruabon F 12
2 Ruan High Lanes F 6
2 Ruan Lanihorne E 6
2 Ruan Minor H 4
15 Ruardean C 9
15 Ruardean Woodside C 9
22 Ribery D 3
39 Ruckcroft A 8
21 Ruckhall Com. H 10
11 Ruckinge E 9
33 Ruckland B 10
21 Ruckley B 10
40 Rudby D 5
45 Rudchester F 9
32 Ruddington G 3
15 Rudford B 11
7 Rudge A 11
15 Rudgeway F 9
9 Rudgwick C 12
15 Rudhall B 9
14 Rudry F 5
41 Rudston H 11
31 Rudyard D 8
49 Ruecastle G 8
34 Rufford F 3
36 Rufforth B 3
45 Ruffside H 8
23 Rugby E 8
31 Rugeley H 9
56 Ruilick E 1
6 Ruishton D 6
18 Ruislip E 1
18 Ruislip Common E 1
44 Ruletownhead B 4
49 Rumbletonlaw E 9
52 Rumblingbridge G 5
27 Rumburgh G 6
2 Rumford C 6
14 Rumney F 5
52 Runacraig F 1
30 Runcorn B 4
9 Runcton F 10
24 Runcton Holme E 7
5 Rundlestone H 4
9 Runfold A 10
26 Runhall E 4
26 Runham D 7
6 Runnington D 5
19 Runsell Green C 8
41 Runswick D 8
57 Runtaleave M 8
19 Runwell D 7
17 Ruscombe F 9
56 Rosehaugh House D 2
19 Rush Green B 11
15 Rushall, Heref. & Worcs. A 9
27 Rushall, Norfolk G 5
22 Rushall, W. Midlands B 4
8 Rushall, Wilts. A 3
27 Rushbrooke J 2
21 Rushbury C 10
25 Rushden, Herts. M 4
25 Rushden, Northants. J 1
27 Rushford G 2
10 Rushlake Green F 5
27 Rushmere G 8
27 Rushmere St. Andrew. K 5
27 Rushmere Street K 5
9 Rushmoor, Surrey B 10
8 Rushmore, Wilts. D 1
22 Rushock E 2
35 Rusholme H 7
30 Rushton, Ches. D 4
23 Rushton, Northants. D 11
21 Rushton, Salop. B 11
31 Rushton Spencer D 8
22 Rushwick G 2
40 Rushyford B 3
52 Ruskie G 1
33 Ruskington E 8
43 Rusko F 7
38 Rusland F 6
10 Rusper D 1
15 Ruspidge C 9
10 Russell's Green G 6
17 Russell's Water E 8
9 Rustington F 11
41 Ruston G 9
37 Ruston Parva A 8
41 Ruswarp D 9
49 Rutherford F 9
47 Rutherglen C 11
3 Ruthernbridge C 7
29 Ruthin D 10
59 Ruthrieston G 7
49 Ruthven, Borders E 10
58 Ruthven, Grampian C 3
56 Ruthven, Highland F 4
57 Ruthven, Highland J 3
53 Ruthven, Tayside B 7
53 Ruthven House B 8
2 Ruthvoes D 6
43 Ruthwell E 11
15 Ruxton Green B 8
30 Ruyton Eleven Towns H 3
45 Ryal F 8
7 Ryall G 7
10 Ryarsh B 5
38 Rydal E 6
9 Ryde G 7
4 Rydon F 2
11 Rye F 8
11 Rye Foreign F 7
11 Rye Harbour F 8
43 Ryemuir D 11
24 Ryhall D 1
37 Ryhill, Humber. E 10
36 Ryhill, W. Yorks. F 2
45 Ryhope H 12
33 Ryland B 7
35 Rylstone A 8
7 Ryme Intrinseca E 9
49 Ryslaw E 10
36 Ryther C 3
15 Ryton, Glos. A 10
41 Ryton, N. Yorks. H 8
21 Ryton, Salop. B 10
22 Ryton, Salop. B 1
45 Ryton, Tyne & Wear G 9
23 Ryton-on-Dunsmore E 7
34 Sabden C 6
18 Sacombe B 3
45 Sacriston H 10
40 Sadberge C 4
46 Saddell F 3
23 Saddington C 10
24 Saddle Bow D 7
8 Saddle Heath E 3
35 Saddleworth F 9
39 Sadgill E 7
25 Saffron Walden L 6
12 Sageston G 4
26 Saham Hills E 2
26 Saham Toney E 2
30 Saighton D 3
50 Sailean C 6
49 St. Abbs C 11
2 St. Agnes, Corn. E 4
2 St. Agnes, Is. of Scilly D 2
18 St. Albans C 2
2 St. Allen E 5
53 St. Andrews E 10
14 St. Andrews Major G 5
34 St. Anne's D 2
43 St. Ann's B 11
3 St. Ann's Chapel, Cornwall C 11
5 St. Ann's Chapel, Devon L 5
2 St. Anthony G 5
10 St. Anthony's Hill H 5
15 St. Arvans E 8
29 St. Asaph C 9
14 St. Athan G 3
3 St. Austell D 7
7 St. Bartholomew's Hill D 12
38 St. Bees D 2
3 St. Blazey D 8
3 St. Blazey Gate D 7
49 St. Boswells F 8
3 St. Breock C 7
3 St. Breward B 8
15 St. Briavels D 9
12 St. Brides F 2
14 St. Brides Major G 2
15 St. Brides Netherwent E 7
14 St. Bride's-super-Ely G 4
14 St. Bride's Wentlooge F 6
38 St. Bridget Beckermet E 3
5 St. Budeaux K 3
2 St. Buryan G 1
15 St. Catherine G 11
51 St. Catherines G 8
12 St. Clears E 6
3 St. Cleer C 9
2 St. Clement E 5
3 St. Clether A 9
46 St. Colmac C 5
2 St. Columb Major C 6
2 St. Columb Minor C 5
2 St. Columb Porth C 5
2 St. Columb Road D 6
58 St. Combs A 8
27 St. Cross South Elmham G 6
49 St. Cuthberts E 11
12 St. David's, Dyfed D 1
52 St. David's, Tayside E 4
2 St. Day E 4
6 St. Decumans B 4
2 St. Dennis D 6
15 St. Devereux A 7
12 St. Dogmaels B 5
12 St. Dogwells D 3
3 St. Dominick C 11
14 St. Donats G 3
16 St. Edith's Marsh H 1
3 St. Endellion B 7
2 St. Enoder D 6
2 St. Erme E 5
3 St. Erney D 10
2 St. Erth F 3
2 St. Ervan C 6
3 St. Ewe E 7
14 St. Faggans F 4
58 St. Fergus B 8
52 St. Fillans E 2
12 St. Florence G 4
2 St. Gennys B 2
29 St. George C 9
15 St. George's, Avon H 7
14 St. George's, S. Glam. G 4
3 St. Germans D 10
4 St. Giles in the Wood D 4
5 St. Giles on the Heath G 2
20 St. Harmon E 5
40 St. Helen Auckland C 2
26 St. Helena D 5
9 St. Helens, I. o. W. G 7
34 St. Helens, Merseyside G 4
2 St. Hilary, Corn. F 3
14 St. Hilary, S. Glam. G 3
10 Saint Hill D 3
14 St. Illtyd D 5
12 St. Ishmael's F 2
2 St. Issey C 6
3 St. Ive C 10
25 St. Ives, Cambs. H 4
2 St. Ives, Corn. F 2
8 St. Ives, Dorset F 3
27 St. James South Elmham G 6
8 St. Joan à Gores Cross A 2
3 St. John D 11
38 St. John Beckermet D 3
22 St. John's, Heref. & Worcs. G 2
38 St. John's, I.o.M. G 1
4 St. John's Chapel, Devon C 4
39 St. John's Chapel, Durham A 11
24 St. John's Fen End D 6
24 St. John's Highway D 6
38 St. Judas F 2
2 St. Just G 1
2 St. Just Lane F 6
58 St. Katherines D 5
2 St. Keverne G 5
3 St. Kew B 7
3 St. Kew Highway B 7
3 St. Keyne D 9
3 St. Lawrence, Corn. C 7
19 St. Lawrence, Essex C 9
9 St. Lawrence, I. o. W. H 7
17 St. Leonards, Bucks. C 10
8 St. Leonards, Dorset F 3
11 St. Leonards, E. Sussex G 7
2 St. Levan G 1
14 St. Lythans G 4
3 St. Mabyn B 7
6 St. Margaret D 4
27 St. Margaret South Elmham G 6
15 St. Margarets, Heref. & Worcs. A 7
18 St. Margarets, Hertfordshire C 4
11 St. Margaret's at Cliffe D 12
64 St. Margaret's Hope E 2
38 St. Mark's H 1
3 St. Martin D 9
52 St. Martins, Tayside D 6
30 St. Martin's, Salop G 2
2 St. Martin's Green G 4
8 St. Mary Bourne A 6
14 St. Mary Church G 3
18 St. Mary Cray G 5
11 St. Mary in the Marsh E 9
18 St. Marylebone F 3
64 St. Marys D 3
11 St. Mary's Bay E 9
15 St. Mary's Grove G 8
19 St. Mary's Hoo F 8
15 St. Maughans C 8
2 St. Mawes F 5
2 St. Mawgan C 6
3 St. Mellion C 11
14 St. Mellons F 6
2 St. Merryn B 6
3 St. Mewan E 7
3 St. Michael Caerhays E 7
2 St. Michael Penkevil E 6
27 St. Michael South Elmham G 6
11 St. Michaels, Kent E 7
21 St. Michaels, Heref. & Worcs. F 11
34 St. Michaels on Wyre C 3
3 St. Minver B 7
53 St. Monans G 10
3 St. Neot C 9
25 St. Neots J 3
12 St. Nicholas, Dyfed C 2
14 St. Nicholas, S. Glam. G 4
11 St. Nicholas at Wade A 11
52 St. Ninians H 3
19 St. Osyth B 11
15 St. Owen's Cross B 8
18 St. Pancras F 3
18 St. Paul's Cray G 5
18 St. Paul's Walden B 2
11 St. Peters A 12
12 St. Petrox G 3
47 St. Quivox G 8
2 St. Stephen D 6
3 St. Stephens, Corn. A 10
3 St. Stephens, Corn. D 11
3 St. Teath B 7
3 St. Tudy B 8
12 St. Twynnells G 3
3 St. Veep D 8
53 St. Vigeans C 11
3 St. Wenn C 7
15 St. Weonards B 8
22 Saintbury H 5
51 Salachail B 8
5 Salcombe M 6
6 Salcombe Regis G 5
19 Salcott C 9
35 Sale H 7
22 Sale Green F 3
33 Saleby B 11
10 Salehurst F 6
20 Salem, Dyfed D 2
13 Salem, Dyfed D 9
28 Salem, Gwynedd E 5
50 Salen, Highland A 4
50 Salen, Mull, Strathclyde C 3
34 Salesbury D 5
23 Salford, Beds. H 12
35 Salford, Manchester G 7
16 Salford, Oxon. A 4
22 Salford Priors G 4
10 Salfords C 2
26 Salhouse D 6
52 Saline H 5
8 Salisbury C 3
26 Sall C 4
51 Sallachan A 7
55 Sallachy, Highland G 3
60 Sallachy, Highland F 6
33 Salmonby C 10
43 Salmond's Muir C 10
21 Salop, Co. B 10
16 Salperton B 2
25 Salph End K 2
48 Salsburgh C 1
31 Salt G 8
3 Saltash D 11
56 Saltburn C 3
41 Saltburn-by-the Sea C 7
32 Saltby H 6
47 Saltcoats E 7
35 Salterforth C 7
24 Salters Lode E 7
30 Satterswall D 5
33 Saltfleet A 11
33 Saltfleetby St. Clements A 11
33 Saltfleetby St. Peter A 11
33 Saltfleetby Saints A 11
15 Saltford G 10
37 Salthaugh Grange E 10
26 Salthouse A 4
36 Saltmarshe E 6
30 Saltney D 3
41 Salton G 7
4 Saltren's D 3
45 Saltwick E 10
11 Saltwood D 10
9 Salvington F 12
22 Salwarpe F 2
7 Salway Ash F 8
22 Sambourne F 4
30 Sambrook H 6
34 Samlesbury D 5
34 Samlesbury Bottoms D 5
6 Sampford B 4
6 Sampford Arundel D 5

4 Sampford Courtenay F 5
6 Sampford Peverell E 4
5 Sampford Spinney H 4
19 Samuel's Corner E 9
49 Samuelston B 7
54 Sanachan F 2
51 Sanahole G 7
2 Sancreed G 1
37 Sancton C 7
64 Sand D 7
36 Sand Hutton A 5
38 Sand Side G 5
55 Sandaig, Highland J 1
55 Sandaig, Highland H 1
35 Sandal Magna E 12
38 Sandale A 5
30 Sandbach D 6
46 Sandbank A 6
8 Sandbanks G 2
58 Sandend A 3
18 Sanderstead H 3
15 Sandford, Avon H 7
39 Sandford, Cumbria D 9
4 Sandford, Devon F 7
8 Sandford, Dorset G 1
9 Sandford, I.o.W. H 7
30 Sandford, Salop H 2
47 Sandford, Strathclyde E 12
16 Sandford-on-Thames D 6
7 Sandford Orcas D 9
16 Sandford St. Martin B 5
58 Sandfordhill C 8
64 Sandgarth C 3
11 Sandgate E 10
58 Sandhaven A 7
42 Sandhead G 2
47 Sandhill H 9
45 Sandhoe F 8
44 Sandholm D 3
36 Sandholme, Humber. D 6
24 Sandholme, Lincs. B 4
17 Sandhurst, Berks. H 9
15 Sandhurst, Glos. B 11
11 Sandhurst, Kent E 7
10 Sandhurst Cross E 6
40 Sandhutton G 4
32 Sandiacre G 2
33 Sandilands B 12
30 Sandiway C 5
16 Sandleigh D 6
10 Sandling B 6
64 Sandness D 6
19 Sandon, Essex C 7
25 Sandon, Herts. M 4
31 Sandon, Staffs. G 8
9 Sandown H 7
3 Sandplace D 9
18 Sandridge, Herts. C 2
15 Sandridge, Wilts. H 12
41 Sandsend D 8
64 Sandside D 1
61 Sandside Hotel A 9
64 Sandsound D 7
36 Sandtoft F 5
11 Sandway, Kent C 7
6 Sandway, Som. C 2
22 Sandwell C 4
38 Sandwick, Cumbria C 6
64 Sandwick, Orkney Is. E 2
63 Sandwick, Highland D 5
64 Sandwick, Shetland Is. E 7
38 Sandwith D 2
25 Sandy K 3
30 Sandy Bank G 4
10 Sandy Cross F 5
12 Sandy Haven F 2
16 Sandy Lane, Wilts. G 1
35 Sandy Lane, W. Yorks. D 9
29 Sandycroft D 12
43 Sandyford, Dumf. & Gall. B 12
47 Sandyford, Strathclyde G 9
38 Sandygate F 2
43 Sandyhills F 9
34 Sandylands A 3
4 Sandymoor Cross F 3
5 Sandypark G 6
44 Sandysike F 2
49 Sandystones G 8
15 Sandyway B 8
50 Sanna A 2
47 Sanquhar H 12
38 Santon Bridge E 4
27 Santon Downham G 1
23 Sapcote C 8
21 Sapey Common F 12
27 Sapiston H 2
15 Sapperton, Glos. D 12
33 Sapperton, Lincs. G 7
24 Saracen's Head C 4
61 Sarclet C 12
12 Sardis F 3
12 Sardis Mountain F 5
8 Sarisbury E 6
28 Sarn, Gwynedd G 2
14 Sarn, Mid Glam. F 2
21 Sarn, Powys C 7
12 Sarnau, Dyfed B 6
13 Sarnau, Dyfed D 8
29 Sarnau, Gwynedd F 9
14 Sarnau, Powys A 3
21 Sarnau, Powys A 8
28 Sarn-back H 2
21 Sarnesfield G 9
13 Saron, Dyfed C 7
13 Saron, Dyfed F 9
28 Saron, Gwynedd D 5
17 Sarratt D 11
11 Sarre B 11
16 Sarsden B 4
8 Sarson B 4
38 Sartfield F 2
40 Satley A 1
4 Satterleigh D 5
38 Satterthwaite F 6
17 Satwell F 8
58 Sauchen F 4
53 Saucher D 7
59 Sauchieburn K 4
47 Sauchrie H 8
44 Saughtree C 4
44 Saughtrees E 3
15 Saul C 10
32 Saundby A 5
12 Saundersfoot F 5
17 Saunderton D 9
17 Saunderton Lee D 9
4 Saunton B 3
33 Sausthorpe C 11
60 Savalmore F 6
31 Saverley Green F 8
50 Savory C 4
18 Sawbridgeworth B 5
41 Sawdon G 9
32 Sawley, Derby G 2
34 Sawley, Lancs. C 6
25 Sawston K 6
25 Sawtry G 3
32 Saxby, Leics. H 5
33 Saxby, Lincs. B 7
37 Saxby All Saints E 7
32 Saxelby H 4
32 Saxilby C 6
26 Saxingham B 3
26 Saxlingham Nethergate F 5
27 Saxmundham J 7
25 Saxon Street J 8
32 Saxondale F 4
27 Saxtead J 6
27 Saxtead Green J 6
26 Saxthorpe C 4
36 Saxton C 3
10 Sayers Common F 2
48 Scabcleuch H 5
40 Scackleton H 6
63 Scadabay H 3
32 Scaftworth A 4
41 Scagglethorpe H 8
50 Scalasaig H 1
36 Scalby, Humber. D 6
41 Scalby, N. Yorks. F 10
23 Scaldwell E 11
44 Scaleby G 3
44 Scalebyhill G 3
38 Scales, Cumb. C 6
38 Scales, Cumbria H 5
34 Scales, Lans. D 3
39 Scales Houses A 8
32 Scalford H 5
41 Scaling D 7
50 Scallastle D 4
64 Scalloway E 7
62 Scalpay House E 5
55 Scamadale K 1
55 Scamodale M 2
41 Scampston H 8
33 Scampton B 7
56 Scaniport F 2
64 Scapa D 2
64 Scar A 4
39 Scar End B 11
63 Scarastavore H 1
41 Scarborough F 10
43 Scarbrae C 9
32 Scarcliffe C 2
35 Scarcroft C 12
54 Scardroy D 6
44 Scare F 3
61 Scarfskerry A 11
40 Scargill D 1
34 Scarisbrick F 3
26 Scarning D 2
32 Scarrington F 4
34 Scarth Hill F 3
37 Scartho G 10
64 Scarwell C 1
56 Scatraig F 3
64 Scatsta C 7
37 Scawby G 7
37 Scawby Brook F 7
40 Scawton G 6
10 Scayne's Hill F 3
14 Scethrog B 4
47 Schaw G 9
31 Scholar Green E 7
35 Scholes, W. Yorks. F 10
35 Scholes, W. Yorks. E 10
36 Scholes, W. Yorks. D 2
40 School Aycliffe C 3
35 Scissett F 11
12 Scleddau D 3
26 Sco Ruston C 6
27 Scole G 4
59 Scolly's Cross J 4
12 Scolton E 3
62 Sconser E 4
53 Scoonie G 8
50 Scoor F 2
33 Scopwick D 8
60 Scoraig G 2
37 Scorborough C 8
47 Scorrieholm F 12
2 Scorrier E 4
5 Scorriton J 6
40 Scorton E 3
34 Scot Lane End F 5
44 Scotby G 3
40 Scotch Corner E 2
34 Scotforth A 4
33 Scothern B 7
45 Scots' Gap D 8
33 Scots Hole D 8
56 Scotsburn D 6
61 Scotscalder Sta. B 10
53 Scotscraig D 9
44 Scotsdike F 2
59 Scotston, Grampian K 5
52 Scotston, Tayside C 4
50 Scotstown A 5
45 Scotswood G 10
53 Scottas J 1
36 Scotter G 6
36 Scotterthorpe G 6
37 Scotton, Lincs. G 7
40 Scotton, N. Yorks. F 2
35 Scotton, N. Yorks. A 12
49 Scoughall A 8
26 Scoulton E 3
60 Scourie C 3
60 Scourie More C 3
64 Scousburgh F 7
61 Scrabster A 10
49 Scraesburgh G 9
33 Scrafield C 10
45 Scrainwood B 8
33 Scramblesby B 10
24 Scrane End A 5
23 Scraptoft B 10
26 Scratby D 8
36 Scrayingham A 5
24 Scredington B 2
6 Screedy D 4
43 Screel F 9
33 Scremby C 11
49 Scremerston D 12
32 Screveton F 4
61 Scriberscross F 8
33 Scrivelsby D 9
35 Scriven A 12
43 Scroggs C 12
32 Scrooby A 4
31 Scropton G 10
33 Scrub Hill E 9
40 Scruton F 3
37 Sculcoates D 8
26 Sculthorpe B 2
37 Scunthorpe F 7
13 Scurlage H 8
26 Sea Palling C 7
7 Seaborough F 8
30 Seacombe A 2
33 Seacroft, Lincs. D 12
35 Seacroft, W. Yorks. D 12
48 Seafield, Lothian C 3
47 Seafield, Strathclyde G 8
10 Seaford H 4
34 Seaforth G 2
63 Seaforth Head E 4
45 Seaham H 12
45 Seahouses D 12
10 Seal B 4
30 Sealand C 2
9 Seale A 10
41 Seamer, N. Yorks. G 10
40 Seamer, N. Yorks. D 5
47 Seamill E 7
37 Searby G 8
11 Seasalter B 9
38 Seascale E 3
33 Seathorne D 12
38 Seathwaite, Cumb. D 5
38 Seathwaite, Cumb. F 5
38 Seatoller D 5
3 Seaton, Corn. D 10
38 Seaton, Cumb. B 3
6 Seaton, Devon G 6
45 Seaton, Dur. H 12
23 Seaton, Leics. B 12
37 Seaton, Humber. B 9
45 Seaton, Northumb. E 11
45 Seaton Burn F 10
40 Seaton Carew B 5
45 Seaton Delaval E 11
36 Seaton Ross C 6
45 Seaton Sluice E 11
58 Seatown, Grampian A 3
58 Seatown, Grampian A 2
7 Seatown, Dorset G 7
40 Seave Green E 6
9 Seaview G 8
43 Seaville F 12
7 Seavington St. Mary E 7
7 Seavington St. Michael E 7
19 Seawick Sands C 11
14 Sebastopol, Gwent E 6
14 Sebastopol, Mid Glam. D 5
38 Sebergham A 6
22 Seckington A 6
60 Second Coast G 1
39 Sedbergh F 9
15 Sedbury E 9
39 Sedbusk F 11
22 Sedgeberow H 4
32 Sedgebrook F 6
40 Sedgefield B 4
24 Sedgeford B 8
7 Sedgehill C 12
22 Sedgley C 2
39 Sedgwick F 7
10 Sedlescombe F 6
10 Sedlescombe St. F 6
15 Seend H 12
15 Seende Cleeve H 12
17 Seer Green E 10
26 Seething F 6
34 Sefton G 2
45 Seghill F 11
31 Seighford H 7
63 Seilebost G 2
22 Seisdon C 2
30 Selattyn G 2
9 Selborne C 9
36 Selby D 4
9 Selham D 10
49 Selkirk G 7
35 Sellack B 9
38 Sellafield Station E 3
64 Sellafirth B 7
11 Sellindge D 9
11 Sellindge Lees D 9
11 Selling B 9
15 Sells Green H 12
22 Selly Oak D 4
10 Selmeston G 4
18 Selsdon H 4
15 Selsey D 11
10 Selsfield Common E 2
39 Selside H 10
11 Selstead D 10
32 Selston E 2
6 Selworthy B 3
64 Semblister D 6
27 Semer K 3
15 Semington H 12
7 Semley D 12
9 Send A 11
9 Sendmarsh A 11
14 Senghenydd E 4
2 Sennen G 1
2 Sennen Cove G 1
14 Sennybridge B 3
43 Senwick Ho. G 7
40 Sessay H 5
24 Setchey D 7
8 Setley F 5
64 Settascarth C 2
64 Setter, Bressay Shetland Is. E 7
64 Setter, Zetland Shetland Is. D 6
64 Setter, Zetland Shetland Is. D 7
35 Settle A 7
45 Settlingstones F 7
41 Settrington H 8
6 Seven Ash C 5
18 Seven Kings E 4
14 Seven Sisters C 2
16 Seven Wells A 2
16 Sevenhampton, Glos. B 1
16 Sevenhampton, Wilts. E 3
10 Sevenoaks C 4
10 Sevenoaks Weald C 4
15 Severn Beach F 8
22 Severn Stoke H 2
11 Sevington, Kent D 9
15 Sevington, Wilts. F 11
25 Sewards End L 7
41 Sewerby H 12
2 Seworgan G 4
32 Sewstern H 6
10 Seyning G 1
17 Shabbington C 7
23 Shackerstone A 7
27 Shadingfield G 7
9 Shackleford B 10
40 Shadforth A 4
11 Shadoxhurst D 8
27 Shadwell, Norfolk G 2
35 Shadwell, W. Yorks. C 12
7 Shaftesbury D 12
36 Shafton F 2
16 Shalbourne H 4
8 Shalcombe G 5
9 Shalden B 8
5 Shaldon J 8
8 Shalfleet G 5
19 Shalford, Essex A 7
9 Shalford, Surrey A 11
19 Shalford Green A 7
52 Shalloch B 3
4 Shallowford B 6
11 Shalmsford Street C 9
23 Shalstone H 9
46 Shalunt B 5
9 Shamley Green B 11
43 Shancastle C 9
47 Shandon A 7
56 Shandwick B 4
23 Shangton C 10
45 Shankhouse E 11
9 Shanklin H 7
46 Shannochie G 5
53 Shanzie B 7
39 Shap D 8
8 Shapwick, Dorset F 1
7 Shapwick, Som. B 7
32 Shardlow G 2
22 Shareshill B 3
35 Sharlston, W. Yorks. E 12
36 Sharlston, W. Yorks. E 2
11 Sharnal Street A 7
25 Sharnbrook J 1
23 Sharnford C 8
34 Sharoe Green D 4
40 Sharow H 3
25 Sharpenhoe M 2
45 Sharperton C 8
15 Sharpness D 10
10 Sharpthorne E 3
26 Sharrington B 3
22 Shatterford D 1
5 Shaugh Prior J 4
7 Shave Cross F 7
30 Shavington E 6
16 Shaw, Berks. G 6
35 Shaw, Lancs. F 8
15 Shaw, Wilts. H 12
34 Shaw Green E 4
35 Shaw Mills A 11
30 Shawbury H 4
45 Shawdon Hill B 9
23 Shawell D 9
8 Shawford D 6
35 Shawforth E 7
43 Shawhead D 9
43 Shawhill E 12
47 Shawood G 10
47 Shawton D 11
7 Shear Cross B 11
43 Shearington E 11
23 Shearsby C 9
4 Shebbear E 3
30 Shebdon H 6
61 Shebster B 9
9 Shedfield E 7
31 Sheen D 9
21 Sheephouse H 7
15 Sheepscombe C 12
5 Sheepstor J 4
4 Sheepwash, Devon E 4
4 Sheepwash, Devon C 7
45 Sheepwash, Northumb. D 10
15 Sheepway G 8
23 Sheepy Magna B 7
23 Sheepy Parva B 7
18 Sheering C 5
11 Sheerness A 8
9 Sheet, Hants. D 9
21 Sheet, Salop E 10
32 Sheffield B 1
25 Shefford L 2
16 Shefford Woodlands G 4
60 Sheigra B 3
43 Sheillahill F 8
21 Sheinton B 11
21 Shelderton E 9
6 Sheldon, Devon E 5
22 Sheldon, War. D 5
11 Sheldwich B 9
35 Shelf D 10
27 Shelfhanger G 4
22 Shelfield, W. Midlands B 4
22 Shelfield, War. F 5
32 Shelford F 4
49 Shellacres E 11
18 Shelley, Essex C 5
35 Shelley, W. Yorks. F 10
16 Shellingford E 4
18 Shellow Bowells C 6
22 Shelsley Beauchamp F 1
21 Shelsley Walsh F 12
32 Shelthorpe H 3
26 Shelton, Norfolk F 5
25 Shelton, Northants. H 1
32 Shelton, Notts. F 5
21 Shelton, Salop A 10
21 Shelve C 9
21 Shelwick H 10
21 Shelwick Green H 10
56 Shenachie F 4
18 Shenfield D 6
23 Shenington H 7
18 Shenley D 2
17 Shenley Brook End A 9
23 Shenley Church End H 11
15 Shenmore A 7
42 Shennanton E 4
22 Shenstone, Heref. & Worcs. E 2
22 Shenstone, Staffs. B 4
57 Shenval G 8
24 Shepeu Stow D 4
18 Shephall B 3
18 Shepherd's Bush F 2
17 Shepherd's Green F 8
11 Shepherdswell C 11
35 Shepley F 10
15 Shepperdine E 9
17 Shepperton G 11
17 Shepperton Grn. G 11
25 Shepreth K 5
32 Shepshed H 2
7 Shepton Beauchamp D 7
7 Shepton Mallet B 9
7 Shepton Montague C 10
10 Shepway C 6
40 Sheraton B 5
7 Sherborne, Dorset E 10
16 Sherborne, Glos. C 3
9 Sherborne St. John A 8
22 Sherbourne F 6
40 Sherburn, Dur. A 3
41 Sherburn, N. Yorks. G 9
40 Sherburn Hill A 4
36 Sherburn in Elmet D 3
9 Shere A 12
26 Shereford C 2
8 Sherfield English D 4
17 Sherfield on Loddon H 7
5 Sherford L 6
36 Sheriff Hutton A 3
26 Sheringham A 4
23 Sherington G 12
24 Shernborne B 8
22 Sherriffhales A 1
8 Sherrington B 1
15 Sherston F 11
4 Sherwood Green D 4
63 Sheshader C 6
47 Shettleston C 11
34 Shevington F 4
34 Shevington Moor F 4
3 Sheviock D 10
55 Shewglie G 8
52 Shian C 3
49 Shidlaw F 10
43 Shiel, Dumf. & Gall. A 8

43 Shiel, Dumf. & Gall. D 7
55 Shiel Bridge H 3
45 Shiel Dykes B 9
54 Shieldaig D 2
54 Shieldaig Lodge (Hotel) C 2
48 Shieldhill, Central B 2
43 Shieldhill, Dumf. & Gall. C 10
43 Shieldhill, Dumf. & Gall. C 11
47 Shieldmuir D 12
50 Shielfoot A 4
58 Shielhill, Grampian B 8
59 Shielhill, Tayside L 2
47 Shieloans F 11
16 Shifford D 5
22 Shifnal A 1
45 Shilbottle B 10
44 Shilburn Haugh D 5
40 Shildon C 3
47 Shillford D 9
6 Shillingford, Devon D 3
17 Shillingford, Oxon. E 7
6 Shillingford Abbot G 2
6 Shillingford St. George G 2
7 Shillingstone E 11
25 Shillington M 2
45 Shillmoor B 7
63 Shiltenish E 4
16 Shilton, Oxon. C 4
23 Shilton, War. D 7
7 Shilvinghampton H 9
27 Shimpling, Norf. G 4
27 Shimpling, Suffolk K 2
27 Shimpling Street K 2
40 Shincliffe A 3
40 Shincliffe Colliery A 3
45 Shiney Row H 11
17 Shinfield G 8
59 Shinfur J 2
43 Shinnelhead B 8
5 Shinner's Bridge J 7
10 Shipbourne C 5
26 Shipdham E 3
7 Shipham A 8
5 Shiphay J 8
17 Shiplake F 8
48 Shiplaw D 5
45 Shipley, Northumb. A 9
22 Shipley, Salop C 2
9 Shipley, W. Sussex D 12
35 Shipley, W. Yorks. C 10
10 Shipley Bridge D 2
26 Shipmeadow F 7
25 Shippea Hill Sta. G 7
16 Shippon D 6
22 Shipston on Stour H 6
16 Shipton, Glos. B 1
21 Shipton, Salop. C 11
36 Shipton, N Yorks A 3
8 Shipton Bellinger B 4
7 Shipton Gorge G 8
9 Shipton Green F 9
15 Shipton Moyne E 12
16 Shipton-on-Cherwell B 6
16 Shipton-under-Wychwood B 4
36 Shiptonthorpe C 6
17 Shirburn E 8
34 Shirdley Hill F 2
22 Shire Oak B 4
32 Shirebrook C 3
32 Shiregreen A 1
15 Shirehampton F 8
45 Shiremoor F 11
15 Shirenewton E 8
32 Shireoaks B 3
4 Shirewell Cross B 5
21 Shirl Heath F 10
32 Shirland D 1
31 Shirley, Derby F 10
8 Shirley, Hants. E 5
22 Shirley, W. Midlands D 5
9 Shirrell Heath E 7
4 Shirwell B 5
46 Shishkine F 4
21 Shobdon F 9
4 Shobrooke F 7
30 Shocklach E 3
19 Shoeburyness E 9
11 Sholden C 12
8 Sholing E 6
4 Shop, Cornwall D 1
2 Shop, Cornwall B 6
27 Shop Street H 5
44 Shopford F 4
18 Shoreditch F 3
10 Shoreham B 4
10 Shoreham-by-Sea G 1
56 Shoremill C 3
49 Shoresdean E 12
49 Shoreswood E 12
56 Shoretown D 2
16 Shornecote E 1
10 Shorne Ridgeway A 6
22 Short Heath, Leics. A 6
22 Short Heath, W. Midlands B 3
22 Short Heath, W. Midlands C 4
5 Shortacombe G 4
10 Shortgate G 4
2 Shortlanesend E 5
47 Shortlees F 9
15 Shortwood G 10
8 Shorwell H 6
7 Shoscombe A 10
30 Shotatton H 2
26 Shotesham F 6
19 Shotgate E 7
45 Shotley Bridge H 9
27 Shotley Gate M 5
27 Shotley Street M 5
45 Shotleyfield H 9
11 Shottenden C 9
9 Shottermill C 10
22 Shottery G 5
23 Shotteswell H 8
27 Shottisham L 6
31 Shottle E 11
29 Shotton, Clwyd C 12
40 Shotton, Durham A 4
49 Shotton, Northumb. F 11
40 Shotton Colliery A 4
48 Shotts C 1
30 Shotwick C 2
38 Shoughlaige-e-Caine G 1
56 Shougle D 8
24 Shouldham E 8
24 Shouldham Thorpe E 8
22 Shoulton F 2
10 Shover's Green E 5
21 Shrawardine A 9
22 Shrawley F 2
17 Shreding Green F 11
22 Shrewley E 5
21 Shrewsbury A 10
8 Shrewton B 2
9 Shripney F 10
16 Shrivenham E 3
26 Shropham F 3
19 Shrub End B 9
31 Shrucknall H 11
25 Shady Camps L 7
63 Shulishader C 6
38 Shundraw C 5
15 Shurdington B 12
17 Shurlock Row G 9
61 Shurrery Lodge B 10
6 Shurton B 5
22 Shustoke C 6
22 Shut End C 2
4 Shute, Devon F 8
6 Shute, Devon F 6
23 Shutford H 7
15 Shuthonger A 12
23 Shutlanger G 10
22 Shuttington B 6
32 Shuttlewood C 2
43 Sibbaldbie C 12
23 Sibbertoft D 10
21 Sibdon Carwood D 9
23 Sibford Ferris H 7
23 Sibford Gower H 7
27 Sible Hedingham M 1
33 Sibsey E 10
24 Sibson, Cambs. F 2
23 Sibson, Leics. B 7
32 Sibthorpe F 5
27 Sicklesmere J 2
35 Sicklinghall B 12
6 Sid G 5
6 Sidbury, Devon G 5
21 Sidbury, Salop D 12
18 Sidcup G 5
38 Siddick B 2
31 Siddington, Ches. C 5
16 Siddington, Glos. D 1
22 Sidemoor E 3
6 Sidford G 5
9 Sidlesham F 10
10 Sidley G 6
10 Sidlow Bridge C 1
6 Sidmouth H 4
5 Sigford H 6
14 Siggiston G 3
37 Sigglesthorne C 9
17 Silchester H 7
23 Sileby A 9
38 Silecroft G 4
20 Silian G 1
24 Silk Willoughby A 2
35 Silkstone G 11
35 Silkstone Com. G 11
44 Silloans C 6
43 Silloth F 11
58 Sillyearn B 3
13 Siloh C 10
41 Silpho F 9
35 Silsden C 9
25 Silsoe M 2
25 Silver End, Beds. L 2
19 Silver End, Essex B 8
11 Silver Street B 7
48 Silverburn C 5
39 Silverdale, Lancs. H 7
31 Silverdale, Staffs. F 7
23 Silverstone H 10
6 Silverton, Devon F 3
47 Silverton, Strathclyde B 9
21 Silvington D 11
45 Simonburn F 7
6 Simonsbath B 1
34 Simonstone D 6
49 Simprim E 11
23 Simpson, Bucks. H 12
12 Simpson, Dyfed E 2
49 Sinclair's Hill D 10
47 Sinclairston H 9
40 Sinderby Quernhow G 4
45 Sinderhope H 7
17 Sindlesham G 8
44 Singdean C 4
17 Singleborough A 8
34 Singleton, Lancs. C 3
9 Singleton, W. Sussex E 10
10 Singlewell or Ifield A 5
30 Singret F 2
58 Sinnahard F 2
41 Sinnington G 7
22 Sinton Green F 2
18 Sipson F 1
14 Sirhowy C 5
11 Sissinghurst D 7
49 Sisterpath E 10
15 Siston G 10
2 Sithney G 3
11 Sittingbourne B 8
58 Sittyton E 6
22 Six Ashes C 2
32 Six Hills H 4
25 Six Mile Bottom J 7
31 Six Roads End G 10
35 Sixhills B 9
27 Sizewell J 8
61 Skail C 7
64 Skail, Egilsay, Orkney Is. B 3
64 Skaill, Mainland, Orkney Is. D 3
64 Skaill, Mainland, Orkney Is. C 1
47 Skares H 10
59 Skateraw, Grampian H 7
49 Skateraw, Lothian B 10
62 Skeabost C 3
40 Skeeby E 2
23 Skeffington B 11
37 Skeffling E 11
32 Skegby D 2
33 Skegness D 12
61 Skelbo G 8
36 Skelbrooke F 3
24 Skeldyke B 4
32 Skellingthorpe C 6
64 Skellister D 7
36 Skellow F 3
35 Skelmanthorpe F 11
34 Skelmersdale F 4
58 Skelmonae D 6
47 Skelmorlie C 7
58 Skelmuir C 7
61 Skelpick B 7
39 Skelton, Cumb. B 7
40 Skelton, Cleveland C 6
36 Skelton, Humber. E 5
36 Skelton, N. Yorks. B 3
36 Skelton, N. Yorks. E 1
40 Skelton, N. Yorks. H 4
38 Skelwirth Bridge E 6
64 Skelwick A 3
33 Skendleby C 11
58 Skene House F 5
15 Skenfrith B 8
37 Skerne B 8
46 Skeroblingarry G 2
61 Skerray B 7
60 Skerricha C 4
34 Skerton A 4
23 Sketchley C 7
13 Sketty H 9
13 Skewen G 10
40 Skewsby H 6
26 Skeyton C 5
60 Skiag Bridge E 4
61 Skibo Castle G 7
33 Skidbrooke A 11
37 Skidby D 8
63 Skigersta A 6
6 Skilgate D 3
32 Skillington H 6
43 Skinburness F 12
62 Skinidin C 1
41 Skinningrove C 7
46 Skipness D 4
37 Skipsea B 9
37 Skipsea Brough B 9
35 Skipton B 8
40 Skipton-on-Swale G 4
36 Skipwith C 4
24 Skirbeck A 4
24 Skirbeck Quarter A 4
48 Skirling E 3
17 Skirmett E 8
36 Skirpenbeck A 5
39 Skirwith, Cumb. B 8
39 Skirwith, N. Yorks. H 9
61 Skirza A 12
44 Skitby F 3
62 Skulamus F 6
60 Skullomie B 6
57 Skye of Curr G 5
35 Slack D 8
31 Slackhall B 9
58 Slackhead A 2
43 Slacks C 11
58 Slacks of Cairnbanno C 6
15 Slad D 12
4 Slade B 4
18 Slade Green F 5
3 Sladesbridge C 7
44 Slaggyford H 5
34 Slaidburn B 6
59 Slains Park K 6
49 Slainsfield E 12
35 Slaithwaite F 9
45 Slaley G 8
48 Slamannan B 1
17 Slapton, Bucks. B 10
5 Slapton, Devon L 7
23 Slapton, Northants. G 9
54 Slattadale C 3
35 Slattcks F 7
10 Slaugham E 1
30 Slaughter Hill E 6
3 Slaughterbridge A 8
15 Slaughterford G 11
23 Slawston C 11
9 Sleaford, Hants. B 9
24 Sleaford, Lincs. A 2
39 Sleagill C 8
21 Sleap A 11
21 Sleapford A 11
15 Sledge Green A 11
37 Sledmere A 7
44 Sleetbeck E 3
39 Sleightholme D 11
41 Sleights D 8
8 Slepe G 1
4 Slerra D 2
61 Slickly A 12
46 Sliddery G 4
62 Sligachan E 4
51 Sligrachan H 9
15 Slimbridge D 10
31 Slindon, Staffs. G 7
9 Slindon, W. Sussex E 11
9 Slinfold C 12
28 Sling D 5
41 Slingsby H 7
58 Slioch D 3
17 Slip End, Beds. B 11
25 Slip End, Herts. L 4
26 Slipper's Bottom D 6
23 Slipton D 12
31 Slitting Mill H 9
57 Slochd G 4
57 Slochnacraig M 7
50 Slockavullin H 5
43 Slogarie E 7
33 Sloothby C 12
17 Slough F 10
6 Slough Green D 6
57 Sluggan G 4
34 Slyne A 4
49 Smailholm F 9
38 Smaithwaite C 5
10 Small Dole G 1
11 Small Hythe E 7
35 Smallbridge F 8
26 Smallburgh C 6
58 Smallburn, Grampian D 8
47 Smallburn, Strathclyde G 11
32 Smalley F 1
10 Smallfield D 2
43 Smallholm D 11
6 Smallridge F 6
8 Smannel A 5
39 Smardale D 9
11 Smarden D 7
6 Smeatharpe E 5
11 Smeeth, Kent D 9
24 Smeeth, Norfolk E 6
23 Smeeton Westerby C 10
35 Smelthouses A 10
61 Smerral D 11
22 Smethwick C 4
31 Smisby H 12
34 Smith Green B 4
44 Smithfield F 3
6 Smithincott E 4
18 Smith's Green B 6
47 Smithston H 9
54 Smithstown B 2
56 Smithtown E 3
32 Smithy Houses E 1
45 Snableazes B 10
43 Snade C 9
21 Snailbeach B 9
25 Snailwell H 7
41 Snainton G 9
36 Snaith E 4
31 Snake Inn A 9
27 Snape, Suffolk J 7
40 Snape, N. Yorks. G 3
34 Snape Green F 3
27 Snape Street J 7
23 Snarestone A 7
33 Snarford B 7
11 Snargate E 8
11 Snave E 9
21 Snead C 8
41 Sneaton D 9
41 Sneaton Thorpe E 9
33 Snelland B 8
31 Snelston F 10
24 Snettisham B 8
45 Snitter C 8
33 Snitterby A 7
22 Snitterfield F 5
21 Snitton E 11
21 Snodhill H 8
10 Snodland B 6
11 Snowdown C 11
16 Snowshill A 2
5 Soar, Devon M 6
13 Soar, Dyfed D 9
14 Soar, Powys A 3
9 Soberton D 7
9 Soberton Heath E 7
25 Soham H 7
12 Solbury F 2
4 Soldon Cross E 2
9 Soldridge C 8
10 Sole Street A 5
11 Solestreet C 9
22 Solihull D 5
21 Sollers Dilwyn G 9
15 Sollers Hope A 9
34 Sollom E 3
12 Solva E 2
44 Solwaybank E 1
23 Somerby, Leics. A 11
37 Somerby, Lincs. F 8
32 Somercotes E 2
8 Somerford G 3
16 Somerford Keynes E 1
9 Somerley F 9
26 Somerleyton F 8
31 Somersal Herbert G 10
33 Somersby C 10
6 Somerset, Co. C 6
25 Somersham, Cambs. H 5
27 Somersham, Suff. K 4
16 Somerton, Oxon. A 6
7 Somerton, Som. C 8
27 Somerton, Suffolk K 1
10 Sompting G 1
17 Sonning G 8
17 Sonning Common F 8
17 Sonning Eye F 8
59 Sootywells K 5
8 Sopley F 3
15 Sopworth F 11
44 Sorbie, Dumf. & Gall. D 2
42 Sorbie, Dumf. & Gall. G 5
44 Sorbietrees E 3
61 Sordale B 10
47 Sorn G 10
47 Sornbeg F 10
48 Sornfallow F 2
47 Sornhill F 10
50 Soroba Farm E 6
61 Sortat B 12
33 Sotby B 9
17 Sotwell E 7
29 Soughton D 11
17 Soulbury A 9
39 Soulby D 9
16 Souldern A 6
25 Souldrop J 1
64 Sound, Zetland, Shetland Is. D 7
64 Sound, Zetland, Shetland Is. E 7
49 Sourhope G 11
64 Sourin B 2
5 Sourton G 4
38 Soutergate G 5
26 South Acre D 1
5 South Allington M 7
52 South Alloa H 4
9 South Ambersham D 10
32 South Anston B 2
17 South Ascot G 10
8 South Baddesley F 5
42 South Balloch B 4
7 South Barrow C 9
28 South Beach G 3
48 South Bellsdyke A 2
19 South Benfleet E 7
9 South Bersted F 10
36 South Bramwith F 4
5 South Brent K 6
7 South Brewham C 10
52 South Bridge-end E 3
45 South Broomhill C 10
26 South Burlingham E 7
7 South Cadbury D 9
42 South Cairn E 1
33 South Carlton C 7
46 South Carrine H 2
37 South Cave D 7
16 South Cerney D 2
7 South Chard F 7
45 South Charlton A 9
7 South Cheriton D 10
36 South Cliffe D 6
32 South Clifton C 5
33 South Cockerington A 11
32 South Collingham D 5
14 South Cornelly F 1
27 South Cove G 8
51 South Creagan C 7
26 South Creake B 1
23 South Croxton A 10
37 South Dalton C 7
10 South Darenth A 4
63 South Dell A 6
58 South Denmore F 7
46 South Druimachro E 2
36 South Duffield D 5
33 South Elkington A 10
36 South Elmsall F 3
17 South End, Berks. G 7
17 South End, Bucks. B 9
34 South End, Cumb. A 1
37 South End, Humber. E 9
54 South Erradale C 1
19 South Fambridge D 8
16 South Fawley F 5
16 South Feorline G 4
37 South Ferriby E 7
58 South Fornet F 5
63 South Galson A 5
46 South Garrochty D 6
14 South Glamorgan, Co. G 4
8 South Gorley E 3
58 South Gorrachie B 5
19 South Green, Essex E 7
11 South Green, Kent B 7
46 South Hall B 5
19 South Hanningfield D 7
9 South Harting D 9
9 South Hayling F 8
45 South Hazelrigg C 11
17 South Heath D 10
10 South Heighton H 3
40 South Hetton A 4
36 South Hiendley F 2
3 South Hill, Corn. B 10
7 South Hill, Som. D 8
16 South Hunksey D 6
4 South Hole D 1
41 South Holme G 7
10 South Holmwood D 1
18 South Hornchurch F 5
47 South Hourat D 8
32 South Hykeham D 6
45 South Hylton G 11
60 South Keanchulish G 3
37 South Kelsey G 8
37 South Killingholme F 9
47 South Kilrusken D 7
40 South Kilvington G 4
23 South Kilworth D 9

36 South Kirkby **F 2**
59 South Kirktown **G 5**
33 South Kyme **E 9**
10 South Lancing **H 1**
16 South Leigh **C 5**
32 South Leverton **B 5**
47 South Limmerhaugh **G 11**
22 South Littleton **G 4**
27 South Lopham **G 3**
23 South Luffenham **B 12**
53 South Mains **B 11**
10 South Malling **G 3**
16 South Marston **E 3**
49 South Middleton **G 12**
36 South Milford **D 3**
5 South Milton **L 6**
18 South Mimms **D 2**
4 South Molton **C 6**
16 South Moreton **E 6**
9 South Mundham **F 10**
32 South Muskham **E 5**
37 South Newbald **D 7**
16 South Newington **A 5**
8 South Newton **C 2**
32 South Normanton **E 2**
18 South Norwood **G 3**
10 South Nutfield **C 2**
18 South Ockendon **F 6**
33 South Ormsby **C 10**
40 South Otterington **F 4**
33 South Owersby **A 8**
18 South Oxhey **E 1**
7 South Perrott **F 8**
7 South Petherton **D 8**
3 South Petherwin **B 10**
26 South Pickenham **E 1**
5 South Pool **M 6**
4 South Radworthy **C 6**
33 South Rauceby **F 7**
26 South Raynham **C 2**
33 South Reston **B 11**
24 South Runcton **E 7**
32 South Scarle **D 6**
63 South Shawbost **B 3**
45 South Shields **F 12**
34 South Shore **D 2**
37 South Skirlaugh **C 9**
33 South Somercotes **A 11**
35 South Stainley **A 1**
18 South Stifford **F 6**
15 South Stoke, Avon **H 10**
17 South Stoke, Oxon. **F 7**
9 South Stoke, W. Sussex **E 11**
11 South Street, Kent **B 9**
18 South Street, London **H 4**
10 South Street E. Sussex **F 3**
4 South Tawton **F 5**
33 South Thoresby **C 11**
8 South Tidworth **A 4**
9 South Town **B 8**
26 South Walsham **D 7**
9 S. Warnborough **A 8**
18 South Weald **E6**
17 South Weston **D 8**
5 South Wheatley, Corn. **G 1**
32 South Wheatley, Notts. **B 5**
7 South Widcombe **A9**
23 South Wigston **B 9**
33 South Willingham **B 9**
32 South Wingfield **E 1**
32 South Witham **H 6**
8 South Wonston **B 6**
19 South Woodham Ferrers **D 6**
24 South Wootton **C 7**
15 South Wraxall **H 11**
36 South Yorkshire, Co. **G 2**
4 South Zeal **F 5**
18 Southall **F1**
16 Southam, Glos **B1**
23 Southam, War. **F 7**
8 Southampton **E 5**
10 Southborough **E 5**
8 Southbourne, Dorset **G 3**
9 Southbourne, W. Sussex **E 9**
26 Southburgh **E 3**
37 Southburn **B 7**
19 Southchurch **E 9**
4 Southcott, Devon **D 3**
16 Southcott, Wilts **H 3**
44 Southdean **B 5**
10 Southease **G 5**
46 Southend, Strathclyde **H 2**
16 Southend, Wilts **G 3**
19 Southend-on-Sea **E 8**
14 Southerndown **G 2**
43 Southerness **F 10**
49 Southernknowe **G 11**
24 Southery **F 7**
41 Southfield **G 7**
10 Southfleet **A 5**
18 Southgate, London **E 3**
24 Southgate, Norfolk **B 8**
26 Southgate, Norfolk **C 4**
13 Southgate, W. Glam **H 9**
25 Southill **L 3**
6 Southleigh **G 5**
19 Southminister **D 9**
45 Southmoor **B 10**
25 Southoe **J 3**
27 Southolt **H 5**
24 Southorpe **E 2**
35 Southowram **E 10**
34 Southport **E 2**
26 Southrepps **B 6**
33 Southrey **D8**
16 Southrop **D 3**
9 Southrope **D 8**
9 Southsea **F 8**
64 Southtown **E 3**
18 Southwark **E 3**
9 Southwater **D 12**
7 Southway **B 8**
7 Southwell, Dorset **H 7**
32 Southwell, Notts **E 4**
45 Southwick, Tyne & Wear **G 12**
9 Southwick, Hants **E 8**
24 Southwick, Northants **F 1**
10 Southwick, W. Sussex **G 1**
7 Southwick, Wilts **A 11**
27 Southwold **H 8**
26 Southwood, Norf **E 7**
7 Southwood, Som. **C 9**
49 Soutra Mains **C 7**
63 Soval Lodge **D 4**
40 Sowerby, N. Yorks. **G 4**
35 Sowerby, W. Yorks. **E 9**
35 Sowerby Bridge **E 9**
38 Sowerby Row **A 6**
6 Sowton **G 3**
44 Spadeadam **F 4**
24 Spalding **C 3**
36 Spaldington **D 5**
25 Spaldwick **H 2**
53 Spalefield **F 10**
32 Spalford **C 5**
24 Spanby **B 2**
26 Sparham **D 4**
38 Spark Bridge **G 5**
7 Sparkford **D 9**
31 Sparklow **D 9**
5 Sparkwell **K 4**
31 Sparrowpit **B 9**
8 Sparsholt, Hants, **C 6**
16 Sparsholt, Oxon **E 4**
45 Spartylea **H 7**
41 Spaunton **F 7**
6 Spaxton **C 6**
55 Spean Bridge **L 6**
8 Spearywell **C 4**
43 Speddoch **C 9**
16 Speen, Berks. **G 5**
17 Speen, Bucks. **D 9**
41 Speeton **H 11**
30 Speke **B 3**
10 Speldhurst **D 4**
18 Spellbrook **B 5**
16 Spelsbury **B 4**
14 Spelter **E 2**
17 Spencers Wood **G 8**
40 Spennithorne **F 2**
40 Spennymoor **B 3**
22 Spetchley **G 2**
7 Spetisbury **F 12**
27 Spexhall **G 7**
58 Spey Bay **A 1**
57 Speybridge **G 6**
56 Speyview **E 8**
33 Spilsby **D 11**
45 Spindlestone **D 11**
32 Spinkhill **B 2**
23 Spinney Hills **B 9**
61 Spinningdale **G 7**
61 Spital **B 11**
33 Spital in the Street **A 7**
45 Spitalford **A 10**
10 Spithurst **F 3**
49 Spittal, Dumf. & Gall. **E 5**
42 Spittal, Dumf. & Gall. **F 4**
12 Spittal, Dyfed **E 3**
49 Spittal, Lothian **B 7**
49 Spittal, Northumb. **D 12**
36 Spittal, Humberside **B 5**
59 Spittal of Glenmuick **J 1**
57 Spittal of Glenshee **M 7**
59 Spittalburn **J 4**
52 Spittalfield **C 6**
26 Spixworth **D 5**
3 Splatt **A 9**
10 Splayne's Green **F 3**
35 Spofforth **B 12**
29 Spon Green **D 12**
32 Spondon **G 1**
26 Spooner Row **F 4**
26 Sporle **D 2**
49 Spott **B 9**
49 Spottiswoode **D 8**
23 Spratton **E 10**
9 Spreakley **B 9**
4 Spreyton **F 6**
33 Spridlington **B 7**
38 Spring Valley **H 2**
47 Springburn **C 10**
44 Springfield, Dumf. & Gall. **F 2**
19 Springfield, Essex **C 7**
53 Springfield, Fife **F 8**
56 Springfield, Grampiam **D 6**
22 Springfield, W. Midlands **D 4**
22 Springhill **B 3**
43 Springholm **E 9**
44 Springkell **E 1**
47 Springside **E 8**
32 Springthorpe **A 6**
45 Springwell **G 11**
32 Springthorpe **A 6**
45 Springwell **G 11**
37 Sproatley **D 9**
30 Sproston Green **C 6**
36 Spotbrough **G 3**
27 Sproughton **L 4**
49 Sprouston **F 10**
26 Sprowston **D 6**
32 Sproxton, Leics. **H 6**
40 Sproxton, N. Yorks **G 6**
30 Spurstow **E 4**
57 Sronlairig Lodge **J 1**
57 Sronpadruig **L 3**
35 Stackhouse **A 7**
12 Stackpole **G 3**
35 Stacksteads **E 7**
5 Staddiscombe **K 4**
36 Staddlethorpe **E 6**
17 Stadhampton **D 7**
39 Staffield **A 8**
62 Staffin **A 4**
31 Stafford **H 8**
31 Staffordshire, Co **H 8**
49 Stagehall **E 7**
24 Stag's Holt **E 5**
25 Stagsden **K 1**
25 Stagsden W. End **K 1**
35 Stainburn **B 11**
32 Stainby **H 6**
35 Staincross **F 12**
17 Staines **G 11**
33 Stainfield, Lincs. **C 8**
24 Stainfield, Lincs. **C 2**
39 Stainforth, N. Yorks. **H 10**
36 Stainforth, S. Yorks. **F 4**
34 Staining **D 2**
35 Stainland **E 9**
41 Stainsacre **D 9**
40 Stainton, Cleveland **D 5**
39 Stainton, Cumb. **B 7**
39 Stainton, Cumbria **G 7**
40 Stainton, Dur **C 1**
40 Stainton, N. Yorks. **F 1**
32 Stainton, S. Yorks. **A 3**
33 Stainton by Langworth **B 8**
37 Stainton le Vale **H 9**
38 Stainton with Agarley **H 5**
41 Staintondale **E 10**
38 Stair, Cumb. **C 5**
47 Stair, Strathclyde **G 9**
41 Staithes **C 8**
34 Stake Pool **B 3**
45 Stakeford **D 11**
7 Stalbridge **D 10**
7 Stalbridge Weston **E 10**
26 Stalham **C 7**
26 Stalham Green **C 7**
11 Stalisfield Green **C 8**
39 Stalling Busk **G 11**
37 Stallingborough **F 9**
34 Stalmine **C 3**
35 Stalybridge **G 8**
25 Stambourne **L 8**
24 Stamford, Lincs **E 1**
45 Stamford, Northumb. **A 10**
36 Stamford Bridge **B 5**
45 Stamfordham **F 9**
38 Stanah **C 6**
18 Stanborough **C 2**
17 Stanbridge, Beds. **B 10**
8 Stanbridge, Dorset **F 2**
35 Stanbury **C 9**
47 Stand **C 12**
48 Standburn **B 2**
22 Standeford **A 3**
11 Standen **D 7**
7 Standerwick **A 11**
9 Standford **C 9**
34 Standish **F 4**
16 Standlake **D 5**
8 Standon, Hants. **C 6**
18 Standon, Herts **B 4**
30 Standon, Staffs. **G 6**
18 Standon Massey **D 6**
27 Standwell Green **H 4**
48 Stane **C 2**
26 Stanfield **C 2**
25 Stanford, Beds. **L 3**
11 Stanford, Kent **D 10**
21 Stanford Bishop **G 12**
22 Stanford Bridge **F 1**
16 Stanford Dingley **G 6**
19 Stanford le Hope **F 7**
23 Stanford on Avon **D 9**
32 Stanford on Soar **H 3**
21 Stanford on Teme **F 12**
18 Stanford Rivers **D 5**
16 Stanford the Vale **E 4**
10 Stnaford's End **D 3**
24 Stranground **F 3**
26 Stanhoe **B 1**
39 Stanhope **A 12**
23 Stanion **C 12**
52 Stank **F 1**
32 Stanley, Derby **F 1**
45 Stanley, Dur. **H 10**
31 Stanley, Staffs. **E 8**
32 Stanley, Tayside **D 6**
16 Stanley, Wilts **G 1**
35 Stanley, W. Yorks. **E 12**
32 Stanley Common **F 1**
21 Stanley Hill **H 12**
35 Stanley Lane Ends **E 12**
10 Stanmer **G 2**
16 Stanmore, Berks. **F 6**
8 Stanmore, Hants. **C 6**
18 Stanmore, London **E 2**
44 Stannersburn **D 5**
45 Stannington, Northumb. **E 10**
31 Stannington, S. Yorks **A 11**
21 Stansbatch **F 9**
27 Stansfield **K 1**
31 Stanshope **E 9**
27 Stanstead **K 1**
18 Stanstead Abbots **C 4**
27 Stanstead Street **K 1**
10 Stansted **B 5**
18 Stansted Mountfitchet **A 5**
31 Stanton, Derby **H 11**
16 Stanton, Glos **A 2**
14 Stanton, Gwent **B 5**
45 Stanton, Northumb. **D 9**
31 Stanton, Staffs. **F 9**
27 Stanton, Suffolk **H 3**
31 Stanton by Bridge **G 12**
15 Stanton by Dale **F 2**
15 Stanton Drew **H 9**
16 Stanton Fitzwarren **E 3**
16 Stanton Harcourt **D 5**
32 Stanton Hill **D 2**
31 Stanton in Peak **D 11**
21 Stanton Lacy **E 10**
21 Stanton Long **C 11**
32 Stanton on the Wolds **G 3**
15 Stanton Prior **H 10**
16 Stanton St. Bernard **H 2**
17 Stanton St. John **C 7**
15 Stanton St. Quintin **F 12**
27 Stanton Street **J 3**
23 Stanton under Bardon **A 8**
30 Stanton upon Hine Heath **H 4**
15 Stanton Wick **H 9**
30 Stanwardine in the Fields **H 3**
19 Stanway, Essex **B 9**
16 Stanway, Glos. **A 2**
17 Stanwell **G 11**
17 Stanwell Moor **G 11**
25 Stanwick **H 1**
41 Stape **F 8**
8 Stapehill **F 2**
30 Stapeley **E 5**
31 Stapenhill **H 11**
11 Staple, Kent **B 11**
6 Staple, Somerset **B 4**
6 Staple Cross, Devon **D 4**
10 Staple Cross, E. Sussex **F 6**
6 Staple Fitzpaine **D 6**
15 Staple Hill **G 9**
10 Staplefield **E 2**
25 Stapleford, Cambs. **K 6**
18 Stapleford, Heref. & Worc. **B3**
32 Stapleford, Leics. **H 5**
32 Stapleford, Lincs **D 6**
32 Stapleford, Notts. **F 2**
8 Stapleford, Wilts. **B 2**
18 Stapleford Abbotts **D 5**
18 Stapleford Tawney **D 5**
6 Staplegrove **D 6**
6 Staplehay **D 5**
10 Staplehurst **D 6**
8 Staplers **G 6**
44 Stapleton, Cumb. **F 3**
21 Stapleton, Heref. & Worc. **F 9**
23 Stapleton, Leics. **B 8**
40 Stapleton, N. Yorks. **D 3**
21 Stapleton, Salop **B 10**
7 Stapleton, Som **D 8**
44 Stapleton Grange **F 1**
6 Stapley **E 5**
25 Staploe **J 2**
12 Star, Dyfed **C 6**
53 Star, Fife **G 8**
15 Star, Somerset **H 7**
39 Starbottom **H 11**
6 Starcross **H 3**
64 Starkigarth **E 7**
25 Starlings Green **M 6**
27 Starston **G 5**
39 Starforth **D 12**
15 Startley **F 12**
30 Statham **B 5**
7 Stathe **C 7**
32 Stathern **G 5**
40 Station Town **B 4**
25 Staughton Green **J 2**
25 Staughton Highway **J 2**
15 Staunton, Glos. **C 9**
15 Staunton, Glos. **A 11**
31 Staunton Harold Hall **H 12**
32 Staunton in the Vale **F 5**
21 Staunton on Arrow **F 9**
21 Staunton on Wye **H 9**
38 Staveley, Cumbria **G 6**
39 Staveley, Cumbria **E 7**
32 Stavely, Derby **C 2**
35 Staveley, N. Yorks. **A 12**
5 Staverton, Devon **J 7**
15 Staverton, Glos. **B 12**
23 Staverton, Northants. **F 9**
15 Staverton, Wilts **H 11**
15 Staverton Bridge **B 12**
7 Stawell **B 7**
5 Stawford **G 3**
6 Stawley **D 4**
61 Staxigoe **B 12**
41 Staxton **G 10**
20 Staylittle **C 4**
34 Staynall **C 2**
32 Staythorpe **E 5**
40 Stean **H 1**
40 Stearsby **H 6**
6 Steart **B 6**
18 Stebbing **B 6**
64 Stebbligrind **D 7**
9 Stedham **D 10**
45 Steel Rigg **E 8**
44 Steele Road **D 4**
21 Steen's Bridge **G 11**
9 Steep **D 9**
7 Steeple, Dorset **H 12**
19 Steeple, Essex **D 9**
7 Steeple Ashton **A 12**
16 Steeple Aston **B 6**
16 Steeple Barton **B 5**
25 Steeple Bumpstead **L 8**
17 Steeple Claydon **A 8**
25 Steeple Gidding **G 2**
8 Steeple Langford **B 2**
25 Steeple Morden **L 4**
35 Steeton **C 9**
62 Stein **C 2**
58 Steinmanhill **C 5**
45 Stelling Hall **F 8**
11 Stelling Minnis **C 10**
3 Stenalees **D 7**
48 Stenhousemuir **A 2**
64 Stenness **C 6**
62 Stenscholl **A 4**
31 Stenson **G 11**
64 Stenswall **D 7**
49 Stenton **B 9**
12 Stepaside **F 5**
43 Stepends **C 9**
18 Stepney **F 4**
25 Steppingley **M 1**
47 Stepps **C 11**
27 Sternfield **J 7**
16 Stert **H 1**
25 Stetchworth **J 7**
18 Stevenage **B 2**
47 Stevenston **E 7**
9 Steventon, Hants. **A 7**
16 Steventon, Oxon. **E 5**
25 Stevington **K 1**
25 Stewarby **L 1**
46 Stewarton, Strathclyde **G 2**
47 Stewarton, Strathclyde **E 9**
17 Stewkley **B 9**
33 Stewton **B 10**
12 Steynton **F 4**
4 Stibb **E 1**
4 Stibb Cross **D 3**
16 Stibb Green **H 3**
26 Stibbard **C 3**
24 Stibbington **F 2**
49 Stichill **F 9**
3 Sticker **F 7**
33 Stickford **D 10**
4 Sticklepath, Devon **F 5**
6 Sticklepath, Som. **E 6**
33 Stickney **D 10**
26 Stiffkey **A 3**
18 Stifford **F 6**
22 Stifford's Bridge **G 1**
10 Stile Bridge **C 6**
36 Stillingfleet **C 4**
40 Stillington, Cleveland **C 4**
40 Stillington, N. Yorks. **H 6**
24 Stilton **F 3**
15 Stinchcombe **D 10**
7 Stinsford **G 10**
21 Stirchley **B 12**
61 Stirkoke House **C 12**
52 Stirling, Central **H 3**
38 Stirling, Grampian **C8**
19 Stisted **A 8**
16 Stitchcombe **G 3**
2 Stithians **F 4**
56 Stittenham **B 2**
23 Stivichall **D 7**
33 Stixwould **D 9**
30 Stoak **C 3**
48 Stobo **F 4**
7 Stoborough **H 12**
7 Stoborough Grn. **H 12**
44 Stobs Castle **B3**
49 Stobswood, Borders **D 9**
45 Stobswood, Northumb. **D 10**
48 Stobwood **D 2**
19 Stock **D 7**
22 Stock Wood **F 3**
58 Stockbridge, Grampian **C 8**
8 Stockbridge, Hants. **C 5**
43 Stockbridgehill **D 12**
47 Stockbriggs **F 12**
11 Stockbury **B 7**
16 Stockcross **G 5**
38 Stockdale Wath **A 6**
23 Stockerston **B 11**
9 Stockholm **B 11**
47 Stockiemuir **A 10**
18 Stocking Pelham **A 4**
23 Stockingford **C 7**
6 Stockland **F 6**
6 Stockland Bristol **B 6**
4 Stockleigh English **E 7**
4 Stockleigh Pomeroy **F 7**
16 Stockley **G 1**
7 Stocklinch **E 7**
31 Stockport **A 7**
35 Stocksbridge **G 11**
45 Stocksfield **G 9**
21 Stockton, Heref. & Worcs. **F 10**
26 Stockton, Norfolk **F 7**
21 Stockton, Salop **B 8**
22 Stockton, Salop **B 1**
23 Stockton, War. **F 8**
8 Stockton, Wilts. **B 1**
30 Stockton Heath **B 5**
40 Stocktonon-Tees **C 4**
22 Stockton on Teme **E 1**
36 Stockton-on-the-Forest **B 4**
11 Stodmarsh **B 11**
26 Stody **B 4**
60 Stoer **D 2**
7 Stoford, Som. **E 9**

8 Stoford, Wilts. **C 2**
6 Stogumber **C 4**
6 Stogursey **B 5**
4 Stoke, Devon **D 1**
8 Stoke, Hants. **A 5**
9 Stoke, Hants **F 8**
11 Stoke, Kent **A 7**
27 Stoke, Suffolk **L 5**
7 Stoke Abbott **F 8**
23 Stoke Albany **C 11**
27 Stoke Ash **H 4**
32 Stoke Bardolph **F 4**
21 Stoke Bliss **F 12**
23 Stoke Bruerne **G 10**
25 Stoke-by-Clare **L 8**
27 Stoke-by-Nayland **L 3**
6 Stoke Canon **F 3**
8 Stoke Charity **B 6**
8 Stoke Climsland **B 10**
21 Stoke Cross **G 11**
17 Stoke D'Abernon **H 12**
25 Stoke Doyle **G 1**
23 Stoke Dry **B 12**
21 Stoke Edith **H 11**
8 Stoke Farthing **D 2**
24 Stoke Ferry **E 8**
5 Stoke Fleming **L 7**
5 Stoke Gabriel **K 7**
15 Stoke Gifford **F 9**
23 Stoke Golding **B 7**
23 Stoke Goldington **G 11**
17 Stoke Green **F 10**
17 Stoke Hammond **A 9**
26 Stoke Holy Cross **E 5**
21 Stoke Lacy **G 11**
16 Stoke Lyne **A 6**
17 Stoke Mandeville **C 9**
18 Stoke Newington **E 3**
31 Stoke-on-Trent **F 7**
15 Stoke Orchard **A 12**
6 Stoke Pero **B 2**
17 Stoke Poges **F 10**
21 Stoke Prior, Heref. & Worcs. **G 10**
22 Stoke Prior, Heref. & Worcs. **E 3**
4 Stoke Rivers **C 5**
32 Stoke Rochford **G 6**
17 Stoke Row **F 8**
7 Stoke St. Gregory **D 7**
6 Stoke St. Mary **D 6**
7 Stoke St. Michael **B 10**
21 Stoke St. Milborough **D 11**
7 Stoke sub Hamdon **D 8**
17 Stoke Talmage **D 7**
7 Stoke Trister **C 10**
30 Stoke upon Tern **G 5**
30 Stoke Wake **F 11**
7 Stokeford **G 12**
32 Stokeham **C 5**
5 Stokeinteignhead **J 8**
17 Stokenchurch **D 8**
5 Stokenham **L 7**
21 Stokesay **D 10**
26 Stokesby **D 1**
40 Stokesley **D 5**
6 Stolford **B 5**
7 Ston Easton **A 9**
17 Stone, Bucks. **C 8**
15 Stone, Glos. **E 10**
22 Stone, Heref. & Worc. **E 2**
10 Stone,Kent **A 4**
11 Stone, Staffs. **G 7**
7 Stone Allerton **A 7**
24 Stone Bridge Corner **E 4**
35 Stone Chair **D 10**
4 Stone Cross, Devon **C 5**
11 Stone Cross, Kent **D 9**
10 Stone Cross, W. Sussex **H 5**
39 Stone House **G 10**
10 Stone Street **C 4**
26 Stonebridge, Norf. **B 6**
22 Stonebridge, W. Midlands **D 5**
32 Stonebroom **D 1**
10 Stonecrouch **E 6**
15 Stone-edge Batch **G 8**
37 Stoneferry **D 8**
47 Stonefield **D 11**
46 Stonefield Castle Hotel **B 4**
44 Stonegarthside **E 3**
10 Stonegate, E. Sussex **E 5**
41 Stonegate, N. Yorks **D 8**
58 Stonegate Crofts **D 8**
41 Stonegrave **G 7**
44 Stonehaugh **E 6**
59 Stonehaven **J 6**
5 Stonehouse, Devon **K 3**
43 Stonehouse, Dumf. & Gall. **E 9**
15 Stonehouse, Glos. **D 11**
44 Stonehouse, Northumb. **G 5**
47 Stonehouse, Strathclyde **E 12**
23 Stoneleigh **E 7**
25 Stonely **J 2**
19 Stone's Green **A 11**
32 Stonesby **H 5**
16 Stonesfield **B 5**
38 Stonethwaite **D 5**
8 Stoney Cross **E 4**
31 Stoney Middleton **C 10**
23 Stoney Stanton **C 8**
7 Stoney Stoke **C 10**
7 Stoney Stratton **B 10**
21 Stoney Stretton **A 9**
48 Stoneyburn, Lothian **C 2**
48 Stoneyburn, Strathclyde **G 2**
23 Stoneygate **B 9**
19 Stoneyhills **D 9**
42 Stoneykirk **F 2**
58 Stoneywood **F 6**
27 Stonham Aspal **J 4**
17 Stonor **E 8**
23 StontonWyville **C 10**
4 Stony Cross, Devon **C 4**
22 Stony Cross, Heref. & Worc. **G 1**
34 Stony Hill **D 2**
23 Stony Stratford **H 11**
4 Stoodleigh, Devon **C 5**
6 Stoodleigh, Devon **D 3**
9 Stopham **D 11**
17 Stopsley **B 12**
30 Storeton **B 2**
35 Storiths **B 9**
63 Stornoway **D 5**
22 Storridge **G 1**
9 Storrington **E 12**
39 Storth **G 7**
36 Storwood **C 5**
56 Stotfield **C 8**
25 Stotfold **L 3**
21 Stottesdon **D 12**
23 Stoughton, Leics **B 9**
9 Stoughton, Surrey **A 11**
9 Stoughton, W.Sussex **E 9**
55 Stoul **K 1**
22 Stourlton **G 3**
7 Stour Provost **D 11**
7 Stour Row **D 11**
22 Stourbridge **D 2**
7 Stourpaine **E 12**
22 Stourport-on-Severn **E 2**
22 Stourton, Staffs **D 2**
22 Stourton, War **H 6**
7 Stourton, Wilts. **C 11**
7 Stourton Caundle **E 10**
64 Stove **B 3**
27 Stoven **G 7**
49 Stow, Borders **E 7**
32 Stow, Lincs. **B 6**
33 Stow Bardolph **E 7**
26 Stow Bedon **F 3**
25 Stow cum Quy **J 6**
25 Stow Longa **H 2**
19 Stow Maries **D 8**
16 Stow-on-the-Wold **B 3**
24 Stowbridge **E 7**
21 Stowe, Salop **E 8**
31 Stowe, Staffs. **G 8**
15 Stowe Green **D 9**
7 Stowell **D10**
27 Stowlangtoft **H 3**
27 Stowmarket **J 3**
11 Stowting **D 10**
27 Stowupland **J 4**
46 Straad **C 5**
57 Straanruie **H 6**
59 Strachan **H 4**
51 Strachur **G 8**
27 Stradbroke **H 5**
25 Stradishall **K 8**
24 Stradsett **E 8**
32 Stragglethorpe **E 6**
43 Strahanna **B 7**
42 Straid **C 2**
43 Straith **C 9**
42 Straiton **A 5**
58 Stralock, Grampian **E 6**
52 Straloch, Tayside **A 5**
31 Stramshall **G 9**
59 Stranathro **H 6**
48 Strand **G 2**
47 Strandhead **G 9**
38 Strands **E 4**
38 Strang **H 2**
41 Stranghow **D 7**
59 Stranog **H 6**
42 Stranraer **E 1**
20 Strata Florida **F 3**
17 Stratfield Mortimer **H 7**
17 Stratfield Saye **H 8**
17 Stratfield Turgis **H 8**
18 Stratford **F 4**
27 Stratford St. Andrew **J 6**
27 Stratford St. Mary **M 3**
8 Stratford sub Castle **C 3**
8 Stratford Tony **C 2**
22 Stratford-upon-Avon **G 5**
52 Strathallan Castle **F 4**
55 Strathan, Highland **K 3**
60 Strathan, Highland **E 2**
60 Strathan, Highland **A 6**
47 Strathaven **E 12**
47 Strathblane **B 10**
54 Strathcarron **E 3**
50 Strathcoil **D 4**
58 Strathdon **F 1**
60 Strathkanaird **F 3**
53 Strathkinness **F 9**
57 Strathmashie Ho **K 2**
53 Strathmiglo **F 7**
61 Strathmore Hotel **C 10**
54 Strathpeffer **D 8**
54 Strathrannoch **B 8**
54 Strathvaich Lo **B 7**
61 Strathy **A 8**
61 Strathy Inn **A 8**
52 Strathyre **E 1**
4 Stratton, Corn **E 1**
7 Stratton, Dorset **G 10**
16 Stratton, Glos. **D 1**
17 Stratton Audley **B 7**
7 Stratton-on-the-Fosse **A 10**
16 Stratton St. Margaret **E 3**
26 Stratton St. Michael **F 5**
26 Stratton Strawless **C 5**
53 Stravithie **F 10**
10 Streat **F 2**
18 Streatham **G 3**
17 Streatley, Beds **A 11**
17 Streatley, Berks. **F 7**
7 Street, Somerset **C 8**
41 Street, Yorks **E 7**
30 Street Dinas **F 2**
11 Street End, Kent **C 10**
9 Street End, W. Sussex **F 10**
36 Street Houses **C 3**
57 Street of Kincardine **H 5**
22 Streethay **A 5**
36 Streethouse **E 2**
40 Streetlam **E 3**
22 Streetly **B 4**
21 Strefford **D 10**
32 Strelley **F 2**
36 Strensall **A 4**
6 Stretcholt **B 6**
5 Strete **L 7**
35 Stretford **H 7**
25 Strethall **L 6**
25 Stretham **H 6**
30 Stretton, Cheshire **B 5**
30 Stretton, Cheshire **E 3**
32 Stretton, Derby **D 1**
23 Stretton, Leics. **A 12**
22 Stretton, Staffs. **A 2**
31 Stretton, Staffs. **G 11**
22 Stretton en le Field **A 6**
21 Stretton Grandison **H 11**
21 Stretton Heath **A 9**
23 Stretton-on-Dunsmore **E 7**
22 Stretton on Fosse **H 6**
21 Stretton Sugwas **H 10**
23 Stretton-under-Fosse **D 8**
58 Strichen **B 7**
6 Stringston **B 5**
23 Strixton **F 12**
15 Stroat **E 9**
54 Stromeferry **F 2**
54 Stromemore **F 2**
64 Stromness **D 1**
51 Stronachlachar **F 11**
55 Stronchreggan Ho **M 4**
63 Strond **H 1**
55 Strone, Highland **L 5**
57 Strone, Highland **G 1**
47 Strone, Strathclyde **A 7**
51 Strone, Strathclyde **H 10**
60 Stronechrubie **E 4**
55 Stronenaba **L 6**
57 Stronetoper **K 4**
51 Stronmilchan **E 8**
50 Strontian **A 5**
50 Strontoiller **E 6**
51 Stronuich **C 12**
10 Strood **A 6**
10 Strood Green **C 1**
15 Stroud, Glos. **D 11**
9 Stroud, Hants. **D 8**
19 Stroud Green **E 8**
17 Stroude **G 11**
32 Stroxton **G 6**
62 Struan **D 3**
33 Strubby **B 11**
26 Strumpshaw **E 6**
54 Struy **F 8**
58 Stuartfield **C 7**
38 Stub Place **F 3**
9 Stubbington **F 7**
35 Stubbins **E 7**
11 Stubbs Cross **D 8**
44 Stubbyknowe **F 2**
8 Stubhampton **E 1**
44 Stublick **G 6**
34 Stubshaw Cross **G 5**
32 Stubton **E 6**
46 Stuck **B 5**
51 Stuckgowan **G 10**
51 Stuckindroin **F 10**
8 Stuckton **E 3**
17 Stud Green **F 9**
45 Studdon **H 7**
39 Studfold **E 9**
17 Studham **C 11**
8 Studland **H 2**
17 Studley, Oxon **C 7**
22 Studley, War. **F 4**
16 Studley, Wilts **G 1**
40 Studley Roger **H 3**
25 Stump Cross **L 6**
25 Stuntney **G 7**
10 Stunts Green **G 5**
31 Sturbridge **G 7**
25 Sturmer **L 8**
7 Sturminster Com. **E 11**
8 Sturminster Marshall **F 1**
7 Sturminster Newton **E 11**
11 Sturry **B 10**
37 Sturton **G 7**
32 Sturton by Stow **B 6**
32 Sturton le Steeple **B 5**
43 Stuston **H 4**
27 Stutton, Suffolk **M 4**
36 Stutton, N. Yorks. **C 3**
31 Styal **B 7**
32 Styrrup **A 3**
58 Succoth, Grampian **D 2**
51 Succoth, Highland **G 10**
21 Suckley **G 12**
25 Sudborough **G 1**
27 Sudbourne **K 7**
15 Sudbrook, Gwent **F 8**
33 Sudbrook, Lincs. **F 7**
33 Sudbrooke **C 7**
31 Sudbury, Derby **G 10**
18 Sudbury, London **E 2**
27 Sudbury, Suffolk **L 2**
56 Suddie **D 2**
15 Sudgrove **D 12**
26 Suffield, Norfolk **B 5**
41 Suffield, N. Yorks. **F 10**
27 Suffolk, County **J 4**
30 Sugnall **G 6**
61 Suisgill **E 9**
62 Suisnish **E 5**
38 Sulby **G 2**
23 Sulgrave **H 9**
17 Sulham **G 7**
17 Sulhamstead **G 7**
17 Sulhamstead Abbots **G 7**
62 Sulishaderbeg **D 4**
9 Sullington **E 12**
64 Sullom **C 7**
14 Sully **G 5**
29 Summer Hill **E 12**
35 Summerbridge **A 10**
2 Summercourt **D 6**
40 Summerhouse **C 2**
15 Summerleaze **F 7**
35 Summerseat **F 7**
16 Summertown **C 6**
35 Summit, Lancs **F 8**
35 Summit, Lancs **E 8**
17 Sunbury on Thames **G 11**
43 Sundaywell **C 9**
38 Sunderland, Cumb **B 4**
34 Sunderland, Lancs **B 3**
45 Sunderland, Tyne & Wear **G 12**
40 Sunderland Bridge **A 3**
48 Sundhope **G 6**
17 Sundon Park **B 11**
10 Sundridge **C 4**
50 Sunipol **B 1**
37 Sunk Island **E 10**
17 Sunningdale **G 10**
17 Sunninghill **G 10**
16 Sunningwell **D 6**
40 Sunniside, Dur. **A 2**
45 Sunniside, Tyne & Wear **G 10**
38 Sunny Bank **F 5**
56 Sunnyhillock **D 4**
52 Sunnylaw **G 3**
10 Sunnyside **D 3**
8 Sunton **A 4**
49 Sunwick **D 11**
18 Surbiton **G 2**
38 Surby **H 1**
24 Surfleet **C 3**
24 Surfleet Seas End **C 4**
26 Surlingham **E 6**
10 Surrey, County **C 2**
26 Sustead **B 5**
36 Susworth **G 6**
4 Sutcombe **E 2**
64 Sutherland **E 2**
26 Suton **E 4**
56 Sutors of Cromarty **C 4**
33 Sutterby **C 11**
24 Sutterton **B 4**
25 Sutton, Beds. **K 3**
17 Sutton, Berks. **F 11**
25 Sutton, Cambs. **G 5**
24 Sutton, Cambs. **F 2**
12 Sutton, Dyfed **E 3**
11 Sutton, Kent **C 12**
18 Sutton, London **H 3**
34 Sutton, Merseyside **H 4**
26 Sutton, Norfolk **C 7**
32 Sutton, Notts. **B 4**
32 Sutton, Notts. **F 5**
16 Sutton, Oxon **C 5**
22 Sutton, Salop **C 1**
30 Sutton, Salop. **G 5**
7 Sutton, Som **C 9**
36 Sutton, S. Yorks **F 3**
30 Sutton, Staffs. **H 6**
27 Sutton, Suffolk **K 6**
10 Sutton, Surrey **B 12**
9 Sutton, W. Sussex **E 11**
23 Sutton Basset **C 11**
10 Sutton at Hone **A 4**
15 Sutton Benger **F 12**
32 Sutton Bonington **H 2**
24 Sutton Bridge **C 6**
23 Sutton Cheney **B 7**
22 Sutton Coldfield **B 5**
16 Sutton Courteney **E 6**
24 SuttonCrosses **C 5**
40 Sutton Grange **H 3**
9 Sutton Green **A 11**
40 Sutton Howgrave **G 3**
32 Sutton in Ashfield **D 2**
35 Sutton-in-Craven **C 8**
23 Sutton in the Elms **C 8**
31 Sutton Lane Ends **C 8**
21 Sutton Maddock **B 12**
7 Sutton Mallet **C 7**
8 Sutton Mandeville **C 1**
7 Sutton Montis **D 9**
37 Sutton-on-Hull **D 9**
33 Sutton on Sea **B 12**
36 Sutton-on-the-Forest **A 4**
31 Sutton on the Hill **G 11**
32 Sutton on Trent **D 5**
24 Sutton St. Edmund **D 5**
24 Sutton St. James **D 5**
21 Sutton St. Michael **H 10**
21 Sutton St. Nicholas **H 10**
8 Sutton Scotney **B 6**
22 Sutton-under-Brailes **H 6**
40 Sutton-under-Whitestonecliffe **G 5**
36 Sutton upon Derwent **B 5**
11 Sutton Valence **C 7**
7 Sutton Veny **B 11**
7 Sutton Waldron **E 12**
15 Sutton Wick **H 9**
33 Swaby **B 11**
31 Swadlincote **H 11**
26 Swaffham **E 1**
25 Swaffham Bulbeck **J 7**
25 Swaffham Prior **J 7**
26 Swafield **B 6**
40 Swainby **E 5**
26 Swainsthorpe **E 5**
15 Swainswick **G 10**
23 Swalcliffe **H 7**
11 Swalecliffe **A 10**
37 Swallow **G 9**
8 Swallowcliffe **C 1**
17 Swallowfield **H 8**
32 Swallownest **B 2**
45 Swalwell **G 10**
30 Swan Green **C 6**
8 Swanage **H 2**
64 Swanbister **D 2**
17 Swanbourne **A 9**
63 Swanibost **A 6**
37 Swanland **D 7**
10 Swanley **A 4**
10 Swanley Village **A 4**
9 Swanmore **D 7**
23 Swannington, Leics. **A 7**
26 Swannington, Norf. **D 4**
10 Swanscombe **A 5**
13 Swansea **H 10**
26 Swanton Abbott **C 6**
26 Swanton Morley **D 3**
26 Swanton Novers **B 3**
32 Swanwick **E 1**
24 Swarby **B 1**
26 Swardeston **E 5**
31 Swarkestone **G 12**
45 Swarland **C 10**
45 Swarland Estate **C 10**
9 Swarraton **B 7**
24 Swaton **B 2**
25 Swavesey **H 5**
8 Sway **F 4**
33 Swayfield **H 7**
8 Swaythling **D 6**
21 Sweet Green **F 12**
4 Sweetham **F 7**
39 Sweetholme **C 8**
49 Sweethope **E 9**
3 Sweethouse **C 8**
27 Swefling **J 6**
23 Swepstone **A 7**
16 Swerford **A 5**
30 Swettenham **C 6**
27 Swilland **K 5**
36 Swillington **D 2**
4 Swimbridge **C 5**
4 Swimbridge Newland **C 5**
16 Swinbrook **C 4**
32 Swinderley **D 6**
15 Swindon, Glos. **B 12**
22 Swindon, Staffs. **C 2**
16 Swindon, Wilts **F 3**
37 Swine **D 9**
36 Swinefleet **E 5**
15 Swineford **G 10**
25 Swineshead, Beds. **J 2**
24 Swineshead, Lincs. **B 3**
24 Swineshead Bridge **A 3**
61 Swiney **D 12**
23 Swinford, Leics. **D 9**
16 Swinford, Oxon **C 5**
11 Swingfield Minnis **D 10**
11 Singfield Street **D 11**
47 Swinhill **D 12**
45 Swinhoe **E 12**
37 Swinhope **G 9**
40 Swinithwaite **F 1**
44 Swinnie **A 5**
31 Swinscoe **E 9**
44 Swinside Hall **A 5**
24 Swinstead **C 1**
49 Swinton, Borders **E 11**
34 Swinton, Manchester **G 6**
41 Swinton, N. Yorks. **H 7**
40 Swinton, N. Yorks. **G 2**
36 Swinton, S. Yorks. **G 2**
49 Swinton Quarter **E 11**
49 Swintonmill **E 10**
23 Swithland **A 9**
56 Swordale, Highland **C 1**
63 Swordale, W. Isles **D 6**
55 Swordland **K 2**
61 Swordly **B 7**
30 Sworton Heath **B 5**
20 Swydd-ffynnon **F 3**
31 Swynnerton **G 7**
7 Swyre **G 8**
20 Sychnant **E 5**
20 Sychtyn **B 5**
15 Syde **C 12**
17 Sydenham **D 8**
5 Sydenham Damerel **H 3**
26 Syderstone **B 1**
7 Sydling St. Nicholas **F 10**
16 Sydmonton **H 6**
32 Syerston **E 5**
35 Syke **F 8**
36 Sykehouse **E 4**
34 Sykes **B 5**
64 Symbister **D 8**
47 Symington, Strathclyde **F 8**
48 Symington, Strathclyde **F 3**
15 Symonds Yat **C 9**
7 Symondsbury **G 8**
13 Synod Inn **B 7**
49 Synton Parkhead **G 7**
61 Syre **C 7**
23 Syresham **H 9**

23 Syston, Leics ....A 9
32 Syston, Lincs. ....F 6
22 Sytchampton ....F 2
23 Sywell ....E 11
54 Taagan ....C 4
47 Tackhouse ....E 11
16 Tackley ....B 6
26 Tacolneston ....F 4
36 Tadcaster ....C 3
31 Taddington ....C 10
4 Taddiport ....D 4
17 Tadley ....H 7
25 Tadlow ....K 4
23 Tadmarton ....H 7
15 Tadwick ....G 10
10 Tadworth ....B 1
14 Tafarnau-bach ....C 4
29 Tafarn-gelyn ....D 11
12 Tafarn-y-bwlch .....D 4
14 Taffs Well ....F 5
20 Tafolwern ....B 4
29 Tai ....D 7
29 Tai-bach, Clwyd ...G 10
13 Taibach, W. Glam .H 11
29 Tai-mawr ....F 9
61 Tain, Highland .....A 11
56 Tain, Highland .....B 3
29 Tainant ....F 12
13 Tairgwaith ....F 10
28 Tai'r-lon ....E 4
18 Takeley ....B 5
18 Takeley Street ......B 5
14 Talachddu ....A 4
29 Talacre ....B 10
6 Talaton ....F 4
12 Talbenny ....F 2
14 Talbot Green ....F 4
8 Talbot Village ......G 2
20 Talerddig ....B 5
13 Talgarreg ....B 7
14 Talgarth ....A 5
20 Taliesin ....C 2
62 Talisker ....E 3
31 Talke ....E 7
44 Talkin ....G 4
48 Talla Linnfoots .....G 4
54 Talladale ....C 3
29 Tallard ....G 8
30 Tallarn Green ....F 3
38 Tallentire ....B 3
13 Talley ....D 9
24 Tallington ....E 2
60 Talmine ....B 6
13 Talog ....D 7
20 Talsarn ....G 1
28 Talsarnau ....G 5
2 Talskiddy ....C 6
28 Talwrn, Gwynedd .....C 4
29 Talwrn, Clwyd ......E 12
29 Talybont, Dyfed ....C 2
28 Tal-y-bont, Gwynedd H 5
28 Tal-y-bont,Gwynedd C 5
29 Tal-y-bont,Gwynedd C 7
14 Talybont, Powys .....B 4
29 Tal-y-cafn ....C 7
15 Tal-y-coed ....C 7
14 Tal-y-garn ....F 4
20 Tal-y-llyn, Gwynedd A 3
14 Tal-y-llyn, Powys ...B 4
18 Tal-y-sarn ....E 4
14 Talywain ....D 6
20 Tal-y-wern ....B 4
40 Tame ....D 5
5 Tamerton Foliot ...K 3
22 Tamworth ....B 5
39 Tan Hill ....E 11
12 Tancredston ....D 2
11 Tanden ....D 8
47 Tandlemuir ....C 8
10 Tandridge ....C 3
45 Tanfield ....G 10
45 Tanfield Lea ....H 10
8 Tangley ....A 5
9 Tangmere ....E 10
64 Tankerness ....D 3
35 Tankersley ....G 12
28 Tan-lan ....F 5
61 Tannach ....C 12
59 Tannachie ....J 5
59 Tannadice ....L 2
27 Tannington ....H 5
31 Tansley ....D 11
31 Tansley Knoll .....D 11
24 Tansor ....F 2
45 Tantobie ....H 10
40 Tanton ....D 5
40 Tanworth in Arden .E 5
28 Tan-y-bwlch ....F 6
29 Tan-y-fron ....F 9
20 Tan-y-graig, Dyfed .E 3
28 Tan-y-graig,
   Gwynedd ....F 3
28 Tan-y-grisiau ....F 6
12 Tan-y-groes ....B 6

29 Tan-y-pistyll ......G 10
17 Taplow ....F 10
46 Tarbert, Strathclyde A 1
46 Tarbert, Strathclyde C 4
63 Tarbert, W. Isles ..G 2
55 Tarbet, Highland ...K 2
60 Tarbet, Highland ...B 3
51 Tarbet, Strathclyde G 10
47 Tarbolton ....G 9
47 Tarbrax ....D 3
30 Tarbuck Green ....A 3
44 Tarcoon ....E 2
22 Tardebigge ....E 3
59 Tarfside ....J 2
59 Tarland ....G 2
34 Tarleton ....E 3
34 Tarlscough ....F 3
15 Tarlton ....D 12
34 Tarnbrook ....B 5
30 Tarporley ....D 4
6 Tarr ....C 4
8 Tarrant Crawford ..F 1
8 Tarrant Gunville ...E 1
8 Tarrant Hinton .....E 1
8 Tarrant Keyneston ..E 1
8 Tarrant Launceston E 1
8 Tarrant Monkton ...E 1
8 Tarrant Rawston ....E 1
8 Tarrant Rushton ....E 1
10 Tarring Neville .....H 3
21 Tarrington ....H 11
62 Tarskavaig ....G 5
58 Tarves ....D 6
54 Tarvie ....D 8
30 Tarvin ....D 4
26 Tasburgh ....F 5
21 Tasley ....C 12
16 Taston ....B 5
31 Tatenhill ....H 10
43 Tath Hill ....B 11
39 Tatham ....H 8
33 Tathwell ....B 10
17 Tatling End ....E 11
10 Tatsfield ....B 3
30 Tattenhall ....D 3
26 Tatterford ....C 2
26 Tattersett ....C 1
33 Tattershall ....D 9
33 Tattershall Bridge .E 9
33 Tattershall Thorpe .D 9
27 Tattingstone ....L 4
27 Tattingstone
   Whitehorse ....L 4
6 Tatworth ....F 6
58 Tauchers ....C 1
6 Taunton ....D 6
26 Taverham ....D 5
12 Tavernspite ....F 5
5 Tavistock ....H 3
4 Taw Green, Devon ..E 5
4 Taw Green, Devon ..F 5
4 Tawstock ....C 4
31 Taxal ....B 8
47 Tayburn ....E 10
51 Taychreggan ....E 7
46 Tayinloan ....E 2
52 Taymouth Castle ....C 3
51 Taynafead ....F 8
15 Taynton, Glos. ....B 10
16 Taynton, Oxon ......C 3
51 Taynuilt ....D 7
53 Tayport ....D 9
46 Tayvallich ....A 2
33 Tealby ....A 8
62 Teangue ....G 6
39 Tebay ....E 8
17 Tebworth ....A 10
4 Tedburn St. Mary ...E 5
16 Teddington, Glos. ..A 1
18 Teddington, London
               G 2
21 Tedstone Delamere
               F 12
21 Tedstone Wafre ....F 12
23 Teeton ....E 10
8 Teffont Evias ....C 1
8 Teffont Magna ....C 2
12 Tegryn ....D 6
23 Teigh ....A 12
7 Teigngrace ....H 7
5 Teignmouth ....H 8
56 Teindland ....D 8
44 Teindside ....B 3
21 Telford ....B 12
10 Telham ....G 6
7 Tellisford ....A 11
10 Telscombe ....H 3
43 Templand ....C 11
3 Temple, Cornwall ...B 7
13 Temple Bar, Dyfed ..B 8
13 Temple Bar, Dyfed ..E 9
48 Temple, Lothian ....D 5
22 Temple Ballsall .....E 5
7 Temple Cloud ....A 9

11 Temple Ewell ....D 11
22 Temple Grafton ......G 5
16 Temple Guiting .....A 2
36 Temple Hirst ....E 4
32 Temple Normanton ...C 1
39 Temple Sowerby .....C 8
7 Templecombe ....D 10
53 Templehall ....H 7
6 Templeton, Devon ...E 2
12 Templeton, Dyfed ...F 4
4 Tempelton Bridge ...E 7
25 Tempsford ....K 3
24 Ten Mile Bank .....F 7
21 Tenbury Wells .....F 11
12 Tenby ....G 5
30 Tendring ....B 11
19 Tendring Green ....A 11
64 Tenston ....C 1
11 Tenterden ....E 7
42 Terally ....G 2
19 Terling ....B 7
30 Ternhill ....G 5
2 Terras ....D 6
17 Terrick ....C 9
41 Terrington ....H 7
24 Terrington St. Clement
               D 6
24 Terrington St. John .D 6
10 Teston ....C 6
8 Testwood ....E 5
15 Tetbury ....E 12
15 Tetbury Upton .....E 12
30 Tetchill ....G 3
4 Tetcott ....F 2
33 Tetford ....C 10
37 Tetney ....G 10
37 Tetney Lock ....G 11
17 Tetsworth ....D 8
22 Tettenhall ....B 2
58 Teuchan ....D 8
58 Teuchar ....C 5
53 Teuchatcroft ....B 9
32 Teversal ....D 2
25 Teversham ....J 6
44 Teviothead ....C 2
59 Tewel ....J 6
18 Tewin ....B 3
15 Tewkesbury ....A 12
11 Teynham ....B 8
11 Teynham Street .....B 8
38 Thackthwaite, Cumb.
               C 4
38 Thackthwaite, Cumb.
               C 6
9 Thakeham ....D 12
17 Thame ....D 8
17 Thames Ditton .....G 12
11 Thanington ....B 10
48 Thankerton ....F 2
26 Tharston ....F 5
16 Thatcham ....F 6
34 Thatto Heath ....H 4
25 Thaxted ....M 7
62 The Aird ....C 3
21 The Bage ....H 8
43 The Barony, Dumf.
   & Gall. ....C 11
64 The Barony, Orkney B 1
31 The Beeches ....H 9
62 The Braes ....C 4
21 The Broad ....F 10
31 The Camp ....C 12
10 The Chart ....C 3
17 The City ....D 8
15 The Cleaver ....A 8
8 The Common ....C 4
21 The Corner ....D 10
60 The Craigs ....D 1
38 The Cronk ....F 2
47 The Den ....D 8
24 The Engine ....E 4
44 The Fauld ....E 4
44 The Flatt ....E 4
11 The Forstal ....E 7
38 The Green, Cumbria G 4
7 The Green, Wilts ..C 12
43 The Grove ....D 10
49 The Hardens ....D 10
9 The Haven ....C 12
27 The Heath ....L 2
10 The Hermitage ......C 1
46 The Highland Hotel .A 5
38 The Howe ....H 1
19 The Hythe ....B 10
43 The Lake ....G 7
11 The Leacon ....E 8
17 The Lee ....D 10
38 The Lhen ....F 2
21 The Marsh ....C 8
45 The Middles ....H 10
10 The Moor ....E 6
10 The Mound ....E 5
47 The Murray ....D 11
64 The Ness ....A 8

59 The Neuk ....H 5
15 The Oval ....H 10
15 The Pill ....F 8
58 The Pole of Itlaw ..B 4
21 The Pound ....E 7
15 The Quarry ....D 10
12 The Rhos ....F 4
9 The Sands ....B 10
16 The Slade ....G 6
11 The Stocks ....E 8
19 The Stone ....C 9
17 The Throat ....G 9
2 The Towans ....F 3
21 The Vauld ....G 10
22 The Wyke ....B 1
14 Theakston ....G 3
37 Thealby ....E 7
17 Theale, Berks. .....G 7
17 Theale, Somerset ...B 8
17 Theale Green ....G 7
43 Theapland ....H 12
24 Thearne ....H 5
27 Theberton ....J 7
23 Theddingworth .....D 10
33 Theddlethorpe
   All Saints ....A 11
33 Theddlethorpe
   St. Helen ....A 11
4 Thelbridge Cross ..E 7
27 Thelnetham ....G 3
26 Thelwall ....B 5
26 Themelthorpe ....C 4
23 Thenford ....H 8
27 Therfield ....L 4
27 Thetford ....G 2
18 Theydon Bois ....D 4
15 Thickwood ....G 11
33 Thimbleby, Lincs. ..C 9
40 Thimbleby, N. Yorks. F 5
40 Thirkleby ....G 5
40 Thirlby ....G 5
49 Thirlestane ....E 8
40 Thirlspot ....C 5
40 Thirn ....G 2
40 Thirsk ....G 4
40 Thistlebottom ......A 5
34 Thistleton, Lancs. .C 3
32 Thistleton,Leics. ..H 6
23 Thistley Green .....H 8
36 Thixendale ....A 6
45 Thockrington ....E 8
24 Tholomas Drove .....E 5
40 Tholthorpe ....H 5
12 Thomas Chapel ......F 4
30 Thomas Close ....A 7
22 Thomas Town ....F 4
58 Thomastown ....D 3
30 Thompson ....F 2
56 Thomshill ....D 8
10 Thong ....A 5
33 Thonock ....A 5
39 Thoralby ....F 12
37 Thoresway ....G 9
32 Thorganby, Lincs. ..G 9
36 Thorganby,
   N. Yorks. ....C 5
41 Thorgill ....E 7
27 Thorington ....H 7
27 Thorington Street ..L 3
35 Thorlby ....B 8
18 Thorley, Herts. ....B 5
8 Thorley, I.o.W. ....G 5
18 Thorley Street, Herts.
               B 5
8 Thorley Street, I.o.W.
               G 5
40 Thormanby ....H 5
11 Thorn ....F 7
30 Thornaby-on-Tees ..C 5
26 Thornage ....B 4
17 Thornborough, Bucks.
               A 8
40 Thornborough,
   N. Yorks. ....G 3
15 Thornbury, Avon ...E 9
4 Thornbury, Devon ..E 3
21 Thornbury, Heref.
   & Worc. ....F 11
23 Thornby ....E 10
31 Thorncliff ....D 8
7 Thorncombe ....F 7
9 Thorncombe Street
               B 11
25 Thorncote Green ....K 3
8 Thorncross ....H 6
11 Thorndon ....H 4
4 Thorndon Cross .....F 4
6 Thorne, Somerset ..D 4
35 Thorne, S. Yorks. ..F 5
35 Thorner ....C 12
24 Thorney, Cambs. ....E 4
35 Thorney, Notts. ....C 6
30 Thorney, Somerset ..D 7
37 Thorney Crofts .....E 9

8 Thorney Hill ....F 4
58 Thorneybank ....D 4
6 Thornfalcon ....D 6
7 Thornford ....E 9
44 Thorngrafton ....F 6
7 Thorngrove ....C 7
37 Thorngumbald ....D 9
24 Thornham ....A 8
27 Thornham Magna ....H 4
27 Thornham Parva ....H 4
24 Thornhaugh ....E 2
52 Thornhill, Central .G 2
38 Thornhill, Cumb. ...D 3
31 Thornhill, Dumf.
   & Gall. ....B 9
8 Thornhill, Hants. ..E 6
14 Thornhill, Mid
   Glam. ....F 5
35 Thornhill, W. Yorks. E 11
37 Thornholme ....A 9
49 Thornielaw ....F 8
49 Thornington ....F 11
40 Thornley, Dur. ....A 4
40 Thornley, Dur. ....B 1
47 Thornliebank ......D 10
25 Thorns ....K 8
35 Thornseat ....H 11
31 Thornsett ....B 8
38 Thornthwaite, Cumb.
               C 5
35 Thornthwaite,
   N. Yorks. ....A 10
17 Thornton, Bucks. ...A 8
40 Thornton,
   Cleveland ....D 5
12 Thornton, Dyfed ...F 2
53 Thornton, Fife ....G 7
36 Thornton, Humber. .C 5
34 Thornton, Lancs. ..C 2
23 Thornton, Leics. ..A 8
33 Thornton, Lincs. ..C 9
34 Thornton,
   Merseyside ....G 2
49 Thornton, Northumb.
              E 12
53 Thornton, Tayside ..C 9
35 Thornton,
   W. Yorks. ....D 9
37 Thornton Curtis ....E 8
18 Thornton Heath ....H 3
30 Thornton Hough ....B 2
35 Thornton in Craven .B 8
39 Thornton in Lonsdale
               H 9
40 Thornton-le-Beans .F 4
36 Thornton-le-Clay ..A 5
41 Thornton-le-Dale ..G 8
37 Thornton le Moor,
   Lincolnshire ......G 8
40 Thornton-le-Moor,
   N. Yorks. ....F 4
30 Thornton-le-Moors .C 3
40 Thornton-le-Street .G 4
47 Thornton Mains ....E 12
39 Thornton Rust .....F 12
40 Thornton Steward ..F 2
40 Thornton Watlass ..G 3
47 Thorntonhall ......D 10
49 Thorntonloch ......B 10
49 Thorntonpark ......E 12
18 Thornwood Com ....C 5
49 Thorndykes ....E 9
38 Thornythwaite .....C 6
32 Thoroton ....F 5
36 Thorp Arch ....C 2
27 Thorp Green ....K 2
31 Thorpe, Derby ....E 10
37 Thorpe, Humberside B 7
33 Thorpe, Lincs. ....B 12
26 Thorpe, Norf. .....F 7
35 Thorpe, N. Yorks. .A 9
32 Thorpe, Notts. ....E 5
17 Thorpe, Surrey ...G 11
27 Thorpe Abbotts ....G 5
32 Thorpe Acre ....H 2
32 Thorpe Arnold .....H 5
36 Thorpe Audlin .....F 3
41 Thorpe Bassett ....H 8
19 Thorpe Bay ....E 9
23 Thorpe by Water ..C 12
22 Thorpe Constantine .A 6
26 Thorpe End Garden
   Village ....D 6
35 Thorpe Hesley ....G 12
36 Thorpe in Balne ...F 4
32 Thorpe in the Fallows
               B 6
23 Thorpe Langton ....C 10
40 Thorpe Larches ....C 5
19 Thorpe-le-Soken ..B 11
36 Thorpe le Street ...C 6
23 Thorpe Malsor .....D 11
23 Thorpe Mandeville .H 9
26 Thorpe Market .....B 5

27 Thorpe Morieux ....K 2
32 Thorpe on the Hill .D 6
26 Thorpe St. Andrew .D 6
33 Thorpe St. Peter ...D 11
32 Thorpe Salvin .....D 2
23 Thorpe Satchville .A 10
40 Thorpe Thewles ....C 4
36 Thorpe Underwood .A 3
25 Thorpe Waterville .G 1
26 Thorpe Willoughby .D 3
27 Thorpeness ....J 8
19 Thorrington ....B 10
7 Thorverton ....F 3
27 Thrandeston ....H 4
25 Thrapston ....G 1
30 Threapwood ....F 3
42 Threave ....A 4
10 Three Bridges .....D 2
2 Three Burrows .....E 4
11 Three Chimneys ....D 7
14 Three Cocks ....A 5
13 Three Crosses .....H 9
10 Three Cups Corner .F 5
40 Three Gates,
   Cleveland ....B 5
8 Three Gates, Dorset E 9
24 Three Holes ....E 6
11 Three Legged Cross .E 3
11 Three Oaks ....G 7
24 Threekingham ......B 2
10 Threelag Cross ....E 6
31 Threelows ....C 8
17 Threemile Cross ...G 8
2 Threemilestone ....E 5
49 Threepwood ....E 8
38 Threlkeld ....C 6
15 Threshfield ....A 8
26 Thrigby ....D 7
39 Thringarth ....C 11
32 Thringstone ....H 2
40 Thrintoft ....F 4
25 Thriplow ....K 5
24 Throckenholt ......E 5
25 Throcking ....M 4
45 Throckley ....F 9
22 Throckmorton ......G 3
45 Throphill ....D 9
45 Thropton ....C 8
5 Throughgate ....B 9
5 Throwleigh ....G 5
11 Throwley ....C 8
11 Throwley Forstal ..C 8
32 Thrumpton ....G 2
61 Thrumster ....C 12
37 Thrunscoe ....F 10
45 Thrunton ....B 9
7 Thrupe ....B 9
15 Thrupp, Glos. ....D 11
16 Thrupp, Oxon ......C 6
5 Thrushelton ....G 3
15 Thrushesbush ......C 5
34 Thrushgill ....A 5
23 Thrussington .....A 10
8 Thruxton, Hants. ..B 4
15 Thruxton, Heref.
   & Worc. ....A 7
36 Thrybergh ....H 3
23 Thurcaston ....A 9
32 Thurcroft ....A 2
4 Thurdon ....E 2
26 Thurgarton, Norf. .B 5
32 Thurgarton, Notts. E 4
35 Thurgoland ....G 11
23 Thurlaston, Leics. .B 8
23 Thurlaston, War. ..E 8
6 Thurlbear ....D 6
24 Thurlby, Lincs. ...D 2
32 Thurlby, Lincs. ...D 6
25 Thurleigh ....J 2
5 Thurlestone ....L 5
35 Thurlstone ....G 11
26 Thurlton ....F 7
23 Thurmaston ....B 10
23 Thurnby ....B 10
26 Thurne ....D 7
11 Thurnham, Kent ....C 8
34 Thurnham, Lancs. ..B 3
26 Thurning, Norf. ...C 4
25 Thurning, Northants.
               G 2
36 Thurnscoe ....G 2
44 Thursby ....H 2
26 Thursford Green ...B 3
9 Thursley ....B 10
61 Thurso ....A 10
61 Thurso East ....A 10
30 Thurstaston ....B 1
27 Thurston ....J 2
44 Thurstonfield .....G 2
35 Thurstonland .....F 10
26 Thurton ....E 6
31 Thurvaston ....F 11

26 Thuxton E 3
27 Thwaite, Suffolk H 4
39 Thwaite, N. Yorks. E 11
26 Thwaite St. Mary F 6
41 Thwing H 10
52 Tibbermore E 5
43 Tibbers B 9
15 Tibberton, Glos. B 10
22 Tibberton, Heref. & Worc. F 3
30 Tibberton, Salop H 5
26 Tibenham F 4
32 Tibshelf D 2
37 Tibthorpe B 7
10 Ticehurst E 6
9 Tichborne C 7
9 Tichfield F 7
24 Tickencote E 1
15 Tickenham G 8
32 Tickhill A 3
21 Ticklerton C 10
31 Ticknall H 12
37 Tickton C 8
22 Tidbury Green E 4
16 Tidcombe H 4
17 Tiddington, Oxon D 7
22 Tidington, War. F 6
10 Tidebrook E 5
3 Tideford D 10
3 Tideford Cross D 10
15 Tidenham E 9
31 Tideswell C 10
17 Tidmarsh G 7
22 Tidmington H 6
8 Tidpit D 2
12 Tiers Cross F 3
23 Tiffield G 10
58 Tifty D 5
59 Tigerton L 3
54 Tighchuig F 8
52 Tighnablair E 3
46 Tighnabruaich B 5
51 Tigh-na-criche G 8
60 Tighnafiline G 1
5 Tigley K 6
25 Tilbrook H 2
18 Tilbury F 6
22 Tile Cross C 5
17 Tilehurst G 7
9 Tilford B 10
10 Tilgate E 2
58 Tillathrowie D 2
35 Tilley G 4
52 Tillicoultry G 4
19 Tillingham D 10
21 Tillington, Heref. &Worc. H 10
9 Tillington, W. Sussex D 11
21 Tillington Com H 10
59 Tillyarblet L 3
59 Tillybardine K 2
58 Tillycorthie E 7
59 Tillydrine House H 4
58 Tillyfar E 7
58 Tillyfourie F 4
58 Tillygrieg E 6
58 Tillyminnate D 2
11 Tilmanstone C 11
24 Tilney All Saints D 7
24 Tilney High End D 7
24 Tilney St. Lawrence D 7
8 Tilshead A 2
30 Tilstock F 4
30 Tilston E 3
30 Tilstone Fearnall D 4
17 Tilsworth B 10
23 Tilton on the Hill B 10
15 Tiltups End E 11
33 Timberland D 8
31 Timbersbrook D 7
6 Timberscombe B 3
35 Timble B 10
49 Timpendean G 9
30 Timperley A 6
15 Timsbury, Avon H 10
8 Timsbury, Hants. D 5
27 Timworth Green H 2
7 Tincleton G 11
44 Tindale G 4
17 Tingewick A 7
35 Tingley D 11
25 Tingrith M 1
5 Tinhay G 3
48 Tinnis F 6
35 Tinshill C 11
3 Tintagel A 7
15 Tintern Parva D 8
7 Tintinhull D 8
35 Tintwistle G 9
43 Tinwald C 11
24 Tinwell E 1
4 Tippacott A 6
58 Tipperty, Grampian E 7
58 Tipperty, Grampian B 4
24 Tipp's End F 6
8 Tiptoe F 4
22 Tipton C 3
6 Tipton St. Johns G 4
19 Tiptree B 9
20 Tarabad H 4
50 Tirghoil E 1
15 Tirley A 11
14 Tir-Phil D 4
39 Tirril C 7
8 Tisbury C 1
9 Tisman's Com C 12
31 Tissington E 10
4 Titchberry C 1
25 Titchmarsh G 1
26 Titchwell A 1
32 Tithby F 4
45 Titlington B 9
21 Titley F 9
10 Titsey C 3
31 Tittensor F 7
26 Tittleshall C 2
15 Tittups End E 11
30 Tiverton, Ches. D 4
6 Tiverton, Devon E 3
6 Tiverton Junction E 4
27 Tivetshall St. Margaret G 4
27 Tivetshall St. Mary G 4
22 Tividale C 3
6 Tivington B 3
31 Tixall H 8
24 Tixover E 1
64 Toab D 3
31 Toadmoor E 12
50 Tobermory B 2
50 Toberonochy G 5
63 Tobson C 2
58 Tocher D 4
16 Tockenham F 2
16 Tockenham Wick F 1
34 Tockholes E 5
15 Tockington F 9
36 Tockwith B 3
7 Todber D 11
17 Toddington, Beds. A 11
16 Toddington, Glos. A 1
22 Todenham H 6
53 Todhall E 8
44 Todhills G 2
35 Todmorden E 8
49 Todrig G 7
32 Todwick B 2
23 Toft, Cambs. K 5
24 Toft, Lincs. D 2
40 Toft Hill B 2
26 Toft Monks F 7
33 Toft Next Newton A 7
49 Toftbarns G 8
26 Toftrees C 2
61 Tofts A 12
26 Toftwood Com D 3
45 Togston C 10
55 Toigal K 1
62 Tokavaig G 5
17 Tokers Green F 8
36 Toll Bar F 3
22 Toll End C 3
58 Toll of Birness D 7
6 Tolland C 4
8 Tollard Royal D 1
7 Toller Fratrum F 9
7 Toller Porcorum F 9
32 Tollerton, Notts. G 3
36 Tollerton, N. Yorks. A 3
19 Tollesbury C 9
19 Tolleshunt D'Arcy C 9
19 Tolleshunt Major C 9
56 Tollie D 1
63 Tolmachan F 2
64 Tolob F 7
7 Tolpuddle G 11
63 Tolstachaolais C 3
57 Tolvah J 4
10 Tolworth B 1
57 Tomatin G 4
57 Tombain J 4
56 Tombreck F 2
55 Tomcrasky H 6
55 Tomdoun J 5
56 Tomich, Highland E 1
55 Tomich, Highland G 7
56 Tomich, Highland C 3
60 Tomich, Highland F 6
57 Tomintoul, Grampian K 7
57 Tomintoul, Grampian H 7
57 Tomintoul, Highland G 2
58 Tomnaven D 2
57 Tomnavoulin G 8
52 Tomphibil B 3
44 Tomishielburn E 2
14 Ton D 6
14 Ton-Pentre E 3
10 Tonbridge C 5
14 Tondu F 2
20 Ton-fanau B 1
63 Tong, W. Iles C 5
22 Tong, Salop A 2
35 Tong, W. Yorks. D 10
32 Tonge H 2
9 Tongham A 10
43 Tongland F 8
60 Tongue B 6
60 Tongue House B 6
14 Tongwynlais F 5
13 Tonna G 11
14 Ton-teg F 4
18 Tonwell B 3
14 Tonypandy E 3
14 Tonyrefail E 3
16 Toot Baldon D 6
18 Toothill D 5
35 Top of Hebers F 7
40 Topcliffe H 4
26 Topcroft F 6
26 Topcroft Street F 5
25 Toppesfield L 8
34 Toppings F 6
6 Topsham G 3
57 Torbain H 7
46 Torbeg, Arran I. F 4
59 Torbeg, Grampian G 1
61 Torboll G 7
56 Torbreck F 3
5 Torbryan J 7
55 Torcastle L 5
5 Torcross L 7
57 Torcroy J 3
55 Torcuileainn J 2
56 Tore D 2
55 Torgyle Bridge H 7
46 Torinturk C 3
32 Torksey B 5
55 Torlundy M 5
15 Tormarton F 11
42 Tormitchell B 3
46 Tormore F 4
56 Tornagrain E 3
57 Tornahaish J 8
59 Tornaveen G 4
57 Torness G 1
40 Toronto B 2
50 Torosay Castle D 4
38 Torpenhow A 4
48 Torphichen B 2
59 Torphins G 4
3 Torpoint D 11
5 Torquay J 8
49 Torquhan E 7
62 Torran, Highland C 5
56 Torran, Highland B 3
47 Torrance B 11
50 Torraneidhinn B 3
50 Torrans E 2
47 Torranyard E 8
5 Torre, Devon J 8
6 Torre, Somerset B 4
54 Torridon D 3
54 Torridon House D 2
62 Torrin F 5
61 Torrisdale B 7
34 Torrisholme A 3
55 Torrlaoighseach H 3
60 Torroboll F 6
58 Torry, Grampian D 2
59 Torry, Grampian G 7
48 Torryburn A 3
58 Torterston C 8
43 Torthorwald D 11
9 Tortington F 11
38 Torver F 5
48 Torwood A 1
32 Torworth B 4
4 Tosberry D 1
54 Toscaig F 1
25 Toseland J 3
34 Tosside B 6
50 Tostarie C 1
27 Tostock J 3
62 Totaig, Highland C 1
55 Totaig, Highland G 2
56 Tote C 3
61 Totegan A 8
8 Totland G 5
31 Totley B 11
7 Totnell E 9
5 Totnes K 7
62 Totscore B 3
18 Tottenham E 3
24 Tottenhill D 7
18 Totteridge E 2
17 Totternhoe B 10
34 Tottington F 6
8 Totton E 5
17 Touchen-end F 9
59 Toucks J 6
6 Toulton C 5
56 Toulvaddie B 4
58 Toux C 7
40 Tow Law A 1
46 Toward C 6
46 Toward Quay C 6
23 Towcester G 10
2 Towednack F 2
18 Tower Hamlets F 4
10 Tower Hill E 1
17 Towersey D 8
58 Towie F 2
58 Towiemore C 1
39 Town End G 7
34 Town Green G 3
10 Town Row E 4
27 Town Street G 1
49 Town Yetholm G 10
43 Townfoot B 10
43 Townhead, Dumf. & Gall. C 10
43 Townhead, Dumf. & Gall. G 8
59 Townhead, Grampian K 5
45 Townhead, Northumb. F 7
42 Townhead, Strathclyde A 3
47 Townhead of Aber A 9
47 Townhead of Gree E 9
43 Town head of Greenlaw E 8
52 Townhill H 6
16 Townsend, Oxon E 5
7 Townsend, Som. A 8
2 Townshend F 3
36 Towthorpe A 4
36 Towton C 3
29 Towyn B 9
33 Toynton All Saints D 11
33 Toynton Fen Side D 11
33 Toynton St. Peter D 11
10 Toy's Hill C 3
47 Trabboch G 9
47 Trabboch Mains G 9
47 Trabbochburn G 9
2 Traboe G 4
56 Tradespark D 4
35 Trafford Park H 7
55 Traigh House K 1
43 Trailtrow D 12
14 Trallong A 3
49 Tranent B 7
30 Tranmere A 2
61 Trantlemore B 8
45 Tranwell E 10
13 Trapp E 10
49 Traprain B 8
48 Traquair F 6
17 Traveller's Rest B 10
35 Trawden C 8
14 Trawscoed A 4
28 Trawsfynydd G 6
13 Tre-Herbert B 9
14 Trelaw E 3
34 Treales D 3
28 Trearddur Bay B 2
62 Treaslane C 3
14 Trebanog E 3
3 Trebartha B 9
3 Trebarwith A 7
2 Trebetheric B 6
6 Treborough C 3
2 Trebudannon D 6
3 Trebullett B 10
3 Treburley B 10
3 Trebyan C 8
14 Trecastle A 2
14 Trecenydd F 5
12 Trecwn D 3
14 Trecynon D 3
30 Tredaule B 9
12 Tre-ddiog D 2
14 Tredegar C 5
22 Tredington H 6
2 Tredizzick B 6
14 Tredomen A 4
12 Tredrissi C 4
15 Tredunnock E 7
14 Tredustan A 5
2 Treen G 1
32 Treeton A 2
12 Trefasser C 2
28 Trefdraeth C 3
14 Trefecca A 5
20 Trefeglwys C 5
20 Trefenter E 2
12 Treffgarne E 3
12 Treffgarne Owen D 2
12 Treffynnon, Dyfed D 2
28 Treffynnon, Gwynedd B 3
14 Trefil C 4
20 Trefilan G 1
29 Trefnant C 10
30 Trefonen G 1
28 Trefor B 3
14 Treforest Industrial Estate F 4
29 Trefriw D 7
29 Tref-y-nant F 12
3 Tregadillet A 10
28 Tregaian B 4
15 Tregare C 7
20 Tregaron F 2
28 Tregarth C 5
3 Tregeare A 9
29 Tregeiriog G 11
28 Tregele A 3
2 Tregeseal F 1
12 Treglemais D 2
2 Tregonetha C 6
2 Tregony E 6
3 Tregoss D 7
2 Tregowris G 5
14 Tregoyd A 5
13 Tre-groes C 7
2 Tregurrian C 5
20 Tregynon C 6
14 Trehafod E 4
14 Treharris E 4
14 Treherbert D 3
3 Trekenner B 10
3 Treknow A 7
3 Trelash A 9
2 Trelassick D 6
29 Trelawnyd B 10
12 Trelach D 6
12 Tre-lech-a'r-Betws D 6
12 Treleddyd fawr D 1
14 Trelewis E 4
3 Treligga A 7
3 Trelights B 7
3 Trelill B 7
2 Trelissick F 5
15 Trelleck D 8
15 Trelleck Grange D 8
29 Trelogan B 10
28 Tremadog F 5
3 Tremail A 8
12 Tremain B 6
3 Tremaine A 9
3 Tremar C 9
3 Trematon D 11
29 Tremeirchion C 10
3 Tremore C 7
2 Trenance, Corn. C 5
2 Trenance, Corn. C 6
2 Trenance, Corn. H 4
3 Trenarren E 7
21 Trench A 12
2 Trenear F 4
3 Treneglos A 9
3 Trenewan D 9
2 Trengune B 2
7 Trent Nether Compton D 2
31 Trentham F 7
4 Trentishoe A 5
14 Treoes F 3
14 Treorchy E 3
3 Trequite B 7
20 Tre'r-ddol C 2
3 Trerule Foot D 10
12 Tresaith B 6
3 Tresayes D 7
22 Trescott B 2
2 Trescowe G 3
15 Tresham E 11
2 Tresillian E 6
12 Tresinwen C 2
2 Treskinnick Cross A 2
3 Tresmeer A 9
2 Tresparrett B 2
2 Tresparrett Posts B 2
52 Tressait A 3
64 Tresta, Zetland B 8
64 Tresta, Zetland D 7
32 Treswell B 5
2 Trethosa D 6
3 Trethurgy D 7
12 Tretio D 1
15 Tretire B 8
14 Tretower B 5
29 Treuddyn D 11
3 Trevadlock B 9
3 Trevalga A 8
30 Trevalyn D 3
3 Trevanson B 7
2 Trevarren D 6
2 Trevarrian C 5
3 Trevarrick E 7
12 Trevaughan, Dyfed E 5
13 Trevaughan, Dyfed E 7
2 Trevellas D 4
3 Trevelmond C 9
2 Treverva F 5
14 Trevethin D 6
3 Trevigro C 10
12 Trevine D 2
2 Treviscoe D 6
3 Trevivian A 9
2 Trevoll D 5
2 Trevone B 6
28 Trevor F 3
2 Trevose B 6
3 Trewarmett A 8
3 Trewassa A 8
2 Trewellard F 1
3 Trewen A 9
2 Trewennack G 4
21 Trewern A 8
3 Trewerthern B 7
3 Trewetha B 7
3 Trewidland D 9
12 Trewilym C 5
2 Trewint B 2
2 Trewithian F 6
3 Trewoon D 7
2 Treyarnon Bay B 6
9 Treyford D 9
35 Triangle E 9
8 Trickett's Cross F 3
44 Triermain F 4
40 Trimdon B 4
40 Trimdon Colliery B 4
40 Trimdon Grange B 4
26 Trimingham B 6
27 Trimley L 6
27 Trimley Heath L 6
22 Trimpley D 1
13 Trimsaran F 8
4 Trimstone B 4
14 Trinant D 5
17 Tring C 10
17 Tring Wharf C 10
6 Trinity, Devon F 3
59 Trinity, Tayside L 4
6 Triscombe C 5
55 Trislaig M 5
2 Trispen E 5
45 Tritlington D 10
52 Trochrie C 5
13 Troedyraur B 7
13 Troed-y-rhiw, Dyfed B 8
14 Troedyrhiw, Mid Glam. D 4
47 Troon, Strathclyde F 8
2 Troon, Cornwall F 4
43 Troqueer D 10
51 Trossachs Hotel G 12
27 Trostan H 2
10 Trottiscliffe B 5
9 Trotton D 9
45 Troughend D 7
38 Troutbeck, Cumbria C 6
38 Troutbeck, Cumbria E 6
38 Troutbeck Bridge E 6
15 Trow Green D 9
32 Troway B 1
15 Trowbridge H 11
32 Trowell F 2
15 Trowle Common H 11
17 Trowley Botton C 11
49 Trows F 9
26 Trowse Newton E 5
7 Trudoxhill B 10
6 Trull D 6
62 Trumpan B 2
21 Trumpet H 12
25 Trumpington K 6
6 Trumps E 4
26 Trunch B 6
2 Truro E 5
3 Truscott A 10
6 Trusham H 2
31 Trusley G 11
33 Trusthorpe B 12
22 Trysull C 2
16 Tubney D 5
5 Tuckenhay K 7
2 Tuckingmill F 4
25 Tuddenham, Suff. H 8
27 Tuddenham, Suff. K 5
10 Tudeley D 5
40 Tudhoe B 3
15 Tudorville B 9
28 Tudweiliog G 2
9 Tuesley B 11
15 Tuffley C 11
12 Tufton D 4
23 Tugby B 11
21 Tugford D 11
45 Tughall E 12
54 Tuirnaig B 3
57 Tulchan M 7
52 Tullibody H 3
51 Tullich, Central D 12
57 Tullich, Highland G 2

54 Tullich, Highland ... E 3
51 Tullich, Strathclyde . F 8
56 Tullich Muir .... B 3
52 Tulliemet .... B 5
59 Tullo of Benholm .. K 5
58 Tulloch, Grampian . D 5
55 Tulloch, Highland ... L 7
52 Tullochan .... D 1
51 Tullochgorm .... H 7
57 Tullochmacarrick ... J 8
58 Tullochs .... C 2
59 Tullochvenus .... G 3
52 Tullybannocher ..... E 2
53 Tullyfergus .... B 7
53 Tullymurdoch ...... B 7
58 Tullynessle .... F 3
13 Tumble .... F 9
33 Tumby .... D 9
33 Tumby Woodside ... D 9
18 Tumford .... C 4
52 Tummel Bridge ..... A 3
10 Tunbridge Wells .... D 5
15 Tunley .... H 10
37 Tunstall, Humber. . D 10
11 Tunstall, Kent ...... B 7
39 Tunstall, Lancs. .... H 8
40 Tunstall, N. Yorks. .. F 2
31 Tunstall, Staffs. ...... E 7
27 Tunstall, Suffolk .... K 6
45 Tunstall, Tyne & Wear .... H 12
26 Tunstall St. Mary ... E 7
9 Tunworth .... A 8
21 Tupsley .... H 10
23 Tur Langton ...... C 10
17 Turgis Green .... H 8
53 Turin .... B 10
16 Turkdean .... B 2
15 Turleigh Freshford H 11
15 Turnastone .... A 7
42 Turnberry .... A 3
31 Turnditch .... F 11
10 Turner's Hill .... E 2
7 Turners Puddle .... G 11
48 Turnhouse .... B 4
7 Turnworth .... E 11
58 Turriff .... C 5
34 Turton Bottoms ..... F 6
49 Turvelaws .... F 12
23 Turvey .... G 12
17 Turville .... E 8
17 Turville Heath ...... E 8
23 Turweston .... H 9
48 Tushielaw .... G 6
31 Tutbury .... G 10
22 Tutnall .... E 3
15 Tutshill .... E 8
26 Tuttington .... C 5
17 Tutts Clump .... G 7
3 Tutwell .... B 11
32 Tuxford .... C 4
64 Twatt, Orkney Is. ... C 1
64 Twatt, Shetland Is. .. D 7
47 Twechar .... B 11
48 Tweeddaleburn .... D 5
49 Tweedmouth ...... D 12
48 Tweedshaws .... H 3
48 Tweedsmuir .... G 4
2 Twelveheads .... E 5
30 Twemlow Green .... C 6
24 Twenty .... C 3
15 Twerton .... H 10
44 Twice Brewed ...... F 6
18 Twickenham .... G 2
15 Twigworth .... B 11
10 Twineham .... F 1
15 Twinhoe .... H 10
27 Twinstead .... L 2
27 Twinstead Green ... L 2
4 Twitchen, Devon ... B 4
4 Twitchen, Devon ... C 7
21 Twitchen, Salop .... D 9
5 Two Bridges .... H 5
31 Two Dales .... D 11
22 Two Gates .... B 5
4 Two Pots .... B 4
23 Twycross .... B 7
17 Twyford, Berks ..... G 9
17 Twyford, Bucks ..... B 7
31 Twyford, Derby ... G 11
8 Twyford, Hants ..... D 6
23 Twyford, Leics. ... A 10
26 Twyford, Norf. ..... C 3
15 Twyford Com .... A 8
13 Twyn Llanan ...... E 11
14 Twyncarno .... C 4
43 Twynholm .... F 7
15 Twyning .... A 12
22 Twyning Green ..... H 3
13 Twyn-mynydd .... F 10
15 Twyn-y-Sheriff ..... D 7
23 Twywell .... D 12
28 Ty-Hen .... G 1
21 Tyberton .... H 9
13 Tycroes, Dyfed ..... F 9
28 Ty-croes, Gwynedd . C 3
29 Tycrwyn .... H 10
24 Tydd Gote .... D 5
24 Tydd St. Giles ...... D 5
24 Tydd St. Mary ...... D 5
29 Tyddininco .... G 9
19 Tye Green, Essex ... B 7
25 Tye Green, Essex ... L 7
12 Ty-hen .... E 6
34 Tyldesley .... G 6
11 Tyler Hill .... B 10
17 Tylers Green, Bucks. E 10
10 Tyler's Grn., Surrey . C 2
14 Tylorstown .... E 3
20 Tylwch .... D 5
29 Ty-nant, Clwyd ..... F 9
29 Ty-nant, Gwynedd .. H 8
20 Tyncwm .... D 4
51 Tyndrum .... E 10
7 Tyneham .... H 12
45 Tyne & Wear, Co. .. F 10
48 Tynehead .... C 6
45 Tynemouth .... F 11
14 Tynewydd .... D 3
49 Tyninghame .... B 8
50 Tynribbie .... C 6
43 Tynron .... B 9
20 Tynswydd .... F 2
29 Ty'n-y-ffridd ...... G 10
28 Ty'n-y-gongl .... B 4
29 Ty'n-y-groes .... C 7
28 Tyn-y-pwll .... B 4
29 Tyn-y-Wern ...... G 10
23 Tyringham .... G 12
4 Tythecott .... D 3
14 Tythegston .... F 2
15 Tytherington, Avon .... E 10
31 Tytherington, Ches . C 7
8 Tytherington, Wilts. . B 1
7 Tytherington, Wilts. B 11
7 Tytherleigh .... F 7
3 Tywardreath .... D 8
3 Tywardreath Highway D 8
29 Tywyn .... B 7
20 Tywyn Mer .... B 2
54 Uags .... F 1
54 Uamh on Triall ..... D 1
27 Ubbeston Green .... H 6
15 Ubley .... H 8
40 Uckerby .... E 3
10 Uckfield .... F 4
15 Uckington .... B 12
47 Uddingston .... C 11
48 Uddington .... F 1
11 Udimore .... F 7
58 Udny .... E 6
47 Udston .... E 12
47 Udstonhead .... E 12
16 Uffcott .... F 2
6 Uffculme .... E 4
24 Uffington, Lincs. ... E 2
16 Uffington, Oxon .... E 4
21 Uffington, Salop .. A 10
24 Ufford, Cambs. ..... E 2
27 Ufford, Suffolk ..... K 6
23 Ufton .... F 7
17 Ufton Green .... G 7
17 Ufton Nervet ...... G 7
46 Ugadale .... F 3
5 Ugborough .... K 5
27 Uggeshall .... G 7
41 Ugglebarnby .... D 9
18 Ugley .... A 5
41 Ugthorpe .... D 8
62 Uig, Skye .... C 1
62 Uig, Skye .... B 3
63 Uig, W. Isles .... D 2
62 Uigshader .... D 4
50 Uisken .... F 1
61 Ulbster .... C 12
33 Ulceby, Humberside F 8
33 Ulceby, Lincs. .... C 11
33 Ulceby Cross ..... C 11
37 Ulceby Skitter ..... F 9
11 Ulcombe .... C 7
38 Uldale .... B 5
39 Uldale House ...... F 9
15 Uley .... D 11
45 Ulgham .... D 10
60 Ullapool .... G 3
22 Ullenhall .... E 5
15 Ullenwood .... C 12
36 Ulleskelf .... C 3
23 Ullesthorpe .... C 8
32 Ulley .... B 2
21 Ullingswick .... G 11
62 Ullinish .... D 2
38 Ullock .... C 3
8 Ullwell .... H 2
38 Ulpha .... F 4
37 Ulrome .... B 9
64 Ulsta .... C 7
49 Ulsoon .... G 9
50 Ulva House .... D 2
38 Ulverston .... G 5
43 Ulzieside .... A 8
62 Umachan .... C 5
4 Umberleigh .... D 5
60 Unapool .... D 4
44 Under Burnmouth .. E 3
10 Under River .... C 4
39 Underbarrow .... F 7
36 Undercliffe .... D 10
47 Underhills .... F 9
64 Underhoull .... A 8
32 Underwood .... E 2
15 Undy .... F 7
64 Unifirth .... D 6
59 Union Croft .... H 6
38 Union Mills .... H 2
32 Unstone .... C 1
32 Unstone Green ..... C 1
35 Unsworth .... F 7
44 Unthank, Cumb. ... H 2
39 Unthank, Cumb. ... A 8
39 Unthank, Cumb. ... B 7
49 Unthank, Northumb. E 12
39 Unthank End .... B 7
7 Up Cerne .... F 10
6 Up Exe .... F 3
15 Up Hatherley ..... B 12
34 Up Holland .... G 4
9 Up Marden .... E 9
9 Up Nately .... A 8
8 Up Somborne ...... C 5
7 Up Sydling .... F 9
8 Upavon .... A 3
11 Upchurch .... A 7
4 Upcott, Devon ..... E 4
21 Upcott, Heref. & Worc. .... G 8
6 Upcott, Somerset ... D 3
17 Updown Hill ...... H 10
48 Uphall .... B 3
48 Uphall Station ...... B 3
4 Upham, Devon ..... E 7
9 Upham, Hants ..... D 7
21 Uphampton, Heref. & Worc. .... F 9
22 Uphampton, Heref. & Worc. .... F 2
14 Uphill .... H 6
47 Uplawmoor .... D 9
15 Upleadon .... B 10
40 Upleatham .... C 6
11 Uplees .... B 8
7 Uploders .... G 8
6 Uplowman .... E 4
6 Uplyme .... G 6
18 Upminster .... E 6
6 Upottery .... E 5
71 Uppat .... F 8
21 Upper Affcott .... D 10
60 Upper Ardchronie . G 6
22 Upper Arley .... D 1
17 Upper Arncott ..... B 7
23 Upper Astrop ...... H 8
42 Upper Barr .... E 5
63 Upper Barvas ...... B 5
17 Upper Basildon .... F 7
63 Upper Bayble ...... D 6
10 Upper Beeding ..... G 1
24 Upper Benefield .... F 1
22 Upper Bentley ..... E 3
58 Upper Boddam ..... E 4
23 Upper Boddington .. G 8
20 Upper Borth .... D 2
9 Upper Bourne ...... B 9
58 Upper Boyndie ..... A 6
22 Upper Brailes ...... H 6
62 Upper Breakish ..... F 6
21 Upper Breinton .. H 10
32 Upper Broughton ... H 4
16 Upper Bucklebury . G 6
8 Upper Burgate ..... D 3
59 Upper Burnhaugh .. H 6
58 Upper Cairnargot .. D 2
25 Upper Caldecote ... L 3
8 Upper Canterton ... E 4
23 Upper Catesby ..... F 8
20 Upper Chapel ...... H 6
6 Upper Cheddon .... C 6
8 Upper Chicksgrove . C 1
14 Upper Church Village F 4
8 Upper Chute .... A 4
8 Upper Clatford ..... B 5
43 Upper Clifton ..... F 10
28 Upper Clynnog ..... F 4
63 Upper Coll .... C 5
20 Upper Corris .... B 3
42 Upper Graigenbay .. D 6
35 Upper Cumberworth F 10
14 Upper Cwmbran .... E 6
13 Upper Cwm-twrch . F 11
58 Upper Dallachy .... A 1
43 Upper Dalveen ..... A 9
25 Upper Dean .... H 1
35 Upper Denby ...... F 11
44 Upper Denton ..... G 4
56 Upper Derraid ..... F 6
54 Upper Diabaig ..... D 2
10 Upper Dicker ...... G 4
61 Upper Dournreay .. A 9
50 Upper Druimfin .... B 2
31 Upper Elkstone .... D 9
31 Upper End .... C 9
56 Upper Ethie .... C 3
15 Upper Framilode .. C 10
22 Upper Gornal ...... C 3
25 Upper Gravenhurst . L 2
16 Upper Green .... H 5
15 Upper Grove Com .. B 9
9 Upper Hale .... A 10
62 Upper Halistra ..... B 2
17 Upper Halliford .. G 11
10 Upper Halling ...... B 6
23 Upper Hambleton . A 12
11 Upper Hardress Court C 10
10 Upper Hartfield .... E 3
36 Upper Haugh ...... G 2
21 Upper Heath ...... D 11
26 Upper Hellesdon ... D 5
36 Uper Helmsley ..... A 5
21 Upper Hergest ..... G 8
23 Upper Heyford, Northants .... F 10
16 Upper Heyford, Oxon B 6
21 Upper Hill .... G 10
44 Upper Hindhope ... B 6
35 Upper Hopton .... E 10
10 Upper Horsebridge . G 5
31 Upper Hulme ...... D 8
16 Upper Inglesham ... D 3
57 Upper Inverbrough . G 4
58 Upper Ironside ..... B 6
53 Upper Kenley ..... F 10
13 Upper Killay .... H 9
58 Upper Kinkell ...... E 5
19 Upper Kirby ...... B 11
58 Upper Knaven ..... C 6
56 Upper Knockando .. E 7
16 Upper Lambourn ... F 4
15 Upper Langford .... H 8
32 Upper Langwith .... C 2
31 Upper Leigh .... F 8
59 Upper Lochton ..... H 4
22 Upper Longdon .... A 4
61 Upper Lybster .... D 11
15 Upper Lydbrook ... C 9
21 Upper Lye .... F 9
62 Upper Milovaig .... C 1
16 Upper Minety ...... E 1
35 Upper Moor Side .. D 11
15 Upper Morton ...... E 9
58 Upper Mulben ..... B 1
44 Upper Mumble ..... E 2
49 Upper Nisbet ...... G 9
17 Upper North Dean .. D 9
52 Upper Obney ...... C 5
62 Upper Ollach ...... E 4
22 Upper Penn .... C 3
36 Upper Poppleton ... B 3
21 Upper Pulley ..... B 10
22 Upper Quinton ..... G 5
8 Upper Ratley ...... D 5
21 Upper Rochford ... F 11
42 Upper Rusko .... E 6
55 Upper Sandaig ..... H 2
21 Upper Sapey ..... F 12
46 Upper Scoulag ..... C 6
16 Upper Seagry ...... F 1
63 Upper Shader ...... B 5
25 Upper Shelton ...... L 1
26 Upper Sheringham .. A 4
48 Upper Side .... D 6
47 Upper Skelmorlie ... C 7
16 Upper Slaughter .... B 3
51 Upper Sonachan .... E 8
15 Upper Soudley .... C 10
15 Upper Stanton Drew H 9
25 Upper Stondon ..... M 3
22 Upper Stonnal ...... B 4
23 Upper Stowe ..... F 10
8 Upper Street, Hants. D 3
26 Upper Street, Norf. . D 7
22 Upper Strensham ... H 3
17 Upper Sundon .... A 11
16 Upper Swell .... B 3
26 Upper Tasburgh .... F 5
31 Upper Tean .... F 8
52 Upper Tillyrie ...... F 6
62 Upper Tote .... B 4
15 Upper Town, Avon . H 8
21 Upper Town, Heref. & Worc. .. G 11
23 Upper Tysoe .... H 7
16 Upper Upham ..... F 3
10 Upper Upnor ...... A 6
23 Upper Wardington .. G 8
23 Upper Weald ..... H 11
23 Upper Weedon ..... F 9
17 Upper Winchendon . C 8
8 Upper Woodford ... B 3
58 Upper Woodhead ... F 4
9 Upper Wootton .... A 7
22 Upper Wyche ...... H 1
44 Upperby .... H 2
35 Uppermill .... G 8
58 Uppertack of Gressiehill .... B 6
35 Upperthong ...... F 10
59 Upperton, Grampian K 5
9 Upperton, W. Sussex D 11
64 Uppertown .... F 2
21 Uppington .... A 11
40 Upsall .... F 5
18 Upshire .... D 4
11 Upstreet .... B 11
17 Upton, Berks ..... F 10
24 Upton, Cambs. ..... E 2
25 Upton, Cambs. ..... G 3
30 Upton, Cheshire .... C 3
4 Upton, Cornwall .... E 1
6 Upton, Devon ...... F 4
8 Upton, Dorset ...... G 1
7 Upton, Dorset .... H 11
8 Upton, Hants. ...... D 5
32 Upton, Lincs. ...... B 2
30 Upton, Merseyside . A 1
26 Upton, Norfolk ..... D 7
23 Upton, Northants .. F 10
32 Upton, Notts. ...... C 5
32 Upton, Notts. ...... E 4
8 Upton, Notts. ...... A 5
16 Upton, Oxon .... E 6
6 Upton, Somerset ... C 3
7 Upton, Somerset ... D 8
22 Upton, War. .... F 5
36 Upton W. Yorks. ... F 3
15 Upton Bishop ...... B 9
15 Upton Cheyney ... G 10
21 Upton Cressett .... C 12
9 Upton Grey .... A 8
4 Upton Hellions ..... F 7
8 Upton Lovel .... B 2
21 Upton Magna ..... A 11
7 Upton Noble ...... B 10
6 Upton Pyne .... F 3
15 Upton St. Leonards C 11
7 Upton Scudamore . A 12
22 Upton Snodsbury ... G 3
22 Upton upon Severn . H 2
22 Upton Warren ...... E 3
9 Upwaltham .... E 10
25 Upware .... H 6
24 Upwell .... E 6
7 Upwey H10
25 Upwood .... G 4
64 Urafirth .... C 6
56 Urchal .... E 3
56 Urchany .... E 4
16 Urchfont .... H 2
63 Urgha Beag .... G 3
40 Urlay Nook .... D 4
34 Urmston .... H 6
56 Urquhart, Grampian C 8
56 Urquhart, Highland . D 1
40 Urra .... E 6
56 Urray .... D 1
40 Ushaw Moor .... A 3
15 Usk .... D 7
37 Usselby .... H 8
56 Ussie .... D 1
64 Ustaness .... D 7
45 Usworth .... G 11
35 Utley .... C 9
4 Uton .... F 7
37 Utterby .... H 10
31 Uttoxeter .... G 9
28 Uwchmynydd ...... H 1
18 Uxbridge .... F 1
64 Uyeasound .... B 8
12 Uzmaston .... F 3
12 Vachelich .... D 1
28 Valley .... B 2
3 Valley Truckle ..... A 8
62 Valtos, Skye .... B 4
63 Valtos, W. Isles .... C 2
20 Van .... D 5
19 Vange .... E 7
14 Varteg Hill .... D 6
62 Vatten .... D 2
14 Vaynor .... C 4
13 Velindre, Dyfed .... C 7
12 Velindre, Dyfed .... C 4
14 Velindre, Powys .... A 5
6 Vellow .... B 4
64 Vementry .... D 6
64 Veness .... B 3
6 Venn Ottery .... G 4
21 Vennington .... A 9
4 Venny Tedburn ..... F 7
9 Ventnor .... H 7
16 Vernham Dean ..... H 4
16 Vernham Street .... H 4
12 Verwig .... B 5
8 Verwood .... E 2
2 Veryan .... F 6
6 Vicarage .... G 5
38 Vickerstown .... H 4
3 Victoria, Corn. ..... D 7
14 Victoria, Gwent .... D 5
64 Vidlin .... C 7
10 Vinehall Street ..... F 6
10 Vine's Cross .... F 5
15 Viney Hill .... D 9
17 Virginia Water .... G 10
5 Virginstow .... G 3
7 Vobster .... A 10
64 Voe .... C 7
15 Vowchurch .... A 7
64 Voxter .... C 7
64 Voy .... C 1
40 Wackerfield .... C 2
26 Wacton .... F 5
22 Wadborough .... G 3
17 Waddesdon .... B 8
37 Waddingham ...... G 7
34 Waddington Lancs. . C 6
33 Waddington, Lincs. . D 7
3 Wadebridge .... B 7
6 Wadeford .... E 6
25 Wadenhoe .... G 1
18 Wadesmill .... B 4
10 Wadhurst .... E 5
31 Wadshelf .... C 11
31 Wadsley .... A 11
32 Wadsley Bridge .... A 1
15 Wadswick .... G 11
36 Wadworth .... G 3
29 Waen Fach ...... H 11
61 Wag .... E 9
33 Wainfleet All Saints D 12
33 Wainfleet Bank ... D 11
45 Wainfordrigg ...... C 7
32 Waingroves .... E 1
2 Wainhouse Corner .. B 2
10 Wainscott .... A 6
35 Wainstalls .... D 9
39 Waitby .... D 10
35 Wakefield .... E 12
24 Wakerley .... F 1
19 Wakes Colne .... A 9
27 Walberswick .... H 8
9 Walberton .... E 11
45 Walbottle .... F 10
24 Walcot, Lincs. ..... B 2
33 Walcot, Lincs. ..... E 8
21 Walcot, Salop .... A 11
21 Walcot, Salop ...... D 9
22 Walcot, War. ...... F 5
16 Walcot, Wilts. ..... F 3
23 Walcote .... D 9
26 Walcott .... B 7
39 Walden Head ..... G 12
36 Walden Stubbs .... E 3
10 Walderslade .... B 6
9 Walderton .... E 9
7 Walditch .... G 8
31 Waldley .... F 9
45 Waldridge .... H 10
27 Waldringfield ...... L 6
10 Waldron .... F 4
32 Wales .... B 2
33 Walesby, Lincs. .... A 8
32 Walesby, Notts. .... C 4
15 Walford, Heref. & Worc. .... B 9
21 Walford, Heref. & Worc. .... E 9
30 Walford, Salop ..... H 3
30 Walford Heath ..... H 3
30 Walgherton .... E 5
23 Walgrave .... E 11
8 Walhampton ...... F 5
35 Walk Mill .... D 7
34 Walkden .... G 6
45 Walker .... G 11
34 Walker Fold .... C 5
48 Walkerburn .... F 6
32 Walkeringham ..... A 5
32 Walkerith .... A 5
18 Walkern .... A 3
21 Walker's Green ... H 10
53 Walkerton .... G 7
8 Walkford .... G 4

5 Walkhampton J 4
37 Walkington C 8
32 Walkley A 1
45 Wall, Northumb. F 7
22 Wall, Staffs. B 4
44 Wall Bowers G 4
21 Wall under Heywood C 10
43 Wallaceton C 9
42 Wallacetown, Strathclyde A 4
47 Wallacetown, Strathclyde G 8
30 Wallasey A 2
38 Wallend, Cumbria G 5
19 Wallend, Kent F 8
17 Wallingford E 7
9 Wallington, Hants. E 7
25 Wallington, Herts M 4
18 Wallington, London H 3
9 Walliswood B 12
64 Walls D 6
45 Wallsend F 11
38 Wallthwaite C 6
48 Wallyford B 6
11 Walmer C 12
34 Walmer Bridge E 3
35 Walmersley F 7
22 Walmley C 5
27 Walpole H 7
24 Walpole Crosskeys D 6
24 Walpole Highway D 6
24 Walpole Island D 6
24 Walpole St. Andrew D 6
24 Walpole St. Peter D 6
22 Walsall B 4
22 Wallsall Wood B 4
35 Walsden E 8
23 Walsgrave on Sowe D 7
27 Walsham le Willows H 3
34 Walshaw F 6
35 Walshford B 12
48 Walston E 3
18 Walsworth A 2
17 Walter's Ash D 9
14 Walterston G 4
15 Walterstone B 7
11 Waltham, Kent C 9
37 Waltham, Humber. G 10
18 Waltham Abbey D 4
9 Waltham Chase E 7
18 Waltham Cross D 4
18 Waltham Forest E 4
32 Waltham on the Wolds H 2
17 Waltham St. Lawrence F 9
18 Walthamstow E 3
23 Walton, Bucks. H 12
24 Walton, Cambs E 3
44 Walton, Cumb. G 3
32 Walton, Derby C 1
23 Walton, Leics C 9
21 Walton, Powys F 8
30 Walton, Salop H 4
7 Walton, Som. C 8
27 Walton, Suffolk L 6
22 Walton, War. G 6
36 Walton, W. Yorks. B 2
35 Walton, W. Yorks. E 12
15 Walton Cardiff A 12
7 Walton Elm D 11
12 Walton East E 4
15 Walton-in-Gordano G 7
34 Walton-Le-Dale D 4
17 Walton-on-Thames G 12
34 Walton on the Hill, Merseyside H 3
31 Walton-on-the-Hill, Staffordshire H 8
10 Walton on the Hill, Surrey C 1
19 Walton on the Naze B 12
32 Walton on the Wolds H 3
15 Walton Park G 7
31 Walton upon Trent H 10
12 Walton West F 2
29 Walwen C 11
45 Walwick F 7
45 Walwick Grange F 7
40 Walworth C 3
12 Walwyn's Castle F 2
6 Wambrook E 6
43 Wamphraygate B 12
9 Wanborough, Surrey A 10
16 Wanborough, Wilts F 3
48 Wandel G 2
45 Wandon C 11
18 Wandsworth F 3
45 Wandylaw A 9
27 Wangford G 8
23 Wanlip A 9
48 Wanlockhead H 2
10 Wannock H 4
24 Wansford, Cambs. F 2
37 Wansford, Humber. B 8
18 Wanstead E 4
7 Wanstrow B 10
15 Wanswell D 10
16 Wantage E 5
23 Wappenbury E 7
23 Wappenham H 9
36 Warcop D 9
10 Warbleton F 5
9 Warblington E 8
17 Warborough E 7
25 Warboys G 4
34 Warbreck C 2
2 Warbstow B 2
30 Warburton A 5
27 Ward Green J 4
11 Warden A 9
31 Wardgate E 11
23 Wardington G 8
48 Wardlaw, Borders H 5
47 Wardlaw, Strathclyde E 8
30 Wardle, Ches. E 5
35 Wardle, Lancs. E 8
23 Wardley B 11
31 Wardlow C 10
45 Wardon F 7
25 Wardy Hill G 6
18 Ware, Herts. C 4
11 Ware, Kent B 11
8 Wareham G 1
11 Warehorne E 8
45 Waren Mill C 12
45 Warenford C 12
45 Warenton C 12
18 Wareside B 4
25 Waresley, Cambs. K 3
22 Waresley, Heref. & Worc. E 2
17 Warfield G 9
5 Warfleet L 7
24 Wargate C 3
17 Wargrave F 9
26 Warham All Saints A 3
26 Warham St. Mary A 2
45 Wark, Northumb E 7
49 Wark, Northumb. E 11
4 Warkleigh D 5
23 Warkton D 12
23 Warkwork H 8
45 Warkworth B 10
40 Warlaby F 4
35 Warland E 8
3 Warleggan C 8
22 Warley C 3
10 Warlingham B 2
35 Warmfield E 12
30 Warmingham D 5
24 Warmington, Cambs. F 2
23 Warmington, War. G 7
7 Warminster B 11
11 Warmlake C 7
15 Warmley G 10
15 Warmley Tower G 10
36 Warmsworth G 3
7 Warmwell H 11
22 Warndon F 2
9 Warnford D 8
10 Warnham E 1
9 Warningcamp E 11
10 Warninglid E 1
31 Warren, Ches. C 7
12 Warren, Dyfed G 3
5 Warren House Inn H 5
17 Warren Row F 9
11 Warren Street C 8
23 Warrington, Bucks. G 12
30 Warrington, Ches. A 5
8 Warsash E 6
31 Warslow D 9
32 Warsop C 3
36 Warter B 6
40 Warthermarske G 2
36 Warthill B 4
10 Wartling G 5
32 Wartnaby H 4
34 Warton, Lancs. D 3
39 Warton, Lancs. H 7
45 Warton, Northumb. C 8
22 Warton, War. B 6
44 Warwick, Cumb. G 3
22 Warwick, War. F 6
44 Warwick Bridge G 3
22 Warwickshire, Co. F 6
44 Warwicksland E 3
64 Wasbister B 2
38 Wasdale Head D 4
16 Wash Common H 5
3 Washaway C 7
5 Washbourne K 7
31 Washerwall E 8
6 Washfield E 3
40 Washfold E 1
6 Washford B 4
4 Washford Pyne E 7
33 Washingborough C 7
45 Washington, Tyne & Wear G 11
9 Washington, W. Sussex E 12
17 Wasing H 7
40 Waskerley A 1
22 Wasperton F 6
40 Wass G 6
6 Watchet B 4
16 Watchfield, Oxon E 3
7 Watchfield, Som. B 7
39 Watchgate E 8
43 Watchill G 12
38 Watendlath D 5
5 Water, Devon H 6
35 Water, Lancs. E 7
18 Water End, Herts. C 2
36 Water End, Humber. C 6
24 Water Newton F 2
22 Water Orton C 5
17 Water Stratford A 7
14 Water Street F 1
38 Water Yeat F 5
25 Waterbeach J 6
44 Waterbeck E 1
26 Waterden B 2
17 Waterend C 11
31 Waterfall E 9
35 Waterfoot, Lancs. E 7
47 Waterfoot, Strathclyde D 10
8 Waterford, Hants. G 5
18 Waterford, Herts. B 3
38 Waterhead, Cumb. E 6
43 Waterhead, Dumf. & Gall. B 12
43 Waterhead, Dumf. & Gall. C 8
47 Waterford, Strathclyde H 10
48 Waterheads D 5
40 Waterhouses, Dur A 5
31 Waterhouses, Staffs. E 9
33 Watering Dyke Houses B 7
10 Wateringbury C 6
64 Wateringhouse E 2
15 Waterlane D 12
32 Waterloo, Derby D 1
8 Waterloo, Dorset G 2
12 Waterloo, Dyfed G 3
34 Waterloo, Merseyside G 2
26 Waterloo, Norf. D 5
62 Waterloo, Skye F 6
48 Waterloo, Strathclyde D 1
52 Waterloo, Tayside C 5
6 Waterloo Cross E 4
9 Waterlooville E 8
48 Watermeetings H 2
17 Waterperry C 7
6 Waterrow D 4
30 Waters Upton H 5
9 Watersfield E 11
44 Waterside, Cumb. H 1
43 Waterside, Dumf. & Gall. D 12
58 Waterside Grampian E 7
42 Waterside, Strathclyde A 5
47 Waterside Strathclyde E 9
47 Waterside, Strathclyde B 11
17 Waterstock D 7
12 Waterston F 3
18 Watford, Herts. D 1
23 Watford, Northants. E 9
40 Wath, N. Yorks. G 3
40 Wath, N. Yorks. H 2
38 Wath Brow D 3
36 Wath upon Dearne G 2
15 Watley's End F 9
24 Watlington, Norf. D 7
17 Watlington, Oxon E 8
32 Watnall Chaworth F 2
61 Watten B 11
27 Wattisfield H 3
27 Wattisham K 3
37 Watton, Humberside B 8
26 Watton, Norf. E 2
18 Watton-at-Stone B 3
47 Wattston B 12
14 Wattstown E 3
55 Wauchan L 3
37 Wauldby D 7
20 Waun Fawr D 2
13 Waunarlwydd G 9
13 Waun-deg D 7
28 Waunfawr D 5
14 Waunlwyd D 5
23 Wavendon H 12
44 Waverbridge H 1
30 Waverton, Ches. D 3
44 Waverton, Cumb. H 1
37 Wawne C 8
26 Waxham C 7
37 Waxholme D 11
6 Way Village E 3
10 Wayfield B 6
7 Wayford F 7
7 Waytown F 8
6 Weacombe B 5
18 Wealdstone E 2
35 Weardley C 11
7 Weare A 7
4 Weare Giffard D 3
39 Wearhead A 11
39 Weasdale E 9
26 Weasenham All Saints C 1
26 Weasenham St. Peter C 1
30 Weaverham C 5
41 Weaverthorpe H 9
22 Webheath E 4
15 Webton A 7
58 Wedderlairs D 6
49 Wedderlie D 9
23 Weddington C 7
16 Wedhampton H 2
7 Wedmore A 8
22 Wednesbury C 3
22 Wednesfield B 3
17 Weedon B 9
23 Weedon Bec F 9
23 Weedon Lois G 9
22 Weeford B 5
4 Week, Devon C 4
4 Week, Devon D 6
4 Week St. Mary F 1
8 Weeke C 6
23 Weekely D 12
37 Weel C 8
19 Weeley B 11
19 Weeley Heath B 11
52 Weem B 3
21 Weeping Cross, Shropshire A 10
31 Weeping Cross, Staffordshire H 8
27 Weeting G 1
34 Weeton, Lancs. D 3
35 Weeton, N. Yorks. B 11
49 Weetwoodhill F 12
35 Weir E 7
15 Weirend B 9
32 Welbeck Abbey C 3
32 Welbeck Colliery C 3
26 Welborne E 4
33 Welbourn E 7
41 Welburn, N. Yorks. G 7
41 Welburn, N. Yorks H 7
40 Welbury E 4
33 Welby F 7
25 Welches Dam G 6
4 Welcombe D 1
23 Weldon C 12
45 Weldon Bridge C 9
16 Welford, Berks. G 5
23 Welford, Northants. D 9
22 Welford-on-Avon G 5
23 Welham C 11
18 Welhamgreen C 2
9 Well, Hants. A 9
33 Well, Lincs. C 11
40 Well, N. Yorks. G 3
7 Well Bottom E 12
17 Well End E 9
10 Well Hill B 4
6 Well Town E 3
22 Welland H 2
53 Wellbank C 9
43 Welldale E 12
22 Wellesbourne Hastings G 6
22 Wellsbourne Mountford G 6
40 Wellfields A 4
59 Wellford L 2
18 Welling F 5
23 Wellingborough F 12
26 Wellingham C 2
33 Wellingore E 7
38 Wellington, Cumb. E 3
21 Wellington, Heref. & Worc. H 10
21 Wellington, Salop A 12
6 Wellington, Som. D 5
21 Wellington Heath H 12
21 Wellington Marsh H 10
15 Wellow, Avon H 10
8 Wellow, I.o.W. G 5
32 Wellow, Notts. D 4
7 Wells B 9
26 Wells-next-the-Sea A 2
58 Wells of Ytham D 4
23 Wellsborough B 7
5 Wellswood J 8
52 Wellwood H 6
24 Welney F 6
4 Welsford D 1
15 Welsh Bicknor C 9
30 Welsh Frankton G 2
12 Welsh Hook D 3
15 Welsh Newton B 8
14 Welsh St. Donats G 4
30 Welshampton G 3
21 Welshpool B 8
7 Welton, Avon A 10
38 Welton, Cumb. A 6
37 Welton, Humberside D 7
33 Welton, Lincs. B 7
23 Welton, Northants E 9
33 Welton le Marsh C 11
33 Welton le Wold B 10
37 Welwick E 11
18 Welwyn B 2
18 Welwyn Garden City C 2
30 Wem G 4
6 Wembdon C 6
18 Wembley E 2
5 Wembury L 4
4 Wembworthy E 5
47 Wemyss Bay B 7
25 Wendens Ambo L 6
16 Wendlebury B 6
26 Wendling D 2
17 Wendover C 9
2 Wendron G 4
25 Wendy K 4
27 Wenhaston H 7
25 Wennington, Cambs. G 3
39 Wennington, Lancs. H 8
18 Wennington, London F 5
31 Wensley, Derby. D 11
40 Wensley, N.Yorks. F 1
36 Wentbridge E 3
21 Wentor C 9
25 Wentworth, Cambs. G 6
35 Wentworth, S. Yorks G 12
14 Wenvoe G 4
21 Weobley G 9
21 Weobley Marsh G 9
24 Wareham E 8
22 Wergs B 2
14 Wern C 4
13 Wernffrwd H 8
15 Wernyrheolydd C 7
24 Werrington, Cambs. E 3
3 Werrington, Corn. A 10
31 Werrington, Suffolk E 8
30 Wervin C 3
34 Wesham D 3
32 Wessington D 1
26 West Acre D 1
16 West Adderbury A 5
6 West Adsborough C 6
49 West Allerdean E 12
45 West Allotment F 11
5 West Alvington L 6
8 West Amesbury B 3
4 West Anstey C 7
4 West Ash D 2
33 West Ashby C 9
9 West Ashling E 9
7 West Ashton A 12
40 West Auckland C 2
41 West Ayton G 10
59 West Balhagarty K 5
6 West Bagborough C 5
33 West Barkwith B 8
41 West Barnby D 8
49 West Barns B 9
42 West Barr G 4
7 West Bay G 8
26 West Beckham B 4
17 West Bedfont G 11
45 West Benridge D 10
19 West Bergholt A 9
7 West Bexington H 9
24 West Bilney D 8
49 West Blackadder D 11
10 West Blatchington G 2
48 West Bold F 6
45 West Boldon G 11
43 West Bowhill D 12
35 West Bowling D 10
26 West Bradenham E 2
34 West Bradford C 6
7 West Bradley C 9
59 West Braidieston K 5
35 West Bretton F 11
32 West Bridgford G 3
22 West Bromwich C 4
47 West Browncastle E 11
4 West Buckland, Devon C 5
6 West Buckland, Som. D 5
64 West Burrafirth D 6
9 West Burton, W. Sussex E 11
39 West Burton, N. Yorks F 12
40 West Butsfield A 1
36 West Butterwick G 6
17 West Byfleet H 11
49 West Byres C 7
26 West Caister D 8
48 West Calder C 3
7 West Camel D 9
58 West Cannahars E 7
47 West Carberth B 10
36 West Carr F 5
47 West Cauldcoats E 11
7 West Chaldon H 11
16 West Challow E 4
7 West Chelborough F 9
45 West Chevington C 10
9 West Chiltington D 12
9 West Chiltington Common D 12
7 West Chinnock E 8
8 West Chisenbury A 3
9 West Clandon A 11
11 West Cliffe D 12
61 West Clyth D 11
7 West Coker E 8
7 West Compton, Dorset G 9
7 West Compton, Som. B 9
36 West Cowick E 4
7 West Cranmore B 10
27 West Creeting Grn. J 4
13 West Cross H 9
44 West Curthwaite H 2
46 West Darlochan G 2
8 West Dean, Hants. C 4
9 West Dean, Sus. E 10
24 West Deeping E 2
30 West Derby A 3
24 West Dereham E 7
45 West Ditchburn A 9
4 West Down B 4
18 West Drayton, London F 1
32 West Drayton, Notts. C 4
45 West Edington E 9
37 West Ella D 8
15 West End, Avon G 8
17 West End, Berks. G 9
28 West End, Gwynedd G 3
8 West End, Hants. E 6
18 West End, Herts C 3
37 West End, Humber. D 7
37 West End, Lincs. G 11
26 West End, Norf. D 8
48 West End, Strathclyde E 2
17 West End, Surrey H 10
8 West End, Wilts. D 1
45 West Fallodon A 10
10 West Farleigh C 6
30 West Felton H 2
10 West Firle G 3
36 West Garforth D 2
16 West Ginge E 5
13 West Glamorgan, Co. G 10
16 West Grafton H 3
17 West Green H 8
8 West Grimstead D 4
10 West Grinstead F 1
36 West Haddlesey D 3
23 West Haddon E 9
16 West Hagbourne E 6
22 West Hagley D 3
44 West Hall F 4
32 West Hallam F 2
37 West Halton E 7
18 West Ham F 4
16 West Hanney E 5
19 West Hanningfield D 7
36 West Hardwick E 2
8 West Harnham C 3
7 West Harptree A 9
45 West Harrington H 11
40 West Hartlepool B 5
6 West Hatch D 6
15 West Hay H 8
24 West Head E 7

17 West Heath . . . . H 9
61 West Helmsdale . . . . E 9
16 West Hendred . . . . . . E 5
41 West Heslerton . . . . . H 9
15 West Hill, Avon . . . . G 8
6 West Hill, Devon. . . G 4
10 West Hoathly . . . . . . E 2
7 West Holme . . . . . . H 12
49 West Hopes . . . . C 8
18 West Horndon . . . . . . E 6
7 West Horrington . . . A 9
9 West Horsley . . . . . A 12
45 West Horton . . . . . . C 11
11 West Hougham . . . . D 11
10 West Humble . . . . . . C 1
6 West Huntspill . . . . . . B 6
17 West Hyde . . . . E 11
11 West Hythe . . . . E 10
16 West Ilsley . . . . F 6
9 West Itchenor . . . . . . F 9
33 West Keal . . . . D 10
16 West Kennett . . . . . . G 2
47 West Kilbride . . . . . . E 7
10 West Kingsdown . . . . B 5
15 West Kington . . . . . . F 11
58 West Kinharrachie . . D 7
58 West Kinnernie . . . . . F 5
30 West Kirby . . . . B 1
41 West Knapton . . . . . . H 9
7 West Knighton . . . . . G 10
7 West Knoyle . . . . . . C 11
45 West Kyloe . . . . B 11
7 West Lambrook . . . . D 7
11 West Langdon . . . . . C 11
61 West Langwell . . . . . . F 7
9 West Lavington, W. Sussex . . . . . . D 10
8 West Lavington, Wiltshire . . . . A 2
40 West Layton . . . . D 2
32 West Leake . . . . G 3
49 West Learmouth . . . F 11
26 West Lexham . . . . . . D 1
36 West Lilling . . . . A 4
45 West Linkhall . . . . . . A 10
48 West Linton . . . . D 4
9 West Liss . . . . C 9
15 West Littleton . . . . G 11
3 West Looe . . . . D 9
6 West Luccombe . . . . B 2
7 West Lulworth . . . . H 11
41 West Lutton . . . . H 9
7 West Lydford . . . . . . C 9
45 West Lyham . . . . . . C 12
7 West Lyng . . . . C 7
24 West Lynn . . . . D 7
45 West Mains, Northumb. . . . . . . B 12
47 West Mains, Strathclyde . . . . D 8
48 West Mains, Strathclyde . . . . . . D 2
10 West Malling . . . . B 5
22 West Malvern . . . . . . G 1
9 West Marden . . . . E 9
32 West Markham . . . . . C 4
37 West Marsh . . . . F 10
35 West Marton . . . . B 8
9 West Meon . . . . D 8
19 West Mersea . . . . . . C 10
22 West Midlands, Co. . C 4
7 West Milton . . . . G 8
11 West Minster . . . . A 8
17 West Molesey . . . . . G 12
8 West Moors . . . . F 2
7 West Morden . . . . . . G 12
49 West Morrison . . . . . . F 8
41 West Ness . . . . G 7
37 West Newton, Humberside . . . . . . C 9
24 West Newton, Norfolk C 8
5 West Ogwell . . . . J 7
7 West Orchard . . . . . E 11
16 West Overton . . . . . . G 2
59 West Park . . . . H 5
8 West Parley . . . . F 2
5 West Panson . . . . G 2
49 West Peaston . . . . C 7
10 West Peckhan . . . . . . C 5
45 West Pelton . . . . H 10
7 West Pennard . . . . B 9
2 West Pentire . . . . D 5
6 West Porlock . . . . B 2
4 West Putford . . . . D 2
6 West Quantoxhead . . B 5
45 West Rainton . . . . . . H 11
33 West Rasen . . . . A 8
26 West Raynham . . . . . . C 2
40 West Rounton . . . . . . E 4
25 West Row . . . . H 8
26 West Rudham . . . . . . C 1
26 West Runton . . . . A 5
49 West Saltoun . . . . C 7
4 West Sandford . . . . . . F 7
64 West Sandwick . . . . . . B 7
40 West Scrafton . . . . . . G 1
48 West Sidewood . . . . . D 3
43 West Skelston . . . . . . C 9
45 West Sleekburn . . . . E 11
26 West Somerton . . . . . D 7
7 West Stafford . . . . . G 10
36 West Stockwith . . . . . H 6
9 West Stoke . . . . E 9
39 West Stonesdale . . . E 11
7 West Stoughton . . . . A 7
7 West Stour . . . . D 11
11 West Stourmouth . . B 11
27 West Stow . . . . H 1
16 West Stowell . . . . H 2
60 West Strathan . . . . . . B 6
8 West Stratton . . . . . . B 6
11 West Street . . . . C 8
40 West Summer Side . . G 2
10 West Sussex, Co. . . . E 1
40 West Tanfield . . . . . . G 3
3 West Taphouse . . . . . C 8
46 West Tarbert . . . . . . C 3
49 West Third . . . . F 9
45 West Thirston . . . . . C 10
9 West Thorney . . . . . . F 9
18 West Thurrock . . . . . . F 6
9 West Tisted . . . . C 8
52 West Tofts . . . . D 6
33 West Torrington . . . . B 8
15 West Town, Avon . . G 8
15 West Town, Avon . . H 8
9 West Town, Hants . . F 8
21 West Town, Heref. & Worc. . . . . F 10
8 West Tytherley . . . . . C 4
16 West Tytherton . . . . G 1
24 West Walton . . . . D 6
24 West Walton Highway . . . . D 6
4 West Warlington . . . . E 6
53 West Wemyss . . . . . . H 8
15 West Wick . . . . H 7
25 West Wickham, Cambs. . . . . K 7
18 West Wickham, London . . . . G 4
12 West Williamston . . . F 4
8 West Willow . . . . D 4
24 West Winch . . . . D 7
8 West Winterslow . . . . C 4
9 West Wittering . . . . . F 9
40 West Witton . . . . F 1
45 West Woodburn . . . . D 7
16 West Woodhay . . . . . H 5
7 West Woodlands . . B 11
9 West Worldham . . . . . B 9
25 West Wratting . . . . . K 7
17 West Wycombe . . . . . E 9
64 West Yell . . . . C 7
35 West Yorkshire, Co. D 10
4 Westacott . . . . C 5
11 Westbere . . . . B 10
32 Westborough . . . . F 6
8 Westbourne, Dorset G 2
27 Westbourne, Suff. . . K 5
9 Westbourne, W. Sussex . . . . E 9
16 Westbrook . . . . G 5
17 Westbury, Bucks. . . . A 7
21 Westbury, Salop . . . . A 9
7 Westbury, Wilts. . . A 12
7 Westbury Leigh . . . A 12
15 Westbury on Trym . . G 9
15 Westbury-on-Severn C 10
7 Westbury-sub-Mendip A 8
34 Westby . . . . D 3
9 Westcatt . . . . A 12
19 Westcliff on Sea . . . . E 8
7 Westcombe . . . . B 10
16 Westcote . . . . B 3
17 Westcott, Bucks . . . . B 8
6 Westcott, Devon . . . . F 4
16 Westcott Barton . . . . B 5
10 Westdean . . . . H 4
57 Wester Aviemore . . . H 4
52 Wester Balgedie . . . . G 6
48 Wester Causewayend C 3
52 Wester Clunie . . . . . . A 4
49 Wester Essenside . . . G 7
58 Wester Fintray . . . . . . F 6
57 Wester Fodderletter G 7
60 Wester Greenyards . G 6
48 Wester Happrew . . . . E 4
49 Wester Housebryres . F 8
56 Wester Lamington . . B 3
56 Wester Milton . . . . . . D 5
53 Wester Newburn . . . G 9
48 Wester Ochiltree . . . B 3
49 Wester Pencaitland . C 7
64 Wester Quarff . . . . . . E 7
56 Wester Rarichie . . . . B 4
57 Wester Shennach . . . G 7
54 Wester Slumbay . . . . F 3
56 Wester Teaninch . . . . C 2
61 Westerdale, Highland . . . . C 10
41 Westerdale, N. Yorks . . . . E 7
27 Westerfield . . . . K 5
9 Westergate . . . . F 10
10 Westerham . . . . C 3
45 Westerhope . . . . F 10
15 Westerleigh . . . . F 10
64 Westermill . . . . E 3
40 Westerton, Dur. . . . . B 3
58 Westerton, Grampian . . . . C 3
53 Westerton, Tayside . . . . B 11
9 Westerton, W. Sussex . . . . E 10
58 Westertown . . . . C 3
38 Westfield, Cumb. . . . B 2
11 Westfield, E. Sussex . F 7
58 Westfield, Grampian E 7
22 Westfield, Heref. & Worc. . . . . G 1
61 Westfield, Highland . . . . B 10
26 Westfield, Norf. . . . . D 3
45 Westfield, Northumb. D 12
7 Westfields . . . . F 10
52 Westfields of Rattray C 6
39 Westgate, Dur. . . . . . A 11
36 Westgate, Lincs. . . . . F 5
26 Westgate, Norf. . . . . . B 3
11 Westgate on Sea . . . A 11
44 Westgillsyke . . . . F 2
27 Westhall . . . . G 7
7 Westham, Dorset . . H10
10 Westham, E. Sussex . H 5
7 Westham, Som. . . . . . B 7
9 Westhampnett . . . . E 10
58 Westhaugh . . . . E 4
7 Westhay . . . . B 8
34 Westhead . . . . F 3
21 Westhide . . . . H 11
59 Westhill . . . . G 6
21 Westhope, Heref. & Worc. . . . . G 10
21 Westhope, Salop . . D 10
24 Westhorpe, Lincs. . . . B 3
27 Westhorpe, Suff. . . . . H 3
34 Westhoughton . . . . . G 5
39 Westhouse . . . . H 9
32 Westhouses . . . . D 2
4 Westleigh, Devon . . . C 3
6 Westleigh, Devon . . . D 4
34 Westleigh, Gtr. Manchester . . G 5
27 Westleton . . . . H 7
21 Westley, Salop . . . . . B 9
27 Westley, Suffolk . . . . J 1
25 Westley Waterless . . K 7
17 Westlington . . . . C 8
44 Westlinton . . . . G 2
11 Westmarsh . . . . B 11
10 Westmeston . . . . G 2
18 Westmill . . . . A 4
18 Westminster . . . . F 3
53 Westmuir . . . . B 8
64 Westness . . . . B 2
43 Westnewton, Cumb. G 12
49 Westnewton, Northumb. . . . . . . F 11
15 Weston, Avon . . . . . H 10
30 Weston, Ches. . . . . . . E 6
30 Weston, Ches. . . . . . . B 4
6 Weston, Devon . . . . . F 5
6 Weston, Devon . . . . . G 5
7 Weston, Dorset . . . . H 7
9 Weston, Hants. . . . . . D 8
18 Weston, Herts. . . . . . A 3
24 Weston, Lincs. . . . . . C 4
35 Weston, N. Yorks. . B 10
23 Weston, Northants . . G 9
32 Weston, Notts. . . . . . C 5
21 Weston, Salop . . . . . C 11
21 Weston, Salop . . . . . . E 9
30 Weston, Salop . . . . . . G 4
31 Weston, Staffs. . . . . . G 8
48 Weston, Strathclyde . E 3
7 Weston Bampfylde . D 9
21 Weston Beggard . . . H 11
15 Weston Birt . . . . E 11
23 Weston by Welland C 11
25 Weston Colville . . . . K 7
31 Weston Coyney . . . . . F 8
23 Weston Favell . . . . . F 11
25 Weston Green . . . . . . K 7
22 Weston Heath . . . . . . A 1
24 Weston Hills . . . . C 4
15 Weston-in-Gordano G 8
30 Weston Jones . . . . . . H 6
26 Weston Longville . . . D 4
30 Weston Lullingfields H 3
22 Weston-on-Avon . . . G 5
16 Weston-on-the-Grn . B 6
9 Weston Patrick . . . . . B 8
30 Weston Rhyn . . . . . . G 1
15 Weston Road . . . . . . G 8
22 Weston Sudedge . . . . H 5
14 Weston-super-Mare H 6
17 Weston Turville . . . . C 9
15 Weston under Penyard B 9
23 Weston under Wetherley . . . . E 7
23 Weston Underwood, Bucks . . . . G 12
31 Weston Underwood, Derbyshire . . . . . . F 11
32 Weston Upon Trent . G 1
22 Weston-under-Lizard A 2
25 Westoning . . . . M 1
7 Westonzoyland . . . . . C 7
36 Westow . . . . A 5
7 Westport, Som. . . . . . D 7
46 Westport, Strathclyde . . . . G 2
16 Westridge Green . . . . F 6
48 Westrigg . . . . C 2
49 Westruther . . . . D 9
24 Westry . . . . F 5
32 Westville . . . . E 2
38 Westward . . . . A 5
4 Westward Ho . . . . C 3
44 Westwater . . . . E 1
11 Westwell, Kent . . . . . C 8
16 Westwell, Oxon . . . . C 3
11 Westwell Leacon . . . C 8
25 Westwick, Cambs. . . . J 5
40 Westwick, Dur. . . . . . D 1
6 Westwood, Devon . . F 4
45 Westwood, Dur. . . . G 9
47 Westwood, Strathclyde . . . . . D 11
15 Westwood, Wilts. . . H 11
36 Westwoodside . . . . . . G 5
40 Wether Cote . . . . F 6
44 Wetheral . . . . H 3
35 Wetherby . . . . B 12
27 Wetherden . . . . J 3
27 Wetheringsett . . . . . . J 4
25 Wethersfield . . . . M 8
64 Wethersta . . . . C 7
27 Wetherup Street . . . . J 4
31 Wetley Rocks . . . . . . E 8
30 Wettenhall . . . . D 5
31 Wetton . . . . E 9
37 Wetwang . . . . A 7
30 Wetwood . . . . G 6
16 Wexcombe . . . . H 4
17 Wexham Street . . . . F 10
26 Weybourne . . . . A 4
27 Weybread . . . . G 5
17 Weybridge . . . . H 11
6 Weycroft . . . . F 6
61 Weydale . . . . A 10
8 Weyhill . . . . B 5
7 Weymouth . . . . G 7
17 Whaddon, Bucks. . . . A 9
25 Whaddon, Cambs. . . K 4
15 Whaddon, Glos. . . . C 11
8 Whaddon, Wilts. . . . . C 3
39 Whale . . . . C 7
32 Whaley . . . . C 2
31 Whaley Bridge . . . . . B 8
32 Whaley Thorns . . . . . C 3
34 Whalley . . . . D 6
45 Whalton . . . . E 9
34 Wham . . . . A 6
24 Whaplode . . . . C 4
24 Whaplode Drove . . . D 4
24 Whaplode St. Catherine . . . . . D 4
39 Wharfe . . . . H 10
34 Wharles . . . . D 3
45 Wharmley . . . . F 7
35 Wharncliffe Side . . . H 11
36 Wharram-le-Street . A 6
30 Wharton, Ches. . . . . D 5
21 Wharton, Heref. & Worc. . . . . G 10
40 Whashton . . . . E 2
39 Whasset . . . . G 7
22 Whatcote . . . . H 6
22 Whateley . . . . B 6
27 Whatfield . . . . K 3
10 Whatlington . . . . F 6
31 Whatstandwell . . . . E 11
32 Whatton . . . . F 5
42 Whauphill . . . . G 5
26 Wheatacre . . . . F 8
18 Wheathampstead . . . C 2
9 Wheatley, Hants. . . . B 9
17 Wheatley, Oxon. . . . D 7
40 Wheatley Hill . . . . . . A 4
35 Wheatley Lane . . . . . C 7
22 Wheaton Aston . . . . A 2
6 Wheddon Cross . . . . . B 3
58 Wheedlemont . . . . . . E 2
17 Wheeler's Green . . . G 8
9 Wheelerstreet . . . . . B 11
30 Wheelock . . . . D 6
30 Wheelock Heath . . . D 6
34 Wheelton . . . . E 5
59 Wheen . . . . K 1
36 Wheldrake . . . . C 4
16 Whelford . . . . D 3
38 Whelpo . . . . A 5
40 Whenby . . . . H 6
27 Whepstead . . . . J 1
27 Wherstead . . . . L 5
8 Wherwell . . . . B 5
31 Wheston . . . . C 10
10 Whetsted . . . . C 5
23 Whetstone . . . . B 9
16 Whichford . . . . A 4
38 Whicham, Cumb. . . . G 4
45 Whickham, & Wear . . . . G 10
5 Whiddon Down . . . . G 6
53 Whigstreet . . . . C 9
23 Whilton . . . . F 9
4 Whimble . . . . F 2
6 Whimple . . . . F 4
26 Whimpwell Green . . C 7
26 Whinburgh . . . . E 3
49 Whinkerstones . . . . E 10
43 Whinnie Liggate . . . . F 8
58 Whinnyfold . . . . D 8
8 Whippingham . . . . . . G 6
17 Whipsnade . . . . B 11
6 Whipton . . . . G 3
23 Whissendine . . . . . . A 11
26 Whissonsett . . . . C 2
17 Whistley Green . . . . . G 9
23 Whiston, Northants. F 11
30 Whiston, Merseyside A 3
32 Whiston, S. Yorks. . . A 2
22 Whiston, Staffs. . . . . A 2
31 Whiston, Staffs. . . . . F 9
30 Whiston Lane Ends . A 3
38 Whitbeck . . . . G 3
21 Whitbourne . . . . G 12
22 Whitbourne Ford . . . F 1
48 Whitburn, Lothian . . C 2
45 Whitburn, Tyne & Wear . . . . G 12
45 Whitburn Colliery . G 12
30 Whitby, Cheshire . . . C 3
41 Whitby, N. Yorks. . . D 9
44 Whitcastles . . . . D 1
15 Whitchurch, Avon . . G 9
17 Whitchurch, Bucks. . B 9
5 Whitchurch, Devon . H 4
12 Whitchurch, Dyfed . D 2
8 Whitchurch, Hants. . A 6
15 Whitchurch, Heref. & Worc. . . . . C 8
17 Whitchurch, Oxon . . F 7
30 Whitchurch, Salop . . F 4
14 Whitchurch, S. Glam. F 5
17 Whitchurch Hill . . . . . F 7
7 Whitcombe . . . . G 10
21 Whitcott Keysett . . . D 8
34 White Chapel . . . . . . C 4
34 White Coppice . . . . . . E 5
7 White Cross, Avon . . A 9
6 White Cross, Devon. G 4
7 White Lackington . . F 10
22 White Ladies Aston . G 3
13 White Mill . . . . E 8
19 White Notley . . . . B 8
33 White Pit . . . . B 11
18 White Roding . . . . . . C 5
21 White Stone . . . . H 11
17 White Waltham . . . . . F 9
56 Whiteacen . . . . E 8
22 Whiteacre Heath . . . C 5
55 Whitebridge . . . . H 8
15 Whitebrook . . . . D 8
49 Whiteburn . . . . E 8
42 Whitecairn . . . . F 3
58 Whitecairns . . . . F 7
48 Whitecastle . . . . E 3
7 Whitechurch Canonicorum . . . . . G 7
48 Whitecraig . . . . B 6
15 Whitecroft . . . . D 9
42 Whitecrook . . . . F 3
48 Whitecross, Central . B 2
3 Whitecross, Corn. . . . B 7
61 Whiteface . . . . G 7
46 Whitefarland . . . . E 4
42 Whitefaulds . . . . A 4
35 Whitefields, Manchester . . . . . . G 7
52 Whitefield, Tayside . D 6
6 Whitefirld, Som. . . . . C 4
58 Whiteford . . . . E 5
6 Whitehall, Devon . . E 5
64 Whitehall, Orkney . . B 4
44 Whitehaugh . . . . B 3
38 Whitehaven . . . . C 2
43 Whitehill, Dumf. & Gall. . . . . D 12
58 Whitehill, Grampian B 3
9 Whitehill, Hants. . . . C 9
47 Whitehill, Strathclyde . . . . D 7
58 Whitehills, Grampian A 4
47 Whitehills, Strathclyde . . . . . D 11
58 Whitehouse, Grampian . . . . F 4
46 Whitehouse, Strathclyde . . . . C 3
49 Whitekirk . . . . A 8
59 Whiteknowes . . . . . . G 3
7 Whitelackington . . . . E 7
49 Whitelaw . . . . D 11
49 Whitelee . . . . F 8
36 Whiteley . . . . E 3
9 Whiteley Bank . . . . . H 7
31 Whiteley Green . . . . . B 8
17 Whiteley Village . . H 11
10 Whitemans Green . . E 2
56 Whitemire . . . . D 5
3 Whitemoor . . . . D 7
31 Whitemore . . . . D 7
8 Whitenap . . . . D 5
8 Whiteparish . . . . D 4
58 Whiterashes . . . . E 6
15 Whiteshill . . . . D 11
48 Whiteside, Lothian . . C 2
44 Whiteside, Northumb. F 5
10 Whitesmith . . . . G 4
6 Whitestaunton . . . . . . E 6
4 Whitestone, Devon . A 4
4 Whitestone, Devon . . F 7
59 Whitestone, Grampian . . . . H 4
58 Whitestones . . . . B 6
15 Whiteway . . . . C 12
6 Whiteway House . . . H 2
34 Whitewell . . . . B 5
5 Whiteworks . . . . J 5
56 Whitewreath . . . . D 8
15 Whitfield, Avon . . . E 10
48 Whitfield, Borders . . D 4
11 Whitfield, Kent . . . D 11
23 Whitfield, Northants. H 9
44 Whitefield, Northumb. G 6
29 Whitford, Clwyd . . . B 10
6 Whitford, Devon . . . G 6
36 Whitgift . . . . E 6
31 Whitgreave . . . . G 7
42 Whithorn . . . . G 5
46 Whiting Bay . . . . G 5
24 Whitington . . . . E 8
12 Whitland . . . . E 5
44 Whitlaw . . . . B 3
47 Whitletts . . . . G 8
17 Whitley, Berks. . . . . . G 8
15 Whitley, Wilts. . . . . H 12
45 Whitley Bay . . . . F 11
45 Whitley Chapel . . . . . G 7
35 Whitley Lower . . . . E 11
22 Whitlock's End . . . . . D 4
15 Whitminster . . . . . . D 11
31 Whitmore . . . . F 7
6 Whitnage . . . . E 4
21 Whitney . . . . H 8
38 Whitrigg, Cumb. . . . . A 4
44 Whitrigg, Cumb. . . . . G 1
44 Whitriggs . . . . B 4
8 Whitsbury . . . . D 3
4 Whitsleigh Barton . . D 4
49 Whitsome . . . . D 11
49 Whitsomehill . . . . . D 11
15 Whitson . . . . F 7
15 Whitson Common . . . F 7
11 Whitstable . . . . A 9
4 Whitstone . . . . F 1
45 Whittingham . . . . B 9
21 Whittingslow . . . . D 9
32 Whittington, Derby. . C 1

16 Whittington, Glos. B 1
22 Whittington, Heref. & Worc. G 2
39 Whittington, Lancs. H 8
30 Whittington, Salop G 2
22 Whittington, Staffs. A 5
22 Whittington, Staffs. D 2
34 Whittle-le-Woods E 5
23 Whittlebury H 10
24 Whittlesey F 4
25 Whittlesford K 6
34 Whittlestone Head E 6
49 Whitton, Borders G 10
40 Whitton, Cleveland C 4
37 Whitton, Humber. E 7
45 Whitton, Northumb. C 9
21 Whitton, Powys F 8
21 Whitton, Salop E 11
27 Whitton, Suffolk K 4
16 Whittonditch G 4
45 Whittonstall G 9
16 Whitway H 6
32 Whitwell, Derby. C 3
18 Whitwell, Herts. B 2
9 Whitwell, I.o.W. H 7
23 Whitwell, Leics. A 12
40 Whitwell, N. Yorks. E 3
41 Whitwell-on-the-Hill H 7
23 Whitwick A 8
36 Whitwood E 2
35 Whitworth E 7
30 Whixal G 4
36 Whixley A 2
22 Whoberly D 6
40 Whorlton, Dur. D 1
40 Whorlton, N. Yorks. E 5
44 Whygate E 6
21 Whyle F 11
10 Whyteleafe B 2
15 Wibdon E 9
23 Wibtoft C 8
11 Wichling B 8
15 Wick, Avon G 10
8 Wick, Dorset G 3
22 Wick, Heref. & Worc. H 3
61 Wick, Highalnd C 12
14 Wick, Mid Glam. G 3
6 Wick, Som. B 5
7 Wick, Som. D 7
9 Wick, W. Sussex F 11
8 Wick, Wilts. D 3
17 Wick Hill H 9
16 Wick Rissington B 3
15 Wick St. Lawrence H 7
25 Wicken, Cambs. H 7
23 Wicken, Northants. H 10
25 Wicken Bonhunt M 6
33 Wickenby B 8
22 Wichenford F 1
32 Wickersley A 2
19 Wickford E 7
16 Wickham, Berks. G 5
9 Wickham, Hants. E 7
19 Wickham Bishops C 8
16 Wickham Heath G 5
27 Wickham Market K 6
27 Wickham St. Paul L 1
27 Wickham Skeith H 4
27 Wickham Street, Suffolk H 4
27 Wickham Street, Suffolk K 1
11 Wickhambreaux B 10
25 Wickhambrook K 8
22 Wickhamford H 4
26 Wickhampton E 7
26 Wicklewood E 4
26 Wickmere B 5
10 Wickstreet G 4
15 Wickwar E 10
25 Widdington M 6
45 Widdrington C 10
45 Widdrington Sta. D 10
45 Wide Open F 10
5 Widecombe in the Moor H 6
3 Widegates D 10
2 Widemouth A 2
64 Widewall E 2
19 Widford, Essex C 7
18 Widford B 4
17 Widmere E 9
17 Widmer End D 9
32 Widmerpool G 4
30 Widnes B 4
6 Widworthy F 5
9 Wield B 7
34 Wigan F 5
8 Wigbeth E 2
6 Wiggaton G 5
24 Wiggenhall St. Germans D 7
24 Wiggenhall St. Mary Magdalen D 7
24 Wiggenhall St. Mary the Virgin D 7
36 Wiggington A 4
17 Wiggington, Herts. C 10
16 Wigginton, Oxon A 5
22 Wigginton, Staffs. A 6
35 Wiggleworth A 7
44 Wiggonby H 1
9 Wiggonholt D 11
36 Wighill B 3
8 Wight, Isle of, Co. G 6
26 Wighton B 2
8 Wigley D 5
21 Wigmore, Heref. & Worc. E 9
11 Wigmore, Kent B 7
32 Wigsley C 6
25 Wigsthorpe G 1
23 Wigston Magna B 9
24 Wigtoft B 4
42 Wigton H 1
42 Wigtown F 5
35 Wigtwizzle G 11
35 Wike C 12
23 Wilbarston C 11
36 Wilberfoss B 5
25 Wilburton H 6
26 Wilby, Norfolk F 3
23 Wilby, Northants E 12
27 Wilby, Suffolk H 5
16 Wilcot H 2
30 Wilcott H 2
15 Wilcrick E 7
31 Wildboarclough C 8
25 Wilden K 2
8 Wildhern A 5
36 Wildsworth G 6
32 Wilford F 3
30 Wilkesley F 5
61 Wilkhaven H 9
48 Wilkieston C 4
18 Wilkin's Green C 2
6 Willand E 4
30 Willaston, Ches. B 2
30 Willaston, Ches. E 5
23 Willen H 12
22 Willenhall, W. Midlands B 3
23 Willenhall, W. Midlands E 7
37 Willerby, Humber. D 8
41 Willerby, N. Yorks. G 10
22 Willersey H 4
21 Willersley H 8
11 Willesborough D 9
18 Willesden E 2
4 Willesleigh C 5
23 Willey Leics D 8
21 Willey, Salop C 12
9 Willey Green A 11
23 Williamscot H 8
18 Willian A 2
18 Willingale C 6
4 Willingcott B 4
10 Willingdon H 5
25 Willingham, Cambs. H 5
32 Willingham, Lincs. B 6
25 Willington, Beds. K 2
31 Willington, Derby. G 11
40 Willington, Dur. B 2
22 Willington, War. H 6
30 Willington Corner D 4
36 Willitoft D 5
6 Williton B 4
44 Willmontswick G 6
33 Willoughby, Lincs. C 11
23 Willoughby, War. E 8
32 Willoughby on the Wolds H 4
23 Willoughby Waterleys C 9
32 Willoughton A 6
19 Willows Green B 7
15 Willsbridge G 10
5 Willsworthy H 4
22 Wilmcote F 5
6 Wilmington, Devon. F 5
10 Wilmington, Kent A 4
10 Wilmington, E. Sussex H 4
31 Wilmslow B 7
22 Wilnecote B 6
34 Wilpshire D 5
35 Wilsden D 9
33 Wilsford, Lincs. F 7
8 Wilsford, Wilts. B 3
16 Wilsford, Wilts H 2
25 Wilshamstead L 2
35 Wilsill A 10
10 Wilsley Pound D 6
15 Wilson, Heref. & Worc. B 9
32 Wilson, Leics. H 1
48 Wilsontown D 2
24 Wilsthorpe D 2
17 Wilstone C 10
44 Wilton, Borders B 3
40 Wilton, Cleveland C 6
38 Wilton, Cumb. D 3
16 Wilton, Hants. H 4
15 Wilton, Heref. & Worc. B 9
41 Wilton, N. Yorks G 8
8 Wilton, Wilts. C 3
16 Wiltshire, Co. G 2
25 Wimbish L 7
25 Wimbish Green M 7
18 Wimbledon G 2
24 Wimblington F 5
8 Wimborne Minster F 1
8 Wimborne St. Giles E 2
24 Wimbotsham E 7
25 Wimpole Lodge K 4
22 Wimpstone G 5
7 Wincanton C 10
9 Winchfield A 9
30 Wincham C 5
48 Winchburgh B 4
16 Winchcombe C 6
11 Winchelsea F 8
11 Winchelsea Beach F 8
8 Winchester C 6
10 Winchet Hill D 6
17 Winchmore Hill E 10
31 Wincle D 8
38 Windermere E 6
23 Winderton H 7
17 Windlesham H 10
31 Windley F 11
31 Windmill B 10
10 Windmill Hill, E. Sussex G 5
6 Windmill Hill, Som. E 6
16 Windrush C 3
44 Windshielknowe C 4
17 Windsor G 10
15 Windsoredge D 11
47 Windy Yet D 9
59 Windyedge H 6
53 Windygates G 8
49 Windywalls F 10
10 Wineham F 1
37 Winestead E 10
35 Winewall C 8
27 Winfarthing G 4
15 Winford, Avon H 8
9 Winford, I.o.W. H 7
21 Winforton H 8
7 Winfrith Newburgh H 11
17 Wing, Bucks. B 9
23 Wing, Leics. B 12
40 Wingate A 4
34 Wingates, Manchester F 5
45 Wingates, Northumb. D 9
32 Wingerworth C 1
17 Wingfield, Beds B 11
27 Wingfield, Suffolk H 5
7 Wingfield, Wilts. A 11
11 Wingham B 11
11 Wingmore C 10
17 Wingrave B 9
32 Winkburn D 4
17 Winkfield G 9
17 Winkfield Row G 10
17 Winkfield Street G 10
31 Winkhill E 9
9 Winklebury A 7
4 Winkleigh E 5
40 Winksley H 3
8 Winkton F 3
45 Winlaton G 10
45 Winlaton Mill G 10
61 Winless B 12
34 Winmarleigh B 3
8 Winnall, Hants. C 6
15 Winnall, Heref. & Worc. A 7
2 Winnard's Perch C 6
17 Winnersh G 8
38 Winscales C 3
15 Winscombe H 7
30 Winsford, Ches. D 5
6 Winsford, Som. C 3
7 Winsham F 7
31 Winshill H 11
13 Winsh-wen G 10
39 Winskill B 8
9 Winslade A 8
15 Winsley H 11
17 Winslow A 8
16 Winson C 2
8 Winsor E 5
38 Winster, Cumbria F 6
31 Winster, Derby. D 11
40 Winston, Dur. D 2
27 Winston, Suff. J 5
15 Winstone C 12
4 Winswell E 4
44 Winter Sheilds F 4
7 Winterborne Clenston F 11
7 Winterborne Herringston G 10
7 Winterborne Houghton F 11
7 Winterborne Kingston F 11
7 Winterborne Monkton G 10
7 Winterborne Stickland F 11
7 Winterborne Whitechurch F 11
7 Winterborne Zelston F 12
15 Winterbourne, Avon F 9
16 Winterbourne, Berks. G 5
7 Winterbourne Abbas G 9
16 Winterbourne Bassett G 2
8 Winterbourne Dauntsey C 3
15 Winterbourne Down F 10
8 Winterbourne Earls C 3
8 Winterbourne Gunner C 3
16 Winterbourne Monkton G 2
7 Winterbourne Steepleton G 9
8 Winterbourne Stoke B 2
35 Winterburn A 8
48 Wintercleugh H 2
37 Winteringham E 7
30 Winterley E 6
35 Wintersett F 12
8 Winterslow C 4
37 Winterton E 7
26 Winterton-on-Sea D 8
33 Winthorpe, Lincs. D 12
32 Winthorpe, Notts. E 5
39 Winton, Cumbria D 10
8 Winton, Dorset G 2
40 Winton, N. Yorks. F 4
41 Wintringham H 9
25 Winwick, Cambs. G 2
34 Winwick, Cheshire H 5
23 Winwick, Northants. E 9
31 Wirksworth E 11
30 Wirswall F 4
24 Wisbech E 6
24 Wisbech St. Mary E 5
9 Wisborough Green C 11
47 Wishaw, Strathclyde D 12
22 Wishaw, War. C 5
17 Wisley H 11
33 Wispington C 9
27 Wissett G 6
21 Wistanstow D 10
30 Wistanswick G 5
30 Wistaston E 5
30 Wistaston Green E 5
25 Wistow, Cambs. G 4
12 Wiston, Dyfed E 4
36 Wistow, N. Yorks. D 4
48 Wiston, Strathclyde F 2
34 Wiswell C 6
25 Witcham G 6
8 Witchampton E 1
25 Witchford G 6
19 Witham B 8
7 Witham Friary B 11
24 Witham on the Hill D 2
33 Withcall B 10
10 Witherenden Hill E 5
4 Witheridge E 7
23 Witherley B 7
33 Withern B 11
37 Withernsea D 11
37 Withernwick C 9
27 Withersdale Street G 6
25 Withersfield K 7
39 Witherslack G 7
3 Withiel C 7
6 Withiel Florey C 3
16 Withington, Glos. C 1
21 Withington, Heref. & Worc. H 11
35 Withington, Manchester H 7
21 Withington, Salop A 11
31 Withington, Staffs. G 9
30 Withington Green C 6
21 Withington Marsh H 11
6 Withleigh E 3
34 Withnell E 5
23 Withybrook D 8
6 Withycombe B 3
6 Withycombe Raleigh H 4
10 Withyham E 4
6 Withypool C 2
9 Witley B 11
27 Witnesham K 5
16 Witney C 5
24 Wittering E 2
11 Wittersham E 7
22 Witton, Heref. & Worc. F 2
59 Witton, Tayside K 3
45 Witton Gilbert H 10
40 Witton le Wear B 2
40 Witton Park B 2
6 Wiveliscombe C 4
9 Wivelrod B 8
10 Wivelsfield F 2
10 Wivelsfield Green F 2
19 Wivenhoe B 10
19 Wivenhoe Cross B 10
26 Wiveton A 3
19 Wix A 11
22 Wixford G 4
25 Wixoe L 8
17 Woburn A 10
23 Woburn Sands H 12
17 Woking H 11
17 Wokingham G 9
5 Wolborough J 7
37 Wold Newton, Humberside G 10
41 Wold Newton, Humberside H 10
10 Woldingham C 3
48 Wolfclyde F 3
24 Wolferton C 7
52 Wolfhill D 6
12 Wolf's Castle D 3
12 Wolfsdale E 3
49 Woll G 7
23 Wollaston, Northants. F 12
21 Wollaston, Salop A 9
30 Wollerton G 5
31 Wolseley H 9
40 Wolsingham A 1
31 Wolstanton E 7
23 Wolston E 7
16 Wolvercote C 6
22 Wolverhampton B 2
22 Wolverley, Heref. & Worc. D 2
30 Wolverley, Salop G 3
23 Wolverton, Bucks. H 11
16 Wolverton, Hants H 6
22 Wolverton, War. F 5
16 Wolverton Com H 6
15 Wolvesnewton D 8
23 Wolvey C 8
40 Wolviston C 5
41 Wombleton G 7
22 Wombourn C 2
36 Wombwell G 2
11 Womenswold C 11
36 Womersley E 3
9 Wonersh B 11
5 Wonsan G 5
17 Wooburn E 10
17 Wooburn Green E 10
17 Wooburn Moor E 10
26 Wood Dalling C 4
25 Wood End, Beds. K 1
25 Wood End, Beds. K 2
18 Wood End, Herts. A 3
22 Wood End, War. B 6
22 Wood End, War. E 4
33 Wood Enderby D 10
18 Wood Green E 3
22 Wood Hayes B 3
26 Wood Norton C 3
25 Wood Walton G 3
4 Woodacott E 3
39 Woodale G 12
32 Woodall D 11
26 Woodbastwick D 6
32 Woodbeck B 5
7 Woodbridge, Dorset. E 10
27 Woodbridge, Suff. K 6
32 Woodborough, Notts. E 3
16 Woodborough, Wilts. H 2
6 Woodbury, Devon G 4
7 Woodbury, Som. B 9
6 Woodbury Salterton G 4
15 Woodchester D 11
11 Woodchurch E 8
6 Woodcombe B 3
17 Woodcote, Oxon. F 7
22 Woodcote, Salop A 1
8 Woodcott A 6
15 Woodcroft E 8
8 Woodcutts D 1
25 Woodditton J 8
16 Woodeaton C 6
38 Woodend, Cumb. F 4
59 Woodend, Grampian H 3
48 Woodend, Strathclyde F 2
23 Woodend, Northants. G 9
8 Woodfalls D 3
44 Woodfield, Dumf. & Gall. F 1
47 Woodfield, Strathclyde G 8
10 Woodfield, Surrey B 1
4 Woodford, Corn. E 1
15 Woodford, Glos. E 10
31 Woodford, Manchester B 7
18 Woodford, London E 4
25 Woodford, Northants. H 1
7 Woodford, Som B 9
23 Woodford Halse G 9
26 Woodgate, Norf. D 3
22 Woodgate, Heref. & Worc. E 3
9 Woodgate, W. Sussex F 10
8 Woodgreen D 3
49 Woodhall, Lothian B 9
45 Woodhall, Northumb. B 9
39 Woodhall, N. Yorks. F 12
33 Woodhall Spa D 9
17 Woodham H 11
19 Woodham Ferrers D 8
19 Woodham Mortimer C 8
19 Woodham Walter C 8
53 Woodhaven D 9
35 Woodhead, Derby G 9
58 Woodhead, Grampian D 5
58 Woodhead House C 5
49 Woodheads E 8
15 Woodhill, Avon G 8
22 Woodhill, Salop D 1
56 Woodholme D 2
45 Woodhorn D 11
45 Woodhorn Demesne D 11
32 Woodhouse, Derby B 1
23 Woodhouse, Leics. A 9
35 Woodhouse, W. Yorks. D 11
23 Woodhouse Eaves A 8
5 Woodhuish K 8
25 Woodhurst H 4
10 Woodingdean G 2
5 Woodland, Devon J 7
40 Woodland, Dur. C 1
58 Woodland, Grampian E 6
58 Woodland, Grampian F 6
8 Woodlands, Dorset E 2
43 Woodlands, Dumf. & Gall. D 11
59 Woodlands, Grampian H 5
8 Woodlands, Hants. E 4
56 Woodlands, Highland D 1
17 Woodlands Park F 9
16 Woodlands St. Mary G 4
31 Woodlane H 10
43 Woodlea C 8
5 Woodleigh L 6
35 Woodlesford D 12
17 Woodley, Berks. G 8
35 Woodley, Manchester H 8
16 Woodmancote, Glos. A 1
16 Woodmancote, Glos. C 1
9 Woodmancote, W. Sussex E 9
9 Woodmancott B 7
37 Woodmansey C 8
9 Woodmansgreen C 10
10 Woodmansterne B 2
8 Woodminton D 2

11 Woodnesborough ..B 11
24 Woodnewton ......F 1
34 Woodplumpton .....D 4
26 Woodrising ....E 3
10 Wood's Green .....E 5
30 Woodseaves, Salop .G 5
30 Woodseaves, Staffs. .H 6
16 Woodsend ....F 3
32 Woodsetts ....B 3
7 Woodsford ....G 11
17 Woodside, Berks. .G 10
43 Woodside, Dumf.
   & Gall. ......D 11
53 Woodside, Fife ....F 9
59 Woodside,
   Grampian ......G 7
49 Woodside, Northants.
   ......E 12
53 Woodside, Tayside ..C 7
59 Woodside of Arbeadie
   ......H 5
44 Woodslee ....F 2
16 Woodstock ....B 5
12 Woodstock Cross ..D 4
12 Woodstock Slop ...D 4
32 Woodthorpe, Derby. C 2
32 Woodthorpe, Leics. .H 3
26 Woodton ....F 6
4 Woodtown, Devon. .C 4
4 Woodtown, Devon. .D 3
59 Woodtown,
   Grampian ......K 3
34 Woodvale ....F 2
31 Woodville ....H 11
8 Woodyates ....D 2
21 Woofferton ....F 10
7 Wookey ....B 8
7 Wookey Hole ......A 9
7 Wool ....H 11
4 Woolacombe ....B 3
11 Woolage Green ...C 11
15 Woolaston ....D 9
7 Wollavington .....B 7
9 Woolbeding ......D 10
6 Woolbrook ....G 5
6 Woolcotts ....C 3
35 Wooldale ....F 10
49 Wooler ....G 12
4 Woolfardisworthy ..E 7
48 Woolfords Cotts ...D 3
8 Woolgarston ......H 2
17 Woolhampton .....G 7
15 Woolhope ....A 9
7 Woolland ....F 11
15 Woollard ....H 9
18 Woollaton ....E 3
4 Woolley, Corn. ....D 1
15 Woolley, Avon ..G 10
25 Woolley, Cambs. ..H 3
35 Woolley, S. Yorks. .F 11
18 Woolmer Green ...B 3
22 Woolmere Green ...F 3
27 Woolpit ....J 3
27 Woolpit Green ....J 3
23 Woolscott ....E 8
4 Woolsey ....D 2
21 Woolstaston ......C 10
32 Woolsthorpe, Lincs. G 5

32 Woolsthorpe, Lincs. H 6
30 Woolston, Cheshire .A 5
5 Woolston, Devon ...L 6
8 Woolston, Hants. ...E 6
21 Woolston, Salop ....D 9
30 Woolston, Salop ....H 2
5 Woolston Green ...J 6
16 Woolstone ....E 4
30 Woolton ....B 3
16 Woolton Hill ......H 5
27 Woolverstone .....L 5
7 Woolverton ....A 11
18 Woolwich ....F 4
21 Woonton ....G 9
45 Wooperton ....A 8
49 Wooplaw ....E 7
30 Woore ....F 6
25 Wootton, Beds. .....L 1
8 Wootton, Hants. ...F 4
37 Wootton, Humber...E 8
11 Wootton, Kent .....C 11
23 Wootton, Northants.
   ......F 11
16 Wootton, Oxon. ....B 5
16 Wootton, Oxon. ....D 6
21 Wootton, Salop ....E 10
31 Wootton, Staffs. ....F 9
31 Wootton, Staffs. ....G 7
16 Wootton Bassett ...F 2
9 Wootton Bridge ...G 7
9 Wootton Com .....G 7
6 Wootton Courtenay .B 3
7 Wootton Fitzpaine ..G 7
16 Wootton Rivers ....H 3
9 Wootton St. Lawrence
   ......A 7
22 Wootton Wawen ...F 5
22 Worcester ....G 2
22 Wordsley ....C 2
22 Worfield ....C 1
64 Work ....C 3
38 Workington ....B 2
32 Worksop ....B 3
37 Worlaby ....F 8
16 World's End, Berks. .F 6
9 World's End, Hants. .E 8
15 Worle ....H 7
30 Worleston ....E 5
26 Worlingham ....F 7
25 Worlington ....H 8
27 Worlingworth .....H 5
27 Wormald Green ...A 11
15 Wormbridge ......A 7
24 Wormegay ....D 8
15 Wormelow Tump ..A 8
31 Wormhill ....C 9
53 Wormiehills ......C 11
27 Wormingford .....M 2
17 Worminghall .....C 7
16 Wormington ......A 1
7 Worminster ....B 9
48 Wormiston ....E 5
53 Wormit ....E 9
23 Wormleighton ....G 8
18 Wormley, Herts. ..C 4
9 Wormley, Surrey ..B 10
11 Wormshill ....B 7
21 Wormsley ....H 9

9 Worplesdon ......A 11
35 Worral ....H 11
35 Worsbrough ......G 12
34 Worsley ....G 6
26 Worstead ....C 6
25 Worsted Lodge ....K 6
35 Worsthorne ....D 7
34 Worston ....C 6
5 Worswell ....L 4
11 Worth, Kent .....C 12
10 Worth, W. Sussex ..D 2
8 Worth Matravers ...H 1
27 Wortham ....H 4
21 Worthen ....B 9
30 Worthenbury ......F 3
26 Worthing, Norf. ...D 3
9 Worthing,
   W. Sussex ......F 12
32 Worthington .....H 1
6 Worthy ....A 2
9 Worting ....A 7
35 Wortley, S. Yorks. .G 11
35 Wortley, W. Yorks. D 11
16 Worton ....H 1
27 Wortwell ....G 6
5 Wotter ....J 4
9 Wotton ....A 12
15 Wotton-under-Edge
   ......E 11
17 Wotton Underwood .C 8
23 Woughton on the
   Green ....H 12
10 Wouldham ....B 6
27 Wrabness ....M 5
58 Wraes ....D 3
4 Wrafton ....C 4
33 Wragby, Lincs. ....B 8
36 Wragby, W. Yorks. .E 2
37 Wragholme ....G 11
26 Wramplingham ...E 4
36 Wrangbrook ......F 3
58 Wrangham, Grampian
   ......D 4
49 Wrangham,
   Northumb. ......F 12
33 Wrangle ....E 11
33 Wrangle Com. ....E 11
33 Wrangle Lowgate ..E 11
6 Wrangway ....D 5
6 Wrantage ....D 6
37 Wrawby ....F 8
15 Wraxall, Avon ....G 8
7 Wraxall, Dorset. ..F 9
7 Wraxhall, Som. ....C 9
39 Wray ....H 8
7 Wrayland ....H 7
37 Wraysbury ....G 11
34 Wrea Green ......D 3
39 Wreay, Cumb. ....C 7
44 Wreay, Cumb. ....H 3
9 Wrecclesham .....B 9
45 Wrekenton ....G 11
11 Wrelton ....F 8
30 Wrenbury ....E 6
26 Wreningham .....F 4
27 Wrentham ....G 8
35 Wrenthorpe ......E 11
21 Wrentnall ....B 9

36 Wressle ....D 5
25 Wrestlingworth ....K 4
24 Wretton ....F 8
30 Wrexham ....E 2
30 Wrexham Industrial
   Estate ....E 2
22 Wribbenhall ....E 2
34 Wrightlington Bar .F 4
30 Wrinehill ....E 6
15 Wrington ....H 8
10 Writhlington .....A 10
19 Writtle ....C 7
21 Wrockwardine ....A 11
36 Wroot ....G 5
10 Wrotham ....B 5
10 Wrotham Heath ...B 5
16 Wroughton ....F 3
22 Wroxall ....E 6
21 Wroxeter ....B 11
22 Wroxhall ....H 7
26 Wroxham ....D 6
23 Wroxton ....H 7
31 Wyaston ....F 10
24 Wyberton ....B 4
25 Wyboston ....K 3
30 Wybunbury ......E 5
10 Wych Cross ....E 3
22 Wychbold ....F 3
22 Wychnor ....A 5
22 Wychnor Bridges ..A 5
40 Wycliffe ....D 1
17 Wycombe Marsh ..E 10
23 Wyddial ....M 5
11 Wye ....C 9
11 Wyerstone ....H 3
11 Wyerstone Street ..H 3
15 Wyesham ....C 8
7 Wyke, Dorset .....D 11
21 Wyke, Salop ....B 12
9 Wyke, Surrey ....A 10
35 Wyke, W. Yorks. .D 10
7 Wyke Champflower C 10
7 Wyke Regis ......H 7
41 Wykeham, N. Yorks. G 9
41 Wykeham, N. Yorks. H 8
30 Wykey ....H 3
45 Wylam ....G 9
15 Wylde Green .....C 5
14 Wyllie ....E 5
8 Wylye ....B 2
14 Wymering ....E 8
32 Wymeswold ......H 3
25 Wymington ....J 1
32 Wymondham, Leics. H 6
26 Wymondham, Norf. E 4
14 Wyndham ....E 3
7 Wynford Eagle ...G 9
40 Wynyard Forest ..C 4
22 Wyre Piddle ......G 3
22 Wysall ....G 3
22 Wythall ....E 4
16 Wytham ....C 6
38 Wythburn ....D 6
31 Wythenshawe ....A 7
25 Wyton ....H 4
32 Wyville ....G 6
54 Wyvis Lodge .....B 8

36 Yaddlethorpe ....F 6
8 Yafford ....H 6
40 Yafforth ....F 4
5 Yalberton ....K 7
10 Yalding ....C 6
16 Yanworth ....C 2
36 Yapham ....B 6
9 Yapton ....F 11
33 Yarburgh ....A 10
6 Yarcombe ....E 6
4 Yard ....D 6
4 Yard Gate ....C 6
22 Yardley ....D 5
23 Yardley Gobion ...H 11
23 Yardley Hastings ..F 12
21 Yardro ....F 8
21 Yarkhill ....H 11
31 Yarlet ....G 7
21 Yarlington ....C 10
40 Yarm ....D 4
8 Yarmouth ....G 5
4 Yarnacott ....C 5
7 Yarnbrook ....A 12
31 Yarnfield ....G 7
4 Yarnscombe ....D 4
16 Yarnton ....C 6
21 Yarpole ....F 10
48 Yarrow ....G 6
48 Yarrow Feus ......G 6
21 Yarsop ....H 9
24 Yarwell ....F 2
15 Yate ....F 10
17 Yateley ....H 9
16 Yatesbury ....G 2
16 Yattendon ....G 6
15 Yatton, Avon .....H 7
15 Yatton, Heref.
   & Worc. ......A 9
21 Yatton, Heref.
   & Worc. ......F 9
15 Yatton Keynell ...G 12
9 Yaverland ....H 7
26 Yaxham ....D 3
7 Yaxley, Cambs. ...F 3
27 Yaxley, Suffolk ....H 4
21 Yazor ....F 9
35 Yeadon ....C 10
39 Yealand Conyers ..H 7
39 Yealand Redmayne .H 7
5 Yealmpton ....K 4
16 Yelford ....D 4
40 Yearby ....C 6
40 Yearsley ....H 6
30 Yeaton ....H 3
31 Yeaveley ....F 10
49 Yeavering ....F 12
16 Yelford ....D 4
25 Yelling ....J 4
11 Yelsted ....B 7
23 Yelvertoft ....E 9
5 Yelverton, Devon ..J 4
26 Yelverton, Norfolk ..E 6
7 Yenston ....D 10
4 Yeo Mill ....C 7
4 Yeoford ....F 6
4 Yeolmbridge .....A 10
7 Yeovil ....D 9
7 Yeovil Marsh .....D 9
7 Yeovilton ....D 9

12 Yerbeston ....F 4
12 Yerbeston Mountain F 4
64 Yesnaby ....C 1
49 Yetholm Mains ....F 11
45 Yetlington ....B 8
7 Yetminster ....E 9
47 Yett, Strathclyde ..G 9
47 Yett, Strathclyde ..C 12
6 Yettington ....H 4
52 Yetts of Muckhart .G 5
25 Yielden ....J 1
48 Yieldshields .....D 2
18 Yiewsley ....F 1
20 Ynys ....F 2
20 Ynys Tachwedd ...C 2
14 Ynys-boeth ....E 4
14 Ynysbwl ....E 4
14 Ynysddu ....E 5
14 Ynyshir ....E 4
13 Ynstawe ....G 10
39 Yockenthwaite ...G 11
21 Yockleton ....A 9
36 Yokefleet ....E 6
47 Yoker ....C 10
58 Yonder Bognie ...C 3
36 York ....B 3
17 York Town ....H 9
11 Yorkletts ....B 9
39 Yockenthwaite ...G 11
21 Yockleton ....A 9
36 Yokefleet ....E 6
47 Yoker ....C 10
58 Yonder Bognie ....C 3
36 York ....B 3
17 York Town ....H 9
11 Yorkletts ....B 9
15 Yorkley ....D 9
48 Yorkeston ....D 6
4 Youldonmoor Cross .E 2
15 Youlgreaves ......D 10
36 Youlthorpe ....B 5
36 Youlton ....A 3
7 Young's End ......B 7
31 Yoxall ....H 10
27 Yoxford ....H 7
29 Ysbyty Ifan ......E 8
20 Ysbyty Ystwyth ...E 3
29 Ysceifog ....C 10
13 Yspitty ....G 9
20 Yspytty Cynfyn ...D 3
13 Ystalyfera ....F 11
14 Ystrad ....E 3
13 Ystrad Aeron .....A 8
20 Ystrad Meurig ....F 3
14 Ystradfellte ......C 3
13 Ystrad-ffin ....B 11
14 Ystradgynlais .....C 1
14 Ystrad-mynach ...E 5
13 Ystradowen, Dyfed F 10
14 Ystradowen,
   S. Glam. ......G 3
20 Ystumtuen ....D 3
58 Ythsie ....D 6
4 Zeal Monachorum ..F 6
7 Zeals ....C 11
2 Zelah ....D 5
2 Zennor ....F 2
64 Zetland, Co. ......D 7

INDEX TO LONDON MAPS

ABBREVIATIONS

App. – *Approach*
Av. – *Avenue*
Bdy. – *Broadway*
Bldg. – *Building(s)*
Br. – *British*
Bri. – *Bridge*
Ch. – *Church*
Cl. – *Close*
Cnr. – *Corner*
Coll. – *College*
Con. – *Convent*
Cres. – *Crescent*
Ct. – *Court*
Dri. – *Drive*
Ex. – *Exchange*
F.C. – *Football Club*
Gdns. – *Gardens*
Gro. – *Grove*
Gt. – *Great*
Ho. – *House*
Hosp. – *Hospital*
Hot. – *Hotel*
Inst. – *Institute*
La. – *Lane*
Lit. – *Little*
Min. – *Ministry*
Mkt. – *Market*
Mt. – *Mount*
Mus. – *Museum*
Nat. – *National*
Nth. – *North*
Pal. – *Palace*
Pk. – *Park*
Pl. – *Place*
Pol. – *Police*
Poly. – *Polytechnic*
Pr. – *Prince*
R.C. – *Roman Catholic*
Rd. – *Road*
Sanct. – *Sanctuary*
Sch. – *School*
Soc. – *Society*
Sq. – *Square*
St. – *Street, Saint*
Sta. – *Station*
Sth. – *South*
Ter. – *Terrace*
Th. – *Theatre*
Wk. – *Walk*
Yd. – *Yard*

The normal abbreviations for the London Postal Districts have been used throughout, e.g., NW10.

73 Abbey Gdns......C 3
73 Abbey Gdns Mews.C 3
79 Abbey Orchard St.D 7
73 Abbey Rd........B 3
80 Abbey St.........D 4
67 Abbey Wood....G 12
80 Abbots La........B 4
76 Abchurch La.....H 3
73 Abercorn Close...C 4
73 Abercorn Pl.......C 3
73 Aberdeen Place....E 5
80 Aberdour St.......E 3
77 Abingdon Rd......D 1
79 Abingdon St......D 8
77 Abingdon Villas...E 1
68 Abridge..........A 1
67 Abridge Rd........A 12
73 Acacia Gdns......B 5
73 Acacia Pl.........B 5
73 Acacia Rd.........B 5
67 Academy Rd.....H 11
70 Acre La. SW2.....B 6
70 Acre La., Carshalton......F 5
66 Acton............F 3
66 Acton Central Sta..G 3
66 Acton La..........F 3
66 Acton (Main Line) Sta.............F 3
66 Acton Park.......G 3
75 Acton St..........D 9
66 Acton Town Sta...G 2
75 Adam St..........J 9
77 Adam & Eve MewsD 2
74 Adams Row ......J 4
71 Addington........F 8
71 Addington G.C....F 8
71 Addington Palace G.C...........F 8
71 Addington Rd., Sanderstead.....G 7
71 Addington Rd., W. Wickham....E 9
80 Addington Square..J 2
79 Addington St.....C 10
71 Addington Village Rd............F 8
71 Addiscombe.......E 7
71 Addiscombe Rd...E 7
71 Addiscombe Sta...E 7
69 Addlestone ....F 2
66 Adelaide Rd......E 5
75 Adelaide St........J 8
75 Adelphi Ter.......J 9
75 Adelphi Theatre...J 9
76 Adler St..........G 6
79 Admiralty........B 8
79 Admiralty Arch ...B 8
73 Adpar St.........F 5
74 Æolian Hall......H 5
75 Agar St...........J 8
75 Agdon St.........E 12
77 Airways Terminal (Europe)........E 3
78 Airways Terminal..F 4
79 Alaska St........B 11
71 Albany Park Sta..C 12
80 Albany Rd.......H 3
74 Albany St.........C 5
74 Albermarle St.....J 5
78 Albert Bridge......J 1
78 Albert Bridge Rd..J 1
77 Albert Court......D 4
79 Albert Embank....F 9
78 Albert Gate ......C 3
77 Albert Memorial ..C 4
77 Albert Place.......D 3
67 Albert Rd.......G 11
74 Albert St..........B 5
74 Albert Ter.........A 3
74 Albert Ter. Mews..A 3
79 Alberta St.......G 12
75 Albery Theatre....J 8
73 Albion Close .....H 6
73 Albion Gate......H 6
73 Albion Mews.....H 6
73 Albion St.........H 6
67 Aldborough Hatch.........C 12
67 Aldborough Rd..C 12
80 Aldbridge St......G 4
66 Aldenham Park ...A 2
66 Aldenham Res.....A 2
65 Aldenham Rd., Bushey.........A 5
66 Aldenham Rd., Watford.........A 2
74 Aldenham St......C 7
76 Aldermanbury....G 2
80 Alderminster Rd...F 6
78 Alderney St.......F 5
67 Aldersbrook.....D 10
67 Aldersbrook Rd..D 10
75 Aldersgate St......F 13
78 Aldford St.........A 3
76 Aldgate...........H 4
76 Aldgate High St...G 5
75 Aldwych..........H 9
75 Aldwych Theatre..H 9
65 Alexander Ave....D 6
77 Alexander Place...E 6
77 Alexander Square..E 6
73 Alexander St......G 2
77 Alexandra Gate....C 5
66 Alexandra Palace..C 6
66 Alexandra Park...C 6
66 Alexandra Park Rd C 6
80 Alexis St.........E 6
74 Alfred Mews.......F 7
74 Alfred Place ......F 7
73 Alfred Rd.........F 1
80 Alice St...........E 3
76 Alie St...........H 6
70 All England Lawn Tennis Club ....C 4
70 All Saints Rd......E 4
75 All Saints St.......B 9
66 All Souls Ave......E 4
77 Allen St...........D 1
76 Allhallows La......J 2
75 Allingham Ter....B 13
78 Allington St.......D 5
73 Allitsen Rd.......B 6
74 Allsop Place......E 3
66 Allum La..........A 2
66 Alma Grove ......F 6
73 Alma Sq...........C 4
66 Alperton ....E 2
77 Alpha Place......H 6
80 Alscot Rd.........E 5
80 Alvey St..........F 3
75 Ambassadors Th. .H 8
79 Ambergate St....G 12
73 Amberley Rd .....E 2
70 Amberwood Rise..E 3
78 Ambrosden Av....E 6
79 Amelia St........F 13
67 Amhurst Park ....D 7
75 Ampton St........D 9
75 Amwell St.......D 11
78 Anderson St.......F 2
73 Andover Pl.......C 2
71 Anerley Rd.......D 7
71 Anerley Sta.......D 7
70 Angel Hill........E 4
67 Angel Rd..........B 8
67 Angel Road Sta....B 8
75 Angel St.........G 13
76 Anglesea St.......E 7
77 Ann La............J 4
76 Anning St.........E 4
77 Ansdell St.........D 3
77 Ansdell Ter........D 2
77 Anselm Rd........H 1
66 Apex Corner.......B 3
78 Apple Tree Yard ..A 7
76 Appleby St........B 5
76 Appolo St.........F 4
78 Apsley House.....C 4
78 Apsley Way ......C 4
71 Aquarius G.C.....B 8
73 Aquila St.........B 5
79 Aquinas St.......B 11
80 Arch St...........E 1
79 Archbishop's Pk..D 10
74 Archer St.........H 7
74 Archery Close .....H 2
66 Archway Rd.......D 6
68 Ardleigh Green ...C 3
68 Ardleigh Green Rd.C 3
77 Argyll Rd, W8 ....D 1
66 Argyle Rd, W13 ...F 1
75 Argyle Square.....D 9
74 Argyll St, W1.....H 6
75 Argyle St. WC1....D 9
66 Arkley...........A 4
66 Arkley La.........A 4
76 Arlington Av......B 2
74 Arlington Rd......B 5
76 Arlington Sq......B 2
78 Arlington St.......B 6
75 Arlington Way...C 11
77 Armadale Rd......J 1
75 Arne St..........H 9
76 Arnold Circus.....D 5
72 Arnolds La........C 3
66 Arnos Grove Sta...B 6
80 Arnside St........H 2
67 Arsenal F.C.......E 7
73 Artesian Rd......H 1
76 Arthur St.........J 3
76 Artillery Ground...E 2
76 Artillery La.......F 4
78 Artillery Row.....D 7
73 Arts Theatre......H 8
75 Arundel St.......H 10
72 Ash..............F 5
73 Ashbridge St......E 6
77 Ashburn Gdns.....E 3
77 Ashburn Mews.....E 3
77 Ashburn Place.....F 3
75 Ashby St.........D 12
69 Ashford Hospital..B 3
69 Ashford La.......D 3
69 Ashford Manor G.C............C 3
69 Ashford Rd, Feltham........C 4
69 Ashford Rd, Laleham ....D 3
69 Ashley Rd., Walton E 4
74 Ashland Place......F 3
69 Ashley Park.......E 4
78 Ashley Place......E 6
70 Ashley Rd, Epsom.........G 3
73 Ashmill St........F 6
79 Ashmole St......H 10
70 Ashtead..........H 2
70 Ashtead Common .G 1
70 Ashtead Park.....H 2
70 Ashtead Sta.......H 1
73 Ashworth Rd......D 3
77 Astell St..........G 6
65 Aston Rd..........B 4
77 Astwood Mews....F 3
77 Atherstone Mews..E 4
79 Atterbury St.......F 8
75 Attneave St......D 10
79 Auckland St. .....G 9
78 Audley St.........B 4
76 Audrey St.........B 6
74 Augustus St.......C 5
76 Austin St.........D 5
76 Austin Friars .....G 3
79 Austral St........E 12
75 Australia House..H 10
75 Ave Maria La....H 12
76 Avebury Estate....D 6
76 Avebury St.........A 3
68 Aveley...........G 4
68 Aveley Rd. ....E 4
79 Aveline St. ......G 10
80 Avely St..........F 3
76 Avenue, The EC3 .H 4
70 Avenue, The SW4..B 5
69 Avenue, The, Sunbury ....D 5
66 Avenue Rd. N14 ..A 6
73 Avenue Rd. NW8..B 6
68 Avenue Rd, Bexleyheath ....H 1
74 Avery Row.......H 5
71 Averyhill Rd......B 11
80 Avon Place ....C 2
80 Avondale Square..G 6
79 Avonmouth St....D 13
74 Aybrook St........F 3
80 Aylesbury Rd.....G 3
75 Aylesbury St. .....E 12
78 Aylesford St.......G 7
80 Ayres St...........C 1
76 Bache's St. ....D 3
76 Back Church La...H 6
75 Back Hill.........E 11
68 Back La...........G 5
80 Bacon Gr..........E 5
76 Bacon St..........E 6
72 Badger's Mount...G 1
80 Bagshot St........G 4
75 Bainbridge St......G 8
74 Baker St...........F 3
74 Baker's Mews.....G 3
75 Baker's Row......E 11
80 Balaclava Rd......F 6
74 Balcombe St.......E 2
74 Balderton St......H 4
75 Baldwin Ter.......B 13
75 Baldwin's Gdns...F 11
65 Baldwin's La......A 4
80 Balfour St.........E 2
68 Balgores La.......C 3
70 Balham...........B 5
70 Balham High Rd...C 5
70 Balham Hill.......B 5
70 Balham Sta........B 5
66 Ballards La. ....C 5
67 Balls Pond Rd.....E 7
76 Baltic Shipping Exchange ......G 4
76 Baltic St..........E 1
67 Banbury Res.......C 8
80 Bank End.........A 2
76 Bank of England..G 3
75 Bankruptcy Court H 10
79 Bankside.........A 13
79 Bankside Power Station........A 13
76 Banner St.........E 2
70 Banstead.........G 4
70 Banstead Downs ..G 4
70 Banstead Downs G.C.............G 4
70 Banstead Hospital.G 4
70 Banstead Rd......G 3
70 Banstead Road South..........F 5
76 Barbican ....F 1
75 Barbican Sta......F 13
75 Barford St........B 11
79 Barge House St...A 11
71 Baring Rd.........C 9
76 Baring St..........A 2
73 Bark Place.........J 2
67 Barking..........E 11
67 Barking Park ....E 11
67 Barking Rd.......F 10
67 Barking Sta.......E 11
67 Barkingside......C 11
77 Barkston Gdns.....F 2
75 Barlett Court....G 11
67 Barley La........D 12
80 Barlow St.........F 3
66 Barn Hill Park....D 2
74 Barnby St.........C 6
72 Barnehurst........A 1
70 Barnes...........A 3
70 Barnes Bridge.....A 3
70 Barnes Bridge Sta..A 3
70 Barnes Common ..A 3
70 Barnes Sta........A 3
66 Barnet...........B 4
66 Barnet Bypass.....A 3
66 Barnet Gate ......A 3
76 Barnet Grove.....D 6
66 Barnet La, Elstree .A 2
66 Barnet La, Totteridge......A 4
66 Barnet Rd.........A 3
66 Barnet Way.......A 3
70 Barnetwood La....H 1
80 Barnham St.......C 4
75 Barnsbury Rd....B 11
75 Baron St.........B 11
76 Baroness Rd.......C 5
79 Baron's Place ....C 11
74 Barrett St.........H 4
73 Barrie St..........H 4
73 Barrow Hill Rd....C 6
67 Barrowell Green...B 7
75 Barter St..........G 9
75 Bartholomew Cl. .F 13
76 Bartholomew La...G 3
80 Bartholomew St....E 3
78 Basil St...........D 2
76 Basing Place......C 4
76 Basinghall Av.....G 2
76 Basinghall St......G 2
75 Bastwick St. .....E 13
72 Bat & Ball Sta.....H 2
75 Batchelor St......B 11
65 Batchworth........B 3
65 Batchworth Hth...B 4
65 Batchworth Heath Hill............B 4
74 Bateman St........H 7
76 Bateman's Row ...D 4
65 Bath Rd, Cranford.H 5
65 Bath Rd, Colnbrook .....H 2
76 Bath St...........D 2
80 Bath Ter..........D 1
66 Bathurst Gdns.....F 4
73 Bathurst Mews ...H 5
73 Bathurst St. ......H 5
70 Battersea.........A 5
77 Battersea Bridge...J 5
70 Battersea Bridge Rd.............A 5
70 Battersea Park....A 5
70 Battersea Park Rd..A 5
70 Battersea Rise.....B 5
80 Battle Bridge La...B 3
75 Battle Bridge Rd...C 8
75 Battlebridge Basin .B 9
76 Batty St..........G 7
76 Baxendale St......C 6
74 Bayham Place......B 6
74 Bayham St.........B 6
65 Bayhurst Wood ...C 3
74 Bayley St..........F 7
79 Baylis Rd.........C 11
66 Bayswater ....F 5
73 Bayswater Rd.....J 4
68 Beacontree Hth....D 1
74 Beak St...........H 6
72 Bean.............C 4
80 Bear Gdns.........A 1
79 Bear La. ....B 12
75 Bear St. ....J 8
74 Beatty St..........B 5
78 Beauchamp Place .D 2
75 Beauchamp St....F 11
78 Beaufort Gdns.....D 2
77 Beaufort St........H 5
74 Beaumont Mews ..F 4
74 Beaumont Place...E 6
74 Beaumont St. .....F 4
71 Beckenham.......D 8
71 Beckenham Hill Rd. C 9
71 Beckenham Hill Sta. C 9
71 Beckenham Junc. Sta. D 8
71 Beckenham Place Park C 9
71 Beckenham Place & Foxgrove G.C...C 9
71 Beckenham Rd....D 8
67 Beckton.........F 11
67 Beckton Rd......F 10
68 Becontree ....D 1
68 Becontree Ave.....D 1
68 Becontree Sta. ....E 1
80 Bedale St.........B 2
70 Beddington.......F 6
70 Beddington Corner E 5
70 Beddington La. ...E 6
70 Beddington Lane Sta. E 5
70 Beddington Park ..E 5
71 Beddlestead La....H 9
69 Bedford Rd, Feltham C 4
69 Bedfont Rd, Stanwell B 3
75 Bedford Av.......G 7
74 Bedford College...D 3
77 Bedford Gdns.....B 2
70 Bedford Hill......C 5
75 Bedford Place.....F 8
75 Bedford Row.....F 10
75 Bedford Square ...F 7
75 Bedford St. ....J 8
75 Bedford Way......E 8
75 Bedfordbury ......J 8
68 Bedford's Park....B 3
72 Bedonwell Rd.....A 1
71 Beech Farm Rd...H 9
76 Beech St..........F 1
72 Beechen Wood....F 1
72 Beechenlea La.....D 2
78 Beeston Place.....D 5
78 Belgrave Mews North D 3
78 Belgrave Mews South D 4
78 Belgrave Mews West D 3
78 Belgrave Place....D 4
78 Belgrave Rd.......F 6
78 Belgrave Square...D 3
66 Belgravia.........G 5
75 Belgrove St.......C 8
68 Belhus Park.......F 4
76 Bell La...........G 5
73 Bell St............F 6
76 Bell Wharf La.....J 2
75 Bell Yard ....H 11
71 Belle Grove Rd...A 11
71 Bellingham ....C 8
71 Bellingham Rd. ...C 9
66 Belmont..........C 1
66 Belmont G.C.......C 1
70 Belmont Rise......F 4
70 Belmont Sta.......F 4
68 Belvedere.........G 2
79 Belvedere Rd.....B 10
75 Bemerton St.......A 9
75 Benjamin St......F 12
70 Benhill Av........F 4
70 Benhill Rd........E 5
68 Bennet Castle La...E 1
74 Bentinck St.......G 4
68 Beredens La.......C 5
78 Berkeley Hotel....B 5
74 Berkeley Mews....G 3
74 Berkeley Square...J 5
78 Berkeley St. ......A 5
67 Bermondsey......G 8
80 Bermondsey Leather Market ....C 3

80 Bermondsey St....C 4
80 Bermondsey Wall East...........C 7
80 Bermondsey Wall West...........C 6
75 Bernard St........E 8
74 Berners Mews ....G 6
74 Berners Place .....G 6
75 Berners Rd.......B 12
74 Berners St. ....G 6
75 Berry St. ....E 12
79 Berryfield Rd. ...G 13
70 Berrylands Sta. ...D 2
71 Berry's Green Rd. H 11
71 Berry's Hill.......G 11
68 Berwick Pond Rd...E 3
74 Berwick St.........H 6
79 Bessborough Gdns.G 7
79 Bessborough Pl....G 7
69 Bessborough Res...D 5
78 Bessborough St....G 7
71 Bethlehem Royal Hospital........E 8
67 Bethnal Green.....E 8
76 Bethnal Green Rd..E 5
67 Bethnal Green Sta..F 8
80 Bethwin Rd.........J 1
72 Betsham ....C 5
75 Betterton St.......G 9
71 Beulah Hill.......C 7
76 Bevan St..........D 2
76 Bevenden St.......C 3
80 Bevington St......D 7
76 Bevis Marks......G 4
72 Bexley ....B 1
71 Bexley Heath G.C.B 12
72 Bexley Hospital...C 1
71 Bexley La........C 12
71 Bexley Rd. SE9...B 11
72 Bexley Rd. Erith...A 1
72 Bexley Sta.........B 1
72 Bexleyheath.......B 1
80 Bianca Rd.........H 6
80 Bibury Close......H 4
74 Bickenhall St......F 3
71 Bickley..........D 10
75 Bidborough St. ...D 8
73 Biddulph Rd.......D 2
71 Biggin Hill.......H 10
71 Biggin Hill Airport G 10
67 Billet Rd. E17......C 8
68 Billet Rd., Chadwell Heath..........C 1
77 Billing Place......J 3
77 Billing Rd.........J 3
77 Billing St..........J 3
76 Billingsgate Market.J 3
76 Billiter St.........H 4
77 Bina Gdns. ....F 3
68 Bind La...........C 4
74 Bingham Place....F 3
71 Bingham Rd. Sta...E 7
74 Binney St..........H 4
72 Birches, The ......F 2
76 Birchin La.........H 3
72 Birchwood Rd.....C 1
74 Bird St...........H 4
78 Birdcage Walk....C 7
80 Bird-in-Bush Rd. ..J 6
80 Birdlip Close......J 4
74 Birkbeck Coll......E 7
71 Birkbeck Sta......D 8
75 Birkenhead St.....C 9
66 Bishops Ave. The..D 5
73 Bishop's Bridge Rd. G 3
79 Bishop's Ter. ....E 11
70 Bishopsford Rd....E 4
76 Bishopsgate ......G 4
69 Bittams La........E 2
67 Black Horse La....C 8
67 Black Horse Rd. Sta. C 8
73 Black Lion Gate...J 3
65 Black Park ....E 1
79 Black Prince Rd. .F 10
76 Blackall St........E 3
66 Blackbird Hill.....D 3
74 Blackburnes Mews.J 3
71 Blackfen..........B 11
71 Blackfen Rd......B 11
75 Blackfriars Bridge.J 12
75 Blackfriars La....H 12
79 Blackfriars Rd....C 12
75 Blackfriars Sta. ..H 12
71 Blackheath ....A 9
67 Blackheath Hill...H 9
67 Blackheath Rd....H 9
71 Blackheath Royal G.C. B 10
78 Blacklands Ter.....F 2
67 Blackwall.........F 9
67 Blackwall Reach ..G 9
67 Blackwall Tunnel..G 9
80 Blackwood St.....G 2
67 Blake Hall.......D 10
80 Blake's Rd........J 4
74 Blandford Estate ..E 1
74 Blandford Place...G 3
74 Blandford Square..E 1
74 Blandford St......G 3
77 Blantyre St.......J 4
71 Blendon Rd......B 12
80 Blendon Row.....F 2
73 Blenheim Rd......B 4
73 Blenheim Ter......B 3
76 Bletchley St.......C 2
77 Blithfield St......E 2
73 Blomfield Rd......F 3
76 Blomfield St. .....G 3
73 Blomfield Vil......F 3
78 Bloomfield Ter. ...F 4
66 Bloomsbury.......F 6
75 Bloomsbury Sq....F 9
75 Bloomsbury St. ...G 8
75 Bloomsbury Way..G 8
76 Blossom St........E 4
69 Blundell La........G 6
75 Boadicea St.......B 9
69 Board La.........C 6
70 Bolingbroke Grove B 5
74 Bolsover St........F 5
70 Bolters La.........G 4
79 Bolton Cres. .....J 12
77 Bolton Gdns.......F 3
78 Bolton St..........B 5
77 Boltons, The......G 3
79 Bondway.........H 9
76 Bonhill St.........E 3
79 Bonnington Sq. ....H 9
76 Boot St...........D 3
67 Borders La.......A 11
66 Borehamwood ....A 3
72 Borough Green...H 5
80 Borough High St...C 2
80 Borough Market...B 2
79 Borough Polytechnic D 12
79 Borough Rd......D 12
79 Borrett Rd........G 13
73 Boscobel St. ......E 5
80 Boss St...........C 5
67 Bostall Hill Rd...G 12
67 Bostall Woods...H 12
66 Boston Manor....G 1
66 Boston Manor Sta.G 1
74 Boston Place......E 2
66 Boston Rd.........G 1
75 Boswell St. ....F 9
78 Botanic Gdns.....H 2
69 Botleys...........E 1
76 Botolph La.........J 3
67 Bounces Rd........B 8
80 Boundary La.......H 2
71 Boundary Rd......G 9
79 Boundary Row...C 11
79 Boundary St. .....D 5
66 Bounds Green Rd. C 6
74 Bourdon St.........J 5
66 Bourne, The......B 6
66 Bourne Hill.......B 6
78 Bourne St..........F 3
73 Bourne Ter........F 2
78 Bournebridge......A 2
68 Bournebridge La...A 2
75 Bouverie St......H 11
67 Bow ....F 9
67 Bow Bridge.......F 9
67 Bow Common.....F 9
76 Bow La. ....H 2
67 Bow Rd...........F 9
75 Bow St...........H 9
66 Bowes Park Sta....C 6
80 Bowles Rd.........H 6
75 Bowling Green La.E 11
79 Bowling Green St.H 11
76 Bowling Green Walk D 3
76 Boyd St...........H 6
79 Boyfield St.......C 12
76 Brackley St.......F 1
79 Brad St...........B 11
73 Braden St.........E 2
79 Braganza St.......G 12
76 Braham St.........G 5
80 Braidwood St......B 4
68 Bramble La.......E 4
77 Bramerton St. ....H 6
77 Bramham Gdns ...F 2
66 Bramley Rd.......A 6
71 Brampton Rd. ...A 12
76 Branch Place......A 3
70 Brand Drive......D 3
80 Brandon St........F 2
72 Brands Hatch .....F 4
72 Brands Hatch Motor Racing Circuit...F 4
71 Brasted Hill.....H 12
71 Brasted La.......H 12
67 Bravel La........B 12
78 Bray Place........F 2
76 Bread St..........H 1
65 Breakspear Rd. North C 3
65 Breakspear Rd. South D 3
75 Bream's Buildings G 11
77 Brechin Place .....F 4
66 Brecknock Rd......E 6
77 Bremner Rd.......D 4
74 Brendon St. ....G 1
66 Brent............D 2
66 Brent Reservoir...D 3
66 Brent Sta.........D 4
66 Brent St..........C 4
66 Brentford.........G 2
70 Brentford Central Sta. A 1
66 Brentford F.C.....H 2
68 Brentwood.........B 6
68 Brentwood Bypass.B 5
68 Brentwood Rd.....D 3
68 Brentwood & Warley Sta...........B 5
78 Bressenden Place..D 5
69 Bretlands.........E 2
74 Brewer St.........H 7
76 Brick La...........E 5
78 Brick St. ....B 4
75 Bride La.........H 12
75 Bridewell Place...H 12
74 Bridford Mews....F 5
69 Bridge Rd. Chertsey E 2
69 Bridge Rd. Esher..D 6
70 Bridge Rd. Chessington F 2
79 Bridge St.........C 8
79 Bridgefoot.........G 8
73 Bridgeman St......C 6
66 Bridgewater Rd....E 2
74 Bridgeway St......C 7
74 Bridle Lane.......H 6
65 Bridle Rd.........D 5
76 Bridport Place ....B 3
67 Bridport Rd.......B 7
73 Bridstow Place....G 1
70 Brighton Rd. Coulsdon H 5
70 Brighton Rd. Croydon G 6
70 Brighton Rd. Sutton F 4
70 Brigstock Rd......D 6
67 Brimsdown Sta....A 8
75 Briset St.........F 12
73 Bristol Gdns.......F 3
73 Bristol Mews......E 3
75 Britannia St.......C 9
75 British Council ...F 10
75 British Medical Association.....D 8
75 British Museum ...F 8
77 Britten St.........G 6
75 Britton St.........F 12
70 Brixton...........A 6
70 Brixton Hill.......B 6
70 Brixton Prison ....B 6
79 Brixton Rd........J 11
70 Brixton Sta........B 6
67 Broad La. N15.....C 8
72 Broad La. Dartford C 2
67 Broad Mead Rd. ..C 10
79 Broad Sanctuary ..D 8
76 Broad Street Sta. ..F 3
77 Broad Walk, The..C 3
74 Broadcasting House G 5
73 Broadley St. ......F 5
73 Broadley Ter.......E 6
74 Broadstone Place..F 3
78 Broadway, SW1...D 7
70 Broadway, SW19..C 4
65 Broadway, Southall G 5
74 Broadwick St......H 6
80 Brockham St......D 2
66 Brockley Hill......B 2
71 Brockley Rise.....B 8
71 Brockley Rd.......B 8
71 Brockley Sta. .....A 8
70 Brockwell Park....B 6
80 Brockworth Close .J 4
75 Bromfield St......B 11
71 Bromley ....D 9
67 Bromley, Tower Hamlets........F 9
67 Bromley-by-Bow ..F 9
71 Bromely Common E 10
71 Bromley Hill......C 9
71 Bromely North Sta. D 9
71 Bromley Rd. SE6...C 9
71 Bromley Rd. Beckenham..D 9
71 Bromley Rd. Chislehurst.....D 11
71 Bromley South Sta. D 9
66 Brompton........G 5
77 Brompton Cemetery H 2
77 Brompton Hospital F 5
78 Brompton Place...D 2
77 Brompton Square .D 6
77 Brompton Rd. ....E 6
66 Brondesbury Park .E 4
66 Brondesbury Park Sta. E 4
66 Brondesbury Sta...E 4
80 Bronti Close......G 2
79 Brook Drive......E 11
71 Brook Fever Hospital A 10
66 Brook Green .....G 4
73 Brook Mews North H 4
74 Brook St..........H 4
75 Brooke St........F 11
69 Brooklands Rd....F 3
74 Brook's Mews....H 5
66 Brookshill........B 1
70 Broom Rd.........C 1
66 Broomfield Park...B 6
72 Broomfield Wood .F 4
74 Brown Hart Gdns. H 4
74 Brown St.........G 2
71 Brownhill Rd......B 9
75 Brownlow Mews .E 10
80 Browning St.......F 2
75 Brownlow St. ....F 10
69 Brox..............F 2
68 Broxhill Rd.......B 3
74 Broxwood Way ...B 1
67 Bruce Castle Park..C 7
67 Bruce Grove Sta. ..C 7
76 Brune St..........F 5
73 Brunel Estate .....F 1
65 Brunel University..F 3
75 Brunswick Centre .E 8
80 Brunswick Court...C 4
77 Brunswick Gdns...B 2
66 Brunswick Park ...B 6
76 Brunswick Place ..D 3
75 Brunswick Square .E 9
76 Brushfield St......F 4
74 Bruton La.........J 5
74 Bruton Place......J 5
74 Bruton St..........J 5
74 Bryanston Mews East G 2
74 Bryanston Mews West G 2
74 Bryanston Place...G 2
74 Bryanston Square .G 2
74 Bryanston St......H 2
68 Bryant Ave. ......C 3
80 Brymer Rd........G 5
76 Buckfast St.......D 6
67 Buckhurst Hill ...B 10
71 Buckhurst Rd....H 11
78 Buckingham Gate .D 6
78 Buckingham Palace C 5
78 Buckingham Palace Gdns...........C 5
78 Buckingham Palace Rd...........E 5
78 Buckingham Place .D 6
79 Buckingham St....A 9
76 Buckland St.......C 3
76 Buckle St.........G 6
76 Bucklersbury .....H 2
75 Bucknall St.......G 8
71 Bug Hill ....H 8
67 Bugsby's Reach ..G 10
79 Bulinga St. ....F 8
68 Bull La...........D 2
74 Bulstrode St. .....G 4
76 Bunhill Fields.....E 2
76 Bunhill Row.......E 2
72 Bunker's Hill La. ..F 5
80 Burbage Close....D 2
70 Burgh Heath .....H 4
70 Burgh Heath Rd...G 3
75 Burgh St.........B 13
69 Burhill G.C. ......F 4
75 Burleigh St. ......H 9
71 Burling La.......H 11
74 Burlington Arcade .J 6
74 Burlington Gdns. ..J 6
73 Burne St..........F 6
77 Burnsall St........G 6
71 Burnt Ash La. ....C 9
66 Burnt Oak........C 3
66 Burnt Oak Sta.....C 3
71 Burntash Hill.....B 9
71 Burntash Rd......B 9
70 Burntwood La. SW17 C 5
71 Burntwood La. Coulsdon ......H 7
79 Burrell St........B 12
78 Burton Court.....G 2
80 Burton Grove.....G 3
75 Burton St.........D 8
69 Burtons Rd.......C 5
73 Burwood Place....G 6
69 Burwood Rd......F 4
76 Bury Court.......G 4
75 Bury Place ....G 8
75 Bury St. EC3. ....G 4
67 Bury St. N9 ......A 7
78 Bury St. SW1......B 6
65 Bury St. Ruislip...D 4
77 Bury Walk........F 6
67 Bury Wood.......A 10
76 Busby St.........E 6
67 Bush Hill.........A 7
67 Bush Hill G.C.....A 7
76 Bush La..........H 2
65 Bushey...........A 6
65 Bushey Hall G.C...A 5
66 Bushey Heath.....A 1
70 Bushey Rd........D 3
65 Bushey & Oxhey Sta. A 5
67 Bushill Park......A 7
67 Bushill Park Sta...A 7
69 Bushy Park.......D 6
77 Bute St...........F 5
76 Buttesland St.....D 3
72 Button St.........D 2
68 Butts La..........D 3
71 Buxton La........H 7
76 Buxton St.........E 6
69 Byfleet ....G 3
69 Byfleet Rd........G 4
69 Byfleet & New Haw Sta.............F 3
74 Byng Place ....E 7
76 Byward St.........J 4
78 Bywater St........F 2
73 Cabbel St.........G 6
76 Cable St..........H 6
71 Cackets La.......G 11
80 Cadbury Rd.......E 6
80 Cadiz St..........G 2
78 Cadogan Gdns. ...E 2
78 Cadogan Gate ....E 3
78 Cadogan La.......E 3
78 Cadogan Pier.....H 1
78 Cadogan Place....E 3
78 Cadogan Square...E 2
78 Cadogan St. ......F 2
67 Cadogan Ter......E 9
76 Caesar St.........C 4
80 Caldew St.........J 2
77 Cale St...........F 6
75 Caledonia St......C 9
75 Caledonian Rd. ...B 9
66 Caledonian Rd. & Barnsbury Sta...E 6
77 Callow St. ....H 4
80 Calmington Rd....H 4
75 Calshot St. ....B 9
75 Calthorpe St. ....E 10
76 Calvert Av........D 4
76 Calvin St. ....E 5
71 Camberwell.......A 7
79 Camberwell New Rd. J 11
80 Camberwell Rd....J 2
75 Cambridge Circus .H 8
67 Cambridge Heath Sta. F 8
67 Cambridge Park. E11 D 10
70 Cambridge Park. Twickenham....B 1
77 Cambridge Place..D 3
70 Cambridge Rd....D 2
73 Cambridge Sq.....G 6
78 Cambridge St......F 5
66 Camden..........E 6
74 Camden High St...B 5
66 Camden Rd.......E 6
74 Camden St........A 6
66 Camden Town....E 6
75 Camden Walk ...B 12
77 Camera Place.....H 4
77 Camlet St.........D 5
76 Camley St. ....B 7
76 Camomile St......G 4
77 Campden Grove ..C 1
77 Campden Hill Rd..C 1
77 Campden St.......B 2
66 Camrose Ave......C 2
79 Canada House....A 8
80 Canal St..........H 3
70 Cane Hill Hospital H 5
67 Cann Hall........D 10
76 Canning Place ....D 3
67 Canning Town....F 10
67 Canning Town Sta..F 9
76 Cannon St.........H 2
76 Cannon Street Sta. .J 2
79 Cannon Row .....C 8
76 Canon St..........A 1
67 Canonbury ....E 7
67 Canonbury Sta. ...E 7
66 Canons Park.......B 2
66 Canon's Park Sta...C 2
67 Capel Rd.........E 10
73 Capland St........E 5
74 Capper St.........E 6
74 Carburton St......F 5
73 Cardigan Rd......D 1
79 Cardigan St.......G 11
74 Cardington St.....D 6
74 Carey La..........G 1
75 Carey St.........G 10
76 Carlisle Av........H 4
79 Carlisle La.......D 10
78 Carlisle Place .....E 6
74 Carlisle St........G 7
74 Carlos Place.......J 4
74 Carlow St.........B 5
66 Carlton Ave. East .D 2
78 Carlton Gdns. ....B 7
73 Carlton Hill ......B 3
79 Carlton House Ter.B 7
73 Carlton Vale......C 1
77 Carlyle Square ....G 5
77 Carlyle's House ...H 6
75 Carmelite St. ....H 11
74 Carnaby St. ......H 6
75 Carnegie St. .....B 10
73 Caroline Place.....J 2
78 Caroline Ter. .....F 2
65 Carpenders Park ..B 5
65 Carpenders Park Sta. B 5
67 Carpenters Rd.....E 9
78 Carriage Drive East J 4
78 Carriage Drive Nth. H 4
78 Carriage Rd., The .C 2
79 Carroun Rd.......J 10
70 Carshalton ....E 5
70 Carshalton Beeches Sta.............F 5
70 Carshalton Ho.....F 5
70 Carshalton on the Hill F 5
70 Carshalton Rd. Wallington .....F 5
70 Carshalton Rd. Woodmansterne G 5
75 Carter La........H 13
80 Carter Place......G 1
79 Carter St........G 13
78 Carteret St.......D 7
75 Carthusian St.....F 13
75 Carting La........J 9
74 Carton St.........G 3
75 Cartwright Gdns. .D 8
76 Cartwright St......J 6
65 Cassiobury Park ..A 4
76 Casson St.........F 6
73 Castellain Rd......E 3
70 Castelnau Rd. ....A 3
66 Castle Bar Park Sta.F 1
75 Castle Baynard St.H 13
66 Cat Hill..........A 5
80 Catesby St........F 3
71 Catford ....B 9
71 Catford Bridge....B 8

71 Catford Hill......B 8
71 Catford Sta.......B 8
77 Cathcart Rd.......H 3
78 Catherine Place...D 6
75 Catherine St......H 9
74 Cato St...........G 1
80 Cator St..........J 5
69 Catos Hill........E 6
75 Catton St.........G 9
79 Causton St........F 7
77 Cavaye Place......G 4
73 Cavendish Av......C 5
73 Cavendish Cl......C 5
78 Cavendish Hotel ..B 6
74 Cavendish Place...G 5
66 Cavendish Rd. NW6 E 4
70 Cavendish Rd. SW12 B 5
74 Cavendish Square .G 5
76 Cavendish St......C 2
76 Caversham St......H 2
78 Caxton Hall.......D 7
78 Caxton St.........D 7
76 Cayton St. ....D 2
70 Caesar's Camp....C 3
79 Cenotaph ....C 8
79 Centaur St.......D 10
75 Central Criminal Court G 12
71 Central Hill .....C 7
68 Central Park......D 2
70 Central Rd. ......D 4
75 Central St.......D 13
68 Chadwell Heath...D 1
68 Chadwell Hth La..D 1
75 Chadwell St......C 11
78 Chadwick St. .....E 7
74 Chagford St.......E 2
65 Chalfont Common B 1
65 Chalfont Park ....C 1
65 Chalfont St. Peter .C 1
66 Chalk Farm Rd. ..E 6
70 Chalk La..........G 3
71 Chalky Hill .....G 11
74 Chalton St........C 7
76 Chamber St........H 6
80 Chambers St.......C 6
76 Chambord St. .....D 5
79 Chancel St.......B 12
75 Chancery La......G 10
75 Chandos Place ....J 8
74 Chandos St........G 5
75 Chantry St.......B 13
80 Chapel Court.....C 2
67 Chapel End........C 9
75 Chapel Market...B 11
73 Chapel Side.......J 2
73 Chapel St. NW1...F 6
78 Chapel St. SW1...D 4
79 Chapter Rd.......G 13
78 Chapter St........F 7
79 Charing Cross Pier.B 9
75 Charing Cross Rd..H 8
79 Charing Cross Sta..A 9
73 Charlbert St.......B 6
73 Charles La........B 6
76 Charles Square....D 3
78 Charles St. ....B 4
78 Charles II St......A 7
80 Charleston St......F 2
74 Charlotte Mews...F 6
76 Charlotte Rd......D 4
74 Charlotte St.......F 6
75 Charlotte Ter.....B 10
67 Charlton.........G 10
67 Charlton F.C. ...G 10
69 Charlton La. .....D 4
67 Charlton Park ...H 10
75 Charlton Place...B 12
67 Charlton Rd. SE7 H 10
69 Charlton Rd. Shepperton.....D 4
67 Charlton Way ....H 9
78 Charlwood Place ..F 6
78 Charlwood St.......G 6
71 Charmwood La...F 12
74 Charrington St. ...B 7
76 Chart St..........D 3
75 Charterhouse .....F 12
75 Charterhouse Sq..F 13
75 Charterhouse St. .F 12
66 Chase Rd.........A 6
66 Chase Side ....A 6
80 Chatham St........E 3
70 Cheam ....F 4
70 Cheam Rd.........F 3
70 Cheam Sta.........F 4
76 Cheapside........H 2
78 Chelsea Barracks..G 4
78 Chelsea Bridge....H 4
78 Chelsea Bridge Rd. G 4
78 Chelsea Embank...H 2
77 Chelsea Hospital for Women.........G 5
77 Chelsea Manor Gdns. C 6
77 Chelsea Manor St..G 6
77 Chelsea Park Gdns.H 5
77 Chelsea PolytechnicG 5
78 Chelsea Reach....H 3
77 Chelsea Square ...G 5
71 Chelsfield Hill....F 12
71 Chelsfield La. Orpington.....E 12
72 Chelsfield La. Orpington......F 1
71 Chelsfield Rd.....E 12
71 Chelsfield Sta.....F 12
71 Chelsfield Village .F 12
71 Chelsham.........H 8
71 Chelsham Ct. Rd..H 9
71 Chelsham Rd.....H 8
78 Cheltenham Ter...F 2
75 Cheney Rd........C 8
74 Chenies Mews ....E 7
74 Chenies St........F 7
77 Cheniston Gdns...D 2
73 Chepstow Cres....H 1
73 Chepstow Place...H 1
73 Chepstow Rd. ....G 1
73 Chepstow Villas...H 1
76 Chequer St........E 2
76 Chequers Rd.......B 3
76 Cherbury St.......C 3
69 Chertsey ....E 2
69 Chertsey Bridge....E 3
69 Chertsey G.C. ....D 2
69 Chertsey La.......D 2
69 Chertsey Rd. Byfleet G 3
69 Chertsey Rd. Feltham C 4
69 Chertsey Rd. Shepperton.....E 3
78 Chesham Mews ...D 3
78 Chesham Place....D 3
78 Chesham St........E 3
76 Cheshire St. ....E 6
70 Chessington ......F 2
70 Chessington Nth. Sta. F 2
70 Chessington Rd....F 2
70 Chessington South Sta. F 2
70 Chessington Zoological Gdns...........F 1
78 Chester Close.....D 4
74 Chester Gate .....D 5
78 Chester Mews ....D 4
74 Chester Place. ...C 5
74 Chester Rd. ....D 4
78 Chester Row......F 3
78 Chester Square....E 4
78 Chester St. ....D 4
74 Chester Terrace ..D 5
79 Chester Way.....F 11
78 Chesterfield Hill...A 4
78 Chesterfield St....B 4
77 Cheval Place......D 6
71 Chevening Park..H 12
77 Cheyne Gdns. .....H 6
77 Cheyne Hospital ..H 6
77 Cheyne Row ......H 6
77 Cheyne Walk.....H 6
79 Chicheley St. ...C 10
73 Chichester Rd.....F 3
78 Chichester St.......G 6
76 Chicksand St......F 6
67 Chigwell ....B 11
67 Chigwell La......A 11
67 Cigwell Rise......B 11
67 Chigwell Rd. ....C 10
67 Chigwell Row.....B 12
68 Childerditch La. ..D 6
77 Child's Place......F 2
77 Child's St.........F 2
70 Chiltern Rd........F 4
74 Chiltern St........F 3
76 Chilton St. ....E 6
73 Chilworth Mews ..H 4
73 Chilworth St......H 4
67 Chingford.........B 9
67 Chingford Hatch ..B 9
67 Chingford La.....B 10
67 Chingford Mount Rd. B 9
67 Chingford Rd.....C 9
73 Chippenham Mews E 1
73 Chippenham Rd...E 1
70 Chipstead ....H 5
70 Chipstead Valley Rd. H 5
71 Chislehurst ......D 11
71 Chislehurst Common C 11
71 Chislehurst G.C. ..C 11
71 Chislehurst Rd. Bromley.......D 10
71 Chislehurst Rd. Orpington .....E 11
71 Chislehurst Sta...D 10
71 Chislehurst West .C 10
76 Chiswell St........F 2
66 Chiswick..........G 3
70 Chiswick Bridge...A 2
66 Chiswick High Rd. G 3
70 Chiswick House....A 3
66 Chiswick Park Sta..G 3
70 Chiswick Sta......A 2
66 Chiswick Steps....H 3
74 Chitty St..........F 6
65 Chorleywood Rd. .A 3
66 Christchurch Ave..C 1
70 Christchurch Rd...B 6
78 Christchurch St....G 2
76 Christian St.......H 7
76 Christina St.......E 4
76 Christopher St.....F 3
80 Chumleigh St.....H 4
68 Church Elm La....E 2
66 Church End ....C 4
72 Church Hill, Dartford C 2
67 Church Hill, Loughton A 11
69 Church Hill, Pyrford H 2
66 Church Hill Rd....A 5
79 Church House....D 9
71 Church La........H 9
71 Church Rd. SE19..D 7
70 Church Rd. SW19.C 4
69 Church Rd. Addlestone .....F 2
69 Church Rd. Ashford C 3
69 Church Rd. Byfleet G 3
71 Church Rd. Chelsfield F 12
68 Church Rd. Noak Hill A 3
65 Church Rd. Northolt E 5
72 Church Rd. Sutton-at-Hone..........C 3
70 Church Rd. Teddington.....C 1
73 Church St. NW8...F 5
67 Church St. Edmonton B 7
67 Church St. Enfield .A 7
70 Church St. Epsom. G 3
69 Church St. Walton .E 4
78 Churchill Gardens Estate ....G 6
78 Churchill Gardens.. Rd..............G 5
74 Churchill Hotel...G 3
75 Churchway.......D 7
79 Churchyard Row.E 12
78 Churton St.........F 6
73 Circus Rd. ....C 5
75 City Garden Row C 13
75 City of London School H 12
75 City Rd. EC1.....C 12
76 City Rd. EC1......D 3
76 City Road Basin ..C 1
75 City University ..D 12
77 City & Guilds College D 5
74 Civil Service Commission ....J 6
78 Clabon Mews......E 2
73 Clanricarde Gdns. .J 2
70 Clapham..........A 6
70 Clapham Common B 5
70 Clapham Common North Side .....B 5
70 Clapham Common South Side......B 5
66 Clapham Junc. Sta. H 5
70 Clapham Park Rd. B 6
70 Clapham Rd.......A 6
70 Clapham Sta.......A 6
67 Clapton Common .D 8
67 Clapton Sta.......D 8
75 Claremont Close .C 11
75 Claremont Square C 11
74 Clarence Gate.....E 3
74 Clarence Gardens .D 5
78 Clarence House...C 6
73 Clarendon Gate...H 6
73 Clarendon Gdns...E 4
74 Clarendon Grove..C 7
73 Clarendon Place ..H 6
78 Clarendon St......G 5
77 Clareville Grove...F 4
77 Clareville St.......F 4
78 Clarges Mews.....B 5
78 Clarges St. ....B 5
74 Claridge's Hotel ..H 4
78 Claverton St......G 6
74 Clay St...........F 3
67 Claybury Hosp...C 11
70 Claygate..........F 1
67 Clayhall.........C 11
67 Clayhall Av.......C 11
67 Clayhall Park ...C 11
75 Claylands Place ..J 10
79 Claylands Rd.....J 10
65 Claypit La........B 4
79 Clayton St.......H 11
79 Cleaver Square..G 11
79 Cleaver St. ......G 11
72 Clement St........C 2
76 Clement's La......H 3
79 Cleopatra's Needle A 9
73 Clere Place ....E 3
76 Clere St. ....E 3
75 Clerkenwell Close E 11
75 Clerkenwell Green E 12
75 Clerkenwell Rd...E 11
73 Cleveland Gdns...H 3
78 Cleveland Row....B 6
73 Cleveland Square .H 3
74 Cleveland St.......F 6
73 Cleveland Terrace .G 4
74 Clifford St. ....J 5
73 Clifton Gdns.......E 3
73 Clifton Hill.......B 3
73 Clifton Place .....H 5
73 Clifton Rd.........E 4
76 Clifton St..........F 3
73 Clifton Villas .....F 3
80 Clink St..........A 2
74 Clipstone St.......F 5
67 Clissold Park.....D 7
78 Cliveden Place ....E 3
76 Cloak La.........H 2
71 Cloack House Sta. D 8
69 Clockhouse La. ...C 3
75 Cloth Fair.......F 13
75 Cloudesley Place .B 11
75 Cloudesley Rd....B 11
75 Cloudesley Sq....A 11
75 Cloudesley St.....B 11
76 Club Row.........D 5
77 Coalbrookdale Gt .C 5
76 Coate St...........C 7
76 Cobb St...........G 5
69 Cobham ....G 5
69 Cobham Park ....H 5
69 Cobham Rd. ......H 6
72 Cobham Terrace Rd. B 4
69 Cobham & Stoke D'Abernon Sta..H 5
80 Cobourg Rd.......H 5
73 Cochrane St.......C 5
76 Cock Hill ....G 4
75 Cock La.........G 12
66 Cockfosters........A 5
66 Cockfosters Sta....A 6
79 Cockspur St.......B 8
76 Code St...........E 6
79 Coin St..........B 11
77 Colbeck Mews ....F 3
68 Colchester Rd.....C 3
72 Coldblow Maypole B 1
70 Coldharbour La. SE5 B 6
65 Coldharbour La. Hayes ....G 5
70 Cole Park ....B 1
80 Cole St...........D 2
75 Colebrooke Row .B 12
80 Colegrove Rd......J 6
77 Coleherne Mews ..G 2
77 Coleherne Rd.....G 2
80 Coleman Rd.......J 4
76 Coleman St.......G 2
75 Coley St.........E 10
65 Colham Green .....F 4
66 Colin Deep La. ...C 3
66 Colindale.........C 3
66 Colindale Av......C 3
66 Colindale Sta......C 3
75 Coliseum Theatre..J 8
76 College Hill ......H 2
75 College of Arms..H 13
74 College Place .....A 6
71 College Rd. SE21..B 7
71 College Rd. Bromley D 9
72 College Rd. Dartford D 1
70 College Rd. Epsom G 3
76 College St........H 2
68 Collier Row ....C 2
68 Collier Row La....C 2
68 Collier Row Rd....C 2
75 Collier St.........C 9
70 Collier's Wood....C 5
77 Collingham Gdns..F 3
77 Collingham Place..F 2
77 Collingham Rd....F 3
79 Collinson St......C 13
65 Colnbrook ....H 2
65 Colnbrook Bypass.H 2
79 Colnbrook St. ...D 12
65 Colney Butts......A 5
66 Colney Hatch.....B 5
66 Colney Hatch La...C 6
79 Colombo St.......B 12
75 Colonnade.........E 8
76 Columbia Rd. .....D 5
74 Colville Place .....F 7
72 Colyers La........A 1
76 Commercial Rd. ..G 6
76 Commercial St.....F 5
67 Commercial Way .H 8
66 Common Rd.......B 1
70 Commonside East.D 5
70 Commonside West D 5
75 Compton St.......E 12
79 Concert Hall Approach B 10
73 Conduit Mews....H 4
73 Conduit Place ....H 5
74 Conduit St........H 5
80 Congreve St.......F 4
74 Connaught Place..H 2
74 Connaught Sq.....H 2
74 Connaught St.....H 6
79 Cons St. ....C 11
78 Constitution Hill..C 5
80 Content St.........F 2
69 Convent Rd.......C 4
74 Conway St.........E 6
79 Cooks Rd. ....H 12
70 Coombe Hill G.C. .C 2
70 Coombe La........D 3
70 Coombe Rd., Kingston.......D 2
70 Coombe Rd. New Malden.........D 3
71 Coombe Rd. Sta...E 7
70 Coombe Wood G.C. C 2
75 Coomb's St......C 13
80 Cooper's Rd......G 5
72 Cooper's Wood...G 4
77 Cope Place........D 1
75 Copenhagen St....A 9
75 Copperfield St....C 13
70 Copse Hill ....D 3
65 Copse Wood.......C 4
69 Copsem La.........F 6
76 Copthall Av. ......G 3
76 Copthall Court ...G 3
75 Coptic St.........G 8
79 Coral St.........C 11
75 Coram St.........E 8
75 Coram's Field Playground......E 9
76 Corbet Place.......F 5
68 Corbets Tey ....E 4
68 Corbets Tey Rd....E 4
74 Cork St............J 6
76 Corn Exchange ...H 4
76 Cornhill ....H 3
77 Cornwall Gdns. ...E 3
79 Cornwall Rd.....B 11
76 Coronet St........D 3
75 Corporation Row.E 11
78 Corsham St.......D 3
79 Cosser St........D 10
73 Cosway St. ....F 6
80 Cotham St.........F 2
77 Cottage Place......D 6
78 Cottage Walk.....D 3
70 Cottenham Park ..D 3
70 Cottenham Park Rd. D 3
77 Cottesmore Gdns..D 3
79 Cottington St.....F 12
70 Coulsdon ....H 6
70 Coulsdon Court G.C. G 6
70 Coulsdon La......H 5
70 Coulsdon North Sta. G 6
70 Coulsdon Rd. ....H 6
78 Coulson St........F 2
79 County Hall......C 9
80 County St.........E 2
71 Court La. ....B 7
79 Courtenay St.....G 10
77 Courtfield Gdns...F 2
77 Courtfield Rd. ....F 3
75 Covent Garden ...H 9
79 Covent Garden Market H 8
74 Coventry St. ......J 7
80 Cowan St.........H 4
75 Cowcross St......F 12
65 Cowley............F 3
79 Cowley St. ....D 8
76 Cowper St.........D 3
70 Craddocks Av.....H 2
80 Crail Row........F 3
74 Cramer St.........F 4
79 Crampton St.....F 13
75 Cranbourn St.....H 8
67 Cranbrook Rd. ..C 11
65 Cranford..........H 4
65 Cranford La.......H 5
68 Cranham..........D 5
74 Cranleigh St. .....C 6
77 Cranley Gdns.....G 4
77 Cranley Mews.....F 4
77 Cranley Place .....F 5
76 Cranwood St.......D 3
73 Craven Hill Gdns..H 3
79 Craven St.........B 8
73 Craven Terrace ...H 4
74 Crawford Place ...G 1
74 Crawford St.......F 2
72 Crayford..........A 2
72 Crayford Rd.......B 2
76 Creechurch La. ...H 4
75 Creed La.........H 12
67 Creekmouth .....F 12
76 Cremer St. ....C 5
77 Crescent Place ....E 6
77 Cresswell Gdns....F 3
77 Cresswell Place ...G 4
75 Crestfield St......C 9
66 Cricklewood ......E 4
66 Cricklewood La...D 4
66 Cricklewood Sta...E 4
80 Crimscott St. .....E 4
75 Crinan St.........B 9
78 Cringle St.........J 6
76 Cripplegate Institute F 1
74 Criterion Theatre..J 7
72 Crockenhill.......E 1
71 Crofton Heath ...E 10
71 Crofton Park Sta. .B 8
71 Crofton Rd......E 11
71 Croham Hurst G.C. F 7
71 Croham Rd........F 7
75 Cromer St.........D 9
73 Crompton St.......E 4
77 Cromwell Cres.....F 1
77 Cromwell Gdns....E 5
77 Cromwell Mews...E 5
77 Cromwell Place ...E 5
77 Cromwell Rd. SW5 & SW7..........E 3
69 Cromwell Rd. Hounslow......B 6
76 Crondall St.......C 3
76 Cropley St........B 2
80 Crosby Row.......C 3
76 Crosby Square....G 4
68 Cross La. ....D 3
70 Crossdeep ....C 1
76 Crosswall ....H 5
66 Crouch End ......D 6
66 Crouch Hill ......D 6
66 Crouch Hill Sta. ..D 6
68 Crow La..........D 2
70 Crown Dale ....C 6
75 Crown Office Row H 11
80 Crown St..........J 2
74 Crowndale Rd.....B 6
65 Croxley Green.....A 4
65 Croxley Green Sta. A 4
65 Croxley Sta.......A 4

71 Croxted Rd......B 7
71 Croydon ....E 7
70 Croydon La.......G 5
71 Croydon Rd.
 Beckenham.....D 8
71 Croydon Rd. Bromley
 E 10
71 Croydon Rd.
 Chelsham......H 9
70 Croydon Rd. Croydon
 E 6
70 Croydon Rd. Mitcham
 D 5
80 Crucifix La. ......C 4
75 Cruden St........B 12
75 Cruickshank St...C 10
76 Crutched Friars...H 4
71 Crystal Palace F.C. D 7
71 Crystal Palace Sta..C 7
71 Crystal Palace Park C 7
75 Cubit St.........D 10
70 Cuddington G.C...G 4
71 Cudham ....G 11
71 Cudham La. Cudham
 G 11
71 Cudham La. Green
 Street Green ...F 11
71 Cudham La. Horns
 Green ....H 11
71 Cudham Rd. ....G 11
78 Culford Gdns.....F 2
76 Culham St........H 4
74 Culross St........J 3
73 Culworth St.......C 6
74 Cumberland Gate .H 2
74 Cumberland Hotel H 3
74 Cumberland Market
 D 5
78 Cumberland St....G 5
74 Cumberland Ter...C 5
75 Cumming St......C 10
80 Cunard St........H 3
78 Cundy St.........F 4
73 Cunningham Pl...E 5
79 Cureton St.......F 8
80 Curlew St........C 5
75 Cursitor St.......G 11
76 Curtain Rd.......E 4
80 Curtis St.........E 5
78 Curzon Gate......B 4
78 Curzon St........B 4
76 Custom House ....J 4
67 Custom House Sta.F 10
79 Cut, The ....C 11
73 Cuthbert St.......F 5
76 Cutler St.........G 4
75 Cynthia St. ......C 10
74 Cypress Place ....F 6
75 Cyrus St.........D 12
78 Dacre St.........D 7
68 Dagenham........E 2
68 Dagenham Av.....E 1
68 Dagenham Dock Sta.
 F 1
68 Dagenham Heathway
 Sta............E 1
68 Dagenham Rd....D 2
68 Dagenham Park..B 4
75 Dallington St....E 12
67 Dalston.........E 7
67 Dalston Junc. Sta. .E 7
68 Dalston La.......E 8
72 Daltons Rd.......E 1
75 Dame St.........B 13
75 Danbury St.......B 12
75 Dane St.........F 9
71 Danson Park ....B 12
79 Danson Rd. SE17 G 13
71 Danson Rd. Bexley
 Heath.........B 12
79 Dante Rd.........F 12
77 Danvers St.......H 5
74 D'Arblay St......H 6
76 Darby St.........J 6
72 Darenth.........C 3
72 Darenth Rd.......B 3
72 Dartford.........B 2
72 Dartford G.C. ....C 2
72 Dartford Heath ...B 2
72 Dartford-Purfleet
 Tunnel........A 3
72 Dartford Rd. Dartford
 B 2
72 Dartford Rd. Hextable
 C 2
66 Dartmouth Park Hill
 D 6
71 Dartmouth Rd. ....C 8

78 Dartmouth St.....D 7
80 Dartnell Rd.......H 4
80 Darwin St........F 3
65 Datchet..........H 1
80 Date St..........G 2
76 Davenant St......F 6
73 Daventry St.......F 6
80 Davey St.........H 5
71 Davidson Rd......E 7
74 Davies Mews......H 4
74 Davies St........H 4
66 Dawes Rd.........H 4
80 Dawes St.........F 3
65 Dawley Rd.......G 4
67 Daws Hill........A 9
73 Dawson Place ....H 1
71 Days La.........B 11
77 De Laune St......G 12
74 De Vere Gdns....D 3
74 De Walden St.....F 4
80 Deacon St........E 1
80 Deacon Way......E 1
76 Deal St..........F 6
78 Dean Bradley St...E 8
78 Dean Farrar St....D 7
79 Dean Ryle St.....E 8
78 Dean Stanley St...E 8
74 Dean St..........H 7
78 Deanery St.......B 4
73 Dean's Buildings..F 3
75 Dean's Court....II 13
66 Dean's La........B 3
78 Dean's Yard......D 8
66 Deansbrook Rd...B 3
67 Debden Sta......A 11
80 Decima St........D 4
70 Deer Park........D 4
79 Defence, Ministry of
 B 8
65 Delaford Park....F 2
73 Delamere Terrace..F 3
74 Delancey St......B 5
73 Delaware Rd......E 2
75 Delhi St.........A 9
75 Denbigh Place ...F 6
78 Denbigh St.......F 6
65 Denham ....D 2
65 Denham Aerodrome
 C 2
74 Denman St.......J 7
75 Denmark Grove..B 11
71 Denmark Hill.....B 7
71 Denmark Hill Sta..A 7
75 Denmark St.......G 8
70 Denning Avenue..F 6
68 Dennises La.......E 4
71 Denny Crescent ..F 11
79 Denny St.........F 11
78 Denyer St........F 2
80 Depot St.........J 2
67 Deptford.........H 8
67 Deptford Sta......H 9
76 Derbyshire St....D 7
76 Dereham Place...D 4
74 Dering St.........H 5
71 Derry Downs .....E 12
77 Derry St.........D 2
80 Deverell St.......E 2
75 Devonia Rd.......B 12
76 Devons Rd........F 9
74 Devonshire Close..F 5
74 Devonshire Mews
 South...........F 4
74 Devonshire Mews
 West...........F 4
74 Devonshire Place..F 4
74 Devonshire Plce. Mews
 F 4
76 Devonshire Row..G 4
76 Devonshire Square G 4
74 Devonshire St.....F 4
73 Devonshire Ter....H 4
75 Dewey Rd........B 11
77 Dial Walk, The ...C 3
74 Diana Place ......E 5
80 Dickens Square...D 2
75 Dignum St........B 11
78 Dilke St.........H 2
76 Dingley Place....D 2
76 Dingley Rd.......D 1
76 Diss St..........C 5
76 Distaff La........H 1
79 Distin St........F 11
70 Ditton Hill.......E 1
65 Ditton Park......G 1
70 Ditton Rd.......E 2
76 Dock St..........J 6
80 Dockhead........C 6
80 Dockley Rd.......D 6

79 Doddington Gr...G 12
79 Dolben St........B 12
79 Dolland St.......G 10
66 Dollis Hill La.....D 4
66 Dollis Hill Sta....E 3
78 Dolphin Square...G 7
75 Dombey St........F 9
76 Dominion St......F 3
80 Domville Grove...G 5
75 Donegal St.......C 10
78 Donne Place......E 1
79 Doon St.........B 10
78 Dorchester Hotel..B 4
74 Doric Way........D 7
70 Dorking Rd.......G 2
75 Dorrington St....F 11
74 Dorset Close.....D 4
76 Dorset Estate.....C 5
78 Dorset Mews .....D 4
78 Dorset Place......F 7
75 Dorset Rise .....H 12
70 Dorset Rd. SW19 .D 4
79 Dorset Rd. SW8..J 9
74 Dorset Square ....E 2
74 Dorset St.........F 3
78 Doughty Mews...E 10
75 Doughty St......E 10
78 Douglas St........F 7
70 Douro Place......D 3
77 Dove Mews.......F 4
76 Dove Row........B 6
78 Dovehouse St.....G 5
70 Dover House Rd..B 3
78 Dover St.........A 5
76 Dowgate Hill.....H 2
78 Down St.........B 4
71 Downe...........G 10
71 Downham Estate..C 9
71 Downham Way...C 9
79 Downing St.......C 8
70 Downs Rd. Epsom G 3
70 Downs Rd. Sutton G 4
72 Downs Rd.
 Swanscombe....C 6
71 Downs Wood.....G 6
71 Downside........H 5
70 Downside Rd......H 5
79 Draco St.........H 13
76 Drant St.........F 5
79 Draper St........E 13
76 Drapers Hall.....G 3
78 Draycott Avenue..F 1
78 Draycott Place....F 2
78 Draycott Terrace..F 2
74 Drayson Mews....C 2
77 Drayton Gdns.....G 4
66 Drayton Green....F 1
67 Drive, The ......D 11
80 Druid St.........C 5
74 Drummond Cres...C,7
74 Drummond St.....D 6
75 Drury La.........H 9
75 Dryden St........H 9
75 Drysdale St.......D 4
77 Duchess of Bedford's
 Walk...........C 1
75 Duchess St.......F 5
75 Duchess Theatre..H 9
79 Duchy St.........B 11
75 Ducks Hill........C 4
65 Ducks Hill Rd....C 4
66 Dudden Hill La....E 3
75 Dufferin St.......E 2
78 Duke of York St...A 6
78 Duke of York's
 H.Q............A 6
75 Duke of York's Th. J 8
78 Duke St. SW1....A 6
74 Duke St. W1.....H 4
80 Duke Street Hill..B 3
77 Duke's La........C 2
78 Duke's Place .....H 4
78 Duke's Rd........D 7
71 Dulwich.........B 7
71 Dulwich College ..C 7
71 Dulwich Common..B 7
71 Dulwich Park....B 7
71 Dulwich Village...B 7
71 Dulwich Wood Pk. C 7
71 Dulwich & Sydenham
 Hill G.C........C 7
76 Dunbridge St.....E 7
75 Duncan St........B 12
79 Duncan Terrace..B 12
76 Dunloe St........C 5
80 Dunlop Place .....E 6
68 Dunning's La.....D 6
74 Dunraven St.......H 3
70 Dunstans Hill.....F 4

76 Dunston Rd. .....A 5
72 Dunton Green ....H 1
80 Dunton Rd.......F 5
78 Duplex Ride......C 3
78 Durant St........C 6
67 Durants Park ....A 8
70 Durham Rd.......D 3
78 Durham St........H 5
73 Durham Terrace ..G 2
66 Durnsford Rd. N11
 C 6
70 Durnsford Rd. SW19
 C 4
78 Dyley St.........E 3
75 Dyott St.........G 8
76 Dysart St.........E 3
78 Eagle St.........F 9
76 Eagle Wharf Rd...B 2
66 Ealing...........F 2
66 Ealing Broadway Sta.
 F 2
66 Ealing Common ..G 2
66 Ealing Common Sta.
 G 2
66 Ealing G.C.......F 1
66 Ealing Rd. Brentford
 G 2
65 Ealing Rd. Greenford
 F 6
66 Ealing Rd. Wembley
 E 2
73 Eamont St........B 6
77 Eardley Cres......G 1
80 Earl Rd..........F 5
76 Earl St..........F 3
75 Earlham St.......H 8
77 Earl's Court ......G 1
77 Earl's Court Gdns. F 2
77 Earl's Court Rd...E 1
77 Earl's Court Sq...G 2
77 Earl's Court Sta...F 2
67 Earl's Path ......A 10
77 Earl's Walk.......E 1
70 Earlsfield Rd......B 4
70 Earlsfield Sta.....B 4
75 Earlstoke St. ....D 12
76 Earnshaw St......G 8
66 East Acton.......G 3
66 East Acton Sta...F 3
66 East Barnet......A 6
69 East Bedfont.....B 4
71 East Croydon Sta..E 7
71 East Dulwich.....B 7
71 East Dulwich Rd..B 7
71 East Dulwich Sta..B 7
66 East End Rd......C 5
70 East Ewell........F 4
66 East Finchley....C 5
66 East Finchley Sta..C 5
71 East Hall Rd.....E 12
71 East Ham ....F 11
75 East Harding St...G 11
72 East Hill, Dartford.B 3
70 East Hill, SW18..B 4
70 East India Dock Rd.
 F 9
70 East La..........D 2
69 East Moseley.....D 6
70 East Putney Sta...B 4
76 East Rd..........D 3
71 East Rochester Way
 B 12
70 East Sheen.......B 2
70 East Sheen Gate..B 2
76 East Smithfield...J 6
80 East St. SE17....F 4
70 East St., Epsom ..G 3
76 East Tenter St....H 6
66 East Wickham...H 12
73 Eastbourne Mews..G 4
73 Eastbourne Ter...G 4
65 Eastbury.........B 4
65 Eastcastle St......G 6
76 Eastcheap........H 3
65 Eastcote.........D 6
65 Eastcote La......E 5
65 Eastcote Rd......D 4
66 Eastern Avenue ..D 10
68 Eastern Avenue East
 C 2, C 3
68 Eastern Avenue West
 C 1
68 Easthall La.......F 3
67 Eastham Manor
 Way...........F 11
75 Eastman Dental
 Hospital ......D 10
75 Easton St........D 11
69 Eastworth........E 2

69 Eastworth Rd......E 2
78 Eaton Gate.......E 3
78 Eaton La.........D 5
78 Eaton Mews North E 3
78 Eaton Mews South.E 4
78 Eaton Mews West .E 4
78 Eaton Place......E 3
78 Eaton Row.......D 4
78 Eaton Square.....E 4
78 Eaton Terrace....E 3
76 Ebenezer St......D 2
78 Ebor St..........E 5
78 Ebury Bridge ....F 4
78 Ebury Bridge Rd..G 4
78 Ebury Mews ......E 4
78 Ebury Mews East .E 4
78 Ebury Square.....F 4
78 Ebury St.........E 4
78 Eccleston Bridge .E 5
78 Eccleston Mews...D 4
78 Eccleston Square .F 5
78 Eccleston Street Mews
 F 5
78 Eccleston Place...E 5
73 Edbrooke Rd......E 1
70 Eden Park........D 8
70 Edge Hill Rd.....F 6
77 Edge St..........B 2
66 Edgware.........B 2
66 Edgware Rd., NW2
 D 3
66 Edgware Rd. NW9 C 3
73 Edgware Rd. W2..F 5
78 Edinburgh Gate...C 2
77 Edith Grove .....J 4
77 Edith Terrace....J 3
80 Edmund St.......J 3
70 Eel Pie Is........B 1
76 Effra Rd.........B 6
78 Egerton Crescent .E 6
77 Egerton Gardens..E 6
77 Egerton Place....E 6
77 Egerton Terrace...E 6
69 Egham..........C 1
70 Elba Place ....E 2
71 Elder Rd.........C 7
76 Elder St.........E 4
76 Eldon Rd.........D 3
76 Eldon St.........F 3
80 Elephant Rd......E 1
80 Elephant & Castle Sta.
 E 1
73 Elgin Avenue ....D 2
75 Elia St. ....C 12
78 Elizabeth Bridge..F 5
78 Elizabeth St......E 4
76 Ellen St.........H 6
79 Elliott's Row .....E 12
76 Ellis St..........E 3
65 Elm Avenue ......D 5
68 Elm Park ....D 3
77 Elm Park Gdns....G 5
77 Elm Park La......G 4
77 Elm Park Rd. SW3 H 4
65 Elm Park Rd., Pinner
 C 5
77 Elm Place ....G 5
75 Elm St. ....E 10
73 Elm Tree Rd......C 5
71 Elmers End......D 8
71 Elms Mews ......J 4
71 Elmstead........C 10
71 Elmstead La. ....C 10
71 Elmstead Wood..C 10
69 Elmwood Avenue .C 5
73 Elnathan Mews ..E 3
66 Elstree..........A 2
66 Elstree Aerodrome..A 1
66 Elstree Hill South..A 2
66 Elstree Rd., Bushey A 1
66 Elstree Rd., Stanmore
 B 2
66 Elstree & Boreham-
 wood Sta......A 2
80 Elsted St.........F 3
71 Eltham ....B 10
71 Eltham Bypass...C 10
71 Eltham Common.A 10
71 Eltham Hill......B 10
71 Eltham Park .....B 11
71 Eltham Park Sta. .B 10
71 Eltham Rd.......B 9
80 Eltham Rd.......F 2
71 Eltham Warren G.C.
 B 11
71 Eltham West Hall Sta.
 B 10
66 Elthorne Heights ..F 1
77 Elvaston Mews ...D 4

77 Elvaston Place ....D 4
70 Elvers Way.......H 3
78 Elverton St.......E 7
76 Elwin St.........C 6
75 Ely Place ....F 11
77 Elystan Place ....F 2
77 Elystan St........F 6
78 Embankment Gdns.
 H 3
69 Ember La........E 6
75 Emerald St.......F 10
68 Emerson Park ....D 3
80 Emerson St.......A 1
78 Emery Hill St. ...E 6
77 Emperor's Gate...E 3
66 Empire Pool......E 2
66 Empress Place ...F 2
75 Endell St.........G 8
69 Endlebury Rd.....B 9
74 Endsleigh Gdns. ..D 7
74 Endsleigh Place ..C 7
74 Endsleigh St.....D 7
71 Endwell Rd.......A 8
67 Enfield..........A 7
67 Enfield Chase Sta..A 7
67 Enfield G.C......A 7
66 Enfield Rd.......A 6
67 Enfield Town Sta..A 7
74 Enford St........F 2
80 Enid St..........D 5
76 Ennismore Gdns...D 6
77 Ennismore Gardens
 Mews..........D 5
77 Ennismore Mews..D 6
77 Ennismore St.....D 6
76 Ensign St........H 6
79 Environment, Dept. of
 B 13
70 Epsom..........G 2
70 Epsom Common ..G 2
70 Epsom District
 Hospital ......G 2
70 Epsom Downs Race
 Course.........H 3
70 Epsom Downs Sta. G 3
70 Epsom G.C.......G 3
70 Epsom La........H 3
70 Epsom Rd., Croydon
 E 6
70 Epsom Rd., Ewell .G 3
70 Epsom Rd.,
 Leatherhead....H 1
70 Epsom Rd., Morden
 E 4
67 Epping Forest
 A 10, C 9
67 Epping New Rd..A 10
76 Epworth St.......E 3
79 Erasmus St.......F 8
72 Erith ....A 2
68 Erith Marshes ...G 1
68 Erith Reach ......G 2
68 Erith Rd., Belvedere
 G 2
68 Erith Rd.,
 Northumberland
 Heath..........H 2
74 Eros............J 7
76 Errol St..........E 2
69 Esher...........F 6
69 Esher Common ..F 6
69 Esher La.........E 6
69 Esher Rd.........F 5
69 Esher Sta........E 6
80 Esmeralda Rd.....F 7
73 Essendine Rd. ....D 1
76 Essex Rd. ....A 12
75 Essex St.........H 10
77 Essex Villas......D 1
72 Eustace Rd.......J 1
74 Euston Centre ....E 5
74 Euston Square....D 7
74 Euston Sta.......D 6
74 Euston Station
 Colonnade.....D 7
74 Euston Rd........E 6
74 Euston Rd........D 6
74 Euston Tower.....E 6
70 Evelyn Gdns......G 4
67 Evelyn St........G 8
75 Everilda St.......A 10
74 Eversholt St......C 6
70 Ewell...........F 3
70 Ewell Bypass.....F 3
70 Ewell East Sta....F 3
70 Ewell West Sta...F 3
79 Ewer St.........B 13
67 Exeter St........H 9
77 Exhibition Rd.....D 5
75 Exmouth Market..D 11

80 Exon St. F 4
79 Exton St. B 11
72 Eynsford E 3
75 Eyre Street Hill E 11
76 Ezra St. C 6
69 Faggs Rd. B 4
80 Fair St. C 4
76 Fairchild St. E 4
71 Fairchildes Rd. G 9
76 Fairclough St. H 7
80 Faircombe St. C 7
67 Fairlop Sta. C 11
67 Fairmead Rd. A 10
69 Fairmile G 5
69 Fairmile La. G 5
70 Fairoak La. G 1
72 Fairseat G 5
71 Falconwood Sta. B 11
76 Falkirk St. C 4
65 Falling La. F 3
80 Falmouth Rd. E 2
76 Fann St. E 1
76 Fanshaw St. C 4
80 Faraday St. H 3
71 Farleigh G 8
71 Farleigh Court Rd. G 8
71 Farley Rd. F 7
77 Farm La. SW6 J 1
70 Farm La., Epsom H 2
74 Farm St. J 4
71 Farnborough F 11
71 Farnborough Bypass F 11
71 Farnborough Common E 10
79 Farnham Place B 13
79 Farnham Royal G 10
72 Farningham E 3
72 Farningham Rd. D 3
72 Farningham Rd. & Sutton-at-Hone Sta. D 3
72 Farningham Wood D 2
75 Farringdon Rd. E 11
75 Farringdon Sta. F 12
75 Farringdon St. G 12
76 Fashion St. F 5
79 Faunce St. G 12
77 Fawcett St. H 3
72 Fawkham Green E 4
72 Featherbed La. F 8
76 Featherstone St. E 2
69 Feltham C 4
69 Feltham Rd. C 4
69 Felthamhill C 5
69 Felthamhill Rd. C 4
76 Fen La. E 6
68 Fencepiece Rd. B 11
76 Fenchurch Avenue H 4
76 Fenchurch Bldgs. H 4
76 Fenchurch St. H 4
76 Fenchurch Street Sta. H 5
80 Fendall St. D 4
79 Fentiman Rd. J 9
75 Fernsbury St. D 11
75 Fernshaw Rd. J 3
67 Ferry La. N17 C 8
68 Ferry La., Rainham F 2
75 Fetter La. G 11
71 Fickleshole G 9
75 Field Court F 10
65 Field End Rd. D 5
75 Field Place C 11
75 Field St. C 9
76 Fieldgate St. G 7
72 Filston La. G 2
77 Finborough Rd. H 3
76 Finch La. H 3
66 Finchley C 5
66 Finchley Central Sta. C 5
66 Finchley G.C. B 4
66 Finchley Rd. E 5
73 Finchley Rd. B 4
66 Finchley Rd. D 4
66 Finchley Road & Frognall Sta. E 5
79 Finck St. D 10
67 Finsbury F 7
76 Finsbury Circus F 3
67 Finsbury Park D 7
67 Finsbury Park Sta. D 7
76 Finsbury Pavement F 3
76 Finsbury Square F 3
76 Finsbury St. F 2
79 Fire Brigade H.Q. F 9
67 Firs La. B 7
78 First St. E 1
70 Firtree Rd. G 4
76 Fish Street Hill J 3
75 Fisher St. F 9
73 Fisherton St. E 5
76 Fishmongers' Hall J 3
79 Fitzalan St. E 10
73 Fitzhardinge St. G 3
66 Fitzjohn's Avenue E 5
78 Fitzmaurice Place A 5
74 Fitzroy Square E 6
74 Fitzroy St. E 6
75 Flaxman Terrace D 8
75 Fleet La. G 12
75 Fleet St. H 11
79 Fleming Rd. H 12
76 Fleur de Lis St. E 4
80 Flint St. F 3
80 Flinten St. F 4
78 Flood St. G 1
77 Flood Walk G 6
75 Floral St. H 8
76 Florida St. D 7
77 Flower Walk, The C 4
76 Flower & Dean St. F 5
76 Fochelle St. D 5
74 Foley St. F 6
76 Folgate St. F 4
71 Foots Cray C 12
71 Foots Cray La. C 12
71 Foots Cray Rd. B 10
76 Forbes St. H 6
69 Ford Bridge Rd. C 3
69 Fordbridge Rd. D 4
76 Fore St. EC2 F 2
67 Fore St. N18 B 8
65 Fore St., Ruislip C 5
79 Foreign Office C 8
67 Forest Gate E 10
71 Forest Hill C 7
71 Forest Hill Sta. C 8
67 Forest Hospital B 10
67 Forest La. E 10
67 Forest Rd. E17 C 9
67 Forest Rd., Ilford C 12
70 Forest Rd., Sutton E 4
67 Forest Side A 10
73 Formosa St. E 3
76 Fornier St. F 5
74 Forest St. G 2
76 Forston St. B 2
80 Fort Rd. F 6
66 Fortis Green Rd. C 5
66 Fortress Rd. E 6
66 Fortune Green Rd. E 4
76 Fortune St. E 2
66 Forty Avenue D 2
66 Forty La. D 3
76 Foster La. G 1
74 Foubert's Place H 6
77 Foulis Terrace F 5
76 Foutain St. D 5
75 Fox Court F 11
69 Fox Hill Rd. F 1
76 Fox La. B 6
68 Foxburrow Wood A 1
69 Foxoak Hill F 4
73 Frampton St. E 5
78 Francis St. E 6
78 Franklin's Row G 3
79 Frazier St. C 11
80 Frean St. D 6
75 Frederick St. D 9
80 Fremantle St. F 4
69 French St. D 5
80 Frensham St. H 6
80 Friary Rd. J 7
75 Friend St. C 12
74 Friends House D 7
66 Friern Barnet B 5
74 Frith St. H 7
71 Frith Wood G 8
75 Frome St. B 13
68 Front La. D 4
66 Fryent Way D 2
70 Fulham F.C. A 3
70 Fulham Palace A 4
66 Fulham Palace Rd. H 4
70 Fulham Rd. SW6 A 4
77 Fulham Rd. SW10 G 5
76 Fuller St. D 6
65 Fulmer E 1
69 Fulwell G.C. C 5
75 Furnival St. G 11
70 Furze Hill H 4
66 Furzehill Rd. A 3
78 Fynes St. E 5
80 Gainsford St. C 5
68 Gale St. E 1
71 Gallery Rd. B 7
72 Galley Hill B 5
67 Galliard Rd. A 8
67 Gallions Reach G 11
68 Gallows Corner C 3
79 Gambia St. B 12
70 Gander Green La. E 4
74 Ganton St. H 6
67 Gants Hill Sta. D 11
74 Garbutt Place F 4
73 Garden Rd. C 4
79 Garden Row D 12
76 Garden Walk D 4
76 Garlick Hill H 2
75 Garnault Place D 11
70 Garratt La. C 4
76 Garrett St. E 1
75 Garrick St. H 8
75 Garrick Theatre J 8
70 Garth Rd. E 3
73 Garway Rd. H 2
76 Gascogne Place D 5
76 Gasholder Place G 10
69 Gaston Bridge Rd. D 4
75 Gate St. G 9
73 Gateforth St. E 6
67 Gates Corner C 10
80 Gateway H 2
78 Gatliff Rd. G 4
75 Gaunt St. D 13
79 Gayfere St. E 8
79 Gaywood St. E 12
79 Gaza St. G 12
75 Gee St. E 13
76 Geffrye Museum C 4
76 Geffrye St. B 5
75 General Post Office G 13
77 Geological Museum E 5
80 George Row C 6
74 George St. G 2
74 George Yard H 4
65 George V Avenue C 6
79 Geraldine Mary Harmsworth Park E 11
79 Geraldine St. E 12
68 Gerpins La. E 4
75 Gerrard Rd. B 12
74 Gerrard St. H 7
65 Gerrards Cross D 1
75 Gerridge St. D 11
77 Gertrude St. H 4
68 Gidea Park C 3
68 Gidea Park Sta. C 3
75 Gilbert Place G 8
79 Gilbert Rd. F 11
74 Gilbert St. H 4
72 Gildenhill Rd. D 3
78 Gillingham St. E 5
77 Gilston Rd. G 4
75 Giltspur St. G 12
66 Gladstone Park E 3
79 Gladstone St. D 12
79 Glass Hill St. C 13
74 Glasshouse St. J 6
79 Glasshouse Walk G 9
75 Glasshouse Yard E 13
77 Glebe Place H 6
77 Gledhow Gdns. F 3
80 Glengall Rd. H 6
80 Glengall Terrace H 5
74 Glentworth St. E 2
67 Globe Rd. F 8
80 Globe St. D 2
80 Globe Theatre, SE1 E 3
74 Globe Theatre, W1 H 7
74 Globe Yard H 5
74 Gloucester Avenue A 4
74 Gloucester Gate B 4
73 Gloucester Mews H 4
73 Gloucester Mews West H 4
74 Gloucester Place F 2
74 Gloucester Place Mews G 3
77 Gloucester Rd. E 3
73 Gloucester Square H 5
78 Gloucester St. G 6
73 Gloucester Terrace G 3
77 Gloucester Walk C 1
75 Gloucester Way D 11
79 Glyn St. G 9
77 Godfrey St. G 6
79 Goding St. G 9
75 Godson St. B 11
71 Godstone Rd. H 7
76 Golden La. E 1
74 Golden Square H 6
66 Golders Green D 4
66 Golders Green Rd. D 4
66 Golders Green Sta. D 5
66 Goldhawk Rd. G 4
74 Goldington Cres. B 7
74 Goldington St. B 7
73 Goldman St. H 13
73 Goldney Rd. E 1
76 Goldsmiths Hall G 1
76 Goldsmiths Row B 6
74 Goodge Place F 6
74 Goodge St. F 6
76 Goodman St. H 6
76 Goodmans Yard H 5
67 Goodmayes D 12
67 Goodmayes Hospital D 12
67 Goodmayes La. D 12
75 Goods Way B 8
76 Gopsall St. B 3
77 Gordon Place C 2
75 Gordon Square E 7
74 Gordon St. E 7
72 Gore Hill C 3
77 Gore St. D 4
71 Gorse Rd. E 12
68 Goresbrook Rd. E 1
76 Gorsuch St. C 5
74 Gosfield St. F 5
66 Gospel Oak Sta. E 6
76 Gosset St. D 6
75 Goswell Rd. D 12
75 Goswell Terrace D 12
76 Goulston St. G 5
75 Gough Square G 11
75 Gough St. E 10
74 Gower Mews F 7
74 Gower Place E 7
74 Gower St. E 7
76 Gowers Walk H 6
76 Gracechurch St. H 3
74 Grafton Mews E 6
74 Grafton Place D 7
74 Grafton St. J 5
74 Grafton Way E 6
67 Graham Rd. E 8
75 Graham St. C 13
78 Graham Terrace F 3
76 Granby St. D 6
74 Granby Terrace C 6
70 Grandstand Rd. H 3
80 Grange, The D 5
67 Grange Hill B 11
67 Grange Park Sta. A 7
80 Grange Rd. SE1 D 4
71 Grange Rd. SE25 D 7
76 Grange St. B 3
80 Grange Walk D 4
80 Grange Yard D 5
71 Grangewood D 7
75 Grantbridge St. B 12
73 Grantully Rd. D 2
74 Granville Place H 3
73 Granville Rd. C 1
75 Granville Square D 10
75 Grape St. G 8
76 Gravel La. E1 G 5
67 Gravel La., Abridge A 12
72 Gravesend G.C. C 6
79 Gray St. C 11
68 Grays H 6
75 Gray's Inn Gardens F 10
75 Grays Inn Rd. D 9
71 Grays Rd. H 11
69 Great Bookham Common H 6
67 Great Cambridge Rd. A 8
74 Great Castle St. G 5
74 Great Central St. F 2
74 Great Chapel St. G 7
70 Great Chertsey Rd. A 2
79 Great College St. D 8
74 Great Cumberland Place H 2
80 Great Dover St. D 2
76 Great Eastern St. E 4
79 Great George St. C 8
79 Great Guildford St. B 13
75 Great James St. F 10
74 Great Marlborough St. H 6
66 Great North Rd. A 5
66 Great North Way C 4
75 Great Ormond St. F 9
75 Great Percy St. C 10
79 Great Peter St. D 8
74 Great Portland St. F 5
74 Great Pulteney St. H 6
75 Great Queen St. G 9
75 Great Russell St. G 8
76 Great St. Helens G 4
79 Great Scotland Yd. B 8
79 Great Smith St. D 8
69 Great South West Rd. B 4
79 Great Suffolk St. C 13
75 Great Sutton St. E 12
76 Great Swan Alley G 3
70 Great Tattenhams H 3
74 Great Titchfield St. F 6
76 Great Tower St. J 4
68 Great Warley C 5
69 Great West Rd. A 5
76 Great Winchester St. G 3
74 Great Windmill St. H 7
68 Great Wood A 1
72 Great Wood G 6
72 Greatness H 2
76 Greatorex St. F 6
75 Greek St. H 7
65 Green, The G 5
72 Green Court E 1
67 Green Dragon La. A 7
80 Green Hundred Rd. H 7
71 Green La. SE9 C 11
70 Green La. SW16 D 6
69 Green La., Addlestone
68 Green La., Goodmayes D 1
69 Green La., Hatton B 5
67 Green La., Ilford D 12
70 Green La., Morden E 4
65 Green La., Northwood B 4
69 Green La., Shepperton D 4
67 Green Lanes, N4 & N16 B 7, D 7
78 Green Park C 5
72 Green Rd. C 3
74 Green St. W1 H 3
72 Green St., Dartford C 3
67 Green St., Newham E 10
69 Green St., Sunbury D 4
72 Green Street Green, Dartford C 4
71 Green Street Green, Farnborough F 11
75 Green Terrace D 11
70 Green Wrythe La. E 5
73 Greenberry St. C 6
78 Greencoat Place E 6
78 Greencoat Row E 6
76 Greenfield Rd. G 7
65 Greenford F 6
66 Greenford Avenue F 1
65 Greenford Green E 6
65 Greenford Rd. F 6
65 Greenford Sta. E 6
66 Greenhill D 1
72 Greenhithe B 4
74 Greenwell St. E 5
67 Greenwich H 9
67 Greenwich High Rd. H 9
67 Greenwich Park H 9
67 Greenwich Reach G 9
67 Greenwich Sta. H 9
79 Greet St. B 11
73 Grendon St. E 6
77 Grenville Place E 3
75 Grenville St. E 9
76 Gresham St. G 2
74 Gresse St. G 7
75 Greville St. F 11
78 Greycoat Place E 7
78 Greycoat St. E 7
76 Greyeagle St. E 5
76 Grimsby St. E 6
73 Grittleton Rd. E 1
78 Groom Place D 4
78 Grosvenor Bridge H 5
78 Grosvenor Cres. C 4
78 Grosvenor Crescent Mews C 3
78 Grosvenor Gdns. D 5
74 Grosvenor Hill J 5
74 Grosvenor House Hotel J 3
80 Grosvenor Park J 1
78 Grosvenor Place D 4
78 Grosvenor Rd. H 6
74 Grosvenor Square H 4
74 Grosvenor St. H 5
80 Grosvenor Terrace H 1
73 Grove End Rd. C 4
71 Grove Park C 10
71 Grove Park Hospital C 10
67 Grove Rd. E2 F 8
67 Grove Rd. E18 C 10
70 Grove Rd., Mitcham D 5
67 Grove Rd., Romford D 12
67 Grovegreen Rd. D 9
68 Gubbins La. C 4
69 Guildford Rd. F 2
76 Guildhall G 2
78 Guildhouse St. F 6
75 Guilford St. E 9
79 Gundulf St. F 10
66 Gunnersbury G 3
66 Gunnersbury Ave. G 2
66 Gunnersbury Park G 2
77 Gunter Grove J 3
80 Guy St. C 3
80 Guy's Hospital C 2
79 Gye St. G 9
71 Gypsey Hill Sta. C 7
76 Haberdasher St. C 3
70 Hackbridge E 5
67 Hackney E 8
67 Hackney Downs E 8
67 Hackney Downs Sta. E 8
67 Hackney Marsh E 8
76 Hackney Rd. C 5
67 Hackney Wick E 9
68 Hacton La. E 4
80 Hadden Hall St. E 3
76 Haggerston Park B 6
76 Haggerston Rd. A 5
67 Hainault C 12
67 Hainault Estate B 12
68 Hainault Forest B 1
67 Hainault Rd., Chigwell B 11
67 Hainault Rd., Hainault C 12
76 Halcomb St. B 4
67 Hale End B 9
75 Half Moon Cres. B 10
75 Half Moon St. B 5
77 Halford Rd. H 1
68 Halfway Reach F 2
71 Halfway St. B 11
70 Haling Park Rd. F 6
78 Halkin Place D 3
78 Halkin St. D 4
73 Hall Gate D 4
67 Hall La. E4 B 9
68 Hall La., Upminster D 4
68 Hall La. D 6
73 Hall Place, W2 F 5
72 Hall Place, Bexley B 1
73 Hall Rd. NW8 D 4
71 Hall Rd., Eltham B 10
75 Hall St. C 12
68 Hall Wood, Brentwood B 6
72 Hall Wood, Fairseat G 6
74 Hallam St. F 5
73 Hallfield Estate G 3
69 Halliford Rd. D 4
78 Halsey St. E 2
72 Halstead G 1
70 Ham C 1
70 Ham Common C 2
70 Ham Cross C 2
70 Ham Gate C 2
70 Ham House B 1
73 Hamilton Close D 4
73 Hamilton Gdns. C 4
78 Hamilton Place B 4
73 Hamilton Terrace C 3
66 Hammersmith G 4
66 Hammersmith Bri. G 4
66 Hammersmith Rd. G 4
66 Hampden Way B 6
65 Hampermill La. A 5
66 Hampstead E 5
66 Hampstead Heath D 5
66 Hampstead Heath Sta. E 5
66 Hampstead La. D 5
66 Hampstead Ponds E 5

74 Hampstead Rd. C 6
69 Hampton D 6
69 Hampton Court Bridge D 6
70 Hampton Court G.C. D 1
70 Hampton Court Palace D 1
70 Hampton Court Park D 1
69 Hampton Court Rd. D 6
69 Hampton Court Way E 6
69 Hampton Rd., Feltham C 5
69 Hampton Rd., Twickenham C 6
79 Hampton St. F 13
70 Hampton Wick D 1
71 Hamsey Green G 8
76 Hanbury St. F 5
75 Handel St. E 8
69 Hangar Hill F 4
66 Hanger Hill F 2
66 Hanger La. F 2
66 Hanger Lane Sta. F 2
80 Hankey St. D 3
79 Hanover Gdns. H 10
74 Hanover Gate D 1
74 Hanover Square H 5
74 Hanover St. H 5
74 Hanover Terrace D 2
74 Hanover Terrace Mews D 2
78 Hans Crescent D 2
78 Hans Place D 2
78 Hans Rd. D 2
78 Hans St. D 2
74 Hanson St. F 6
74 Hanway Place G 7
74 Hanway St. G 7
66 Hanwell G 1
69 Hanworth C 5
69 Hanworth Park C 5
69 Hanworth Rd., Hanworth C 5
69 Hanworth Rd., Hounslow B 6
73 Harbet Rd. F 5
74 Harcourt St. F 1
77 Harcourt Terrace G 3
69 Hardwick La. E 2
75 Hardwick St. D 11
69 Hare Hill F 2
70 Hare La. F 1
68 Hare Street C 3
76 Hare Walk B 4
65 Harefield C 3
65 Harefield Hospital C 3
65 Harefield Place G.C. D 3
65 Harefield Rd. B 3
74 Harewood Avenue E 1
68 Harewood Hall La. E 4
74 Harewood Place H 5
73 Harewood Row F 6
66 Harlesden E 3
66 Harlesden Sta. F 3
77 Harley Gdns. G 4
74 Harley Place G 4
74 Harley St. F 4
79 Harleyford Rd. H 9
79 Harleyford St. H 11
65 Harlington H 4
65 Harlington Rd. F 4
69 Harlington Road East B 5
65 Harmondsworth H 3
65 Harmondsworth La. H 3
79 Harmsworth St. G 12
68 Harold Hill B 3
79 Harold Place G 10
68 Harold Wood C 4
80 Harper Rd. D 2
75 Harper St. F 9
67 Harringay Stadium D 7
67 Harringay Stadium Sta. D 7
67 Harringay West Sta. D 7
77 Harrington Gdns. F 3
77 Harrington Rd. E 5
74 Harrington Square B 6
74 Harrington St. C 6
75 Harrison St. D 9
66 Harrow C 1
66 Harrow on the Hill D 1
66 Harrow on the Hill Sta. D 1
76 Harrow Place G 4
73 Harrow Rd. W9 F 1
71 Harrow Rd., Chelsham G 8
66 Harrow Rd., Wembley E 2
66 Harrow School D 1
66 Harrow Weald C 1
66 Harrow & Wealdstone Sta. C 1
74 Harrowby St. G 2
76 Hart St. H 4
72 Hartley E 5
72 Hartley Wood D 5
65 Hartsbourne G.C. B 6
76 Harvey St. A 3
65 Harvil Rd. D 3
78 Hasker St. E 2
67 Haslebury Rd. B 7
65 Haste Hill G.C. C 4
75 Hastings St. D 8
65 Hatch End C 6
65 Hatch End Sta. C 6
67 Hatch La. B 9
69 Hatchord Park H 4
76 Hatfield St. E 1
79 Hatfields B 12
73 Hatherley Grove G 2
69 Hatton B 4
69 Hatton Cross Sta. B 4
75 Hatton Garden F 11
69 Hatton Rd. B 4
73 Hatton St. E 5
75 Hatton Wall F 11
75 Havelock St. A 9
68 Havering D 3
68 Havering Park B 2
68 Havering Rd. B 2
68 Havering-atte-Bower B 2
66 Haverstock Hill E 5
75 Haverstock St. C 13
72 Hawley C 3
72 Hawley Rd. C 3
71 Hawsted La. F 12
74 Hay Hill J 5
70 Haydon's Rd. Sta. C 4
65 Hayes G 4
71 Hayes, Bromley E 9
71 Hayes Common E 9
65 Hayes End F 4
71 Hayes La., Beckenham D 9
71 Hayes La., Bromley E 9
70 Hayes La., Coulsdon H 6
73 Hayes Place F 6
65 Hayes Rd. G 5
65 Hayes & Harlington Sta. G 4
79 Hayles St. E 12
65 Hayling Rd. B 5
74 Haymarket J 7
74 Haymarket Theatre J 7
80 Haymerle Rd. H 6
75 Hayne St. F 13
78 Hay's Mews A 4
75 Hayward's Place E 12
71 Hazel Wood G 11
75 H.Q.S. Wellington J 10
78 Headfort Place D 4
70 Headley Rd. H 2
65 Headstone C 6
66 Headstone Drive C 1
65 Headstone La. C 6
65 Headstone La. Sta. C 6
76 Hearn St. E 4
72 Heath La. C 2
68 Heath Park D 3
68 Heath Park Rd. D 3
69 Heath Rd. B 6
69 Heath Row F 3
68 Heath Way E 1
66 Heathbourn Rd. B 1
75 Heathcote St. D 9
69 Heathrow Airport London A 3
72 Heaverham H 4
74 Heddon St. J 6
67 Hedge La. B 7
68 Hedgemans Rd. E 1
79 Heiron St. H 13
75 Hemingford Rd. A 10
76 Hemming St. E 7
80 Hemp Row F 3
76 Hemsworth St. B 4
77 Hemus Place G 6
66 Hendon C 4
66 Hendon Central Sta. D 4
66 Hendon G.C. C 4
66 Hendon Way D 4
66 Hendon Wood La. A 3
80 Hendre Rd. F 4
76 Heneage F 6
76 Heneage La. G 4
77 Henniker Mews H 4
74 Henrietta Place G 4
75 Henrietta St. J 9
76 Henriques St. H 7
80 H.M.S. *Belfast* B 4
75 H.M.S. *Chrysanthemum* J 11
75 H.M.S. *Discovery* J 10
75 H.M.S. *President* J 11
75 Herbal Hill E 11
75 Herbrand St. E 8
79 Hercules Rd. D 10
77 Hereford Square F 4
73 Hereford Rd. G 1
76 Hereford St. E 6
75 Hermes St. C 10
75 Hermit St. C 12
80 Hermitage Wall B 7
71 Herne Hill B 7
70 Herne Hill Sta. B 6
79 Herrick St. F 8
69 Hersham F 5
69 Hersham Rd. E 5
69 Hersham Sta. E 5
67 Hertford Rd. A 8
78 Hertford St. B 4
71 Heseirs Hill H 9
71 Heseirs Rd. H 9
77 Hesper Mews F 2
65 Heston H 5
65 Heston Rd. H 5
76 Hewett St. E 4
71 Hewitts Rd. F 12
72 Hextable D 2
79 Heyford Avenue J 9
80 Heygate St. F 1
78 Hide Place F 7
66 High Barnet Sta. A 4
75 High Holborn G 10
66 High Rd. N2 C 5
67 High Rd. N17 C 7
66 High Rd. N20 A 5
66 High Rd. NW10 E 3
69 High Rd., Byfleet G 3
67 High Rd., Chigwell B 11
72 High Rd., Dartford C 2
65 High Rd., Eastcote D 5
67 High Rd., Ilford D 12
67 High Rd., Leytonstone D 9
67 High Rd., Loughton A 10
71 High Rd., Orpington E 11
67 High Rd., Woodford Bridge C 10
67 High Rd., Woodford Green B 10
67 High St. E11 D 10
67 High St. E15 F 9
66 High St. N8 C 6
67 High St. SE15 H 8
70 High St. SE27 C 6
70 High St. SW18 B 4
70 High St., Merton, SW19 D 4
70 High St. SW19 C 4
68 High St., Aveley G 4
70 High St., Banstead G 4
71 High St., Beckenham D 8
71 High St., Bexley Heath A 12
65 High St., Bushey A 6
70 High St., Carshalton F 5
71 High St., Croydon E 7
70 High St., Epsom G 2
69 High St., Feltham C 4
65 High St., Harlington G 4
66 High St., Harrow C 1
68 High St., Hornchurch D 3
69 High St., Hounslow A 6
70 High St., New Malden D 3
67 High St., Ponders End A 8
65 High St., Rickmansworth A 3
69 High St., Shepperton E 4
71 High St., Sidcup C 12
69 High St., Stanwell B 3
70 High St., Sutton F 4
70 High St., Teddington C 1
69 High St., Walton E 4
65 High St., Watford A 5
71 High St., West Wickham E 8
70 High St., Colliers Wood C 5
67 High St. North E 10
67 High St. South F 11
67 Higham Hill C 8
67 Highams Park B 9
67 Highams Park, Hale End Sta. B 9
67 Highbury E 7
67 Highbury & Islington Sta. E 7
66 Highgate D 6
66 Highgate G.C. D 5
66 Highgate Ponds D 5
66 Highgate Rd. E 6
66 Highgate Sta. D 6
66 Highgate Wood D 6
76 Highway, The J 7
66 Highwood Hill B 3
77 Hildyard Rd. H 1
66 Hilfield La. A 1
66 Hilfield Reservoir A 1
65 Hill End B 3
65 Hill End Rd. C 3
73 Hill Rd. C 4
78 Hill St. A 4
80 Hillery Rd. F 3
77 Hillgate Place B 2
77 Hillgate St. B 2
65 Hillingdon E 4
65 Hillingdon G.C. F 3
65 Hillingdon Heath F 4
65 Hillingdon Hill F 3
65 Hillingdon Rd. E 3
65 Hillingdon Sta. E 4
79 Hillingdon St. H 13
67 Hillreach G 10
71 Hilly Fields B 8
78 Hilton Hotel B 4
70 Hinchley Wood E 1
74 Hinde St. G 4
71 Hither Green B 9
78 Hobart Place D 4
77 Hobury St. H 4
76 Hocker St. D 5
68 Hoe La. A 1
67 Hoe Street D 9
66 Hogarth House H 3
77 Hogarth Rd. F 2
71 Hogtrough Hill H 11
78 Holbein Mews F 3
78 Holbein Place F 3
75 Holborn G 11
75 Holborn Circus G 11
75 Holborn Viaduct G 12
75 Holborn Viaduct Sta. G 12
68 Holden's Wood C 5
66 Holders Hill C 4
66 Holders Hill Rd. C 4
75 Holford Gdns. C 10
66 Holland Avenue G 4
66 Holland Rd. G 4
77 Holland St. C 1
74 Hollen St. G 7
74 Holles St. G 5
67 Hollow Pond D 9
66 Holloway Rd. D 6
76 Holloway St. G 6
72 Hollows Wood F 1
70 Holly La. H 4
77 Hollywood Rd. H 3
71 Holmwood Park F 10
79 Holyoake Rd. F 12
80 Holyrood St. B 4
76 Holywell La. E 4
76 Holywell Row E 3
79 Home Office C 8
72 Home Rd. C 2
74 Homer Row F 1
74 Homer St. F 1
67 Homerton E 8
67 Homerton High St. E 8
67 Homerton Rd. E 8
79 Hone Parade E 10
66 Honeypot La. C 2
71 Honor Oak Park B 8
71 Honor Oak Park Sta. B 8
71 Honor Oak & Forest Hill G.C. B 8
70 Hook E 2
72 Hook Green, Meopham E 6
72 Hook Green, Southfleet C 5
72 Hook Green E 6
72 Hook Green C 5
72 Hook Green Rd. C 2
71 Hook La., Bexley Hth B 11
68 Hook La., Stapleford Abbotts A 2
70 Hook Rise E 2
70 Hook Rd., Chessington E 2
70 Hook Rd., Epsom G 2
70 Hook Rd., Horton F 2
71 Hookwood Rd. G 12
76 Hooper St. H 6
76 Hopetown St. F 6
74 Hopkins St. H 7
79 Hopton St. A 12
76 Horatio St. C 6
66 Horn La. G 3
68 Hornchurch D 3
68 Hornchurch Marshes F 2
68 Hornchurch Rd. D 3
68 Hornchurch Stadium E 4
71 Horns Green H 11
67 Horns Rd. D 11
66 Hornsey D 6
66 Hornsey La. D 6
66 Hornsey Rise D 6
66 Hornsey Rd. D 6
77 Hornton Place C 2
77 Hornton St. C 1
79 Horse Guards B 8
79 Horseferry Rd. E 7
79 Horseguards Av. B 8
80 Horselydown La. B 5
66 Horsenden Hill E 1
80 Horsley St. H 2
77 Hortensia Rd. J 3
70 Horton, Ewell F 2
69 Horton, Staines A 1
70 Horton Hospital G 2
72 Horton Kirby D 3
70 Horton La. G 2
69 Horton Rd., Horton A 1
69 Horton Rd., Stanwell B 2
75 Hosier La. G 12
69 Hospital Bridge Rd. B 6
74 Hospital for Nervous Diseases G 4
75 Hospital for Sick Children E 9
73 Hospital of St. John C 5
79 Hotspur St. F 10
75 Houghton St. H 10
76 Houndsditch G 4
69 Hounslow A 6
69 Hounslow Central Sta. B 6
69 Hounslow East Sta. B 6
69 Hounslow Heath B 5
69 Hounslow Rd. C 5
69 Hounslow Sta. B 6
69 Hounslow West Sta. A 5
79 Houses of Parliament D 9
70 Howell Hill G 3
78 Howick Place E 6
74 Howland St. F 6
73 Howley Place F 4
76 Hows St. B 5
67 Hoxton E 7
76 Hoxton Square D 4
76 Hoxton St. B 4
78 Hugh Mews F 5
78 Hugh St. F 5
76 Hull St. D 1
80 Humphrey St. G 5
79 Hungerford Railway Bridge B 9
74 Huntley St. E 7
65 Huntsmoor Park F 3
74 Huntsworth Mews E 2
76 Hunton St. E 6
79 Hurlbutt Place F 13
70 Hurlingham House A 4
69 Hurst Rd., Molesey D 5
71 Hurst Rd., Sidcup B 12
66 Hyde, The C 3
78 Hyde Park Barracks C 3
78 Hyde Park Corner C 4
73 Hyde Park Cres. H 6
73 Hyde Park Gdns. H 5
73 Hyde Park Gdns. Mews H 5
77 Hyde Park Gate D 4
78 Hyde Park Hotel C 2
73 Hyde Park Square H 6
73 Hyde Park St. H 6
76 Hyde Rd. B 3
69 Hythe C 2
69 Hythe End C 1
65 Ickenham D 4
76 Idol La. J 4
77 Ifield Rd. H 3
72 Ightham H 5
73 Ilchester Gdns. D 11
67 Ilford E 11
67 Ilford Football Club D 11
67 Ilford G.C. D 11
67 Ilford La. E 11
79 Iliffe St. F 13
76 Imber St. B 2
77 Imperial College D 5
77 Imperial College of Science D 5
65 Imperial Drive D 6
75 Imperial Hotel F 8
77 Imperial Institute D 5
77 Imperial Institute Rd. D 4
79 Imperial War Museum E 11
76 India St. H 5
74 Ingestre Place H 6
75 Inglebert St. C 11
68 Ingrave B 6
68 Ingrave Green B 6
74 Inner Circle D 3
77 International Hotel E 2
73 Inverness Place H 3
73 Inverness Terrace H 3
73 Inverness Terrace Gate J 3
80 Inville Rd. G 3
76 Ironmonger La. G 2
76 Ironmonger Row D 1
76 Ironmonger St. D 2
76 Ironmonger's Hall F 1
75 Irving St. J 8
75 Isabella St. B 12
69 Island Barn Res. E 6
67 Isle of Dogs G 9
70 Isleworth B 1
70 Isleworth Sta. A 1
67 Islington E 7
75 Islington Green B 12
75 Islington High St. B 12
79 Italian Walk G 9
65 Iver F 2
65 Iver Heath E 2
65 Iver La. F 2
77 Iverna Court D 2
77 Iverna Gdns. D 2
66 Iverson Rd. E 4
75 Ives St. E 1
74 Ivor Place E 2
76 Ivy St. B 4
72 Ivyhouse La. H 1
77 Ixworth Place F 6
71 Jackass La. F 10
80 Jacob St. C 6
71 Jail La. G 10
80 Jamaica Rd. D 6
75 James St. WC2 H 9
74 James St. W1 G 4
77 Jameson St. B 2
80 Jardin St. H 4
77 Jay Mews D 4
78 Jermyn St. A 6
73 Jerome Crescent E 6
76 Jerome St. F 5
69 Jersey Rd. A 6
76 Jewry St. H 5
79 Joan St. B 12
75 Jockey's Fields F 10
65 Joel St. C 5
75 John Adam St. J 9
75 John Carpenter St. H 12

76 John Fisher St. . . . . J 6
79 John Islip St. . . . . F 8
74 John Princess St. . . G 5
79 John Ruskin St. . . J 13
75 John St. . . . . E 10
79 Jonathan St. . . . . . F 9
75 John's Mews. . . . . E 10
72 Joyce Green Hosp. A 3
72 Joyce Green La. . . . A 3
72 Joyden's Wood. . . . C 1
67 Jubilee Park. . . . . A 8
78 Jubilee Place. . . . . G 1
75 Judd St. . . . . D 8
73 Junction Mews. . . . G 6
66 Junction Rd. . . . . . D 6
77 Justice Walk. . . . . H 6
79 Juxon St. . . . . E 10
67 Katherine Rd. . . . . E 10
74 Kay St. . . . . B 6
75 Kean St. . . . . H 9
75 Keeley St. . . . . G 9
77 Kelso Place. . . . . . D 2
75 Kemble St. . . . . . . H 9
77 Kempsford Gdns. . G 2
79 Kempsford Rd. . . F 12
80 Kempshead Rd. . . . G 4
69 Kempton Park Race Course. . . . . C 5
72 Kemsing. . . . . H 3
73 Kendal Street. . . . . H 6
71 Kenley. . . . . H 7
79 Kennings Way . . . G 12
79 Kennington Grove H 10
79 Kennington La. . . G 10
79 Kennington Oval H 10
79 Kennington Park. H 11
79 Kennington Park Gdns. . . . . H 12
79 Kennington Park Place H 12
79 Kennington Park Rd. G 12
79 Kennington Rd. . . E 11
74 Kenrick Place . . . . . F 3
66 Kensal Green. . . . . F 4
66 Kensal Green Sta. . F 4
77 Kensington Church St. B 2
77 Kensington Court . C 3
77 Kensington Court Place . . . . D 3
77 Kensington Gdns. . B 3
73 Kensington Gardens Square. . . . . H 2
77 Kensington Gate . . D 3
77 Kensington Gore. . C 4
77 Kensington High St. D 1
77 Kensington Mall . . B 2
77 Kensington Palace. B 2
77 Kensington Palace Barracks . . . . C 2
77 Kensington Palace Gdns. . . . . B 2
77 Kensington Palace Green. . . . . C 2
73 Kensington Park Rd. J 1
77 Kensington Place . . B 2
77 Kensington Rd. . . C 3
77 Kensington Square D 2
66 Kensington & Chelsea G 4
71 Kent House Sta. . . D 8
76 Kent St. . . . . B 5
74 Kent Terrace. . . . . D 2
66 Kentish Town. . . . . E 6
66 Kentish Town Sta. . E 6
66 Kenton . . . . D 2
66 Kenton La. . . . . C 2
66 Kenton Rd. . . . . . . C 2
75 Kenton St. . . . . E 8
77 Kenway Rd. . . . . . . F 2
66 Kenwood . . . . D 5
71 Keston. . . . . F 10
71 Keston Mark . . . . E 10
70 Kew. . . . . A 2
66 Kew Bridge . . . . . . G 2
70 Kew Bridge Rd. . . . A 2
66 Kew Bridge Sta. . . G 2
70 Kew Gardens Sta. . A 2
70 Kew Palace. . . . . . . A 2
70 Kew Rd. . . . . A 2
80 Keyse Rd. . . . . E 5
75 Keystone Crescent. C 9
75 Keyworth St. . . . . D 12
71 Kidbrooke. . . . . A 9
71 Kidbrooke Sta. . . A 10
66 Kilburn . . . . E 4
66 Kilburn High Rd. Sta. E 5
73 Kilburn Park Rd. . . D 1
66 Kilburn Sta. . . . . . . E 4
73 Kildare Terrace . . . G 2
75 Killick St. . . . . C 9
79 King Charles St. . . . C 8
75 King Edward St. . G 13
79 King Edward Walk D 11
67 King George V Dock G 11
69 King George VI Res. B 2
67 King George's Res. A 9
79 King James St. . . . D 12
76 King John's Court . E 4
76 King St. EC2. . . . . . G 2
78 King St. SW1 . . . . . B 6
75 King St. WC2 . . . . H 8
66 King St. W6. . . . . . G 3
76 King William St. . . H 3
80 King & Queen St. . . F 2
69 Kingfieldgreen . . . . H 1
80 Kinglake St. . . . . . . G 4
74 Kingly St. . . . . H 6
76 King's Arms Yard . G 2
79 King's Bench St. . . C 12
75 King's Bench Walk H 11
75 King's College . . . H 10
75 King's Cross Rd. . D 10
75 King's Cross Sta. . . C 8
67 King's Head Hill . . A 9
80 King's Head Yard . B 3
75 King's Mews. . . . . F 10
80 King's Place . . . . . . D 1
78 King's Rd. SW1. . . E 4
77 King's Rd. SW3 . . G 6
67 King's Rd., Chingford B 9
78 King's Scholars' Passage . . . . E 6
74 King's Terrace . . . . B 6
66 Kingsbury. . . . . C 3
66 Kingsbury Green. . D 3
66 Kingsbury Rd. . . . . D 3
66 Kingsbury Sta. . . . D 2
72 Kingsdown . . . . F 4
65 Kingshill Avenue . . F 5
67 Kingsland . . . . E 7
76 Kingsland Rd. . . . . C 4
69 Kingsley Rd. . . . . . . A 6
73 Kingsmill Terrace . B 5
70 Kingston Bridge . . D 1
70 Kingston Bypass . . D 3
70 Kingston Gate . . . . C 2
70 Kingston Hill . . . . . C 2
65 Kingston Lane . . . . F 3
70 Kingston Rd. SW15 B 3
70 Kingston Rd. SW20 D 4
70 Kingston Rd., Leatherhead . . . . H 1
70 Kingston Rd., New Malden . . . . D 2
69 Kingston Rd., Staines C 3
70 Kingston Rd., Teddington . . . . . C 1
70 Kingston Rd., Tolworth . . . . F 3
70 Kingston upon Thames D 2
70 Kingston Vale . . . . C 2
75 Kingsway . . . . G 9
70 Kingswood Sta. . . . H 4
78 Kinnerton St. . . . . . C 3
80 Kipling St. . . . . C 3
79 Kipton St. . . . . D 3
80 Kirby Grove. . . . . . C 3
75 Kirby St. . . . . F 11
71 Kirkdale . . . . C 7
78 Kirtling St. . . . . J 6
79 Kirwyn Way. . . . . J 13
80 Kitson Rd. . . . . J 2
71 Kitto Rd. . . . . A 8
77 Knaresborough Place F 2
70 Knight's Hill. . . . . C 6
69 Knights Res. . . . . . D 5
78 Knightsbridge. . . . . C 2
69 Knipp Hill . . . . G 5
77 Knivet Rd. . . . . J 1
71 Knockholt . . . . . . H 12
71 Knockholt Main Rd. H 11
71 Knockholt Pound G 12
71 Knockholt Rd. . . . G 12
71 Knockholt Sta. . . . F 12
69 Knowle Green . . . . C 2
74 Knox St. . . . . F 2
77 Kynance Mews. . . . E 3
77 Kynance Place . . . . D 3
76 Laburnum St. . . . . . B 5
76 Lackington St. . . . . F 3
66 Ladbroke Grove. . . F 4
80 Lafone St. . . . . C 5
69 Laleham . . . . D 3
69 Laleham Rd., Shepperton . . . . D 3
69 Laleham Rd., Staines C 2
76 Lamb Passage. . . . . E 2
76 Lamb St. . . . . F 5
80 Lamb Walk . . . . . . C 4
70 Lambeth . . . . B 6
79 Lambeth Bridge. . . . E 9
79 Lambeth High St. . . E 9
79 Lambeth Hospital F 12
79 Lambeth Palace . . . E 9
79 Lambeth Palace Rd. D 9
79 Lambeth Pier . . . . . E 9
79 Lambeth Rd. . . . . E 10
76 Lambeth St. . . . . . . H 6
79 Lambeth Walk . . . E 10
75 Lamb's Conduit. . . E 9
69 Lammas La. . . . . . . F 6
77 Lamont Rd. . . . . . . H 4
69 Lampton . . . . A 6
69 Lampton Rd. . . . . . A 6
73 Lanark Place . . . . . E 4
73 Lanark Rd. . . . . D 3
73 Lancaster Gate . . . . J 4
78 Lancaster House . . C 6
73 Lancaster Mews . . . H 4
75 Lancaster Place. . . . J 9
79 Lancaster St. . . . . C 12
73 Lancaster Terrace . H 5
73 Lancelot Place . . . . D 2
74 Lancing St. . . . . D 7
75 Land Registry Office G 10
70 Landor Rd. . . . . A 6
73 Langford Place. . . . B 4
74 Langham Place . . . G 5
74 Langham St. . . . . . . F 5
65 Langley . . . . G 1
79 Langley La. . . . . H 9
71 Langley Park, Eden Park . . . . E 9
65 Langley Park, Slough F 1
71 Langley Park G.C. . E 9
75 Langley St. . . . . H 8
70 Langley Vale . . . . . H 3
75 Langton Close. . . . D 10
77 Langton St. . . . . J 4
73 Lanhill Rd. . . . . E 1
67 Lansdowne Rd. . . . C 8
79 Lant St. . . . . C 13
80 Larcom St. . . . . F 2
70 Latchmere Rd. . . . . A 5
71 Lathams Rd. . . . . . . F 9
80 Latona Rd. . . . . H 6
79 Laud St. . . . . G 9
73 Lauderdale Rd. . . . D 2
77 Launceston Place. . D 3
68 Launders La. . . . . . F 3
76 Laurence Pountney La. J 3
67 Lausanne Rd. . . . . H 8
70 Lavender Hill. . . . . B 5
77 Laverton Place. . . . F 2
79 Lavington St. . . . B 13
75 Lavinia Grove . . . . B 9
80 Law St. . . . . D 3
79 Lawn La. . . . . H 9
70 Lawn Rd. . . . . H 1
66 Lawrence St. NW7. B 3
77 Lawrence St. SW3 . H 6
71 Layhams Rd. . . . . . G 9
75 Laystall St. . . . . . . E 10
70 Layton Rd. . . . . F 1
67 Lea Bridge . . . . D 8
67 Lea Bridge Rd. . . . D 8
67 Lea Bridge Sta. . . . D 8
67 Lea Valley Rd. . . . . A 9
76 Leadenhall Market H 3
76 Leadenhall St. . . . . H 4
79 Leake St. . . . . C 10
71 Leas Rd. . . . . H 8
75 Leather La. . . . . . . F 11
70 Leatherhead Bypass H 1
70 Leatherhead Common H 1
70 Leatherhead G.C. G 1
70 Leatherhead Rd., Chessington. . . . . F 1
70 Leatherhead Rd., Leatherhead . . . . H 1
80 Leathermarket St. C 3
71 Leaves Green . . . . G 10
71 Leaves Green Rd. . F 10
71 Ledgers Rd. . . . . . . H 8
71 Lee . . . . B 9
71 Lee High Rd. . . . . . B 9
71 Lee Rd. . . . . A 9
75 Leeke St. . . . . C 9
74 Lees Place . . . . H 3
71 Leesons Rd. . . . . . D 11
75 Leicester Square . . . J 7
80 Leigh Hunt St. . . . . C 1
70 Leigham Court Rd. C 6
73 Leinster Gdns. . . . . H 3
73 Leinster Mews . . . . J 4
73 Leinster Rd. . . . . . . C 1
73 Leinster Square . . . H 2
73 Leinster Ter. . . . . . . J 3
76 Leman St. . . . . H 6
78 Lennox Gdns. . . . . . E 2
78 Lennox Gardens Mews E 2
76 Leonard St. . . . . E 3
79 Leopold Walk . . . . G 9
80 Leroy St. . . . . E 4
68 Lessness Heath . . . G 2
76 Lever St. . . . . D 1
71 Lewisham . . . . B 8
71 Lewisham High St. . B 9
71 Lewisham Rd. . . . . A 9
79 Lewisham St. . . . . C 7
77 Lexham Gdns. . . . . E 2
77 Lexham Mews . . . . E 1
74 Lexington St. . . . . . H 6
67 Ley St. . . . . D 11
76 Leyden St. . . . . G 5
67 Leyton . . . . D 9
67 Leyton High Rd. . . D 9
67 Leyton Marshes . . . D 8
67 Leyton Midland Road Sta. . . . . D 9
67 Leytonstone High Rd. Sta. . . . . D 9
67 Leytonstone Rd. . . E 9
69 Liberty La. . . . . F 2
79 Library St. . . . . . . D 12
74 Lidlington Place . . . C 6
76 Ligonier St. . . . . . . D 5
73 Lilestone St. . . . . . . E 6
66 Lillie Rd. . . . . H 4
79 Lillington Gardens Estate . . . . F 7
76 Lime St. . . . . H 4
67 Limehouse. . . . . F 9
67 Limehouse Reach . G 9
77 Limerston St. . . . . . H 4
71 Limpsfield Rd. . . . . G 7
67 Lincoln Rd. . . . . . . A 7
78 Lincoln St. . . . . F 2
75 Lincoln's Inn. . . . . G 10
75 Lincoln's Inn Fields G 10
73 Linden Gdns. . . . . . J 1
75 Lindsey St. . . . . . . F 13
74 Linhope St. . . . . E 2
80 Linsey St. . . . . E 6
76 Linton St. . . . . B 2
74 Lisle St. . . . . H 7
73 Lisson Green Estate E 6
73 Lisson Grove . . . . . E 6
73 Lisson St. . . . . F 6
74 Little Albany St. . . . D 5
77 Little Boltons, The. G 3
75 Little Britain . . . . G 13
65 Little Bushey La. . . A 6
78 Little Chester St. . . D 4
74 Little Edward St. . . C 5
66 Little Ealing . . . . . . G 2
66 Little Gaynes La. . . E 4
79 Little George St. . . C 8
65 Little Green La. . . . A 4
74 Little Marlborough St. H 6
75 Little New St. . . . . G 11
65 Little Oxhey La. . . . B 5
74 Little Portland St. . G 6
75 Little Russell St. . . . G 8
78 Little St. James's St. B 6
76 Little Trinity La. . . H 2
70 Little Woodcote . . G 5
70 Little Woodmansterne La. . . . . G 5
69 Littleton . . . . D 3
69 Littleton La. . . . . . . D 3
80 Liverpool Grove . . G 2
75 Liverpool Rd. . . . . B 11
76 Liverpool St. . . . . . G 3
76 Liverpool Street Sta. F 4
74 Livonia St. . . . . H 6
76 Lizard St. . . . . D 2
80 Llewellyn St. . . . . . C 6
75 Lloyd Baker St. . D 10
75 Lloyd Square . . . . D 10
75 Lloyd St. . . . . C 11
76 Lloyd's Avenue . . . H 4
76 Lloyd's Buildings . H 3
75 Lloyd's Row. . . . . D 12
71 Loampit Hill . . . . . A 8
69 Lock La. . . . . H 3
66 Locket Rd. . . . . C 1
71 Locksbottom . . . . E 10
67 Lockwood Res. . . . C 8
67 Lodge Avenue . . . E 12
71 Lodge La. . . . . F 9
73 Lodge Rd. . . . . D 5
80 Loftie St. . . . . C 7
77 Logan Mews. . . . . . E 1
77 Logan Place . . . . . . E 1
76 Lolesworth St. . . . . G 5
79 Lollard Place. . . . . F 11
79 Lollard St. . . . . . . F 10
79 Loman St. . . . . . . C 13
75 Lombard La. . . . . . H 11
76 Lombard St. . . . . . H 3
80 London Bridge. . . . A 3
80 London Bridge Station B 3
80 London Bridge St. . B 3
74 London Clinic . . . . E 4
74 London College of Music . . . . H 6
79 London College of Printing. . . . . . E 12
67 London Fields Sta. . E 8
74 London Planetarium E 3
79 London Rd. SE1 . D 12
71 London Rd. SE23 . B 7
68 London Rd., Aveley G 4
72 London Rd., Badger's Mount . . . . G 1
65 London Rd., Batchworth . . . . . B 3
70 London Rd., Croydon E 6
72 London Rd., Dunton Green . . . . H 1
67 London Rd., Enfield A 7
70 London Rd., Hackbridge . . . . . E 5
70 London Rd., Kingston D 2
70 London Rd., Mitcham D 5
70 London Rd., Morden D 4
70 London Rd., Norbury D 6
68 London Rd., Romford D 2
68 London Rd., Shenfield A 6
69 London Rd., Staines C 3
66 London Rd., Stanmore B 2
72 London Rd., Swanscombe. . . . B 4
68 London Rd., W. Thurrock . . . H 5
75 London School of Economics . . . . H 10
70 London School of Hygiene. . . . . F 7
70 London Scottish G.C. C 3
76 London St. EC3 . . H 4
73 London St. W2. . . . G 5
69 London St., Chertsey E 2
68 London Tilbury Rd. G 4, G 5
76 London Wall . . . . . G 3
75 London Weather Centre. . . . . . . G 10
75 Long Acre . . . . H 8
70 Long Ditton . . . . . . E 1
65 Long Elmes. . . . . . . C 6
70 Long Grove Hospital F 2
70 Long Grove Rd. . . . F 2
75 Long La. EC1 . . . . F 13
80 Long La. SE1 . . . . . C 3
71 Long La., Bexley Heath. . . . . A 12
71 Long La., Croydon D 8
69 Long La., Staines . . B 3
65 Long La., Uxbridge E 4
77 Long Ridge Rd. . . . F 1
76 Long St. . . . . C 5
80 Long Walk . . . . D 4
77 Long Water, The. . B 5
75 Long Yard . . . . E 9
67 Longbridge Rd. . . . E 11
80 Longcroft Rd. . . . . H 4
70 Longdown Road North G 3
72 Longfield. . . . . D 5
72 Longfield Hill. . . . . D 6
72 Longfield Rd. . . . . . D 5
65 Longford . . . . H 3
74 Longford St. . . . . . . E 5
71 Longlands. . . . . . . C 11
67 Longleigh La. . . . . H 12
80 Longley St. . . . . F 6
66 Longmore Avenue. A 5
78 Longmore St. . . . . . F 6
67 Longwood Gdns. . C 11
73 Lord Hills Bridge. . G 2
73 Lord Hills Rd. . . . . F 2
79 Lord North St. . . . . E 8
73 Lord's Cricket Ground D 5
67 Lordship La. N17. . C 7
71 Lordship La. SE22. B 7
67 Lordship Rd. . . . . . D 7
75 Lorenzo St. . . . . . C 10
79 Lorrimore Rd. . . . H 13
79 Lorrimore Square H 13
76 Lothbury. . . . . G 3
73 Loudon Rd. . . . . . . B 4
65 Loudwater La. . . . . A 3
79 Loughborough St. G 10
70 Loughborough Junc. Sta. . . . . A 6
67 Loughton . . . . A 11
67 Loughton Way. . . A 10
76 Lovat La. . . . . J 3
76 Love La. EC2. . . . . . G 2
70 Love La., Morden . E 4
80 Lovegrove St. . . . . . G 7
71 Lower Addiscombe Rd. . . . . E 7
70 Lower Ashtead . . . H 1
68 Lower Bedford Rd. C 2
78 Lower Belgrave St. . E 4
67 Lower Clapton Rd. E 8
67 Lower Edmonton. . B 8
69 Lower Feltham . . . C 4
69 Lower Green . . . . . E 6
69 Lower Green Rd. . . E 6
78 Lower Grosvenor Place . . . . D 5
79 Lower Marsh . . . . C 11
70 Lower Morden La. . E 4
70 Lower Mortlake Rd. B 2
70 Lower Richmond Rd. A 3
67 Lower Rd. . . . . G 8
78 Lower Sloane St. . . . F 3
69 Lower Sunbury Rd. D 5
71 Lower Sydenham. . C 8
71 Lower Sydenham Sta. C 8
76 Lower Thames St. . . J 3
72 Lowfield St. . . . . . . B 3
66 Lowlands Rd. . . . . D 1
78 Lowndes Place. . . . D 3
78 Lowndes Square . . D 3
78 Lowndes St. . . . . . . D 3
77 Lucan Place . . . . . . F 6
80 Lucey Rd. . . . . E 6
75 Ludgate Circus . . H 12
75 Ludgate Hill. . . . . H 12
76 Luke St. . . . . E 3
72 Lullingstone Castle F 2
72 Lullingstone Park. . F 1
74 Lumley St. . . . . H 4
71 Lunghurst Rd. . . . . H 8
78 Lupus St. . . . . G 6
79 Luscombe Way. . . . J 8
71 Lusted La. . . . . . . H 10
73 Luton St. . . . . E 5
74 Luxborough St. . . . F 3
71 Luxted Rd. . . . . . . G 10

78 Lyall St. E 3
80 Lydney Close J 4
80 Lynton Rd. F 6
73 Lyons Place E 5
80 Lytham St. G 2
66 Lyttelton Rd. C 5
75 Mabledon Place D 8
75 Macclesfield Rd. D 13
73 Mackennal St. B 6
75 Macklin St. G 9
80 Macks Rd. E 6
74 Mackworth St. C 6
80 Macleod St. G 2
65 Mad Bess Wood C 4
74 Madame Tussaud's E 3
74 Maddox St. H 5
80 Madron St. F 4
80 Magdalen St. B 4
79 Magee St. H 11
80 Maguire St. C 5
73 Maida Avenue F 4
73 Maida Vale D 3
75 Maiden La. J 9
71 Maidstone Rd. C 12
71 Main Rd., Biggin Hill H 10
71 Main Rd., Sidcup C 11
72 Main Rd., Sutton-at-Hone D 3
78 Makins St. F 1
70 Malden E 3
70 Malden Manor Sta. E 3
70 Malden Rd., Cheam F 4
70 Malden Rd., New Malden D 3
70 Malden Rushett G 1
70 Malden Way E 3
74 Malet Place E 7
74 Malet St. E 7
78 Mall, The B 7
77 Mallord St. H 5
73 Mallory St. E 6
76 Mallow St. E 2
80 Malt St. H 6
75 Malta St. D 12
80 Maltby St. D 5
73 Malvern Mews D 1
73 Malvern Rd. D 1
67 Manchester Rd. G 9
74 Manchester Square G 4
74 Manchester St. G 3
80 Manciple St. D 3
74 Mandeville Place G 4
75 Manette St. H 7
80 Mann St. G 3
71 Manor Avenue A 8
70 Manor Hospital G 2
67 Manor Park E 11
79 Manor Place G 13
67 Manor Rd. N16 D 7
67 Manor Rd., Buckhurst Hill A 10
68 Manor Rd., Hainault B 1
70 Manor Rd., Mitcham D 5
70 Manor Rd., Wallington F 5
67 Manor Rd., Woodford Bridge B 11
70 Manor Rd. North E 1
77 Manresa Rd. G 6
76 Mansell St. H 5
67 Mansfield Hill B 9
74 Mansfield St. F 5
76 Mansfield St. C 7
71 Mansion, The B 12
76 Mansion House H 2
76 Mansion House Place H 2
77 Manson Place F 4
75 Mantell St. B 11
72 Maplescombe F 3
70 Marble Hill Park B 1
75 Marchmont Ter. E 8
80 Marcia Rd. F 4
74 Margaret St. G 6
77 Margaretta Ter. H 6
75 Margery St. D 11
76 Mark La. H 4
76 Mark St. E 3
78 Market Mews B 4
74 Market Place G 6
79 Markham Square G 2
78 Markham St. G 2
67 Markhouse Rd. D 9
68 Marks Gate C 1
68 Marks Gate Rd. C 1
76 Marlborough Av. A 6
73 Marlborough Gate J 5
80 Marlborough Grove G 6
78 Marlborough House B 7
73 Marlborough Hill B 4
73 Marlborough Pl. B 4
78 Marlborough Rd. B 6
77 Marlborough St. F 6
74 Marle St. F 6
77 Marloes Rd. E 2
70 Marlpit La. H 6
66 Marsh La., Highwood Hill B 3
66 Marsh La., Stanmore B 2
65 Marsh Rd. C 5
67 Marsh Side B 8
74 Marshall St. H 6
80 Marshalsea Rd. C 2
79 Marsham St. E 8
79 Marsland Rd. G 13
75 Mart St. H 9
76 Martin La. H 3
69 Martindale Rd. B 5
78 Marriet Walk D 2
70 Martin Way D 4
76 Mary St. A 2
74 Mary Terrace B 5
67 Maryland Sta. E 9
73 Marylands Rd. E 1
66 Marylebone F 6
73 Marylebone Flyover F 5
74 Marylebone High St. F 4
74 Marylebone La. G 4
74 Marylebone Mews G 4
74 Marylebone Rd. F 2
74 Marylebone Sta. E 2
74 Marylebone St. F 4
68 Mascalls La. B 5
80 Mason St. E 3
71 Masons Hill D 9
80 Massinger St. F 4
79 Mathew Parker St. D 8
75 Matilda St. A 10
78 Maunsel St. E 7
80 Mawbey Place G 6
69 Maybury H 1
67 Mayesbrook Park E 12
66 Mayfair G 6
78 Mayfair Hotel A 5
78 Mayfair Place B 5
75 Maygood St. B 10
68 Mayney Rd. C 2
71 Maypole Rd. F 12
66 Mays La. A 4
67 Maze Hill Sta. H 9
79 Mead Row D 11
79 Meadcroft Rd. H 12
79 Meadow Rd. J 9
80 Meadow Row E 1
74 Meard St. H 7
75 Mecklenburg Place E 9
75 Mecklenburg Sq. E 9
75 Medical College of St. Bartholomew's E 13
78 Medway St. E 7
75 Melbourne Pl. H 10
74 Melbury Terrace E 2
74 Melcombe Place E 2
74 Melcombe St. E 2
70 Melfort Rd. D 6
73 Melina Place D 4
80 Melior St. C 3
80 Menshaw St. E 2
72 Meopham E 6
72 Meopham Green E 6
72 Meopham Sta. D 6
79 Mepham St. B 10
75 Mercer St. H 8
76 Mercers Hall H 2
76 Merchant Taylor's Hall H 3
75 Meredith St. D 12
75 Merlin St. D 11
80 Mermaid Court C 2
75 Mermaid Theatre H 12
80 Merrick Square D 2
80 Merrow St. G 3
65 Merry Hill B 6
65 Merryhill Rd. A 6
70 Merton Park Sta. D 4
70 Merton Rd., SW18 B 4
70 Merton Rd., SW19 C 4
79 Methley St. G 11
78 Metropolitan Police H.Q. D 7
69 Metropolitan Police Training School E 6
79 Metropolitan Tabernacle E 12
79 Meymott St. B 12
76 Micawber St. C 1
77 Micklethwaite Rd. H 1
75 Middle St. F 13
75 Middle Temple La. H 11
74 Middlesex Hosp. F 6
75 Middlesex St. G 5
71 Midfield Way D 12
75 Midland Rd. C 8
77 Milborne Grove G 4
69 Milbourne La. F 6
72 Mildmay Forest G 1
76 Mildmay Miss. Hosp. D 5
67 Mile End Rd. F 8
69 Miles La. G 5
79 Miles Street H 8
75 Milford La. H 10
76 Milk St. G 2
66 Mill Hill B 3
66 Mill Hill (Broadway) Sta. B 3
66 Mill Hill East Sta. C 4
66 Mill Hill G.C. A 3
69 Mill La., Chertsey D 2
68 Mill La., Dagenham G 4
76 Mill Row B 4
80 Mill St. SE1 C 6
74 Mill St. W1 H 5
79 Millbank E 8
79 Millbank Barracks F 8
74 Miller St. B 5
67 Millers La. B 12
75 Millman St. E 10
67 Millwall G 9
67 Millwall Dock G 9
67 Millwall F.C. H 8
77 Milmans St. J 5
78 Milner St. E 2
69 Milton Park C 1
76 Milton St. F 2
79 Milverton St. G 11
80 Mina Rd. G 4
76 Mincing La. H 4
78 Minerva Mews E 4
80 Minnow St. F 4
76 Minories H 5
80 Mint St. C 1
76 Mintern St. B 3
70 Mitcham D 5
70 Mitcham Common D 5
70 Mitcham G.C. D 5
70 Mitcham Junc. Sta. D 5
70 Mitcham La. C 5
70 Mitcham Rd. SW17 C 5
70 Mitcham Rd., Croydon E 6
70 Mitcham Sta. D 5
76 Mitchell St. D 1
71 Mitchley Av. G 7
71 Mitchley Hill G 7
79 Mitre Rd. C 11
76 Mitre St. H 4
66 Moat Mount A 3
69 Molesey Rd. E 5
74 Molyneux St. G 2
79 Monck St. E 7
79 Monkton St. E 11
73 Monmouth Rd. H 2
75 Monmouth St. H 8
80 Monnow Rd. F 6
80 Montagu Close B 2
74 Montagu Mansions F 3
74 Montagu Mews North F 2
74 Montagu Mews South G 2
74 Montagu Mews West G 2
74 Montagu Place G 2
74 Montagu Row F 3
74 Montagu Square G 2
74 Montagu St. G 3
75 Montague Place F 8
67 Montague Rd. B 8
75 Montague St. F 8
76 Montclare St. D 5
79 Montford Place G 11
77 Montpelier Place D 6
77 Montpelier Square D 6
77 Montpelier St. D 6
77 Montpelier Walk D 6
66 Montrose Avenue C 3
78 Montrose Place D 4
76 Monument St. J 3
76 Moor La. EC2 F 2
68 Moor La., Hornchurch C 5
65 Moor La., Rickmansworth B 3
70 Moor La., Surbiton F 2
65 Moor Park G.C. B 4
65 Moor Park Sta. B 4
78 Moore St. E 2
76 Moorfields F 2
76 Moorfields Eye Hosp. D 2
65 Moorfields Rd. D 3
76 Moorgate G 2
73 Moorhouse Rd. G 1
76 Mora Place D 2
72 Morants Ct. Rd. H 1
70 Morden E 4
70 Morden G.C. E 4
70 Morden Hall Rd. D 4
70 Morden Park E 4
70 Morden Rd. D 4
70 Morden Road Halt D 4
70 Morden South Sta. D 4
70 Morden Sta. D 4
80 Morecambe St. F 2
75 Moreland St. D 13
78 Moreton Place G 6
78 Moreton St. G 6
78 Moreton Terrace G 6
80 Morgan's La. B 4
71 Morland Rd. E 7
79 Morley St. D 11
74 Mornington Cres. C 6
74 Mornington Place B 5
74 Mornington St. B 5
74 Mornington Ter. B 5
80 Morocco St. C 4
78 Morpeth Ter. E 6
73 Morshead Rd. D 2
74 Mortimer St. G 6
70 Mortlake B 2
70 Mortlake Rd. A 2
74 Morwell St. G 7
73 Moscow Rd. J 2
78 Mossop St. E 1
70 Mostyn Rd. D 4
78 Motcomb St. D 3
70 Motspur Park D 3
71 Mottingham C 10
71 Mottingham Rd. C 10
75 Mount Pleasant, WC1 E 10
65 Mount Pleasant, Southall F 6
74 Mount Row J 4
74 Mount Royal Hotel H 3
72 Mount Rd. B 4
74 Mount St. J 4
65 Mount Vernon Hospital B 4
74 Moxon St. F 3
76 Mulberry St. G 6
77 Mulberry Walk H 5
70 Mulgrave Rd. F 4
74 Munster Square D 5
80 Munton Rd. E 2
75 Muriel St. B 10
79 Murphy St. D 11
76 Murray Grove C 2
75 Museum of London F 13
75 Museum St. G 8
66 Muswell Hill C 6
66 Muswell Hill G.C. C 6
66 Muswell Hill Park Rd. C 6
75 Myddleton Passage C 11
75 Myddleton Square C 11
75 Myddleton St. D 11
68 Nags Head La. C 4
67 Nags Head Rd. A 8
76 Napier Grove B 2
71 Nash F 9
72 Nash Street D 6
74 Nassau St. F 6
74 National Dental Hospital F 5
79 National Film Theatre B 10
79 National Gallery A 8
74 National Heart Hospital F 4
77 National History Museum E 5
75 National Hospital E 9
67 National Maritime Museum H 9
79 National Theatre B 10
76 Navarre St. D 5
68 Navestock Common A 3
75 Neal St. H 8
66 Neasden E 3
66 Neasden Sta. E 3
80 Neate St. H 4
80 Neckinger D 5
66 Nelson Gdns. C 7
75 Nelson Place C 12
69 Nelson Rd. B 6
79 Nelson Square C 12
75 Nelson Terrace C 12
79 Nelson's Column A 8
66 Nether St. C 4
66 Netherland Rd. A 5
77 Netherton Grove H 4
74 Netley St. D 6
77 Nevern Place F 1
77 Nevern Square F 1
77 Neville St. F 5
71 New Addington F 9
72 New Barn D 5
71 New Barn La., Cudham H 11
72 New Barn La., Swanley Village D 2
71 New Beckenham C 8
71 New Beckenham Sta. C 8
74 New Bond St. H 5
75 New Bridge St. H 12
76 New Broad St. G 3
74 New Burlington St. H 6
74 New Cavendish St. F 5
76 New Change H 1
67 New Charlton G 10
80 New Church Rd. J 2
75 New Compton St. H 8
67 New Cross Gate Sta. H 8
67 New Cross Rd. H 8
67 New Cross Stadium H 8
67 New Cross Sta. H 9
72 New Cut H 1
65 New Denham E 3
71 New Eltham C 10
75 New Fetter La. G 11
69 New Haw F 3
69 New Haw Rd. F 3
76 New Inn St. E 4
76 New Inn Yard E 4
80 New Kent Rd. E 2
70 New King's Rd. A 4
70 New Malden D 3
70 New Malden G.C. D 3
76 New North Place E 4
76 New North Rd. N1 B 2
67 New North Rd., Hainault B 12
75 New North St. F 9
75 New Oxford St. G 8
79 New Palace Yard C 8
74 New Quebec St. H 3
78 New Ride C 2
67 New Rd. E4 B 9
65 New Rd., Croxley Green A 4
68 New Rd., Dagenham F 2
69 New Rd., Littleton D 4
69 New Rd., W. Molesey D 6
75 New Row J 8
66 New Southgate B 6
66 New Southgate & Friern Barnet Sta. B 6
75 New Square G 10
76 New St. G 4
75 New Wharf Rd. B 9
71 New Years La. G 11
69 Newark La. H 2
74 Newburgh St. H 6
79 Newburn St. G 10
67 Newbury Park D 11
75 Newbury St. F 13
73 Newcastle Place F 5
77 Newcombe St. B 2
80 Newcomen St. C 2
73 Newcourt St. C 6
80 Newent Close J 4
75 Newgate St. G 13
67 Newham F 10
67 Newham Way F 10
80 Newhams Row D 4
79 Newington Butts F 12
79 Newington Causeway D 13
79 Newington Cres. F 12
74 Newman Passage G 7
74 Newman St. G 6
75 Newport Place H 8
79 Newport St. F 10
76 Newton Grove B 3
73 Newton Rd. G 2
75 Newton St. G 9
76 Nicholas La. H 3
79 Nicholson St. B 12
70 Nightingale La. B 5
67 Nightingale Rd., Edmonton A 8
70 Nightingale Rd., Wallington E 5
76 Nile St. C 2
80 Nile Terrace G 5
78 Nine Elms La. J 7
68 Noak Hill B 3
68 Noak Hill Rd. B 3
76 Noble St. G 1
65 Nockhill Wood C 2
67 Noel Park C 7
75 Noel Rd. B 12
74 Noel St. G 6
70 Nonsuch Park F 3
76 Norah St. D 7
70 Norbiton D 2
70 Norbiton Sta. D 2
70 Norbury D 6
70 Norbury Cres. D 6
70 Norbury Hill D 6
73 Norfolk Cres. G 6
73 Norfolk Place G 5
79 Norfolk Row E 10
73 Norfolk Rd. A 5
73 Norfolk Square G 5
76 Norman St. D 1
66 North Acton Sta. F 3
74 North Audley St. H 3
73 North Bank D 6
66 North Circular Rd. N3 C 5
66 North Circular Rd. NW2 D 3
66 North Circular Rd. NW10 E 2
67 North Circular Rd., Wood Green B 7
71 North Cray C 12
72 North Cray Rd. C 1
74 North Crescent F 7
75 North Down St. C 9
70 North Cheam E 4
66 North Ealing Sta. F 2
71 North End, Croydon E 7
72 North End, Erith A 2
71 North End La. F 10
66 North End Rd., NW11 D 5
66 North End Rd., W14 G 4
66 North End Way D 5
66 North Finchley B 5
74 North Gower St. D 6
65 North Harrow Sta. D 6
66 North Hill D 6
65 North Hyde G 5
65 North Hyde La. H 5
75 North Mews E 10
66 North Middlesex G.C. B 5
67 North Middlesex Hospital B 7
68 North Ockendon E 5
65 North Orbital Rd. C 2
76 North Place E 6
73 North Ride J 4
66 North Rd. N6 D 6
68 North Rd., Purfleet G 4
68 North Rd., Romford B 2
74 North Row H 3
70 North Sheen Sta. B 2
68 North St. C 2

70 North Sugden Rd. ... E 1
76 North Tenter St. ... H 5
77 North Terrace ... E 6
65 North View ... D 5
66 North Wembley Sta. E 2
74 North West Poly. ... A 5
66 North Western Av. A 1
73 North Wharf Rd. ... G 5
67 North Woolwich . G 11
67 North Woolwich Rd. G 10
75 Northampton Rd. E 11
75 Northampton Sq. D 12
70 Northborough Rd. D 6
75 Northburgh St. ... E 12
66 Northfields Av. ... G 2
66 Northfields Sta. ... G 2
72 Northfleet ... B 6
75 Northington St. ... F 10
65 Northolt ... E 5
65 Northolt Aerodrome E 4
65 Northolt Park ... E 6
65 Northolt Park Sta. . E 6
65 Northolt Rd. ... E 6
71 Northover Rd. ... C 9
76 Northport St. ... B 3
76 Northumberland Alley H 4
79 Northumberland Av. B 8
72 Northumberland Heath ... A 1
67 Northumberland Park Sta. ... C 8
73 Northumberland Place G 1
79 Northumberland St. A 8
73 Northwick Close .. E 5
66 Northwick Park Hospital ... D 1
66 Northwick Park Sta. D 1
73 Northwick Terrace E 4
65 Northwood ... B 4
65 Northwood G.C. ... C 4
65 Northwood Hills Sta. C 5
65 Northwood Rd. ... C 3
76 Norton Folgate ... F 4
76 Norwich Rd. ... A 6
75 Norwich St. ... G 11
71 Norwood ... C 7
65 Norwood Green ... G 6
71 Norwood Junc. Sta. D 7
70 Norwood Rd. SE27 C 6
65 Norwood Rd., Southall G 5
66 Notting Hill ... F 4
77 Notting Hill Gate .. A 1
74 Nottingham Place F 3
74 Nottingham St. ... F 3
74 Nottingham Ter. ... E 3
73 Nugent Terrace ... C 4
71 Nunhead ... A 8
71 Nunhead La. ... A 7
80 Nursery Row ... F 2
74 Nutford Place ... G 2
76 Nuttall St. ... B 4
69 Oak Avenue ... C 5
73 Oak Tree Rd. ... D 5
79 Oakden St. ... E 11
70 Oaken La. ... F 1
65 Oakend Wood ... C 1
72 Oakfield La. ... C 2
73 Oakington Rd. ... E 1
66 Oakleigh Park ... A 5
66 Oakleigh Park South B 5
66 Oakleigh Park Sta. .. A 5
75 Oakley Crescent .. C 12
77 Oakley Gdns. ... H 6
80 Oakley Place ... G 5
74 Oakley Square ... B 6
77 Oakley St. ... H 6
67 Oakwood Hill ... A 11
66 Oakwood Park ... A 6
66 Oakwood Sta. ... A 6
79 Oar St. ... B 13
76 Oat La. ... G 1
69 Oatlands Av. ... F 4
69 Oatlands Chase ... E 4
69 Oatlands Drive ... E 4
69 Oatlands Park ... E 4
79 Occupation Rd. .. G 13
68 Ockendon Rd. ... E 5
69 Ockham Common H 4
69 Ockham La. ... H 3
69 Ockham Park ... H 3
80 Odell St. ... G 5
79 Offley Rd. ... J 11
74 Ogle St. ... F 6
67 Okehampton Cres. H 12
75 Old Bailey ... G 12
74 Old Bond St. ... J 6
76 Old Broad St. ... G 3
77 Old Brompton Rd. F 3
74 Old Burlington St. . J 6
76 Old Castle St. ... G 5
74 Old Cavendish St. . G 5
67 Old Church Rd. E4 B 9
68 Old Church Rd., Romford ... D 2
77 Old Church St. ... G 5
74 Old Compton St. .. H 7
70 Old Coulsdon ... H 6
77 Old Court Place ... C 2
70 Old Deer Park ... A 1
71 Old Farleigh Rd. .. G 8
67 Old Ford Rd. ... E 8
75 Old Gloucester St. . F 9
80 Old Jamaica Rd. .. D 6
76 Old Jewry ... G 2
80 Old Kent Rd. ... F 4
69 Old La. ... H 4
73 Old Marylebone Rd. G 6
76 Old Montague St. . F 6
76 Old Nichol St. ... E 5
79 Old Paradise St. .. E 10
78 Old Park La. ... B 4
78 Old Pye St. ... D 7
74 Old Quebec St. ... H 3
79 Old Queen St. ... C 7
65 Old Redding ... B 6
72 Old Rd. ... B 1
67 Old Royal Observatory H 9
75 Old Seacoal La. .. G 12
76 Old St. ... D 3
79 Old Vic Theatre .. C 11
69 Old Woking Rd. .. G 2
74 Oldbury St. ... F 4
65 Oldfield La. ... F 6
70 Oldfield Rd. ... E 4
80 Olmar St. ... H 6
80 Olney Rd. ... H 1
66 Olympia ... G 4
80 Omeara St. ... B 2
77 Ongar Rd. ... H 1
77 Onslow Gdns. ... F 4
77 Onslow Square ... F 5
79 Ontario St. ... D 13
79 Opal St. ... F 12
74 Open Air Theatre .. D 3
75 Orange St. ... J 7
77 Oratory, The ... E 6
80 Orb St. ... F 2
74 Orchard St. ... H 3
73 Orchardson St. ... E 5
75 Orde Hall St. ... F 9
73 Ordnance Hill ... B 5
67 Orient Football Club D 9
79 Orient St. ... E 12
73 Orme Court ... J 2
73 Orme La. ... J 2
73 Orme Square ... J 2
73 Orme Square Gate . J 2
73 Ormond Yard ... A 6
78 Ormonde Gate ... G 2
76 Ormsby St. ... B 5
71 Orpington ... E 12
71 Orpington Bypass, Orpington ... E 12
71 Orpington Bypass, St. Paul's Cray . D 12
71 Orpington Rd. ... D 11
73 Orsett Mews ... G 3
79 Orsett St. ... F 10
73 Orsett Terrace ... G 3
73 Orsman Rd. ... A 4
76 Osborn St. ... G 6
66 Osidge La. ... A 6
74 Osnaburgh St. ... E 5
73 Ossington St. ... J 2
80 Ossory Rd. ... H 6
74 Ossulston St. ... C 7
77 Osten Mews ... E 3
70 Osterley ... A 1
66 Osterley La. ... G 1
65 Osterley Park ... G 6
69 Osterley Park Ho. . A 6
79 Oswin St. ... E 12
72 Otford ... H 2
72 Otford La. ... G 1
69 Ottershaw ... F 2
79 Otto St. ... H 12
70 Ottways La. ... H 1
74 Outer Circle B 2, D 2, C 4
75 Outram St. ... A 9
70 Outwood La. ... H 4
79 Oval Cricket Ground, The ... H 10
74 Oval Rd. ... A 4
79 Oval Way ... G 10
71 Ovenden Rd. ... H 12
78 Ovington Gdns. ... D 1
78 Ovington Square .. E 2
78 Ovington St. ... E 2
74 Oxendon St. ... J 7
74 Oxford Circus ... G 5
65 Oxford Rd. ... D 1
73 Oxford Square ... H 6
74 Oxford St. ... G 6
65 Oxhey ... A 5
65 Oxhey Drive ... B 5
65 Oxhey La. .. A 5, B 6
71 Oxlea Wood ... A 11
69 Oxshott ... G 6
69 Oyster La. ... G 3
75 Packington St. ... A 13
66 Paddington ... F 5
73 Paddington General Hospital ... F 1
73 Paddington Green . F 5
73 Paddington Recreation Ground ... C 2
73 Paddington Sta. ... G 4
74 Paddington St. ... F 3
68 Padnall Corner ... C 1
79 Page St. ... E 7
80 Page's Walk ... E 4
75 Paget St. ... C 12
67 Painters Rd. ... C 12
75 Pakenham St. ... D 10
73 Palace Court ... J 2
77 Palace Gate ... D 3
77 Palace Gardens Mews B 2
77 Palace Green ... B 2
75 Palace Hotel ... H 9
71 Palace Parade ... C 7
70 Palace Rd. ... B 6
78 Palace St. ... D 6
75 Palace Theatre ... H 8
76 Palissy St. ... D 5
78 Pall Mall ... B 7
79 Pall Mall East ... A 7
74 Palladium Theatre H 6
78 Palmer St. ... D 7
66 Palmer's Green, ... B 6
67 Palmers Green, Southgate Sta. .. C 7
67 Palmerston Rd. .. B 10
70 Pampisford Rd. ... F 6
75 Pancras La. ... H 2
75 Pancras Rd. ... B 7
74 Panton St. ... J 7
73 Parade, The ... J 3
78 Paradise Walk ... H 2
70 Parchmore Rd. ... D 6
80 Pardoner St. ... D 3
76 Parfett St. ... G 7
79 Paris Garden ... B 12
67 Park Avenue ... A 7
74 Park Crescent ... E 5
74 Park Crescent Mews East ... E 5
74 Park Crescent Mews West ... E 4
68 Park Farm Rd. ... E 4
71 Park Hill Rd. ... B 12
71 Park Hospital ... B 9
78 Park La. W1 ... B 4
70 Park La., Ashtead . H 2
67 Park La., Tottenham C 8
78 Park Lane Hotel .. B 5
78 Park Place ... B 6
73 Park Place Villas .. F 4
74 Park Rd. NW1 ... D 1
70 Park Rd., Banstead G 4
71 Park Rd., Fickleshole G 9
69 Park Rd., Stanwell . B 3
70 Park Rd., Teddington C 1
69 Park Rd., Twickenham C 6
66 Park Royal ... F 2
66 Park Royal Sta. ... F 2
70 Park Side ... C 3
74 Park Square East .. E 5
74 Park Square West .. E 4
80 Park St. SE1 ... B 2
74 Park St. W1 ... J 3
74 Park Village East .. B 5
74 Park Village West . B 5
77 Park Walk ... H 4
73 Park West Place ... G 6
65 Park Wood ... C 4
75 Parker St. ... G 9
80 Parker's Row ... C 6
75 Parkfield St. ... B 11
72 Parkfield Wood ... E 4
80 Parkhouse St. ... J 3
71 Parklangley ... D 9
74 Parkway ... A 5
65 Parkway, The ... G 5
66 Parliament Hill ... E 5
79 Parliament Square . C 8
79 Parliament St. ... C 8
76 Parr St. ... B 2
79 Parry St. ... H 9
68 Parsloes Avenue ... E 1
68 Parsloes Park ... E 1
66 Parson St. ... C 4
69 Parvis Rd. ... G 3
79 Pascal St. ... J 8
79 Pasley Rd. ... G 13
78 Passmore Terrace .. F 3
75 Patent Office ... G 11
77 Pater St. ... D 1
75 Paternoster Square G 13
76 Paton St. ... D 1
76 Paul St. ... E 3
77 Paulton's Square .. H 5
77 Paultons St. ... H 5
73 Paveley St. ... D 6
78 Pavilion Rd. ... D 2
68 Pea La. ... E 5
78 Peabody Avenue . G 5
76 Peace St. ... E 7
79 Peacock St. ... F 13
75 Pear Tree Court .. E 11
75 Pear Tree St. ... D 13
79 Pearman St. ... D 11
69 Pears Rd. ... A 6
76 Pearson St. ... B 5
71 Peckham ... A 7
80 Peckham Hill St. .. J 6
80 Peckham Park Rd. . J 6
71 Peckham Rd. ... A 7
71 Peckham Rye ... B 7
71 Peckham Rye Common B 7
71 Peckham Rye Park . B 7
71 Peckham Rye Sta. . A 7
76 Pedley St. ... E 6
77 Peel St. ... B 2
76 Peerless St. ... D 2
77 Pelham Crescent ... F 6
77 Pelham Place ... F 5
77 Pelham St. ... E 5
80 Pelier St. ... H 1
73 Pembridge Gdns. .. J 1
73 Pembridge Place .. H 1
73 Pembridge Rd. ... J 1
73 Pembridge Square .. J 1
73 Pembridge Villas .. H 1
77 Pembroke Close ... C 4
77 Pembroke Place ... D 1
77 Pembroke Rd. W8 . E 1
65 Pembroke Rd., Ruislip D 4
77 Pembroke Square .. E 1
77 Pembroke Villas ... E 1
70 Pen Ponds ... B 2
73 Penfold Place ... F 5
73 Penfold St. ... E 5
71 Penge ... C 7
71 Penge East Sta. ... C 8
71 Penge West Sta. ... C 7
71 Penhill Rd. ... B 12
76 Penn St. ... A 3
80 Pennack Rd. ... H 5
77 Pennant Mews ... E 2
76 Pennington St. ... J 7
79 Penrose Grove ... G 13
79 Penrose St. ... G 13
74 Penryn St. ... B 7
79 Penton Place ... G 13
75 Penton Rise ... C 10
75 Penton St. ... B 10
75 Pentonville Rd. .. C 10
77 Penywern Rd. ... F 2
80 Pepler Rd. ... G 5
70 Pepys Rd. ... D 3
76 Pepys St. ... H 4
75 Percival St. ... D 12
75 Percy Circus ... C 10
73 Percy Rd. NW6 ... C 1
69 Percy Rd., Hampton C 6
69 Percy Rd., Twick. .. B 6
74 Percy St. ... G 7
66 Perivale ... E 2
78 Perkins Rents ... D 7
71 Perry Hill ... C 8
71 Perry St. ... C 11
77 Peter Pan Statue .. A 5
74 Peter St. ... H 7
75 Peters La. ... F 12
70 Petersham ... B 2
77 Petersham La. ... D 3
77 Petersham Mews .. E 4
77 Petersham Place ... D 4
74 Peto Place ... E 5
76 Petticoat Square .. G 5
71 Petts Wood ... D 11
71 Petts Wood Rd. .. D 11
78 Petty France ... D 6
78 Petyward ... F 1
80 Phelp St. ... H 2
77 Philbeach Gdns. ... F 1
67 Philip La. ... C 7
77 Phillimore Gdns. .. D 1
77 Phillimore Place ... D 1
77 Phillimore Walk ... D 1
76 Phillipp St. ... B 4
76 Philpot La. ... H 3
76 Phipp St. ... E 4
75 Phoenix Place ... E 10
74 Phoenix Rd. ... C 7
75 Phoenix St. ... H 8
78 Piccadilly ... B 5
74 Piccadilly Circus ... J 7
74 Piccadilly Hotel ... J 6
74 Piccadilly Theatre .. J 7
75 Pickard St. ... C 13
71 Pickford La. ... A 12
71 Pickhurst La. ... E 9
74 Picton Place ... G 4
68 Pike La. ... E 5
75 Pilgrim St. ... H 12
80 Pilgrimage St. ... D 2
68 Pilgrims Hatch ... A 5
71 Pilgrims Way, Knockholt ... H 12
72 Pilgrims Way, Otford H 2
78 Pimlico Garden ... H 7
78 Pimlico Rd. ... F 4
76 Pinchin St. ... H 6
76 Pindar St. ... F 4
73 Pindock Mews ... E 3
75 Pine St. ... E 11
66 Pinkham Way ... C 6
65 Pinner ... C 5
65 Pinner Green ... C 5
65 Pinner Hill G.C. ... C 5
65 Pinner Hill Rd. ... C 5
65 Pinner Rd. ... D 6
76 Pitfield St. ... C 3
77 Pitt St. ... C 1
78 Pitts Head Mews .. B 4
67 Plaistow ... F 10
71 Plaistow La. ... D 10
67 Plaistow Sta. ... F 10
72 Platt ... H 5
74 Platt St. ... B 7
74 Plender Place ... B 6
74 Plender St. ... B 6
69 Plough La. ... H 5
76 Plough Yard ... E 4
75 Plum Tree Court . G 12
76 Plumbers Row ... G 6
67 Plumstead ... G 11
67 Plumstead Common H 11
67 Plumstead Common Rd. ... H 11
67 Plumstead High St. G 12
67 Plumstead Marshes G 12
67 Plumstead Rd. ... G 11
67 Plumstead Sta. ... G 11
73 Plympton St. ... E 6
79 Pocock St. ... C 12
69 Pointers Rd. ... H 4
72 Pol Hill ... G 1
74 Poland St. ... H 6
66 Police College ... C 3
76 Pollard Row ... D 7
74 Polygon Rd. ... C 7
74 Polytechnic of London F 3
67 Pomeroy St. ... H 8
77 Pond Place ... F 6
67 Ponders End ... A 8
79 Ponsonby Place ... F 9
79 Ponsonby Terrace . F 8
78 Pont St. ... E 2
76 Poole St. ... B 2
80 Pope St. ... D 4
67 Poplar ... F 9
67 Poplar High St. ... F 9
73 Poplar Place ... J 2
73 Porchester Gdns. .. H 3
73 Porchester Place .. H 6
73 Porchester Rd. ... G 2
73 Porchester Square . G 3
73 Porchester Square Mews ... G 3
73 Porchester Terrace H 3
73 Porchester Terrace Gate ... J 3
73 Porchester Terrace North ... G 3
80 Porlock St. ... C 3
68 Porters Avenue ... E 1
73 Porteus Rd. ... F 4
71 Portland Rd. ... D 7
80 Portland St. ... G 3
74 Portman Close ... G 3
74 Portman Hotel ... G 3
74 Portman Mews South H 3
74 Portman Square ... G 3
74 Portman St. ... H 3
69 Portmore Park Rd. E 3
70 Portnalls Rd. ... H 5
75 Portpool La. ... F 11
74 Portsea Place ... H 2
69 Portsmouth Rd., Esher F 6
70 Portsmouth Rd., Thames Ditton .. E 1
69 Portsmouth Rd., Wisley ... H 3
75 Portsmouth St. ... G 10
76 Portsoken St. ... H 5
75 Portugal St. ... H 10
74 Post Office Tower .. F 6
80 Potier St. ... E 3
65 Potter St. ... C 5
80 Potter's Fields ... B 4
65 Potterstreet Hill ... B 5
76 Poultrey ... H 2
71 Pound La. ... G 12
71 Poverest Rd. ... D 11
69 Powdermill La. ... B 5
76 Pownall Rd. ... A 6
69 Poyle ... A 2
70 Poynders Rd. ... B 6
73 Praed St. ... G 5
74 Pratt Mews ... A 6
74 Pratt St. ... A 6
79 Pratt Walk ... E 10
71 Pratt's Bottom ... F 12
76 Prebend St. ... A 1
76 Prescot St. ... H 6
66 Preston ... D 2
66 Preston Rd. ... D 2
66 Preston Rd. Sta. .. D 2
65 Prestwick Rd. ... B 5
79 Price's St. ... B 12
75 Prideaux Place ... D 10
79 Prima Rd. ... J 11
66 Primrose Hill ... E 5
66 Primrose Hill Sta. .. E 5
76 Primrose St. ... F 4
74 Prince Albert Rd. .. B 2
75 Prince Charles Theatre H 7
77 Prince Consort Rd. D 4
77 Prince of Wales Gate C 6
74 Prince of Wales Theatre ... J 7
67 Prince Regents La. F 10
76 Princelet St. ... F 5
70 Princes Coverts ... G 1
77 Prince's Gdns. ... D 5
77 Prince's Gate ... C 5
77 Prince's Gate Mews D 5
73 Princes Mews ... H 2
72 Princes Rd. ... B 2
73 Princes Square ... H 2
76 Princes St. ... G 2
77 Princess Beatrice Hospital ... G 2
73 Princess Rd. ... C 1
75 Princeton St. ... F 10
80 Prioress St. ... E 3
70 Priory La. ... B 3
66 Priory Rd. ... C 6
77 Priory Walk ... G 4

76 Pritchards Rd. . . . . B 7
80 Priter Rd. . . . . D 6
75 Procter St. . . . . F 9
75 Provence St. . . . . . B 13
76 Provost St. . . . . C 2
69 Pryford Rd. . . . . . . G 2
75 Public Record Office G 11
75 Public Trustee Office G 9
76 Pudding La. EC3 . . J 3
67 Pudding La., Chigwell A 12
75 Puddle Dock . . . . H 12
72 Puddledock La. . . . C 1
80 Purbrook St. . . . . . D 4
76 Purcell St. . . . . B 4
74 Purchese Rd. . . . . . C 7
68 Purfleet . . . . G 4
68 Purfleet Bypass . . . . G 4
68 Purfleet Rd. . . . . . . G 4
70 Purley . . . . G 6
71 Purley Downs . . . . G 7
71 Purley Downs G.C. G 7
71 Purley Downs Rd. . G 7
71 Purley Oaks Sta. . . F 7
80 Purley Rd. . . . . J 7
70 Purley Way . . . . E 6
70 Putney . . . . B 3
70 Putney Bridge . . . . . A 4
70 Putney Bridge Rd. . B 4
70 Putney Heath . . . . . . B 3
70 Putney High St. . . B 4
70 Putney Hill . . . . B 4
70 Putney Sta. . . . . B 4
69 Pyrcroft . . . . E 2
69 Pyrford . . . . H 2
69 Pyrford Common Rd. H 2
68 Pyrgo Park . . . . B 3
76 Quaker St. . . . . E 5
79 Queen Alexandra Military Hospital F 8
74 Queen Anne Mews G 5
74 Queen Anne St. . . . G 4
78 Queen Anne's Gate D 7
77 Queen Elizabeth College . . . . C 1
79 Queen Elizabeth Hall B 10
70 Queen Elizabeth Hospital . . . . H 4
80 Queen Elizabeth St. C 5
69 Queen Elizabeth II Res. E 5
69 Queen Mary Res. . . D 3
74 Queen Mary's Gardens D 3
71 Queen Mary's Hospital C 12
70 Queen Mary's Hospital for Children . . . . . F 5
75 Queen Square . . . . . F 9
76 Queen St. EC4 . . . . H 2
78 Queen St. W1 . . . . B 5
78 Queen Victoria Memorial . . . . . . C 6
75 Queen Victoria St. H 13
74 Queen's College . . . G 4
73 Queen's Gdns. . . . . H 4
77 Queen's Gate . . . . . D 4
77 Queen's Gate Gdns. E 4
77 Queen's Gate Mews D 4
77 Queen's Gate Place E 4
77 Queen's Gate Place Mews . . . . E 4
77 Queen's Gate Ter. . D 4
73 Queen's Grove . . . . A 5
75 Queen's Head St. . A 12
73 Queen's Mews . . . . H 2
66 Queen's Park Rangers F.C. . . . . G 4
66 Queen's Park Sta. . . F 4
67 Queen's Rd. SE15 . H 8
70 Queen's Rd., Richmond . . . . . . B 2
70 Queens Rd., Teddington . . . . . C 1
69 Queens Rd., Weybridge . . . . . . F 4
67 Queen's Rd., Peckham Sta. . . . H 8
70 Queen's Rd. Sta. . . . A 5
80 Queen's Row . . . . . H 2
73 Queen's Terrace . . . B 5
74 Queen's Theatre . . H 7
66 Queen's Wood . . . . D 6
77 Queensberry Way . E 5
73 Queensborough Ter. H 3
76 Queensbridge Rd. . B 6
66 Queensbury . . . . C 2
77 Queensbury Place . E 4
70 Queensmere Rd. . . C 4
78 Queenstown Rd. . . . J 4
73 Queensway . . . . H 3
75 Quick St. . . . . C 12
80 Quilp St. . . . . C 2
76 Quilter St. . . . . C 6
77 Racton Rd. . . . . H 1
77 Radley Mews . . . . . E 2
73 Radnor Mews . . . . H 5
73 Radnor Place . . . . . H 6
80 Radnor Rd. . . . . . . J 6
76 Radnor St. . . . . D 2
79 Radnor Terrace . . . J 9
78 Radnor Walk . . . . . G 2
71 Rag Hill . . . . H 10
80 Railway Approach . B 3
76 Railway Place . . . . H 4
75 Railway St. . . . . C 9
80 Rainbow St. . . . . . . J 4
68 Rainham . . . . F 3
68 Rainham Marshes . F 3
68 Rainham Rd. . . . . . . E 2
73 Rainsford St. . . . . . G 6
75 Raleigh St. . . . . . . B 13
80 Ralph St. . . . . D 2
74 Ramillies Place . . . . H 6
74 Ramillies St. . . . . . . H 6
78 Rampayne St. . . . . G 7
76 Ramsey St. . . . . D 6
79 Randall Road . . . . . F 9
79 Randall Row . . . . . F 9
70 Randalls Rd. . . . . . . H 1
73 Randolph Avenue . D 3
73 Randolph Crescent E 3
73 Randolph Gdns. . . . C 2
73 Randolph Mews . . . E 4
73 Randolph Rd. . . . . . E 4
73 Ranelagh Bridge . . . G 3
78 Ranelagh Gardens . G 4
78 Ranelagh Grove . . . F 4
67 Rangers Rd. . . . . . A 10
73 Ranston St. . . . . . . F 6
78 Raphael St. . . . . C 2
74 Rathbone Place . . . G 7
74 Rathbone St. . . . . . G 7
71 Ravensbourne Sta. . D 9
66 Ravenscourt Park G 3
66 Ravenscourt Pk. Sta. G 4
76 Ravenscroft St. . . . C 5
79 Ravensdon St. . . . G 11
76 Ravey St. . . . . E 4
78 Rawlings St. . . . . . . F 2
75 Rawstorne St. . . . D 12
75 Ray St. . . . . E 11
65 Rayners La. . . . . . . D 6
70 Raynes Park . . . . . . D 3
70 Raynes Park Sta. . . D 3
76 Rector St. . . . . A 1
69 Rectory La., Byfleet G 3
67 Rectory La., Loughton A 11
70 Rectory La., Mitcham C 5
70 Rectory La., Sutton G 5
67 Rectory Rd. Sta. . . . E 8
70 Red La. . . . . F 1
80 Red Lion Row . . . . H 2
75 Red Lion Square . . F 9
75 Red Lion St. . . . . . F 10
71 Red Lodge Rd. . . . E 9
74 Red Place . . . . H 3
73 Redan Place . . . . . H 2
67 Redbridge . . . . C 12
67 Redbridge La. . . . D 10
67 Redbridge Sta. . . . D 10
78 Redburn St. . . . . . . G 2
76 Redchurch St. . . . . . E 5
77 Redcliffe Gdns. . . . G 3
77 Redcliffe Mews . . . G 3
77 Redcliffe Place . . . . H 3
77 Redcliffe Rd. . . . . . G 4
77 Redcliffe Square . . G 2
77 Redcliffe St . . . . . . H 3
80 Redcross Way . . . . C 2
78 Redesdale St. . . . . . G 2
77 Redfield La. . . . . . . E 2
69 Redhill Rd. . . . . G 4
74 Redhill St. . . . . C 5
80 Redmead La. . . . . . . B 6
77 Reece Mews . . . . . . F 4
68 Reede Rd. . . . . E 2
79 Reedworth St. . . . . F 11
76 Rees St. . . . . A 2
74 Reeves Mews . . . . . J 4
74 Regal La. . . . . A 4
76 Regan Way . . . . C 4
78 Regency St. . . . . E 7
74 Regent Palace Hotel J 6
75 Regent Square . . . . D 9
74 Regent St. . . . . H 6
74 Regent's Park . . . . . C 3
74 Regent's Park Barracks . . . . C 5
66 Regent's Park Rd. N3 C 4
74 Regent's Park Rd. NW1 . . . . A 4
76 Regents Row . . . . . A 6
70 Reigate Avenue . . . E 4
70 Reigate Rd. . . . . . . G 3
75 Remington St. . . . C 12
75 Remnant St. . . . . . . G 9
79 Renfrew Rd. . . . . . F 12
79 Rennie St. . . . . A 12
80 Rephidim St. . . . . . D 3
77 Reston Place . . . . . D 3
80 Reveroy Rd. . . . . . . F 6
78 Rex Place . . . . A 4
75 Rheidol Terrace . . B 13
78 Richard's Place . . . E 1
65 Richings Park . . . . G 2
70 Richmond . . . . B 2
70 Richmond Bridge . . B 1
70 Richmond Gate . . . B 2
70 Richmond G.C. . . . . C 2
74 Richmond Mews . . H 7
70 Richmond Park . . . B 2
70 Richmond Park Public G.C. . . . . B 3
70 Richmond Rd. . . . . C 2
79 Richmond Terrace C 8
77 Rickett St. . . . . H 1
71 Ricketts Hill Rd. . H 10
65 Rickmansworth . . . A 3
65 Rickmansworth Rd., Croxley Green . . A 4
65 Rickmansworth Rd.. Harefield . . . . C 3
70 Riddlesdown Rd. . . G 6
71 Riddlesdown Sta. . G 7
67 Ridge Avenue . . . . . A 7
70 Ridge Rd. . . . . E 4
72 Ridge Wood . . . . . . F 6
74 Ridgmount Gdns. . F 7
74 Ridgmount St. . . . . F 7
67 Ridgeway . . . . B 9
70 Ridgway . . . . C 3
74 Riding House St. . . G 6
80 Riley Rd. . . . . D 4
77 Riley St. . . . . J 5
73 Ring, The . . . . H 4
69 Ripley . . . . H 3
68 Ripple Rd. . . . . E 1
79 Rita Rd. . . . . J 9
75 Ritchie St. . . . . B 11
78 Ritz Hotel . . . . B 6
75 River St. . . . . C 11
79 Riverwalk Gdns. . . G 8
76 Rivington St. . . . . . D 4
74 Robert Adam St. . . G 3
74 Robert Mews . . . . . D 6
74 Robert St. . . . . D 5
76 Roberta St. . . . . D 6
70 Robin Hood Gate . C 3
70 Robin Hood Way . C 3
78 Rochester Row . . . . E 6
78 Rochester St. . . . . . E 7
71 Rochester Way, SE9 A 10
72 Rochester Way, Bexley B 1
75 Rockcliffe St. . . . . C 12
80 Rockingham St. . . . E 1
67 Roding La. E18 . . C 10
67 Roding La., Buckhurst Hill . . . . B 11
67 Roding Lane South C 10
67 Roding Valley . . . B 10
74 Rodmarton St. . . . . G 3
80 Rodney Place . . . . . E 2
80 Rodney Rd. . . . . . . F 2
75 Rodney St. . . . . . . B 10
70 Roehampton . . . . . . B 3
70 Roehampton Gate . B 3
70 Roehampton G.C. . B 3
70 Roehampton Vale . C 3
75 Roger St. . . . . E 10
77 Roland Gdns. . . . . G 4
77 Roland Way . . . . . . G 4
80 Rolls Rd. . . . . F 5
72 Roman Villa Rd. . . C 3
68 Romford . . . . D 2
68 Romford G.C. . . . . C 3
68 Romford Rd., Aveley F 4
68 Romford Rd., Chadwell Heath D 1
68 Romford Rd., Chigwell Row . . . B 1
67 Romford Rd., Ilford D 11
67 Romford Rd., Stratford . . . . . . E 10
75 Romilly St. . . . . H 7
79 Romney St. SW1 . . E 8
72 Romney Street, Kent G 3
76 Rood La. . . . . H 4
74 Roosevelt Memorial H 4
76 Ropemaker St. . . . . F 2
77 Rosary Gdns. . . . . . F 4
76 Roscoe St. . . . . E 2
80 Rose Alley . . . . A 1
70 Rose Hill . . . . E 4
68 Rose La. . . . . C 1
75 Rosebery Avenue . E 11
78 Rosemoor St. . . . . . F 2
71 Rosendale Rd. . . . . B 7
75 Rosoman St. . . . . D 11
74 Rossmore Rd. . . . . E 1
79 Rotary St. . . . . D 12
67 Rotherhithe . . . . . . G 8
67 Rotherhithe New Rd. G 8
67 Rotherhithe St. . . . G 8
80 Rothsay St. . . . . D 3
78 Rotten Row . . . . . . C 2
80 Rouel Rd. . . . . E 6
77 Round Pond . . . . . . B 3
70 Roundshaw . . . . F 6
67 Roundway, The . . . C 7
79 Roupell St. . . . . . . B 11
65 Rousebarn La. . . . . A 4
69 Row Hill . . . . F 2
69 Row Town . . . . F 2
70 Rowan Rd. . . . . D 6
80 Rowcross St. . . . . . G 5
76 Rowland St. . . . . . . F 7
66 Rowley Bank . . . . . A 3
66 Rowley La. . . . . A 3
66 Roxeth . . . . D 1
65 Roxeth Green Av. . D 6
74 Royal Academy of Arts . . . . J 6
74 Royal Academy of Music . . . . E 4
66 R.A.F. Museum . . . C 3
67 Royal Albert Dock G 11
77 Royal Albert Hall . C 4
79 Royal Army Medical College . . . . F 8
78 Royal Automobile Club . . . . B 7
78 Royal Avenue . . . . G 2
70 Royal Botanical Gardens . . . . A 2
77 Royal Cancer Hospital F 5
77 Royal College of Art D 5
77 Royal College of Music D 5
74 Royal College of Physicians . . . . . . E 5
77 Royal College of Science . . . . D 5
75 Royal College of Surgeons . . . . . . G 10
74 Royal College St. . . B 7
75 Royal Courts of Justice . . . . H 10
74 Royal Ear Hospital E 7
76 Royal Exchange . . H 3
79 Royal Eye Hospital D 12
79 Royal Festival Hall B 10
75 Royal Free Hospital, N1 . . . . A 11
75 Royal Free Hospital, WC1 . . . . D 10
77 Royal Geographical Society . . . . C 5
78 Royal Horticultural Society Hall . . . . E 7
78 Royal Hospital . . . . G 3
78 Royal Hospital Rd. G 3
74 Royal Institute of British Architects F 5
73 Royal Lancaster Hotel H 5
78 Royal Mews, The . . D 5
67 Royal Military Academy . . . . H 11
69 Royal Military School of Music . . . . B 6
76 Royal Mint . . . . J 5
76 Royal Mint St. . . . . J 5
67 Royal Naval College G 9
75 Royal Opera House H 9
79 Royal Rd. . . . . H 12
74 Royal Society . . . . . J 6
79 Royal St. . . . . D 10
74 Royal Veterinary College . . . . A 7
67 Royal Victoria Dock G 10
79 Royal Waterloo Hospital . . . . . . B 10
70 Royal Wimbledon G.C. . . . . C 3
74 Royle St. . . . . H 6
65 Royston Park . . . . . B 6
67 Ruckholt Rd. . . . . . E 9
73 Rudolf Rd. . . . . C 2
76 Rufus St. . . . . D 4
70 Rugby Union Football Ground . . . . B 1
65 Ruislip . . . . D 4
65 Ruislip Common . . C 4
65 Ruislip Gardens Sta. E 5
65 Ruislip G.C. . . . . . . D 4
65 Ruislip Lido . . . . . . C 4
65 Ruislip Manor Sta. D 5
65 Ruislip Rd. . . . . F 6
80 Runham St. . . . . . . G 3
74 Rupert St. . . . . H 7
68 Rush Green . . . . . . D 2
68 Rush Green Rd. . . D 2
70 Rushett La. . . . . . . G 1
71 Rushey Green . . . . . B 8
71 Rushmore Hill Rd. G 12
76 Rushton St. . . . . B 3
79 Rushworth St. . . . C 12
71 Ruskin Park . . . . . . B 7
75 Russell Hotel . . . . . E 8
66 Russell La. . . . . B 5
75 Russell Square . . . . F 8
75 Russell St. . . . . H 9
80 Rust Square . . . . . . J 2
78 Rutherford St. . . . . E 7
77 Rutland Gdns. . . . . C 6
77 Rutland Gate . . . . . C 6
77 Rutland Mews . . . . D 6
77 Rutland St. . . . . D 6
79 Rutley Close . . . . H 12
69 Ruxbury Rd. . . . . . E 2
70 Ruxley La. . . . . F 2
69 Rydens Rd. . . . . E 5
78 Ryder St. . . . . B 6
73 Ryders Terrace . . . . B 3
71 Rye La. . . . . A 7
74 Sackville St. . . . . J 6
75 Saffron Hill . . . . . . F 11
75 Saffron St. . . . . F 11
79 Sail St. . . . . E 10
79 St. Agnes Place . . H 12
77 St. Alban's Grove . D 3
74 St. Alban's St. . . . . . J 7
76 St. Alphage Gdn. . . F 2
75 St. Andrew St. . . . G 11
75 St. Andrew's Gdns. D 10
75 St. Andrew's Hill . H 12
67 St. Ann's Rd. N15 . D 7
69 St. Ann's Rd., Chertsey . . . . E 2
79 St. Ann's St. . . . . . . D 7
73 St. Ann's Terrace B 5
78 St. Barnabas St. . . . F 4
75 St. Bartholomew's Hospital . . . . . . G 12
66 St. Bernard's Hanwell Hospital . . . . G 1
76 St. Botolph St. . . . . G 5
75 St. Bride St. . . . . . G 12
75 St. Chad St. . . . . . . C 9
75 St. Chad's Place . . . C 9
76 St. Clare St. . . . . . . H 5
75 St. Clement Dane's Church . . . . H 10
76 St. Clement's Church H 3
75 St. Clement's La. . H 10
75 St. Cross St. . . . . . F 11
71 St. Denham Hill . . C 7
76 St. Dunstan's Hill . J 4
74 St. Edmund's Ter. . B 2
79 St. Gabriel St. . . . . E 12
74 St. George St. . . . . . H 5
69 St. George's Av. . . . F 4
79 St. George's Cathedral D 11
79 St. George's Circus D 12
78 St. George's Drive . F 5
75 St. George's Gdns. D 9
69 St. George's Hill G.C. F 4
78 St. George's Hospital C 4
79 St. George's Rd. . D 12
78 St. George's Square G 7
80 St. George's Way . . H 4
75 St. Giles High St. . . G 8
75 St. Helena St. . . . . D 11
76 St. Helen's Place . . G 4
70 St. Helier . . . . E 5
70 St. Helier Avenue . E 4
70 St. Helier Hospital . E 4
70 St. Helier Sta. . . . . . E 4
67 St. Jame's Street Sta. D 8
74 St. James's Terrace Mews . . . . B 2
78 St. James's . . . . B 6
70 St. James's Drive . . B 5
78 St. James's Palace . . B 6
78 St. James's Park . . . C 7
78 St. James's Place . . . B 6
80 St. James's Rd. SE16 E 7
71 St. James's Rd., Croydon . . . . . . E 7
75 St. James's Row . . E 12
78 St. James's Square . B 7
78 St. James's St. . . . . B 6
75 St. John St. . . . . . . D 12
70 St. John's Hill . . . . B 5
75 St. John's La. . . . . F 12
75 St. John's Square . E 12
67 St. John's Sta. . . . . H 9
66 St. John's Wood . . . F 5
73 St. John's Wood Barracks . . . . B 5
73 St. John's Wood High St. . . . . C 5
73 St. John's Wood Park A 5
73 St. John's Wood Rd. D 5
73 St. John's Wood Terrace . . . . B 6
80 St. Katherine's Way B 6
67 St. Leonard St. . . . . F 9
76 St. Leonard's Hospital B 4
78 St. Leonard's Ter. . G 2
78 St. Loo Avenue . . . H 2
77 St. Luke's Hospital G 6
77 St. Luke's St. . . . . . G 6
79 St. Margaret St. . . D 8
70 St. Margarets . . . . . B 1
79 St. Margaret's Church D 8
75 St. Mark's Hospital C 13
75 St. Martins in the Fields Church . . . J 8
75 St. Martin's La. . . . J 8
75 St. Martin's le Grand G 13
79 St. Martin's Place . A 8
75 St. Martin's St. . . . . J 8
75 St. Martin's Theatre H 8
77 St. Mary Abbots Hospital . . . . E 2
76 St. Mary at Hill . . . . J 3
76 St. Mary Axe . . . . . G 4
71 St. Mary Cray . . . . D 12
76 St. Mary-le-Bow Church . . . . H 2
79 St. Mary's Gdns. E 11
73 St. Mary's Hospital, W2 . . . . G 5
68 St. Mary's La. D 4, D 5
70 St. Mary's Rd. . . . . E 1
73 St. Mary's Terrace . F 4
79 St. Mary's Walk . . E 11

78 St. Matthew St. . . D 7
76 St. Matthew's Row D 6
73 St. Michael's St. . . G 5
71 St. Mildred's Rd. . . B 9
79 St. Oswald Place . G 10
74 St. Pancras Gardens
      B 7
74 St. Pancras Hospital
      B 7
75 St. Pancras Sta. . . . . C 8
74 St. Pancras Way . . A 7
76 St. Paul St. . . . . . . A 1
75 St. Paul's Cathedral
      H 13
75 St. Paul's Churchyard
      H 13
71 St. Paul's Cray . . D 12
71 St. Paul's Cray Rd.
      D 11
75 St. Paul's Pier . . . . J 12
67 St. Paul's Rd. . . . . E 7
79 St. Paul's Terrace H 12
71 St. Paul's Wood Hill
      D 11
76 St. Peter's Avenue . C 6
76 St. Peter's Close. . . C 7
75 St. Peter's St. . . . B 12
73 St. Petersburgh Mews
      J 2
73 St. Petersburgh Pl. . J 2
76 St. Philip Way . . . A 2
66 St. Quintin Av. . . . F 4
73 St. Stephen's Gdns. G 1
77 St. Stephen's Hospital
      H 4
65 St. Thomas Drive . C 5
80 St. Thomas St. . . . . B 3
79 St. Thomas's Hospital
      D 9
79 Salamanca St. . . . . . F 9
73 Sale Place. . . . . G 6
73 Salem Rd. . . . . H 2
75 Salisbury Court . . H 12
74 Salisbury Place . . . . F 2
80 Salisbury Row . . . . F 3
73 Salisbury St. . . . . . . E 6
66 Salmon St. . . . . D 3
71 Salmons La. . . . . . . H 7
73 Samford St. . . . . . . E 5
79 Sancroft St. . . . . . F 10
80 Sanctuary St. . . . . . C 2
71 Sanderstead . . . . . . G 7
71 Sanderstead Hill . . G 7
71 Sanderstead Rd. . . . F 7
71 Sanderstead Sta. . . . F 7
80 Sandford Row . . . . G 3
71 Sandhurst Rd. . . . . B 9
75 Sandland St. . . . . . F 10
80 Sandover Rd. . . . . . C 4
69 Sandown Park Race
      Course . . . . E 6
75 Sandwich St. . . . . . D 8
68 Sandy La., Dagenham
      G 4
69 Sandy La., Esher . G 5
70 Sandy La.,
      Twickenham. . . . D 1
70 Sandy Lane South . F 6
65 Sandy Lodge G.C. B 4
65 Sandy Lodge La.
      B 4
65 Sandy Lodge Rd. . B 4
76 Sandy Row . . . . F 4
70 Sandycombe Rd. . . A 2
71 Sangley Rd. . . . . . . B 9
75 Sans Walk . . . . . . E 12
73 Sardinia St. . . . . G 9
79 Saunders St. . . . . . E 10
76 Savage Gdns. . . . . . H 4
74 Saville Row . . . . . . J 6
75 Savoy Hill . . . . J 9
75 Savoy Place . . . . . . J 9
75 Savoy St. . . . . J 9
75 Savoy Theatre . . . . J 9
79 Sawyer St. . . . . . . C 13
71 Scadbury Park . . C 11
74 Scala St. . . . . F 6
76 Scarborough St. . . . H 5
80 Scarsdale Rd. . . . . . H 4
77 Scarsdale Villas . . . E 1
69 School La. . . . . F 2
75 School of Arts &
      Crafts. . . . . F 9
77 Science Museum . . D 5
75 Sclater St. . . . . D 6
79 Scoresby St. . . . . . B 12
71 Scotshall La. . . . . . G 9
73 Scott Ellis Gdns. . . D 5
80 Scott Lidgett Cres. . D 6

71 Scotts La. . . . . D 9
71 Scotts Lodge . . . . H 11
66 Scovell Rd. . . . . C 4
66 Scratchwood. . . . . . A 3
66 Scrubs La. . . . . F 4
76 Scrutton St. . . . . . . E 3
72 Scudders Hill . . . . . D 4
75 Seacoal La. . . . . . . G 12
77 Seagrave Rd. . . . . . H 1
80 Seal . . . . H 3
80 Searles Rd. . . . . E 3
80 Sears St. . . . . J 2
78 Sebastian St. . . . . . D 12
79 Secker St. . . . . B 11
80 Secretan Rd. . . . . . . H 4
78 Sedding St. . . . . F 3
71 Sedlescombe Rd. . . H 1
75 Seething La. . . . . . . J 4
76 Sekforde St. . . . . . E 12
76 Selby St. . . . . E 7
71 Selhurst. . . . . D 7
71 Selhurst Rd. . . . . . . D 7
79 Sellow Mews. . . . . F 10
74 Selous St. . . . . A 6
71 Selsdon . . . . F 8
71 Selsdon Park G.C. . G 7
71 Selsdon Park Rd. . . F 8
71 Selsdon Rd. . . . . . . F 7
71 Selsdon Sta. . . . . . . F 7
71 Selsdon Wood. . . . . G 8
77 Selwood Place . . . . G 5
77 Selwood Terrace . . . G 5
78 Semley Place. . . . . . F 4
75 Senate House . . . . . F 8
73 Senior St. . . . . F 2
77 Serle St. . . . . G 10
77 Serpentine, The . . B 6
77 Serpentine Bridge. . B 5
78 Serpentine Rd. . . . . B 2
80 Setchell Rd. . . . . . . E 5
76 Settles Rd. . . . . G 7
75 Seven Dials . . . . . . H 8
67 Seven Kings . . . . . D 12
67 Seven Sisters Rd. . . D 7
67 Seven Sisters Sta. . . C 7
71 Sevenoaks Rd. . . . . F 12
69 Severnhills Rd. . . . . F 4
78 Seville St. . . . . C 3
73 Sevington St. . . . . . E 2
75 Seward St. . . . . . . D 13
67 Sewardstone Rd. . . A 9
67 Sewardstonebury . . A 9
74 Seymour Hall. . . . . G 2
74 Seymour Mews . . . G 3
74 Seymour Place . . . . G 2
74 Seymour St. . . . . . . H 2
74 Seymour Walk . . . . H 4
80 Shad Thames . . . . . C 5
74 Shaftesbury Av. . . . H 7
76 Shaftesbury St. . . . . C 2
77 Shalcomb St. . . . . . H 4
80 Shand St. . . . . C 4
68 Sharsted St. . . . . . . G 12
71 Shaw La. . . . . H 7
78 Shawfield St. . . . . . G 2
70 Sheen Common. . . . B 2
70 Sheen Rd. . . . . B 2
69 Sheerwater Rd. . . . . G 2
77 Sheffield Terrace . . B 2
77 Sheldrake Place . . . C 1
71 Shelleys Hill . . . . . H 11
76 Shelton St. . . . . H 8
68 Shenfield . . . . A 6
66 Shenley Rd. . . . . . . A 2
78 Shepherd Market. . B 5
78 Shepherd St. . . . . . . B 4
76 Shepherdess Walk . C 2
67 Shepherd's Bush . . G 4
66 Shepherd's Bush Rd.
      G 4
66 Shepherds Hill . . . . D 6
69 Shepperton . . . . . . E 4
69 Shepperton Rd. . . . D 3
74 Sheraton St. . . . . . . H 7
76 Sherborne La. . . . . . H 3
71 Sherwood Park Av.
      B 12
71 Ship Hill. . . . . H 10
68 Ship La., Aveley. . . F 5
72 Ship La., Dartford . D 3
72 Shipton St. . . . . C 6
71 Shire La. . . F 10, F 11
73 Shirehall Rd. . C 2, C 3
73 Shirland Rd. . . . . . . E 2
71 Shirley. . . . . E 8
71 Shirley Park G.C. . E 7
71 Shirley Rd. . . . . E 8
75 Shoe La. . . . . G 11
67 Shooter's Hill. . . . H 11

67 Shooter's Hill G.C.
      H 11
67 Shooter's Hill Rd. H 10
67 Shoreditch. . . . . E 7
76 Shoreditch High St. E 4
76 Shoreditch Park. . . B 2
72 Shoreham . . . . G 2
80 Shorncliffe Rd. . . . . G 5
79 Short St. . . . . C 11
71 Shortlands . . . . D 9
75 Short's Gdns. . . . . . H 8
71 Shortlands G.C. . . . D 9
71 Shortlands Rd. . . . . D 9
71 Shortlands Sta. . . . . D 9
73 Shroton St. . . . . D 9
74 Shouldham St. . . . . G 2
73 Shrewsbury Mews . G 1
73 Shrewsbury Rd. . . . G 1
73 Shroton St. . . . . F 6
71 Sidcup . . . . C 11
71 Sidcup Bypass . . . . C 11
71 Sidcup G.C. . . . . . C 12
71 Sidcup Hill . . . . . . C 12
71 Sidcup Rd. . . . . . . C 11
74 Siddons La. . . . . . . E 2
79 Sidford Place . . . E 10
75 Sidmouth St. . . . . . D 9
70 Sidmouth Wood. . . B 2
79 Silex St. . . . . C 12
67 Silver St. . . . . B 7
67 Silver Street Sta. . . B 7
70 Silver Thorne Rd. . A 5
67 Silvertown. . . . . . . G 10
67 Silvertown Way . . F 10
76 Singer St. . . . . D 3
79 Single St. . . . . G 11
65 Sipson . . . . H 4
65 Sipson Rd. . . . . G 4
69 Sixth Cross Rd. . . . C 5
71 Skeet Hill La. . . . . E 12
71 Skibbs La. . . . . . . E 12
76 Skinner La. . . . . . . H 2
76 Skinner St. . . . . . . D 11
76 Skinners Hall . . . . H 2
72 Slade Green . . . . . A 2
71 Slaidburn St. . . . . . J 4
71 Slines New Rd. . . . H 8
71 Slines Oak Rd. . . . H 8
71 Slingsby Place . . . . H 8
78 Sloane Avenue . . . . F 1
78 Sloane Court East . G 3
78 Sloane Court West . G 3
78 Sloane Gardens . . . F 3
78 Sloane Square. . . . . F 3
78 Sloane St. . . . . D 2
78 Sloane Terrace . . . F 3
65 Slough . . . . G 1
78 Smith Square . . . . E 8
78 Smith St. . . . . G 2
78 Smith Terrace . . . . G 2
70 Smitham Sta. . . . . . G 6
75 Smithfield Central
      Market. . . . . F 12
75 Smithfield St. . . . . G 12
80 Smyrk's Rd. . . . . . . G 4
67 Snaresbrook . . . . . C 10
67 Snaresbrook Rd. . . C 9
75 Snow Hill . . . . . . G 12
78 Snowden St. . . . . . . F 4
80 Snowfields. . . . . . . C 3
66 Soho. . . . . F 6
74 Soho Square. . . . . . G 7
74 Soho St. . . . . G 7
73 Somers Cres. . . . . . H 6
73 Somers Mews. . . . . G 6
66 Somers Town . . . . . F 6
75 Somerset House . . H 10
80 Sondes St. . . . . H 3
66 South Acton Sta. . . G 3
79 South Africa House A 8
74 South Audley St. . . H 7
67 South Bermondsey Sta.
      G 8
77 South Bolton Gdns. G 5
74 South Crescent . . . . F 7
70 South Croydon. . . . F 6
71 South Croydon Sta. F 7
71 South Croxted Rd. . C 7
72 South Darenth . . . . D 3
66 South Ealing Rd. . . G 2
66 South Ealing Sta. . . G 2
78 South Eaton Place . E 4
71 South Eden Park . . D 8
71 South End, SE9 . . B 11
77 South End, W8. . . . D 2
71 South End, Croydon F 7
68 South End Rd. . . . . E 3
77 South End Row . . . D 2
66 South Greenford Halt
      F 1

66 South Hampstead Sta.
      E 5
65 South Harrow . . . . C 1
66 South Herts G.C. . A 5
68 South Hornchurch.
      E 3
66 South Kenton Sta. . D 2
79 South Lambeth Rd. H 9
70 South La. . . . . E 3
70 South Merton Sta. . D 4
74 South Molton La. . H 4
74 South Molton St. . . H 4
71 South Norwood. . . . D 7
71 South Norwood Hill
      D 7
68 South Ockendon . . F 5
69 South Oxhey. . . . . . B 5
77 South Parade . . . . . G 5
67 South Park Drive E 12
76 South Place. . . . . . . F 3
65 South Ruislip Sta. . E 5
68 South Stifford . . . . H 5
70 South St., W1. . . . . A 4
72 South Street,
      Meopham . . . . . . F 6
67 South St., Ponders End
      A 8
68 South St., Romford D 2
76 South Tenter St. . . H 5
77 South Terrace . . . . . E 6
67 South Tottenham Sta.
      D 7
68 South Weald. . . . . . B 4
68 South Weald Common
      B 4
73 South Wharf Rd. . . G 5
67 South Woodford Sta.
      C 10
65 Southall. . . . . G 5
65 Southall Green. . . . G 6
65 Southall La. . . . . . . H 5
75 Southampton Bldgs.
      G 10
75 Southampton Place G 9
75 Southampton Row. F 9
75 Southampton St. . . J 9
70 Southampton Way H 7
71 Southborough,
      Bromley. . . . . . . D 10
70 Southborough,
      Surbiton . . . . . . E 2
71 Southborough La. D 10
71 Southborough Rd. D 10
67 Southbury Rd. . . . . A 7
70 Southcroft Rd. . . . . C 5
70 Southend. . . . . C 9
67 Southend Rd. E18 C 10
68 Southend Rd.,
      Romford. . . . . . . C 4
75 Southern St. . . . . . . B 9
70 Southfields Sta. . . . B 4
77 Southfleet . . . . C 5
66 Southgate. . . . . A 6
67 Southwark . . . . G 7
67 Southwark Bridge. . J 2
79 Southwark Bridge Rd.
      C 13
80 Southwark Cathedral
      B 2
67 Southwark Park. . . G 8
80 Southwark Park Rd.
      E 6
79 Southwark St. . . . . B 13
77 Southwell Gdns. . . . E 3
73 Southwick Mews . . G 5
73 Southwick Place . . H 6
73 Southwick St. . . . . . G 6
71 Spa Hill . . . . C 7
80 Spa Rd. . . . . E 5
65 Spaniards Rd. . . . . . D 5
65 Sparrowsherne . . . . A 6
77 Spear Mews . . . . . . F 1
76 Spelman St. . . . . . . F 6
75 Spencer St. . . . . . . D 12
78 Spenser St. . . . . D 6
71 Spinney Hill . . . . . . F 2
68 Spital La. . . . . H 5
76 Spital Square. . . . . . F 4
76 Spital St. . . . . E 6
67 Spitalfields. . . . . . . F 8
76 Spitalfields Market. F 5
79 Sprimont Place . . . . F 2
78 Spring Gdns. . . . . . B 8
70 Spring Grove . . . . . A 1
71 Spring St. . . . . H 5
67 Springfield Park . . D 8
73 Springfield Rd. . . . . A 3
71 Spur Rd. . . . . E 12
80 Spurgeon St. . . . . . D 2

69 Squires Bridge Rd. D 3
68 Squirrels Heath . . C 3
66 Squirrels Heath Rd. C 4
76 Squirries St. . . . . . . D 6
75 Stacey St. . . . . H 8
78 Staff St. . . . . D 3
78 Stafford Place. . . . . D 6
73 Stafford Rd. NW6 . C 1
70 Stafford Rd.,
      Beddington. . . . . F 6
78 Stafford St. . . . . A 5
78 Stafford Terrace . . . D 1
66 Stag La. . . . . C 3
78 Stag Place . . . . D 6
69 Staines . . . . C 2
69 Staines Bridge . . . . C 2
69 Staines Central Sta. C 2
69 Staines La. . . . . D 2
69 Staines Reservoirs . B 3
69 Staines Rd., Hounslow
      B 5
69 Staines Rd., Laleham
      D 2
69 Staines Road East D 5
69 Staines Rd., West. . C 4
69 Stamford Brook Sta.
      G 3
67 Stamford Hill. . . . . D 7
67 Stamford Hill Sta. . D 7
79 Stamford St. . . . . . B 11
70 Stanford Rd. . . . . . D 3
77 Stanhope Gdns. . . . E 4
78 Stanhope Gate. . . . B 4
77 Stanhope Mews East
      E 4
77 Stanhope Mews West
      E 4
74 Stanhope Place . . . H 2
74 Stanhope Place Gate
      H 2
78 Stanhope Row . . . . B 4
76 Stanhope St. . . . . . . D 6
73 Stanhope Terrace . . H 5
70 Stanley Park Rd. . . F 5
70 Stanley Rd. . . . . . . C 1
75 Stanley Passage . . . C 8
66 Stanmore. . . . . B 2
66 Stanmore Hill. . . . . B 1
66 Stanmore Sta. . . . . . B 2
79 Stannary St. . . . . . G 11
78 Stanstead Rd. . . . . . B 8
72 Stansted . . . . F 5
76 Stanway St. . . . . C 4
66 Stanwell. . . . . B 3
69 Stanwell New Rd. . C 2
69 Stanwell Rd., Staines
      C 3
69 Stanwell Rd.,
      W. Bedfont. . . . . B 4
69 Stanwellmoor . . . . B 2
80 Staple St. . . . . D 3
68 Stapleford Abbotts A 2
68 Staples Corner. . . . D 4
73 Star St. . . . . G 5
70 Star & Garter Home
      B 2
72 Star Hill Rd. . . . . . H 1
74 Starcross St. . . . . . . D 6
74 Station Avenue . . . E 4
67 Station La. . . . . D 3
69 Station Rd.,
      Addlestone. . . . . E 3
66 Station Rd., Harrow
      C 1
65 Station Rd., Hayes G 4
66 Station Rd., New
      Barnet. . . . . A 5
71 Station Rd., Orpington
      E 11
71 Station Rd., Sidcup
      C 11
75 Stationers' Hall . G 12
80 Stead St. . . . . F 2
79 Steedman St. . . . . F 13
69 Steels La. . . . . G 6
69 Stephen St. . . . . . . G 7
74 Stephenson Way . . D 6
67 Stepney . . . . F 8
76 Stepney East Sta. . . F 8
77 Sterling St. . . . . D 6
80 Sterry St. . . . . C 2
76 Steward St. . . . . F 4
77 Stewart's Grove . . . F 5
68 Stifford . . . . G 6
68 Stifford Rd. . . . . . . G 4
78 Stillington St. . . . . . E 6

76 Stock Exchange . . . G 3
65 Stockley Rd. . . . . . . G 4
67 Stockwell Rd. . . . . . A 6
69 Stoke D'Abernon . H 5
67 Stoke Newington. . D 7
67 Stoke Newington Rd.
      E 7
67 Stoke Newington Sta.
      D 7
69 Stoke Rd. . . . . G 5
72 Stone. . . . . B 4
72 Stone Buildings . G 10
72 Stone Crossing Halt
      B 4
66 Stone Grove . . . . . . B 2
72 Stone Marshes . . . . A 3
66 Stonebridge Park Sta.
      E 2
70 Stonecot Hill. . . . . E 4
69 Stonehill Rd. . . . . . F 1
71 Stonehouse La.,
      Orpington . . . . . F 12
68 Stonehouse La.,
      W. Thurrock. . . . G 4
70 Stoneleigh Sta. . . . . F 3
80 Stones End St. . . . . D 1
80 Stoney La. . . . . G 4
80 Stoney St. . . . . B 2
72 Stony Corner . . . . . D 6
76 Stopford Rd. . . . . . G 13
74 Store St. . . . . F 7
79 Storey's Gate. . . . . . D 8
80 Storks Rd. . . . . D 7
74 Stourcliffe St. . . . . . G 2
68 Straight Rd. . . . . . . C 3
76 Strand . . . . J 9
75 Strand Theatre . . . . H 9
67 Stratford . . . . E 9
67 Stratford New Town
      E 9
74 Stratford Place. . . . H 4
77 Stratford Rd. . . . . . E 1
67 Stratford Sta. . . . . . E 9
73 Strathearn Place . H 5
80 Strathnairn St. . . . . F 7
78 Stratton St. . . . . B 5
70 Strawberry Hill G.C.
      C 1
70 Strawberry Hill Sta.
      C 1
70 Strawberry Vale. . . C 1
66 Streatfield Rd. . . . . C 2
70 Streatham . . . . C 6
70 Streatham
      Common. . . . . . . C 6
70 Streatham Common
      North. . . . . C 6
70 Streatham Common
      Sta. . . . . C 5
70 Streatham High Rd.
      C 6
70 Streatham Hill . . . . B 6
70 Streatham Hill Sta. C 6
70 Streatham Rd. . . . . D 5
70 Streatham Sta. . . . . C 6
75 Streatham St. . . . . . G 8
70 Streatham Vale . . C 6
70 Street, The. . . . . H 2
69 Stroud Green Rd. . D 7
69 Stroude. . . . . D 1
78 Strutton Ground . . D 7
78 Strype St. . . . . G 5
73 Stuart Rd. . . . . D 1
68 Stubbers La. . . . . . . E 4
69 Stukeley St. . . . . . . G 9
79 Sturgeon Rd. . . . . G 13
76 Stutfield St. . . . . . . H 7
66 Sudbrook Park . . . . C 2
66 Sudbury G.C. . . . . . E 2
66 Sudbury Hill Sta. . E 1
66 Sudbury Hill &
      Harrow Sta. . . . . E 1
66 Sudbury Town Sta. E 2
66 Sudbury & Harrow
      Rd. Sta. . . . . E 2
75 Sudeley St. . . . . . . C 12
75 Sudrey St. . . . . C 13
76 Suffolk La. . . . . J 2
76 Suffolk Rd. . . . . A 6
80 Suffolk St. SE1 . . . C 1
79 Suffolk St. SW1 . . A 7
80 Sultan St. . . . . J 1
80 Summer Rd. . . . . . . D 1
66 Summers La. . . . . . . B 5
77 Summer Place . . . . F 5
76 Sumner Rd. . . . . J 5
79 Sumner St. . . . . . . B 13
76 Sun St. . . . . F 3
69 Sunbury . . . . D 4

69 Sunbury Sta. ... D 4
73 Sunderland Ter. ... G 2
71 Sundridge Hill Rd. H 12
71 Sundridge Park G.C. C 10
71 Sundridge Park Sta. D 9
72 Sundridge Rd. ... H 1
68 Sunnings La. ... E 4
70 Surbiton ... E 2
70 Surbiton G.C. ... E 1
73 Surrendale Place ... E 2
80 Surrey Canal ... H 4
79 Surrey Row ... C 12
80 Surrey Square ... F 4
75 Surrey St. ... H 10
80 Surrey Terrace ... F 4
73 Sussex Gardens ... H 5
73 Sussex Place ... H 5
73 Sussex Square ... H 5
78 Sussex St. ... G 5
73 Sutherland Avenue E 2
73 Sutherland Place ... G 1
80 Sutherland Square. G 1
78 Sutherland St. ... G 5
80 Sutherland Walk G 2
70 Sutton ... F 4
72 Sutton-at-Hone ... D 3
72 Sutton at Hone Rd. C 2
68 Sutton Avenue ... D 3
70 Sutton Common Rd. E 4
70 Sutton Common Sta. E 4
69 Sutton La., Hounslow A 5
70 Sutton La., Sutton. G 4
74 Sutton Row ... G 7
70 Sutton Sta. ... F 4
65 Swakeleys ... E 4
74 Swallow St. ... J 6
80 Swan Mead ... E 4
80 Swan St. ... D 2
78 Swan Walk ... H 2
72 Swancombe Marshes A 5
76 Swanfield St. ... D 5
72 Swanley ... D 2
72 Swanley La. ... D 2
72 Swanley Village ... D 2
72 Swanley Village Rd. D 2
72 Swanscombe ... B 5
72 Swanscombe Halt . B 5
72 Swanscombe Park . C 5
80 Sweeney Crescent . D 5
75 Swinton St. ... D 9
66 Swiss Cottage Sta. . E 5
76 Swithin's Hall ... H 2
71 Sydenham ... C 7
71 Sydenham Hill Sta. C 7
71 Sydenham Rd. ... C 8
71 Sydenham Sta. ... C 8
77 Sydney Place ... F 5
77 Sydney St. ... G 6
78 Symons St. ... F 3
70 Syon La. ... A 1
70 Syon Lane Sta. ... A 1
70 Syon House ... A 1
80 Tabard St. ... D 2
76 Tabernacle St. ... E 3
78 Tachbrook St. ... F 6
73 Talbot Rd. ... G 1
73 Talbot Square ... H 5
80 Talbot Yard ... B 2
75 Tallis St. ... H 11
77 Tamworth St. ... H 1
68 Tank La. ... G 4
80 Tanner St. ... C 4
76 Taplow St. ... C 2
79 Tarver Rd. ... G 13
79 Tate Gallery ... F 8
71 Tatsfield ... H 10
71 Tatsfield La. ... H 10
70 Tattenham Corner Rd. H 3
70 Tattenham Corner Sta. H 3
70 Tattenham Way ... H 4
80 Tatum St. ... F 3
74 Taunton Place ... E 2
75 Tavistock Place ... E 8
75 Tavistock Square ... E 8
75 Tavistock St. ... H 9
74 Taviton St. ... E 7
76 Teale St. ... B 7
70 Teddington ... C 1
78 Tedworth Square . G 2
75 Temple, The ... H 11
75 Temple Avenue ... H 11
75 Temple Bar ... H 11
75 Temple Gardens . H 11
75 Temple Place ... H 10
70 Temple Rd. ... G 2
77 Templeton Place ... F 1
80 Tennis St. ... C 2
65 Tentelow La. ... G 6
78 Terminus Place ... E 5
69 Terrace Rd. ... E 5
77 Thackeray St. ... D 2
70 Thames Ditton ... E 1
70 Thames Ditton Sta. E 1
75 Thames Water Authority ... D 11
68 Thamesmead ... G 1
75 Thanet St. ... D 8
75 Thavies Inn ... G 11
74 Thayer St. ... G 4
75 Theatre Royal ... H 9
79 Theed St. ... B 11
66 Theobald St. ... A 2
75 Theobald's Rd. ... F 9
78 Thirleby Rd. ... E 6
69 Thistlecroft ... F 5
79 Thomas Doyle St. D 12
80 Thomas More St. . A 6
76 Thorburn Square ... F 6
76 Thoresby St. ... C 1
68 Thorndon Park ... C 6
68 Thorndon Park G.C. C 6
65 Thorney La. ... F 2
79 Thorney St. ... E 8
73 Thorngate Rd. ... E 2
70 Thornton Heath ... D 6
74 Thornton Place ... F 2
70 Thornton Rd. ... E 6
69 Thorpe ... D 2
69 Thorpe Rd., Chertsey D 2
69 Thorpe Rd., Staines C 2
80 Thrale St. ... B 2
75 Thrawl St. ... G 5
76 Threadneedle St. ... H 3
74 Three Kings Yard . H 4
80 Three Oak La. ... C 5
76 Throgmorton Avenue G 3
76 Throgmorton St. ... G 3
79 Thrush St. ... G 13
80 Thurland Rd. ... D 6
77 Thurloe Place ... E 5
77 Thurloe Square ... E 5
77 Thurloe St. ... E 5
80 Thurlow St. ... G 3
76 Thurtle Rd. ... B 5
70 Tibbetts Corner ... B 4
78 Tilney St. ... B 4
79 Tinworth St. ... F 9
80 Tisdall Place ... F 3
73 Titchborne Row ... H 6
74 Titchfield Rd. ... B 2
78 Tite St. ... H 2
79 Tiverton St. ... D 13
76 Token House Yard G 3
66 Tollington Park Rd. D 6
74 Tolmers Square ... D 6
65 Tolpits La. ... A 4
70 Tolworth ... E 2
70 Tolworth Rise ... E 2
70 Tolworth Rd. ... E 2
67 Tomswood Hill ... C 11
75 Tonbridge St. ... D 8
80 Tooley St. ... B 4
70 Tooting Bec Rd. ... C 5
70 Tooting Bec Sta. ... C 5
70 Tooting Common . C 5
70 Tooting Graveney . C 5
70 Tooting Graveney Common ... C 5
70 Tooting High St. ... C 5
70 Tooting Sta. ... C 5
79 Topaz St. ... E 10
75 Topham St. ... E 11
77 Tor Gdns. ... C 1
73 Torquay St. ... F 2
75 Torrens St. ... C 12
74 Torrington Place ... F 7
67 Tottenham ... C 7
74 Tottenham Court Rd. F 6
67 Tottenham Hale ... C 8
67 Tottenham Hale Sta. C 8
67 Tottenham Hotspur F.C. ... C 8
66 Tottenham La. ... D 6
74 Tottenham St. ... F 6
66 Totteridge ... A 4
66 Totteridge La. ... B 4
66 Totteridge & Whetstone Sta. ... B 5
79 Toulmin St. ... C 13
76 Tower, The ... J 5
80 Tower Bridge ... B 5
76 Tower Bridge Approach ... J 5
80 Tower Bridge Rd. . D 4
67 Tower Hamlets ... F 8
76 Tower Hill ... J 5
75 Tower St. ... H 8
69 Town La. ... B 3
71 Townley Rd. ... B 12
80 Townsend St. ... F 3
73 Townshend Rd. ... B 6
76 Toynbee St. ... G 5
79 Trade, Dept. of ... D 7
80 Trafalgar Avenue . H 5
67 Trafalgar Rd. ... G 9
79 Trafalgar Square ... A 8
80 Trafalgar St. ... G 3
73 Transept St. ... F 6
80 Tranton Rd. ... D 7
67 Traps Hill ... A 11
70 Traps La. ... D 3
79 Treasury ... C 8
75 Treaty St. ... B 9
77 Trebovir Rd. ... F 1
77 Tregunter Rd. ... G 3
73 Tresham Crescent . D 6
79 Treveris St. ... B 12
78 Trevor Place ... D 1
78 Trevor Square ... D 2
78 Trevor St. ... C 2
79 Trigon Rd. ... J 10
80 Trinity Church Square D 2
76 Trinity House ... H 5
70 Trinity Rd. ... B 5
76 Trinity Square ... J 4
80 Trinity St. ... D 2
80 Trothy Rd. ... F 7
74 Triton Square ... E 5
72 Trottiscliffe ... G 6
78 Tryon St. ... F 2
71 Tubbenden La. ... E 11
70 Tudor Drive ... E 4
74 Tudor Place ... G 7
69 Tudor Rd. ... C 6
75 Tudor St. ... H 11
66 Tufnell Park Rd. ... E 6
79 Tufton St. ... E 8
70 Tulse Hill ... B 6
70 Tulse Hill Sta. ... C 6
70 Turin St. ... D 6
78 Turk's Row ... G 3
66 Turnham Green Sta. G 3
75 Turnmill St. ... F 12
67 Turnpike La. ... C 7
69 Twickenham ... B 6
70 Twickenham Bridge B 1
70 Twickenham Park . B 1
70 Twickenham Rd., Teddington ... C 1
69 Twickenham Rd., Twickenham ... C 5
74 Tyburn Way ... H 2
80 Tyers Gate ... C 4
79 Tyers St. ... G 9
79 Tyers Terrace ... G 10
75 Tysoe St. ... D 11
78 Udall St. ... F 6
79 Ufford St. ... C 12
76 Underwood Rd. ... E 6
76 Underwood St. ... C 2
76 Union Square ... B 1
79 Union St. ... B 12
76 Union Walk ... C 4
74 University College . E 7
74 University College Hospital ... E 6
75 University of London F 8
74 University St. ... E 6
80 Unwin Close ... H 6
73 Upbrook Mews ... H 4
68 Upminster ... D 4
68 Upminster Bridge Sta. D 4
68 Upminster G.C. ... D 4
68 Upminster Rd., Rainham ... F 3
68 Upminster Rd., Upminster ... D 4
67 Upney ... E 12
67 Upney La. ... E 11
67 Upney Sta. ... E 12
78 Upper Belgrave St. . D 4
74 Upper Berkeley St. . G 2
74 Upper Brook St. ... J 3
77 Upper Cheyne Row H 6
67 Upper Clapton ... D 8
67 Upper Clapton Rd. D 8
67 Upper Edmonton . B 8
71 Upper Elmer End. . E 8
74 Upper Grosvenor St. J 3
79 Upper Ground ... A 11
69 Upper Halliford Halt D 4
69 Upper Halliford Rd. D 4
74 Upper Harley St. ... E 4
66 Upper Holloway Sta. D 6
79 Upper Marsh ... D 10
74 Upper Montagu St. F 2
70 Upper Norwood ... D 6
77 Upper Phillimore Gdns. ... C 1
68 Upper Rainham Rd. D 3
70 Upper Richmond Rd., East Sheen ... B 2
70 Upper Richmond Rd., Putney ... B 3
75 Upper St. Martins La. H 8
75 Upper St. ... B 12
69 Upper Sunbury Rd. D 5
71 Upper Sydenham. . C 7
76 Upper Thames St. . H 2
70 Upper Tooting Rd. C 5
67 Upper Walthamstow C 9
71 Upper Warlingham Sta. ... H 7
71 Upper Wickam La. A 12
74 Upper Wimpole St. F 4
67 Upton ... E 10
67 Upton La. ... E 10
67 Upton Park Sta. ... E 10
71 Upton Rd. ... B 12
80 Urlwin St. ... H 1
65 Uxbridge ... E 3
66 Uxbridge Rd., Acton G 3
69 Uxbridge Rd., Feltham C 5
65 Uxbridge Rd., Harefield ... D 3
65 Uxbridge Rd., Hatch End ... C 6
66 Uxbridge Rd., Hanwell G 1
65 Uxbridge Rd., Hayes End ... F 4
65 Uxbridge Rd., Maple Cross ... B 2
65 Uxbridge Rd., Pinner C 5
65 Uxbridge Rd., Southall ... F 5
66 Uxbridge Rd., Stanmore ... B 1
77 Uxbridge St. ... B 2
77 Vale, The, SW3 ... H 5
66 Vale, The, W3 ... G 3
73 Vale Close ... D 3
68 Valence Avenue ... D 1
79 Valentine Place ... C 11
67 Valentines Park ... D 11
76 Vallance Rd. ... E 7
78 Vandon St. ... D 6
76 Vandy St. ... E 3
77 Vanston Place ... J 1
74 Varndell St. ... D 6
80 Vauban St. ... E 5
75 Vaudeville Theatre. J 9
79 Vauxhall Bridge ... G 7
78 Vauxhall Bridge Rd. E 6
79 Vauxhall Grove ... H 9
79 Vauxhall Park ... H 9
79 Vauxhall Sta. ... G 8
79 Vauxhall St. ... G 10
79 Vauxhall Walk ... G 9
73 Venables St. ... F 5
71 Verdant La. ... B 9
74 Vere St. ... H 4
75 Vernon Rise ... C 10
75 Verulam St. ... F 11
71 Vesta Rd. ... A 8
76 Vestry St. ... C 3
69 Vicarage Farm Rd. A 5
77 Vicarage Gate ... B 2
67 Vicarage La., Chigwell ... B 11
68 Vicarage La., South Weald ... B 4
69 Vicarage Rd. ... C 4
78 Victoria Coach Sta. F 4
67 Victoria Dock Rd. F 10
70 Victoria Drive ... B 4
79 Victoria Embankment B 9
79 Victoria Embankment Gdns. ... A 9
73 Victoria Gate ... J 5
77 Victoria Grove ... E 5
78 Victoria Hospital H 3
78 Victoria Palace Theatre D 5
67 Victoria Park ... E 8
67 Victoria Park Rd. ... E 8
66 Victoria Rd. NW10 F 3
77 Victoria Rd. W8 ... D 3
68 Victoria Rd., Romford D 2
65 Victoria Rd., Ruislip D 5
78 Victoria Square ... D 5
80 Victory Place ... E 2
80 Victory Square ... J 3
78 Victoria Sta. ... E 5
78 Victoria St. ... D 6
77 Victoria & Albert Museum ... E 5
74 Vigo St. ... J 6
80 Villa St. ... G 3
67 Village Way, Enfield A 7
65 Village Way, Harrow D 5
79 Villiers St. ... A 9
76 Vince St. ... D 3
78 Vincent Square ... E 7
79 Vincent St. ... F 7
75 Vincent Terrace ... B 12
75 Vine Hill ... E 11
80 Vine La. ... B 4
76 Vine St. ... H 5
73 Violet Hill ... C 4
79 Virgil St. ... D 10
79 Victoria Tower Gardens ... D 9
76 Virginia Rd. ... D 5
69 Virginia Water Sta. D 1
80 Wadding St. ... F 2
70 Waddington ... H 6
70 Waddon ... E 6
70 Waddon Marsh Halt E 6
67 Wadham Rd. ... C 9
80 Waite St. ... H 5
75 Wakefield St. ... D 9
75 Wakley St. ... C 12
76 Walbrook ... H 2
79 Walcot Square ... E 11
70 Waldgrave Rd. ... C 1
71 Waldram Park Rd. . B 8
77 Walham Grove ... J 1
74 Wallace Collection. G 3
67 Wallend ... E 11
77 Wallgrave Rd. ... F 2
70 Wallington ... F 5
79 Walnut Tree Walk E 11
78 Walpole St. ... F 2
73 Walterton Rd. ... D 1
67 Waltham Forest ... C 9
67 Walthamstow ... D 8
67 Walthamstow Avenue C 9
67 Walthamstow Central Sta. ... C 9
67 Walthamstow Marshes ... D 8
67 Walthamstow Queen's Rd. Sta. ... C 9
69 Walton Bridge ... E 4
70 Walton Downs ... H 3
78 Walton Place ... D 2
69 Walton Rd. ... D 5
78 Walton St. ... E 1
69 Walton-upon-Thames E 5
67 Walworth ... G 7
80 Walworth Place ... G 2
80 Walworth Rd. ... F 1
80 Wansey St. ... F 1
67 Wanstead ... D 10
67 Wanstead Flats ... D 10
67 Wanstead G.C. ... D 10
67 Wanstead Park ... D 10
67 Wanstead Park Sta. E 10
67 Wanstead Sta. ... D 10
70 Wandsworth ... B 4
70 Wandsworth Bridge A 4
70 Wandsworth Bridge Rd. ... A 4
70 Wandsworth Common B 5
70 Wandsworth Common Sta. ... B 5
70 Wandsworth Prison B 5
79 Wandsworth Rd. ... H 8
70 Wandsworth Rd. Sta. A 6
70 Wandsworth Town Sta. ... B 4
67 Wapping ... G 8
80 Wapping High St. . B 6
74 Wardour St. ... H 7
70 Warham Rd. ... F 6
79 Warham St. ... J 12
68 Warley Barracks ... B 5
68 Warley Rd. C 4, C 5
71 Warlingham ... H 8
75 Warner St. ... E 11
76 Warner Place ... C 6
68 Warren La., W. Thurrock ... G 5
69 Warren La., Woking H 2
71 Warren Rd. F 11, F 12
74 Warren St. ... E 6
73 Warrington Cres. ... E 3
73 Warwick Avenue ... E 3
73 Warwick Crescent . F 3
73 Warwick Estate ... F 2
79 Warwick House St. B 7
75 Warwick La. EC4. G 12
68 Warwick La., Rainham F 4
73 Warwick Place ... F 3
67 Warwick Res. ... D 8
77 Warwick Rd. ... F 1
78 Warwick Row ... D 5
78 Warwick Square ... F 6
74 Warwick St. ... J 6
78 Warwick Way ... F 5
71 Wash Pond Rd. ... H 9
67 Water La. ... D 12
67 Waterden Rd. ... E 9
75 Watergate ... H 12
70 Waterhouse La. ... H 4
75 Waterloo Bridge. . J 10
75 Waterloo Pier ... J 10
78 Waterloo Place ... B 7
79 Waterloo Rd. ... C 11
79 Waterloo Sta. ... C 10
66 Waterlow Park ... D 6
76 Waterson St. ... D 4
69 Watersplash Rd. ... D 3
65 Watford ... A 5
66 Watford Bypass ... A 2
65 Watford F.C. ... A 5
65 Watford Heath ... A 5
65 Watford High St. Sta. A 5
66 Watford Rd., Harrow E 1
65 Watford Rd., Rickmansworth . A 3
66 Watford Way, NW4 C 4
66 Watford Way, Edgware ... B 2
65 Watford West Sta. . A 4
66 Watling Avenue ... C 3
76 Watling St. EC4 ... H 1
72 Watling St., Swanscombe ... C 4
72 Watling St. ... B 1
71 Watts La. ... D 11
73 Waverley Place ... B 4
78 Waverton St. ... B 4
79 Waxwell Terrace . D 10
68 Weald Park ... A 4
66 Wealdstone ... C 1
76 Weaver St. ... E 6
80 Weaver's La. ... B 4
80 Webb St. ... E 4
79 Webber Row ... D 11
79 Webber St. ... C 12
74 Welbeck St. ... G 4
74 Welbeck Way ... G 4
74 Weigh House St. ... H 4
75 Weirs Passage ... D 8
72 Well Hill ... F 1
76 Wellclose Square. . H 6

80 Weller St. ....C 1
76 Wellesey Terrace ..C 2
71 Welling ....A 12
71 Welling Way.....A 11
78 Wellington Arch ..C 4
78 Wellington Barracks
                       D 6
73 Wellington Pl. ....C 5
73 Wellington Rd. ...C 5
69 Wellington Rd. South
                       B 5
76 Wellington Row ..D 6
78 Wellington Square. G 2
75 Wellington St. ....H 9
74 Wells Mews ......G 6
74 Wells Rise........B 2
74 Wells St. ....G 6
80 Wells Way........H 3
80 Welsford St. ......F 6
66 Wembley ....E 2
66 Wembley Central Sta.
                       E 2
66 Wembley Hill Sta. .E 2
66 Wembley Stadium .E 2
76 Wenlock Basin....C 1
76 Wenlock Rd. ......C 1
76 Wenlock St. ......C 2
68 Wennington ......F 3
68 Wennington Marshes
                       G 3
68 Wennington Rd....F 3
76 Wentworth St.....G 5
74 Werrington St.....C 7
76 Wesley's Chapel. .E 3
66 West Acton Sta....F 2
69 West Bedfont.....B 3
69 West Byfleet......G 2
69 West Byfleet G.C..G 2
69 West Byfleet Sta...G 2
75 West Central St. ..G 8
71 West Common Rd. E 9
77 West Cromwell Rd. F 1
71 West Croydon Sta.
                       E 7
65 West Drayton ....G 3
65 West Drayton Rd..F 4
65 West Drayton &
    Yiewsley Sta...G 3
71 West Dulwich Sta..C 7
66 West Ealing Sta....F 1
78 West Eaton Place ..E 3
69 West End, Esher ..F 6
65 West End, Southall F 5
66 West End La......E 5
65 West End Rd. D 4, E 5
70 West Ewell ....G 3
67 West Ferry Rd....G 9
66 West Finchley Sta..B 5
67 West Green.......C 7
67 West Green Rd....C 7
69 West Grove.......F 5
78 West Halkin St....D 3
67 West Ham........F 10
67 West Ham F.C....E 10
67 West Ham Park ..E 10
67 West Ham Stadium
                       F 10
66 West Hampstead Sta.
                       E 5
65 West Harrow.....D 6
66 West Heath, NW3 .D 5
68 West Heath, SE2..H 1
72 West Hill.........B 2
68 West Horndon Sta. D 6
67 West India Docks .G 9
71 West Kent G.C...G 11
77 West Mall........A 1

66 West Middlesex G.C.
                       F 1
69 West Molesey ....D 6
71 West Norwood....C 7
70 West Norwood Sta. C 6
70 West Park Hospital G 2
78 West Rd..........G 3
65 West Ruislip Sta...D 4
75 West Smithfield...F 12
79 West Square.....E 12
75 West St..........H 8
70 West Sutton Sta...F 4
76 West Tenter St....H 5
78 West Thurrock ...H 5
68 West Thurrock
    Marshes ....H 5
71 West Wickham....E 9
71 West Wood La....B 11
73 Westbourne Bridge G 3
73 Westbourne Cres. .H 4
73 Westbourne Gdns..G 2
73 Westbourne Gate ..J 5
73 Westbourne Grove H 2
73 Westbourne Park Rd.
                       G 1
66 Westbourne Park Sta.
                       F 4
73 Westbourne Park
    Villas ....G 2
73 Westbourne St. ..H 5
73 Westbourne Ter. ..G 4
73 Westbourne Ter. Rd.
                       F 3
74 Westbury Hotel ..J 5
67 Westcombe Park Sta.
                       H 10
79 Westcott Rd.....H 12
69 Westend La.......F 5
71 Westerham Rd. ..F 10
66 Western Avenue,
    Greenford......F 1
65 Western Avenue,
    Uxbridge.......E 4
77 Western Hospital .H 2
70 Western Rd., Mitcham
                       F 4
65 Western Rd., Southall
                       G 5
77 Westgate Terrace. .H 3
71 Westhall Rd......H 7
71 Westhorne Av....B 10
76 Westland Place ...D 2
76 Westmead Rd. ....F 5
66 Westminster ......G 6
79 Westminster Abbey D 8
79 Westminster Bridge C 9
79 Westminster Bridge
    Rd............D 11
78 Westminster Chapel
                       D 6
79 Westminster Hall .D 8
79 Westminster Hospital
                       E 8
79 Westminster Pier . .C 9
78 Westminster R.C.
    Cathedral ......E 6
79 Westminster School D 8
78 Westminster Theatre
                       D 5
78 Westmoreland Place
                       G 5
80 Westmoreland Rd.
    SE17 ....H 2
80 Westmoreland Rd.
    SE17 ....G 4
71 Westmoreland Rd.,
    Bromley........D 9

74 Westmoreland St...F 4
78 Westmoreland Ter. G 5
70 Weston Green ....E 1
70 Weston Green Rd..E 1
75 Weston Rise......C 10
80 Weston St........C 3
73 Westway ....F 3
72 Westwood........C 5
71 Westwood Hill....C 7
77 Wetherby Gdns...F 3
77 Wetherby Place ..F 4
69 Weybridge........E 4
69 Weybridge Rd....E 3
69 Weybridge Sta....F 3
76 Weymouth Mews..F 5
76 Weymouth Ter. ..B 5
74 Weymouth St.....F 5
74 Whalebone La.....C 1
68 Whalebone La. South
                       D 1
75 Wharf Rd. ......C 13
75 Wharfdale Rd.....B 9
75 Wharton St......D 10
76 Wheler St........E 5
66 Whetstone.......B 5
75 Whetstone Park ..G 10
75 Whidborne St.....D 9
67 Whipps Cross....D 9
75 Whiskin St.......D 12
76 Whiston Rd......B 5
76 Whitby St........E 5
66 Whitchurch La. ...C 2
75 Whitcomb St.....J 7
76 White Church Lane G 6
66 White City Stadium F 4
75 White Conduit St. B 11
79 White Hall Place...B 8
67 White Hart La. N17 C 7
68 White Hart La.,
    Collier Row ....C 2
67 White Hart Lane Sta.
                       C 7
80 White Hart Yard ..B 2
65 White Hill........B 4
72 White Hill La......F 6
71 White Horse Hill .C 10
78 White Horse St....B 5
76 White Kennett St. .G 4
75 White Lion Hill . .H 13
70 White Lodge.....B 2
67 Whitechapel ......F 8
76 Whitechapel High St.
                       G 5
76 Whitechapel Rd. ..G 6
76 Whitecross St. ....F 2
71 Whitefoot La......C 9
75 Whitefriars St....H 11
79 Whitehall........B 8
79 Whitehall Court...B 8
67 Whitehall Rd.....B 9
79 Whitehall Theatre. B 8
79 Whitehart St....G 11
78 Whiteheads Grove .F 1
71 Whitehorse Rd....D 7
69 Whiteley Village..F 4
80 White's Grounds . .C 4
76 White's Row......F 5
74 Whitfield Place...E 6
74 Whitfield St......F 6
75 Whitgift St.......F 9
76 Whitmore Rd.....A 3
78 Whittaker St......F 3
75 Whittlesey St.....B 11
69 Whitton.........B 6
65 Whitton Avenue...E 6
69 Whitton Rd......B 6

71 Whyteleafe......H 7
71 Whyteleafe Rd....H 7
71 Whyteleafe South Sta.
                       H 7
67 Wick Rd.........E 8
67 Wickham La.....H 12
71 Wickham Rd. SE4 .A 8
71 Wickham Rd.,
    Beckenham.....D 8
71 Wickham Rd.,
    Croydon.......E 8
79 Wickham St. ...G 10
71 Wickham Way....D 9
75 Wicklow St.......C 9
76 Widegate St......F 4
73 Widley Rd........D 1
67 Widmore Rd......D 10
67 Wightman Rd....D 7
71 Wigmore Hall ...G 4
74 Wigmore Place...G 5
74 Wigmore St......G 4
75 Wilbraham Place..E 3
67 Wilbury Way .....B 7
75 Wild Court.......G 9
75 Wild St..........A 9
80 Wild's Rents.....D 3
66 Willesden........E 4
66 Willesden Green...E 4
66 Willesden Green Sta.
                       E 4
66 Willesden Junc. Sta.F 3
66 Willesden La......E 4
67 William Girling Res.
                       B 8
78 William Mews ....C 3
74 William Rd.......D 5
74 William St........C 3
75 William IV St......J 8
71 Willoughby La....C 8
71 Willow Grove....C 10
78 Willow Place......E 6
75 Willow St.........D 3
80 Willow Walk .....E 4
65 Willowbank ......E 3
80 Willowbrook Rd...J 5
76 Wilmer Gdns.....B 4
70 Wilmerhatch La...H 2
75 Wilmington......C 2
75 Wilmington Square
                       D 11
76 Wilson St........F 3
76 Wiltshire Row....A 3
78 Wilton Crescent...D 3
78 Wilton Mews.....D 4
78 Wilton Place......C 3
78 Wilton Rd........E 5
78 Wilton Row......C 3
76 Wilton Square....A 2
78 Wilton St........D 4
78 Wilton Terrace...D 3
70 Wimbledon.......C 4
70 Wimbledon Chase .D 4
70 Wimbledon Common
                       C 3
70 Wimbledon G.C...C 3
70 Wimbledon Hill Rd.
                       C 4
70 Wimbledon Park ..C 4
70 Wimbledon Park G.C.
                       C 4
70 Wimbledon Park Rd.
                       B 4
70 Wimbledon Park Sta.
                       C 4
70 Wimbledon Stadium
                       C 4

70 Wimbledon Sta....C 4
76 Wimbolt St.......C 6
76 Wimbourne St....B 2
74 Wimpole Mews ...F 4
74 Wimpole St.......G 4
78 Winchester St.....G 5
80 Winchester Walk..B 2
67 Winchmore Hill...A 7
79 Wincott St.......F 11
66 Windmill La.......G 1
74 Windmill St.......F 7
79 Windmill Walk ..C 11
70 Windsor Terrace ..C 2
74 Winfield House ...C 1
68 Wingletye La......D 4
76 Winkworth Rd....G 4
73 Winsland Mews...G 5
73 Winsland St.......G 5
74 Winsley St........G 6
69 Wisley...........G 3
69 Wisley Common ..H 3
69 Wisley La.........G 3
69 Woburn Hill......E 3
75 Woburn Place....E 8
75 Woburn Square...E 8
69 Woking..........H 1
71 Woldingham Rd...H 8
80 Wolseley St.......C 6
65 Wolsey Way......B 4
65 Wood End, Hayes .F 4
65 Wood End, S. Harrow
                       E 6
67 Wood Grange Park
    Sta............E 10
66 Wood Green......C 6
66 Wood Green Sta...C 6
70 Wood La. W12...F 4
68 Wood La., Becontree
                       E 1
68 Wood La., Dagenham
                       E 3
66 Wood La., Stanmore
                       B 2
67 Wood St. E17.....C 9
76 Wood St. EC2....G 2
66 Wood St., Barnet..A 4
67 Wood Street Sta. ..C 9
75 Woodbridge St. ..E 12
73 Woodchester Sq...F 2
70 Woodcote Grove Rd.
                       G 6
70 Woodcote La. ....G 5
70 Woodcote Park G.C.
                       G 5
70 Woodcote Park G.C.
    (R.A.C.).......H 3
70 Woodcote Rd.....F 5
70 Woodfall St.......G 2
70 Woodfield La.....H 2
67 Woodford........C 10
67 Woodford Bridge. B 10
67 Woodford Green .B 10
67 Woodford New Rd. C 9
67 Woodford Wells. .B 10
69 Woodham........G 2
69 Woodham La.....G 2
69 Woodland Park...H 6
72 Woodlands.......G 3
69 Woodlands La.....H 6
70 Woodmansterne ..G 5
70 Woodmansterne La.
                       G 5
70 Woodmansterne Rd.
                       F 5
70 Woodmansterne Sta.
                       G 5
65 Woodridings......C 6

74 Woods Mews .....J 3
76 Woodseer St......F 6
71 Woodside ....E 7
66 Woodside Avenue .C 5
65 Woodside Park Sta. B 5
70 Woodstock La.....E 1
74 Woodstock St.....H 4
69 Woodthorpe Rd...C 3
80 Wooler St........G 3
66 Woolwich........G 11
67 Woolwich Arsenal Sta.
                       G 11
67 Woolwich Church St.
                       G 11
67 Woolwich Common
                       H 10
67 Woolwich Dockyard
    Sta............G 11
67 Woolwich Reach .G 11
67 Woolwich Rd. SE7
                       G 10
68 Woolwich Rd.,
    W. Heath ....G 1
79 Wootton St......B 11
70 Worcester Park ...E 3
70 Worcester Park Sta. E 3
79 Worgan St........G 9
66 Wormwood Scrubs. F 3
76 Wormwood St. ...G 4
73 Woronzow Rd. ...A 5
70 Worple Rd. SW19 .D 3
69 Worple Rd., Staines
                       D 2
76 Worship St.......E 3
69 Wraysbury ....B 1
69 Wraysbury Res....B 2
75 Wren St..........E 10
80 Wright's Buildings .E 4
77 Wright's La.......D 2
72 Wrotham.........H 5
76 Wrotham Heath. .H 6
72 Wrotham Heath G.C.
                       H 6
72 Wrotham Hill Park G 5
72 Wrotham Rd..C 6, D 6
70 Wrythe, The......E 5
70 Wrythe La........E 5
74 Wybert St........D 5
75 Wyclif St.........D 12
66 Wyke Green G.C. .G 1
73 Wymering Rd.....D 2
75 Wynatt St........D 12
75 Wyndham Place ..F 2
74 Wyndham St......F 2
75 Wyndham's Theatre
                       J 8
75 Wynford Rd. ....B 10
77 Wynnstay Gdns. ..D 1
74 Wythburn Place...G 2
79 Wyvil Rd. ....J 8
76 Yalding Rd........E 6
65 Yeading ....F 5
65 Yeading La.......F 5
67 Yeoman's Row ...E 6
65 Yiewsley.........F 4
74 York Bridge .....E 3
75 York Buildings ...J 9
74 York Gate........E 3
77 York House Place .C 2
79 York Rd.........C 10
74 York St..........F 2
74 York Terrace .....E 4
75 York Way........B 9
76 Yorkton St.......C 6
77 Young St.........C 2
74 Zoological Gardens
                       B 3

PRINTED IN GREAT BRITAIN BY GEORGE PHILIP PRINTERS LTD,, LONDON.